State & Local Tax Revolt

NEW DIRECTIONS FOR THE '80s

State & Local Tax Revolt

NEW DIRECTIONS FOR THE '80s

Edited by

Dean Tipps
Executive Director
Citizens for Tax Justice

Lee Webb
Executive Director
Conference on Alternative State & Local Policies

Assistant Editor

Cameron Duncan

Contributing Editors

Diane Fuchs	Robert D. Ebel	Steven D. Gold
Leonard Goldberg	Gerald Kaufman	Bob Kuttner
James C. Rosapepe	Jonathan Rowe	

Conference on Alternative State & Local Policies

2000 Florida Avenue NW, Washington, DC 20009 (202) 387-6030

State and Local Tax Revolt
New Directions for the '80s

Production Director: Jim Higgins

Production Assistants:
Michael Atkin, Pat Konopka, Marsha Isley,
Gary Palmatier, Alvin Jones, Mitchell Rosenfeld

Special Thanks to Carol Baldwin for editorial assistance
in the early stages of production.

The illustrations in this book are by Larry Gonick,
247 Missouri Street, San Francisco 94107

Cover design by Andrew Bornstein

The research and writing of this book was
funded in part by the Shalan Foundation. Their
assistance was greatly appreciated.

The Conference on Alternative
State & Local Policies
2000 Florida Avenue NW
Washington, DC 20009

Printed by Union Printers

The Editors:

Cameron Duncan is a research economist for the Center to Protect Workers' Rights, the research organization of the Building Trades Department, AFL-CIO. Formerly he was coordinator of the Tax Reform Project of the Conference on Alternative State and Local Policies. He received a B.A. from Stanford University and a M.A. in economics from the University of Texas. He taught economics at Inter-American University in Puerto Rico and worked as a labor economist in the research department of the American Federation of State, County and Municipal Employees. His articles on public policy, the labor movement and plant closings have appeared in *In These Times, WIN, Seven Days, Southwest Economy & Society, Guardian* and *Dollars & Sense.*

Diane Fuchs is an attorney and a partner in Rosapepe, Fuchs, and Associates, a Washington-based public policy consulting firm that specializes in taxes, energy, and other economic issues. Currently, she is an adjunct professor at the Washington College of Law, American University, and a member of the Financial Stress and Public Management Project, a non-profit public administration consulting firm. Ms. Fuchs was previously the state and local tax specialist with the Tax Reform Research Group in Washington. Prior to that she worked for several years as a litigator with various Legal Services programs providing free legal assistance to low income families.

Robert D. Ebel received his B.A. in economics from Miami University in 1964 and his Ph.D. from Purdue University in 1971. Currently he is on leave from the faculty of the University of the District of Columbia and is serving as a full time consultant to the U.S. Advisory Commission on Intergovernmental Relations.

Dr. Ebel has taught at the University of Hawaii (1969-1974) and at Miami, Purdue, and American Universities. His administrative and research work has included the Chairmanship of the State Income and Business Taxation Committee of the National Tax Association—Tax Institute of America, and the Executive Directorship of the Washington D.C. Tax Revision Commission.

While at the University of Hawaii, Dr. Ebel also worked as the economic advisor to the Legislative Coalition (a lobby group for low-income persons in Honolulu), the Hawaii Council of Public Sector Unions, and the University of Hawaii's Environmental Center.

Dr. Ebel's most recent books include *The Michigan Business Activities Tax, An Evaluation of a Value Added Tax for the State of Hawaii,* and *Who Pays Hawaii's Taxes: A Study of the Incidence of State and Local Taxes in Hawaii.*

Steven D. Gold is Professor of Economics at Drake University. He received a B.A. from Bucknell University in 1966 and a Ph.D. from the University of Michigan in 1972. He has served as a consultant on taxes, budgeting, and collective bargaining to cities and unions of their employees and as an adviser to the Iowa Legislature.

His scholarly research has focused on two areas: the distributional effects of government services and taxes, and state and local tax issues. His articles have appeared in the *National Tax Journal, Public Finance Quarterly,* and other journals. He has directed projects in 1977-78 and 1979-80 to improve the understanding of Iowa citizens about local government finance and authored a book, *A Citizen's Guide to Local Government Finance: Iowa at the Property Tax Crossroads.* During 1978-79 he was a Visiting Scholar at The Urban Institute as a recipient of a Science Faculty Professional Development Fellowship from the National Science Foundation.

He is author of *Property Tax Relief* published by D.C. Heath in 1979. The book describes and analyzes all major types of property tax relief currently in use.

Leonard Goldberg is an economist currently on the staff of California Assemblyman Tom Bates, where he is developing legislation in the areas of renter policy, housing, solar energy, oil and gas, and labor policy. He is currently a visiting instructor at California State University, San Francsico, and has worked as a consultant to the California Director of Employment Development and Community Economics, Inc., in Oakland. He is a co-author of *The Cities Wealth,* and has published in *Working Papers* and various Bay Area weeklies.

Gerald Kaufman is an attorney and consultant to the city of Hartford, Connecticut, in the areas of school finance and state and local tax reform. Mr. Kaufman was previously in private practice in Pittsburgh for ten years, and served for six years (1967-1972) in the Pennsylvania House of Representatives.

Bob Kuttner is the editor of *Working Papers for a New Society.* He has recently completed work as a Fellow at the Institute for Politics at Harvard University, and written a book on the tax revolt entitled *Revolt of the Haves.*

He has worked as staff director of the National Commission on Neighborhoods, chief investigator for the U.S. Senate Banking Committee, national staff writer for the *Washington Post,* Washington editor of the *Village Voice* and has written for several national magazines. He has also worked as a reporter in public radio and television.

Mr. Kuttner holds an A.B. from Oberlin and a M.A. from the University of California at Berkeley, both in political science. He has also studied at the London School of Economics.

James C. Rosapepe is a partner in Rosapepe, Fuchs, and Associates, a Washington-based public policy consulting firm that specializes in taxes, energy, and other economic issues. A former Legislative Assistant to Sen. Fred Harris (D, Okla.) and Rep. Andrew Maguire (D, N.J.), he has lobbied on Capitol Hill and in state legislatures on behalf of the Multistate Tax Commission, the League of Women Voters, the Interfaith Center on Corporate Responsibility, and other clients. He has worked as a policy consultant to a variety of public and private groups including the National Governor's Conference, the Service Employees International Union, the Energy Action Committee, the Small Business Administration, the National Commission on Neighborhoods, and the COIN Campaign. Rosapepe's articles on tax policy issues have appeared in *The New York Times, The Washington Monthly,* and *Elected Public Official.* He is a director of Consumer Congress of Virginia, a member of the Steering Committee of the Conference's Agriculture Project, and a member of the National Petroleum Council.

Dean C. Tipps is executive director of Citizens for Tax Justice, a national citizen-labor coalition headquartered in Washington, D.C. As legislative advocate for the California Tax Reform Association, he was actively involved in the legislative battles for property tax reform before Proposition 13, the Proposition 13 campaign, and its aftermath. Educated at Whittier College, he has a master's degree from the University of California, Berkeley, where he was Regents Fellow in Sociology, and an Honorary Woodrow Wilson Fellow. In addition to drafting and lobbying tax legislation, he has authored many articles on Proposition 13 and tax policy in California.

Jonathan Rowe has degrees from Harvard College and the University of Pennsylvania Law School. For four and one-half years he was state and local tax specialist for Ralph Nader. He has been counsel to the Finance and Revenue Committee of the District of Columbia City Council, and Deputy Director of the Multistate Tax Commission, an organization of states working for better enforcement of state taxes on large multinational corporations and to keep the federal government from dictating tax policies to the states.

Currently Mr. Rowe is Associate Director of Citizens for Tax Justice, a coalition of labor and civic organizations working for fair distribution of the tax burden, especially at the state and local levels.

Mr. Rowe is co-author of *Tax Politics,* co-editor of *New Directions in State and Local Tax Reform* and the author of articles appearing in numerous periodicals. He has spoken on state and local taxes in many forums, including the continuing education programs of the American Law Institute/American Bar Association, and at the Kennedy Institute of Politics.

Lee Webb is an economist and executive director of the Conference on Alternative State and Local Policies. For seven years, he taught economics and public policy at Goddard College, Vermont. While in Vermont, he was appointed a member of the Governor's Commission on Electric Energy, a member of the Board of Directors of the Vermont—New Hampshire Blue Cross, and a trustee of the Vermont Historical Society. He was also elected Justice of the Peace.

On the national level, Lee Webb has been a special assistant to Senator George McGovern, and was recently appointed a member of the National Consumer Advisory Committee to the Department of Energy.

Lee Webb is the author and editor of a number of books including, *New Directions in State and Local Public Policy, Public Policies for the 1980's, Public Policy Reader, New Directions in Farm, Land and Food Policy, Public Employee Pension Funds: New Strategies for Investment,* and *State and Local Tax Revolt: New Directions for the '80s.*

Mr. Webb has an M.A. in economics and a Ph.D. in economics and public policy.

Contents

I. Introduction | 2
  1 Principles of Tax Reform | 4

II. The Property Tax: What's Wrong With It | 16
  2 The Property Tax: An Overview | 19
  3 Reforming Assessment Practices | 35
  4 Collecting Delinquent Taxes | 55

III. The Property Tax: Homeowner Relief | 64
  5 California's Tax Revolt | 67
  6 Property Classification | 107
  7 Circuit Breakers and Homestead Exemptions | 119

IV. Tax Relief for Tenants | 136
  8 Tenants and the Property Tax | 136

V. Taxes and Land Use | 146
  9 Protecting Agricultural Land | 149
  10 Taxing Urban Speculation | 159

VI. Structural Inequities and Local Finance | 172
  11 Exempt Property | 175
  12 Wealth Related Disparities in School Finance | 183
  13 Metropolitan Tax Base Sharing | 191

VII. Alternative Strategies for Taxing Wealth | 198
  14 Intangible Property | 203
  15 Inheritance, Estate and Gift Taxes | 211

VIII. Taxing Consumption | 218
  16 Sales and Use Tax | 221
  17 User Charges | 237

IX. Taxing Personal Income | 248
  18 The Income Tax: A Progressive Alternative | 248

X. Taxing Business | 270
  19 The Economic Impact of State and Local Business Taxes | 273
  20 Taxing Corporate Profits | 291
  21 Severance Taxes | 309

XI. The Limits of Tax and Spending Limitations | 316
  22 Tax Expenditure Reform | 319
  23 Truth in Taxing/Full Disclosure | 327
  24 Tax and Expenditure Limitations | 332

XII. New Directions for the '80s | 346
  25 New Directions for the '80s | 346

Statistical Appendix | 361

Introduction
By Dean Tipps — Lee Webb 2

1—Principles of Tax Reform 4
RULES FOR REFORM: TAX POLICY IN A NUTSHELL 6
Robert Stumberg, Harrison Institute for Public Law, Georgetown University

WHAT IS FAIR TAXATION? 13
Brandon, Rowe and Stanton, *Tax Politics*, Random House Inc., 1976

I. The Property Tax: What's Wrong With It 16
By Steven Gold

2—The Property Tax: An Overview 19
TAXES: HOW THEY WERE 20
Brandon, Rowe and Stanton, *Tax Politics*, Random House Inc., 1976

PROPERTY TAX OVERVIEW 23
District of Columbia Tax Revision Commission, *Financing An Urban Government*, 1978

THE REGRESSIVITY ISSUE 28
Public Policy Department, *AFSCME Action Plan for State and Local Taxes*, American Federation of State, County and Municipal Employees, 1977

CORRECTING THE PROPERTY TAX RECORD 29
Allen D. Manvel, *Tax Notes*, Taxation with Representation Fund, December 18, 1978

BEHIND THE 'TAX REVOLT' 31
Robert Kuttner, *The Washington Post*, September 9, 1979

3—Reforming Assessment Practices 35
ASSESSING AND THE ASSESSOR 36
Brandon, Rowe and Stanton, *Tax Politics*, Random House Inc., 1976

PROPERTY TAX IS OFTEN POORLY RUN 39
Diane Fuchs, *People and Taxes*, Public Citizen Tax Reform Research Group, October 1976

SMALL HOMES HERE TAXED HARDEST 42
Ed McManus, *The Chicago Tribune*, August 30, 1978

WHITES GET LOWER LEVY REGULARLY 43
Ed McManus, *The Chicago Tribune*, April 14, 1979

PROPERTY ASSESSMENT A DISGRACE 44
David Yepsen, *The Des Moines Register*, October 18, 1977

CITY ASSESSMENTS HIT COMMERCIAL BUILDINGS LIGHTLY 46
LaBarbara Bowman, *The Washington Post*, May 11, 1977

TAXES: WHO'S NOT PAYING? 47
Public Action News, Illinois Public Action Campaign, November 4, 1978

WE DO NEED ASSESSMENT REFORM 49
Mason Gaffney, *Property Tax Reform*, Urban Institute, 1973

TAPES—TAXPAYER ASSISTED PROPERTY EVALUATION SYSTEM 52
Office of Ken Johnston, Pierce County, Washington, Tax Assessor, July 16, 1976

A PLAN FOR REFORM 53
Derek Shearer, *Public Policies for the 80's*, Conference on Alternative State and Local Policies, 1978

4—Collecting Delinquent Taxes 55
REAL PROPERTY TAX DELINQUENCY AND URBAN LAND POLICY 56
John J. Lawlor, Lincoln Institute of Land Policy, 1978

BOSTON ORDERED TO TELL WHO OWES BACK TAXES 62
Walter V. Robinson and Fletcher Roberts, *The Boston Globe*, May 20, 1977

III. The Property Tax: Homeowner Relief 64
By Robert Kuttner

5—California's Tax Revolt 67
CALIFORNIA'S GREAT PROPERTY TAX REVOLT: THE ORIGINS AND IMPACT OF PROPOSITION 13 68
Dean Tipps, Citizens for Tax Justice, 1979

PROP. 13's BIGGEST BOOSTER WAS INFLATION 91
William Schneider, *The Los Angeles Times*, June 11, 1978

HOMEOWNER SHARE OF PROPERTY TAX RISES 93
Claire Speigel, *The Los Angeles Times*, February 1, 1979

GRASS ROOTS BURNING AGAIN: THIS TIME IT'S RENT CONTROL 94
Bill Boyarsky, *The Los Angeles Times*, February 1, 1979

THE RICH GOT RICHER THROUGHOUT THE STATE 95
Tom Furlong, *Long Beach Independent Press Telegram*, June 14, 1979

ONE CITY'S STORY: OAKLAND AFTER PROP. 13 97
Roger L. Kemp, *The Taxes Ranger*, California Tax Reform Association, May 4, 1979

IDAHO TAX SHIFT SPURS TAX REBELLION 98
Robert Kuttner

IMPACT OF A PROP. 13 TYPE AMENDMENT IN ARIZONA 102
Harold Scott and Paul Waddell, *Arizona Realtors Digest*, July-August 1979

6—Property Classification 107
CLASSIFIED PROPERTY TAX SYSTEMS IN THE U.S. 108
International Association of Assessing Officers, April, 1979

WHAT 100 PER CENT REVALUATION MEANS FOR MASSACHUSETTS 112
Massachusetts Fair Share

TURNING TAX REBELLION INTO TAX REFORM 115
Bob Kuttner, *The Washington Post*, November 5, 1978

7—Circuit Breakers and Homestead Exemptions 119
THE RESIDENTIAL CIRCUITBREAKER 120
Steve Gold, *Property Tax Relief*, 1980

CIRCUIT BREAKER: YOUR PROTECTION AGAINST PROPERTY TAX OVERLOAD 129
FOCUS, Ohio AFL-CIO, February, 1979

Index to Resources

REASSESSING THE CIRCUITBREAKER   130
Elizabeth Bass. Massachusetts Fair Share

HOMESTEAD EXEMPTION PROGRAMS   133
Abt Associates. *Property Tax Relief Programs for the Elderly.* 1975

IV. Tax Relief for Tenants   136
By Leonard Goldberg

8—Tenants and the Property Tax   137

THE MCKINSEY REPORT: TOWARD A NEW DEAL FOR RENTERS   140
Peter Marcuse. *New York Magazine.* November. 1972

GOVERNOR SIGNS 120M RENTER'S TAX CUT   143
New York Daily News. July 7. 1978

BILL LETS RENTERS TAKE DEDUCTIONS   143
Associated Press. June 2. 1978

RENTERS: NO BREAK ON TAXES   144
Kenneth R. Harney. *The Washington Post.* April 21. 1979

REMEMBERING CALIFORNIA'S FORGOTTEN TAXPAYERS   145
Jonathan Lewis and Steven Spencer. *The Los Angeles Times.* February 26. 1979

V. Taxes and Land Use   146
By Lee Webb

9—Protecting Agricultural Land   149

PROTECTING FARM LAND THROUGH NEW TAX POLICIES   150
Lee Webb. *New Directions in Farm. Land and Food Policies: A Time for State and Local Action.* 1979

THE PROGRESSIVE LAND TAX   152
Byron L. Dorgan. North Dakota Tax Commissioner. 1978

PROPERTY TAX RELIEF FOR FARMERS: NEW USE FOR CIRCUIT BREAKERS   154
Advisory Commission on Intergovernmental Relations. 1974

10—Taxing Urban Speculation   159

TAX REFORMERS GO AFTER LAND SPECULATION   160
Lee Webb. *Ways and Means.* Conference on Alternative State and Local Policies. July/August. 1978

MYTHS AND FACTS ABOUT REAL ESTATE SPECULATION IN SAN FRANCISCO   161
David Prowler. *Public Policies for the 80's.* Conference on Alternative State and Local Policies. 1978

RESTORING A CITY: WHO PAYS THE PRICE?   162
Carol Richards and Jonathan Rowe. *Working Papers.* Winter. 1977

SITE VALUE TAXATION MAY BE A WAY TO STIMULATE HOUSING CONSTRUCTION AND REHABILITATION   168
Walter Rybeck. *Journal of Housing*

VI. Structural Inequities and Local Finance   172
By Gerald Kaufman

11—Exempt Property   175

EXEMPTED AMERICA: TAXPAYERS PAY $15 BILLION EXTRA EACH YEAR BECAUSE MAJOR PROPERTIES ARE GOING UNTAXED   176
Lee Mitgang. *The Washington Post.* February 4. 1978

SOME PAY . . . SOME DON'T: EVALUATING PROPERTY TAX EXEMPTIONS   178
Richard Pomp. *People and Taxes.* Public Citizen Tax Reform Research Group. September. 1978

CONNECTICUT ADOPTS P.I.L.O.T. LEGISLATION FOR SCHOOLS AND HOSPITALS   181
Lee Webb. Conference on Alternative State and Local Policies. 1978

12—Wealth Related Disparities in School Finance   183

PUBLIC SCHOOL FINANCE: FINE TUNING THE SYSTEM   184
Allan Odden. *State Government.* Winter. 1978

MONEY AND EDUCATION: WHERE DID THE $400 MILLION GO? THE IMPACT OF THE NEW JERSEY PUBLIC SCHOOL EDUCATION ACT OF 1975   189
Margaret E. Goertz. Educational Testing Service. 1978

13—Metropolitan Tax Base Sharing   191

MINNESOTA HELPS ITS METROPOLIS SHARE THE TAX BASE   192
Peter Nye. *Nation's Cities.* November. 1977. National League of Cities

VII. Alternative Strategies for Taxing Wealth   198
By Jonathan Rowe

14—Intangible Property   203

TAXING WEALTH—A NEW SOURCE OF GOVERNMENT REVENUE   204
Jonathan Rowe. *Public Interest Economics.* August. 1977

TAX INTANGIBLES FOR HOMEOWNER RELIEF   208
Leonard Greenberg

15—Inheritance, Estate and Gift Taxes   211

INHERITANCE AND ESTATE TAXES   212
Dr. L.L. Ecker-Racz. *The Politics and Economics of State and Local Finance.* Prentice Hall. 1970

DEATH AND TAXES. THE AMERICAN ESTATE TAX: A DEATH PENALTY   215
Byron L. Dorgan. *State Government.* Spring. 1976

VIII. Taxing Consumption
By Robert Ebel
218

16—Sales and Use Tax
221

A LOOK AT THE SALES TAX
222
Diane Fuchs, *People and Taxes*, Public Citizens
Tax Reform Research Group, January, 1978

RETAIL SALES AND USE TAX
224
District of Columbia Tax Revision Commission,
Financing an Urban Government, 1978

EXEMPTING NECESSITIES FROM THE SALES
230
TAX: THE ARKANSAS CASE
Larry Ginsburg, Association of Community
Organizations for Reform Now (ACORN)

LOUISIANA'S ADVANCE SALES TAX LAW:
234
HISTORY, APPLICATION AND CURRENT STATUS
J. Eugene Martin and Donald L. Dawson,
Louisiana Department of Revenue

17—User Charges
237

USER CHARGE FINANCING
238
Advisory Commission on Intergovernmental
Relations, *Local Revenue Diversification*, 1974

PROPOSITION 13 FORCES SHIFT TO USER FEES
244
Jonathan Lewis, *The Taxes Ranger*, California
Tax Reform Association, 1979

DEVELOPMENT CHARGES
245
Donald G. Hagman, *Financing State and Local
Government: Trends, Policies and Law*,
American Law Institute, 1977

IX. Taxing Personal Income
By Dean Tipps
248

18—The Income Tax— A
Progressive Alternative
249

RATING A RATE
251
Allen D. Manvel, *Tax Notes*, Taxation with
Representation Fund, April 24, 1978

FOUR ADVANTAGES OF
253
PROGRESSIVE INCOME TAXES
Milton Taylor, et al., 1977

INCOME TAXES AND INFLATION
254
Advisory Commission on Intergovernmental
Relations, *Inflation and Federal and State
Income Taxes*, 1976

CAPITAL GAINS BENEFITS FAVORS RICH
258
Martin Helmke, *Tax Back Talk*, California Tax
Reform Association, July, 1976

IMPROVING THE CALIFORNIA PERSONAL
260
INCOME TAX
Martin Huff, *Taxation: A California Perspective*,
California Tax Reform Association, 1978

TANGLED TAX LAW STRANGLES
261
CALIFORNIANS
Martin Huff, *Los Angeles Times*
February 11, 1980

ATTENTION TAXPAYERS!
262
California Tax Reform Association, February
1980

THE LOW-INCOME COMPREHENSIVE TAX
263
REBATE: NEW MEXICO'S BROAD-BASED TAX
RELIEF PROGRAM
Charles D. Turpen, *Revenues Review*, March,
1977

THE POSSIBILITY OF A LOCAL INCOME TAX IN
268
NEW YORK STATE
*The New York Temporary State Commission on
State and Local Finance*, 1975

X. Taxing Business
By James Rosapepe
270

19—The Economic Impact of State
and Local Business Taxes
273

BATTLING FOR BUSINESS
274
Jerry Jacobs, *People and Taxes*, Public Citizens
Tax Reform Research Group, September, 1978

BUSINESS LURES USELESS, NADER SAYS
276
Larry Kramer, *The Washington Post*, August 2,
1979

THE POLITICAL ECONOMY OF STATES' JOB-
277
CREATION BUSINESS INCENTIVES
Bennett Harrison and Sandra Kanter, *AIP
Journal*, October, 1978

TAX ABATEMENT: THE BIG GIVEAWAY
289
Ohio AFL-CIO, *Focus*, March, 1978

20—Taxing Corporate Profits
291

A TUSSLE OVER TAXES: BUSINESS VS. THE
292
STATES
Linda Hudak, *The Washington Post*, August 13,
1978

HOW THE CORPORATION DODGED ITS TAXES,
296
AN UNJUST-SO STORY
Larry Gonick

STATEMENT FOR MISSOURI LEGISLATURE
299
CONCERNING BILL TO ESTABLISH UNIFORM
RULES FOR CORPORATIONS REPORTING
INCOME TO MISSOURI
Jonathan Rowe, Multistate Tax Commission,
February 16, 1979

VAT: IT'S BROCCOLI, DEAR
302
Charles Kingson, *Tax Notes*, Taxation with
Representation Fund, March 12, 1979

THE MICHIGAN SINGLE BUSINESS TAX: A STATE
304
VALUE ADDED TAX?
Alan Schenk, *Tax Notes*, Taxation with
Representation Fund, April 9, 1979

21—Severance Taxes
309

STATE SEVERANCE TAXES: DIGGING FOR
310
DOLLARS
Kay Christensen, *State Legislatures*, September/
October, 1977

TAXING COAL
311
Byron L. Dorgan, *The Coal Industry Meets Its
Match in the West*, November 4, 1977

LINCOLN COUNTY, W. VA.
313
The Elements, Public Resource Center, April,
1978

XI. The Limits of Tax and
Spending Limitations
316
By Diane Fuchs

Index to Resources

22 — Tax Expenditure Reform — 319

TAX EXPENDITURES — 320
Edmund G. Brown. *Governors Budget for 1979-1980.* January 10, 1979

LIMITS MAY ENCOURAGE TAX EXPENDITURES — 326
Russell M. Lidman. *An Analysis of Initiative 62.* Washington Association of Community Action Agencies. 1978

23 — Truth in Taxing/ Full Disclosure — 327

FULL DISCLOSURE OF PROPERTY TAX INCREASES—TRUTH IN TAXATION — 328
Advisory Commission on Intergovernmental Relations. *State Constitutional and Statutory Restrictions on Local Taxing Powers.* 1978

PROPERTY TAX ISSUE REALLY NOTHING NEW — 330
Jane Bryant Quinn. *The Washington Post.* June 19, 1978

24 — Tax and Expenditure Limitations — 332

THE GREAT TAX LIMITS DEBATE — 334
Diane Fuchs. *People and Taxes,* April 1978

AN IMPRESSIONISTIC EVALUATION OF SEVERAL WAYS TO SLOW DOWN STATE AND LOCAL SPENDING — 336
John Shannon. Advisory Commission on Intergovernmental Relations, September, 1978

STATE TAX AND SPENDING LIMITATIONS — 337
Public Policy Department, American Federation of State, County and Municipal Employees. 1978

NEW JERSEY's 5% CAP ON MUNICIPAL BUDGETS — 338
Sanford L. Jacobs. *Boston Sunday Globe.* November 5, 1978

AFTER JARVIS: TOUGH QUESTIONS FOR FISCAL POLICYMAKERS — 340
John Shannon and Carol Weissert. *Intergovernmental Perspective.* Summer, 1978

XII. New Directions for the '80s — 346
By Dean Tipps

25 — New Directions for the '80s — 347

THE MASSACHUSETTS FAIR SHARE TAX CAMPAIGN — 348
Elizabeth Bass. Massachusetts Fair Share

RENEGADE TAX REFORM: TURNING PROP 13 ON ITS HEAD — 354
David Osborne. *Saturday Review.* May 12, 1979

WE CAN HAVE FAIR TAXES, IF THE CORPORATIONS PAY THEIR FAIR SHARE — 357
Ohio Public Interest Campaign. 1979

REFASHIONING OHIO'S TAX STRUCTURE — 359
Steve Wilson. *The Cincinnati Enquirer.* March 30, 1980

Statistical Appendix — 361

STATE AND LOCAL GOVERNMENT REVENUES AND EXPENDITURES, 1927-1977 — 362
Economic Report of the President. January 1979

TRENDS IN STATE-LOCAL TAX REVENUES — 363
Allen D. Manvel. *Tax Notes.* Taxation with Representation Fund. May 29, 1978

STATE-LOCAL TAX TRENDS — 364
Allen D. Manvel, *Tax Notes.* Taxation with Representation Fund. November 20, 1978

STATE AND LOCAL TAX IS SURPRISINGLY UNIFORM — 366
Theodore J. Stroll, *Tax Notes.* Taxation with Representation Fund. January 15, 1979

AVERAGE STATE AND LOCAL TAXES BY STATE — 368
Money Magazine. February 1979

THE TAX REVOLT — 369
Everett C. Ladd Jr., *Public Opinion.* American Enterprise Institute. July/August 1978

In 1977, the Conference published its first book on tax issues, *New Directions in State and Local Tax Reform*. Since then, taxpayer anger over unfair taxes has seized center stage in the nation's political arena.

The tax revolt came as no surprise to readers of *New Directions*. Taxpayers have much to be angry about: property tax shifts from business onto home-owners; assessments and tax bills which vary from neighborhood to neighborhood, from city to city, and frequently fail to recognize the difference between properties which are residences and properties which are businesses; income taxes which, if they are progressive at all, usually apply progressive rates to the low and middle income working families, but not to the wealthy; loophole riddled tax laws which subsidize the rich while soaking the rest of us; heavy reliance on regressive sales taxes which often tax such necessities as food and medicine while allowing many of the services consumed largely by the wealthy to go untaxed; and massive corporate tax avoidance which is officially sanctioned in the form of tax abatements and unofficially sanctioned by lax tax enforcement.

An Historic Watershed

The tax revolt sparked by California's Proposition 13 marks an historic watershed for our country. Rising taxpayer anger over the many inequities perpetuated by our tax system could fuel political movements moving in two dramatically different directions.

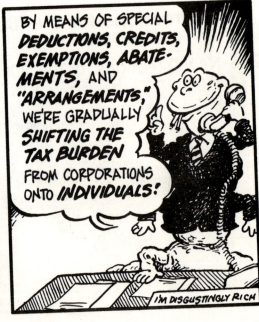

Introduction

By Dean Tipps
and Lee Webb

On the one hand, Proposition 13 style legislation could be passed in a number of states. The result would be a new and larger set of inequities in our tax system, local governments crippled by unacceptable budget cuts and left unable to respond to the needs of their communities, a public further angered and embittered, and continued political momentum for the right wing and its corporate allies.

On the other hand, the tax revolt could spawn progressive political movements aimed at providing real solutions to taxpayer grievances. Instead of dividing middle income workers and the poor against each other, such a movement would show people that they can have both lower taxes and better schools and other public services by means of tax reforms aimed at forcing the wealthy and the corporations to start paying their share.

This second path is the one which motivates this volume. Faced with a massive property tax shift from business properties onto homeowners, Californians turned to Proposition 13 only after the state's legislature failed to pass a compromise version of the Tax Justice Act — featured in *New Directions* — on the last day of its 1977 sessions. This is one of the most important lessons of Proposition 13: the success of Jarvis and his right wing allies in capturing the tax issue in California came only after efforts to achieve a progressive solution to taxpayer grievances fell short. Obviously, the best way to oppose Proposition 13 and its offspring is by providing a better solution to taxpayer grievances and by providing it first.

A Comprehensive Approach

Of course, in order to provide better solutions we must know what the problems are and how to go about solving them. Our search for the answers to these questions has guided the preparation of this volume. We have attempted to be comprehensive without pretending to be exhaustive. There is no one problem, nor is there any single solution. Each state and locality is different, posing its own problems which require their own solutions.

The list of topics covered in the volume's twelve sections and twenty-five chapters reflects this diversity of concerns. The property tax receives extensive treatment because it is the focal point of the tax revolt in so many states. Other sections focus on sales taxes, user charges, personal and corporate income taxes, and taxing natural resources. Proposition 13 and efforts to impose tax and spending limitations on state and local government are the subjects of two separate chapters (Chapter 5 and Chapter 24, respectively).

Each chapter uses a variety of sources from news clippings and campaign flyers to government reports and original articles to identify the critical problem areas which are generating taxpayer anger and to offer real solutions. We have attempted as best we could — and as available materials permitted — to combine the technical side of understanding taxes with the political and practical. For ultimately there is no other way to achieve a fair tax system than to make good tax policies into good politics as well.

While tax reform comes in many shapes and sizes, there nonetheless are recurring themes. In this first section of the reader, two articles present some of the basic standards or principles commonly used by tax reformers to diagnose what's wrong with our tax laws and prescribe remedies. The basic concepts they define and explain surface repeatedly throughout the volume.

In the first article — **Rules for Reform: Tax Policy in a Nutshell** — Robert Stumberg outlines five basic goals of tax reformers, with fairness heading the list, followed by comprehensiveness, neutrality, simplicity, and accountability. He likens the battle to achieve these goals to a shell game in which the "pea" is who pays and who doesn't and the goal of the opponents is to hide the pea from taxpayers through diversionary tactics.

In the second article — **What is Fair Taxation?** — Robert Brandon, Jonathan Rowe, and Thomas Stanton expand upon Mr. Stumberg's discussion of fairness — the notion that taxes should reflect the ability to pay — as a goal of tax reform. They trace some of its historical roots and take on the competing arguments and principles frequently advanced by its opponents. They conclude that "Despite the long tradition of the ability to pay principle, the lip service we pay to it, and its supposed embodiment in the federal income tax, the tax system we have today falls far short of this ideal."

One word of caution is in order concerning the "language" introduced in this section. Concepts such as progressivity, regressivity, neutrality, and so on are tools which help us understand our tax system and how it should be changed. However, in the political arena they need to be translated into terms which define issues clearly and concretely for tax reformers and taxpayers alike. We need to talk less about "progressivity" and "regressivity" and more about "who pays and who doesn't."

CHAPTER 1

Principles of Tax Reform

Tax Shifts and the Tax Revolt

The issue of "who pays" is another common theme that unites the varied sections of this volume. It is the critical issue which allows us to capture the tax debate from the right wing proponents of Proposition 13 and its offspring.

It is the one issue they don't want to talk about. And for good reason. The evidence is overwhelming that the real origins of the tax revolt can be found in massive tax shifts from business onto homeowners. As articles by Dean Tipps in Chapter 5 and Bob Kuttner in Chapter 2 and Chapter 5 demonstrate, the tax revolt in California was preceded by just such a shift, as was the case in Idaho, the only other state to actually adopt a Proposition 13 of its own in 1978. Moreover, these shifts are by no means unique to California and Idaho.

The devices which have generated these tax shifts are varied, and their effects are not limited to the property tax. The chapters of this volume chronicle the many ways in which wealthy corporations and individuals avoid paying their fair share while average taxpayers — working families, senior citizens, the poor, homeowners, renters, family farmers, and small business owners — are forced to shoulder more and more of the load.

Loopholes and "incentives", lax enforcement of corporate tax codes and other devices for shifting tax burdens are wrong not just because they allow the corporations to pay less, but because they force the rest of us to pay more. This message is the key to converting taxpayer anger over rising taxes into a political movement for progressive change.

New Directions for the '80s

Proposition 13 clearly was a major victory for conservative right wing forces in California and nationally. But aggressive campaigns are being mounted by citizen coalitions in many states and cities which could turn around the political momentum created by Proposition 13.

These campaigns have succeeded in putting the right wing and the corporations on the defensive by focusing taxpayer anger on who is responsible for their unfair tax burdens — the wealthy corporations and individuals who aren't paying their fair share.

But they aren't just defining the problem, they're also providing solutions. Their answer to rising homeowner taxes is to give tax relief to homeowners, not the corporations. Their answer to increasing tax burdens on renters is to give tax relief to tenants, not landlords. Their answer to unfair taxes on family farmers and small business is to tailor tax reforms to meet their needs, not those of the Fortune 500. Their answer to unresponsive government and corporate bureaucracies is not less government, but rather better, more democratic government. And their answer to corporate pleas for new tax abatements and incentives is to reduce taxes for the average taxpayer by forcing wealthy corporations and individuals to start paying their fair share.

The tax battles of 1978-9 were only the first skirmishes in a long war which will continue so long as taxpayers continue to be victimized by unfair taxes. The tax revolt is only one expression of the struggle of people to regain control over their lives. As with this larger struggle, the tax revolt will take a reactionary or a progressive direction depending upon who succeeds in organizing it.

The challenge facing tax reformers is to tell taxpayers the truth about taxes, to provide real solutions to their grievances, and to organize taxpayer protest movements around solutions which encompass working families, senior citizens, minority communities, homeowners, renters, the poor, family farmers, and small business owners.

If this second Conference book on state and local tax reform aids this cause, it will have served its purpose well.

Rules for Reform: Tax Policy in a Nutshell

By Robert Stumberg

I. Introduction: The Tax Reform Shell Game

In the hands of a skilled con artist, three nutshells and a pea become a game of chance. "Keep your eye on the pea." The pea, of course, is hidden. The movement of the shells is rapid and disguised by slight-of-hand. The goal of the con artist is confusion, forcing the victim to guess, increasing the odds to 2 to 1 (assuming the pea is still there).

A. Confusion as a Political Strategy

Ninety-five percent of the families in Massachusetts would reap an income tax reduction if the state shifted from a proportional (flat rate) to progressive (graduated tax table) income tax.[1] A constitutional amendment to implement this tax burden shift was placed before the voters in 1972, an amendment that would have reduced income taxes for all families then earning below $23,000. Such a tangible economic reward should have triggered a landslide for tax reform.

But the opponents knew that if they used the shell game strategy, they could shift the odds against tax reform simply by injecting two more issues.

The two issues thrown in by opponents were: (1) progressive rates mean higher taxes (which was true, but only for 5 percent of the taxpayers), and (2) big spending is the real issue — tax reform just feeds the appetite of government for more taxes.[2] To illustrate, an anti-reform poster read:

> **DON'T BE FOOLED**—The graduated Income Tax is just another tax increase. It means much more for them and less for you . . . again!

The author is deputy director of the Harrison Institute for Public Law, Georgetown University Law Center. Work on this article was funded by a National Science Foundation grant entitled "Implementation of Urban Policy Through Law." (APR-7604329)

Before the election, a tax reform coalition poll showed that 90 percent of the people felt that a progressive tax was more fair.[3] But so many people felt that they had to choose between tax reform and spending reduction, that a majority voted against the proposal, apparently as an expression of protest against spending. The Massachusetts election is a textbook example of how opponents of change can use confusion as a political strategy.

B. How to Play the Game

This is a simple article about a complex subject. It does not consider such important issues as media campaigns or organizing strategies for tax reform. This article is a summary of concepts which are useful in reducing confusion about tax reform. It is, in effect, a set of general rules for playing (or, more accurately, avoiding) the shell game.

(1) Rule No. 1: Understand the Object of the Game (Shifting the Tax Burden)

The effect of any tax change is to shift the burden of paying taxes from one group to another. If a few people pay less, the rest will have to pay more. For example, the job of a corporate tax lobbyist is to promote passage of exemptions, deductions, lower rates, etc. which reduce the corporations' tax burden. If these changes occur, however, the cost of government is not reduced—someone else will have to make up the difference.

The object of the tax game is to shift the burden of who pays and who does not. The corporate lobbyist and tax reformer alike are out to shift the tax burden. The difference is that the shifts resulting from real tax reform promote broad public interests rather than narrow private interests—shifts which promote such goals as fairness, comprehensiveness and neutrality. Tax reform also promotes other goals which are essential if taxpayers are to understand where the tax burdens actually lie. All too often the tax laws are so complicated or their impact so disguised that the real burdens are obscured.

(2) Rule No. 2: Keep Your Eye on the Pea (Tax Reform Goals in a Nutshell)

The reasons for shifting the tax burden one direction or another can themselves lead to confusion. The labels are vague (e.g., "fairness") and there are different reasons for tax reform which sometimes compete with one another. A clever opponent will use these sources of confusion to frustrate tax reform.

The tax reformer can counter potential confusion by identifying these multiple goals of tax reform and offering a common-sense definition for each. The following are offered as one way to portray tax reform goals:

(a) *Fairness* is defined in terms of people's ability to pay. A tax can be linked to ability to pay through rates which are "progressive." As a taxpayer's wealth or income increases, each incremental or progressive amount is taxed at a higher rate. Progressive rates serve a number of economic objectives such as income transfer and economic trend stabilization.

(b) *Comprehensiveness* refers to the number of taxpayers or the amount of wealth, income or consumption being taxed: in other words, the "tax base." The degree of comprehensiveness of a tax base has a direct bearing on a tax rate. The broader the base, the lower the rate necessary to yield a certain amount of revenue. A "loophole" occurs when the tax base is reduced (*e.g.*, someone's income is excluded or deducted) and the rate must go up to yield the same amount of revenue as before the loophole occured.

(c) *Neutrality* is the goal of evenhanded treatment of taxpayers in similar situations. It throws light not only on the fact that there are different tax burdens, but the reasons for the differences as well. Property tax assessments are often attacked on this ground for being at different percentages of real value for no justifiable reason.

(d) *Simplicity* is a goal with two dimensions. One is mechanical—the ease of administration which makes a tax cheaper to both pay and collect. The other aspect is psychological; public confidence and compliance depends upon understanding how the tax system works. The greater the complexity, the less the understanding.

(e) *Accountability* is a goal for how tax laws are made. It means that the tax system should be answerable to the people in terms of notice when tax decisions are implicitly or explicitly being made. The public should be notified when the tax burden goes up, even though rates remain the same (as in the case of increasing property assessments). Accountability means putting a price tag on the special treatment given to any group so that a tax break can be subjected to cost/benefit analysis.

(3) Rule No. 3: Play One Game at a Time (Tax Reform vs. Spending Limitation)

When opponents of tax reform in Massachusetts wanted to confuse the issue, they asserted that tax reform would divert attention from putting a lid on excess spending. Spending and budgetary accountability of public officials is obviously a popular and timely reform issue. But these two concerns should not and need not be played off against each other. The first step toward avoiding civil war among citizen activists is to recognize the differences between fundamental issues.

Equity of the tax system is a concern no matter how much is being spent. The demand for public services and the crush of inflation guarantee that taxes will remain a significant percentage of family budgets. And no matter how much is being spent, the tax shift game will continue and its losers will pay higher taxes even if the services they are paying for stay the same or are reduced. The real questions will always be those posed by the above goals: Is the tax base fair? comprehensive? neutral? simple? accountable?

Most of the confusion comes when spending reformers seek to control the size of the state budget by first reducing tax revenues, as in the case of Proposition 13. The purpose of such tax limitations is not tax structure reform. It is tax reduction.

Tax *reform* may result in tax reduction for some people. (Example: The proposed Massachusetts graduated income tax would have reduced the total tax burden of 95% of the people and increased it for 5%.) But when a tax burden is shifted due to a tax *limitation*, someone else may have to pick up the tab. Tax limitation in one area, however, may result in undesirable tax shifts. (Example: Limitation of the property tax burden may force a state to increase a sales tax, an even greater percentage of which is carried by the poor.) Any time a limitation is placed on a single tax, a shift in the overall tax burden can be expected even if spending is also limited by the same amount of revenue loss. And when spending through the appropriated budget is limited, it is more obvious who will suffer from the resulting "spending shift".

II. Tax Reform and the Tax Burden

The impact of tax reform should be a shift of tax burdens among taxpayers in the direction of a broader tax base, more progressive rates, etc. Creation of a loophole also causes a shift of tax burden, but in an undersirable direction. Because the concept of tax burden is the crux of the tax reform debate, it is important to discuss the mechanics of burden shifting.

A. Nominal vs. Effective Tax Rates

Tax rates are not necessarily a good indicator of the kind of comparative burden a particular tax places on the individual taxpayer. The stated rates in a statute are referred to as "nominal" because they exist in name only. The rate which a taxpayer should be most concerned about is referred to as the "effective" rate. The difference between the two can be shown by calculating the actual tax liability and then figuring the percentage of total income or wealth represented by that tax liability. The effective rate can be lowered by any reduction in the income or wealth by which the rate is multiplied.

Example: Assume a nominal income tax rate of 10 percent (a flat or proportional rate). If there is a standard deduction of $5,000, the effective rate for different income levels would be as follows:

$ 6,000 income . . . . rate = 1.6 percent
$25,000 income . . . . rate = 4.0 percent
$55,000 income . . . . rate = 9.0 percent

The effect of the deducton for all income groups in this example is to reduce the effective rate. If additional deductions were factored in, they would also reduce the effective rate, but only for those income levels receiving the deduction. Preferential treatment of capital gains doesn't benefit most wage earners and deductions for interest payments are not available to taxpayers who do not itemize deductions.

Changes in the effective rate can be used as an indicator of a tax shift. For example, if a new deduction for solar equipment is enacted, it is an expense which relatively higher-income taxpayers can afford. Use of the deduction will reduce their effective income tax rate. The tax shift away from those upper-income taxpayers can be expressed in terms of the percentage change in their effective rate. If a taxpayer's effective rate drops from 9 to 6 percent, it represents a 33 1/3 percent drop in the rate.

B. Passthrough of the Tax Burden

Who pays a tax? Quite possibly, it is not the person or corporation which pays the government, at least in the final analysis. Take the corporate income tax, for example. The corporation may be able to pass through the tax, either to the public which buys its products or uses its services, or to its stockholders, by reducing the dividends they receive. Who pays the property tax on farms? Quite likely, the consumers of farm products. The term "tax incidence" refers to the actual burden a tax imposes, and whether this burden can be passed through to others.

As a matter of economics, a tax is not necessarily passed through. It depends on a number of factors including the market power of individual firms and the extent of demand for the goods or services which "bear" the additional cost of the tax.

Proposition 13 can be used to illustrate the importance of passthroughs in cumulative burden analysis. Approximately 25 percent of the rent dollar goes toward paying the property tax. An across the board reduction in property tax results in a savings for landlords. While there is an incentive to pass through a tax cost, there is no incentive to pass through a tax saving. Although tenants indirectly pay the property tax (housing is an inelastic package of goods and services),

few of them will receive the benefits of the tax reduction. Furthermore, if the property tax reduction in California ultimately results in the increase of other taxes, tenants will bear a double cumulative burden: a savings not realized plus the later tax increase.

Business taxpayers sometimes argue that since taxes of business may be passed through to consumers, businesses should not be taxed at all. But consider the alternatives. In the course of producing goods and services, businesses—like individuals—benefit from public services. To the extent prices reflect the cost to businesses of those services (that is, taxes), then that cost is eventually picked up by the consumers of the goods and services they produce. Thus, the passthrough of taxes is no different than the passthrough of other production costs for capital, materials, labor, etc. The alternative is to ask the general taxpayer to bear the cost of public services benefitting businesses through higher taxes, thereby subsidizing the price of goods and services to their consumers or the profits of business.

C. Exporting Taxes

It is becoming more and more popular among state and local officials to export their tax burden. This means the taxation of non-residents directly or indirectly. *Examples:* non-resident income tax (frequently called a "commuter tax"), parking lot taxes, hotel and resort sales taxes, and severance taxes on natural resources which are themselves exported from the state. Recently, the development of casino gambling has generated interest because the gambling tax burdens are substantially exported.

D. The Burden of Inflation

There is an inflation-induced burden injected into most taxes. This results in a comparative tax burden shift when the wealth being taxed (especially real property) is inflating in value faster than the general rate of inflation. With progressive rate income taxes, inflation not only increases the taxable income (while not increasing purchasing power), it escalates the taxpayer into a higher tax bracket.

The tax sting from inflation can be removed. In the case of income taxes, proposals for "indexing" at the state and federal levels would reduce either taxable income or the tax table rates to compensate for the past years rate of inflation. With property taxes, the tax rate can be calculated to produce the prior year's level of revenue as is done in the District of Columbia. As assessments increase, the tax rate automatically decreases. It then requires an act of the legislative body to increase the rate level above this level.

E. The Cumulative Burden on Individual Taxpayers

The buck literally does stop with the individual taxpayer. There is no one to whom the individual can pass through the tax burden. The real tax burden for the individual taxpayer, therefore, is not only the taxes directly paid by the individual. It also includes all of the taxes indirectly paid through the cost of goods and services.

This cumulative burden must be carefully considered when evaluating a tax reform proposal. For ex-

8

ample, consider a proposal which would shift future tax increases from individual income taxpayers to a state franchise tax. Some of the business franchises in the state probably do business with people from other states. Part of the tax would be exported along with the goods and services. But a great deal of business is done within the state, with the tax being passed right back to the individuals in the form of higher prices. The point of this example is simply that a proposal which may look like it causes a progressive tax shift, may in fact fall short of its promise.

Another crucial factor influencing the cumulative burden is the the way in which one tax may affect another through credits, exemptions or deductions. This is sometimes referred to as "tax interaction."

Example: The federal income tax allows a deduction for certain state taxes paid, including the property tax. Proposition 13 resulted in a property tax reduction in California, but it also took away a federal income tax deduction for those taxpayers. For a California taxpayer in the 25 percent federal tax bracket, a federal tax increase of 25 cents must be subtracted from every dollar of property tax saved in order to calculate the "cumulative" impact of Proposition 13.

III. Tax Reform Goals: A Closer Look

A. Fairness and Progressivity

Ability to pay is usually thought of in terms of progressive tax rates. Actually, the *effective* rate of a tax can be progressive even though the nominal rate is not. This was illustrated earlier. This kind of progressivity is an increase in the tax rate (effective or nominal) in relation to increments of that tax base (more income or more wealth).

A tax can also be considered progressive in terms of the cumulative tax burdens of rich people compared to poor people. A sales tax on luxury items would be a progressive tax in terms of cumulative tax burdens. So too would be a general sales tax which exempts staple items like food and medicine.

The same factors can make a tax regressive, that is, a tax which takes a higher percentage of income from low-income people than from higher-income people. A sales tax only on staple items is an example. A tax with a flat (or proportional nominal) rate, or even with a progressive nominal rate, can be made regressive if deductions and exemptions are only available to upper-income taxpayers.

There are important policies regarding progressive rates that have to do primarily with concepts of social and economic justice. There are also some negative criticisms leveled at progressive rates. Both of these perspectives are briefly summarized below.

(1) Social/Economic Policies Supported by Progressivity

Minimized Sacrifice. This is the essence of ability to pay: The last dollar earned theoretically means less to a rich person than to a poor person, and hence is more appropriate for taxation. It is also argued that those with greater income actually benefit from the governmental and economic system to a greater degree.

Life Cycle Adjustment of Tax Burdens. Except for the very wealthy, the income or wealth of families usually reaches a peak and subsequently declines. Retirement comes immediately to mind, but the early death of wage earner, unemployment, disability, and divorce are all everyday occurrences which adversely affect the ability to pay taxes. Progressive taxes not only increase tax burdens when the ability to pay increases, but reduces them when it declines.

Economic Equalization. Progressive tax rates, if still effective after all preferences have their impact, can redistribute income or wealth by having the wealthy shoulder more of the tax burden, and by rechanneling tax revenues by transfer payments such as welfare and housing subsidies.

Decision-Making Equalization. Great concentrations of wealth tend to concentrate political influence as well. It is argued that if the tax policy supports economic equalization, it will promote political equalization as well.

Economic Trend Stabilization. Progressive taxes are sensitive to economic conditions in the following manner: During times of depression, as incomes drop, the tax rates for individuals fall as well. This leaves taxpayers with a greater percentage of take-home income for purposes of consumption. During times of inflation, as incomes are inflated, higher rates serve as an economic depressant, and provide the government with more revenue to meet its inflated costs.

In short, progressivity is tax policy shorthand for a cluster of policies in addition to promoting fairness (defined as the ability to pay). Tax reformers may find it advantageous to abandon the shorthand at times and use the underlying policy rationales for which their proposals stand.

(2) Negative Factors Regarding Progressivity

Complexity. The refinements necessary for equitable and neutral tax classifications, time periods and income definitions tend to make progressive taxes difficult to administer and understand compared to flat rate or proportional taxes.

Inflation Windfalls. As noted before, inflation not only increases taxable income (without increasing purchasing power), it boosts the taxpayer into higher brackets. The gradual effect is to undermine progressivity as lower-income taxpayers are pushed into higher brackets. More taxpayers fall into the highest bracket after which all additional income is taxed at the same rate. This problem can be cured by indexing the tax rates to compensate for inflation.

Political Domination. An argument against progressivity is that a majority of taxpayers set the rates for a minority (those in the highest income brackets). The Massachusetts rejection of progressive income tax rates cited earlier suggests this argument should not be given too much weight.

Impaired Economic Productivity. Critics argue that progressive rates impair capital formation by reducing the amount of income which can be saved. It also increases risk in business ventures by reducing the estimated possible gain when compared to the potential for loss.

B. Comprehensiveness

Generally speaking, taxes are levied on wealth, income, or consumption (transactions). As the base of wealth, income or consumption expands, the tax rate necessary to raise a certain amount of revenue decreases. Conversely, when the tax base is eroded, the tax rates must increase to keep revenue constant. The goal of comprehensiveness is a basic commitment to keep the tax base as broad as possible so that the rates can be kept as low as possible.

Erosion of the tax base can be described in several ways. The categories below are the technical means by which a "loophole" occurs.

(1) Exclusions and Exemptions

Before a tax base can be taxed, it must be built. That requires a basic definition of income which is a subjective judgement. Sometimes exclusions or exemptions from income are not even listed in the tax laws.

With an income tax, exclusion is defined as an item not included in gross taxable income (such as social security, welfare payments, or imputed income from taxpayers' assets like the homeowner's "rent"). Property tax exemptions are typically property owned by charitable organizations, churches, and governments. The sales tax base frequently is reduced by exemptions of specific commodities and services from taxation.

(2) Deductions and Credits

With an income tax, deductions constitute subtractions from gross income once it is calculated, such as charitable contributions, major medical expenses, business expenses, depreciation/depletion, and business investment. Property tax deductions (or credits) are usually incentive for special purposes, such as rehabilitation. The foremost reform issue raised here, aside from erosion of the tax base, is that deductions are available to some (wealthy people and large businesses) and not others. Furthermore, when tax rates are progressive, deductions bestow a greater dollar benefit on high bracket than on low bracket taxpayers.

Credits, dollar-for-dollar, are an even greater tax break because they are subtracted from the actual tax, rather than from taxable income. However, they avoid two problems frequently encountered with deductions: taxpayers need not itemize deductions to enjoy the benefit of a credit, and the value of the credit is not dependent on the tax bracket of the taxpayer.

(3) Differential Tax Rates

Differential rate issues really concern the class being taxed and why it deserves a lower or higher rate. The most notorious income tax "class" is capital gains. Property tax classes are usually governed by the state constitution. The Tennessee constitution, for example, provides different rates for utility, industrial, commercial, farm and home property. It could well be argued that such differentials constitute an expansion of the former tax base — not an erosion. (It is important to note that rate differentials are meaningless if assessment practices vary.) Sales tax rate differentials are pervasive — each commodity having its own tax niche.

(4) Timing of Taxation

The comprehensiveness of the tax base is a function of time as well as scope: There are many postponement devices in income tax laws which permit income earned in one period to be taxed in a later period. This has numerous "erosion" consequences. First, because of gross income levels, the taxpayer may be in a lower tax bracket when the income is finally taxed. Secondly, a tax deferral is tantamount to an interest free loan obtainable at the borrower's will. Thirdly, the impact of inflation erodes the value to the government of the taxes deferred. Timing devices which tend to erode the tax base include "carry forward" accounting procedures, income averaging, non-realization of appreciation prior to transfer, tax free exchanges and conversion of assets.

The categories listed above help identify when the tax base has eroded from the high plateau which theorists refer to as the "comprehensive tax base" (CTB). There are often significant, even compelling policy reasons for eroding great canyons in the comprehensive tax base. Nonetheless, the abolition of even the most sacred tax preferences, despite their appeal, is a major thrust of tax reform.

The result would be much lower rates, and surplus revenues to legislate direct subsidies for the purposes formerly served by tax preferences should such subsidies prove justified. Discussion of tax loopholes usually focuses on the policies behind the particular provision in question. But even seemingly valid preferences may be added until the whole structue is too cumersome and fiscally weak.

Tax base arguments for tax reform do not have to be followed to a logical conclusion to be useful in everyday practice however. They can be used instead to establish a norm: the desirability of the most comprehensive tax base possible. Then, basic rules can be set for departing from that norm (to be applied strictly): (1) any departure from the comprehensive base must serve a major national or state objective; (2) the tax mechanism must be the most efficient method of achieving the objective; and (3) the cost/effectiveness of any departure must be subjected to periodic legislative review.

C. Neutrality

Like comprehensiveness, neutrality is a goal which opposes special treatment for any group, but on equitable as opposed to economic grounds. It is simply a recognition that beyond ability to pay, there are few, if any, "fair" reasons for the tax system to give favored status to any taxpayer. This goal of similar treatment for similar taxpayers is often called "horizontal equity" (as opposed to "verticle equity" which refers to the ability to pay).

It is important to note that horizontal equity problems can result not only from special treatment knowingly given certain taxpayers, but from faulty administration. The most flagrant example is tax assessment practices which allow some neighborhoods to be taxed according to recent values, while others are taxed at values which are several years old. (This is distinct from flat-out bias in assessment of different neighborhoods.)

D. Simplicity

The goal of simplicity goes hand-in-hand with neutrality. The reason is that most of the complicated provisions of a tax code are needed to ensure neutrality in the application of special preferences. Complexity becomes the telltale shadow of special preferences; its presence breeds cynicism among the majority of citizens who are not affected by the provisions directly in question. A recent commentator put it this way:

> ...the public's impression of the tax system results not only from its impact on them personally, but from what they hear and read about its impact on others. Thus the integrity and fairness of the tax system is more significant than the substantial revenues it collects; any weakening of the fabric affects the attitude of the public toward the entire system of government.[4]

Tax complexity also has tangible costs of administration. First, it simply takes more auditors to oversee provisions which are more complicated. Secondly, it takes more legal and accounting services for taxpayers to comply with complicated tax laws. Thirdly, the more complicated the laws are, the more likelihood there is of taxpayer error, or even fraud disguised as error. The final cost is perhaps the most serious: Given our voluntary system of assessment and payment (at least with income taxes), a breakdown in public understanding of and confidence in the tax system can mean a breakdown in compliance.

E. Accountability

Accountability in taxation is possible only when taxpayers have information about the actual impact of the tax system on themselves and other taxpayers who are treated differently. Without full disclosure about comprehensiveness, the real degree of progressivity, and shifts in the cumulative tax burden, voters have no way of holding their legislators accountable. Moreover, without such information, legislators themselves cannot make knowing decisions about tax policy.

Several accountability mechanisms have been mentioned before, including the "truth in taxation" laws which disclose hidden increases due to inflation. These laws automatically reduce the tax rates to yield prior levels of revenue. The legislature must then vote in order to increase the rates. Inflation indexing for the income tax has a similar effect.

One of the most important accountability mechanisms is disclosure of the revenue loss caused by exemptions, deductions, and other special preferences. This loss was well named a "tax expenditure" by Stanley S. Surrey, who coined the phrase during his tenure as Treasury Assistant Secretary for Tax Policy under the Johnson administration:

> the phrase, "tax expenditures" (illustrates that) ...provisions of the federal income tax containing special exemptions, exclusions, deductions, and other tax benefits (are) really methods of providing governmental financial assistance. These special provisions (are) not part of the structure required for the income tax itself, but (are) instead Government expenditures made through the tax system. They (are) similar in purpose, therefore, to the direct expenditures listed in the regular budget. But since they provided their assistance through the route of tax reduction rather than direct aid, I called them "tax expenditures."[5]

Surrey's thesis is that the federal (and likewise any state) tax system consists of two parts: one part necessary to implement a tax on individuals or business; the other designed to provide government assistance through the tax system instead of through direct subsidies. Hence, in addition to the government's program budget, there is an implicit tax expenditure budget.

> "It is true that these provisions exist side by side, or rather are intertwined, and without guidance cannot be told apart. The Tax Expenditure Budget provides that guidance, for it seeks to separate the apparatus of expenditure policy from the inherent structure of the income tax itself...tax reform is quite another matter if it means examining a program of financial assistance to a particular group to decide whether that assistance should be given, in what amount, and on what terms. It really is not tax reform but 'expenditure reform,' and the issues and answers to be explored both involve different premises and require different experts...[6]

The tax expenditure budget to which Surrey refers must be extracted by the tax reformer—whether it pertains to only selected provisions, or whether it encompasses an entire tax code. Once tax expenditures are identified, the difficult task of analysis begins. The principal questions involve:

- whether the tax assistance is necessitated by local, state or national priorities
- if so, whether tax assistance is more efficient than direct assistance, taking into account complexity of administration
- if direct assistance is most efficient, how should the program be structured; how would it be integrated into existing executive departments; and what kind of legislative committee strategy would be required to achieve the switch from tax assistance to direct assistance
- if a tax expenditure is most efficient, whether its effectiveness can be evaluated on a continuing basis to assure that it is accomplishing the purpose for which it was enacted (and, indeed, whether that purpose is still a priority)

IV. Conclusion

Tax reform is complex, which makes it vulnerable to opponents who use confusion as a political strategy. Tax reformers need to develop their proposals in a way which is capable of explanation in terms which are both basic and systematic. The following three "rules" have been suggested as an antidote to confusion over tax policy:

- Focus the debate in terms of who is shifting the tax burden onto whom.

- Explain the need for tax reform in terms of the most basic and common-sense goals possible: fairness (ability to pay), comprehensiveness, neutrality, simplicity, and accountability.

- Distinguish between tax reform and tax or spending limitation. The "pea" in the tax reform game is "who pays and who doesn't." The issue of government spending is a different game altogether.

In the final analysis, whether tax reform has democratic impact will depend not only on the economics of changes in the tax system, but upon whether citizens understand and participate in the debate.

Footnotes

[1]Sclar, Behr, Torto and Edid, "Taxes, Taxpayers and Social Change: The Political Economy of the State Sector," in *New Directions in State and Local Tax Reform*, Jonathan Rowe, ed., Conference on Alternative State and Local Public Policies, Washington, 1977, p. 12.

[2]*Id.*, p. 20.

[3]*Id.*, p. 21.

[4]Roberts, *et al.*, A Report on Complexity and the Income Tax, 27 Tax Law Review 325 at 328 (1972).

[5]Surry, *Pathways to Tax Reform*, Harvard University Press (Cambridge, Mass. 1973), p. vii.

[6]*Id.*, p. 31.

What is Fair Taxation?

The principle for allocation of the tax burden that the authors choose is ability-to-pay. People and corporations should contribute to the commonwealth in the proportion that they are able. This view is neither radical nor novel. No less an apostle of free enterprise than Adam Smith argued in 1776 that "the subjects of every state ought to contribute towards the support of the government as nearly as possible in proportion to their respective abilities."

Smith pointed to a basis for the ability-to-pay principle that isn't always remembered. "The expence of government to the individuals of a great nation," he said, "is like the expence of management to the joint tenants of a great estate, who are all obliged to contribute in proportion to their respective interests in the estate." The more one has, Smith was saying, the bigger one's stake in the social order, and therefore the more expense of maintaining and protecting that order the taxpayer should bear.

The ability-to-pay principle is the simplest and most direct. Thinkers in all ages have espoused it and without pretending to clairvoyance, we would venture that to most people "tax justice" means taxation according to ability-to-pay.

Opponents of this principle advance others on which a tax system could be based. Some of these merit attention and are discussed below. But the objections most commonly raised are little more than apologies of the wealthy in the guise of argument. For example, they will try to debunk taxation according to ability as a "soak-the-rich" scheme, yet most tax reformers are moved not by a desire to hurt anyone, rich or otherwise, but rather by a desire to protect and do justice to those less well-off. "If anyone bears less than his fair share of the burden," wrote John Stuart Mill in his *Principles of Political Economy*, "some other person must suffer more than his share, and the alleviation to the one is not, on the average, so great a good to him as the increased pressure upon the other is an evil."

Opponents of tax reform also try to tarnish the ability-to-pay ideal by twisting it into a "penalty on success." The suggestion is that taxes might cause the poor beleaguered leaders of business and industry to lose heart, causing free enterprise and the ship of state to founder as a result. The life styles of those who make such claims, opulent even by America's habit—let alone the world's—leave one wondering where and how their success has been penalized. Sociologists tell us, moreover, what we already know, that beyond a certain level of income people strive more for power and prestige than for the last dollar. And even if taxes did clip a bit the ambition of the few at the top, the effect could be to open up more opportunities for those further down, making the whole system more competitive, open, and democratic.

An alternative to the ability-to-pay principle worthy of more respect is called the benefits principle. Under this theory, people should pay taxes only to the extent that they benefit from public expenditures. The theory is not without surface appeal. "Why should I pay school taxes when my kids are grown up and married?" some people ask; or, "Why should I pay for libraries when I buy my own books?"

In practice the benefits principle has less to recommend it. Trying to determine exactly who benefits from a given public expenditure is a task to which medieval theologians might well have turned. For example, even people with no children benefit significantly from a good local school system when the time comes to sell their home—as real estate brokers are only too well aware.

Besides, if Adam Smith was correct that a person's over-all stake in the system—his or her income and wealth—is the true measure of benefit from government, then the circle comes full turn, right back to ability-to-pay.

This is not to say that the benefits principle is completely useless. It is used today when property owners are charged "special assessments" for particular items—such as sidewalks and sewers—which uniquely benefit their own property, and special taxes or service charges might well be levied upon such groups as commuters who use a city's streets and other facilities but do not help support them, and upon sports promoters whose functions require extra police protection. The benefits principle has a place, in special charges for special service, but as a touchstone for the tax system it will not stand up.

In recent years a new element has entered the tax debate, almost eclipsing all others. It is called economic policy. The federal government has seized upon the tax system as a way to manipulate economic activity, heating it up, cooling it down, encouraging investment in this industry or that. Yoking the tax system to economic planning and policy has had a number of regrettable effects:

1. It has completely sidetracked discussion of taxes from matters of fairness and justice to those of economic policy, real or fabricated.

2. It has made tax matters hopelessly complex, beyond the grasp of most taxpayers and, in fact, of most representatives in Congress. This has stripped the public of any effective voice on taxes, while enhancing the power of a handful of congressmen, senators, and executive branch officials.

3. It has made the tax system even more vulnerable to loopholes

and exemptions. Business pressure groups who would not have a prayer of justifying loopholes on equity grounds have been only too ready to cast them in terms of "boosting the economy." A perpetual run on the Treasury has emerged, with one industry after another arguing that it adds to the Gross National Product, and that it too is therefore deserving of some favor. The larger the industry, the more forcefully it can make such claims, and the tax laws that ensue confirm again the old saw that the richer you are, the richer you become.

The result of turning taxes over to the economic policymakers and those who use economic policy to justify their own tax breaks has been a multibillion-dollar under-the-table subsidy system, largely for the rich and unneedy. These subsidies are often called "tax expenditures," since they are funds the public has given up just as much as if they had been collected and spent. Those who receive these tax subsidies greatly prefer them to outright grants. Lawmakers review their above-board expenditures every year or every few years, and while the probe is not always thorough, the special benefits at least see the light of day. By contrast, once a tax loophole is enacted, it lies buried in the tax laws until some inquisitive lawmaker troubles to question it—which in most cases is never.

There are three additional grounds on which taxes—or the failure to tax—are sometimes justified. Some taxes, called "sumptuary," are supposed to discourage people from certain behavior. In the past these reflected rigid moral judgments against such things as smoking and drinking. More recently they have been proposed for social concerns more broadly defined, such as pollution and the excessive use of automobiles. Taxes on cigarettes and liquor exist in virtually every state, and considering the revenues they generate — over $4 billion in 1971 — it is worth noting that the danger of taxing social ills is that government can come to depend on the

revenues and thus encourage the continuation of such activities.

A related reason some taxes are imposed is to give the government a special handle for controlling certain illegal activities, or for simply gathering data. The U.S. Supreme Court has greatly curtailed the former, but as to the latter, many states impose land transfer taxes not for the revenue but so that a record of the sales price will appear on the deed.

Lawmakers and officials in particular are keen on still another way of looking at taxes—called "elasticity." A tax is "elastic" if, as economic activity expands, revenues grow even faster. Officials like elastic taxes because the bigger revenues come in without increases in the tax rate.

By the same token, however, elastic taxes dip even faster than does the economy when economic activity slows down. During the long boom following World War II this drawback was not of great concern. It appears to be looming larger now.

In general, income taxes with truly progressive rates are the most elastic taxes, because people move into higher rate brackets as their income rises. Revenues increase more rapidly than does the personal income on which it is based. Sales taxes have low elasticities, because the more people make, the smaller the portion of it they spend on goods. Property taxes are between the two, but their elasticity has been greatly underrated because assessors do not keep assessments in line with changing property values.

The benefits principle and the economic policy justifications have genuine and disinterested adherents. But the arguments are most often raised as window dressing for a rear-guard effort to erode policy decisions made long ago and stemming from traditions that go all the way back to our colonial beginnings. Early on, our nation opted for ability-to-pay as its ideal for tax justice. The earliest colonial enactments expressed it, the state constitutions adopted it directly or indirectly, and with

the Sixteenth Amendment the tradition found expression in the U.S. Constitution.

Further, when the U.S. Congress passed an income tax in keeping with the Sixteenth Amendment, it made certain the tax included progressive rates as many state income taxes had done before it. Progressive taxes are a direct attempt to embody the ability-to-pay principle. The phrase arises constantly in discussions of tax reform. We should try to understand what it means.

A tax is progressive if it is larger on those who have a lot of the thing taxed than it is on those who have a little. The more the taxpayer has, the higher the rate becomes.

The reason for progressive taxes is simple and was well stated by the political philosopher Montesquieu, writing about the tax system in ancient Athens:

It was judged that each had equal physical necessities, and that those necessities ought not to be taxed; that the useful came next, and that it ought to be taxed, but less than what was superfluous; and lastly, that the greatness of the tax on the superfluity should repress the superfluity.

In other words, as applied to income taxes, people need a certain amount to acquire their basic necessities, and this amount should not be taxed. The more they have above this amount, the less they need it, and thus the more heavily it can be taxed. It bears repeating that the intent of progressive taxes is not to afflict the rich, but rather to put the tax burden where it will cause the least suffering.

Progressivity should not just be measured in terms of income. A property tax is progressive if it taxes people with lots of property at higher rates than people with little. It is common, however, to rate the progressivity of taxes solely in terms of how the taxes affect taxpayers at different income levels. This is a major blind spot in our thinking about taxes and is a reason why wealth taxes have made so little headway in the United States.

The federal income tax illutrates a progressive rate structure. The rates on unmarried individuals (in 1974) rose from 14 percent on the first $500 of taxable income, to 15 percent on the next $500, 16 percent on the next $500, on up to 70 percent on all income over $100,000. Note that the very rich do not pay the highest rates on *all* of their income, but only on the income above set levels.

The opposite of a progressive tax is a *regressive tax*, when the less a person has of the thing taxed, the higher is the rate he pays. The social security tax is a perfect example of a regressive tax. Workers making $15,000 a year pay $825, which is 5.5 percent of their income. Meanwhile an executive pulling in $100,000 a year pays the same $825, which is less than one-tenth of 1 percent of his or her income.

A tax which is neither progressive nor regressive is called proportional. This means that everyone, rich and poor alike, is taxed at the same rate. A tax rate which goes neither up nor down, but stays the same for everyone, is called a *flat rate*.

The income tax is not the only tax that can be progressive. A sales tax could be progressive, with rates increasing according to the size of the sale. A permit fee could be progressive if the fee increased according to the size of the business applying. A property tax could be progressive, with people paying a rate that was high or low according to how much property they owned. The Australians have such a progressive property tax, and in the United States it could be the most progressive tax of all, since property ownership in this country is more concentrated among a wealthy few than is income.

Similarly, progressive rates are not the only way to make a tax progressive. A tax can also be progressive or regressive according to what it taxes. For example, a sales tax could be progressive in a rough sense if food and medicines were exempted but attorneys', real estate brokers', and other professional service fees were taxed. An income tax would be roughly progressive, even with flat rates, if workers' earnings were exempted but income from stocks, bonds, and sales of property were fully taxed.

By the same token, we should not be fooled by tax rate structures. They tell only half the story. Exemptions and loopholes are the other half. The most progressive rate structure in the world is not worth much if special provisions allow the most well-off to slip through untouched. The key is not the statutory tax rate but the rates people actually pay, taking into account all exemptions, deductions, and other special provisions. This tax rate that people actually pay is called the "effective" tax rate. As we shall see, there is a vast difference between the rates listed in the Internal Revenue Code and the effective rates that taxpayers end up paying.

Despite the long tradition of the ability-to-pay principle, the lip service we pay to it, and its supposed embodiment in the federal income tax, the tax system we have today falls far short of this ideal. Nationwide, and all taxes considered, the very wealthy pay taxes at virtually the same rate as that imposed on people far less well-off.

Three trends bring this result. First, we are replacing taxes that tend to be progressive with regressive ones; raising little from estate taxes, for example, while leaning heavily on sales and payroll taxes. Second, we are undeteriming our supposedly progressive taxes with special favors and loopholes, and third, weak administration of the tax laws further erodes progressivity.

How this happened is the subject of the next section.

We will be talking about tax "loopholes," so we should say what we mean by the term. Many tax experts insist that the term "loopholes" should refer only to unintended slips in the wording of the tax laws, slips that particular taxpayers can contrive to exploit. Special favors deliberately granted they dignify with the polite label "preferences."

We consider such niceties misleading. As we use the term and as we think most taxpayers understand it, loopholes are special provisions which depart from the normal pattern and give any taxpayer or group of taxpayers benefits not enjoyed by others. Whether enacted deliberately by Congress (as most are), or unintended gaps left by sloppy wording, they are still loopholes.

In large measure, the tax revolt has been a revolt against the property tax. The reasons are not hard to find. Residential property taxes, like sales taxes on food and medicine, tax a basic necessity of life—shelter. And they do so without regard to ability to pay, placing the heaviest burden on low and fixed income taxpayers and inflation-plagued wage earners. Exemptions and abatements gradually have converted the property tax from a broad-based wealth tax into a tax aimed increasingly at homes. This property tax shift onto homeowners has been accelerated in many states by court decisions mandating uniform valuation of all property and the dramatic inflation of home values during the 1970's.

This section provides an overview of the property tax and why it has become the focal point of a tax revolt. The first of its three chapters surveys the history of the property tax in the United States, how it works, and the basic inequities which long have made it a target of tax reformers and, more recently, of a grassroots tax revolt in California and a number of other states. The last two chapters focus in more detail on the inequities caused when the property tax is not administered fairly. Taken together, these three chapters establish a framework for the discus-

sion of California's Proposition 13 and strategies for relieving homeowners from unfair property taxes contained in section III.

Achieving a fairly administered property tax is a prerequisite to all other reforms. At first glance, the subject of property tax administration may appear dull and complicated. But it can provide a valuable banner around which to organize because it touches everyone. And the fundamental concepts of unequal assessments and uncollected taxes are something which anyone can grasp, even if the technical details are more elusive. While the reforms presented in Chapters 3 and 4 will not necessarily reduce property tax collections, they can make the tax much fairer.

Assessment Inequities

The basic problem is that the administration of the property tax falls far short of what it could be and what the law says it should be. Early in the 1970's, a survey of the members of the International Association of Assessing Officers (most of whom are assessors) found that two-thirds rated the quality of assessment administration as either "relatively poor" or "very poor".[1] If assessors themselves judge the system to be poor, there is little doubt that it is.

The Property Tax: What's Wrong With It?

By Steven Gold

Inaccurate assessments cause many types of inequities. One of the most common problems is for homes with high values to be assessed at a lower percentage of their market value than more inexpensive homes, causing the rich to bear a smaller share of the tax load than they legally should. Another situation which occurs frequently is for businesses to receive a break on their assessments.

Unequal treatment of homes can easily be documented by comparing the prices of homes which have been sold with their assessments. The same comparison can be made when business properties are sold, although such sales are much less frequent. The press often jumps to publicize the results of studies which provide evidence of inequities. Legal actions also can be pursued. The procedure for appealing overassessment is often straightforward and can be used as an organizing vehicle. Reports issued by state agencies frequently contain incriminating information about assessments which goes unnoticed. A well-informed public interest group may find it surprisingly easy to prove that serious inequities exist. Thus, this is one area in which a bad situation can often be improved by direct citizen action.

The ideal situation is for property to be assessed at a uniform percentage of its market value. The real world can never attain this ideal, but it could come much closer than it does in most places.

One reason uniform assessments are difficult to achieve is that different methods often are used to determine the value of different types of property. For homes, market values can be established fairly easily and accurately by looking at sales data for similar properties. But this "comparable sales" approach works less well for large commercial and industrial properties which change hands far less frequently than homes. For these properties, values often are determined on the basis of their current and future income-producing capability (using the "capitalization of income" approach). Thus, an important "ability to pay" component frequently is incorporated into the assessments of large commercial and industrial properties which is distinctly missing in the assessment of homes, although homes yield their owners no income out of which taxes can be paid.

Two words of caution are necessary about assessment reform. First, the property tax situation varies greatly from state to state and within states. A serious tax inequity in one city (such as overassessing

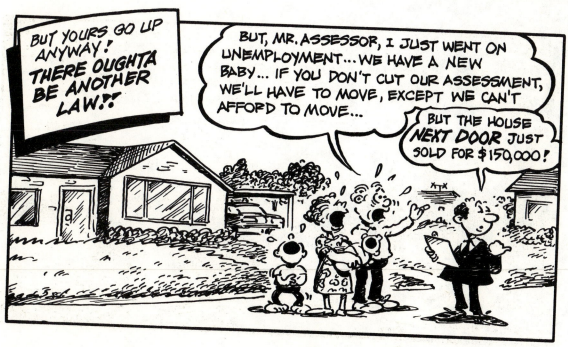

BUT YOURS GO UP ANYWAY! THERE OUGHTA BE ANOTHER LAW!!

BUT, MR. ASSESSOR, I JUST WENT ON UNEMPLOYMENT... WE HAVE A NEW BABY... IF YOU DON'T CUT OUR ASSESSMENT, WE'LL HAVE TO MOVE, EXCEPT WE CAN'T AFFORD TO MOVE...

BUT THE HOUSE NEXT DOOR JUST SOLD FOR $150,000!

property in poor neighborhoods) may not be a problem at all in a second one, where a different problem may be found instead (such as undertaxation of business property). Many assessors are competent, adequately-financed, hard-working, free from politics, and honest; but many others lack one or more of these five important characteristics.

Second, assessment reform should be viewed as only a first step in achieving a fair property tax. It is an essential step, but it is not sufficient. A fairly administered assessment system will reduce but not eliminate the regressivity of the property tax. Nor will it prevent massive shifts in the property tax burden from business properties onto homeowners when runaway inflation forces up home values. In fact, assessment reform may actually contribute to such shifts. As a result, the impact of assessment reforms must be carefully evaluated, and they should be coupled with other reforms outlined in Section III in order to assure a fair distribution of the property tax burden.

Delinquencies

Much of what has been said about assessments also applies to tax collection. Delinquencies are a serious problem in some areas but not in others. They may be a problem which no one has noticed. Community groups can mobilize to force a clamp-down on business and wealthy property owners who are tax delinquents. There is one other similiarity: if one group's taxes are too low, another's must be higher in order to recoup lost revenue. Self-interest can be a powerful organizing tool; and in these areas it is not necessary to change laws but simply to have them enforced.

Conclusion

Polls consistently rate the property tax as the most unpopular major tax in America, but progressive tax reformers should not have a knee jerk reaction in favor of reducing it across the board. One important role of the property tax in our tax system is to force those who take advantage of income tax loopholes to contribute to the cost of government. During the past decade, some of our wealthy politicians (Rockefeller, Reagan, Carter, Nixon) all found it possible in at least one year to reduce their income tax to practically nothing. But they could not avoid the property tax. This is one reason why the property tax must be retained.

The progressive approach should be to reform the property tax by improving assessment and collection procedures, opposing business exemptions and abatements that shift more and more of the property tax burden onto homeowners and renters, and helping families which need relief through circuitbreakers or similar policies. Reform may be complex but it is vital. We have only to look to California to see what can happen when progressive reforms are rejected and legitimate taxpayer grievances ignored.

[1]Richard Almy, "Rationalizing the Assessment Process", in George E. Peterson, ed., *Property Tax Reform* (The Urban Institute, 1973), p. 175.

CHAPTER 2

The Property Tax: An Overview

The five selections in this chapter provide a summary description of what the property tax is, how it got that way, what its effects are, and how experience with it has varied from state to state.

The first article, **Taxes: How They Were**, is from *Tax Politics* by Messrs. Brandon, Rowe, and Stanton. It sketches the history of the property tax from colonial times. During the 1800s the tax evolved from a partial to a general one, with the ideal of uniform treatment of all property enshrined in law though never approached in practice. In this country, the tax base eroded as most property other than land and buildings was increasingly exempted. Thus, the tax is now to a great extent a levy on real estate.[1]

The distribution of property tax burdens among income groups is the major concern of the next two articles. **Property Tax Overview**, a report from the District of Columbia Tax Revision Commission, explains why economists have altered their views on this issue (as well as discussing other aspects of the tax). It shows that regardless of what assumptions are made, the property tax is regressive for the majority of households. The next article, by the AFSCME Public Policy Department entitled **The Regressivity Issue**, points out how the deductibility of the property tax when computing income tax liability aggravates this regressivity of the property tax.

Correcting the Property Tax Record by Allen Manvel analyzes trends in the proportion of personal income going for the property tax during the 1972—77 period and demonstrates that in most states the rise in income outpaced the increase of property taxes. However, because he looks at the property tax as a whole, Mr. Manvel misses the important fact that the proportion of taxes on homeowners increased in many states due to the more rapid increase in the assessments of homes than other types of property. Thus, in states such as California, the property tax rose as a proportion of the income of homeowners while it fell as a fraction of total personal income.

The chapter concludes with Bob Kuttner's article, **Behind the Tax Revolt**, which documents the origin and extent of this property tax shift in California and other states. He attributes this shift not only to rapidly inflating home values, but also to differences in the methods by which residential and business properties are assessed and the growth of business tax abatements. These influences have been compounded, he notes, by the willingness of the courts to mandate implementation of constitutional or statutory requirements that all property be assessed uniformly. Mr. Kuttner concludes that who pays what share of the property tax burden will emerge as a larger and larger issue as voters continue to feel the effects of rising taxes and declining services.

---

[1]For more on the erosion of the property tax base see the articles in Chapter 11, *Exempt Property*, Chapter 14, *Intangible Property*, and Chapter 19, *The Economic Impact of State and Local Business Taxes*.

Taxes: How They Were

In the early colonies, state and local expenses were met largely through voluntary contributions and through revenues from the public lands and enterprises. The religious origins of many of the colonies cast a churchly hue over public functions and made contributions to them akin to giving at church. Thus in 1644 in New Haven, Connecticut, each resident "whose heart is willing" was asked to give a peck of wheat to support "poor scholars at Harvard College."

Such contributions were requested with ever-increasing regularity, and their "voluntary" nature became largely a nicety of theory. In 1680, Maryland imposed "equal assessments" on inhabitants of a county who refused to contribute to a local charity. Around the time of the Revolution, people in Maryland who would not pay a share were cited as "enemies of America" in resolutions published in the *Maryland Gazette*, and were reported to local committees of observation.

Still, the spirit of voluntary assistance to the common cause remained strong during this period. Ben Franklin left a fund of £1,000 to the city of Philadelphia to be loaned to young married couples in amounts up to £60. Stephen Girard, another wealthy Philadelphian, left his large estate to the city to help "diminish taxation."

Publicly run enterprises were another way the early colonists diminished the need for taxes. Philadelphia, for example, raised considerable revenue by renting wharves, market stalls, and other city-owned property. By 1710 the city did not even have the power under its charter to levy taxes. In the nineteenth century, gas works, water works, and like facilities were often publicly owned. The state of New York operated a salt works. Massachusetts reclaimed over one hundred acres of marsh land in Boston's Back Bay and sold it for a $4 million profit (although critics charged the property could have been leased for up to

$2 million per year). Savannah, Georgia, had a plan that was even more ambitious. The city was extended only when and where the city itself had acquired the proposed new section. After making certain improvements the city would auction the lots at a profit.

Fines were a third way the colonies kept their taxes low. With taboos covering so many forms of behavior, the opportunities for such revenues were ample, as Mary Stebbins of Springfield, Massachusetts, discovered when, in 1667, she was fined ten shillings for wearing silks contrary to law.

When contributions, public enterprise, and fines could no longer carry the load, the colonies began to levy a wide assortment of license and permit fees, excise and poll taxes. But the bulwarks of their tax systems defied the rigid classifications of "income" taxes, "property" taxes, and "sales" taxes that we have today. The early colonists appear to have been much more concerned with taxpaying ability. Legal historian Arthur Lynn points to the English Poor Tax as a major model in the minds of the early settlers on this continent. The Poor Tax eventually evolved toward a fixed-rate levy, but for a long time tax officials tried to take each taxpayer's total financial circumstances into account. This attitude was epitomized by the "faculty" tax, a combination of income and property tax designed to reach the individual's taxpaying ability, whether it resided in revenue-producing land, a business, or a profession.

Thus assessors in New Plymouth Colony were instructed in 1643 to assess all inhabitants "according to their estates or faculties, that is, according to goods, lands, improved faculties, and psonal abillities" (sic). This mandate to reach all sources of taxpaying ability persisted up to 1777, when the instruction to tap non-real-estate sources of property and wealth was made even more explicit.

Vermont, by 1796, had, in addition to its regular property tax, an optional levy on lawyers, traders, and owners of mills, in proportion to their profits. Included in the Massachusetts tax were shops, mills, industrial works, tonnage of vessels, government securities, stock in banks, and plate. Connecticut taxed the profits of any and all gainful professions, trades, and occupations, with exemptions for public officeholders, farmers, and common labor for hire.

The taxes were often progressive even among members of the same profession. Connecticut attorneys paid a tax on their practices, the "least practitioners" at £50 and others "in proportion to their practice."

In New England in the 1700s property taxes constituted about two-thirds of direct taxes, and poll taxes only about one-third.

The pattern was quite different in the South, however, due mainly to the concentrated landownership there and the political power arising from it. The southern plantation owners stoutly resisted property taxes, promoting instead poll taxes, license fees and permits and duties on imports. Virginia, for example, levied property taxes briefly, in 1645-48, and then not again until the French and Indian War in 1755. In 1763 less than one-third of Virginia's revenues came from the land and over two-thirds from polls. Maryland did not have a tax on real estate until 1756. This tax was extended to all property in 1777, but was used little in the late eighteenth and early nineteenth centuries.

Standards used for valuing property were different as well. The "market value" standard common today was not then so widely used, in part because real estate did not change hands as frequently. Often land was assessed instead at a set amount per acre, depending roughly on how productive it could be. It was also common to classify land according to its nature and use. In

Ohio, for example, there were three classes, and observers deplored the trend by which more and more land gravitated to the lowest taxed category.

To ameliorate this trend, state after state adopted laws and constitutional amendments requiring that all property be assessed and taxed uniformly. Historian Lynn points to Ohio as typical. In 1825 the state abandoned the system of classifying land and began to assess real estate according to its market value—what a "willing buyer" would pay a "willing seller." In 1846, the period of broadening the tax base was capped by the so-called Kelly Act, under which all property not specifically exempt was to be taxed according to market value.

To **pro**tect the "uniformity" clause nineteenth-century Ohio lawmakers embedded it into the state constitution three years later. "The legislature," wrote Jens Peter Jensen, the late dean of property tax scholars, "had become disturbed in Ohio as well as in other states. It was charged with favoring certain corporations in selecting the list of taxables. It was deemed necessary to free 'man, as such, his business, occupation, and profession, from legislative caprice.' " Thus the new section of the Ohio constitution asserted that "Laws shall be passed, taxing by a uniform rule, all monies, credits, investments in bonds, joint stock companies, or otherwise, and also all real and personal property according to its true value in money."

In a like spirit, New Jersey Governor Daniel Haines exclaimed to the state legislature in his 1851 message that the tax "burden, whether great or small, shall be borne as equally as possible by all; and no proposition of political economy can be more obvious or just, than that everyone should contribute toward the support of the government in proportion to the amount of his property protected by it. The passage of a law equalizing taxation seems to be imperatively demanded by the people, and I respectfully but earnestly commend it to your early consideration, and prompt and efficient action."

After this message the New Jersey legislature enacted the state's first general property tax, subjecting all property, real, personal, and intangible, to taxation "upon an equal ratio according to actual value."

At this time property taxes provided the bulk of revenue for state as well as for local governments (New Jersey was an exception), so that the states took some role in the administration of the tax. Assessing, however, remained a local matter and the thousands of local assessors, many part-time and untrained, often lacked the ability, inclination, or both to make the ideal of uniform taxation of all property a fact in practice. Uniform assessment of real estate was rare, and much property, especially personal property and intangibles, never even got onto the tax rolls.

Viewing this failure, many observers took the stance—one still accepted widely and uncritically—that the ideal of uniform taxation, and not the paltry efforts taken to achieve it, was at fault. Thus E. R. A. Seligman's early twentieth-century denunciation of the property tax:

Practically, the general property tax as actually administered is beyond all doubt one of the worst taxes known in the civilised world. Because of its attempt to tax intangible things it sins against the cardinal rules of uniformity, of equality and of universality of taxation. It puts a premium on dishonesty and debauches the public conscience; it reduces deception to a system and makes a science of knavery; it presses hardest on those least able to pay; it imposes double taxation on one man and grants entire immunity to the next. In short the general property tax is so flagrantly inequitable that its retention can be explained only through ignorance or inertia. It is the cause of such crying injustice that its alteration or its abolition must become the battle cry of every statesman and reformer.

Two other developments around this time practically killed any hope that the states would provide adequate property tax administration. One was the way school financing evolved. "Our early schools," Lynn writes, "were essentially private and . . . prior to 1825, even public schools often derived much of their revenue from non-tax sources." Some states enacted laws permitting localities to impose school property taxes, but the states remained under pressure to put school finance on a dependable basis. At the same time, powerful conservatives were objecting to mandatory public schooling and the accompanying taxes as an intrusion of government upon individual rights—and incidentally, upon their pocketbooks. To squirm out of this bind, the state lawmakers went ahead with compulsory schools, but put the burden of running and paying for them onto the local governments. The main revenue source the localities had for meeting this burden was the property tax, and even today schools consume more property tax revenues than does any other public function. Having passed the buck to the localities, the states—which alone had the constitutional power to improve faltering property tax administration—could conveniently look the other way.

A related development was the rise of new sources of state revenue, such as motor fuel and vehicle taxes and, later, sales and income taxes. Scholars began to advance a theory of "separation of revenue sources." This theory held that states and localities should impose completely different taxes instead of sharing revenue from the same taxes. Accordingly the states would withdraw from the property tax and leave it more or less completely to local governments. In large measure this has happened. In 1902 the states still raised a full 51 percent of their revenue from property taxes, but by 1937 this figure had declined by half, to 26.8 percent. Ten years later only 8.7 percent of state revenues came from property taxes, and the decline has continued to just a little over 2 percent today.

Ironically, one promised result of this "separation of revenue sources" was to be better property tax administration. But the opposite has occurred. No longer relying on property taxes for revenue, state lawmakers were not greatly concerned. To this day they answer property tax complaints from constituents with a cold "I'm sorry, that's a local matter." Local officials and politicians for their part welcomed state neglect and often turned the property tax into an adjunct of their patronage machines.

Though study commissions recommended reforms and scholars like Professor Seligman harangued long into the night, the political impetus for improved property tax administration just did not arise. The alternative to reform was to throw in the towel and cease even trying to tax those forms of property that presented the most difficulty.

Assessing according to market value, in place of standards based on the yield of the property, had already made it difficult to include occupations and professions in the property tax and helped pave the way to the strict cleavage we now have between "income" taxes and "property" taxes. Now a further claim was advanced that special exemptions for business were necessary to promote industry, employment, and "growth." These arguments suited neatly, and gave respecta-bility to, the desires of the wealthy and the special interests that otherwise could lay little claim to relief.

As a result, there has been during our century a steady erosion of the property tax base, shifting the burden more and more to residential real estate. Most states have undone the work of the colonists and the mid-nineteenth-century tax reformers and have eliminated stocks and other "intangible" property partially or entirely from the tax base.

Though the actual number of states that in theory levy taxes on at least some kinds of intangibles increased from fifteen in 1962 to twenty-seven in 1969, only a few—Ohio, Florida, and Connecticut among them—levy taxes on intangibles with some success.

A parallel erosion has taken place regarding personal property. When assessed and taxed, property falling into this category can make up a substantial part of the property tax base—about 20 to 25 percent. Some twenty-six states exempt household personal property, not without good reason. But at least five states—Delaware, Hawaii, Idaho, New York, and Pennsylvania—exempt business personal property entirely, while at least nine more are in the process of phasing out part or all of their property taxes on business inventories and/or equipment and machinery. Most of the other states have at least partial exemptions for business property of some kinds.

The outright exemption of business property and the intangible property of the wealthy, moreover, is just a more obvious form of property tax erosion. Subtler forms, such as underassessment, back-door exemptions gained through leasing government property, and low-tax zones and industrial "tax havens," have evolved in tandem. In just ten years, from 1957 to 1967, the portion of property taxes falling initially on business dropped from 45.1 percent of the total to 39.5 percent.

The over-all result of this century-long process of tax-base erosion is that the burden of property taxes is falling increasingly on real estate and individual taxpayers. "Assessed value data from the 1957, 1962, and 1967 Censuses of Governments," says the Advisory Commission on Intergovernmental Relations (ACIR), "indicate a steady growth in the proportion that is attributed to residential assessments, and a steady drop in industrial and commercial assessments."

"The property tax," the ACIR concludes, "is increasingly a tax on housing."

"Taxes: How They Were" is reprinted by permission from *Tax Politics*, Brandon, Row and Stanton, ed., © 1976 by Pantheon Books, a division of Random House, Inc.

Property Tax Overview

THE PROPERTY TAX BASE

The property tax can be either general or specific in its application. A *general property tax* would be imposed on all classes of property *e.g.*, land, improvements, machinery, household goods, automobiles, business inventories, etc.—in an identical manner irrespective of the nature of the asset, its use or its ownership. The property tax levy would be determined by applying a constant tax rate uniformly to the estimated value of all assets. A *specific property tax* would be imposed on a well defined subset of all classes of property. Depending on the type of asset, its use or its ownership, its value may be totally or partially excluded from the property tax base—*e.g.*, specific government-owned land, homestead exemp-

Historically, the property tax in the United States was initially a specific property tax imposed on selective classes of wealth easily identifiable in an agrarian economy—*e.g.*, land, improvements, cattle, etc. During the early nineteenth century the variety of forms of tangible wealth multiplied and intangible property made its appearance. In an effort to broaden its base to include these new forms of wealth, the property tax was gradually transformed into a general property tax uniformly applied to all varieties of property independent of form.

However, the main component of the property tax base continued to be *real property* consisting of two separate elements—land (residential, commercial, agricultural) and improvements (buildings, structures, and other capital improvements). *Personal property*—tangible and intangible—was an expanding component of the base. Tangible personal

property—business inventories, automobiles, machinery, jewelry, livestock, household furnishings, etc.—was generally divided into business and household categories. Intangible personal property—corporate stocks and bonds, bank deposits, mortgages, etc.—represent claims on real and/or tangible personal property. To avoid double taxation, intangible personal property is generally excluded from the property tax base. However, some forms of intangible personal property—*e.g.*, cash or government bonds—do not represent claims on other physical assets and, ignoring administrative complexities, could theorically be included in the base.

Over time, however, as the variety of assets continued to grow, wealth became more concentrated and the administrative difficulties of assessing the various forms of personal property became apparent. So the tide turned once again toward a selective property tax. Personal property—tangible and intangible—declined in relative importance as a component of the property tax base.

In reality, the property tax base is often only a fraction of the estimated full market value of these different assets. However, the ratio between market value and the portion of that value subject to the tax—*i.e.*, the assessment ratio—varies between jurisdictions, property types, and, in some instances, between individual properties. Therefore, the actual —or effective—property tax rate will also vary between jurisdictions, types of property or individual properties.

The legislated property tax rate, or *nominal rate* (expressed in dollars per hundred dollars assessed value), when multiplied by the assessment ratio for each property, equals the *effective tax rate*. For example, if the legislated property tax rate (the nominal rate) was $1.83 per $100 assessed value, and the assessment ratio was legislated to be 100 percent, the entire market value of the property is subject to taxation, the nominal rate will equal the effective rate, $1.83 per $100 market value. This is the actual situation in the District. However, if the assessment ratio had been 50 percent, the effective rate would be half the legislated rate $.92 per $100 market value.

BASIC FEATURES OF THE PROPERTY TAX

The property tax, in part, is consistent with both the 'ability to pay' and the 'benefits' principle of taxation. In the first case, it is argued that the property tax—essentially a tax on wealth[1]—closely approximates an individual's ability to contribute to the cost of local services. This argument is a carry over from the colonial days when a tax per acre was assessed on land in an attempt to reach income—a preferred measure of 'ability to pay'—indirectly. While this may have been a necessary approach in an agrarian economy, it is not as important today since the income tax has become a rather well defined and widely used source of revenue at all levels of government.

Nevertheless, the property tax still provides a most effective, albeit indirect, means of taxing one component of income which most income taxes ignore—*i.e.*, the real estate component of unrealized capital gains. By tapping this source of income which avoids traditional income taxation, the property tax provides a vehicle for some equity improvement in an ability to pay sense. Additionally, it provides a mechanism to reach the specific problem of the land speculator who, in the current period, holds property off the open market in the expectation of realizing a future capital gain. During the holding period, such idle (vacant or under-utilized) land can entirely escape income taxation—thus increasing the incentive to hold the land idle—but not property taxation

The property tax is also consistent with the 'benefits' principle of taxation. It is argued that property taxes, in general, are primarily used to finance local government expenditures—police, fire, sewer, water, etc.—which are site oriented services, benefitting local property owners[2] and thereby increasing the value of their properties.

This argument, however, implicitly assumes

1.) that the benefits of local government expenditures are distributed across properties in direct proportion to the value of the property;

2.) that these benefits are, in fact, capitalized in the value of the properties; and

3.) that the benefit to each property owner equals, in dollar terms, their property tax liabilities.

These assumptions may not be true for all goods and services provided by local government. For example, the direct benefits of education are not likely to be distributed across all properties in proportion to property values, but rather according to the number of school age children in the household.

REVENUE PRODUCTIVITY

The absolute dollar amount produced by the property tax in any single year is calculated as the product of the property tax rate times the property tax base. Normally, the nominal (legislated) property tax rate can be changed only by legislative action.[3] The property tax base—the assessed value—changes as a result of a change in the level of assessment. This, in turn, is largely a function of the frequency of assessment and the degree to which assessed values capture changes in market values resulting from real and/or nominal economic growth. Thus, given a constant assessment ratio and annual assessment, the base increases in direct proportion to the growth in market values. Therefore, since the rate is constant, the property tax is generally regarded as having a high degree of revenue stability.[4]

A feature of revenue stability is the relative lack of growth in revenue in response to economic growth and the accompanying growth in the demand for public service. That is, as income and property values increase, the tax base would grow proportionally with income while expenditures would grow at a faster pace. A tax is defined to be an 'income elastic' revenue source if revenues increase relatively faster than the growth in income and 'income inelastic' in the opposite case. In general, depending on assessment procedures and the efficacy with which increased property values are reflected in the property tax base, the property tax is characterized as being a unitary elastic revenue source.[5] Thus, if a jurisdiction relies heavily (100%)on the property tax as a source of revenue, it would continually face a fiscal gap as the economy grows since the demand for services is income elastic, but property tax revenues are not. Alternatively, to the extent a jurisdiction diversifies its revenue structure by de-emphasizing the property tax in favor of more income responsive revenue sources— *e.g.*, the income tax—this problem becomes less critical.

INCIDENCE: WHO PAYS THE PROPERTY TAX?

Each year property owners pay local governments an amount equal to their property tax liability. This transfer of funds—from the property owner to the local government—represents the *initial burden* of the property tax. Depending on the use associated with each property, the property owner may shift all or part of the property tax to others through changes in the prices of things he sells and/or buys. Therefore, the *ultimate burden* (incidence) of the property tax is likely to differ from the initial burden.

Land

The property tax base includes a variety of property types—land, improvements and personal property. The assumptions about the potential for shifting that portion of the property tax falling on each component differ. Economists generally agree that a tax on land results in a decrease in the land's value and a capital loss to the land owner at the time the tax is imposed or increased.

The supply of land is, for all practical purposes (especially in the case of the District),ᶜ considered to be fixed. As a result of the fixed supply of land, potential renters need bid no more for the land than they did before the imposition of the property tax. Therefore, since the owners of the land must pay the tax, the potential net rental income is reduced—by the amount of the tax—and potential buyers will bid less for the land. It turns out that the reduction in the land's value would be exactly equal to the (increased) property tax liability capitalized at the appropriate rate. Therefore, in this case, the owner ultimately pays the property tax—*i.e.*, the initial and final burden coincide and thus fall on the owners of land (capital).⁷ There is also a consensus that that portion of the property tax derived from tangible personal property owned by individuals (not businesses) is borne by the individual.

Improvements and Tangible Personal Property

The tax on improvements and tangible personal property owned by business is more complicated. Therefore, the outcome is less clear. According to the traditional view the renter ultimately pays the property tax on improvements in the form of higher rents. The property tax is viewed as reducing the rate of return on capital improvements, thereby slowing the rate of investment in the taxed good—*e.g.*, new structures, rehabilitation, and maintenance. As a result, the stock of structures becomes less valuable and the user pays higher rents for a restricted stock. This restriction on supply will continue until the after tax rate of return is equal to the rate of return existing before the imposition (increase) of the tax. Therefore, rents will increase by the amount of the tax.

The ability of business to shift that portion of the property tax falling on improvements and personal property depends on

1.) the market structure of the industry,
2.) the availability of substitutes for the product and
3.) the degree of influence the firm has in determining factor input prices.

As opposed to the 'traditional view', the 'new view' starts from the premise that there is a portion of the property tax which is common to all jurisdictions. The analysis treats this portion of the tax as a uniform general property tax. In this case, the initial and ultimate burdens again coincide and fall on the owner of capital since all forms of capital are subject to a uniform rate and there is no opportunity for shifting resources to non-taxed areas.

The second dimension of the 'new view' of property tax incidence is an analysis of the effects of that portion of the tax which is not common to all jurisdictions—*i.e.*, the effective tax rate differential. This portion of the tax is treated as a non-uniform property tax—*i.e.*, a tax on all property, but applied at different rates for different sectors. It is argued that, in response to these tax differentials, resources shift from high to low taxed sectors in an effort to maximize the after tax rate of return.

The impact on profits in each sector is uncertain and depends on

1.) the mix of capital and labor in each sector, and
2.) the degree to which capital and labor are substitutable.

In addition, the flow of resources away from high taxed products to low taxed products results in a more or less balanced pattern of price increases (in high taxed sectors) and price decreases (in low taxed sectors) with no change in the general price level. Thus, the consumers' share of the property tax burden is regarded as progressive, regressive or proportional depending on the degree to which the consumption of high-taxed products are concentrated in high income groups and to which low-taxed products are consumed by low income groups. In any event, this general equilibrium approach to tax incidence suggests that a larger portion of the ultimate burden falls on the owners of capital than previously thought.

The differential tax rate feature of the 'new view' can also be presented in a regional context. In this case the differential tax rates do not differ between various sectors of the economy, but differ on a regional basis. That is, the situation is analogous to the case of a uniform property tax levied at different rates in different regions. The high interregional mobility of capital will equalize the after tax rates of returns to capital in ventures of similar risk by reducing supply in high tax regions and increasing it in low tax regions. Thus, taxpayers in areas where the tax rate is relatively high will have to pay high before-tax prices to owners of capital while the reverse is true in low tax regions.

Also, because of the high degree of mobility of workers, households and shoppers, within any given metropolitan region, it follows that intraurban property tax differentials will be born by land owners. That is, the movement of capital (workers, households, and shoppers) out of the high tax area depresses land values and rents because of the reduced demand. If labor and capital are perfectly mobile, one would expect land rents in the high tax area would be reduced by the full amount of the tax. Thus, according to the 'new view', intraurban property tax differentials are borne by land owners in the form of capital losses which arise when the property tax is imposed or increased.

In summary, the 'new view' leads to a number of implications which extend those associated with the 'traditional view.' First, that portion of the property tax common to all property across jurisdictions falls on the owners of capital in the form of lower rates of return than would be expected in the non-tax situation. Second, in addition to their share of the average nationwide property tax burden, property owners bear a major portion of the above-average tax rate differentials in urban areas. Third, that portion of the property tax which is shifted to consumers is much less important than believed according to the 'traditional view.'

It should be emphasized that the 'new' and 'traditional' views are complementary and not competing views. If the concern is a change in the national average property tax the 'new' view leads to the correct conclusion that the tax change is primarily borne by the owners of capital. If, however, the concern is the relative change in a local property tax,

the 'traditonal view' provides the appropriate framework for analysis focusing on the 'excise' effects of local differentials.

Table 6-1 expresses the ultimate property tax burden, under various assumptions, as a percent of annual income by income class. It is important to note, regardless of whether one believes in the 'new' or 'traditional' view, that in every case the property tax is regressive (the tax liability accounts for a larger percentage of income as income falls) below $15,000. Thus, there is a strong basis for policy-makers' concern with property tax relief for the low income.

FOOTNOTES

[1] The tax is currently applied to gross wealth and might more appropiately be applied to net wealth, *e.g.*, the equity one has in a home, not the total market value of the home.

[2] If all jurisdictions provided the same set of public goods (including the distribution of tax burdens) differential property values would not be influenced by the level of expenditures. Only differential benefit levels or differential distribution of tax burdens are capitalized into property values.

[3] Because of the provisions in the Real Property Tax Revision Act of 1974, this is not true for the District. In fact, without legislative action the District's tax rate would be automatically reduced as property value increased so that the property tax would generate the same amount of revenue, exclusive of new construction, as produced last year. For 1976, if the City Council had not actively voted to maintain the $1.83 rate, the rate would have been automatically reduced to an estimated $1.69.

[4] Actual property tax collections usually do not grow as rapidly as implied by the growth in market values; in part, because new exemptions and/or exclusions have the direct result of reducing the base. On the other hand, property taxes are generally very responsive to inflationary pressures, especially when assessments are made on a timely basis using modern techniques. See David Greytak and Bernard Jump, *The Effect of Inflation on State and Local Government Finances*, 1967-74, occasional paper # 25, Syracuse University, 1975.

[5] In general, the various components of the real property tax base have different income (GNP) elasticities which, over the years, have been estimated to fall in the following ranges: Non-farm residential ranges from .8 to 1.2; non-farm non-residential, .5 to 1.8; farm property, .6 to 1.0; weighted averages for all real property .7 to 1.4. An income elasticity of 1.0 indicates a proportional revenue source (revenues rising at the same rate as income), a value greater than one indicates an elastic revenue source and a value of less than one indicates an inelastic revenue source.

[6] Typically, the supply of land can be increased by annexation, land fill or similar activities. This option does not exist for the District of Columbia so the assumption of a fixed supply of land seems most appropriate here.

[7] This theoretical discussion assumes a static land market to the extent that there is *bona fide* unmet demand, the owner of the land would be in a position to shift some of the property tax to the renter (consumer).

Table 6-I
Incidence of the Property Tax Under Alternative Assumption, 1972

PROPERTY TAX BURDEN AS PERCENT OF INCOME ASSUMING THAT THE TAX ON IMPROVEMENTS IS BORNE BY INCOME CLASS

	Capital Only[1] A	Intermediate Cases B	Renters and Consumers Only[2] C
$ 0-2,999	7.2%	10.1%	13.0%
3,000-4,999	5.4	6.7	8.0
5,000-9,999	3.6	4.8	5.9
10,000-14,999	2.6	3.8	5.9
15,000-19,999	2.9	3.8	4.9
20,000-24,999	3.7	3.8	4.7
25,000-49,999	5.7	4.1	4.4
50,000-99,999	14.1	5.1	4.4
100,000-499,999	22.4	8.9	3.7
500,000-999,999	24.5	13.0	3.5
1,000,000 and Over	18.2	13.8	3.0
All Incomes	**5.0**	10.2	2.1
		5.0	**5.0**

Note: Property taxes include all levies by state and local governments on automobiles; livestock; commercial, industrial, and residential property; etc. Income is equal to the sum of federal adjusted gross income, transfer payments, state and local government bond interest and long-term capital gains excluded from federal income taxation. The tax on land is distributed on the basis of income from capital under all sets of assumptions. (The exclusion of imputed income from owner-occupied homes from the definition of income somewhat overstates the estimated progressivity of the tax in columns A and B. Imputations in the national income accounts for interest, net rent, and proprietors' income associated with owner-occupied homes amount to some 18 percent of local proprietors' income, rents, dividents and interest).

[1] Property taxes other than levies on non-farm motor vehicles and agriculture property are distributed on the basis of total property income; the tax on cars is distributed using the value of cars owned by the family; and agriculture taxes are distributed on the basis of gross farm value.

[2] It is assumed that the tax on owner-occupied homes falls on the owner-occupier and that the tax on apartments rests on tenants in proportion to rents paid. The tax on commercial and industrial improvements is allocated on the basis of general consumption, and the tax on farm improvements is allocated among farmers and consumers in general.

Source: Charles L. Schultze, Edward R. Fried, Alice M. Rivlin, and Nancy H. Teeters, *Setting National Priorities, The 1973 Budget,* Brookings Institution, Washington, 1972). Columns A and C are from p. 445. Other column from ACIR staff computations based on p. 445 and p. 447. See *Financing Schools and Property Tax Relief — A State Responsibility,* The Advisory Commission on Intergovernmental Relations, Washington, D.C., January 1973 and based on data contained in *The 1973 Budget,* Brookings Institution, Washington, D.C. 1972.

The Regressivity Issue

The property tax -- as currently structured -- does fall heavily on lower income families. Since property taxes are levied as a flat dollar amount per $100 of assessed value, they bear no relationship to the homeowner's income. It is therefore inevitable that the property tax is a major burden on lower income families.

Additionally, when placed in the context of the overall burden of federal, state and local taxes combined, this regressivity is heightened for two reasons. First, in most states, renters -- a large segment of whom are low income families -- are not permitted to deduct any portion of the property taxes which they pay indirectly as part of their rent from their income tax liability. Second, in calculating federal or state income tax liability, property taxes paid are generally deducted from a taxpayer's gross income. The fact that these taxes are deducted rather than converted to a tax credit results in relatively greater benefits going to high income households -- the exact opposite of the desired impact.

This deduction vs. credit debate is best clarified by an example. Compare the tax break that is received on the basis of $1,000 in property taxes paid by a lower middle income wage earner in a large city (on a $15,000 house in Newark, New Jersey, for example) with the same $1,000 paid by a wealthy suburban resident (on a $50,000 house in Bergen County, New Jersey). Under the present tax deduction system the worker in Newark would save $140 on his federal income tax liability. The wealthy suburbanite from Bergen County would realize as much as $700 in savings on his federal taxes from the same property tax payment.

The inequity results from the fact that the value of a tax deduction depends upon an individual's income tax bracket. Individuals in the high tax brackets -- with incomes over $100,000 per year -- are able to achieve savings of as much as 70 percent of the property taxes they pay in the form of reduced income tax obligation. Individuals in the lowest tax brackets -- with incomes of less than $10,000 per year -- can reduce their income tax by only 14 percent of their property taxes paid.

"The Regressivity Issue" is reprinted by permission from *AFSCME Action Plan for State and Local Taxes*, Public Policy Department, American Federation of State, County and Municipal Employees, 1977.

CORRECTING THE PROPERTY TAX RECORD
by Allen D. Manvel

The usual explanation of the "taxpayers' revolt" that led to sweeping popular ratification of Proposition 13 in California, and that has politicians everywhere competing for a chance to "save the poor property taxpayer," goes about like this: With the tax base bloated by rapid inflation of real estate values, local officials everywhere have been

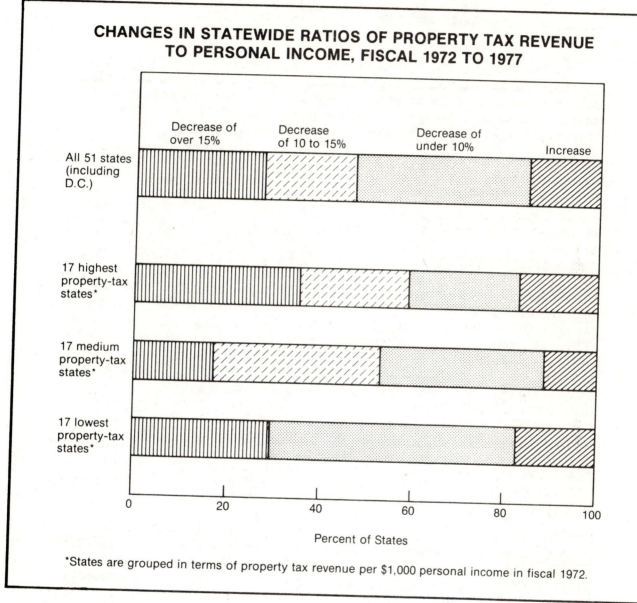

CHANGES IN STATEWIDE RATIOS OF PROPERTY TAX REVENUE TO PERSONAL INCOME, FISCAL 1972 TO 1977

*States are grouped in terms of property tax revenue per $1,000 personal income in fiscal 1972.

encouraged to raise property tax exactions to a point where they represent an impossible burden for the average homeowner.

Recently issued census statistics, however, tell a different story, about both California and the rest of the nation.

In the five years before Proposition 13 was adopted, the officially assessed property tax base in California grew 50 percent, and property tax revenue rose 49 percent. During the same five-year interval, however, the personal income of Californians went up 63.5 percent. Accordingly, the ratio of property taxes to personal income in that statute

dropped off nine percent, from $71.50 per $1,000 income in fiscal 1972 to $65.14 per $1,000 in fiscal 1977.[1]

In the nation as a whole, similarly, property tax revenue went up 46 percent between fiscal 1972 and fiscal 1977. But with personal income raising 60 percent, the ratio of property taxes to personal income went down nine percent, from $50.02 per $1,000 to $45.63 per $1,000.[1]

Nor was this nationwide change traceable to only a few major states. In fact, as shown by the accompanying chart, the ratio of property taxes to personal income dropped off in all but eight states between 1972 and 1977. And, as the chart also shows, this trend has prevailed not only among states which in 1972 had a relatively high level of property taxation, but also among those whose average rate was in the intermediate range and these with a relatively low 1972 rate.

Totals and averages, of course, conceal underlying diversity. There can be no doubt that, for many householders and other property owners, property tax bills have taken a larger proportion of current income during recent years. But the hard statistical record suggests that for a majority of property owners, the shift has been in the other direction — i.e., that in most instances, the rise in property tax liability has been outpaced by income growth.

_____

[1]Tax base data are from *Assessed Valuations for Local General Property Taxation* (Preliminary Report No. 2 of the 1977 Census of Governments) and *Taxable and Other Property Values* (Vol. 2, Part 1 of the 1972 Census of Governments). Tax revenue and income data are from Bureau of the Census, *Preliminary Report — Governmental Finances in 1976-77* (September 1978) and *Compendium of Government Finances* (Vol. 4, No. 5 of the 1972 Census of Governments).

Summary statistics that underlie the chart are as follows:

Change in property tax per $1,000 personal income, 1972 to 1977	Number of states, grouped by 1972 property tax level [a]				Percent of states, grouped by 1972 property tax level [a]			
	All states	High level	Medium level	Low level	All states	High level	Medium level	Low level
Total...............	51	17	17	17	100.0	100.0	100.0	100.0
Increase	8	3	2	3	15.7	17.6	11.8	17.6
Decrease:								
Less than 10 percent ...	19	4	6	9	37.3	23.5	35.3	52.9
10 to 15 percent	10	4	6	–	19.6	23.5	35.3	—
Over 15 percent	14	6	3	5	27.5	35.3	17.6	29.4

Sources: See detailed tabulation below.
a Including the District of Columbia as a state.

Supporting individual-state figures for the three tax-level groups of states are as follows:

17 highest property tax states				17 medium property tax estates				17 lowest property tax states			
	Property tax per $1,000 income				Property tax per $1,000 income				Property tax per $1,000 income		
State	1972	1977	% change	State	1972	1977	% change	State	1972	1977	% change
Calif.	$71.50	$65.14	-8.9	Ariz.	$54.04	$55.29	+2.3	Ala.	$15.31	$11.76	-23.2
Conn	63.52	55.92	-12.0	Colo.	51.47	49.47	-3.9	Alaska	25.00	134.81	+439.2
Ind.........	59.02	39.21	-33.6	Fla.........	38.81	35.19	-7.9	Ark.........	24.95	22.56	-9.6
Iowa	59.85	46.71	-22.0	Idaho......	43.95	37.45	-14.8	Del.........	21.42	19.06	-11.1
Maine	66.06	44.94	-32.0	Ill..........	50.88	45.09	-11.4	D.C.	32.00	29.28	-8.5
Mass.	72.79	74.24	+2.0	Kans.......	54.41	46.57	-14.4	Ga.	33.22	34.70	+4.5
Minn.	57.78	43.94	-24.0	Md.	40.39	38.54	-4.6	Hawaii	26.60	24.07	-9.6
Mont.	73.52	64.30	-12.5	Mich.......	52.67	49.28	-6.4	Ky.	22.57	21.11	-6.5
Nebr.	59.27	58.94	-0.6	Mo.	40.06	32.54	-18.8	La..........	26.91	18.73	-30.4
N.H.	73.38	65.70	-10.5	Nev.	43.96	41.39	-5.8	Miss.	28.08	26.03	-7.3
N.J.........	66.67	63.36	-5.0	N.D.	48.46	38.82	-19.9	N.M.	26.38	21.71	-17.7
N.Y........	57.69	63.30	+9.7	Ohio	44.44	38.34	-13.7	N.C.	28.39	25.88	-8.8
Ore.	61.56	57.53	-6.5	Pa.	34.30	31.03	+4.0	Okla.	29.27	23.99	-18.0
S.D.	70.08	60.19	-14.1	R.I.	50.05	52.06	-7.6	S.C.	26.43	25.17	-4.8
Vt.	73.02	61.97	-15.1	Tex.	41.74	38.55	-14.4	Tenn.	29.31	26.89	-8.3
Wis.	71.72	49.29	-31.3	Utah	43.00	36.79	-18.8	Va.	31.11	31.26	+0.5
Wyo.......	58.75	62.98	+7.2	Wash.	46.86	38.04	-9.8	W.Va.	24.76	20.98	-15.3

Sources: Bureau of the Census, *Preliminary Report, Governmental Finances in 1976-77* (September 1978), and *Compendium of Government Finances* (Vol. 4, No. 5 of the 1972 Census of Governments.)

_____

"Correcting the Property Tax Record" is reprinted by permission from the December 18, 1978 issue of *Tax Notes*, Taxation with Representation Fund.

Behind the 'Tax Revolt': A Shift of the Burden From Business to Homeowners

By Bob Kuttner

I F ONE HAD to pick the political myth of the decade, the leading candidate could easily be what lay behind "the great tax revolt of 1978."

Business conservatives, muttering about government spending and ending up as the biggest beneficiaries of Proposition 13 and its clones, have managed to convince people that taxpayers were rebelling against growth in public outlays. But the real problem, it turns out, was that businesses were already *getting* too big a tax break, that property taxes increasingly were being shifted *away* from them and onto homeowners.

Though the idea might give a Howard Jarvis apoplexy, in reality the tax revolt of 1978 was created largely by business tax relief at the expense of homeowners.

Consider what happened in California, incubator of the revolt. Taxes on homes there increased about 110 percent between 1975 and 1978 — while business assessments rose only 26 percent. By 1978, when Proposition 13 was ratified, single-family homeowners were carrying about 44 percent of California's property tax load; five years earlier they had paid only 32 percent. Small wonder that California homeowners were angry, especially since their excessive share of tax payments was contributing indirectly to a massive state budget surplus.

Why has the tax revolt been misunderstood, continuing to provide pressure for reduced government spending?

First, Jarvis & Co. shrewdly focused attention strictly on the rising homeowner taxes — rather than on the growing inequity of the tax burden, on who was carrying what load. Second, there is wide misunderstanding of government spending statistics, which can indeed be misleading; while government takes in more dollars every year, largely because of inflation, government spending as a fraction of real income leveled off around 1974. Federal spending as a portion of gross national product actually has declined slightly, while state and local spending has remained about constant.

Moreover, the tax-burden shift away from business and onto homeowners has been difficult to detect because most states don't keep statistics on who pays what share of the property tax. To get those estimates, you have to compile figures on total assessments by type of property and then apply average rates, factoring out credits and exemptions.

One thing you come up with is the fact that local government did not grow fat from property tax revenues. On the average, property taxes *declined* as a fraction of personal income in all but eight states in the five years preceding the tax revolt. But try telling that to homeowners whose property taxes just doubled — a blow arriving on top of the steadily growing share individuals also have been paying of state and federal income taxes.

It didn't matter to Idaho homeowners, for example, that in their low-tax, low-spending state, total property taxes had been rising far less than the rate of inflation. Despite this, Idaho was the one state last November where voters ratified a Proposition 13 clone, placing the blame on government spending. The homeowners didn't realize that their property tax rise really reflected a major shift in that burden away from business and onto them.

That shift, in fact, was even more extreme than California's. In 1969, Idaho homeowners shouldered about 24 percent of the property tax burden. By 1978, the year of the revolt, they were carrying more than 44 percent, a nearly doubled share of the load.

A confluence of accidents

The shifting tax burden has largely eluded policymakers as well, in part because it was not deliberate.

Some of it was produced by inflation; as the value of homes increased faster than the value of railroads or factories, housing came to absorb a heavier share of the tax load. But the shift is also the result of other independent trends.

First, homes and businesses are assessed under different formulas. In most states, residences are assessed according to their actual market value, while businesses are assessed by converting the income they generate into a presumed capital worth. This is reasonable enough in a period of stable prices, but during a period of inflation this formula protects businesses against inflationary increases in assessment — while homes pay full freight.

Second, the spurt in inflation coincided with a little-noticed series of state court decisions and legislative reforms that had the effect of increasing homeowner taxes.

Since colonial times, local tax assessors customarily valued homes and small farms at far below their actual worth. During the 19th century, when states began to levy property taxes on business plant and equipment and on paper wealth, many state constitutions were amended to require that all property be assessed and taxed uniformly.

These so-called "uniformity clauses" were honored mostly in the breach. Local assessors are usually elected, and when property taxes on homes rise disproportionally, they are not re-elected. Until very recently, the tax assessor's survival instinct amounted to a crude, extra-legal check against a tax shift onto homeowners.

But beginning in the late 1950s, state courts showed a new willingness to wade into this legal thicket, and they gradually agreed to lower assessments on businesses that were over-appraised relative to homes. By the late 1960s, some courts grew bold enough to dictate comprehensive reassessments.

In California, the state legislature passed a 1966 law requiring all property to be assessed at a uniform 25 percent of value. A year later the Idaho supreme court ruled for a group of utilities claiming to be over-valued. Courts in Massachusetts in 1974 and New York in 1975 held the customary system of "fractional assessment" invalid and ordered reassessments. In all, some 20 states revised their assessment formulas.

The local assessor was thus stripped of his fail-safe role just when housing prices were climbing through the roof. As a result, higher prices translated into higher taxes. In mandating new uniform assessment ratios, most legislatures failed to appreciate how this might mix with inflation. Ironically, in California, where the 1966 reform was stimulated by an assessment scandal that sent several assessors to jail for taking bribes from businesses, it was assumed that the new system would lower residential taxes.

Third, in the past decade state rivalries to attract industry have intensified. In particular, older industrial states are locked in a fierce competition to lure or retain business through the tax system. New York, Missouri and Ohio have led the way in offering a profusion of abatements and exemptions that forgive all or some of the taxes that otherwise would apply to new industry. In downtown Boston and New York, for example, virtually nothing has been built in recent years without some tax concession.

Among public officials, Cleveland's scrappy mayor, Dennis Kucinich, is virtually alone in resisting these business tax preferences. While there is much controversy over whether business tax inducements have their intended effect of stimulating development that would not have occurred anyway, there is no doubt that as business pays a declining share of the tax load, other taxpayers must make up the difference.

As part of their moves to improve "business climate," many states also have repealed taxes dating to the 19th century on business inventory or industrial plant and equipment. While these taxes were administratively cumbersome and may have penalized capital-intensive or high-inventory businesses, they nonetheless contributed a large portion of tax revenues. Though a few states such as Michigan replaced these traditional taxes with other taxes on business, others like Ohio just repealed them.

A look at other states

Taxes on housing, then, have come to carry an ever-increasing share of the tax load at a time when the net worth of most ordinary people is increasingly concentrated in their homes. Consequently, the wealth of middle-income and lower-income Americans is heavily taxed, while most other wealth, such as stocks, bonds and luxury commodities, escapes taxation as property.

Besides California and Idaho, a survey of tax assessment and collection data reveals that:

• Oregon homeowners paid 53 percent of the property tax load in 1978, up from 45 percent in 1974. The commercial and industrial share dropped sharply. Oregon voters narrowly rejected two different tax reduction initatives, leading the state legislature to enact a comprehensive tax relief package.

• Wisconsin homeowners paid 58.2 percent of the property taxes in 1978, compared to 50.8 percent in 1971. The industrial share dropped from 17.7 percent to 8.5 percent. In Wisconsin, the new Republican governor sponsored a two-month moratorium in income taxes and a onetime homeowners' tax credit.

• Ohio homeowners paid 39.9 percent of property taxes in 1978, up from 36.7 percent in 1973. In Ohio, an even greater tax shift is forecast in future years, because a state supreme court decision enforcing equal assessment ratios has not yet taken full effect, and because a legislative action intended to offset increases in taxes produced by inflation inadvertently gives greater reductions to business.

It is estimated that in 1980, Cuyahoga county (Cleveland) residential taxpayers will pay $108 more in property taxes on average, while commercial and industrial taxpayers will pay $362 less. At the current rate of inflation, Cleveland taxpayers will pay an estimated 80 percent of the property tax load by 1982.

• Minnesota homeowners paid 49.3 percent of property taxes in 1977, up from 41.5 percent in 1973. The industrial and commercial share fell proportionately.

In some cases, the tax shift that would have occurred was offset by deliberate policy. Michigan, for example, was one state that kept shares of the tax load relatively stable by enacting a 'circuit-breaker' law, which refunds a portion of the property tax when the tax exceeds a percentage of income. This approach makes the property tax more progressive, as well as stabilizing the residential share. Last November, Michigan voters rejected a Proposition 13 look-alike and approved a more moderate spending 'cap,' limiting future government growth to the rate of growth in Michigan's personal income. Oregon, Minnesota and Wisconsin would have had even sharper tax shifts without their circuit-breaker programs. Colorado and Nebraska, which rejected tax limitation initiatives, also apparently did not suffer tax shifts.

Ironically, states like California, Idaho and Oregon, which pioneered 'reforms' intended to modernize property tax administration, produced as by-products higher residential taxes and voter rebellion. In 1975, Idaho's state tax commission got tired of waiting for local assessors to comply with its equalization orders and brought in an out-of-state consulting firm to do the job. The firm, oblivious to local political needs, equalized assessment ratios in a single year — producing a 50 percent hike in residential taxes in the state's largest county.

Ironically too, states with antiquated tax systems have managed to avoid the shift. In many Massachusetts cities, assessments bear little resemblance to actual values. Tax rates in Boston are an astronomical $252 per $1,000 of assessed value, but assessments on homes have lagged well behind market values. In 1974, however, the Massachusetts supreme court ordered all cities to comply with the constitutional requirement of uniform assessments at full value. This would have shifted an estimated $265 million in tax burdens onto homeowners. The voters responded by approving an amendment legalizing different rates for different types of property.

New York got a similar court ruling in 1975. Like Massachusetts, New York homeowners in the past were protected against a tax shift by horse-and-buggy assessment practices. In the wake of the court ruling, known as *Hellerstein*, the legislature has not been able to agree on what to do to head off a tax shift. But if New York fails to either enact homeowner tax relief or legalize split rates, a state assembly committee estimates that compliance with the *Hellerstein* standard will increase taxes on New York City homeowners by 113 percent — while property taxes on business will drop about 26 percent. The same kind of shift will also occur in Albany, Buffalo, Rochester and Yonkers. Devising a remedy is especially difficult because the effects will not be uniform throughout the state.

Attempting to stabilize shares of the tax load can be very tricky business. For instance, South Carolina in 1976 sought to compensate for a tax shift onto homeowners by authorizing split rates, assessing industrial property at 10.5 percent of its actual value and homes at 4 percent — only to find after the fact that the historic gap between assessment on homes and businesses in many countries had been far wider. The 'reform' may turn out to exaggerate the burden on homeowners.

Changing the focus

Even though the tax shift to homeowners was the largely hidden cause of taxpayer protest, the tax revolt has taken on a life of its own as a reaction to "big government."

Only in Ohio, where a statewide consumer group, the Ohio Public Interest Campaign, and Mayor Kucinich vociferously campaigned against business abatements — and in Massachusetts, where mayors and consumer organizations recognized the probable effect of the state supreme court's assessment decision — did the distribution of the tax load catch on as a pressing issue.

Elsewhere, conservatives have largely succeeded in focusing attention on the total tax load rather than on who is and should be paying it. Thus balanced-budget amendments and conservative assertions about excessive taxation strangling business have dominated the tax policy debate. Spenders and taxers are on the defensive. After Jarvis, the 1978 federal tax reform bill, intended to close loopholes, was transformed into a measure to reduce capital gains rates.

The generally conservative fiscal mood has inspired several state laws limiting taxes and expenditures, which will certainly force government to be more deliberate in its priorities. But as the more stringent of these limits translate into cuts in public services, the voters may begin to pay more attention to the distribution of the tax load, as well as its size, to control their tax bills.

"Behind the 'Tax Revolt'" is reprinted by permission from the September 9, 1979 issue of *The Washington Post*.

CHAPTER 3

Reforming Assessment Practices

This chapter explains how property is assessed, illustrates some of the problems which frequently make assessments unfair, and suggests some ways of improving the quality of assessment.

After **Assessing and the Assessor** by Brandon, Rowe, and Stanton, which describes the procedures used in assessing property, Diane Fuchs' article, **Property Tax Is Often Poorly Run**, summarizes many of the problems which plague the administration of the property tax. She suggests improvements through upgrading the qualifications of assessors, increased utilization of computers, and more diligent tax collection efforts.

A series of six articles tell of studies which document assessment inequities. The first two, **Small Homes Here Taxed Hardest** and **Whites Get Lower Levy Regularly**, by Ed McManus of *The Chicago Tribune,* report the results of a study of home assessments in Chicago by Professor Arthur Lyons of the University of Illinois at Chicago Circle. Professor Lyons' research reveals that lower value homes are assessed at higher ratios than more expensive homes and that homes in Chicago's Black neighborhoods are being over assessed while homes in predominantly White neighborhoods generally are underassessed. Next, David Yepsen of the *Des Moines Register* in the article, **Iowa Assessments a Disgrace**, reports the results of a survey of home assessments in Iowa by Professor Steven Gold. According to Professor Gold, "two people who have

the same house are likely to pay different property taxes and that isn't fair."

The next two articles shift the focus to assessment of commercial and industrial properties. **City Assessments Hit Commercial Buildings Lightly**, by LaBarbara Bowman of *The Washington Post*, reports on a study of assessed values in Washington D.C. which concludes that "several of the major commercial properties of the District have been given a free ride for property tax purposes over the last several years." **Taxes: Who's Not Paying**, by The Illinois Public Action Campaign, tells the story of assessor Pat Hartley's fight against underassessment of industrial properties in Will County.

The last article in this series is an excerpt from an essay by Mason Gaffney called **We Do Need Assessment Reform**, which draws attention to the underassessment of land and natural resources. **Severance Taxes**, in Chapter 21, further explores the taxation of natural resources.

The chapter concludes with two proposals for reform. Pierce County, Washington, assessor Ken Johnston in **TAPES—Taxpayer Assisted Property Evaluation System**, describes a very successful system for verifying assessments with direct citizen input. Derek Shearer's **A Plan for Reform** outlines a comprehensive program for reforming the Los Angeles County assessor's office which he submitted to the County's Board of Supervisors in 1977.

Assessing and the Assessor

The assessor's job is as important as it is difficult. A good assessor must know how to keep abreast of the real estate market in his community. He must be an expert on construction costs and on the economics of buying, selling, and operating real estate for profit. In many places he must understand the economics of the mining or timber industries as well. An assessor needs to understand corporate accounting and, increasingly, modern computer techniques. He must be a lawyer, amateur if not actual. An assessor must be able to organize and manage a staff of assistants and mountains of records and paperwork. He must be competent in dealing with the public and the press, and he must be able to navigate the stormy political waters through which his work can take him. He is responsible for thousands of separate parcels of property. If he does not get these onto the tax rolls and assess them properly, then local functions and taxpayers will suffer. How does an assessor carry out his responsibilities?

listing

Listing is the process of finding all the property in a jurisdiction and putting it on the tax rolls. The assessor can draw on three main sources of information. One is taxpayer reporting forms, the system the IRS uses. These are common for personal property, less common for real estate; some states—Texas and Kentucky are among them—require taxpayers to file reports on all their property. The second source is the data network which good assessors establish. They check—or even get copies of—deeds, building permits, zoning changes, and other records which show where property is and what is happening to it. The third source is actual field inspections. These are especially important for buildings under construction and inventories.

Once he has these data, the assessor must assemble them in a useful form. Changes in real estate are recorded on *tax maps*. These are carefully drawn maps showing the location, size, and tax map number for each parcel of real estate in the jurisdiction. Tax maps sometimes include buildings on the property as well. Many smaller jurisdictions do not have these tax maps and have no way of being sure that they have all real estate on the tax rolls.

In many jurisdictions, property data for both real and personal property go onto *property record cards* which list all the information about each property that the assessor needs to determine its value. More advanced assessing offices use computers to transfer the raw property data from the various sources to property record cards.

valuing

The assessor's next step is to ascertain the value of the property on his assessment roll. An assessor is a special kind of appraiser. Private, or *fee* appraisers, determine property values for many different purposes—insurance, corporate mergers, condemnation lawsuits. Assessors determine property values for just one purpose: property taxes. Unlike fee appraisers who can take painstaking care with every property, assessors have a whole community full of properties to appraise. They lack the time and the staff to do a full-fledged appraisal on each. Out of necessity, they have developed techniques to handle large numbers of property on a mass, or assembly-line basis.

It is these so-called *mass appraisal* techniques which really set assessors apart from other appraisers. These techniques can be admirably resourceful and accurate. They can also be utterly fallacious short-cuts that extend or conceal favored treatment for particular taxpayers or enable a lazy or incompetent assessor to get by with little work.

The keystone of assessing is the concept of *market value*, which one court defined as "the price it [the property] would bring if offered on an open market under conditions in which neither buyer nor seller could take advantage of the exigencies of the other." This is the value the assessor is charged by law to find. The word "find" is important; the assessor is not supposed to dream up a value, but rather to arrive at one from factual data about the actual real estate market. There are a few instances, such as farmland assessing, in which the law permits assessors to depart from the market value concept. Such cases are the ex-

ception, however, and even here the idea of market value is only modified, not cast out.

Implicit in the market value concept is the standard of "highest and best use." This standard is the source of much confusion. It means that assessors are to look to the most intense and profitable use to which buyers are apt to put the property. A farm surrounded on four sides by residential subdivisions would be assessed at its value for subdividing, not farming; a vacant lot in a downtown business district would be assessed at its value for highrise development, or rather, at the price someone might pay to put a building on it.

In this sense the market value concept is biased towards development. "Highest and best" use is really "most fully developed and profitable" use. Whether most profitable always means best is matter for dispute.

Since market value is the key, why don't assessors merely look at what properties are selling for and be done? Sales prices are probably the best evidence of market value, but they cannot do the job alone. For one thing, there are not always enough sales of a particular kind of property to give the assessor reliable evidence as to value. This is especially true of commercial and industrial properties which tend to be unique, so that the sales price for one does not say much about the value of another. More important, sales *price* does not always reflect market *value*. Speculators often take advantage of uninformed sellers, buying inner-city rowhouses and farmland in the

path of development for much less than they are worth. Sellers can also take advantage of buyers. A landowner who knows that a developer needs his parcel to complete a subdivision tract is likely to hold out for the very last dollar. In such cases, it can be argued, the sales price does not truly reflect the value of the property.

For these reasons, assessors consider sales prices just one indicator of value. They use two other methods of finding value called the *cost approach* and *income approach*. In using these approaches the assessor puts himself into the shoes of a prospective buyer and asks himself how much he would be willing to pay for the property in question.

the comparable sales or market data approach

The assessor simply looks up what the particular property, or properties like it, called *comparables*, have sold for recently. He ignores sales that were not "arm's length"—those that were between two family members, for example, or in which the buyer or seller was in special distress, such as a sale of a home after a divorce or death of a spouse. Then the assessor makes adjustments for minor differences between the comparables and the property he is assessing. Adjustments might be for location, the land area, or the condition of the property.

The market data or comparable sales approach works best in assessing homes, which are bought and sold often, and which are sufficiently alike to be useful as comparables. Many assessors think it is the best test, because it is objective.

the cost approach

Under this approach, the assessor figures out how much buildings cost. Then he subtracts an amount to cover wear-and-tear or depreciation. Also called the *summation approach*, the cost approach is often the first assessors use. It involves a detailed description of the property—its size, shape, how it is constructed, its condition and age—because only such a description makes possible an accurate cost estimate. Once down on paper, these details can be used in the other approaches to value as well.

There are three different kinds of costs which assessors use: *historical cost*—what it actually cost to build the particular building; *reproduction cost*—what it would cost today to build exactly the same building; and *replacement cost*—what it would cost to construct a building that would perform the same functions as the one in question, using today's materials and technology. For example, someone building a downtown office building today would be more likely to use glass and aluminum than granite and marble.

There are also three different kinds of depreciation which assessors take into account: *physical deterioration*, which is simple wear-and-tear; *functional obsolescence*, which describes an old factory with loading docks built to receive horse-drawn wagons instead of trucks; and finally, *economic obsolescence*, which is a decline in value due to events apart from the building itself. For example, if an airport were built

next to a drive-in movie theater the value of the theater would probably go down.

There is a fourth kind of depreciation which assessors are not supposed to consider. *Accountant's depreciation* is a special, rapid form of depreciation that is usually used for income tax purposes. It has little or nothing to do with the actual condition or value of the property. But assessors have slipped this form of depreciation into their calculations to give particular building owners an assessment break.

Assessors cannot afford to investigate fully the actual cost of every building they appraise. Instead they use tables which purport to show the cost of different building components per square or cubic foot of building space. For example, the excavation for a typical ranch house might be computed at 65 cents per square foot of total floor area, the exterior walls at $2.49 per square foot, and so on. There is nothing wrong with such shorthand methods so long as they are based on actual cost data and are up to date. This is not always the case, however.

The cost approach can be very convenient to use. The assessor simply takes the cost of building components from a manual (which he may or may not have prepared himself) and plugs these into the property in question. Training assistants to use the cost approach is also easy. These are reasons assessors tend to use the cost approach more than any other.

the income approach

Assessors often use this approach to value office buildings and other properties that produce income for the owners. In this

approach, the assessor tries to reckon the value of the property from the income it produces currently and which it can be expected to produce in the future.

The basic premise is that people who invest in real estate are looking to the income it will yield. An investor interested in buying an office building would want to know how much rental income the building was bringing in and its maintenance cost. He would check the condition of the building and of the neighborhood to see how long it would produce this much income. Then he would figure out how much he should pay. Assessors have reduced these questions down to a system:

1. Estimate the gross annual income.

2. Substract rent loss due to vacancies and "bad debts."

3. Subtract operating expenses.

4. Estimate how many more years this "income stream" will last.

5. Choose a "capitalization rate" and a "capitalization technique." These are formulas for figuring out how much an investor would pay now to get the future income of the building.

Assessors, however, do not have the authority in all states to make property owners submit detailed statements of their costs and income. Nor do they always use this authority. And building owners often ignore requests for data while most assessors lack the legal staffs to put teeth in their requests. Assessors can use the table which real estate trade groups and mortgage lenders prepare to make an educated guess on how much income specific kinds of buildings should produce though many, unfortunately, accept without question oral statements from the owners.

Property Tax Is Often Poorly Run

By Diane Fuchs

It is no secret that the property tax is the least popular of all taxes. Recent polls taken by the Advisory Commission on Intergovernmental Relations (ACIR) indicate that 33% of the nationwide respondents thought that the property tax is the "least fair."

The property tax system suffers with this poor public image because it is antiquated, varies from locality to locality and often is arbitrarily administered.

With a strong tradition of local administration, some 65,000 units of government levy their own property taxes. The rates of taxation, standards for assessing property, the practices of assessors, as well as levels of property valuation vary from district to district. The administration of the tax on the whole has failed to keep current with technological advances leading the ACIR to characterize modern property tax administration as a "treasured relic of pioneer days."

According to Henry Aaron, author of *Who Pays the Property Tax?*, "the impact of the property tax depends on the vagaries of administration more than does that of any other tax." If assessments don't keep pace with market fluctuations in property values, if property is assessed infrequently, and if assessors are not accurate in valuing property and fail to provide uniform valuations in accordance with statewide standards, the effect will almost certainly be inequitable assessments and unfair tax bills.

A 1971 survey conducted by the U.S. Bureau of the Census which compared assessment levels of single family non-farm residential property (the easiest kind of property to assess) to actual sales prices (thereby arriving at what is known as an "assessment sales ratio") found that roughly only half of all tax jurisdictions had "acceptable" administration and only one in sixteen had "excellent" administration. At the other end of the scale, large numbers of jurisdictions (one in eleven) had extremely large discrepancies in their assessments. Interestingly, in a 1973 poll, about 2/3 of the members of the International Association of Assessing Officers (a professional organization for tax assessors) sided with their critics by rating the overall quality of tax assessment as "poor" or "very poor."

Valuation

The real property tax is a tax on the value of property. It is the job of the assessor to give a value to each property – a job that is necessarily subjective.

Naturally, the subjectivity of their jobs gives assessors a great deal of discretion which invites abuse. The assessing process is often used to pursue a variety of political and economic goals and can be used for dispensing favors as well as punishments. For this reason, assessor discretion can and does lead to assessments which fall short of legally mandated standards.

As tax rates have increased, assessment inequities have been the focus of a number of challenges. Frustrated taxpayers facing higher bills base their attacks on the failure of assessments to meet the standards required by state law. These battles waged in the courts and legislatures have led some states to pursue full value assessments (assessments that represent 100% of the full value of the property) while others have assessments based on a uniform fixed fraction of actual value.

Another variation of the fractional standard adopted by some states is known as "classification." By this standard homes are assessed at one percent of full market value while businesses, utilities, and farms are assessed at other fixed percentages. This, of course, leads to the problem of separate interest groups pressuring for separate classifications and preferred (low) levels of assessments.

Regardless of whether a jurisdiction follows full valuation, fractional valuation or classification, none of the systems necessarily solve the problem of assessment inequality because the underlying problem of finding a uniform basis for evaluating the property still remains. The debates concerning which standard is better fail to deal directly and effectively with the basic cause of assessment discriminations, namely the quality of the original assessment of the property.

Although none of the three systems guarantees proper assessments most authorities favor full valuation as a standard for assessment because it is a more meaningful figure for the taxpayer. Under full valuation, it is easier for the taxpayer to find out if his or her property has been improperly valued. Hence, the full value standard induces more active taxpayer participation leading to more accurate assessments. Recent studies back this position up by showing that assessments are more uniform when they are closer to actual value.

It is agreed that many valuations are unfair and that full valuation is a way to make them fairer. Ironically, the biggest deterent to assessing at full value and the more uniform valuations this would bring is the taxpayers themselves. Taxpayers fear that full value assessments will result in higher taxes. However, this fear has been proven exaggerated. In states where full valuation has been tried, for example in Oregon, tax rates have been lowered to keep tax payments at about the same level as before the full valuation.

In New York State where a full value standard is about to be implemented, the State Board of Equalization and Assessment indicates that, statewide, nearly 60% of residential homeowners will experience a decrease, no change, or a minimal increase in their current tax liability after full valuation is implemented. The report also shows that the greatest tax shift will be *intra*- rather than *inter*-class, with the shift being within the residential class. This indicates that a significant result of full valuation assessment in New

York will be the reduction of the tax burden of many thousands of homeowners who have, in effect, been paying portions of their neighbor's tax bills.

Consolidation and State Involvement

Legal attacks on the local basis of school financing have also had a significant impact on property tax administration. The impact of this litigation has been to make the states take a more significant and responsible role in assisting localities in the administration of the tax. In California and Oregon where the state's role is most pronounced, the property tax is more fairly and efficiently administered.

In recent years, over one-third of the states have overhauled their state tax agencies to strengthen the state role in enforcing fair assessments. Most of these reforms involve supplanting multiheaded agencies with a single director appointed by and responsible to the governor. Three states, Hawaii, Montana, and Maryland have centralized portions of their property tax administration at the state level. Maryland, for example, now requires that assessments be done annually by state officials.

Furthermore, thirteen states, including California, have taken the initiative in encouraging and giving assistance to small taxing and assessing districts to consolidate. Larger districts have the advantage of using more efficient computer techniques, equipment, and professional training. Consolidation of taxing jurisdictions or statewide administration does not necessarily mean better administration but there are obvious advantages. Day-to-day assessment procedures can be carried out at the local level, while research, training, equalization and review can be conducted at the state level.

Assessor Competence

The quality of assessors is obviously an important component to proper administration of the property tax. An assessor must have a working knowledge of building and construction costs to be able to keep up with the real estate market. He or she must be knowledgeable in corporate accounting and, to an increasing extent, must grasp computer techniques. He or she must have the capacity to manage a staff of assistants and clerical workers and must possess the ability to work well with the press and changing political currents in state and local government.

Many states have made notable progress in upgrading the quality of assessors and in standardizing their assessment practices and have either initiated or improved their training programs for assessors. All but

one of these states (Massachusettes) requires the certification of its assessors — a requirement that was almost non-existent fifteen years ago. In addition, 26 states have launched some kind of mandatory training program ranging from year long sessions to an occasional conference on current assessing and appraisal techniques. Professional societies such as the International Association of Assessing Officers and the National Association of Tax Administrators also offer courses and research on the newest innovations in assessing.

To assure that stiffer standards are met, states are moving in the direction of requiring that tax assessors be appointed rather than elected. According to Paul V. Corusy, Executive Director of the IAAO, about half of the nation's 14,000 assessors are elected.

Computers

Computers have had an impressive record in boosting the quality and efficiency of the administration of the property tax. The computer simplifies a number of tasks such as the preparation of the tax role showing property ownership, description of property and the preparation of the billing. Automating these procedures speeds up the assessment process and allows for easy access to information.

Computers also have been programmed to aid in the actual appraisal of property. Variables such as living space, area of a house, number of bedrooms, quality of construction, and so on are fed into the computer. The computer then calculates the value of all the property using a standardized formula. Although the initial cost is substantial, the efficiency of a well programmed automated appraisal system is impressive. The use of typical data processing equipment can cost much less per appraisal than the comparable cost of a traditional appraisal system. California was one of the first states to pioneer automated appraisal systems for assessing single family homes. Due to its favorable results, the state has had implemented or is developing the use of computerized appraisal systems in nearly half of its 58 counties.

Nationwide, despite the prodding by professional assessor associations, the trend to automate has been slow. Of about 83 million taxable properties, less than 10% are assessed by computer systems. At last count, 14 states have implemented or are in the process of introducing computer technology in their assessing procedures.

The computer, boosting the efficiency

of the assessment process, allows the assessor to follow market trends more closely and to update more frequently. The assessor is then able to make more accurate, and hence fairer property tax assessments. One survey in Orange County, California, showed computerized residential assessments to be more than twice as accurate as some of the nation's most qualified assessors.

Although computers may boost the efficiency of appraising property, there are some drawbacks. Robert Brandon, Jonathan Rowe, and Thomas Stanton, authors of *Tax Politics*, warn of the potential for alienation of the assessor from the taxpayer, making it more difficult for property owners to complain. "You can sit down and argue with an appraiser," they maintain, "but who can fight with a third generation IBM?" Furthermore, computer systems are only as good as those who design and use them. An effective automated assessment system requires accurate sufficient data collection and qualified personnel who are able to properly program and interpret the computer information.

Full Disclosure

In addition to being fair and efficient, a tax should be comprehensible to the taxpayer. The inability of property owners to be able to gauge the effective rate of tax is one of the main reasons why property owners have little confidence in the property tax.

Although some state and local taxing jurisdictions have moved toward more openness, property tax bills are still mystifying to most property owners. At a minimum property owners should receive: 1) annual notification of the full value ascribed to their property; 2) notification of the statutory ratio of assessed value to full value (if the state is a fractional rather than a full value state); and 3) notification of the average ratio of assessed value to true value of all property in their locality, class (if in a state that classifies property) and state.

Actually about a third of the states have moved in the direction of sending more explicit explanations to taxpayers on how their tax bills are computed and how they can be appealed.

Some states have gone even further. In some jurisdictions in Illinois, Washington, and Wisconsin, under a Taxpayer Assisted Property Evaluation System (TAPES), property owners are sent a form similar to the assessor's worksheet listing information about the property and showing the tentative value of the land and improvements. The property owner is asked to review the worksheet, correcting any errors in assessment and to return it to the taxing authorities. If there are any major disagreements, the assessor will then reassess the property. This system does not supplant the assessor's role in valuing property. Rather, it attempts to verify the data collected by the assessor, similar to banks sending out a monthly statement for customers to review.

Exemptions

Properties that are exempt from taxation diminish an already dwindling tax base. Given the harsh impact of exemptions on the remaining property taxpayers, assessors should value and publish lists of exempt properties regularly so the community can periodically reconsider the social value of exempting such properties. When exempt property changes its use, it should no longer be exempt. For example in Tacoma, Washington, the property of the Church of the Latter Day Saints was recently placed back on the tax rolls because it was found that the buildings were being occupied by persons other than pastors which the law required for the exemption.

Lax Tax Collection

Lastly a major area in which local tax administration often flounders is in the area of tax collections. Delinquent tax-payments shift the burden onto the remaining taxpayers who must absorb the loss of revenues through higher tax rates.

Delinquencies are neither petty nor uncommon. In New York City alone, $570.8 million of property taxes were uncollected as of June 1976. This was at a time in its history when New York City was borrowing at astronomically high rates to keep financially afloat. According to Jack Newfield in his recently published book, *The Abuse of Power*, among those who were delinquent were the largest commercial landlords in the city. Similarly, as of this year, delinquent taxpayers in Boston owe $107 million in property taxes.

Lax enforcement and lenient punishment are two reasons why so many potential tax dollars remain in the pockets of tax delinquents. Even when the locality does impose penalties, fines may be so minimal as to actually encourage delinquency. In New York City, for example, interest charged on arrears is lower than that charged for commercial bank loans. By not collecting back taxes the city is, in effect, making a low interest loan to its biggest property owners.

The property tax can be made more equitable if property is valued at its full value, made uniform throughout districts and classes, and assessed annually using updated techniques. Full disclosure of information to taxpayers will stimulate taxpayer scrutiny of their tax bills and encourage taxpayer confidence. Tightening up administration in the area of collections by regularly reviewing exempt properties and removing policies and attitudes which cultivate delinquencies will provide an abundant new source of revenues. These sums can then be channeled to finance better administration and lower tax rates.

"Property Tax is Often Poorly Run" is reprinted by permission from the October 1976 issue of *People and Taxes*, Public Citizen Tax Reform Research Group.

Small homes here taxed hardest

By Ed McManus

Urban affairs editor

MOST SMALL homes in Cook County are being assessed at a dramatically higher rate than large, expensive homes, according to a study of assessments by Prof. Arthur Lyons of the University of Illinois at Chicago Circle.

Computerization in the assessor's office has made the problems in assessments worse, Lyons said, and some homes have been assessed at a rate nine times higher than more expensive homes in a neighboring township.

Lyons' study also showed that in South Township—a portion of Chicago's South Side that includes the politically powerful 11th Ward—typical homes were assessed at no more than 17 per cent of market value for the 1976 tax year.

No other township had such a low maximum, the study said. The rate mandated by law at that time was 22 per cent.

"Steps should be taken immediately to eliminate both the unfair burden on the owners of lower value residential properties in almost every township of the county, and the serious nonuniformities that exist among areas for similarly valued properties," the report said.

"ALTHOUGH THE computer-assisted assessment procedure has made progress in dealing with the latter problem at some price levels, it appears actually to have accentuated the former problem."

Lyons said in an interview Tuesday that he "can only guess" why there is so much nonuniformity. "But in the North Quadrant, the patterns are so devastatingly consistent, it's almost as if the [computer] program was written to discriminate against lower-value homes," he said.

The study was based on assessments in the Northwest Quadrant of the county

for the tax year 1974, in the Southwest Quadrant for 1975, in the South Quadrant for 1976, and in the North Quadrant for 1977. Only the North Quadrant was assessed by computer.

The Northwest Quadrant and part of the Southwest subsequently have been reassessed by computer, but Lyons said he did not have access to the data.

ASSESSOR THOMAS M. TULLY has refused to permit examination of his computer program, but he submits data annually to the State Department of Local Government Affairs. The department passed last year's data on to the Cook County Real Estate Tax Study Commission, which gave it to Lyons.

The commission, appointed by County Board President George W. Dunne, also provided some financial assistance for Lyons' five-month study. Most of it was supported by a grant from the Wieboldt Foundation.

Under the new assessment procedure, data on recent sale prices of homes is fed into a computer. The value of each home is determined by selling prices of comparable homes in the same neighborhood.

So if 3-bedroom, 20-year-old, brick homes in a given neighborhood are selling for $100,000 and you have that kind of home, the computer should determine that your home is worth $100,000. The assessed valuation of your property under the newly-enacted rate—16 per cent of market value—would be $16,000.

That figure is adjusted by the State Department of Local Government Affairs in an effort to make assessments more uniform, and the tax rate of each local government is applied to the adjusted assessment to determine how much tax you pay.

According to the study, homes in Barrington Township valued at $20,000 were assessed at 38 per cent of market value when that township was assessed for the

1977 tax year. [The legally-mandated rate was 17 per cent.]

Homes in Schaumburg Township valued at $70,000 were assessed at only 4 per cent when Schaumburg was assessed for the 1974 tax year, the report said. [The legal rate at that time was 22 per cent.]

IN MOST OF the North Quadrant townships, the rates show a steady decline linked to increasing value. For instance, while New Trier and Barrington Township homes valued at up $40,000 were assessed at a higher rate than the mandated 17 per cent for 1977, homes worth $80,000 or more were assessed at only 13 per cent in those townships.

Daniel Pierce, Tully's chief deputy, said the data Lyons used had some misleading aspects that could have distorted the results of the study. One example Pierce cited was partial assessments on homes not fully built at the time their value was determined by the assessor.

"I can't accept that there are homes assessed at 38 per cent," he said. "I can't say strong enough how wrong that is—there's no way. And if there were, that's what the appeal system is all about. I think the study was sort of skewed to get a desired result."

LYONS MADE four recommendations in the report:
● The assessor should hire a "highly qualified statistician" to develop a better computer program.
● The assessor should provide greater public access to its data.
● There should be a more comprehensive annual monitoring of assessments "to insure that inequities of the type uncovered in this report, once corrected, do not unintentionally reappear."
● The appeals process should be changed to make it easier for homeowners to complain about assessments.

"Small Homes Here Taxed Hardest" is reprinted by permission from the August 30, 1978 issue of *The Chicago Tribune*.

Whites Get Lower Levy Regularly

By Ed McManus
Urban affairs editor

HOMES IN THE Chicago's black neighborhoods are taxed consistently at a much higher level than those in white communities, a study by researchers at the University of Illinois at Chicago Circle has found.

The study discovered that the Cook County assessor's office has underestimated the value of almost all residential property in four predominantly white neighborhoods of Chicago and two white suburbs.

On the other hand, the value of a major portion of the homes in five black neighborhoods of Chicago and one black suburban areas has been overestimated, according to the study.

The result has been higher taxes in black neighborhoods—sometimes three times higher than on comparable property in white neighborhoods, the research team said.

THE TAX BILL last year on a $20,000 home in North Lawndale was $411 higher than in Bridgeport, according to the study; the bill on a $30,000 home in South Shore was $299 higher than in Bridgeport; and the bill on a $50,000 home in South Shore was $295 higher than in Portage Park.

The study is the first of its kind in the nation. No other comprehensive analysis comparing black and white assessments has been conducted here or elsewhere.

"We don't think the disparities are due to a conscious effort by the assessor's office to discriminate," said Prof. Arthur Lyons, who supervised the study, "but the evidence is here. We have no idea why it is happening because we haven't been granted access to the assessors' procedures."

TONI MAHAN, one of five graduate students who conducted the research, said the group did not expect to find nearly as much variation between black and white assessments.

"We expected a hint of it, but this is a lot more than a hint," she said. "We hope it embarrasses them enough to clean up the assessment process."

Daniel Pierce, chief deputy to Assessor Thomas Hynes, said, "The inference that blacks are being discriminated against by some systematic activity is 100 per cent wrong—it's just not true. The assessments are done by computer, and the computer is literally color blind."

Pierce said the graphs in the report "optically look very dramatic" but assessments of homes values at $20,000 to $40,000 are fairly similar in most of the neighborhoods studied.

MOST OF THE overassessment, according to the study, is in low-priced black homes and most of the underassessment is in high-priced white homes. Pierce said any variation that occurs in assessment rates is related to the value of the properties, not the race of the occupants.

Mahan, Fred Bremer, Ed Dolan, Thelma Karson, and Larry Wenderski spent an estimated 1,250 hours over the last six months studying sale prices and assessments of 3,915 properties of one to four units in the 12 target communities.

The black communities were Austin, West Englewood, North Lawndale, Chatham-Avalon Park, South Shore, and central Evanston. The white areas were Bridgeport, Marquette Park-Gage Park, Portage Park, Sauganash-Edgebrook, Lincolnwood, and Hometown.

"Only one white community, Marquette Park-Gage Park, has overassessment at any level of market value," the report said. "This occurs in the $20,000-$27,000 range and affects only about 35 per cent of the homes in the neighborhood. All the other white areas are underassessed.

"Bridgeport has the lowest assessments of any of the 12 neighborhoods, about 50 to 60 per cent of what they should be."

Bridgeport, South Shore, and Chatham-Avalon Park were assessed in 1975 before the assessment process was computerized. The other nine communities were assessed by computer.

WITHIN EACH of the black neighborhoods and three of the white neighborhoods, the study found small homes assessed at a higher rate than larger, more expensive homes.

Only Bridgeport, Lincolnwood, and Sauganash-Edgebrook have fairly uniform assessments for high- and low-priced homes, according to the study.

A study conducted by Lyons last year concluded that most small homes throughout the county were being assessed at a much higher rate than more expensive homes.

The new report made several recommendations, including:

● The County Board or the Illinois legislature should enact legislation requiring the assessor to disclose the computer program he is using.

● The legislature should give the State Department of Local Government Affairs authority to equalize assessments among subdivisions if necessary to achieve uniformity.

● The legislature should give the department authority to order reassessments in specific neighborhoods when necessary and to conduct the reassessments itself if the local assessor fails to conduct them.

All the assessments studied were made when Thomas Tully was assessor. Hynes replaced Tully in December.

"Whites Get Lower Levy Regularly" is reprinted by permission from the April 14, 1979 issue of *The Chicago Tribune*.

Iowa property assessment a disgrace: Economist

By DAVID YEPSEN
Register Staff Writer

The way Iowa residential property is assessed remains "a disgrace," Drake University economist Steven Gold told a state meeting of local assessors Monday.

And Gold suggested the state might want to start revising local assessments each year instead of every two years or fire assessors who aren't doing an accurate job. .

"The quality of assessment in 1976 was not significantly different than it was in 1975," Gold said.

"Last year I characterized it as a disgrace. I see no reason to change that conclusion now," he said.

On the average, he said, assessments in Iowa are 23 per cent off. "I don't expect it to be perfect, but 23 per cent is very serious," he said. "All property should be assessed at the same per cent of its real value. Two people who have the same house are likely to pay different property taxes and that isn't fair."

He said some homeowners think that because their assessments are lower than the market value of their homes they are getting a break. They may be, he said, but homeowners should not tolerate inaccurate assessments "because they don't know how big a break their neighbors are getting. It could be more."

Gold also told the assessors it is "deplorable that most of you in effect give a tax break to the owners of high value property."

Conducted Survey

Gold based his findings on comparisons of the sale prices of residential properties against the assessed valuation of those properties.

Gold's survey did not include farm sales because "there are simply not enough usable sales of farmland to permit a study of them," he said.

Gold, who earned the ire of many assessors with his report last year, emphasized he is "measuring the quality of assessment, not necessarily how good a job the assessor is doing."

In prepared remarks deleted from his speech, Gold said "the places with more accurate assessments do tend to pay higher salaries, and this probably has an effect on the caliber of person who serves as assessor."

Gold said he omitted the comment from his speech because it was "too insulting" and "wouldn't be very tactful."

Many of the assessors were angered at Gold's statements anyway.

"Have you ever been an assessor or walked in our shoes?" Buchanan County Assessor Lawrence Jacobs asked.

"No, but you don't have to be a chef to tell if the soup tastes good," Gold retorted.

Legislators Accused

Fort Madison's assessor, Willis Holland, suggested Iowa legislators are unwilling to make changes in property tax laws because the changes might not benefit their own land holdings.

Gold said some legislators don't say they are farmers but "they do have a little farm or a feedlot on the side. There are a few closet farmers" in the legislature.

But one assessor, who was not immediately identified, stood up and thanked Gold.

"You did us a great service because without the statistics and rankings you did and that ran in The Des Moines Register I don't believe I would have got the county conference board to vote a reappraisal," the assessor said.

Conference boards are groups of officials from local governments. Members govern the assessors offices and approve money for reappraisal studies.

Gold said the dismal quality of the assessments is bad because "assessments are the basis of how much

property tax we pay and the idea behind the property tax is that your tax should depend on the value of your property."

He said "the quality of assessment is best in cities and metropolitan areas, a notch lower in urban and mostly rural counties and far worse in the completely rural counties."

He also said "the commonly accepted minimum for an acceptable" variation between sale prices and assessed valuations is 20 per cent.

"By this standard, only 35 (of 118) assessment jurisdictions are adequate .... This means almost three-fourths of all jurisdictions' assessments are not adequately accurate."

"We should not be satisfied," Gold said, until the difference is "10 per cent or lower in most places."

Gold also listed several reasons for the differences in the quality of assessments among jursdictions. He said:

● Assessors do not have adequate office budgets.

● Some city and county boards of review "may change assessments set by assesors. Some of the blame for inaccurate assessments may belong to the board."

● If an outside firm has recently completed a revaluation of property, it would tend to make the assessments look more accurate.

● Twelve assessors also revalued the property in their districts during 1977 — not a year in which state officials ordered a revaluation.

"While I applaud them for being conscientious, I deplore the result: The property taxpayers in their jurisdictions were not treated fairly .... Their school property tax was too high because school aid from the state was reduced due to the higher assessments," Gold said.

● Some assessors have been in office only a short period of time and may have inherited problems from their predecessor or not had time to correct inaccuracies.

Gold said new assessors were hired in 1975 and 1976 in Hancock, O'Brien, Fremont, Cedar, Clark, Clinton, Taylor and Woodbury counties and in Mason City and Boone.

● Luck may make assessments look better or worse than they actually are. "It would be good luck if most of the houses sold were ones where the assessor was close to the mark while the ones on which he had erred were not sold," Gold said.

"Despite all of these qualifications, I stated last year and I still believe that the rankings probably do in most cases reflect how well individual assessors are doing their jobs," Gold said.

He said most assessors are "at about the same place they were last year" which indicates to him that "luck" plays little part in the quality of assessments.

He said there is a "noticeable difference" among the rankings for different areas.

But "no type of assessment jurisdiction has a monopoly on good assessments," he said.

Among the top 20 jurisdictions, nine are from mostly rural counties, six from cities, three from metropolitan counties and two from urban counties.

Defends Statement

Gold, who admits he touched off a political storm when he called assessments a "disgrace" a year ago, defended that term again Monday.

"Frankly, when I used the term I was borrowing from President Carter who often has called the federal income tax a 'disgrace to the human race.' I would submit that if the income tax is a disgrace, the property tax is a double disgrace," Gold said.

Gold offered the following suggestions for improving the system of Iowa's property tax assessments:

● The "automatic removal of assessors whose performance is consistently inadequate ...." This suggestion brought an angry retort from Des Moines City Assessor Andrew S. Regis who said it would be "unconstitutional."

● The establishment of "minimum levels of funding (for assessor's offices) partially supported by state aid."

● The "consolidation of (assessment) districts that are now too small to provide efficient and accurate assessment."

● An "annual adjustment of assessed property values to keep up with inflation."

● Offering "monetary incentives to assessors who perform well."

● Enactment of "a law requiring accurate reporting of sales prices."

● Passage of "a requirement to select assessors from among the most qualified applicants along with a provision for periodic retesting."

● Increased use of computers — probably with help from state government — to help determine property values and reduce the paperwork in assessors offices.

Following is Gold's ranking of the performance of city assessors in Iowa based upon how close assessed values are to market values.

1. Cedar Rapids, 2. Iowa City, 3. Ames, 4. Newton, 5. Dubuque, 6. Fort Madison, 7. Sioux City, 8. Davenport, 9. Muscatine, 10. Marshalltown, 11. Clinton, 12. Des Moines, 13. Fort Dodge, 14. Boone, 15. Waterloo, 16. Mason City, 17. Keokuk, 18. Ottumwa, 19. Oskaloosa.

Following is a ranking of "metropolitan counties" in Iowa. These are the counties containing cities with populations over 50,000.

1. Scott, 2. Polk, 3. Linn, 4. Black Hawk, 5. Dubuque, 6. Pottawattamie, 7. Woodbury.

Following is Gold's ranking of "urban counties." These are counties just below the seven largest ones. "Urban counties" must have 50 per cent of their population living in communities with populations larger than 2,500 and contain a city larger than 10,000 population.

1. Johnson, 2. Clay, 3. Clinton, 4. Muscatine, 5. Marshall, 6. Wapello, 7. Lee, 8. Cerro Gordo, 9. Story, 10. Des Moines, 11. Mahaska, 12. Webster.

Following is the ranking for "mostly rural" counties. These counties contain at least one town of at least 2,500 people.

1. Fayette, 2. Jackson, 3. Floyd, 4. Henry, 5. Delaware, 6. Mills, 7. Cherokee, 8. Buena Vista, 9. Howard, 10. Warren, 11. Dallas, 12. Greene, 13. Hardin, 14. Buchanan, 15. Plymouth, 16. Emmet, 17. Allamakee, 18. Bremer, 19. Winneshiek, 20. Washington, 21. Sioux, 22. Davis. 23. Winnebago, 24. Hamilton, 25. Cedar, 26. Crawford, 27. Shelby, 28. Kossuth, 29. Boone, 30. Benton, 31. Harrison, 32. Clarke, 33. Osceola, 34. Palo Alto, 35. Montgomery, 36. Dickinson, 37. Cass, 38. Page, 39. Grundy, 40. Union, 41. Jones, 42. Jefferson, 43. Humboldt, 44. Franklin, 45. Chickasaw, 46. Marion, 47. Tama, 48. Lucas. 49. Sac, 50. Poweshiek, 51. Wright, 52. Audubon, 53. Monroe, 54. Madison, 55. Decatur, 56. Jasper, 57. Monona, 58. Carroll, 59. Lyon, 60. Mitchell, 61. Appanoose, 62. O'Brien.

Gold ranked the "completely rural" counties (those with no town with a population larger than 2,500) as follows:

1. Hancock, 2. Adair, 3. Worth, 4. Iowa, 5. Adams, 6. Ida, 7. Pocahontas, 8. Clayton, 9. Guthrie, 10. Van Buren, 11. Butler, 12. Calhoun, 13. Fremont, 14. Keokuk, 15. Louisa, 16. Wayne, 17. Taylor, 18. Ringgold.

City Assessments Hit Commercial Buildings Lightly

By LaBarbara Bowman
Washington Post Staff Writer

The assessed value of some of Washington's most expensive commercial real estate has declined or remained the same in the past four years while assessments on most single-family dwellings have soared, according to a report issued yesterday by the D.C. auditor.

While the assessed value of all residential property has jumped an average of 66 per cent since 1974, the assessed value of business properties has increased only 23 per cent, according to the report.

In addition, assessments on the city's 20 most valuable properties as of 1974, have risen an average of only 16 per cent in the past four years, the report says.

"It is quite apparent...that several of the major commercial properties of the District have been given a free ride for property tax purposes over the last several years," stated the report prepared by Carl Bergman, deputy D.C. auditor. The auditor's office is an arm of the D.C. City Council.

Donald Beach, chief of the city's real estate property assessment tax administration, said he had not read the report and could not explain why the assessments of almost half of the 20 most valuable properties from 1974, including the Washington Post building and the Capital Hilton Hotel, had declined or remained constant.

As a general rule, he said, residential assessments have leaped ahead of commercial assessments because intown living has become increasingly popular, accelerating the turnover of homes, while commercial development continues to lag with many old line city businesses still leaving for the suburbs.

Beach denied there is a government policy to give businesses a tax break. The disparity in commercial and residential assessment changes is simply the result of open market dynamics, he said.

He noted, for example, that two large downtown stores—Kann's and Lansburgh's—have closed down in the last few years, and until very recently office buildings had been plagued with vacancies.

In addition, Beach said, the assessed value of office buildings and hotels is determined primarily by the amount of rent collected or the income produced from the building.

"To raise the assessment (of a commercial building) $1 million takes a gross income increase of $250,000," he said. Most office building tenants are on long-term leases, and rents are not increased annually, he said.

The assessed value of single-family homes, by contrast, is determined by the price of comparable homes sold in the same neighborhood, Beach said.

Bergman said the city tax rolls show assessments actually declined in the last four years for the following properties: The Washington Post, Sheraton Park Hotel, the office building at 1025 Connecticut Ave. NW, The Towers apartment building at 4201 Cathedral Ave. NW, the Mayflower Hotel, the apartment building at 4000 Massachusetts Ave. NW and the National Press Building.

The Capitol Hilton Hotel had the same $12.1 million assessment this year as it held in 1974. The Van Ness Center, a large shopping and apartment complex on upper Connecticut Avenue, had its assessed value increase only 1 per cent in the four-year period.

Of the remaining 11 properties among the top 20 in value in 1974, all had their assessments increased, Bergman said, but many of the increases occurred because the buildings were still under construction in 1974 and subsequently acquired greater value on completion.

L'Enfant Plaza, for example, which contains an underground shopping mall, had its assessment increased by 85 per cent in four years from $37.1 million to $68.9 million upon comple-

tion. The owners now are appealing their 1978 assessment, Beach said.

Bergman prepared the report for a public hearing held yesterday by City Council member Marion Barry, chairman of the Council's finance and revenue committee.

Barry held the hearing to gain citizen and official opinion on several bills that have been introduced to ease the whopping property tax increases that have hit many homeowners this year.

Barry said the disparity in the rate of increases between businesses and single-family homes did not surprise him but he asked Beach to send him a written report explaining how the assessors arrived at the 1978 assessments for the top 20 commercial properties cited by Bergman.

The lag in commercial and apartment building assessments "is the reason that home owners are bearing an increasing proportion of the total burden," Barry said.

Bergman said that in 1974, single-family homes and commercial property each accounted for 39 per cent of the city's tax base of $6.8 billion. By this year, single family homes accounted for 49 per cent of what is now a $9 billion base, while commercial property has slipped to 36 per cent, he said.

Overall, the assessed value of apartment houses in the city has declined 11 per cent since 1974, Bergman said.

Beach attributed the decline to rent control. The assessed value of an apartment building is determined by the income produced by the building, and when rent control holds down the rents, the value also goes down, Beach said.

Bergman attributed part of the decline to the widespread conversion of apartment units to condominiums in recent years.

"City Assessments Hit Commercial Buildings Lightly" is reprinted by permission from the May 11, 1977, issue of *The Washington Post*.

The Texaco plant, located in Lockport Township, is grossly underassessed at $18 million.

Taxes: Who's Not Paying?

Property taxes are skyrocketing here in Illinois and nationwide. Not as well known is the fact that large commercial and industrial properties are not paying their fair share of the property tax load.

No one can be absolutely certain of exactly how much revenue is lost every year through tax breaks for business and industry, or how many dollars these breaks add to the tax bill of the average homeowner and renter. Recent articles and studies have speculated on the loss of hundreds of millions of dollars through tax exemptions and non-collection of corporate taxes. One

escape route from taxation for big business is manipulating the underassessment of their properties through appeals and political pressure.

In Illinois, the assessment of large commercial or industrial property is the responsibility of the local assessor in whose jurisdiction the property lies. Local assessors gather the necessary facts and figures needed to assess the industry's fair market value, tax it at 33 1/3% (40% in Cook County) and submit their findings to the Supervisor of Assessments in their area for approval.

Whereas the "fair market value" of

a home can be well approximated by comparing it to recent sales of similar homes in the same locality, commercial and industrial property is rarely sold and therefore comparisons are impossible. Assessment of "value" must rely upon complicated calculations of the income-producing capacity of the property or the cost of replacing it at current construction prices.

Too often the local assessor is not supplied with the complex and highly technical information needed to calculate a proper and fair assessment. Instead, they are forced to take the word of the industry itself regarding its market value. The Supervisor of Assessments (often subject to political pressures) has the power to change the local assessor's figures and many times does so without any explanations. In addition, the corporations have top-notch attorneys and tax experts who appear before the board of review and tax appeal board to discredit the local assessor's figures. The result has been the unfair assessment of complex properties at the expense of the average taxpayer.

In Will County, Lockport township assessor Pat Hartley has not only documented difficulties in assessing large industry, but also feels the gross underassessment of commercial and industrial property in her jurisdiction is responsible for the intolerably high residential property taxes.

For instance, a Texaco refinery is located in her township, one of the most modern refineries in the world. In 1971 its assessment dropped from $26 million to $16 million as a result of appeals to the Supervisor of Assessments citing "obsolescence" and "deterioration." Yet, the refinery is upgraded every 3 to 4 years and production *has not* dropped. In fact, Texaco spent over $30 million in 1973 for improvements and announced to its stockholders that production *increased* by 25,000 barrels a day. However, the township has never realized a penny in increased taxes because Texaco received an exemption from the state for the improvements, claiming that they were pollution control devices and *did not* increase production.

An even more disturbing fact is that the Texaco refinery, which lies within the city limits of Lockport, pays no city taxes and yet receives electricity, water and use of city roads. One would think that in exchange for these services Texaco would gladly contribute to the city's growth in various other ways. But during Texaco's 55 years in Lockport, the company has yet to contribute even one book to the public library.

The job situation at Texaco isn't much brighter. It would seem to make sense that the township would be more willing to put up with the underassessment of the refinery if it were able to supply numerous jobs for people in the community. But the number of jobs at Texaco has declined over the past few years due to mechanization from over 2,000 to just about 700. As Pat Hartley points out, "Nobody really cares. Texaco is only interested in money, not the people of Lockport. They don't care about paying their fair share to our community."

In 1970, Union Oil built a refinery right next door to the Texaco plant in Will County. Its area is substantially smaller than the 1000 acres Texaco holds and yet was assessed at $62 million. Today, Texaco is presently assessed at $18 million—an outstanding difference of $44 million. According to Hartley, "The scrap value alone of the Texaco refinery is worth more than the $18 million figure."

Although she is virtually certain that the Texaco plant is grossly underassessed, Ms. Hartley cannot arrive at an exact figure because she does not have the productivity figures upon which an accurate assessment would depend.

The enormous resources available to the industrial taxpayer become a significant issue in many instances. in the case of Texaco, Assessor Hartley has tried year after year to set their assessment at reasonable levels ($25 million in 1975; $30 million in 1976) only to find her figures lowered by the Supervisor of Assessments and discredited by the industry's lawyers and tax experts.

However, the Texaco refinery is not the only culprit of underassessed property in Will County. The Sanitary District is also grossly underassessed. The plant is continually accumulating land, selling power to Commonwealth Edison and yet its assessed value keeps dropping. Ms. Hartley calculates the assessed value of the Sanitary District at a modest $5 million instead of its official assessment figure of under $1 million. The stories are similar; no one knows exactly how much the Sanitary District plant is worth.

Industries are not required to reveal cost figures of production which aid the assessor in determining the proper assessment value of their property. There are also no penalties for refusing to reveal those figures. As a result, commercial and industrial properties can keep their true worth a secret among their stockholders and provide the assessor with an assessment figure they want to pay without receiving any trouble from the state.

The Illinois Department of Local Government Affairs (DLGA) was established to provide fair and just property taxation in this state. The Department has the power to formulate and recommend legislation for the improvement of the tax system, request the institution of proceedings, actions and prosecutions to enforce the laws and to order reassessments.

Over the last two years, Public Action has consistently pressed the DLGA to fulfill its responsibilities and provide technical assistance to local assessors on request. However, the Department has remained miserably deficient in processing requests. Presently it has a staff of only "3 and ½ or 4" expert appraisers, whose duties include the upgrading of educational programs as well as providing expert appraisals.

"It is clear that the State Department of Local Government Affairs has completely abandonned any attempt to improve industrial and commercial assessment," said Ms. Hartley. "The DGLA will have to be forced by the legislature to substantially improve their staff and services to local assessors in order to enforce fair assessments on industrial and commercial properties in Illinois. It is also clear that if we are to see any real improvement in the fairness of the system in the near future, industry will have to be required to disclose to local assessors all information pertinent to the accurate appraisal of the real value of their properties."

"Taxes: Who's Not Paying?" is reprinted by permission from the November 4, 1978 issue of *Public Action News,* Ilinois Public Action Campaign.

We Do Need Assessment Reform

The U.S. Census of Governments' quinquennial report on assessment ratios is persuasive and general evidence that we need assessment reform, but it understates how much we need reform. In respect to industrial property, it omits ownerships whose value is judged to surpass a quarter of a million dollars: that is, most industrial property. It is unfortunate that this is pointed out in a part of the Census most users don't get around to reading, even though perhaps they should, so that it took Nader's Raiders to ferret this out.

So many economists are mistaken, I believe, to cite the Census to show that industrial property is not underassessed. The Census is simply not in on the action here, and Nader's data, non-random though they may be, have more to tell us than the Census.

Much of Nader's data are consistent with and supplement and reaffirm the general principle that land is underassessed. He has focused on industrial landholdings: oil in Texas, coal in the Appalachians, copper in Montana, timber in Georgia and Maine. I know of no reason to doubt the generality of these findings, and many reasons to believe it.

Census Study Omission

The Census study omits the class of land most underassessed, that is unsubdivided acreage inside SMSAs. Much of that is speculative; much is in estates held by the very (and the very very) rich; and much is industrial.

I studied some of this industrial land in Milwaukee. It was not only underassessed, but regressively assessed. The large tracts were given a wholesale rate, allegedly because large tracts sell for less per unit. At the same time, the city was assembling and/or holding large tracts in an industrial land bank, allegedly because the market put a premium on large tracts. It makes an interesting contrast. I have published some of my findings on this question elsewhere.[8] Similar findings by Armin Jocz in Beloit, Wisconsin and by Alene Ammond in Cherry Hill, New Jersey, were published recently as testimony presented to the Senate Subcommittee on Intergovernmental Relations.[9]

Professor Samuel Loescher of Indiana University has written me that his students' study "confirms the substantial underassessment of industrial land relative to adjacent residential land, measured on a per-acre basis, in the area of every major industrial property in Monroe County, Indiana."[10]

Beyond Revenue Productivity

The value of assessment reform is much greater than the gain of revenue, however great or small that may be. Increased taxpayer confidence and acceptance are equally important. I do not think that people who countenance corruption and maladministration have any inkling of how destructive these are to the morale of citizens who are outraged first by the facts, and then outraged again by the complaisance and laxity of responsible officials who have the power and duty to act.

The revenue productivity of a tax is limited by the suffering of those most impacted, i.e. those overassessed and paying the highest effective rates. These become the widows and orphans trotted out to damn the entire system.

Easy Half Step

We can move halfway from here to the site value tax without changing any law, simply by obeying the laws we already have and assessing land at market the way we do buildings. I do not exaggerate. Listen to what people say when an assessor moves toward bringing assessed valuation up to market value. "The assessor has gone hog-wild." "He's trying to tell people how to use their land." "The assessor is taking over the planning function." "This vicious radical theory of market value." "Our community is unique." Sound familiar? It gives a notion how time has withered and custom staled the notion that all property should be assessed on the same basis according to law.

I invite your close attention to what has happened in a few jurisdictions whose assessors have brought land up to market: Rosslyn, Va.; Southfield, Michigan; Sacramento, California. I further invite your attention to the cities of Canada, especially western Canada, where assessors traditionally value land more heavily than they do here. These cities compare favorably in most respects with the remains of many of ours.

The underassessment of land is worse than the Census shows, at least in my experience. *Building the American City*, the final report of the Douglas Commission (National Commission on Urban Problems), cites Allen D. Manvel to the effect that 40 percent of urban real estate value is land value, and I believe the true figure is at least that high. But in most city assessment rolls it is down nearer 20 percent or 25 percent.

In sylvan areas, every forest owner likes to overstate the value of stumpage for federal tax purposes (to transfer profit to timber culture, which gets capital gains) and to understate it for state and local excise and property tax purposes. All that is needed here is for state and federal tax officers to exchange information and demand the same valuations be used, although of course immature timber must be discounted from its maturity value.

The most underassessed of all properties are mineral reserves. Producing properties are underassessed; reserve properties are not assessed as mineral-bearing land at all. This has something to do with the problem of measuring reserves, but not very much. It has more to do with differential political power and constitutes, in my opinion, one of the worst breakdowns of the democratic process that we suffer. If one *really* means to help those poor widows, here is a place to start. If the Watergate catharsis is used merely to review the way we play cops-and-robbers, the newsprint lavished on the affair will have been largely wasted. The point is rather how dependence on campaign contributions biases and subverts politicians of both parties at all levels in favor of large contributors. Federal income tax loopholes for mineral owners are matched by local assessors and courts who underassess mineral reserves to the point of exemption.

In West Virginia, for example, the United States Geological Survey maps of coal reserves have been available for a long time, but not used. Recently the State Department of Assessment has begun staff work to help local assessors use these maps, and to win the court cases that inevitably follow. They need help.

Congress should instruct the U.S.G.S., Bureau of Mines, and other federal agencies to cooperate actively with state and perhaps local agencies in the process of valuing mineral reserves. This entails not just ascertaining the physical volume and grade of the reserves; it entails valuation, an economic art.

If it be anticipated that states might not cooperate, I suggest that no state—until it shall have done so—be allowed to plead poverty in Washington. I predict few of them would have reason to plead poverty afterwards.

If it be anticipated that the agencies might not cooperate, or would represent the assessed parties instead of the public, then a new agency may be called for. Whether in a new or old agency, new personnel are needed with new skills and a sense of the new mission.

---

8. *"What Is Property Tax Reform?"* American Journal of Economics and Sociology, April 1972, and "Adequacy of Land as a Tax Base," in Daniel Holland, Ed., The Assessment of Land Value, Madison, University of Wisconsin Press, 1970.

9. Hearings before the Subcommittee on Intergovernmental Relations, The Impact and Administration of the Property Tax, Washington, D.C., Government Printing Office, 1973.

10. John Goss and Dave Hill, "An Examination of Property Tax Assessments in Monroe County," MS.

"We Do Need Assessment Reform" is reprinted by permission from *Property Tax Reform,* George E. Peterson, ed, © 1973 by The Urban Institute.

PIERCE COUNTY

COUNTY-CITY BUILDING

TACOMA, WASHINGTON

Office of Pierce County Assessor
KEN JOHNSTON

N E W S   R E L E A S E

July 16, 1976

Pierce County's radical owner-involvement method of revaluing residential and open-land properties has saved the county money, showed that all of a county can be revalued in a year, and proved that 99 per cent of property owners are honest, according to Ken Johnston, Pierce County Assessor.

Johnston detailed the program's successes in it's first year, saying that the cost benefits and accuracy of his county's unique assessment plan proved that the property owners did a better job of appraisal than either complex computer systems or mass physical appraisals.

Under the Taxpayers Assisted Property Evaluation System or TAPES program, property owners got mailings of computer data concerning their property. They corrected the data where appropriate and returned the form.

Johnston said that random checks showed only about one percent of taxpayers can be suspected of falsifying data intentionally.

"The cost per appraisal was reduced from $16 to $8. We turned in 28 county vehicles because we no longer needed them for extensive on-site appraisals." Johnson said land itself still gets personal appraisals, however.

The program has made it possible for Pierce County to reappraise and revalue annually, Johnston said. The necessity of yearly revaluation of all property stems from the "Valentine case," in which the State Supreme Court affirmed that it was discriminatory for counties to be revalued district by district over a period of years.

Next step for Pierce County, says Johnston, is to continue annual revaluations with TAPES and to extend the program to commercial properties.

Development of the system has won Pierce County two national awards, one from the International Association of Assessing Officers and another from the National Association of Counties.

A Plan for Reform

Most citizens will bear a reasonable tax burden in exchange for government services if they feel that the tax system is fair and equitable, and that taxation officials give no special favor to any individual or interest. In order to restore public confidence, the following policies should be applied:

(1) Disclosure and Conflict of Interest

Full disclosure of possible conflict of interest should be required of all management personnel, and these disclosure statements should be open for public view and updated annually. Let me add that if selected Assessor, I would ask the Board to require that all employees of the office divest themselves of all investment real estate related holdings to assure the public beyond any doubt of the absence of conflict of interest. In this regard, the current operation of the office's Ethics Committee has been inadequate.

(2) Office of the Public Advocate

As Assessor, I would immediately follow the innovative practice begun in Montgomery County, Maryland and recommend that the Board establish the Office of Public Advocate in the Assessor's department, staffed by a lawyer of great integrity and a small support staff of no more than two or three. This office would not handle individual appeals. Rather, it would serve the much needed function of Ombudsperson. Any employee within the department who suspected unfair practices could go directly to the public advocate without fear of retribution. No employee in my office would be punished for following his or her conscience about questionable activities. Any citizen who suspected tax avoidance, tax favoritism, or any other problem with the Assessor's office could go directly to the public advocate.

(3) Use of the Assessor's Powers and Out-of-County Cooperation

Only full use of the Assessor's power to require provision of economic data will insure that business pays its fair share of taxes. As Assessor, I would cooperate fully with the state Board of Equalization and with the Multistate Tax Commission, and with other state and federal agencies to insure that no enterprises are escaping their fair share of taxes.

Related, is the necessity of all "stipulations" and settlements of a significant size being sent to the Board for their information and review.

(4) Public Information

Most citizens are confused and angry about the property tax assessment system. The system appears not only unjust, but mysterious as well. The Assessor's office does not have adequate material for public distribution on the operation of the office and the basic principles of tax assessment. A simple statement explaining the new three year system should be included in each assessment mailing; new easy-to-read publications on the Assessor's office should be available in libraries, markets, and all public buildings in the county.

In addition, as Assessor I would take a close look at the TAPES system in operation in other jurisdictions. This stands for Taxpayer Assisted Evaluation System which is now in operation in Illinois, Wisconsin, and Washington. This is a data verification system which involves the citizen in correcting and updating information about property.

(5) Operating a Public Interest Office

As Assessor I would take the following administrative steps:

A. Cut back unnecessary administrative staff and get more appraisers into the field.

I would request that the Board bring the total appraisers in the field to 350. I would specifically add 20 to the Personal Property division and 20 to Commercial and Industrial, and I would lower the ceiling at which Personal Property returns are audited from $100,000 to $50,000.

B. Conduct a national talent search for top flight aides.

There is a new generation of highly qualified tax experts around the country, working in other assessors' offices and with such bodies as the Multistate Tax Commission. I would choose whatever field deputies are available to me from among such trained individuals.

C. Annual Report on Tax Trends

Ten years ago it was evident to some experts that the burden of the property tax in Los Angeles was falling unevenly on residential property. It should be the job of the Assessor to alert the Board to such trends, whatever their cause. As Assessor, I would have a trained economist prepare an annual report to the Board and to the public on taxation trends in the County and indicate any possible future revenue problems. This would involve adding at least two economists to the Department's Special Services unit.

D. Tax Reform Options and Economic Impact

As an elected official, it should be the duty of the Assessor to serve as a *resource* for the Board on tax reform and relief options. The Assessor should report annually to the Board on tax proposals, both legislative and administrative, which have been put forward in the state legislature and in other states and counties, as well as at the Federal level. This report should also include an estimate of the economic impact of such measures, if enacted, for the county. For example, if the inventory tax is repealed what would be the short and long run economic impact on the county?

(6) Building a Fair Share System

Finally, I would like to offer my views on ways that the Assessor might generate or help to generate new sources of revenue. It is likely that the property tax as currently defined and administered *even if business did pay its fair share* is too restrictive and homeowners and renters will always bear too high a burden, which, in the long run, can only lead to a tax revolt. This is not my judgement alone. Donald Hagman, professor of law at UCLA and one of the country's leading experts on property taxes has stated:

Taxes on property now taxed are five times what they would be if all property were uniformly burdened. The $5.6 trillion (in exempt property) loophole is getting bigger. Legally and illegally, the property tax base is being shrunk. And the faster it shrinks, the faster it will shrink, for one property owner's exemption translates into the nonexempt property owner's increased tax, which leads him too, to seek relief. Gone—in fact if not always in law—is the principle of the sweeping constitutional and statutory provisions of the nineteenth century that all property was to be assessed at a uniform and full value.

How can the shrinkage of the property tax base be reversed?

As Assessor, I would investigate the following avenues:

A. Exempt Property

I would conduct a special audit to examine all exempt property in the county, just as the reform-minded assessor, Ken Johnson, did in the state of Washington. If illegal exemptions were found, this property would be placed on the roles. If it appeared that exemptions were unjustified or out-of-date, yet legal, payments-in-lieu of taxes might be recommended. The city of Newark, N.J., as the result of a special mayor's task force on exempt property, has advocated such a course of action for that city.

B. Intangible Property

Originally the property tax included *all* property, which in the nineteenth century meant mainly land. Today much wealth is held in the form of stocks and bonds. Some economists such as Lester Thurow of MIT and Lester Snyder of the University of Connecticut have advocated taxing intangible wealth. According to a report of the Securities and Exchange Commission, intangible property amounts to over *half* of all private assets. A tax rate of 2%, typical for property taxes, on intangibles would generate over $80 billion—almost twice what property taxes currently yield. Modern computers and IRS reporting requirements now make administration of an intangibles tax feasible.

"A Plan for Reform" is reprinted from *Public Policies for the 80's*, Conference on Alternative State and Local Policies, 1978.

C. Tax Relief from the State

SB 154 introduced earlier this year in the state legislature by Senator Nicholas Petris would have provided property tax relief to both homeowners and renters by making the state income tax more progressive and closing such tax loopholes as the capital gains exemption. Such reform measures, when linked to property tax relief, merit special attention from the Board.

D. Anti-Speculation Measures

One of the causes of the dramatic inflation in residential housing in Los Angeles is speculation. Measures have been introduced in other jurisdictions such as Washington, D.C. to discourage speculation through stiff taxes on short term sales of residential property.

E. Classified Tax System

There is a built-in bias in favor of commercial property in the assessment process because of the use of different assessment methods for residential and commercial property. Other jurisdictions in Illinois, Minnesota, and other states have different rates for different kinds of property. Such a system should be considered by the state legislature, perhaps with a graduated rate for business, so that small business was not unduly penalized and burdened.

A Tax Assessor is, and should be, a politician—a publicly accountable official who sets a standard of behavior for society.

CHAPTER 4

Collecting
Delinquent Taxes

Increasingly, cities have experienced difficulty in collecting the property taxes which have been levied. The first article, **Real Property Tax Delinquencies and Urban Land Policy**, by John Lawlor documents the extent of this problem and outlines a number of creative policies which cities have adopted to combat it.

Campaigns aimed at identifying and forcing payment of delinquent tax bills by wealthy corporate and individual tax avoiders can play an important role in focusing taxpayer protest on the critical issue of who pays and who doesn't. The chapter concludes with **Boston Ordered to Tell Who Owes Back Taxes**, by Walter V. Robinson and Fletcher Roberts, which reports on one such successful campaign mounted by Boston Fair Share. Elizabeth Bass also discusses the Fair Share Campaign against tax delinquents in Chapter 25.

Real Property Tax Delinquency and Urban Land Policy

By John J. Lawlor

Ross, Hardies, O'Keefe, Babcock & Parsons

I.   INTRODUCTION

In July of 1977, the Lincoln Institute of Land Policy commissioned John J. Lawlor of the Chicago law firm of Ross, Hardies, O'Keefe, Babcock & Parsons to organize a research effort which would make a preliminary investigation of (a) the scope of the real property tax delinquency problem facing American cities in terms of lost revenues and affected buildings and parcels; (b) legal obstacles which impede efforts to reutilize delinquent property; and (c) current governmental efforts to reutilize delinquent buildings and parcels.

This report is an attempt to summarize the Lincoln Institute's research effort. What is unique about the Lincoln Institute's undertaking is that, for the first time, an attempt was made to permit real property tax collection officials from all over the United States to share their common problems and perspectives. While assessment can certainly result in delinquency, it was decided to isolate this factor due to the great amount of research already available on the subject. Insofar as tax collection and land utilization practices are concerned, the Lincoln Institute would like to point out the preliminary nature of its work and the need for further research into the basic integrity of the real property tax assessment and collection system in light of the growing levels of real property tax delinquency being reported throughout the country.

One of the most troublesome aspects of this new wave in real property tax delinquency is the problem posed by occupied residential buildings. In Cleveland, for example, 52% of the city's tax delinquent parcels contained occupied residential structures. This percentage represents 10,000 housing units.[1] In New York City, 6,000 delinquent parcels presently house over

20,000 families.[2] There are reports from these and other cities of "squatters" who refuse to leave delinquent buildings once the municipality has acquired title through tax enforcement procedures. In short, contemporary urban real property tax delinquency has a peculiar aspect which was not present during the Depression, when delinquency most often occurred with vacant, prematurely subdivided land. In the words of Robert Shur, a New York City-based housing consultant, "The growing volume of multi-family dwelling so passing into city ownership...is an end-product of owner disinvestment and abandonment...(and) is today more a social problem than a matter of replenishing the city treasury."[3]

Despite the poignant social problem posed by low income residents living in tax delinquent structures, municipalities have been very reluctant to serve as receivers of these buildings, given the risky economics of housing low and moderate income people in an inflationary period. Some cities are reluctant to bring real property tax enforcement proceedings against any tax delinquent property in the first place, for fear that once the city acquires title it will be unable to market the property elsewhere. Fifteen respondants to the Lincoln Institute survey indicated that no governmental agency in their jurisdiction attempts to market and/or land bank delinquent buildings or parcels.

In short, there are two different ways to describe the impact of increasing levels of delinquency in developed portions of the central cities. The most obvious way is in terms of revenue.[4] As taxpayers throughout the country suffer increased levels of assessment and increased tax levies, it may not be surprising if political pressure mounts which demands that action be taken against tax delinquent property owners.

The second type of impact is more subtle. Tax delinquency is usually -- and correctly -- viewed as a symptom of other urban problems.[5] Those familiar with the dynamics of inner city housing markets, however, may also view real property tax delinquency as a causal agent in the further deterioration of existing housing stock. For example, lax real property tax enforcement permits buildings to deteriorate in the hands of an owner who no longer sees his property as an assett but who, nevertheless, be unwilling to sell and sustain capital losses on his investment. Too often, the tragedy is that these slow tax enforcement proceedings and lengthy redemption periods which accrue to the benefit of the tax delinquent property owner make it impossible for would-be rehabilitators to acquire delinquent property quick enough to be able to restore it at a reasonable cost. This gives the fledgling "back to the city" movement still another obstacle. The presence of large accrued tax liens can discourage not only rehabilitation efforts, but large scale redevelopment as well. The burden of clearing large tax liens can prevent a private party from assembling parcels for commercial, industrial or residential development within central city areas.

Data collected by the Lincoln Institute survey reveals that cities throughout the country are beginning to address the phenomenon of increasing levels of real property tax delinquency. Much of this activity is in the form of straightforward efforts to simply recoup as much of the real property tax levy as possible. These efforts have taken the form of:

(a) Increasing Penalty Rates. Municipal officials in New Haven, Connecticut, for example, recently noted that low penalty rates for non-payment of taxes encouraged "borrowing" at the expense of the city, given the high interest rates in the private sector in today's inflationary economy. As a result the City raised its penalty rate from 6% to 12%.[6]

(b) Improving the Performance of Tax Sales. In Newark, New Jersey, for example, an attempt has been made to market tax delinquent property through the distribution of catalogs which describe available buildings in a manner very similar to the usual brokerage listing. This technique has been helpful in marketing delinquent structures adjacent to viable ethnic areas.

(c) Streamling the Foreclosure Process. Many cities have been frustrated by the delays entailed in foreclosing upon tax delinquent property. By declaring foreclosures to be "in rem" actions against tax delinquent parcels, rather than "in personam" actions against property owners themselves, statutory amendments recently passed in New York City, Newark, Cleveland and St. Louis have streamlined notice requirements and cut litigation costs.[7] In Newark, for example, what was formerly a two year tax foreclosure process can now be accomplished within six months. St. Louis now takes foreclosure action within two years of the initial incidence of delinquency rather than four.

(d) Utilization of In Personam Lawsuits. All too often, a tax delinquent property owner will abandon his building secure in the knowledge that a municipality will not be able to reach his personal assets in atempting to recover unpaid tax and demolition liens. The "in rem" foreclosure process, referred to above, does not entitle a municipality to satisfy its judgment out of any asset other than the tax delinquent structure or parcel. In cases where unpaid accrued tax liens are particularly high, the result is that municipalities will be unable to recoup their losses.

According to Lincoln Institute survey data, at least ten American jurisdictions can impose personal liability upon tax delinquent property owners for non-payment of real property taxes. In Chicago, Boston and Baltimore, municipal corporations are bringing "in personam" actions against tax delinquent property owners as a means to recoup revenue and put the "bite" back into the real property tax cellection system.

In addition to initiating programs designed to recoup unpaid tax dollars, a number of cities have initiated programs and statutory amendments designed to facilitate the rehabilitation or redevelopment of tax delinquent buildings and parcels. The programs which attempt to preserve or reutilize delinquent buildings and structures have taken the following forms:

(a) <u>Shortening the Redemption Period</u>. Private developers, community groups and municipalities interested in restoring the existing housing stock are often frustrated by the existence of a lengthy redemption period which prevents the would-be rehabilitator from entering a tax delinquent parcel subsequent to its sale. Periods of redemption accruing to the benefit of tax delinquent property owners can extend for as much as six years (Phoenix, Arizona) to as little as sixty days (Wilmington, Delaware). The length of the average redemption period in the Lincoln Institute survey sample was approximately two years and three months. Several cities have undertaken to shorten this statutory redemption period so that it would no longer pose an obstacle to redevelopment. Other cities have made innovations which attempt to address delinquency in its present urban context. Troy, New York, has bifurcated its redemption period for owner occupied as opposed to non-owner occupied structures, while the City of Boston can restrict foreclosure rights where the property is abandoned.<u>8</u>/

(b) <u>Receivership Programs</u>. Another technique which can be used to preserve the quality of tax delinquent housing stock during the period of the tax delinquent owner's right of redemption is the imposition of a receivership upon the building. Seven Lincoln Institute survey respondents indicated that receiverships have been imposed on tax delinquent property within their jurisdiction. In Phoenix, the state is currently serving as a receiver on eighty-eight parcels. In Wilmington, a private party is serving as receiver on eight multi-family dwellings and 100 single family homes. Similarly, a Hartford, Connecticut, private receiver is managing nine multi-family structures. In St. Louis, Kansas City and Milwaukee, governmental units serve in receivership roles in appropriate cases. St. Louis limits its management role by refusing to accept new tenants when former tenants leave.<u>9</u>/

(c) <u>Encouraging Tenant Management and Rehabilitation</u>. In New York City an attempt has been made to solve

the problem posed by tax delinquent buildings by initiating a program which encourages tenants to manage their own
structures, and which presents the possibility that a
viable tenant group with a sound housing management record
can acquire title to tax delinquent structures. Where
successful, the "Community Management Program" solves two
problems for the City of New York: (1) the problem of
managing a large number of tax delinquent buildings by
means of utilizing municipal employees, and (2) the problem of finding a market for delinquent multi-family structures.

(d)   <u>Initiating Homesteading Programs</u>. St. Louis,
Pittsburgh, Philadelphia and other cities have initiated
"homesteading programs" which encourage the reutilization
of tax delinquent single family structures. Most often,
these programs require a rehabilitator to make a down payment, live in the structure and restore it to housing code
specifications within a given period of time. Philadelphia
acquires title to many buildings by accepting deeds in
lieu of tax foreclosure.[10/]

(e)   <u>Facilitating the Assembly of Tax Delinquent</u>
<u>Parcels</u>. The St. Louis and Cleveland land reutilization
authorities are in a position to acquire title and assemble
large tracts of tax delinquent land. The ability to clear
title to parcels which formerly had large accrued tax
liens can serve to promote redevelopment. For example,
45% of a newly constructed industrial park is built upon
land acquired and assembled by the St. Louis Land Reutilization Authority.

(f)   <u>Enacting Anti-Arson Statutes</u>. The fate of
improved parcels within the American inner city is all
too familiar. Abandonment, destruction by fire, demolition and continued tax delinquency impose staggering
social and economic costs upon central cities. Several
jurisdictions are attempting to recoup some of these
costs by the enactment of statutes which give a governmental lien holder a first claim to any insurance proceeds paid out under any fire insurance policy.

Summary

The initiation of the above described programs, many
of which are still in experimental stages, has led many municipal officials to more fully appreciate the nature of inner city
housing markets and the problem of housing low and moderate income people during an inflationary period. In short, there is
a growing awareness of the impact of not only tax assessment

on the quality of inner city housing stock, but also the impact of tax enforcement activity. Before launching an ambitious program to recoup real property tax dollars, a municipal tax collection official had best inquire into:

      (a)   The nature and causes of real property tax delinquency within his jurisdiction, and

      (b)   Whether increased tax collection activity can prevent abandonment and deterioration, or actually accelerate by forcing landlords to cut their other major expense -- maintenance -- and hope to escape housing code enforcement.

FOOTNOTES

1. Linner, John, "Cleveland is Banking Tax Delinquent Land," *Practicing Planner*, June 1977, p. 12.

2. Schur, Robert, "Foreclosure for Non-Payment of Taxes in New York City: A Brief Introduction" (unpublished manuscript) p. 10.

3. *Id.*

4. Figures reported by Lincoln Institute survey respondents.

5. Sternlieb and Lake, "The Dynamics of Real Estate Tax Delinquency," *National Tax Journal* 29 (September 1976).

6. Back Tax Task Force, City of New Haven, "Controller's Report on Delinquent Taxes," July 27, 1977, p. 5.

7. See Part VI. D.I., *infra*, for a more detailed discussion of "*in rem*" tax foreclosures.

8. See Ch. 60, Sec. 81A, Mass. Gen. Laws.

9. Olson, Susan and Lachman, M. Leanne, *Tax Delinquency in the Inner City: The Problem and Its Possible Solution*, Lexington, Mass.: D.C. Heath, 1976. p. 60.

10. See Chapter 16-400 of the Philadelphia Code.

"Real Property Tax Delinquency and Urban Land Policy" is reprinted by permission from the Lincoln Institute of Land Policy, 1978.

Boston Ordered To Tell Who Owes Taxes

A governor's councillor, a major theater chain. A taxi firm owner. The Socialist Workers Party and the Democratic State Committee. They have one thing in common.

According to City of Boston records, they are among thousands of individuals and businesses which owe the city a total of more than $50 million in property taxes. The city has been ordered by the state to publicly release the list. The listings cover the last three fiscal years.

The precedent-setting step, according to city fiscal officials, is likely to prompt quick payment by some delinquent taxpayers embarrassed by possible public disclosure and provoke demonstrations by some community groups to force others to pay.

In fact, Boston Fair Share, the political organization whose request for the records led to the state order for their release, has already announced that it will mount a campaign to force payment.

It will have no shortage of targets.

A brief glimpse by The Globe at some of the real estate, excise and personal property tax delinquent records in the City Collector's office last night turned up the names of scores of prominent businessmen, lawyers, elected public officials and well-known businesses, organizations and landlords who, the records show, have not paid their taxes.

According to those records they include:

—Executive Councilor Herbert Connolly, who has unpaid property tax bills of approximately $40,000.

—E.M. Loew's Theatres, Inc., which has an unpaid 1977 property tax bill of $25,200 on a building at 164 Tremont St.

—Frank Sawyer, the owner of Checker Taxi Co., 20 Gainsboro St., who has an unpaid $25,000 tax bill on a Brighton parcel.

—Boston landlord Nick Haddad of Haverty Realty Trust, who owes more than $42,000 in real estate taxes on two Back Bay apartment buildings.

Newell Cook, the city's first assistant collector-treasurer who will be meeting today with Fair Share representatives to work out the details of the release, said he hoped "the disclosure would embarrass some significant fraction of the delinquents into paying up."

Cook called the release order by John J. McGlynn, the state's supervisor of public records, "a positive step" and noted that the privacy previously afforded the records "has allowed some delinquents to hide their lack of citizenship."

He expressed concern, however, that the computerized records might be misinterpreted. For example, the property tax delinquent lists contain the names of at least two of Boston's leading banks, which are several hundred thousand dollars in arrears.

However, Cook noted, they have paid their taxes for the first half of the fiscal year, have applied for abatements and are therefore entitled to withhold second half payments pending abatement decisions.

Unfortunately, the largest delinquent is unlikely to blush and pay up. The bankrupt Penn Central Railroad owes the city between $1 million and $2 million, Cook explained. But under Federal Railroad Bankruptcy law, the city can do little to collect.

Also heavily delinquent are other bankrupt firms, including the Boston & Maine railroad and Kasanof's Bakery.

McGlynn ordered the disclosure of the records after Fair Share appealed to his office in April. Prior to that, Fair Share was denied access by Herbert P. Gleason, the city's corporation counsel. A similar request by The Globe was also denied.

Carolyn Lucas of Hyde Park, secretary of Fair Share's Property Tax Coalition, said Fair Share will study the lists and release names of delinquents at neighborhood and citywide meetings that will precede a campaign to force payment.

Lucas said she believes that the city's property taxpayers, who were subjected to a $56.20 tax increase last year and who face the probability of another increase this year, will join actively in any effort to force delinquents to pay.

Last September, Fair Share members demonstrated outside Jimmy's Harborside Restaurant on Northern Avenue after learning that it owed $60,000 in property taxes. The money was paid within 30 days.

"Boston Ordered To Tell Who Owes Back Taxes" is reprinted by permission from the May 20, 1977 issue of *The Boston Globe.*

The popular mythology has depicted the great 1978 tax revolt as a voter protest against the rising cost and size of government. Some political leaders such as California Governor Jerry Brown chose to interpret it as a revolt against government itself.

Yet a careful state-by-state analysis of tax politics shows that most taxpayer grievances were the result of abuses within the taxation system. Where these inequities were effectively remedied by state government, there was no revolt. Where they festered while political leadership abdicated, the revolt was extreme. And, despite the generally conservative flavor of tax protest, in at least three states progressive coalitions have been able to mobilize voter frustrations around reforms that distribute tax burdens more fairly, rather than simply attacking government.

California's Tax Revolt

California's Proposition 13 was the extreme case of a quite valid grievance which the state legislature failed to remedy. It was also, of course, the most extreme solution.

The roots of the Jarvis-Gann amendment are multiple. They include a reform in assessment procedures in the late Sixties, which unwittingly set in motion a massive tax shift, as well as the soaring inflation in housing prices. Tax limitation initiatives had been presented to California voters repeatedly, including one backed by then-Governor Reagon. But it took the right combination of explosive property tax increases and a political default in Sacramento before this movement succeeded.

The assessment 'reform' deserves particular attention, because it points to the need to carefully analyze seemingly innocent procedural changes, for hidden consequences. In the late Sixties, a series of assessment scandals led the state legislature to overhaul California's assessment system. The new procedure eliminated the traditional element of local assessor discretion, which historically had functioned as a kind of crude, unlegislated circuit-breaker, keeping homeowner assessments (and taxes) within tolerable limits. The new legislation required periodic, comprehensive reassessments, and uniform assessment ratios among all classes of property. Though it did not become serious until the inflation of the mid-Seventies, one result of this procedure was to shift tax burdens onto homeowners.

A moderate homestead exemption, which was in-

The Property Tax: Homeowner Relief

By Robert Kuttner

creased to $1,750 ($7,000 full value) in 1972, was dwarfed by the rapid increase in California housing prices that accelerated after 1975. Between 1975 and 1978, assessed valuation of all owner-occupied homes in California went up by 110.9%, compared to 32.4% for apartment buildings, and 26.4% for businesses. As data in the Tipps article in this section documents, the result of this was to shift the share of total taxes borne by single family homes from 31.2% in 1973-74, the year after the homestead exemption was increased, to 44.3% in 1978-79.

In addition, the progressive character of the California state income tax and the strength of the California economy combined with inflation to produce windfall revenues for the State government; and as local property tax revenues increased with rising property values, the share of state aid dropped, fattening the state's budgetary surplus even further.

Thus, at a time of stagnating real income, and oppressive housing costs, California taxpayers saw their taxes rising much faster than their income or the benefits they received from government. What they didn't see was that business was paying a decreasing share of tax burdens. Adding insult to injury was the huge state surplus.

When the state legislature and Governor Brown failed to pass a tax relief package by the end of the 1977 session, Howard Jarvis's success was almost guaranteed. A very inept campaign by the anti-Jarvis coalition only widened Proposition 13's margin. With big business supporting (and largely bankrolling) the anti-13 coalition, it was not politic to emphasize that the alternative to Proposition 13, Proposition 8, would have provided more relief to middle and low income homeowners, and less to business. Instead of responding to the very valid tax grievances, the anti-13 coalition resorted to scarce tactics that became less plausible to voters as the state surplus continued to grow.

The 1977 tax relief package, which passed the Assembly and failed by only 2 votes in the Senate, combined a circuitbreaker with a property tax revenue limitation tied to a split roll, and targeted substantial tax relief to moderate income homeowners and to renters (who got nothing out of Proposition 13). That bill, which was backed by a broad coalition of labor, urban, good-government, and tax reform groups, almost surely would have headed off Proposition 13. Its defeat was largely the result of Gov. Brown's failure to support it decisive-

ly. The fact that the pocketbook issues which produced Proposition 13 have also fueled a rent control movement refutes the claim that Proposition 13 was simply a right wing reaction against government. Basic economic discontent underlay the tax revolt in California; politically, this discontent is still up for grabs.

The Business-Homeowner Tax Shift

The shift in tax burdens from business onto consumers was not restricted to California. The same shift is occurring in numerous other states, as the result of three trends: court decisions, inflation, and business tax abatement. During the past twenty years, state courts have increasingly ruled that the informal practice of under-assessing homeowners violates the provision found in most state constitutions requiring uniform assessment of all classes of property. Combined with the higher rate of inflation in residential property values and the fact that homes change hands more often than businesses, the move to uniform assessment ratios has increased the consumer share of property taxes. As the table in Chapter 2 prepared by Allen Manvel suggests, total property taxes as a percent of personal income actually fell in most states (including California) during the Seventies. But the property taxes paid by homeowners tended to rise, because business taxes were slipping. Another factor contributing to this shift is the erosion of the business tax base in many Northeast and Midwestern states caused by lucrative abatements and exemptions offered to influence locational decisions of businesses.

The one state, curiously, to pass a virtual copy of Proposition 13 in the November 1978 elections, was Idaho, which had a lower-than average aggregate property tax level, and a low level of government services. Looking behind these aggregates, however, it turns out that Idaho had the most extreme tax shift of any state. A 1968 court decision required the state's assessors to value all types of property uniformly. As a consequence, homeowners who had been paying only 24% of all property tax bills in 1969, were paying 44.5% by 1978.

Significantly, however, where state legislatures acted decisively to head off the tax shift by passing circuitbreaker relief for homeowners, the tax revolt either failed or took a much more moderate form. Two of the states that decisively defeated Jarvis-type limits, Oregon and Michigan, are among the six states with broad-based circuit-breaker programs. Colorado, where a more extreme constitutional limitation on spending was defeated in the 1978 initiative, had enacted a more moderate statutory limit in 1977.

Property Classification

Tax classification can be an effective approach to reform, but it will be portrayed by business groups as an attempt to shift tax burdens to them. The fact is that a shift in the other direction has already ocurred, and tax classification simply restores the old system of taxing homeowners at less onerous rates. Minimally, classification can be used to prevent further shifts onto homeowners even if it isn't politically feasible to redress the effects of past business-to-homeowner tax shifts.

Depending on local political circumstances, tax relief can be provided through classification, circuit breakers, homestead exemptions or a combination. As the readings suggest, each of these has advantages and disadvantages. Circuitbreakers target relief to the neediest, but this can be a political liability. They can also be administratively cumbersome. Homestead exemptions provide benefits to all taxpayers, but this can be so expensive that the benefits are diluted to those who really need them; and, as in California, the value of a homestead exemption can be eroded quickly by inflation. Classification solves these problems, but in older states that are trying to attract or retain industry, there is likely to be great political resistence to the idea of taxing business at a higher rate, even though this was the historic practice.

One other reform is worth considering, but it can also be a double-edged sword. So-called truth in taxation is a form of tax limitation that prevents localities from taking advantage of rising assessments to collect increased revenues without raising nominal rates. Under Florida's Truth-in-Taxation law, which Common Cause and the Advisory Commission on Intergovernmental Relations hold up as a model, rates must drop in proportion to the rise in assessments, unless explicitly increased by the local taxing authority after due public notice.

This approach is preferable to arbitrary tax limits, because it retains the right to raise taxes when necessary. It also makes government more accountable, since it forces increases to be deliberate rather than accidental. But in an inflationary climate where home assessments are rising faster than businesses, truth in taxation can reinforce the tax shift because it cuts rates uniformly across-the-board. It is important, therefore, that split tax rates or some other form of relief be provided along with truth-in-taxation, or the effect can be to give disproportionate benefits to business at the expense of homeowners.

Beyond Assessment Reform

Often, a 'first-generation' reform such as California's attempt to clean up assessment practices, can produce 'second generation' problems. The remedy to spiraling inflation in California was not to restore the haphazard, old system of tax assessment, but to temper the impact of inflation by enacting a circuitbreaker, homestead exemption, or split roll.

There is no cook-book of tax reform remedies. Devices need to suit local circumstances. Conservatives have a very simple explanation for tax grievances: the government is wasting money. Their equally simple remedy is to cut taxes and starve government. But this freezes in place tax inequities and deprives people of services. A better approach is to research and explain how tax burdens are actually distributed, and provide alternative strategies that produce enough revenues for services, and a fair distribution of the tax load.

CHAPTER 5

California's Tax Revolt

Proposition 13 was one of the most misunderstood happenings in the history of American politics. Conservative groups, the national media, and California Governor Jerry Brown interpreted the Jarvis amendment as an outcry against government. In fact, it was an outcry against a property tax system that went out of control as business property tax burdens shifted to homeowners and the state legislature and Governor Brown failed to agree on a remedy.

In **California's Great Property Tax Revolt,** Dean Tipps locates the principal cause of that state's property tax crisis in a previous shift from business property tax burdens to homeowners. Taxes on California homes increased about **92 percent** between 1975 and 1978—while business assessments rose only **14** percent. By 1978, when Proposition 13 was ratified, single-family homeowners were carrying about 44 percent of California's property tax load; five years earlier they had paid only 32 percent. Tipps also analyses the impact of Proposition 13 on the state's tax system and on state and local government.

Only a small minority of those who supported Proposition 13 told poll takers that they were protesting the size of government, according to the article by William Schneider, **Prop 13's Biggest Booster Was Inflation,** based on *Los Angeles Times* Survey of voters.

The further shift in the property tax burden from business to homeowners as a result of Proposition 13 is documented in Claire Speigel's **Homeowner Share of Property Tax Rises.** In Los Angeles County during 1978-79, there was ''a substantial 8% shift'' in the tax burden from commercial-industrial to residential properties.

The Jarvis amendment had a number of unintended side effects. New fees imposed by governments made housing more expensive. Much local control has been shifted to Sacramento. Proposition 13 has created a kind of county-wide tax-base sharing, but under state control. Under the state's ''bail-out'' formula to local government, the cuts are shared *pro rata*. Those communities that were ''rich'' in service

levels will stay rich. Those that were poor will stay poor. Unintentionally, Jarvis, who represented apartment owners, and Gann, a retired realtor, have given birth to a rent control movement, described in Bill Boyarsky's article, **Grass Roots Burning Again.**

The impact of the $6.1 billion tax reduction under Proposition 13 has benefitted corporations more than individuals, landlords more than renters, and rich homeowners more than poor ones. Much of the tax savings went to shareholders of corporations who were not even California residents. As Tom Furlong's article, **The Rich Got Richer Throughout The State,** indicates, business has been slow to pass along its savings to the public.

Proposition 13 has hurt the recipients of public services, especially the poor, who are suffering disproportionate cuts in health services, education, recreation, and previously free services like museums and libraries. Roger Kemp's article, **One City's Story: Oakland After Prop. 13,** describes how Proposition 13 ''has redirected the focus of the city away from positive action and towards survival.''

Bob Kuttner's **Idaho Tax Shift Spurs Tax Rebellion** analyses the underlying business-to-homeowner tax shifts in Idaho which preceeded approval of a ''close imitation of Proposition 13'' in November, 1978. He shows that the Idaho vote was similar to that in California, where the general public was not aware that rising homeowner taxes were actually the result of the tax shift rather than of a ballooning government bureaucracy.

Finally, Harold Scott and Paul Waddell analyze an upcoming vote on a property tax limitation initiative in **Impact of a Prop. 13 Type Amendment in Arizona.** They emphasize that passage of a Proposition 13 measure in Arizona would effectively eliminate the state's progressive programs for homeowner property tax relief—a classified property tax system favoring homeowners and a direct homeowners' tax reduction program. In addition, homeowners would experience only a modest cut in taxes under Proposition 13, while business properties would enjoy a $350 million tax cut.

California's Great Property Tax Revolt:

The Origins and Impact of Proposition 13

by Dean C. Tipps

On June 6, 1978, Californians voted in overwhelming numbers to cut their property tax bills in half. Their vote reduced property tax levies by $5.5 billion and radically restructured California's tax system. It also sparked a national tax revolt as tax and spending limitation proposals became the central political issue of 1978 in states from Oregon to Maine and reached even to the federal level.

What Californians voted for was Proposition 13, the Jarvis-Gann Initiative. Proposition 13 limits tax rates to 1% of market value (or $4.00 per $100 of assessed value under California's system of assessing property at 25% of full value). The only allowable exception is for tax rates levied to pay for existing voter-approved debt. These provisions reduced the average 2.67% (or $10.68) tax rate for the 1977-1978 fiscal year to 1.18% (or $4.73) in 1978-1979, a reduction of 55.7%.

Proposition 13 also rolls back assessed values to 1975-1976 levels and limits adjustments for inflation to 2% a year. Property that has been sold or newly constructed after 1975-1976 can be reassessed to reflect its actual full market value. Despite the assessment rollback, the reassessments permitted by Proposition 13 combined with California's expanding economy and speculative real estate market to produce a 1978-1979 increase in net (after exemptions) taxable assessed value of 6.6%.

Finally, Proposition 13 prohibits imposition of any new taxes on property and places constraints on the ability of the state and local governments to increase other taxes by requiring a ⅔ vote of the electorate to impose "special taxes" at the local level.

The Jarvis-Gann Initiative was not the first tax limitation measure to appear on the California ballot. Over the last decade, Californians had rejected three limitation measures by decisive margins — two property tax limitation initiatives sponsored by Los Angeles County Assessor Phillip Watson in 1968 and 1972, and a spending limitation proposal by then-Governor Reagan in 1973. But 1978 was different. This time Californians enthusiastically embraced a tax limitation measure far more radical than any of the three earlier proposals.

This article offers an explanation of why Proposition 13 happened and how it affected California in the first year after it passed. The first section identifies the principal causes of California's property tax crisis.

Section II analyzes the politics of the property tax crisis in Sacramento and the reasons for the political stalemate which left the Legislature unable to produce a solution. The third section discusses the election campaigns of the two sides and interprets the vote. Section IV looks at Proposition 13's impact on California's tax system. The final section briefly surveys the effects of Proposition 13 on state and local government.

I. CALIFORNIA'S PROPERTY TAX CRISIS

Uniform Assessments

The seeds of California's property tax crisis can be found in the assessment reforms adopted by the Legislature more than a decade earlier. Uniform assessments have been required in California since the Constitution of 1850. But despite periodic efforts at reform, substantial assessment inequities persisted into the 1960's.

Finally, amid increasing public concern over corruption and irregular assessment practices, the Legislature enacted AB 80, the Assessment Reform Act of 1966. A key provision of this legislation required that all property be assessed at a uniform 25% of full value by the March 1, 1971, lien date. Although assessment differentials were not eliminated entirely, AB 80 did result in an assessment system widely regarded as a model of equal and uniform administration. It also created an assessment system that responded fairly accurately to fluctuations in property values.

Prior to AB 80, business properties in some areas of the state, particularly in the larger urban counties, traditionally had been assessed at higher percentages of their full value than residential property. By requiring a uniform 25% assessment ratio, AB 80 forced a shift in the property tax burden in these areas from business properties to homeowners. However, the effects of this shift were offset by the introduction of a homeowners' exemption of the first $750 in assessed value (equal to $3,000 of full value) in 1969, followed by a 1973 increase in the exemption to the first $1,750 of assessed value (or $7,000 of full value).

Inflated Home Prices

The full consequences of having a relatively well-administered property tax system based on uniform assessments became apparent only with the explosion

Table 1

Average Resale Prices of Single Family Homes 1974 - 1978

	Southern California	National
April, 1974	$37,800	$37,800
April, 1978	83,200	56,100
Change		
$	+45,400	+18,300
%	+120%	+48%

Source: "Existing Home Prices Still Rising...," *Los Angeles Times,* Part X, November 19, 1978.

Table 2B

Increase of Property Tax Levies by Property Type, 1975-1978 (dollar amounts in millions)

	Property Tax Levies		
Type of Property	1975	1978[a]	% Change
Owner-Occupied Residential	$2,149	$4,117	+91.6%
Renter-Occupied Residential	1,729	2,110	+22.0
Commercial, Industrial, Agricultural	4,419	5,031	+13.8
TOTAL	$8,297	$11,258	+35.7

[a]Estimate prepared prior to Proposition 13.
Source: see Table 2A.

of home prices in California after 1974. Home prices began increasing at rates far in excess of increases in other property values or the Consumer Price Index. Between 1974 and 1978, the average sales price of existing homes in southern California increased by 120%, while the national average was increasing by only 48%. During 1977, the average price of a re-sale home in the Los Angeles area increased by 18.6%; in the San Francisco Bay Area, it increased by 18.7%. By contrast, the California Consumer Price Index increased by a comparatively modest 7.1% that same year.

As home prices skyrocketed, assessment increases followed quickly behind. Between 1975 and 1978, homeowner assessments increased almost three and one-quarter times faster than assessments on renter-occupied residential property and well over four times as fast as assessments on commercial, industrial, and agricultural property (see Table 2A). While owner-occupied homes represented 24.8% of the net assessment roll in 1975, by 1978 this inflation-induced shift

increased owner-occupied homes to 35.2% of total net assessed value. Data compiled by William H. Oakland (see Table 3) shows the share of property taxes paid by single family homes — owner and renter occupied — increasing from 32.1% in 1973-74 to 44.3% in 1978-79 if Proposition 13 had not passed.

Thus, the uniformity and accuracy of California's assessment system combined with the sharp escalation of home prices to produce a dramatic shift of the property tax burden onto homeowners. As Table 2B indicates, if Proposition 13 had not passed, homeowner property taxes would have increased by 92% between 1975 and 1978 while taxes on commercial, industrial and agricultural property would have increased by only 14% during the same period.

The impact of this shift on homeowners was further magnified by the lag in assessments resulting from the three to five year reassessment cycle prac-

Table 2A

Increase of Net Assessed Values by Property Type, 1975-78 (dollar amounts in millions)

	NET ASSESSED VALUE[a]		
TYPE OF PROPERTY	1975	1978[b]	% CHANGE
Owner-Occupied Residential	$18,198	$38,371	+110.9%
Renter-Occupied Residential	14,646	19,661	+34.2
Commercial, Industrial, Agricultural	40,402	51,056	+26.4
TOTAL	$73,246	$109,088	+48.9%

[a]Net assessed value is assessed value net state- reimbursed exemptions for homeowners and business inventories.

[b]Estimate prepared prior to adoption of Proposition 13.

Source: Legislative Analyst, *Budget Analysis, 1977-1978*, p. A-32, and idem., *An Analysis of Proposition 13* (May, 1978), p. 25.

Table 3

Distribution of Net* Assessed Value and Property Tax Burden on Single-Family Dwellings in California, 1964-65 to 1978-79

| Period | Share of Total Net Assessed Value | | | | Share of Property Taxes of Single-Family Dwellings (5) | Taxes on Single-Family Dwellings as a Percent of Personal Income (6) |
	Single-Family Residences (1)	Other Residences (2)	Non-Residential (3)	State Assessedf (4)		
1964-65	34.8%	12.3%	40.8%	12.1%	36.2%	1.97%
65-66	34.5	12.6	41.4	11.5	34.8	2.01
66-67	34.0	13.3	41.8	10.9	35.3	2.04
67-68	33.6	13.7	42.6	10.1	35.0	2.05
68-69a	34.0	13.8	42.6	9.7	35.4	2.11
69-70b	32.3	14.4	44.0	9.5	33.5	1.98
70-71c	33.5	14.8	42.9	8.8	34.8	2.24
71-72	33.7	14.5	43.8	8.1	35.0	2.37
72-73	34.0	13.9	44.4	7.6	35.2	2.35
73-74d	31.6	13.8	46.9	7.7	32.1	1.88
74-75e	32.9	13.4	46.4	7.3	33.9	1.98
75-76	35.2	13.2	44.7	6.9	36.2	2.16
76-77	39.5	12.9	41.0	6.6	40.4	2.48
77-78	41.0	12.6	39.6	6.7	42.2	2.53
78-79	43.0	12.6	38.3	6.4	44.3	2.60

* Net of exemptions
a First significant "open space" assessments.
b Introduction of $750 homestead exemption; 15-percent inventory exemption.
c With 30-percent inventory exemption.
d With $1,750 homestead exemption; 45-percent inventory exemption.
e With 50-percent inventory exemption.
f State-assessed property is mainly personal property of utilities. Beginning in 1964 and ending in 1974, the assessment ratio on this class was lowered until it reached the ratio applying to other classes.
Source: California Board of Equalization: author's estimates for years 1975-76 to 1978-79.

From William H. Oakland, "Proposition 13—Genesis and Consequences", Federal Reserve Board of San Francisco, *Economic Review*, Winter, 1979, p. 22.

ticed by most county assessors. When home values were increasing 2% to 3% per year as they were throughout the 1960's, the lag between reassessments had little impact on homeowners. But when home values began increasing in many areas by 20% or more annually, the lag time between reassessments had a cumulative impact which produced extraordinary tax increases in the year when homes finally were reassessed.

The effect of this inflation-induced tax shift on individual homeowners was dramatic. A Los Angeles family whose home was assessed at $45,000 in 1974 paid a fiscal year (FY) 1976-77 property tax of $1,310 based on that assessment. If that same home was reassessed in FY 1977-78 to $90,000 — an increase typical of those experienced in many areas of Los Angeles — that family's property tax bill increased to $2,860. That amounts to a one-year tax increase of $1,550. The impact of such increases was especially traumatic because they were aimed at people's homes. As a result, they were perceived as threatening a fundamental value of American culture: the ability of families to own their own homes.

State's Relief Programs Inadequate

The state had adopted two programs designed to provide property tax relief to homeowners prior to the property tax crisis of the 1970's: a senior citizens' property tax assistance law adopted by the Legislature in 1967 and the homeowners' exemption approved by the voters in November, 1968. Although the Legislature subsequently increased the benefits offered by these programs, neither was able to effectively curb the rapid escalation of homeowner property taxes—despite state expenditures of $760 million for its homeowners' exemption program and another $78 million on property tax rebates for senior citizen homeowners in FY 1977-78.

As noted earlier, the original homeowners' $750 assessed value exemption was expanded in 1973 to exempt from taxation the first $1,750 assessed value (or $7,000 full value) of an owner-occupied residence. Because the exemption is based upon a fixed property value, the tax relief it provides to homeowners increases as tax rates increase and declines as tax rates decline. So long as home values remained fairly stable and tax rates were rising, the homeowner exemption provided homeowners some measure of relief.

However, when homeowner assessments began taking off in the mid-1970's, tax rates levelled off and then began to decline. As a result, many homeowners saw the relief they received from the homeowners' exemption actually decline in the face of dramatic increases in their property tax bills. Since inflationary assessments — not rising tax rates — were the cause of California's property tax crisis, the homeowners' exemption proved to be an ineffective mechanism of homeowner property tax relief.

California's circuit-breaker property tax rebate program for senior citizens was more effective, but it also had major limitations. Under this program, homeowners age 62 or older with incomes of $12,000 or less receive rebates on the property taxes they pay on the first $34,000 of their home's value after allowing for the $7,000 homeowners' exemption. Like the homeowners' exemption, its benefits have also been expanded since it was first introduced. Presently, the rebate varies from 96% of the eligible property tax for seniors with incomes under $3,000 to 4% for seniors with incomes between $11,500 and $12,000. This program clearly benefitted low income seniors owning homes valued under $41,000. However, its assessed value and income restrictions during a period when both assessments and incomes were under intense inflationary pressures undermined its effectiveness for many senior homeowners. In addition, seniors only received the rebate after they had used their own funds to pay their property tax bills. Participation was also discouraged by the program's application procedure. And, of course, the age restriction denied the program's benefits to most California homeowners.

No Relief from Tax Rates

Nor did tax rate reductions provide homeowners with protection from rising assessments. In 1972, the Legislature imposed maximum tax rate restrictions on cities and counties and property tax revenue limits on school districts. However, tax rate limitations had little effect. While property tax levies increased by almost $2 billion — or 24% — between 1975-76 and 1977-78, the statewide average property tax rate declined during the same period from $11.33 per $100 assessed value (or 2.83% full value) to $10.68 (or 2.67% full value). Tax rates were able to decline while levies increased because of rising assessments, especially rising assessments on homes.

In fact, reductions in tax rates frequently reinforced the shift onto homeowners. Like assessments, tax rates in California are applied uniformly to all classes of property. When local governments sought to offset inflated home assessments by reducing tax rates, they were using excess revenues coming largely from homeowners to reduce tax rates on all classes of property, not just homeowners. In effect, tax increases on the 35% of the tax rolls made up of homeowners were being used to finance tax reductions for the other 65% of the tax rolls made up of various types of income-producing properties.

The interaction between rising assessments and tax rates also created an opportunity for fiscal manipulations which contributed to the undercurrent of political resentment which was fueled by California's property tax crisis. Rising assessments produced tempting windfall revenues which allowed many local officials to claim that they were being frugal by lowering tax rates even though tax revenues were increasing and they were spending more money than ever before. However, homeowners soon caught on to this political shell game as their tax bills continued to escalate despite modest decreases in their tax rate.

Local Cost Squeeze

Local officials were also caught in a very real cost squeeze that left them little alternative but to rely increasingly on property tax revenues. The double-digit inflation of the mid-1970's affected the cost of delivering local services just as it affected the cost of other goods and services. This inflation-induced cost squeeze was compounded by the state's practice of mandating programs that local governments had to pay for out of local, primarily property tax revenues.

Another factor in the local cost squeeze was "slippage" — a decline in the state's share of the cost of programs funded jointly by state and local revenues. Here, again, the culprit was increasing assessed values. State-established formulas for determining the relative contribution of local property taxpayers and the state to the funding of local school districts, Medi-Cal, and aid to aged, blind, and disabled (SSI/SSP) were tied directly to assessed values. As assessments increased, the local share of the cost of these programs went up automatically while the state share declined. In the case of schools — which receive almost 53¢ of every property tax dollar — this "slippage" caused local property tax bills to soar despite state-imposed revenue limitations.

Homeowner Reaction

From the viewpoint of homeowners, the dramatic shift in the property tax burden from income properties onto homeowners and the cost squeeze on local government were largely invisible. What was visible were the outrageous increases in their property tax bills — increases which bore no relationship to their ability to pay or any perceptible improvement in the quality or quantity of the services they were receiving from local government. Faced with massive increases in their tax bills and no visible evidence that they were getting anything more for their money, homeowners were left to draw only one conclusion: they were being crucified on a cross of overtaxation and government waste.

The State's Growing Surplus

California's mounting state surplus only served to reinforce this impression. Many critics of government spending contend that "if you give politicians a dollar, they'll spend it." But in Jerry Brown's California, they were almost as likely to accumulate it. The last Reagan budget, for fiscal year (FY) 1974-75, ended with a General Fund surplus of $757 million.

By the end of FY 1977-78 — just three years later — that surplus had grown to an astonishing $3,969.9 million.

The origins of this surplus can be traced in large part to the fiscal policies of the Reagan administration. Although Reagan left office with an untarnished reputation as a fiscal conservative, the eight Reagan budgets produced an increase in General Fund expenditures of 177% while the California Consumer Price Index grew by just 48% and the state's personal income by 94%. As a result of major increases in sales, personal income, and corporation tax rates, General Fund revenues grew even faster than expenditures — by 198% over the same period.

During Jerry Brown's first term as Governor, the revenues yielded by the tax increases of the Reagan years far exceeded even the most optimistic fiscal forecasts as a result of skyrocketing inflation and an

extraordinary economic expansion. In the first three budget years of the Brown administration (FY 1975-76 through FY 1977-78), General Fund revenues increased by 59%. Price inflation and the growth of taxable sales as a percent of income resulted in a 49% increase in sales tax revenues. Inflation and a 38% increase in personal income increased the yield of California's progressive personal income tax by 81% during the same three-year period. Together, these two taxes — the sales tax and the personal income tax — accounted for 71% of General Fund revenues in FY 1977-78.

The impact of these increases on taxpayers was exacerbated by a massive income tax shift from corporate to individual income taxpayers. As indicated in Table 5, during the early and mid-1960s California's bank and corporation tax yielded almost as much revenue as the personal income tax. But by the late 1970s, the bank and corporation tax was contributing only 45% as much as personal income taxes to the state treasury.

The accumulating state surplus was a classic and highly visible example of overtaxation — a point not overlooked by outraged homeowners looking to the state for relief from soaring property tax bills. While homeowners were paying more and more of their incomes to the state, these increasing tax burdens produced no visible benefits in return. State taxes were not cut to bring revenues in line with expenditures, nor were expenditures increased to provide taxpayers with a higher level of state services. Most importantly, the state failed to seize the opportunity provided by the surplus to substantially reduce residential property taxes. This failure was the most important single factor contributing to the success of Proposition 13.

Table 4

California's General Fund Surplus[1]

Fiscal Year	Ending Surplus ($Millions)	Annual Change ($Millions)	(Percent)
1974-1975	$ 756.6	$ +390.1	+106.4%
1975-1976	947.2	+190.6	+ 25.2
1976-1977	1,955.7	+1,008.5	+106.5
1977-1978	3,969.9	+2,014.2	+103.0
1978-1979	2,961.2	−1,008.7	− 25.4

[1]Federal revenue sharing funds available for General Fund appropriation are included

Source: California Department of Finance

Table 5

CALIFORNIA'S INCOME TAX SHIFT

Average Revenues from Personal Income and Bank and Corporation Taxes During Three Administrations ($ Millions)

Administration	Personal Income (P.I.)	Bank and Corporation (B&C)	B&C as % of P.I. Revenues
Brown Sr.			
FY 1960 - FY 1963	$284,184	$281,584	99.1%
FY 1964 - FY 1967	$439,290	$427,642	97.3%
Reagan			
FY 1968 - FY 1971	$1,117,654	$572,070	51.2%
FY 1972 - FY 1975	$2,020,806	$959,876	47.5%
Brown Jr.			
FY 1976 - FY 1979	$4,066,552	$1,824,305	44.9%

Beginning in fiscal 1967, most state revenues were placed on an accrual basis. Since fiscal 1974, only accounts receivable are accrued. Revenues for fiscal 1979 are estimates prepared by the Department of Finance.

Averages are calculated for the terms of each Governor based on

the fiscal years for which they approved the state budget. For example, Ronald Reagan took office in 1967, but the first budget he signed was for fiscal 1968. Thus, fiscal 1967 is attributed to Brown Sr.'s last term and fiscal 1968 to Reagan's first term.

Source: California Department of Finance

II. THE LEGISLATURE FAILS TO ACT

In his 1977 "State of the State" message, Governor Jerry Brown identified the property tax as "number one on the agenda." Legislative leaders echoed this sentiment. The word from Sacramento was that 1977 would be the year the Legislature finally responded to growing taxpayer unrest over rising property taxes. Yet when the session ended on September 15th, legislators went home empty-handed. The Legislatures' failure to act spurred irate taxpayers by the thousands to take pen and petition in hand and rally around the flag of Howard Jarvis and Paul Gann. The initiative process allowed Californians to do for themselves what the Legislature apparently was unwilling to do for them.

Three Major Bills

Early in 1977, there was little hint of the Legislature's eventual paralysis. Of the many bills introduced on the subject, three comprehensive property tax reform proposals emerged as the principle foci of debate. All three proposed major "circuit-breaker" programs designed to prevent property tax "overloads" by providing homeowner rebates in the form of refundable income tax credits based on household income and the size of homeowners' property tax bills. The bills differed in the amount and distribution of the rebates, emphasis given to renter relief, methods of funding, and inclusion or absence of local property tax revenue limitations. They also differed in constituency appeal and political support.

Senate Bill 154 (Nicholas Petris, D-Oakland), the Tax Justice Act of 1977, provided the greatest dollar amounts of relief to both homeowners and renters. It used highly progressive distribution formulas and was funded by a combination of income tax reforms — closing the capital gains loophole and adding high income tax brackets — and the growing state surplus. Co-sponsored by the California Tax Reform Association (CTRA) and Citizens' Action League (CAL), SB 154 enjoyed broad support from organized labor, senior citizens, tax reformers, community organizations, political clubs, consumer groups, and local government officials.

Senate Bill 12 (Jerry Smith, D-Saratoga) provided the least relief to the fewest homeowners and renters using the least progressive formula of any of the three bills. Unlike the other bills, it contained no tax reforms but instead relied exclusively on the state surplus for funding. Unlike SB 154, it contained a property tax revenue limitation formula based upon a price index and tied to passage of a constitutional amendment — Senate Constitutional Amendment 6 — which permitted separate tax rates for homeowners and owners of other types of property. The revenue limitation formula was elaborately constructed to protect homeowners from the effects of rising assessments while assuring business property owners that homeowner taxes would not be shifted back onto them. SB 12 was supported by the Governor and some elements of the business community who were also pushing another Brown-backed bill by Senator Smith which would have repealed the remaining 50% of California's business inventory tax at a cost of $450 million — approximately the same cost as the homeowner and renter relief contained in SB 12.

The third major bill, Assembly Bill 999 (Willie Brown, D-San Francisco), was a compromise plan worked out within the Assembly's Democratic Caucus after negotiations between Democratic and Republican members collapsed. It fell between SB 154 and SB 12 in both the amount and distribution of homeowner and renter rebates. Like SB 154, its funding came from a combination of tax reforms and state surplus. Like SB 12, it contained a split tax rate property tax revenue limitation on local governments, though in contrast to SB 12 it also provided local governments with alternative revenue sources and imposed a revenue cap on the state as well. AB 999 also would have phased out the business inventory tax over five years (with the cost offset by an increase in the state bank and corporation tax) and adjusted the state's personal income tax for inflation by widening the existing eleven brackets and adding four new ones. As a compromise struck among legislators, it had little visible support outside the Legislature.

AB 999 cleared the Assembly easily. Both SB 154 and SB 12 were passed by the Senate, the former largely with Democratic support — only two of the Senate's fourteen Republicans voted for it — and the latter with a mixture of support from seventeen Democrats and ten Republicans.

The SB 154 Conference Committees

Late in June, SB 154 took center stage when the Assembly amended into it the contents of AB 999 and passed it back to the Senate where the Assembly amendments were rejected. A conference committee then was appointed to work out a compromise version.

After a summer of negotiations among its members and with the Governor, the conference committee finally submitted its report to both houses of the Legislature on September 2. The report proposed $550 million in circuit-breaker relief for homeowners and $285 million for renters; a split tax rate property tax revenue limit on local government offset in part by a grant of limited new taxing authority; a state revenue limit; a full repeal of the business inventory tax in 1979-80 partially offset by a 1% increase in the bank and corporation tax rate; a watered down real estate speculation tax; and modest reforms reducing the preference given capital gains and closing several other loopholes.

The report was widely criticized for providing inadequate relief to homeowners. The California Tax Reform Association, an original sponsor of SB 154, withdrew its support, citing its overemphasis on relief for business at the expense of homeowners, a weakening of reforms contained in earlier versions, and its lack of fiscal balance based on available projections of revenues and expenditures. The report was adopted in the Assembly but was defeated in the Senate where ten Democrats joined thirteen Republicans voting against it.

A second SB 154 conference committee was formed to attempt a new compromise. It added $100 million of additional relief targeted to middle income homeowners to the $550 million contained in the first report. Other changes included upping the price tag to business for ending the inventory tax, strengthening several reform provisions, an improved formula for renter relief, and a controversial increase in vehicle license fees to replace provisions opposed by business on alternative local revenue sources contained in the first report.

The second conference committee report was submitted to the Senate for approval on September 15, the last day of the 1977 session. Twenty-one Senators — all Democrats — voted for the report. This was a bare majority of the forty member Senate, but a ⅔ vote was required for passage. All fourteen Republicans and one Democrat voted no (ironically, the Democrat represented Kern County, one of only three counties in which voters subsequently were to reject Proposition 13). Four Democrats abstained, but agreed to vote for the report if the other two votes needed to reach the ⅔ mark could be found. The two votes were not found and the Legislature adjourned at midnight without delivering on the property tax relief promised so confidently by the Governor and legislative leaders nine months before.

Many reasons could — and have — been cited for the Legislature's failure to act. However, the following factors certainly were the most critical: first, the requirement of an extraordinary majority to pass SB 154; second, the intrusion of partisan politics into the deliberations; third, the absence of significant debate over the relative advantages and disadvantages of the circuit-breaker and the homeowners' exemption; fourth, the waning of focused public pressure on the Legislature during the summer months leading up to the critical vote; and, finally, Governor Brown's failure to provide the leadership needed to force a compromise.

Minority Rule

A vote of ⅔ of each house of the Legislature was required to pass SB 154. This requirement was imposed because the bill contained an urgency clause so it could take effect immediately in the current fiscal year, because it contained an appropriation, and because its repeal of the business inventory tax amended personal property tax codes, all of which triggered constitutional provisions mandating a ⅔ vote for passage.

The effect of this requirement was to allow only 14 Senators out of 120 legislators to veto the will of the majority. While well over ⅔ of the Assembly and a majority of the Senate were on record in support of SB 154, a small band of 15 members of the Senate were able to overrule their support and block passage of the bill.

Partisan Politics Intrude

Although the property tax debate attracted the normal amount of partisan wrangling early in the session, party differences didn't appear decisive. Both AB 999 and SB 12 had received bipartisan support and even SB 154 had picked up two Republican votes in the Senate.

However, these earlier bipartisan votes proved to be misleading in the final weeks of the session as Senate Republicans seized the opportunity afforded them by the ⅔ vote requirement to vote as a solid 14-vote bloc against property tax relief in 1977. They now began attacking features they had voted for in earlier bills in order to justify voting against the second SB 154 conference report.

Senate Minority Floor Leader George Deukmejian, who led the attack on the report, charged that it was unfair because it failed to provide relief across the board to all homeowners. Yet Senator Deukmejian had made the motion to pass SB 12 out of the Senate Revenue and Taxation Committee and later supported it on the floor despite the fact that its circuit-breaker provided far less relief to many fewer homeowners than the circuit-breaker in the second SB 154 conference committee report. Likewise, he attacked the report for not providing enough relief to middle income homeowners even though it provided substantially more relief to middle income homeowners than SB 12. In fact, 75% of the report's $650 million in homeowner relief went to families with incomes between $10,000 and $42,000.

The Republican vote blocking property tax relief reflected a political strategy based on the coming 1978 elections. Seventeen Democratic seats in the Senate were up for election in 1978 and all three of the incumbent Republicans who faced reelection intended to retire. Of the Assembly's eighty members, only twenty-three were Republicans and several of them intended to retire or seek other offices. Republicans held only one statewide office and the incumbent, Attorney General Evelle Younger, was running for Governor. Thus, if taxpayers became sufficiently irate at the failure of politicians to deliver on their

Wipe off our fingerprints, Deuk, and we'll blame it on the Democrats!

promises of property tax relief and decided to "throw the bums out," the "bums" they would throw out were far more likely to be Democrats than Republicans.

The November, 1978, election confirmed the logic of this strategy in the "year of the tax revolt." Although Republicans gained only one seat in the Senate, they unseated two liberal Democrats. They also picked up another Democratic seat in a subsequent special election. Republican gains in the Assembly were more dramatic. Their strength increased from 23 to 30 seats, denying Democrats the ⅔ control necessary to pass appropriations and other measures requiring an extraordinary majority. A Republican also defeated a Brown appointee running for a full term on the state Board of Equalization which oversees administration of the property tax. Republicans also gained a statewide office when Mike Curb defeated the Democratic Lt. Governor Mervyn Dymally. And Senator George Deukmejian was elected California's new Attorney General.

Circuit-breaker vs. Homeowner Exemption

Early in the session all three major property tax bills had adopted the circuit-breaker approach to property tax relief. As a result, debate during most of the session focused on how the circuit-breaker formula should be designed, with little serious discussion of the basic advantages and disadvantages of the circuit-breaker compared to other approaches. There was a widespread assumption that, whatever its shape, the final property tax bill would contain a circuit-breaker.

This assumption was not really put to the test until the Republican assault on the second SB 154 conference committee report. As an alternative to the report's $650 million homeowner circuit-breaker, Senator Deukmejian and his colleagues proposed a $570 million increase in the state's existing homeowner exemption program, raising the value of the exemption from $7,000 ($1,750 assessed value) to $12,000 ($3,000 assessed value).

Rhetorical pleas from Deukmejian and his allies on behalf of "the middle income homeowner" and "giving relief to everyone" masked the fundamental weaknesses of his proposal. In the name of "across the board" relief, the Deukmejian plan would have provided only token reductions to overburdened middle income homeowners, and even these would have been quickly eroded by rising assessments.

The contrast with the second SB 154 conference committee report was dramatic. Consider the comparison in Table 6. Taking a family with $25,000 income—clearly a "middle income" family—living in an $83,000 home (the average sale price for Southern California homes in April, 1978) and paying a $12.40 tax rate (the 1977-78 average for Los Angeles County), SB 154 would have resulted in a $906 reduction compared to a $155 reduction provided by the Deukmejian plan. Even if Deukmejian had proposed spending another $80 million to match the $650 million for homeowners in SB 154, the additional in-

Table 6

Illustrative Comparison of the Homeowner Relief Provided by the Second SB 154 Conference Committee Report and the Deukmejian Alternative Proposal

L. A. County Family with $25,000 Household Income	SB 154	Deukmejian
Home Value (April, 1978, Av. So. Cal. Resale Price)	$83,200	$83,200
Tax Rate (1977-78 Av. for L. A. County)	$12.40	$12.40
Tax Under Current Law	$2,362	$2,362
Tax After SB 154/ Deukmejian	$1,455	$2,207
Tax Savings	$907	$155

crease in the homeowners' exemption would have resulted in only another $22 in relief for the family in our comparison.

Moreover, the relief offered by the exemption would have continued to depend on tax rates instead of changes in homeowner tax bills, since the Deukmejian plan did not call for indexing the homeowner's exemption to provide for annual adjustments based on average increases in assessments. By contrast, the circuit-breaker's "overload protection" offered permanent "tax insurance" guarding homeowners against excessive property tax bills caused by inflated home assessments since the rebates it provided went up as tax bills — not tax rates — increased.

Unfortunately, the pervasive assumption during the session that the circuit-breaker mechanism itself was not at issue had left its supporters in the Legislature and Administration unprepared to respond effectively when it came under attack during the final days of the session. Despite the many inadequacies of the Deukmejian plan — not the least of which was that it simply failed to provide very much tax relief — the Democratic majority supporting SB 154 failed to mount an effective counterattack to put the Republican opposition on the defensive. Perhaps a major debate on the merits of the two approaches earlier in the session would have left them better able to respond.

The Organizing Campaign Falters

The success of the original SB 154 in moving through two committees and off the Senate floor was a surprise to many Sacramento observers who, when it was introduced, had predicted its early demise. The key to its success was a massive statewide organizing effort that produced hundreds of organizational endorsements and effective local organizing campaigns in targeted legislative districts. The statewide campaign was highlighted by three mass demonstrations in Sacramento: one in January sponsored by the Service Employees International Union, the second and largest in April organized by Citizens' Action League, and in May a major rally sponsored by the state's senior citizen network.

In retrospect, it is clear that the organizing campaign "peaked too soon." The momentum of the Spring was not sustained through the Summer. In part, this reflected a natural relaxation of energies after a long, sustained period of organizing activity which built toward the mass "lobby day" demonstrations in Sacramento and was rewarded by some major initial victories when SB 154 passed the Senate floor and eventually became the "vehicle" that was sent to conference committee.

The conference committee process also proved to be an obstacle to sustained momentum. The proceedings of the first conference committee dragged on far longer than anyone anticipated. The ebb and flow of issues, the political in-fighting, the bargaining, and the uncertain pace of progress toward agreement — none of these staples of the conference committee process lent themselves to gearing up a new organizing campaign, particularly since the conference committee members all had well established views and represented "safe" districts. Moreover, it was no longer possible to organize support for "SB 154" since no one would know what it was until the conference committee completed its work.

Finally, the compromises struck in the conference committee reports eroded support within the coalition responsible for the early successes of SB 154 and attracted new opposition from sources that were on the sidelines during most of the year.

Both conference committee reports contained property tax revenue limitations on local government which were unacceptable to public employee unions and the California Labor Federation. In order to soften the impact of the revenue limits, each conference report contained new alternative revenue sources for local governments which provoked more opposition. The first report contained provisions from AB 999 authorizing counties and cities to impose utility user and business license taxes that attracted strong opposition from industry lobbyists. The second report dropped these provisions in favor of an increase in motor vehicle licensing fees that drew fire from the highway lobby and agricultural interests.

Both reports also contained tax reforms designed to raise additional funds for property tax relief beyond what would have been possible within the limits of official estimates of the state surplus. These, too, attracted opposition. The electronics industry opposed a modest capital gains reform. The oil companies opposed a reform subjecting intangible drilling costs to the minimum tax on preference income. The mining industry opposed a reform of the mineral depletion allowance. An assessment reform allowing new construction to be assessed upon completion drew the opposition of the construction industry and the building trades.

As noted earlier, even the California Tax Reform Association (CTRA) — a co-sponsor of the original SB 154 — withdrew its support from the first conference committee report, although it worked actively for passage of the second report.

The slackening of the organizing campaign and the erosion of support within the original SB 154 coalition obviously contributed to the defeat of the second conference committee report. When the fate of SB 154 came down to the need to get two votes — specifically, two Republican votes — on the last night of the 1977 session, those votes were not delivered. Ironically, the two Republican Senators most likely to vote for the report — the two who had voted earlier in the year for the original SB 154 — represented districts in San Francisco and Contra Costa County where the SB 154 coalition had been strongest. Yet neither Senator felt compelled to vote for property tax relief before returning home to their districts for the year.

No Leadership from the Governor

Whatever the loss of organizing momentum or the inadequacies of the early debate over the circuit-breaker may have contributed to the defeat of the second conference committee report, they were not decisive. What was decisive was the failure of Governor Jerry Brown to provide leadership when it was needed.

Throughout 1977, Brown frequently seemed more concerned about providing tax breaks to business than in the plight of California's homeowners and renters. He consistently supported legislation giving the least residential property tax relief and the greatest tax relief to business, although California business was enjoying record profits and was the primary beneficiary of a massive shift in the state and local tax burden over the preceding decade.

The Brown Administration's political management of the mounting state surplus was a major

BUSINESSMAN'S BEST FRIEND

obstacle to a successful legislative compromise. Official estimates consistently understated the rate of growth of the General Fund surplus. Brown viewed the surplus as a political asset providing tangible evidence of the frugality of his Administration while protecting against the necessity of a general tax increase at some future date.

Residential property tax relief was also competing with other Brown spending priorities: eliminating the business inventory tax, low and moderate income housing, tax breaks for foreign-based multinational corporations, reforestation, and energy conservation and development. Many of these projects were proposed in January, 1978, when the Governor presented his budget proposals to the Legislature and *after* Jarvis and Gann had filed their 1.2 million signatures. For Brown, the homeowner property tax was an issue, but it was not *the* issue in 1977 and early 1978.

The Brown Administration's tight control over the amount of surplus funds it was willing to commit to property tax relief meant that Brown's "surplus-only" approach could only finance levels of property tax relief many legislators considered grossly inadequate. To fund additional relief, the Legislature was forced to add revenue-raising provisions which eroded support for the conference committee reports both inside and outside the Legislature. None of these controversial provisions would have been necessary had the Brown Administration been more forthcoming in its management of the surplus and had it given property tax relief the priority it deserved.

Even in the final hours of the second conference committee's deliberations, the Administration was pressuring the committee to cut back on homeowner and renter relief, citing the sudden discovery of hundreds of millions of dollars of Medi-Cal cost overruns — a "crisis" which disappeared just as suddenly as it appeared after the conference committee's report was defeated. Unknown to the committee's members and other legislators, at the same time they were being pressured to reduce homeowner and renter benefits, the Brown Administration was quietly moving to support a tax treaty with the United Kingdom under consideration in the U.S. Senate which would have provided millions of dollars in California tax breaks to British-based multinational corporations doing business in the State.

But Brown's greatest contribution to the defeat of property tax relief legislation in 1977 came with his reaction to the events of the last night of the session. If the Republicans can be credited with blocking property tax relief in the Senate, then Jerry Brown must also be credited with letting them get away with it.

When SB 154 fell two votes short of passage on the last day of the session, California homeowners and renters were denied tax reductions on their 1977-78 property tax bills and protection against future property tax increases. Despite a year of promises, the Legislature went home empty-handed. The credibility of the state's political leaders was on the line.

Moreover, the solid phalanx of Republican opposition was a high risk strategy since it left them vulnerable to the charge that they were placing partisan politics ahead of the needs of California homeowners.

At this critical time requiring decisive and forceful leadership, Governor Brown was unable or unwilling to supply it. By denouncing the partisan Senate vote, calling an immediate special session of the Legislature, and urging the people of California to help him get the two additional votes needed to make property tax relief a reality in 1977-78, the Governor could have forced a legislative solution to the property tax crisis. But Brown refused to attack the Republicans for putting partisan politics ahead of property tax relief. Nor did he answer Republican attacks on SB 154 or attack the Republicans' "alternative" which would have placed increasing reliance on the widely discredited homeowners' exemption program.

Instead, the Governor suggested that "Senators should go home and meditate." Worse yet, Brown and his advisors began publicly echoing the Republican rhetoric attacking SB 154. By thus granting credibility to the Republican position, Brown threw away a year's worth of compromises and foreclosed the possibility of achieving property tax relief in 1977-78 through a special session.

Brown's failure to act aggressively to break the legislative stalemate reflected, in part, his own inability to grasp the depth of public feeling caused by the continued escalation of homeowner property taxes. If the Legislature failed to act in 1977, it could always pass an election year tax cut in 1978 — when the Governor would be running for reelection. And, of course, the state would have accumulated an even larger surplus.

When Brown submitted his budget proposal to the Legislature in January, 1978 — after Jarvis and Gann already had qualified their initiative for the June ballot with a record-breaking 1.2 million signatures — he still seemed to lack a real sense of urgency on the issue. The new budget proposed $1 billion for property tax relief — just $85 million more than the first year cost of the defeated second SB 154 conference report. At the same time, he proposed spending $800 million of the state's surplus on new housing, energy, and reforestation programs, all of which were subsequently rejected by the Legislature. Meanwhile, the new budget projected a 1977-78 surplus of $2.9 billion compared to a $2 billion estimate used three months earlier during the deliberations of the second SB 154 conference committee (the actual 1977-78 surplus ended up at $3.7 billion).

Brown's failure to act also reflected his unwillingness to engage in a partisan confrontation with the Republicans. Faced with no serious challenge from within the Democratic party, Brown saw the key to a landslide reelection victory in 1978 hinging on his ability to compete with the Republicans for their own constituency. Partisan confrontation risked alienating that constituency. On the other hand, by echoing Republican attacks on SB 154, Brown could effectively undercut the ability of any future Republican opponent to use the property tax issue against him, particularly if the Legislature succeeded in passing a bill in 1978. What these calculations ignored, of course, was the initiative petition being circulated by Mssrs. Jarvis and Gann.

Too Little, Too late

After the defeat of the second SB 154 conference committee report, many legislators commented on the lack of apparent public reaction. The key word is "apparent." The public had given up on Sacramento. Too many promises had been made and broken. Instead of writing letters and demonstrating in Sacramento, they decided to take matters into their own hands. In November, Howard Jarvis and Paul Gann — who had teamed up after each had failed separately earlier in the year to get enough signatures to place property tax limitation measures on the ballot — filed their 1.2 million signatures with the Secretary of State.

These signatures were an inevitable response to Sacramento's failure to enact a property tax bill. In California's media-oriented society, politicians have many ways of communicating with the people through electronic and print media, computerized mailings, and legislative newsletters. But there are few ways in which the people can communicate with the politicians in a way that forces them to respond. Signing an initiative is one way. The 1.2 million Californians who signed the Jarvis-Gann initiative sent a message the Legislature could not ignore.

By the time Sacramento finally got the message, the opportunity to provide property tax relief before the June primary election had slipped away. While the Legislature could pass a bill, it could not be implemented in time to get property tax relief into the pockets of taxpayers before June 6. When the Legislature met again in January, it had to achieve a new consensus in order to produce a property tax bill that could gain the support of two-thirds of its members. After two months of deliberations, the result was a lowest-common-denominator compromise — Senate Bill 1, the "Behr bill." The key features of this $1.4 billion compromise were a 30% across-the-board homeowner property tax reduction, a property tax revenue limitation based on split tax rates similar to the one contained in both SB 154 conference committee reports, and modest increases in the state's income tax credit for renters and senior citizens property tax relief programs.

SB 1 was a classic case of too little, too late. By the time the Legislature finally acted — clearly an eleventh hour reaction to the Jarvis-Gann initiative — the public's skepticism could not easily be overcome. At the very least, a skillful campaign would be required to win the public over. But such a campaign never materialized.

III. THE PROPOSITION 13 LANDSLIDE

A Los Angeles Times poll taken in mid-March

showed 35% of respondents favoring Proposition 13 and 27% opposed. Its fate rested in the hands of the 35% who were undecided. By June 6, they had made their decision: 4,280,689 (or 64.8%) voted in favor of Proposition 13 and only 2,326,167 (or 35.2%) voted against it. The Legislature's alternative — Proposition 8 — was defeated, but more narrowly (47% yes to 53% no). The margin of Proposition 13's victory clearly reflected the dimensions of the property tax crisis in California and the public's reaction to the state's failure to respond. It also reflected the approaches of the two sides to the election campaign.

An Effective "Yes" Campaign

The proponents of Proposition 13 staged a highly effective campaign. Their message was simple: cut your property tax by 60% and show the politicians who's boss! It was a message that struck a responsive chord among taxpayers angered by excessive and apparently uncontrollable property tax increases and frustrated by the failure of government officials to act.

The campaign's message also was skillfully delivered. Heavy reliance was placed on personalized mailings detailing individual tax savings and paid media spots featuring Howard Jarvis, economist Milton Friedman and others reinforcing the basic message and assuring the public that the opponents' "scare tactics" were unfounded. The campaign also benefitted from its ability to make effective use of free media time — radio talk shows, news programs, and letters to the editor. Howard Jarvis became a news personality. For three solid weeks in May, Jarvis appeared nightly on the highest rated television news program in Los Angeles to debate a different opponent.

The "Yes" campaign was well financed. Altogether, the supporters of Proposition 13 spent $2.2 million, of which $1.6 million was spent by the central Yes on 13 campaign managed by the Orange County public relations firm of Butcher and Forde. Large contributions came primarily from real estate-related interests, but most of the fund were from small contributions raised by direct mail appeals.

An Inept "No" Campaign

The campaign mounted by the opponents of Proposition 13 was as inept as the proponents' campaign was effective. Californians were mad about taxes, but Winner/Wagner and Associates — the public relations firm managing the "No" campaign — refused to talk about taxes. Property taxes were too complicated—people wouldn't understand.

Instead, Winner/Wagner ran exactly the campaign which the proponents of Proposition 13 had prepared the voters to expect: one based on "scare tactics" threatening massive reductions in police, fire, and other essential services should Proposition 13 pass. The "No" campaign ignored the tax shifts that created California's property tax crisis. It also failed to emphasize the additional tax shifts that would victimize homeowners over the long term should Proposition 13 pass and the multi-billion dollar tax windfalls it would give to business. In fact, while the Winner/Wagner office in Los Angeles was running the ''No on 13'' campaign, its lobbyists in Sacramento were representing corporate clients attempting to undermine California's corporate income tax. The campaign also failed to emphasize any of the advantages to the homeowner of the Legislature's tax relief plan when contrasted with Proposition 13. Indeed, the superiority of Proposition 13 as a means of providing home-owner tax relief was virtually conceded by many of the ''No'' campaign's radio and television ads which ended with the tag line, ''it may look good, but it costs too much.''

Instead of asking voters to choose between approaches to reducing property taxes, the ''No'' campaign asked them to choose between the risk of reduced public services or the certainty of a substantial property tax reduction. For obvious reasons, voters chose the latter.

That choice was made easier by the state surplus. With the state sitting on a projected $5 billion surplus — plus another $800 million the state would pick up in reduced property tax relief costs and increased income tax revenues if Proposition 13 passed — people simply did not believe that a $6.1 billion reduction in property tax levies would have the devastating impact on essential services predicted by the initiative's opponents. And, of course, they were right. After Proposition 13 passed, the Legislature gave local governments $4.4 billion to offset their revenue loss. Moreover, revisions to the state budget increased the available surplus for 1978-79 eventually to $8.3 billion.

While the state's surplus undercut the apparent risk to services, news of 1978 homeowner assessed value increases made immediate and substantial tax reduction a necessity. The pressure of the campaign resulted in the early release of 1978 assessments in several counties during the weeks before the election. In Los Angeles County, the impact was dramatic: homes reassessed in 1978 increased an *average* of 120% over the prior year. Homeowner ''horror stories'' were front page news.

The Los Angeles Board of Supervisors and Governor Brown responded to the new assessments by asking county assessors to freeze assessments at 1977-78 levels — in direct violation of state law. This ploy only confirmed what the proponents of Proposition 13 had been saying all along: In their desperation, the politicians would attempt to use every device possible to manipulate the people into voting against Proposition 13. Moreover, it obscured the fact that SB 1 — the Legislature's plan — actually offered homeowners greater long term protection against the effects of assessment increases than Proposition 13 because its revenue limitation would have gradually forced homeowner property taxes not just to 1% of market value — as provided in Proposition 13 — but below 1% when assessments went up.

News of 1978 assessments made taxes the unavoidable issue during the last month of the campaign. But Winner/Wagner had no strategy for cam-

paigning on tax issues. By ignoring the weaknesses of Proposition 13 as a tax measure earlier in the campaign, they now had no basis on which to counterattack. Polls taken late in May showed a dramatic shift of support in favor of Proposition 13. The ''No'' campaign staged no last minute media blitz attempting to stem the tide. By the final week before the election, Winner/Wagner had conceded defeat.

In the end, the ''No'' committee's strategy of building a broad coalition of opposition to Proposition 13 encompassing business, labor, public interest groups and political leaders backfired. While the ''leaders'' were opposing Proposition 13, their members and employees were supporting it. The ''No'' coalition itself became a target in the campaign, representing the ''establishment'' opposing the will of the people — an impression inadvertently reinforced by the style and themes of the ''No'' campaign. The role of big business in the opposition campaign also sent confusing messages to the voters concerning who really benefitted from Proposition 13 and placed constraints on Winner/Wagner's ability to make Proposition 13's tax breaks to business a major issue.

The opposition to Proposition 13 spent $2 million, with the Winner/Wagner-directed ''No'' campaign spending $1.8 million of that total. Large contributions came from major business interests — particularly in the financial sector — and public employee groups.

The Vote

On June 6, Proposition 13 won easily. Despite the landslide proportions of the Proposition 13 victory, its yes vote equalled only 43.1% of all registered voters, and only 28.4% of California's voting age population.

Still, the scale of Proposition 13's victory was impressive. It was successful in 55 of California's 58 counties, meeting defeat only in San Francisco, Yolo, and Kern. San Francisco is a city of renters, and renters had little to gain from Proposition 13. Yolo is a predominantly rural county whose voters favored Proposition 13, except for the residents of Davis who supplied the margin of its defeat. Davis is the home of a branch of the University of California and a bedroom community for state employees working in neighboring Sacramento. Kern is California's wealthiest agricultural county and also contains valuable oil and gas resources which only recently had been reassessed upward. Home values and homeowner taxes were relatively low. Resentment of Los Angeles, its neighbor to the south, runs high and Proposition 13 was seen — quite correctly — as benefitting Los Angeles far more than Kern.

Interpretations of the Proposition 13 vote must distinguish its meaning for voters on election day from its subsequent political impact. Proposition 13 was a major organizing victory for longstanding ideological critics of government spending, many of whom — like Howard Jarvis — had previously been relegated to the political fringes. Thus, the post-13 debate over its meaning has focused less on what's wrong with the tax system than on what's wrong with government. Conservatives have used the tax revolt as a cutting edge to open up a broader attack on government spending and regulation. While this conservative response to Proposition 13 has created a reality of its own, it is not necessarily what shaped the thoughts of California voters as they went to the polls on June 6, 1978.

The best available evidence concerning the meaning of Proposition 13 for the people who voted for it comes from the Los Angeles Times-Channel 2 News Survey of 2,482 voters as they left their polling places on election day. The Survey's findings indicate that taxes were uppermost in the minds of voters, and those voters most adversely affected by the property tax were most likely to vote for Proposition 13.

Senior citizens and homeowners were two groups most directly threatened by California's property tax crisis. Among seniors, 76% voted for Proposition 13. Among homeowners, 72% voted for Proposition 13; of homeowners without a government employee in their household, 81%. By contrast, only 28% of renters with a government employee in their household voted yes. When asked to explain their vote, more than half the supporters of Proposition 13 cited the statement that "property taxes are too high."

The Survey also revealed the predictable ideological differences. Conservatives (82%) were almost twice as likely to vote for Proposition 13 as liberals (45%). However, among homeowners who had no government employees in their household — who made up more than half the voters — the majority voted yes whether they identified themselves as liberal, moderate, or conservative.

There also was remarkably little evidence of strong support for the traditional conservative agenda of cutbacks in government services. Only 22% of Proposition 13's supporters gave "government provides too many services" as a reason for their vote. In addition, 71% of the voters for Proposition 13 believed they could benefit from its cut in property taxes without a significant reduction in the level of government services. This finding was confirmed by a survey conducted immediately after the election by Opinion Research Corporation for Arthur D. Little, Inc. It found that 85% of its respondents believed that current service levels could be maintained if government were made more efficient.

Although voters expressed little enthusiasm for reducing government services, there was nonetheless a strong undercurrent of dissatisfaction with the performance of government. In addition to lowering property taxes and "squeezing the fat out," Proposition 13 also was intended to "send a message." Forty percent of the voters who supported Proposition 13 agreed that one reason for their vote was that "it's a way to show what people want." However, one interesting finding of the Opinion Research Corporation survey was that 55% of those who voted for Pro-

Table 7	
How Californians Voted on Proposition 13	
	% Voting Yes
PROPERTY	
Owners	70 %
Renters	41
PUBLIC EMPLOYEES	
In Household	43
Not in Household	74
IDEOLOGY	
Conservatives	82
Moderates	65
Liberals	45
PARTY	
Republicans	78
Democrats	57
EDUCATION	
No High School	72
High School Grad	76
Some College	66
College Grad	54
INCOME	
Under $8,000	55
$8,000 - $15,000	67
$15,000 - $25,000	68
Over $25,000	63
ETHNIC	
Blacks	40
Whites	67
TOTAL	65

Source: The Los Angeles Times—Channel 2 News Survey.

position 13 (compared to 43% of those who voted against it) believed that government officials would act sensibly when implementing any spending cuts it might require. Of voters living in households containing a government employee, only 37% exhibited a similar degree of confidence.

There was, of course, a hard core of ideological conservatives supporting Proposition 13 — among them its chief sponsors. But they were incapable of supplying the margin of victory. That came instead from outraged homeowners — of all ideological persuasions — who simply wanted the property tax off their backs.

Based upon what the voters said as they left the polls, the evidence is clear that California's tax revolt was just that — a revolt against taxes, not a revolt against government. Most Californians wanted cheaper government, more efficient government, but not reduced government services. Given the massive property tax shift that was victimizing homeowners and the equally massive tax shifts and fiscal mismanagement at the state level, their motivation was not unreasonable. They knew they had a problem, and Proposition 13 appeared to be the only choice they had to do anything about it.

IV. THE IMPACT ON TAXES

Who Got What

Proposition 13's most obvious impact was on the tax bills received by California property owners for the 1978-1979 fiscal year: a dramatic $5.5 billion reduction from the previous year. This massive tax reduction was accompanied by an equally dramatic, though far less visible tax shift. While reducing property tax bills by an average of 52%, Proposition 13 also shifted the remaining property tax burden among property owners and shifted much of the responsibility for financing local services from property taxpayers onto other taxpayers.

The consequences of this shift for the individual taxpayer were not readily apparent. The immediacy of Proposition 13's property tax cuts contrasted with the longer term effects of the accompanying shifts. Moreover, these reductions were "prepaid" in the form of excessive state taxes *before* Proposition 13 which created a huge state surplus so that other taxes did not have to be raised *after* it passed to prevent catastrophic cuts in essential local services.

Any discussion of the impact of Proposition 13 on California's tax system must begin by identifying "who got what". California's property tax crisis was really a homeowner property tax crisis. Proposition 13 responded to this crisis by providing homeowners with a $2 billion property tax reduction. However, since Proposition 13 reduced property taxes across the board for all types of property, not just homes, the "price" of this $2 billion homeowner reduction was another $3.5 billion in tax reductions for the owners of business properties—a sum large enough to have eliminated the entire homeowner property tax with money to spare. Although homeowner property taxes were increasing more than six times as rapidly as taxes on business property, Proposition 13 gave the owners of business properties approximately $1.80 in property tax relief for every $1.00 going to homeowners.

The windfalls to individual businesses were staggering. The oil companies were among the largest beneficiaries: Standard Oil of California got $47 million; Shell Oil, $16 million; Getty Oil, $12.3 million; and ARCO, $10 million. The Bank of America netted $7.2 million after taxes, or 7¢ per share. After tax gains to other banks included $2.9 million to Security Pacific Corporation and $1.2 million to Wells Fargo. Large corporate landholders also fared well. Southern Pacific Co. saved $20 million and the privately-held Irvine Co. $4.5 million.

The state's utilities were forced by the California Public Utilities Commission to return their $264.4 million in savings back to their customers. However, in its February 13, 1979, story on Proposition 13's "Business Bonanza," *The Wall Street Journal* points out that "much of the savings go to large industrial and commercial customers because they generally use more power than homeowners."

THE PROPOSITION 13 PAYOFF

The *Wall Street Journal* calls it a "business bonanza": Proposition 13 led to a $3 billion tax cut on commercial and industrial properties in California. Politicians ranging from California Governor Jerry Brown to Ronald Reagan and Proposition 13 author Howard Jarvis have called on the state's businesses to use the tax savings to lower prices or to create more jobs in California. So far, it hasn't happened.

After Proposition 13 passed, Crocker National Bank took out full page newspaper ads promising to use its tax savings to make job-creating loans. But the bank now admits that "We obviously don't know that the money goes directly for that [job creation], although we feel and hope that most of it does." A similarly hollow promise came from Safeway Stores, which announced that its tax cut would be passed on in lower prices; a spokeswoman said, "You can't say we've done it yet, and I can't give you any idea of the size of the cuts." And the folks at Disneyland just said, "We hope we won't have to raise ticket prices as fast."

California's public utilities were forced by the state regulators to lower prices, passing on $264 million of Proposition 13 savings to customers. However, a lot of that goes to other businesses, who have the biggest utility bills. Southern California Edison cut its average residential customer's bill by all of 1%.

A number of banks seem to have cast a nervous glance over their shoulders at the impact of Proposition 13: the Bank of America, United California Bank and Wells Fargo have given away all of their first year's savings to charitable causes — some of it to the United Way to help social agencies that lost public funds in the cutbacks. But many see this as a one-time-only sop to keep things quiet until the issue dies down. "I think that after this year," said the chairman of the United California Bank, "it will be business as usual."

Elsewhere, business as usual didn't even have to wait a year. Southern Pacific is using its tax cut to buy more locomotives and freight cars, but could not say if it was buying any more than it would have without the cut. Tele-

dyne Co. was able to reveal that, "We have revenue and we have income, and whatever we have left after taxes we handle like we usually do."

Some simply pretend ignorance. Texaco, which saved $6.8 million in Los Angeles County alone, claimed not to know how much the tax cut was worth. And MCA, which saved at least $1.6 million in taxes on its Universal Studios, felt the tax savings were insignificant.

Perhaps the most candid comment came from Carl Hartnack, chairman of Security Pacific, a major bank. "We sincerely believe that it's wrong to make public the so-called savings figure," he said. "In the emotional and political environment of Proposition 13, there's a good possibility that isolating these numbers could produce misleading conclusions."

For example, people might conclude that Carl Hartnack and his friends were laughing all the way to the bank.

Dollars & Sense
March 1979

While a property tax reduction measured in hundreds of dollars may have been significant to homeowners struggling to protect their homes and families from the ravages of inflation, corporate executives seemed unimpressed with their millions. "In the overall scheme of things," said one oil company executive, "the savings aren't that big a thing." As another executive put it, "The savings to us may sound like a lot, but it's really only a drop in the bucket."

Another billion dollar "drop in the bucket" went to the federal government. It ended up with about $1.5 billion of the $5.5 billion tax break because of the higher federal taxes California individual and corporate taxpayers paid as a result of lower property tax deductions.

Shift to Individual Taxpayers

But while business taxpayers were reaping almost two-thirds of the benefits of Proposition 13's property tax cut, individual taxpayers were forced to bear most of the cost of the state's bailout of local government. By providing $4.4 billion to pay for local services formerly funded by property taxes, the state shifted the cost of these services onto those taxpayers whose tax dollars contributed to the state's surplus — for the most part, sales and income tax-

Table 8
The Distribution of Proposition 13
Property Tax Reductions by
Type of Ownership

Type of Owner	Property Tax Reduction $ Billions	Percent
Homeowners	$2.0	36%
Residential Landlords	1.0	19
Commercial, Industrial, and Agricultural Owners	2.5	45
Total Reduction	$5.5	100%

Based upon an estimate of the distribution of the property tax burden by type of ownership in the Legislative Analyst, *An Analysis of Proposition 13* (May, 1978), p. 203, and data on actual 1978-1979 property tax levy reductions supplied by the California Board of Equalization.

payers. Since business taxpayers contribute only 32% of the sales tax and 11% of the income tax, the effect was to substitute state tax revenues coming from homeowners and renters for property tax revenues formerly paid by business.

With California business already benefitting from massive pre-Proposition 13 property and income tax shifts, with the California economy already booming and business profits at record-breaking levels, the Proposition 13 tax shift away from business was nothing other than a tax giveaway. But to California voters it was a politically acceptable giveaway because the source of the giveaway — Proposi-

tion 13 — was the only means they saw of putting an end to the threat of runaway homeowner property taxes. Besides, they were already paying the state taxes piling up in the surplus. If giving away two-thirds of a loaf was necessary to get one-third, that still was better than no loaf at all.

Shift to User Charges

Proposition 13 also caused other tax shifts as local governments moved to substitute new user fees and taxes for lost property tax revenues. According to a California Department of Finance survey, local governments imposed over $200 million in new charges immediately after Proposition 13 passed. The largest increases were imposed by cities ($103 million of 15.8% of the revenues lost under Proposition 13) and special districts engaged in enterprise activities.

Business license taxes and fees paid by land developers have been two of the most popular sources of new revenue. Homeowners have been hit with new or increased fees for such property-related services as fire protection, flood control, sewers, sidewalk repair, and the lighting, sweeping, and maintenance of streets. Local governments have increased bus fares, water rates, trash collection and dumping fees, utility user charges, and municipal parking rates and fines. Still other new revenues have come from admissions taxes, recreation and library fees, animal license fees, hotel-motel bed taxes, and paramedic and ambulance fees.

The shift from property taxes to user charges allows local governments to continue providing a variety of services jeopardized by the loss of property tax revenues, although at a heavy cost to most homeowners and renters. For homeowners, this shift means that they are paying for government services through charges which are no longer deductible on state and federal income tax returns. By contrast, owners of business properties continue to enjoy state and federal subsidies of their local tax burden since for them user charges, like property taxes, are deductible business expenses.

Ironically, the wealthiest taxpayers who have the greatest ability to pay user fees frequently are also least likely to be affected by them. Increased bus fares, library fees, or charges for public recreational facilities (swimming pools, tennis courts, playgrounds, parks, golf courses, etc.) mean little to taxpayers who ride in their own cars, buy their own books, and "recreate" in private country clubs. On the other hand, these tax increases have a real impact on taxpayers who do use such public services. Moreover, for services which are discretionary (such as libraries, museums, and recreation facilities), higher user charges are often self-defeating since public use of these services may drop, revenues decline, and their quality deteriorate. For services which are not really discretionary (for example, sewers, bus rides to work, or emergency medical fees), these charges simply are regressive tax increases forcing middle and low income taxpayers to pay a larger share of the costs of government.

Property Tax Shifts

Proposition 13 also has shifted California's remaining property tax burden in a variety of ways. Unfortunately, one thing it has not changed is the basic regressivity of the tax, although it has substantially reduced the role of this regressive tax in California's tax system. Still, wealthy homeowners continue to pay a smaller proportion of their incomes in property taxes than lower income homeowners. Nonetheless, Proposition 13 has fundamentally altered who pays the property tax in California. As a result, it clearly has benefitted some property owners far more than others.

Obviously, taxpayers living in communities with high tax rates benefitted the most from Proposition 13's 1% limit. In the year before Proposition 13 passed, communities in Alameda County paid the highest tax rates, averaging $12.59 per $100 assessed value (or 3.1% of full value), while the lowest rates were paid by property owners in tiny Alpine County, whose tax rates averaged $4.98 (or 1.2% of full value). After Proposition 13, average tax rates were reduced by 58.8% in Alameda County, but only by 14.3% in sparsely populated Alpine County. As indicated in Table 9, the effect was to eliminate tax effort disparities between high tax rate urban areas and suburban and rural areas where tax rates tended to be lower. But while urban property owners benefitted most from the 1% limitation, the local governments who levied high rates to compensate for a poor tax base (that is, low per capita assessed values) or to meet the needs of their communities also suffered the greatest revenue losses.

At the same time, however, the impact of the state bailout tended to favor urban taxpayers at the expense of the suburbs. Table 10 illustrates the urban-suburban shift which accompanied the state bailout. While 37.8% of the Proposition 13 bailout went to local governments in Los Angeles County, Los Angeles residents account for less than 34% of the state's income tax revenues and less than 32% of its taxable sales. By contrast, Orange County jurisdictions received 6.3% of the bailout while Orange County taxpayers account for 9% of the state's income tax revenues and 8.8% of its taxable sales. Since suburban Orange County residents are contributing more to the state surplus than they are getting back in bailout funds and their urban Los Angeles neighbors are contributing less, one effect of Proposition 13 has been to shift some of the tax burden from urban Los Angeles to suburban Orange County.

The assessment provisions of Proposition 13 also resulted in significant property tax shifts. Since homeowner assessments were increasing almost four times as fast as assessments on other property, homeowners generally benefitted most from the rollback of assessments to 1975 levels, and homeowners living in areas with the most rapid increases in home values

benefitted most of all—especially if they bought their homes before 1975.

However, as time passes, the initial savings enjoyed by homeowners as a result of the assessment rollback will be eroded by another feature of the initiative. Under Proposition 13, property is to be reassessed to its actual market value only when it changes ownership. According to the California Association of Realtors, the average home is sold once every four to six years. Oil refineries, manufacturing plants, and office buildings are sold far less frequently. As a result, homes will be reassessed more often than other properties, and homeowners therefore will be taxed on a larger share of the actual market value of their property than will other property owners. Thus, while Proposition 13 cut the property tax burden in half, it continues to perpetuate the pre-

Table 9

Reductions in Average County Tax Rates, 1978-1979

	Average Tax Rates		
County	1977-1978	1978-1979	% Reduction
Urban			
Alameda	$12.59	$5.19	58.8%
Los Angeles	12.40	4.78	61.5
San Francisco	11.82	5.06	57.2
Suburban			
Orange	8.83	4.98	43.6
San Mateo	8.61	4.39	49.0
Marin	8.92	4.56	48.9
Rural/Agricultural			
Kern	8.60	4.47	48.0
Alpine	4.98	4.27	14.3
San Joaquin	10.80	4.56	57.8
Statewide Average	$10.68	$4.79	55.1%

Source: California Board of Equalization

Table 10

Proposition 13's Suburban-Urban Tax Shift An Illustration Comparing Los Ange and Orange Counties

	County Share of Statewide Totals	
Comparison	*Los Angeles*	*Orange*
Proposition 13 Tax Reduction (1978-1979)	39.6%	6.8%
State Bailout Funds (1978-1979)	37.8	6.3
Personal Income Taxes (1976)	33.7	9.0
Taxable Sales (1978)	31.8	8.8

Proposition 13 shift of more and more of the remaining property tax burden from owners of business property onto homeowners. Los Angeles County Assessor Alexander Pope found that one-sixth of the county's properties changed ownership or were improved by construction during the first year of Proposition 13. As a result of reassessing these 300,000 parcels, the County's assessment roll increased by 12% and residential property assessments (homeowner and rental units) grew from 64% of the roll to 72%. Pope predicts that within five years residences will be paying 80% of the property tax, leaving commercial, industrial and other properties with only 20%.

Renters Left Out

Perhaps the greatest victims of Proposition 13's redistribution of the tax burden are California's renters, now almost one-half the state's population. The median income of California's renters is roughly half that of homeowners, yet renters typically pay a larger share of their income for housing. While Proposition 13 gave landlords a $1 billion tax break, a tight rental market has continued to force post-Proposition 13 rents higher. Despite the campaign rhetoric of Howard Jarvis and other Proposition 13 advocates about lower rents, few California renters have benefitted from its passage. However renters continue to contribute to the state's surplus, pay many of the newly imposed local fees and taxes, and suffer the effects of service cutbacks along with everyone else.

With most landlords retaining their Proposition 13 savings and rents continuing to rise, angry renters and sympathetic homeowners have made rent control a major issue in California. While the landlord lobby in Sacramento was able to block legislation introduced soon after Proposition 13 passed requiring landlords to pass through 80% of their Proposition 13 savings to their tenants, they have been less successful locally. Although some efforts to require pass throughs or rent controls have failed, others have succeeded—including proposals in the city and the unincorporated areas of Los Angeles, Santa Monica, Beverly Hills, San Francisco, Davis, Berkeley, and Cotati—often with the sympathetic support of homeowners.

Another of the many ironies of Proposition 13 is that Howard Jarvis, executive director of the Los Angeles Apartment Owners Association, may prove — quite unintentionally — to be the father of rent control in California.

V. THE IMPACT ON STATE AND LOCAL GOVERNMENT

The State's Response

In sharp contrast to the pre-Proposition 13 legislative stalemate on property tax relief, less than three weeks after the election the Legislature and the governor were able to reach agreement on legislation to "bail out" local governments on a one-year

basis by substituting $4.4 billion in state surplus for much of their property tax revenue loss. Ironically, the legislative vehicle for achieving their agreement was a third conference committee on SB 154 — the bill whose defeat nine months earlier contributed so mightily to the success of Jarvis-Gann.

Altogether, SB 154 and subsequent legislation provided $4,375 million of surplus funds to the state's schools, counties, and special districts for fiscal 1978-79. More than half of this bailout went to California's 1,114 school and community college districts. In addition, the state picked up the local county share of costs for major health and welfare programs (Medi-Cal, AFDC, and SSI-SSP). Block grants for general support also went to California's 58 counties, 413 cities, and more than 4,700 special districts. Another $30 million in loans was made available to local governments facing cash flow problems as a result of Proposition 13. Along with its offer of funds, the state also imposed a number of "strings", including a freeze on local government salaries (subsequently invalidated by the courts where employee raises were called for by labor agreements already in effect) and a mandate that police and fire services be maintained at pre-Proposition 13 levels.

Sacramento's response to the fiscal crisis precipitated by Proposition 13 has been shaped by two political objectives: first, preventing the massive cutbacks in essential services which, before the election, it had predicted would result from Proposition 13's passage; and, second, avoiding a state tax increase in the foreseeable future.

Table 11

The 1978-1979 Local Government Bailout ($ Millions)

Schools		$2,461.0
K-12	$2,201.0	
Community Colleges	260.0	
Counties		1,503.8
Health & Welfare Buyout	$1,079.6	
Block Grants	424.2	
Cities		220.6
Special Districts		190.0
TOTAL		$4,375.4

These objectives were heartily embraced by Governor Jerry Brown, a new convert to the ranks of Jarvis-Gann advocates. Brown's presidential ambitions have him a critical stake in making Proposition 13 work. In order to claim national credit as a fiscal conservative who successfully implemented Proposition 13, he had to avoid a "big bang" crisis resulting from sudden and massive cutbacks in police, fire, educational, and other high visibility services, while hanging onto sufficient funds to insure against a future tax increase. Legislators also shared these concerns. They feared that massive service cuts would result in charges they were "sabotaging" Proposition 13, while they viewed the prospect of having to raise taxes in the face of Proposition 13's landslide victory as political suicide.

The key to steering a successful course through this political minefield was the state surplus and the growing annual gap between state revenues and expenditures which produced it. The surplus provided the immediate funds necessary for the local governments with replacement revenues on a permanent basis without resorting to a state tax increase.

California ended the 1977-1978 fiscal year (24 days after Proposition 13 was adopted) with a General Fund surplus of $3,969.9 million. This surplus was further increased with a General Fund budget for fiscal 1978-1979. Back in January of 1978, Governor Brown had proposed a General Fund budget of $13,482.5 million for 1978-79. After Proposition 13 passed, the Legislature cut $1,197.5 million from the January budget proposal, and the Governor vetoed another $153.7 million himself, leaving the 1978-1979 General Fund budget at $12,131.3 million, or $1,351.2 million below the original budget proposal.

The largest reductions resulted from lower state property tax relief costs due to Proposition 13 ($696 million), a state employee pay freeze ($254.4 million), and a partial freeze on welfare grant levels ($114.5 million). Even after these cuts, the state didn't spend all of the money it was budgeted to spend. In the last month of the 1978-1979 fiscal year, the Department of Finance estimated that actual General Fund expenditures for the year were $11,875.4 million, $255.9 million less than budgeted.

The effect of these spending cuts was to further widen the revenue-expenditure gap, leaving the state's General Fund awash in a sea of money. As a result, the Legislature not only gave local governments $4,405 million in "bailout" funds for 1978-1979, but also adopted a major $930 million cut in income tax revenues—the largest in the state's history—which included a partial indexing of the state's personal income tax and a $615 million one-year only increase in the personal credit. Even with these two major programs, the state still was left with a 1978-1979 year-end surplus of $2,961.2 million.

Altogether, the bailout, the income tax cut, and the surplus amounted to $8,296 million. That's a total "excess" equal to 70% of the state's $11,875 million General Fund budget. Of this, the $615 million one-

However, the real key to permanently implementing Proposition 13 while avoiding a massive fiscal crisis is the annual gap between state revenues and expenditures. As Table 13 indicates, that gap grew to almost $4 billion in fiscal 1978-1979 — just $417 million less than the $4.4 billion price tag of the first Proposition 13 bailout. By holding the line on expenditure tax cut, the $30 million loaned to local governments in the bailout, and the $2,961 million surplus all represented funds not permanently committed and therefore available to help fund future bailouts.

ditures and the cost of the bailout so that state revenues would continue to outpace costs, the Brown Administration hoped to gradually widen the revenue-expenditure gap until it could provide enough money on an annual basis to fund the bailout. Meanwhile, the accumulated surplus could be "spent down" to offset annual shortfalls until this objective could be achieved.

This fiscal game plan worked well during the first year of Proposition 13. A tight lid was kept on state spending, and revenues continued to grow rapidly. But whether the Brown Administration will be similarly successful in the future is less certain. In January 1979 Brown proposed a state budget for 1979-80 which called for $13.2 billion in General Fund expenditures, holding the local government bailout to almost $4.4 billion, and increasing the annual revenue-expenditure gap to just under $4.4 billion — almost exactly the cost of his proposed second year state bailout. But mounting pressures for "catch-up" spending compounded by double digit inflation forced Brown to abandon this course. The budget and other fiscal legislation he signed into law for the 1979-1980 fiscal year will cost the state $13.8 billion, not $13.2 billion, and the state bailout will cost $4.9 billion, not $4.4 billion. As a result, the annual revenue-expenditure gap will hold steady at $3.9 billion—down a modest $14.5 million from the prior year—instead of increasing by $500 million to $4.4 billion. This means that the state surplus will be spent down another year with the state moving no closer to being able to fund the bailout on an annual basis out of the revenue-spending gap. At this rate, the surplus will be depleted by the end of 1981 and the "real" Proposition 13 will begin to emerge.

Clearly, Proposition 13 would have been every bit the disaster its opponents predicted without the surplus and the revenue-expenditure gap which produced it. Of course, in the absence of the political mismanagement of the state's finances which created the surplus and allowed the property tax shift onto homeowners to continue unchecked Proposition 13 might never have happened.

The Impact on Local Government

Proposition 13 cut local government property tax revenues in California from $11,710 million in 1977-1978 to $5,562 million in 1978-1979, a loss of $6,149 million. The impact of this dramatic reduction

Table 12

Excess State Funds, 1978-1979

	$ Millions
Proposition 13 "Bailout"	$4,405
State Income Tax Reduction	930
Remaining General Fund Surplus	2,961
Total Funds in Excess of General Fund Expenditures	$8,296

was offset by state bailout funds and a combination of other factors including the "spending down" of local reserves, revenues from new user fees, and rapid growth of other non-property tax revenues—especially the sales tax—in response to the continuing economic boom that was well underway before Proposition 13 passed. As a result, instead of the highly visible "big bang" crisis which was predicted by Proposition 13's opponents before the election, local governments were faced with a quiet, more gradual, incremental crisis.

A survey of local governments conducted by the Department of Finance midway through the 1978-1979 fiscal year found that their overall budgeted revenues were 1.4% below the prior year's levels. An estimate prepared by the Department in June 1979 placed the net local revenue loss at 4.4%, with schools down 2.8%; counties, 2.9%; and cities, 3.2%. Special districts were down 34%, but in their case the analysis failed to include offsetting increases in revenues beyond the state bailout.

Despite these revenue reductions, the Department's mid-year survey found that local government budgets for 1978-79 actually called for modest increases in spending. Using deferrals, reserves, and other revenue sources, counties budgeted spending increases of 9.5%, while cities and community colleges upped their budgets by 3.8%. School district (K-12) spending remained at roughly the same level as 1977-78, increasing by only 0.7%.

But even with the use of state bailout funds and other resources, Proposition 13 did force many cuts in local spending and services. With revenues severely restricted, rising costs due to inflation and legal mandates had to be compensated for by reducing spending elsewhere. Thus, locally initiated "discretionary" programs tended to be hit hardest. Moreover, the numbers portraying overall impacts are deceptive because they mask the wide range of variations between individual jurisdictions, reflecting differences in their dependence on property tax revenues, their ability to develop replacement revenue sources, and the needs of their communities.

Table 13

The Gap Between California State Revenues and Expenditures, 1974-1975 — 1979-1980

Fiscal Year	Revenues $ Millions	Revenues % Increase	Expenditures $ Millions	Expenditures % Increase	Excess Revenues $ Millions
1974-1975	$ 8,617.3	23.7%	$ 8,340.2	14.3%	$ 277.1
1975-1976	9,612.8	11.6	9,500.1	13.9	112.7
1976-1977	11,380.6	18.4	10,467.1	10.2	913.5
1977-1978	13,695.0	20.3	11,785.6	12.6	1,909.4
1978-1979 est.[1]	15,833.5	15.6	11,875.4	0.8	3,958.1
1979-1980 est.	17,781.0	12.3	13,837.4	16.5	3,943.6

1. Revenues include $615 million in uncollected personal income tax revenue due to a one-year increase in personal credits.

Source: Legislative Analyst, *Analysis of the Budget Bill*, 1979-1980, p. A-74; Department of Finance, Governor's Budget 1980-81.

Table 14

The Impact of Proposition 13 on Property Tax Revenues

	1977-1978 ($Millions)	1978-1979 ($Millions)	Reduction Millions	Reduction Percent
Schools	$ 6,094	$2,937	$3,157	51.8%
Counties	3,404	1,476	1,928	56.6%
Cities	1,168	534	634	54.3%
Special Districts	1,044	615	429	41.4%
Total	$11,710	$5,562	$6,149	52.5%

Source: Board oi Equalization

For California's schools, the property tax is the only locally-generated source of revenue. Since 53¢ of every property tax dollar goes to the schools, Proposition 13 had a major impact on school funding. Locally raised funding was reduced to roughly 25% of school budgets. As a result, schools were more dependent on the state for funding than most other agencies and had less flexibility in responding to Proposition 13's impact. One immediate effect of Proposition 13 on the schools was the widespread cancellation of summer school classes. Other budget-cutting responses included reductions in the range of elective course offerings and after-school activities, deferral of maintenance and capital outlays, and charging tuition fees for formerly free adult education courses.

In contrast to the schools, counties received only 37% of their pre-Proposition 13 revenues from the property tax and therefore were somewhat less dramatically affected. Funding for major mandated health and welfare programs was left intact by the state assumption of the county share of their costs. However, the buyout failed to cover all mandated health and welfare programs or the cost of other mandates in areas such as public safety and criminal justice. The state also provided counties $436 million in addition to the health and welfare buyout, but they still were forced to make cutbacks in many discretionary programs. Library and recreation programs were favorite targets of budget-cutting. General hiring freezes and layoffs meant that fewer people were trying to cope with growing workloads. Fees were imposed on a variety of formerly free services. In Los Angeles, the county began imposing fees at public museums and gardens, but found that projected revenues failed to materialize when attendance declined sharply.

Cities were less affected by Proposition 13 than either the schools or the counties. Only 22% of their pre-Proposition 13 revenues came from the property tax, although the degree of property tax dependence among cities varied from almost 60% to zero. While the cities received only $250 million in the bailout, they were able to capitalize on booming sales tax revenues and their access to a broad range of alternative revenue sources in order to offset much of the effects of Proposition 13. The Department of Finance midyear survey found that cities had budgeted $103 million in revenues from new taxes, permits, licenses, fines, and service charges. Still, many cities were forced to impose hiring freezes and layoffs, cut service levels (especially in discretionary recreational and cultural programs), and defer maintenance and capital spending.

The impact of Proposition 13 on California's more than 4700 special districts is more difficult to judge. For those districts engaged in enterprise activities (for example, electric or water utilities, port authorities, hospitals, airports, etc.), the impact was minimal since they were already funded largely through service charges and, to the extent they did levy property taxes, much of the revenue was used to service debt payments which were exempt from Proposition 13's 1% limitation. Moreover, any reduction in property tax revenues could be offset easily by increases in service charges.

The same could not be said of California's non-enterprise special districts (e.g., fire protection, recreation and parks, flood control, libraries, cemetery, lighting, pest control, etc.). Most of these districts relied heavily on property taxes for revenues; some were funded exclusively by the property tax. Since their ability to raise substitute revenues through service fees generally was limited, they had to rely on the state for assistance. Unfortunately, the state was largely unaware of their needs, and the initial bailout funds proved woefully inadequate, with most of the money going to the state's 597 fire protection districts. Even after supplemental legislation, many districts were still faced with major revenue shortfalls, layoffs, and service cutbacks.

Proposition 13 also had a significant impact on public employment at the local level. Between May 1978 and May 1979, state and local government employment declined by 103,600 or 6.8% due to layoffs, hiring freezes, and above-average rates of attrition — particularly in skilled occupations in high demand in the private sector. Actual layoffs accounted for 16,911 of these reductions. Fortunately, Proposition 13 passed in the midst of a major expansion of the California economy. As a result, the economic impact of these job losses in the public sector was offset by the continued growth of employment in the private sector, although the loss of public sector jobs did reduce somewhat the overall rate of employment growth.

While the first-year $4.4 billion bailout saved local governments from a massive and highly visible crisis, it was not large enough to prevent the beginnings of a less visible incremental crisis which could prove just as disastrous over the longer term. Ironically, the long term cumulative impact of Proposition 13 may be to turn its sponsors' attacks on government inefficiency and unresponsiveness into self-fulfilling prophesies.

Instead of the greater efficiency which many voters expected along with their property tax reductions, Proposition 13 resulted in lower service levels and deferred maintenance and capital outlays, threatening a gradual deterioration of public facilities. Hiring and pay freezes have resulted in a loss of many highly skilled employees to the private sector, the destruction of employee morale, and an erosion of local government's ability to cope with the effects of inflation and the demands placed on it by the economy. Finally, Proposition 13 has transferred power over local fiscal decisions to state government—whose inability to resolve California's property tax crisis legislatively was responsible for the very tax revolt it symbolizes.

The Impact of New Construction

Over the long term, Proposition 13's impact on public and private sector construction could prove to be the most damaging of all its many side-effects.

According to one investment analyst quoted in *The Wall Street Journal* (11/29/79), general obligation bonds — the most popular and cheapest form of municipal financing — are "deader than a dodo bird" as a result of Proposition 13. Unless Proposition 13 can be modified to allow voters to approve overrides of the 1% limit for new bond issues, local governments soon will deplete their reserves and bond funds approved prior to Proposition 13 and will be unable to finance new schools, parks, prisons, courts, libraries, street improvements, fire houses, police stations, senior citizens centers and other municipal construction needs. Already, California schools report a backlog of more than $740 million in maintenance work. As another municipal finance specialist commented to *The Wall Street Journal*: "Things will begin to wear out faster, and new construction to handle growth and orderly replacement of old facilities won't take place."

Tax allocation bonds used to finance redevelopment projects also have been hit hard. According to an analyst for Merrill Lynch, Pierce, Fenner and Smith, a total of $79 million in bonds issued by 13 different redevelopment agencies are in danger of going into default before July, 1983. Moreover, the market for new issues has dried up since the agencies which rate new bonds refuse to give a rating to new tax allocation bonds from California.

But the effects of Proposition 13 are not limited to public sector construction. Residential construction — which accounted for 69% of all California construction activity in 1977 — also is threatened by Proposition 13. A study prepared by the San Francisco-based consulting firm Gruen and Gruen Associates concludes that unless Proposition 13 can be modified, "the net effect will almost certainly be fewer and more expensive homes." Among the specific effects it cites are: a decrease in the supply of buildable land and an increase in its cost, further encouragement of restrictive local government zoning and building regulations to discourage new housing developments, and as much as $4,000 in additional costs for each new housing unit due to increased user and developer charges.

As a result of Proposition 13, local governments have little incentive to facilitate new residential con-

DID PROPOSITION 13 SPUR CALIFORNIA'S ECONOMY?

Evidence is now mounting that Proposition 13 did not spur growth in California's economy.

Howard Jarvis claims Proposition 13 created a half-million new jobs and lowered inflation in California.

The facts tell a much different story:

New Jobs Down

According to the Bureau of Labor Statistics, 461,000 new private jobs were created in California during the first year of Proposition 13.

That sounds pretty good.

But it ignores one fact. During the year *before* Proposition 13, the California economy created 634,000 new private sector jobs.

If Proposition 13 was so good for California, why were almost 40% more private sector jobs created in the year before Proposition 13 than were created in the year after?

Housing Starts Down

A housing shortage in California drove up home prices and with them homeowner property taxes. The result: Proposition 13.

But has Proposition 13's lower property taxes on homes encouraged the construction of more new housing? No!

In fact, new housing starts as measured by the Bank of America have been declining. Between June 1977 and June 1978 — the year before Proposition 13 — new housing starts increased from 252,000 to 302,000, a gain of almost 20%. By June 1979 — the end of the first year

under Proposition 13 — new housing starts had dropped to 218,000, a 28% decline.

Inflation Up

Howard Jarvis likes to boast that Proposition 13's property tax cuts kept inflation in California below the national level. For 1978, he was right. Inflation as measured by the Consumer Price Index was up 7.4% in California vs. 9.0% nationally.

It turns out, however, that he wasn't right for long.

A year later, the CPI in California had increased an astronomical 15.7% compared to a national inflation rate of 13.3%.

And why was inflation so much higher in California? One reason was Proposition 13. The California CPI shot up dramatically in the last quarter when new property tax bills came out, reflecting tax increases on properties which had been resold during the year (when properties are sold, Proposition 13 requires assessors to increase assessments to reflect the value established by the sales price).

Proposition 13: No Economic Miracle

The situation in California was unique because of the state's multibillion dollar surplus — itself the product of a booming economy. The surplus allowed the state to enter into a deficit spending situation to soften the impact of Proposition 13, thereby providing some additional stimulus to the state's economy.

Even so, new jobs are down, new housing starts are down, and inflation is soaring. The evidence is clear: Proposition 13 produced no economic miracle in California.

struction. In most cases they are unable to meet the needs of their existing residents out of current revenues. They are prevented from issuing new general obligation bonds required to finance the capital improvements demanded by residential growth. And Proposition 13 severely restricts the new property tax revenues they will receive from new construction. Even if developers pay the cost of capital improvements and pass them on to their customers in the form of higher sales prices, new housing developments will not produce enough revenues to pay for the public services they require. Consequently, existing services, already spread thin, must be spread even thinner if the housing needs of an expanding population and economy are to be met. As surpluses are exhausted and budgets squeezed, local officials and their constituents are likely to take an increasingly dim view of proposals for new residential construction which force major redistributions of already scarce local services.

VI. COUNTERING THE TAX REVOLT MYTHOLOGY

California taxpayers had good reason to revolt. Homeowners were being victimized by a massive property tax shift while the state was accumulating an enormous surplus which it neither spent nor returned to the taxpayers. When a small group of fifteen state senators successfully blocked a progressive legislative response to the property tax crisis and the Governor responded by calling for meditation instead of action, political leadership of the tax revolt passed to the right-wing sponsors of the Jarvis-Gann Initiative.

The success of Proposition 13 allowed its sponsors to create their own tax revolt mythology. This mythology ignored the business-homeowner tax shift in favor of an interpretation of the property tax crisis which attributes high taxes to excessive government spending. But it would be a mistake to characterize the success of Proposition 13 and California's tax revolt in terms of this mythology rather than the reality which created it.

There is little evidence that California voters wanted to make radical cuts in government spending. Election day polls indicate that Proposition 13's supporters had three basic beliefs about what it would accomplish: first and foremost, they believed it would get the property tax off their backs; second, it would force government to eliminate waste and "fat"; and, finally, they believed both could be accomplished without jeopardizing the present level of services government was providing. Thus, Californians agreed with the claims of Proposition 13's proponents that government waste and inefficiency were the source of their problem. But they refused to swallow the mythology whole by advocating major cutbacks in government services — a portion of the mythology whose appeal was never really tested because of the state surplus.

The two major elements of Calfornia's tax crisis—

the property tax shift onto homeowners and the state surplus—both affected taxpayers in ways which appeared to confirm the right-wing explanation of the crisis. For a family which saw their tax bills doubling or more than doubling from one year to the next, explanations attributing such increases to wasteful government spending seemed plausible. Their property tax bill was increasing far beyond any change in their ability to pay. With inflation increasing faster than their income, such a sudden and dramatic increase in property taxes posed a direct threat to their economic security.

But while their property tax bill had doubled, nothing they received from government had increased by 100%—the schools weren't 100% better, nor were police or fire protection or any other service provided by government. In short, homeowners were being asked to pay more—substantially more—while receiving nothing more in return. Government, they could only conclude, must be wasting their hard-earned tax dollars on a truly massive scale. For them, cutting property taxes in half, eliminating fat in government, and continuing to receive basically the same levels of service from government appeared neither contradictory nor unworkable.

Underlying these perceptions, of course, was the reality of the business-homeowner tax shift. As with any tax shift, the victims of the shift could not receive more from government in return for their higher taxes since they were now paying someone else's share of the tax burden. What homeowners perceived as waste was their tax dollars being substituted for those of business taxpayers. But they only saw what they paid, not what others didn't pay.

The state's multi-billion dollar General Fund surplus also created the same impression. Inflation and economic expansion combined with the highly elastic tax system inherited from the Reagan Administration to produce extraordinary increases in state revenues. Meanwhile, state spending was increasing more slowly. In contrast to the 1950's and 1960's when California embarked upon major public investment projects—the state highway system, the state college and university system, and the California Water Project—which produced tangible, visible benefits in exchange for higher taxes, the 1970's were marked by no such major policy initiatives as both Governors Reagan and Brown touted their fiscal conservatism. Taxes, however, continued to rise. But while Reagan punctuated tax increases with tax cuts to prevent the accumulation of a large surplus, Brown continued to nourish a surplus which eventually provided the state with a $4 billion surplus in 1977-78 and over $8 billion in excess funds during the first year of Proposition 13.

Like the property tax shift, the surplus left taxpayers with higher tax bills and nothing from government to show for them. Once again, however, the perception of wasteful government spending was misplaced. Neither spent nor returned to the taxpayers, the surplus was indeed a monumental example of waste, but of wasteful taxation, not wasteful spending.

The right succeeded in capturing the tax issue in California only after the Legislature and the Governor proved unable to respond to the state's tax crisis. Not only did they fail to produce a solution to the crisis, but they shrank from making the business-homeowner tax shift a central issue of the tax debate out of fear of alienating the state's business community. California taxpayers saw no other means of forcing a resolution of the state's tax crisis than by adopting the solution offered by the advocates of Proposition 13—and with it their definition of the problem in terms of wasteful government spending.

The Proposition 13 mythology should not be turned into a self-fulfilling prophecy by dismissing the tax revolt as a right-wing movement. When people are mad about taxes, their anger can take progressive or reactionary directions depending upon who defines the issues and provides the solutions. Organizing on taxes is fundamentally a matter of providing pocketbook solutions to pocketbook problems. The basic issue — which the right prefers to ignore — is who pays and who doesn't. The chronicle of California's path to Proposition 13 demonstrates both the inherent opportunities for progressive action and the potential consequences of failing to respond to taxpayer anger over unfair taxes.

Prop. 13's Biggest Booster Was Inflation, Not Anger Against All Government

BY WILLIAM SCHNEIDER

"The baby got hold of the hammer." That's the way one commentator saw the results of the Proposition 13 vote as the figures came rolling out of the computer on Tuesday night.

On Wednesday, Sen. Alan Cranston remarked that "Jarvis-Gann is like that two-by-four you're supposed to hit a mule with to get its attention." And Patricia Harris, President Carter's Secretary of Housing and Urban Development, said that the vote in California was "rather like burning down a barn to roast a pig when there are some easier ways to do it."

The judgment of most moderate and responsible politicians is that the voters of California behaved in an immoderate and irresponsible manner by turning out in record numbers to pass Proposition 13, the "Jarvis-Gann" Property Tax Initiative, by a window-rattling 65% to 35% majority.

Just what were the voters trying to say?

There is no question that the voters knew exactly what they were doing. Proposition 8, the more "moderate and responsible" property-tax relief measure supported by Gov. Brown and the state Legislature, was rejected, 53%

William Schneider, an associate professor of government at Harvard who is working at the Hoover Institution in Palo Alto this summer, was a consultant to The Times during the June 6 primary.

to 47%. Indeed, The Los Angeles Times-Channel 2 News Survey, in which almost 2,500 voters filled out questionnaires as they left the polls Tuesday, revealed that Propositions 8 and 13 were seen by most voters as mutually exclusive alternatives, even though it was entirely possible for voters to play it safe by voting for both measures.

Among those who voted for Proposition 13, only one in five also voted for Proposition 8, while Proposition 8 was endorsed by fully 91% of those who voted "no" on Proposition 13. Proposition 13 was advertised as a stronger tax-relief measure than Proposition 8. That is exactly how the voters saw it, and that is exactly what they wanted.

A careful inspection of the survey results turns up two factors which explain the vote on Proposition 13.

One is self-interest. It was in the interest of most voters to have their property taxes lowered. We knew this because the survey allowed us to separate out those voters who did not have such an interest. The latter included renters, who do not pay property taxes directly, and public employes, for whom Proposition 13 meant a possible loss of employment.

Voters whose households included public employes and who lived in rental housing voted only 28% in favor of

Proposition 13—and 80% in favor of Proposition 8. Voters for whom only one of these conditions applied—either rental housing or public employment—split their votes almost evenly on both measures. And voters who owned their own homes and who had no public employes in their households voted overwhelmingly for Proposition 13—81% "yes," 19% "no"—and rejected Proposition 8 by almost as decisive a margin.

The problem for opponents of Proposition 13 was that two thirds of the voters on June 6 owned their own homes and two thirds had no public employes in the family. Over half of the electorate June 6 fell into the category where these two conditions intersected—homeowners with no public employes in the family. This group, of course, had the highest interest in property-tax relief. Fewer than one voter in 10 fell into the category with the opposite characteristics, that is, the category which had a very low interest in property-tax relief.

The self-interest component of the vote can be seen in the county returns as well. There were three counties which Proposition 13 failed to carry. One was San Francisco, a county dominated by renters. Another was Yolo, a county dominated by state employes. The third was Kern, a wealthy agricultural county in which property taxes have not increased at nearly the rate found in other, more suburban and residential counties.

The second factor that explains the Proposition 13 vote is ideology. The Los Angeles Times-Channel 2 News Survey asked voters to describe their political views as either liberal, moderate or conservative. The vote for Proposition 13 increased from 45% among self-described liberals, to 65% among moderates, to 82% among conservatives. The vote for Proposition 8 increased in the opposite direction. Only 2% of self-described conservatives voted for Proposition 8, but the percentage of "yes" ballots on Proposition 8 rose to 47% among moderates and 63% among liberals. Thus, the effect of ideology was strong and consistent: Proposition 13 was the "conservative alternative," while Proposition 8 appealed disproportionately to liberals.

Still, it is worth emphasizing that 45% of the liberals did vote in favor of Proposition 13, and so did 40% of blacks for that matter. Clearly, self-interest cross-cut ideology and brought many blacks and liberals over to the "yes on 13" side.

When one takes both interest and ideology into account, the vote on Proposition 13 has been largely explained. Voters in the high self-interest category (homeowners with no public employes in the household) gave Proposition 13 a majority of their votes, whether they were liberal, moderate or conservative.

And Proposition 13 carried among all conservatives, even those who rented and worked for the government.

The vote among conservatives who owned their homes and did not work for the government was almost unanimous—90% in favor of Proposition 13. The vote among liberals who were renters and public employes was at the opposite extreme—only 19% favorable.

Proposition 13 created a coalition of interest and ideology. Interest was by far the more important factor however. Over half of the voters fell into the high interest category as described above. But only 28% of the voters called themselves conservatives.

The evidence also suggests that these groups had different reasons for supporting Proposition 13. In both The Times-Channel 2 polls and a similar survey taken on election day by NBC News and the Associated Press, two reasons for their stand were most frequently given by supporters of Proposition 13: High property taxes and waste in government. Over half of the respondents who voted for Proposition 13 in The Times-Channel 2 poll explained their vote with the statement "Property taxes should be lowered." Only 22% gave the reason, "Government provides many unnecessary services."

The view that "property taxes should be lowered" tended to be much stronger among homeowners as compared with renters for obvious reasons. But liberals, moderates and conservatives did not differ very much on this point. The difference between liberals, moderates and conservatives was much greater over the issue of whether "government provides many unnecessary services." Conservatives were much more likely than liberals to feel that this was the case.

It appears that the primary concern of the "self-interested" voters, who made up most of the "yes on 13" coalition, was to lower taxes. Conservatives shared this concern, but added to it a strong hostility to government. Conservatives saw Proposition 13 as a way to do what conservatives have been trying to do for almost 50 years—stop the growth of government. The telling point is that when respondents were asked "Do you think local services will be reduced if Proposition 13 passes?" less than a quarter of those who voted for Jarvis-Gann said "yes."

Seventy-one percent of the "yes on 13" voters thought that they could obtain drastic property tax reductions without any significant reductions in government services—unrealistic perhaps, but hardly indicative of a deep antipathy toward government.

Thus, it would be a mistake to interpret the Proposition 13 vote as more than what it was. It was a vote against high taxes. The property tax is a particularly good target because it is billed and not withheld, because its rate of increase in most areas has been truly outrageous, and because it taxes what most Americans regard as an essential component of success and security—owning your own home.

The "yes on 13" forces pointedly advertised their campaign as one to "save the American Dream."

Conservatives oppose high taxes like everyone else, but they also oppose government spending and the expansion of public services in principle. Inflation—the increase in the cost of everything, including the cost of government—has given conservatives a powerful ally in their anti-government crusade: the mass of homeowners, taxpayers and consumers who "are mad as hell and aren't going to take it anymore."

There is no evidence that these voters are opposed to government in principle. They are simply opposed to more government than they can afford. Voters respond to the choices available to them. The choice presented by Proposition 13 was, "Do you want to achieve a massive reduction in property taxes or not?" The answer, not surprisingly, was a defiant "yes." Proposition 13 was the first major ballot issue anywhere in America which asked voters to respond to inflation in clear and direct terms. It may well represent the first in a nationwide wave of anti-inflation protest votes. It is not surprising that the anti-inflation protest is taking the form of a tax revolt: Taxes are the only "prices" that people can vote on. All other price increases, like postal rates, are simply declared, and people are forced to live with them.

Thus, it would be a mistake to read the vote on Proposition 13 as a massive crusade against government or as a conversion of the voters to conservatism. But it would also be a mistake to underestimate this landslide. The voters want—indeed, demand—that some way be found to alleviate the tax burden. Elimination of waste and frills in government is certainly called for. But few voters really want to eliminate the wide variety of government services which they regard as essential. This was not clear from the Proposition 13 vote simply because it was not asked on the ballot. Elimination of government services, The Times-Channel 2 poll showed, was much more on the minds of opponents of Proposition 13 than on those of its supporters.

Thus, the issue raised by Jarvis-Gann is more technical and economic than it is ideological. Gov. Brown would be well advised to come up with a solution—and fast.

"Proposition 13's Biggest Booster was Inflation" is reprinted by permission from the June 11, 1978, issue of *The Los Angeles Times;* © 1978, the Times-Mirror Company.

Homeowner Share of Property Tax Rises

BY CLAIRE SPIEGEL
Times Staff Writer

Although Proposition 13 will keep a lid on this year's property taxes, it will force homeowners to shoulder a larger share of the tax burden and allow big business to pay proportionately less, Los Angeles County Assessor Alexander Pope said Thursday.

Pope made the observation as he announced completion of a $154 billion property assessment roll for 1979-80. The roll, up 12% from last year, will form the base for computing tax bills that will be mailed in late October.

The annual press conference called by Pope to announce the new county roll was a lackluster affair, in contrast to previous years when disclosures of rapidly escalating property assessments—foreshadowing higher taxes—came under heavy fire and ultimately helped lead to passage of Proposition 13.

Proposition 13 generally limited property taxes to 1% of market value, based on 1975 values, and provided for updating annually after that with increases of no more than 2% per year. However, any change of ownership or new construction on the property triggers reappraisal—and higher taxes—based on current value.

Pope explained that because residential property changes hands more frequently than commercial and industrial property, it is reappraised more frequently.

Thus, Pope explained, "the homeowner is bearing an ever-increasing share of the property tax burden while business is paying, and will predictably continue to pay, a smaller share."

In 1978, residential properties accounted for 64% of total real property value in the county. Commercial-industrial properties accounted for 36%.

This year, the share of residential properties has climbed to 72% and commercial has dipped to 28%. Pope called the increase "a substantial 8% shift." In five years, he predicted, residential will rise to 80%.

About 300,000 parcels of property—or one-sixth of the county's total—changed ownership or were improved by construction between March, 1978, and March, 1979.

These properties have been reappraised, Pope said, and largely account for the 12% increase in the assessment roll. Owners will receive their notices of reappraisal next week and have until Oct. 1 to appeal them.

Pope said he "strongly opposed" Proposition 13 last year, but now accepts it as "a fact of life." He said that the initiative needs "a couple modifications to make it more workable and fair."

"There needs to be a regular cyclical reappraisal of commercial and industrial properties," Pope said, to ensure that big business pays its fair share of property taxes.

CITY HALL FIGHT RESUMES TODAY

Grass Roots Burning Again: This Time It's Rent Control

BY BILL BOYARSKY
Times City-County Bureau Chief

Few people in City Hall favor strong rent control.

Deep down, all Mayor Bradley wants is some form of voluntary regulation. Only two members of the 15-member City Council advocate strong measures.

Yet, within a few weeks, the Los Angeles City Council is likely to pass, and the mayor sign, a control law stronger than almost anyone wants.

Why?

Because the real power in the rent control struggle has passed from City Hall to the grass roots, to the growing number of renters who have become a political force since the wave of post-Proposition 13 rent increases last year.

That is the assessment of advocates and opponents of strong rent control given in interviews as the rent fight is renewed today at a hearing before the council's Government Operations Committee.

Foes of strong rent control have given up outright opposition and retreated to a position of merely phasing out, over a long period of time, the present Los Angeles moratorium on rent increases.

"If we don't do something on a phaseout basis, we will blow this city wide open," said City Councilman David Cunningham, acknowledging the growing power of pro-rent control political organizations. Cunningham is against strict control and originally opposed any mandatory control.

"If they took controls off, there would be rent hikes and a tenant explosion," said Tom Hayden, who heads the pro-rent control Campaign for Economic Democracy. That group and the Coalition for Economic Survival have done the bulk of the tenant political organization.

In the view of some political observers, rent control is another example of the grass roots taking the initiative on major domestic policy with elected officials following behind.

It happened with taxes. Legislators and governors ignored an unfair tax structure for years until finally voters did the overhauling themselves with the approval of Proposition 13.

Grass-roots organizations in Los Angeles forced insurance companies to modify auto insurance rates. Other organizations forced passage of legislation against the banks'

redlining—or refusing to lend money—in poor minority residential areas.

In this case, grass-roots power began when tenants were shocked with rent increases from landlords who had benefited from Proposition 13, according to Cary Lowe of the Center for Public Policy, research arm of Hayden's CED organization.

City Hall politicians still are talking about what happened.

Bus loads of renters, many of them angry senior citizens, came downtown. Council members faced angry tenants in community meetings. Mayor Bradley was besieged by phone calls, letters and personal complaints.

Despite his personal reservations about rent control, the mayor joined Councilman Joel Wachs and Ernani Bernardi, the two strongest rent control advocates, in backing a one-year moratorium on rent increases last fall.

It passed. Today, the council and mayor are trying to determine what to do when the moratorium expires in the spring. The memory of all those angry tenants shapes their actions.

In the past, political campaigners, trying to sign up voters for presidential, governorship or legislative candidates, have tended to find renters unresponsive.

That was true even on issues that directly affected them. On the same day that Proposition 13 passed, for example, Santa Monica, a city with an electorate dominated by renters, rejected a rent control measure on the ballot.

But that was before the post-Proposition 13 rate increases. Along with an important, but little noticed, change in the economic status of renters, those increases have changed the political situation. Inflation and high costs of single family homes—once the favorite Southern California dwelling—have affected politics. Today, the renter is apt to be a family member who once would have owned a home but can no longer afford one.

"We are seeing the onset of tenant consciousness," said Lowe. "They realize they will be tenants for some time to come and they realize it's to their economic advantage to make things better for tenants. It's a subtle and very little analyzed phenomenon."

Rich Got Richer Throughout State

Proposition 13, the tax-cut quake that rattled California to the core last year, is a splendid example of the wealthiest getting a little wealthier.

Though much of the attention prior to the June 6 initiative was riveted to potential property tax savings for homeowners and landlords, much of the subsequent gains went to businesses with the largest landholdings in the state.

In Southern California, that has meant an unprecedented windfall for the oil, aerospace, real estate and utility industries.

But as year-later follow-ups show, the big kahunas of the private sector aren't inclined to pass along savings with nearly the same alacrity as increased costs.

In their own defense, spokesmen for many of the windfall recipients point out that the tax savings, though very large when viewed in a vacuum, aren't that significant compared with year-end profit totals.

Additionally, they reason, the money saved will be better utilized by investing it in job-creating projects than by passing it along to the consumer.

Tax collection figures in Southern California show that the 10 largest taxpayers in Los Angeles County and the 10 largest in Orange County saved a total of $170 million on their 1978-79 tax bills because of Proposition 13. That's about 2½ percent of the total statewide savings of $7 billion.

In Los Angeles County alone:
— The 1978-79 tax bills for the county's seven largest oil firms were $42 million less than in 1977-78.
— The tax bill for McDonnell Douglas, which employs almost 30,000 people in the Long Beach area, dropped 50 percent in one year.
— Pacific Telephone, far and away the county's largest taxpayer, saw its property taxes drop 62 percent, or $45.4 million.

In Orange County:
— The Irvine Co., which owns 77,000 acres of land and is the county's largest single property taxpayer, saved $3.3 million.
— Disneyland's vast expanse in Anaheim saved $1.2 million for

---

'In the overall scheme of things, the savings aren't that big'
—Manny Jiminez
Atlantic Richfield

Walt Disney Productions.
In California:
— The state's largest oil company, Chevron U.S.A., saved $47 million, while the nation's biggest bank, the Bank of America, saved $7.2 million.

In one particular area, the savings did trickle down in a systematic way from those on the Top 10 lists.

The state's public utilities, as required by the California Public Utilities Commission, passed along the entire windfall in the form of lower rates or monthly credits on customers' bills.

Four of the five largest taxpayers in Los Angeles County and three of the five in Orange County are public utilities.

In the case of Southern California Edison Co., its first-year tax savings statewide from Proposition 13 amounted to $54 million. That averages out to a monthly saving of $1.50 for each of the company's 3 million customers.

With one exception, none of the largest firms in this area made any significant commitment to charity with their savings.

United Way of Los Angeles County, which represents about 250 agencies, reports that it has received $320,000 in the past year as a direct result of Proposition 13, and almost all of that came from two Los Angeles banks.

The one exception was Chevron U.S.A., the domestic subsidiary of Standard Oil Co. of California, which has a specially earmarked fund to help out Proposition 13-devastated agencies.

About 40 gifts totaling $250,000 — including a $5,000 donation to the Cedar House child-abuse treatment facility in Long Beach — have been made to date, said Henry Brett, Chevron's coordinator of corporate contributions. (That $250,000 is about 5 percent of the firm's first-year Proposition 13 savings.)

How the "Top 10" in Los Angeles and Orange counties spent their Proposition 13 savings — or did not spend — gives a mild headache to those public relations executives paid to answer such bothersome questions.

"Our people here didn't want to get into it," said McDonnell Douglas' Harry Calkins. "So the answer is: No comment."

In the case of the Lockheed Corp., with its huge aircraft construction complex in Burbank, "the tax savings were minor compared with our losses last year," said spokesman Ross Hopkins.

Indeed, Lockheed's Burbank operations lost $100 million in 1978, or almost 17 times the company's $6 million savings in Los Angeles County.

Spokesmen for the oil companies tended to minimize their savings, saying the money doesn't amount to much compared with total profits.

A typical reaction came from Atlantic Richfield Co.'s Manny Jiminez:

"In the overall scheme of things, the savings aren't that big a thing." ARCO saved $10 million on its property tax bill this year. That's about 1.2 percent of its 1978 worldwide net income of $804 million.

THUMS, the five-company consortium running oil drilling operations for the city of Long Beach, saved a whopping $7.4 million on its tax bill, a reduction of 63 percent. That's 9 percent of its 1978 earnings, but most of that will go to the state.

Under its agreement with the city, THUMS (Texaco, Humble-Exxon, Union, Mobil and Shell) gets 4.4 percent of the net income, while the state gets the rest.

Houston-based Shell Oil Co. saved about $16 million last year in real estate taxes in California, about 2 percent of its worldwide profits of $814 million in 1978.

"Those savings will be reinvested here," says Shell's Bill Wicker, based at the firm's refinery in Carson. "They aren't going back to Houston."

Wicker pointed out that Shell was investing millions in two Long Beach-area projects — an offshore oil platform near Huntington Beach and an oil tanker terminal in Long Beach.

However, Wicker declined to specify how much Shell was planning to invest. He also admitted that the Proposition 13 savings had no relation to Shell's decision to put up the money for the projects.

The single real estate firm among the Big Winners was the Irvine Co., which owns 3,300 rental units throughout Orange County.

The privately held firm saved about $4.5 million on Proposition 13 this year and did pass along savings worth more than $1 million to its tenants in the form of rent credits, said company spokesman Martin Brower.

"The savings to us may sound like a lot, but it's really only a drop in the bucket," he said.

Indeed, the Irvine Co. is not at all happy about Proposition 13, Brower said, because it has reduced government funding of local projects.

In one case, Brower said, the Irvine Co. is going to spend about $10 million in off-ramp highway construction, because the California Department of Transportation won't do it.

Another large real estate owner and operator, R&B Development Co. of Los Angeles, also passed along 80 percent of its real estate tax savings to renters, as called for by initiative co-sponsor Howard Jarvis.

R&B, which has about 900 units in Long Beach and 12,400 units statewide known as the Oakwood Garden Apartments, gave its tenants rebate checks and also rolled back the rents a small amount.

Because of inflation, though, R&B has since resumed its regular, once-a-year rent increases,

said Larry Carlin, marketing director.

In general, said Eugene Zeichmeister, director of a large Southern California landlord association, "the larger the owner, the more likely it was that he pass on some kind of savings."

However, none of the landlord associations in Southern California had figures on what percentage of their members actually passed through rent benefits to their tenants.

"I wouldn't tell you even if I knew," said Chuck Fierce, head of an Orange County landlord group. "If I said it was 50 percent, then the other 50 percent of the renters would be calling us up wanting to know where their rebate is."

In the end, the enduring benefits to the area's largest landowners — and indeed all landowners — may not be the first-time, 1978-79 tax savings, but the quiet, long-range savings accrued year-in and year-out as long as the 1 percent of market value tax ceiling holds.

Under the terms of Proposition 13, in general, property can be taxed at only 1 percent of fair market value, and tax valuations can appreciate only 2 percent a year for as long as the land does not change ownership. This will prevent the wild rises in property taxes that preceded — and to large extent caused — the passage of the tax initiative.

By Tom Furlong
Staff writer

"The Rich Got Richer Throughout the State" is reprinted by permission from the June 14, 1979 issue of *The Long Beach Independent Press Telegram*.

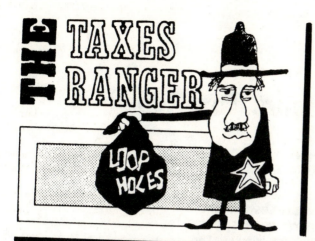

One City's Story:

Oakland After Prop. 13

by Roger L. Kemp

Proposition 13 was passed by California's electorate on June 6, 1978, and became effective on July 1 — only three weeks later. Here is how one municipality — Oakland, California — dealt with the ramifications of Prop. 13 on their community.

First, city officials increased selected revenue sources to mitigate estimated losses rather than merely reducing public services en masse. And the City Council subsequently raised additional revenues by increasing the Business License Tax, the Real Estate Transfer Tax, and the city's Transient Occupancy Tax.

Coupled with the state's surplus funds, these tax revenues reduced Oakland's deficit from $35 million to slightly over $14 million. The city "spread" its losses under Prop. 13 over a two-year period, thereby minimizing service reductions and cutting the number of city employees to be laid off. In actuality, slightly more than 70 employees were laid off; 244 positions were wiped out.

Like in most parts of the state, the impact of Proposition 13 in Oakland has probably not yet been noticed by most citizens. The city's politicians have managed to disperse the cutbacks.

Fire alarm boxes have been removed on a city-wide basis. The maintenance crew responsible for their upkeep has been eliminated. In the fire department, 17 chief's operator positions were eliminated. Batallion chiefs are without an assistant to aid in coordinating fire supression duties.

The City Hall switchboard has been eliminated so that calls are made directly to city departments. Information assistance and after-hours service have been eliminated.

Machine street sweeping is now done less frequently in residential areas. Streets are cleaned once every 4-5 weeks, instead of every 3-4 weeks. Hand sweeping in West and North Oakland has been eliminated. An increase in street litter is expected to result.

A reduction in the Weed Abatement Program will increase response time in handling citizen complaints. The accumulation of weeds and debris on vacant lots will increase fire hazards in such areas.

The Park Ranger Force has been reduced by one-half. Park security and fire protection activities have been reduced accordingly.

Eight gardener positions have been eliminated, resulting in a decrease in maintenance and litter control at city parks and recreation centers.

Hours at the Main Library have been reduced during the summer months from 62 to 50 hours per week. Hours have been reduced by 20 per cent at branch libraries. The two bookmobiles have been eliminated in the Spanish-speaking and Asian communities.

Museum hours have been reduced by 13 per cent, eliminating the only evening hours the facility is open to the public (i.e., Friday nights). The Museum aquarium has been closed and all aquatic exhibits cancelled.

Taken together, these cuts may not seem too severe, but Oakland was a city just on the verge of overcoming some of its traditional big city problems, such as unemployment, housing deterioration, high crime, poor schools and inadequate health care. Now, Proposition 13 has redirected the focus of the city away from positive action and towards survival.

(The Taxes Ranger is a twice-monthly column on tax policy published as a public service by the California Tax Reform Association Foundation.)

"One City's Story: Oakland After Proposition 13" is reprinted by permission from the May 4, 1979 issue of *The Taxes Ranger*, California Tax Reform Association.

Idaho Tax Shift Spurs Tax Rebellion

Robert Kuttner

Idaho is one of the most unlikely states in the union to experience a tax revolt, yet it was the one state where voters ratified a close imitation of Proposition 13 in the November 1978 election.[1] The Idaho initiative limits property taxes to 1% of actual value, though it is statutory while California's is constitutional. The statistics portray Idaho as a low-tax, low-spending state. Tax levels are well below the U. S. average. Per pupil public school expenditure ranks 50th in the country, according to the Idaho Education Association.

Total state and local taxes per capita in Idaho in 1977 were $639.00 compared to the U.S. average of $813.00. And property tax collections per capita were about 40% below average. As a percentage of Idaho personal income, property tax revenue has declined steadily from 4.7% in 1957 to 4.3% in 1967 to 3.7% in 1977.[2]

Given the absence of gross indicators that might otherwise explain Idaho's tax revolt, it is not surprising to learn that Idaho during the last decade has experienced one of the sharpest tax shifts of any state.

In 1969, Idaho commercial, industrial and utility property contributed about 42% of the property tax. By 1978, the percentage had fallen to 32%, but the residential share rose from 24% to 44.5%. The prime cause of rising taxes on homes, therefore, was not the growth in total property tax revenue, but an increase in the residential share.

Idaho does not tabulate actual taxes paid by class of taxpayer, but assessed valuation is a good proxy, (relief from low income elderly home-owners' credit has totaled less than $2 million in recent years).

The Idaho experience is a more extreme version of the national trends. Prior to 1967, according to state taxation officials, residences were assessed at an extremely low fraction of actual market value. In 1965, the legislature attempted to legalize classified fractional assessment. In 1967, a group of utilities filed suit, arguing that they were over assessed under the state's uniformity clause. The state Supreme Court agreed with the plaintiffs, and subsequently the legislature put all county assessors on a timetable to equalize assessment ratios over a 13 year period, at 20%. At the time utility property was assessed at more than 30% of value. Consequently, this decision caused a significant shift. According to one county assessor we interviewed, some residential properties in 1967 were appraised at as little as 5% of their actual value, and then <u>assessed</u> at 10% of that.

Idaho - Estimated Real and Personal Property Taxes (circuit breaker not netted out).

Taxes Collected	1969	1978	% increase
Residential			
Amount	$23.8m	$112.5m	366%
Share	24.5%	44.5%	
Commercial & Industrial			
Amount	$13.1m	$ 44.3m	
Share	14.3%	17.5%	212%
Utility			
Amount	$27.2m	$ 37.6m	
Share	28.0%	14.9%	36%
Agricultural			
Amount	$32.1m	$ 58.2m	
Share	33.1%	23.0%	78%
Total	$96.2m	$252.6m	162.5%

SOURCE: Idaho Tax Commission. Figures - our compilation.

The utilities companies that brought the suit especially benefitted from the shift, dropping from 28% of the 1969 total to only 14.9% in 1978.

A second cause of the shift onto residential property is the preferential method of assessment used to assess commercial and farm property. While homes are assessed based on their genuine market value, commercial property and farms are assessed according to a "band of investment"[3] formula that calculates the presumed return on equity to the owner. This produces a nominal value that is typically less than half of the market value. The 20% assessment ratio is then applied to the nominal 'value', which of course is far less than the true value. According to the assessor of Ada County (Boise), farmland that would cost between two and three thousand dollars to buy on the open market is typically appraised at $500 or $600 an acre.[4]

At a time when property values are inflating, Idaho's version of an income capitalization approach to valuing farmland has sheltered agricultural property from inflationary increases in the property tax, while non-farm residences have borne the full brunt of inflation.

Finally, in 1976 and 1977, the impact of this tax shift was sharply accelerated in three of Idaho's largest counties, with nearly half the state's population, in a manner that canfuriated taxpayers. In these three counties, assessors were slow to follow the legislature's mandate to gradually equalize assessment ratios on all classes or property. Assessors are elected in Idaho and find themselves in trouble with the voters when taxes rise sharply. As in California prior to the 1967 assessment reform, locally elected assessors had sought to play their traditional role of preventing taxes on homes and small farms from paying a disproportionate share. When the assessors failed to keep to the equalization schedule, businesses filed suit again. Eventually, the state tax commission lost patience, and ordered comprehensive reassessments, bringing in an out-of-state appraisal firm, Max Arnold Associates.

The effect of the state tax commission's order was to telescope into a single year what the legislature had wisely attempted to spread over a 13 year period. As it turned out, many properties in several counties had not been reappraised at all. Although the state law required residential property to be assessed at 20% of its full value, the supposed full value carried by the assessor in many instances was less than half the actual value, which reduced the nominal 20% ratio to 10% or even below.

When the Arnold firm came into Idaho, therefore, its reassessment concentrated on underassessed residential properties.

Since commercial and industrial property is valued according to the income it generates, these assessments were kept fairly stable; but the reassessment did count the recent inflation in housing prices. Many homeowners found their assessments doubled and even tripled in a single year.

On average, property taxes in Ada County (Boise) increased about 50% in one year. In addition, the Arnold firm reclassified many small farms as residential development land, ending their preferential assessment. Some small farmers found their marginal acreage appraised as potential subdivisions at a supposed market value of $5,000 per acre, which sharply increased their taxes, too.

Usually, in Ada County, about ten property owners appeal their assessments in a year. After the 1976 tax notices went out, no fewer than 7,000 Ada County taxpayers filed appeals. Another 4,000 appealed in 1977.[5]

With the overload on the appeals process, appeals were rushed through at the rate of one every five minutes, which added insult to the injury many taxpayers felt. Although some reductions were granted, many homeowners felt denied an opportunity to fully explain their case. Thus the Idaho tax revolt was mainly a protest by non-farm homeowners and small farmers, whose traditional tax shares were increased because of the reassessment.

Although there was widespread recognition among policy makers that the rising taxes were largely caused by a tax shift, this conclusion largely escaped the general public. Politically, Idaho is a conservative state, and there were no serious proposals for raising business taxes or for changing the assessment ratios to protect homeowners. Since the Idaho legislature is also especially sensitive to farmers, there was no support for changing the preferential approach to valuing farms. Indeed, the reclassification of some small farms as residential land by Arnold Associates helped fuel the tax revolt, (as long as the land was classified agricultural, most farmers benefited from the tax shift).

Idaho has no general circuit breaker or homeowner exemption--other than a small credit for the elderly to take the sting out of this tax shift. Nor was there support for amending the state constitution to classify taxes. Thus, citizen anger was at full boil in early 1978, when Howard Jarvis began getting national publicity. Proposition 13 looked like a remedy, and Idaho's one percent initiative was a deliberate copy of the Jarvis initiative, according to the leader of the Idaho tax revolt, Don Chance.

Effects

Unlike California, Idaho had only a minimal revenue surplus to redistribute to localities. Since the Idaho 1% initiative was statutory rather than constitutional, the state legislature postponed the effective date for one year to give local government time to adjust to the anticipated 60% reduction in property tax revenues. In 1979, Idaho had a small state surplus of about $25 million, most of which was redistributed to local public schools. But most observers expect that the state will face an increase next year in other taxes if services are to be maintained at traditional levels.

As a tax revolt in response to a tax shift, Idaho presents a classic case of a remedy that was not effectively suited to a grievance, since the problem was not excessive overall levies, but a shift in the distribution of the tax load.

Ironically, a group of homeowners recently filed suit under the state's uniformity clause, claiming that use of the income approach to assessing commercial property and farmland and the use of market value for homes assesses residences in a discriminatory manner. If they are upheld, this could help prevent a future shift.

Footnotes

[1] Nevada voters gave preliminary approval to a Proposition 13 imitation, subject to final voter approval before becoming law.

[2] ACIR, Significant Features of Fiscal Federalism.

[3] This is a capitalization approach.

[4] Ada County, Idaho, interview with a county assessor, May, 1979.

[5] Ada County Assessor, interview.

Impact of a Proposition 13 Type Amendment in Arizona

*Harold Scott

**Paul Waddell*

California's electorate in June of 1978 approved a constitutional amendment that places limits on total property taxes and on the growth of these taxes. Approval of Proposition 13 (Jarvis-Gann initiative) has set off similar actions in other states attempting to emulate California.

For example, in Arizona currently there are two initiatives being circulated. One initiative is being circulated by Robert Shaw and the other by William Heuisler; the Heuisler initiative is a carbon copy of Proposition 13.

Given the high probability that one or both of these initiatives will appear on the ballot for potential approval by Arizona's voters, it is important to begin to evaluate Proposition 13 in terms of what it means to Arizona.

There are a host of possible impacts associated with this initiative. In this article we will discuss two potential impacts. Proposition 13 and its Arizona imitators have been touted as being a vehicle for massive property tax reductions. We will examine both the magnitude and pattern of possible tax reductions that could result from implementation of Proposition 13 in Arizona. Secondly we will examine the possible impact on Arizona's residential real estate market if Proposition 13 or a similar proposal were to be adopted in Arizona. The major provisions are contained in Exhibit One.

We will examine both the magnitude and pattern of possible tax reductions that could result from implementation of Proposition 13 in Arizona. Secondly we will examine the possible impact on Arizona's residential real estate market if Proposition 13 or a similar proposal were to be adopted in Arizona.

The Heuisler initiative is different. The California proposition is directed exclusively at real property. The Heuisler initiative is worded in terms of a limitation on taxes on all forms of property. One could argue that the initiative applies to taxes on automobiles for example. However, the analysis in this paper is restricted to analyzing the impact on real property only.

To date there have been very few studies completed which seek to analyze the impact of Proposition 13 in Arizona. One comprehensive study completed is a staff report prepared for the Governor's Citizens Commission on Tax Reform and School Finance. The study is very broad in its coverage. Included in the report is a detailed evaluation of some of the possible tax reductions or tax shifts that may result from implementation of Proposition 13 in Arizona. The numbers presented in this article are drawn from that report.

To understand the possible pattern of tax reductions which would occur in Arizona, if Proposition 13 were implemented here, it is necessary to understand two basic elements of Arizona's property tax structure. First, unlike California, Arizona has a so-called classified property tax system. This is a euphemism for placing different properties on the tax rolls at varying percentages of their market value depending upon what type of property it is.

For example, producing mine property is on the tax roll in Arizona at 60 percent of its so-called full cash value or market value. Homes, on the other hand, are on the tax rolls at 15 percent of their market value. Other types of property are on the tax rolls at varying percentages ranging from 18 percent to 50 percent of market value. What this means for Arizona is that even without Proposition 13 we have an assessment and tax system which favors homes over other classes of property.

A second distinction between Arizona and California is that Arizona has a direct tax reduction program for homeowners. Around the state capitol, this is the program which is affectionately referred to as the rebate. In fiscal year 1978-79 $57.5 million was appropriated for this program. State-wide the rebate reduced homeowners' taxes 21 percent in 1978-79. California has had no such program. Proposition 13 has been held up as an alternative to the rebate. In this article, we assume that if Proposition 13 were adopted, the rebate would be eliminated.

Thus, currently the State of Arizona has two programs designed to lower homeowners' taxes. A classified property tax system favoring homeowners and a direct homeowners' tax reduction program.

With these two programs in mind, Illustration One presents the possible tax reduction that would have occurred in 1978 had Proposition 13 been in effect. These tax reductions are displayed for the six most common legal classes of property in Arizona. In both percentage terms and absolute dollar terms the most dramatic cuts in taxes occur for non-residential property. This is especially the case for railroads/mines and utilities properties.

In total, property tax levies would have been cut from $776.7 million to $428.2 million — a $348.5 million reduction in taxes. Non-residential properties would receive a reduction of $337.6 million while residential properties would receive a $10.9 million cut in taxes. A tax cut of almost $350 million will make it impossible for the state to continue the homeowners'

tax reduction program.

Remember currently Arizona has a classification system which places mining property on the tax rolls at 60 percent of their full cash value, and utilities on the tax rolls at 50 percent of their full cash value. Under Proposition 13 taxes on properties would be limited to one percent of full cash value plus debt service. Proposition 13 makes no distinction between classes of property. Implementation of Proposition 13 would in effect eliminate Arizona's classification system. Thus the pattern of possible tax reduction emerging from implementation of Proposition 13 is not surprising.

Homes, as can be seen in Illustration One, would have received a very modest cut in taxes as compared to other classes of property had Proposition 13 been in effect in 1978. The legislature recently raised the

homeowners' rebate to $95 million for 1979 — a 65 percent increase over 1978. Had this level of rebate been granted in 1978, homeowners would have actually paid more taxes if Proposition 13 had been in effect.

One could possibly argue that these business tax reductions will be largely passed on to consumers in the form of lower prices for goods and services. Even if this were true, it is important from a state perspective to identify where those customers live. For example, to the extent taxes imposed on mines are shifted to customers, those customers virtually all live outside of Arizona. Arizona consumes very little copper. This phenomenon is true for all other business classes of property also. All the business classes are characterized in varying degrees by out-of-state ownership of Arizona property and many Arizona businesses sell pro-

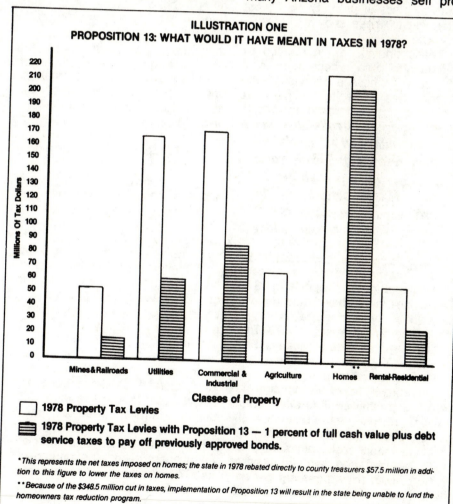

ILLUSTRATION ONE
PROPOSITION 13: WHAT WOULD IT HAVE MEANT IN TAXES IN 1978?

Millions Of Tax Dollars — Classes of Property: Mines & Railroads, Utilities, Commercial & Industrial, Agriculture, Homes*, Rental-Residential**

☐ 1978 Property Tax Levies

▦ 1978 Property Tax Levies with Proposition 13 — 1 percent of full cash value plus debt service taxes to pay off previously approved bonds.

*This represents the net taxes imposed on homes; the state in 1978 rebated directly to county treasurers $57.5 million in addition to this figure to lower the taxes on homes.

**Because of the $348.5 million cut in taxes, implementation of Proposition 13 will result in the state being unable to fund the homeowners tax reduction program.

ducts out-of-state. For example, approximately 40 percent of the Palo Verde nuclear plant under construction in west Phoenix is owned by out-of-state companies. If implementing Proposition 13 in Arizona cuts consumer prices, many of these cuts will occur outside Arizona.

There is one qualification to bear in mind in reviewing the results presented in Illustration One. The analysis in Illustration One was based upon 1978 data. There was no attempt made to roll back property values to the 1975 level as called for in Proposition 13. However, a recently completed study prepared by legislative staff for the Joint Select Committee on Tax Reform and School Finance did simulate the effects of rolling back values to 1975. The conclusions of the legislative study with regard to the size of tax cuts and pattern of tax cuts by class of property are almost identical to those shown in Illustration One.

These findings are reinforced by the results of a recent study conducted in Tennessee. Tennessee, like Arizona, has a classified property tax

---

Proposition 13 rolls back full cash values to 1975 levels and then restricts full cash value growth to two percent per annum. If a property is sold the property can be placed on the tax rolls at its current selling price.

---

system which benefits homeowners. Implementation of Proposition 13 in Tennessee would have caused many residential properties' taxes to increase were it in effect in 1978. This would have occurred because Proposition 13 would eliminate the classification system.

One provision of Proposition 13 which has received little attention in Arizona, to date, is the restriction on full cash value growth. Proposition 13 rolls back full cash values to their 1975 level and then restricts full cash value growth to two percent per annum. However, if a property is sold the property can be placed on the tax rolls at its current selling price.

ILLUSTRATION TWO
Effect of Roll Back of Values on Two Identical Homes Under Proposition 13

Year	Unsold Home Full Cash Value For Tax Purposes*	Home Sold Yearly** Full Cash Value For Tax Purposes
1980	$45,000	$45,000
1981	45,900	65,000
1982	46,818	71,500
1983	47,754	78,650
1984	48,709	86,515

*Limited to two percent growth per year.
**Increase of approximately ten percent per year.

According to the latest *Inside Phoenix* published by Phoenix newspapers, the Phoenix metropolitan area has experienced a 45 percent growth in resident population since 1970. The same publication reports that 58 percent of the metro Phoenix households moved in the past five years. With high mobility and rapid population growth, implementation of Proposition 13 in Arizona would bring along with it dramatically unequal treatment of essentially identical citizens and possibly cause distortions in the residential real estate market.

Under Proposition 13 when a house is sold it can be placed on the tax rolls at its true market value. If a house is unsold its growth in full cash value is limited to two percent per year growth compounded on its 1975 full cash value. A long time resident who stays in the same house could, over time, be taxed at a far lower level than his newly arrived next door neighbor. Even though both taxpayers could be identical in all other respects and live in identical houses.

Illustration Two shows hypothetical full cash value calculations on two identical homes. House A is assumed to have been rolled back to its 1975 full cash value by Proposition 13 for the 1980 tax year and as of 1985 (five years) the house will not be sold. House B, on the other hand, is assumed to be rolled back to its 1975 value in 1980 and then is sold in 1981 for $65,000. House B is resold every year at ten percent over its prior selling price each year from 1981

through 1984.

With these assumptions in mind, Illustration Two shows that a $45,000 house if unsold through 1984 under Proposition 13 would have a full cash value for tax purposes of $48,709. An identical house located next door which sells frequently or at the end of the fifth year, would have a full cash value substantially higher — $86,515. House B would have a value for tax purposes 78 percent above house A. In turn, taxes on house B would be 78 percent higher than on house A. Even if house B only sold at the end of the fifth year, it would still be placed on the tax rolls at its true market value. That is, 78 percent higher than house A.

Over time there would be widely varying taxes imposed on identical homes depending upon when the property last sold. These same effects would apply to other types of properties but the inequities would not be as great because homes sell much more frequently than do other types of property.

Obviously, widely divergent taxes on identical homes presents an interesting set of implications for the residential real estate market. One major implication which screams out of Proposition 13 is that property owners will have a tremendous incentive to hold on to what they have. For example, for a homeowner, there would, after a few years, be a significant increase in taxes if the homeowner moved. A homeowner may desire a more convenient location for work but may choose not to relocate because of higher taxes. Or a couple who would like a smaller home because their children have left home may forego moving because the taxes on a smaller home are likely to be far higher. Also, the upwardly mobile young executive may think more than twice about upgrading homes in the face of a dramatic jump in taxes. Adjusting recently sold homes to full market value for tax purposes will dampen the resale real estate market significantly. This will force real estate firms and residential development firms to adopt marketing strategies tied much more closely to new entrants into the housing market and newly arrived residents.

Real estate firms which specialize largely in resale of existing homes may, over time, be severely impacted by Proposition 13. These effects on the real estate market would probably not be felt immediately. However, extending the limit on full cash value over say ten years clearly will lead to very major tax differences imposed on identical properties. At that time the resale market may be dramatically impacted.

To summarize the discussion in this article, if Proposition 13 had been implemented in Arizona in 1978, there would have been almost a $350 million cut in taxes. Almost all of this cut would have accrued to business properties. Homes would have experienced only a modest cut in taxes. Under the provisions of Proposition 13 when a property sells it is moved to its market value on the tax rolls. If a property does not sell its full cash value growth is limited to two percent per year. Over time identical properties will end up with widely varying taxes depending upon whether they have recently been sold. This will probably damage the resale real estate market. At a minimum it will necessitate different marketing strategies on the part of the real estate industry.

Harold Scott is the Special Assistant to the Director of the Arizona Department of Revenue.

**Paul Waddell is the Assistant Director for Administration of the Arizona Department of Revenue... The views expressed in this article are those of the authors and should not be interpreted as representing official views of the Arizona Department of Revenue.*

''Impact of Proposition 13 Type Amendment in Arizona'' is reprinted by permission from the *Arizona Realtor's Digest,* July-August, 1979.

CHAPTER 6

Property Classification

State and local governments have long taxed different kinds of property at different rates, beginning in colonial times when a cow was taxed at one rate and a pig another. In the nineteenth century, as part of good-government campaigns, many states enacted a "uniformity clause", requiring all property to be taxed at the same rate. During that period of history, however, many states literally taxed *all* property—stocks, bonds, household furniture, industrial machinery, watches, and the family silver. The so called general property tax was an administrative monstrosity, but had the advantage of taxing actual wealth, and therefore taxing those who could best afford to pay. As states gradually ceased taxing personal property in this century, the property tax has increasingly become a tax on housing, and it has been borne more and more heavily by the great mass of people whose only real wealth is in their homes.

In recent years, state courts have begun to enforce the uniformity clauses, and this has had the effect of increasing the effective share of property taxes paid by homeowners. To prevent this shift from occuring, several states have authorized a *classified* property tax, sometimes known as a split roll, which explicitly permits different kinds of property to be taxed at different rates. The first article in this chapter, **Classified Property Tax Systems in the U.S.,** presents a survey of the current property tax classification provisions in effect throughout the country. A Massachusetts tax reform coalition in 1978 made tax classification the centerpriece of its successful campaign, described in the Massachusetts Fair Share article, **What 100 Percent Revaluation Means for Massachusetts.**

Business groups, and state administrations sympathetic to them, will usually oppose tax classification on the grounds that it "discriminates" against business. It can be useful to research the historic share of property taxes paid by business. If they are falling, as has been the case in many states recently, then classification does nothing more than restore the historic share. This was the case in Massachusetts, and tax reform groups effectively made the case that without classification, homeowners would pay more and more of business's tax load, as discussed by Bob Kuttner in **Turning Tax Rebellion Into Tax Reform.**

Classified Property Tax Systems in the U.S.

A classified property tax system is a scheme in which various classes of property are either assessed for tax purposes at different established percentages of market value or taxed at different established rates. The objective of classification is to influence the proportion of taxes allocable to each of the various classes. Residential and farm properties ordinarily constitute the most-favored clases, while business properties usually comprise the least-favored.

Nine states and the District of Columbia have comprehensive classified property tax systems. These are (with the date of implementation): Minnesota (1913), Montana (1917), Arizona (1968), Alabama (1972), Tennessee (1973), South Carolina (1976), Louisiana (1978), District of Columbia (1979), and Massachusetts (1980). West Virginia (1934) achieves much the same by applying different levy rates to different property types. Hawaii (1961), which really has a graded property tax, achieves something of the effect of a classified system with its assessment practices and different levy rates; however, by 1980, all real property in Hawaii will be taxed at the same rate. In 1971, Illinois amended its constitution to allow counties of 200,000 or more to adopt their own classification schemes, and in 1973 Cook County (Chicago) did so. In addition, legislation or constitutional amendments to adopt classification have been introduced from time to time in a number of states. Twenty-seven states have implemented at least partial classification schemes, usually for tangible and intangible personal property. In many cases, these systems involve the use of different levy rates rather than assessment at varying percentages of value.

Alabama, Illinois, Louisiana, Massachusetts, Minnesota, South Carolina, and Tennessee found it necessary to adopt constitutional amendments in order to implement classification. Some states have constitutional authority to classify property, but have only done so with certain kinds of property, e.g., Missouri and South Dakota.

Assessment Levels by Property Types

It is generally conceded that business properties are often assessed at higher levels than real property in general, and it appears, at least in recent instances, that classified property tax systems are designed to give legal foundation to existing practices.

Just how large the differences are in overall assessment levels applied to business and other real property is hard to say. The 1977 **Census of Governments** reports an aggregate assessment-sales ratio for com-

mercial and industrial property of 34.6 percent as compared to a ratio of 31.3 percent for all types of property. [1]

In thirty states, the assessment ratio reported for commercial and industrial properties is higher than the ratio reported for real property in general, although in many states the two ratios are within a few percentage points of each other. In eleven states the ratio reported for commercial and industrial properties is the lower of the two. In only one state were the ratios the same. [2] It is questionable as to how accurately the ratios reported for commercial and industrial properties actually represent overall real world ratios. This is primarily because all sales of $500,000 or more are (for good reason) excluded from the **Census of Governments.** Most of these sales would presumably fall into the commercial-industrial category so that it is difficult to speculate how the total picture might look.

In several states, the adoption of classified property tax systems has been prompted by court orders to equalize assessments between property classes. In 1960, the Southern Pacific Railroad Company challenged Arizona's "discriminatory" assessment of railroad and utility properties, and in 1963 the Arizona Supreme Court ruled that assessments by property type would have to be brought more closely into line. Arizona consequently initiated a four-year reassessment program. When the impact of the reassessment became realizable, the legislature passed a classified property tax law. The story in Tennessee is similar. In 1966, the Tennessee property tax structure was ruled discriminatory in both a state and a federal court in lawsuits brought by railroad companies. As a result, however, the people of Tennessee approved a constitutional amendment providing for classification, and the legislature subsequently passed the "Property Assessment and Classification Act of 1973."

Current Provisions: Comprehensive Classification

Alabama: As of 1978, four classes have been established: Class I, utility property is assessed at 30 percent of market value; Class II, property not otherwise classified, 20 percent; Class III, agricultural, forest, single-family, owner-occupied residential property, and historic buildings and sites, 10 percent; and Class IV, automobiles and trucks owned and operated by an individual not used for hire, 15 percent. Owners of Class III property may apply for assessments based on current use value, rather than fair market value. After 9/30/79, transportation property will not be assessed as Class I property to the extent required by the federal Railroad Revitalization and Regulatory Reform Act of 1976 (which forbids railroad property to be taxed or assessed at higher levels than other commercial/industrial property in those states with classified property tax systems). Presumably, such property would then be considered Class II. Under certain conditions, counties may raise or lower the percentages, but in no case may property in any one class be assessed at less than 5 percent nor more than 35 percent of market value.

Arizona: Seven classes have been established: Class I, flight property, all property of private car companies, all property of railroads, all property of producing mines and mining claims, and standing timber are asssesed at 60 percent of full cash value; Class II, all property of telephone, telegraph, and pipeline companies and gas, water, and electric utilities, 50 percent; Class III, commercial and industrial property (other than property in Classes I, II, IV, V(b), V(c), or VI), 27 percent; Class IV, all property used for agricultural purposes and all other property not included in Classes I, II, III, V, or VI, 18 percent; Class V, (a) all property used for residential purposes not otherwise included in Classes I, II, III, IV or VI; (b) all property used to operate nonprofit residential housing or health care facilities for the care of handicapped persons or persons 62 or older, 15 percent; Class VI, all property not included in Classes I, II, III, IV or V devoted to use as leased or rented residential property, 23 percent for the 1978 tax year, 21 percent thereafter; and Class VII, historic property, 8 percent. Mobile homes are considered personal property and may be considered as Class III, IV, V or VI property.

District of Columbia: Two classes of property are established for tax rate purposes. Class I consists of single-family residences and cooperative residential property; Class II consists of all other property. Personal property is also taxed at different rates.

Hawaii: Hawaii permits land to be taxed at higher rates than buildings and different rates are also imposed on different types of buildings and on different types of land. However, by 1980, all realty will be taxed at the same rate. Agricultural and residential properties may qualify for use-value assessment.

Illinois-Cook County: In 1973, Cook County adopted a classified system as allowed by a 1971 amendment to the Illinois Constitution permitting counties of 200,000 or more local option in this matter. Cook County has created five classes; (1) unimproved land other than farmland, 22 percent; (2) single-family residential property (including condominiums, cooperative apartment buildings, and apartment buildings of six units or less) and farmland, 16 percent; (3) rental residential property of seven units or more, 33 percent; (4) taxable property owned by non-profit organizations, 30 percent, and (5) all other property, 40 percent. Illinois also provides for agricultural use-value assessments.

Louisiana: Three classes have been established: (1) land is assessed at 10 percent of its market value; (2) residential improvements, 10 percent; (3) all other property, 15 percent. Qualified farm, horticultural, marsh, and timber lands are assessed at 10 percent of their use-value.

Massachusetts: Voters in 1978 approved a constitutional amendment that authorizes the classification of property into not more than four classes. The ratios established are applicable to property taxes assessed for the first year beginning 1980. The classes and the percentage of market value to be used are: (1) residential real property, 40 percent; (2) commercial real property, 50 percent; (3) industrial or manufacturing real property, 55 percent; and (4) open space property, 25 percent. Use-value assessments may be applied to agricultural lands.

Minnesota: At least fourteen classes of property have been established with percentages of market value ranging from 5 to 50 percent. In addition, a homestead base value has been established and the amount of market value over the base value is assessed at a different percentage (generally higher) than the base value amount. Residential and agricultural property is generally assessed at lower percentages than other property types. Agricultural land is also eligible for use-value assessment.

Montana: Eighteen classes of property have been established with percentages of market value ranging from 2.4 to 100 percent. Some classes specify nonmarket value bases, e.g., agricultural land is assessed at 100 percent of productive capacity and taxed at 30 percent of that figure, moneyed capital and shares of banks are assessed at 100 percent of book value, etc. Certain municipalities may adopt a tax scheme based on site value taxation, e.g., vacant commercial land could be taxed at 150 percent (after a phase-in period) until such land is developed for commercial use.

South Carolina: Seven classes have been established in South Carolina: (1) all property owned or leased to utilities and manufacturers is assessed at 10.5 percent of market value; (2) business inventories and farm machinery, 6 and 5 percent, respectively; (3) residences (including up to 5 contiguous acres), 4 percent; (4) agricultural realty owned or leased by individuals, partners and certain small corporations (as specified by law), 4 percent; agricultural realty owned or leased by other corporations, 6 percent; (5) property owned or leased by transportation companies, 9.5 percent; (6) all other realty, 6 percent; (7) all other personalty; 10.5 percent. Fair market value of agricultural land is defined as the "productive earning power based on soil capability to be determined by capitalization of typical cash rents or by capitalization of typical net income of like soil in the locality, etc." (Acts of 1975, Act 208 2(d)(2)).

Tennessee: Agricultural, forest, open space lands may be asessed at use value. Residential and farm real property is assessed at 25 percent of market value; industrial and commercial real property (including residential real property of two or more rental units) at 40 percent; public utility real property at 55 percent. Commercial and industrial tangible personal property is assessed at 30 percent; tangible personal property of utilities at 55 percent; and all other tangible personal property at 5 percent. (Ch. 337, Laws 1977 declared that tangible personal property (other than utility, commercial, and industrial personalty) has no value.)

West Virginia: Different tax rates (limited by statute) are applied to four basic classes of property: (1) tangible personal property used in agricultural and all intangible personal property, $.50 per $100; (2) residential property and farms, $1.00 per $100; (3) all other real and personal property situated outside of municipalities, $1.50 per $100; and (4) all other real and personal property located inside municipalities, $2.00 per $100. Actual rates may exceed those in many jurisdictions since debt service requirements are not covered by the statutory limitations. The legislature may also increase the maximum rates. The value of agricultural and residential property may also be determined by considering the possible rental income of such property.

Relation to Homestead Exemptions

Homestead, veteran's, and other partial exemptions for homeowners have an effect similar to classified property tax systems in that they shift part of the tax burden allocable to these groups of taxpayers to other groups. It has been estimated that homestead exemptions have reduced the tax base as follows in the six states that make primary use of them:[3]

Florida	18.0%
Georgia	18.8%
Hawaii	9.4%
Louisiana	20.8%
Mississippi	23.9%
Oklahoma	15.5%

Relationship to Use-Value Farmland Assessments

Use-value farmland assessment is the assessment of farmland upon the basis of its agricultural value rather than upon the basis of its market value. It is designed primarily to preserve urban-fringe farmlands in open space by reducing large tax burdens. Unfortunately, there has been developed a tendency in the literature to view classified tax systems as similar to use-value farmland assessments in their effects upon farm tax burdens. According to this view, each represents an alternative means of accomplishing the same objective. This, however, is a largely misguided analysis. Whereas in the classified tax system the assessment rate applicable to farmland is fixed, in a use-value system it is variable, i.e., increases in market value do not necessarily imply a proportional increase in assessed value.

Furthermore, in a classified tax system, agricultural property is not treated favorably in relation to residential property (the bulk of the tax base) as is the case with use-value farmland assessments. In short, farmlands subject to non-farm market influences can often be expected to receive considerable tax concessions under use-value assessment, but only marginal consideration under a classified system. However, most states with classification systems have made provisions for use-value assessment of farm and open space land.

Administration

Although a classified property tax system poses no new valuation problems for the assessor, some administrative considerations arise. First,, there is the problem of borderline cases. Is a cottage an owner-occupied residential property? When does a parcel of farmland held primarily for speculative purposes and producing only a nominal agricultural return cease to be a bona fide farm property? Do condominium units owned by a real estate investor and rented to tenants qualify as residential or commercial property? Such cases must, of course, be explained to taxpayers and defended against appeals. Second, the enumeration of various property classifications compounds the amount of recording and bookkeeping that must be undertaken. Perhaps most important, however, is a tendency for the number of classes to change and multiply over the years. Arizona has gone through several changes since 1970 and the Minnesota system has been expanded or otherwise modified at least thirty-two times since 1933. Alabama enacted classification in 1972 and revised the scheme in 1978; Montana went from eleven to eighteen classes in 1977. This is not to imply that such changes are necessarily good or bad. While critics charge that such changes are primarily related to lobbying power, proponents argue that they improve the equitability of the property tax structure. In any case, revisions entail administrative complications.

It is worthwhile to note the conclusions reached by the Property Taxation Committee of the National Tax Association concerning classified property tax systems:[4]

> In addition to the lack of any sound theoretical basis for a classified tax, the practical problems are overwhelming. In the first place, the differential treatment that will be enacted initially will very likely represent the political strengths of various property users, and not what is assumed to be in the public interest in terms of equity or economics.
>
> ...The classified property tax lends itself to an erosion of the tax base that is even greater than if the property tax had adhered to the uniformity role.[5]

The U.S. Advisory Commission on Intergovernmental Relations suggests that classification *per se* will not ensure an equitable tax system. Equity "can only be guaranteed if at the same time action is taken to strengthen and supervise assessment administration, and to define valuation standards with greater precision."[6]

Economic Considerations

One criticism of a classified property tax system is

that it tends to discourage commerce and industry from entering the state. This is a valid point to the extent that differential tax rates affect commercial and industrial locational decisions. However, despite much verbiage, this issue has never been satisfactorily resolved. It is commonly agreed, however, that property tax considerations weigh relatively little among those factors affecting locational decisions.[7] Nevertheless, if rates applied to a particular type of property are quite discriminatory, the effect might be significant. In any case, the effect will vary with (1) the over all effective tax rate, the extent to which the state relies upon the property tax, and (2) the extent to which the affected industry relies on property as a factor input; thus, capital-intensive enterprises (railroads, utilities, refineries, etc.) will be more adversely affected than labor-intensive enterprises (most small manufacturers).

The extent to which a classified tax system actually redistributes property taxes from homeowners to businesses can also be debated. Homeowners, of course, are also consumers, and the bulk of any increase in fixed business expenses across an entire state can be expected to be passed on to the consuming public. Since lower-income homeowners and farmers generally pay a higher percentage of income in property taxes than higher-income homeowners, the end effect might well constitute more of a redistribution of tax incidence among types of homeowners themselves than between homeowners and business. Renters of classified commercial property, however, constitute one group that is certain to be adversely affected. This group will probably pay higher property taxes indirectly in the form of increased rents **and** increased consumer prices.

Future of Classification

It would appear that in recent years classification has been regarded as a more politically feasible alternative to full value assessments, which have been the subject of much litigation and which have been mandated by several court-ordered reassessment programs. Classification, at least on the surface, appears to provide relief for homeowners whose property generally constitutes the bulk of a locality's tax base. Whether or not homeowners actually realize any savings under a classified property tax is debatable. Classification has little support from economists, tax scholars, and groups such as the U.S. Advisory Commission on Intergovernmental Relations, who generally favor full value assessment as an important factor for ensuring more equitable property taxes. From this viewpoint, property tax relief is best provided by tax credits or abatements, rather than by abolishing a uniform market value assessment standards. Indeed, a recent research project has shown that there is some evidence to support the assertion that higher levels of assessment have a salutary effect on overall assessment accuracy, and therefore, tax equity.[8] However, tax incidence is a complex issue not perfectly understood even by tax scholars; classification may become even more politically attractive in an era of tax limitations.

Some states will undoubtedly be affected by new federal legislation enacted in 1976. U.S. Public Law 94-210 (S.2718, approved 2/5/76, effective 2/5/79) prohibits states, from taxing or assessing interstate railroad property any more heavily than all other property generally, except in states with classified systems where what is prohibited is less favorable treatment than that given to other commercial and industrial property generally. As a result, some states with classification laws may have to amend them.[9] Whether additional states will be inspired to pass classification laws is impossible to say.

---

[1] This report combines and updates two previous publications—"Classified Property Tax Systems in the U.S.," Research and Information Series, Chicago: IAAO, Research and Technical Services Department, February 1977, 9pp.; and "Classified Property Tax," Bibliographic Series, Chicago: IAAO, Research and Technical Services Department, February 1977, 6pp. Persons holding these two earlier publications should discard them; they have been completely superseded.

[2] U.S. Bureau of the Census, **1977 Census of Governments**, volume 2 (Washington, D.C.: distrib. by Supt. of Docs., U.S. Govt. Print. Off., 1978), p. 60.

[3] Ibid, pp. 60-65; eight states had insufficient data for comparison.

[4] New Jersey Tax Policy Committee, **Report** (Trenton, 1972), vol. 2, p. 26.

[5] National Tax Association, Property Taxation Committee, "The Erosion of the Ad Valorem Real Estate Tax Base," **Tax Policy** 1 (1973):29-30.

[6] U.S. Advisory Commission on Intergovernmental Relations, **Financing Schools and Property Tax Relief: A State Responsibility**, A-40 (Washington, D.C.: distrib. by the Supt. of Docs., U.S. Govt. Print. Off., 1973), p. 74. This is in keeping with earlier recommendations of the Commission in its report, **The Role of the States in Strengthening the Property Tax**, A-17 (Washington, D.C.: distrib. by the Supt. of Docs., U.S. Govt. Print. Off., 1963), vol. 1, pp. 8-12.

[7] Two good summaries of such well-designed research as has been undertaken are John F. Due, "Studies of State-Local Tax Influences on Location of Industry," **National Tax Journal** 14 (June 1961): 163-173; and U.S. Advisory Commission on Intergovernmental Relations, **State-Local Taxation and Industrial Location**, A-30 (Washington, D.C.; distrib. by Supt. of Docs., U.S. Govt. Print. Off., 1967). Other industry-oriented studies of comparative state taxes, issued periodically by Federal Reserve Banks, state economic development commissions, and others, are generally either unscientific or too narrowly focused to be very enlightening.

[8] See Richard R. Almy, "The Impact of Assessment Practices Upon Assessment Performance", in **Analyzing Assessment Equity: Techniques for Measuring and Improving the Quality of Property Tax Administration** (Chicago: International Association of Assessing Officers, 1977), pp. 156-157.

[9] P.L. 94-210 has been challenged in Tennessee where public utility property is assessed at a higher level than commercial and industrial property; see **State of Tennessee et al.** v. **Louisville and Nashville Railroad Co. et al.**, No. 79-3025 (U.S. Middle District of Tennessee, Nashville Division, filing date not known).

What 100% Revaluation Means for Massachusetts

There may be no more critical issue confronting Massachusetts residents today than the effect of 100 percent revaluation. While many people are talking about property tax reform this year 100 per cent revaluation will not only affect every renter and property owner in the state, but will significantly raise residential property taxes and rents. Unless it is stopped, 100 per cent will spell disaster for homeowners and will make any property tax reform won in 1978 meaningless.

Background to 100 Per Cent

Under the Massachusetts Constitution, property is supposed to be assessed at 100 per cent of value, what is known as full and fair cash value (or how much property would sell for on the open market). However, due to the depression, in practice, assessors began valuing property at a fraction of full value. Over the years a system developed under which different communities were assessing property at different values while within communities, and this is most important, residential property was generally valued at a lower rate than income producing business or utility property.

Although throughout the sixties and early seventies some communities were forced to go to 100 per cent, the Sudbury case handed down by the Massachusetts Supreme Judicial Court on Christmas eve of 1974 mandates that all cities revalue property at 100 per cent, and the State Tax Commissioner is responsible to ensure that all municipalities comply with this decision. Although the Court is merely enforcing the provision of the Massachusetts Constitution requiring 100 per cent revaluation, enforcement of this provision will wipe out what has been in practice—although not in law—preferential treatment for residential property by local assessors.

While the tax rate goes down under 100 per cent, since previously residential property as a class was assessed lower than commercial and industrial, the effect of going to 100 per cent and assessing everyone at the same rate is that the property tax burden shifts from business onto residential, or in dollars and cents, tax bills for homeowners go up, and for businesses go down.

Impact of 100 Per Cent Revaluation

Two recent studies have been done which clearly document the impact of 100 per cent revaluation in the Commonwealth. According to the Federal Reserve Bank of Boston[1] study completed in 1975, under 100 per cent revaluation the tax burden shifts from business to residential property in 251 of the 257 municipalities studied. As the summary table below indicates, under 100 per cent revaluation, homeowners' tax bills will increase by 16 per cent, while utility property tax bills drop by 32 per cent.

Statewide Average Shift in the Property Tax Burden

Homeowner tax bills:	up	16%
Industrial property tax bills:	down	23%
Commercial property tax bills:	down	12%
Utility property tax bills:	down	32%

More importantly, the Federal Reserve Study demonstrates that the older urban communities will be the hardest hit under 100 percent.

"The average impact, however, conceals an important trend across the Commonwealth. In almost all cases, it is the larger, older industrial cities and towns that are effected most by revaluation. Boston, Cambridge, Somerville, Chelsea, Revere, Everett, Fall River, Haverhill, Lawrence, Lowell, Lynn, Malden, New Bedford, Quincy, Salem, Watertown and Worcester are the major urban industrial centers of Massachusetts and all will experience more than a 20% shift in tax burdens.

"It was felt in the beginning of this study that such urban industrial centers also possess a large share of the Commonwealth's lower income residents and hence revaluation would force a disproportionately heavy burden on them.

"The figures clearly support the proposition that the effect of revaluation across communities is regressive. Wealthier towns, on average, contain less industry and hence will undergo less tax shifting than communities with a larger share of low income residents."

Fair Share has just completed a city by city analysis of the impact of 100 per cent revaluation and the results are startling. Although the increase on tax bills will be greater on homeowners in cities rather than towns, tax bills will generally increase on single family homeowners between 10 to 25 percent, or from $125 to $300. As the table below indicates, the increase in many communities will be much greater as taxes in Boston will jump by $841, taxes in Lawrence 43%, Lynn 47%, Worcester $380, and Springfield 38%.

[1]*The Statewide Impact of Full Property Revaluation in Massachusetts*, Federal Reserve Bank of Boston, 1975.

Increase in Taxes
For Single Family Homeowner
Under 100 Per Cent Revaluation

	Dollar Increase	Percentage Increase
Amherst	$ 80	6.2
Beverly	136	10.2
Boston	841	76
Brookline	233	.07
Cambridge	779	40.4
Chicopee	268	40.7
Fall River	272	23.9
Haverhill	138	13
Holyoke	464	47
Lawrence	357	43
Lowell	301	35
Lynn	523	47
Malden	342	31
Natick	104	.09
North Adams	151	19
Pittsfield	121	12
Quincy	319	31
Salem	546	
Springfield	294	38
Worcester	380	40.7

Based on 1976 Equalized Valuation for Cities and Towns in Mass. as determined by the Department of Corporations and Taxation.

But enough of numbers. Let me describe a few real life stories of what happened when 100 percent was implemented in Massachusetts.

"Homeowners tax bill in Woburn tripled under 100 per cent." **Woburn Times**, September 30, 1976.

"Woburn is up in arms over revaluation". **Boston Globe**, June, 1977.

When Worcester sent out its estimated tax bills, the Worcester Telegram wrote on February 2, 1975, "Receipt of the tax bill is causing havoc with Worcester taxpayers."

"People didn't want to buy in Worcester because they were afraid 100 per cent revaluation would happen. Now that it has, Worcester will become a ghost town," a real estate agent commented on February 18, 1975 in the **Worcester Telegram**.

While the Telegram reported on December 11, 1976: "Under revaluation the average tax on a single family home would increase about $400, while the personal property tax paid by New England Telephone Company would decline by $1.8 million.

The Newton Graphic reported that Newton stands to lose $2 million in property tax revenue from revaluation, and on May 1, 1975 the Graphic wrote, "Revaluation has inspired fear and panic and outrage among many people here. Residents have taken one look at their tax bills and said, 'We can't afford to live in Newton anymore.' "

Revaluation causes such panic among homeowners in Newton and Worcester that the courts were forced to grant these cities a delay in implementation.

Not only will homeowners' tax bills increase, but tenants can expect their rents to skyrocket as landlords pass along their tax increases. Particularly hard hit will be the elderly and those on a fixed income, as widows, senior citizens and veterans will lose a substantial amount of the property tax abatements they now receive.

While 100 percent will hurt older urban communities the most, it will also have an extremely adverse impact on Cape Cod and other rural communities throughout the state. These communities with a great deal of open space will face huge tax increases on this open space under 100 per cent. Many owners of this land will be forced to sell to developers. For many towns that want to preserve their open space, rather than have haphazard development, 100 per cent is disastrous.

100 per cent revaluation will not mean more money for municipalities. Cities and towns will still collect the same amount of money in property taxes. But they'll collect much more of it from the renter and homeowner—and much less of it from business, industry and utilities.

Classification: The Only Alternative to 100 Per Cent Development

There is only one way to minimize the impact of 100 percent revaluation and that is passage of a constitutional amendment to allow for classification of property. Under this amendment, which is printed below and will be on the November 1978 ballot, property could be placed into no more than four classes according to its use, and property would be valued differently between classes, while property within a class would be assessed at the same rate.

Classification Amendment

Article IV of Part the Second of the Constitution is hereby amended by inserting after the words "and to impose and levy proportional and reasonable assessments, rates and taxes, upon all the inhabitants of, and persons resident, and estates lying, within said Commonwealth" the words:—, except that, in addition to the powers conferred under Articles XLI and XVIX of the Amendments, the general court may classify real property according to its use in no more than four classes and to assess, rate and tax such property differently in the classes so established, but proportionately in the same class; and except that reasonable exemptions may be granted.

So, for example, commercial property could be assessed at 40 per cent and residential property at 20 per cent of value. The amendment would legitimatize the de facto classification system which has operated up to now, preserving the status quo of assessing commercial and industrial property above residential and preventing the devastating impact of 100 per cent revaluation, while correcting the inequities of assessing within classes.

The classification issue has two equally important parts: winning passage of the amendment on the November 1978 ballot, and winning good classification rates from the legislature. Thus it could be possible to win the amendment, but bad classification rates could just shift the tax burden on to homeowners anyway.

Currently before the legislature is House Bill 1900, which would propose a set of classification rates that would go into effect if the voters approve the referendum this fall. Under this bill, residential property would be assessed at 40%, commercial at 50%, industrial at 55% and open space at 25% of value. In addition, the bill will establish a residential partial exemption of $5,000 to be subtracted from the assessed value. Although this bill represents an approach, it would clearly establish classification rates which would prevent a shift of taxes from business to residential property, equalizing assessments within each of the four classes while saving homeowners from the disastrous impact of 100 per cent.

Classification: Here and Elsewhere

Classification is not a new issue either in Massachusetts or in many other states across the country. In 1970, the classification amendment was on the ballot and lost. It lost both because at that time 100 per cent was not a concrete threat to many communities in the Commonwealth, (despite losing 2 to 1 statewide, with one quarter of the voters abstaining, in Quincy, which was facing a separate court order, classification won

16,528 to 14,754) and it was opposed bitterly by the business coummunity, which stands to benefit by a tremendous tax break under 100 per cent reevaluation. Already, the business community is preparing a massive campaign to defeat classification on the November 1978 ballot.

Today, eight other states have comprehensive classification systems covering all real and personal property. These are (with the date of implementation): Minnesota (1913); Arizona (1968), Alabama (1972), Tennessee (1973), South Carolina (1976), and Louisiana (1978). Montana (1917) and West Virginia (1934) have achieved the same result by applying different tax rates to different classes of property. In 1971, Illinois amended its constitution to allow counties of 200,000 or more to adopt their own classification schemes, and in 1973 Cook County did so. Since 1961, 14 states have eliminated 100% valuation from their constitution because they have found it to be unreasonable and unfair. Twenty-two states have partial classification or have constitutional provisions permitting classification, and since 1968 alone, five states have adopted these provisions.

In conclusion, classification is not the answer for Massachusetts' need for property tax relief. But it will soften the devastating impact of 100 per cent revaluation.

Over the coming months we will hear a great deal about classification and 100 per cent. The issue will not go away. The choice is either 100 per cent revaluation, which will shift the tax burden from business on to homeowners and tenants, or passage of the classification amendment on the November ballot, which will protect the residential property owner and provide for fair taxation. The choice is yours.

"What 100 Percent Revaluation Means for Massachusetts" is reprinted by permission from Massachusetts Fair Share.

Turning Tax Rebellion Into Tax Reform

Massachusetts coalition fights to preserve assessment system which can benefit homeowners

By Bob Kuttner

BOSTON — Agnes Tomaszycki pays $1,500 in property taxes on her modest Dorchester house, or about one-sixth of the family income. She enjoys a lower tax than some of her Boston neighbors, largely because assessors have valued her property well below its actual worth. If her assessment is raised to full value, as the Massachusetts Supreme Court recently decreed, "We'll lose the house. We couldn't even sell it. Who's going to buy a $30,000 house with a $3,000 tax bill?" she asks.

The tax revolt has come to Massachusetts, and Agnes Tomaszycki is part of it. So are the citizens of New Bedford, where several thousand recently stormed City Hall to protest increased assessments.

But there's an unusual wrinkle to the Massachusetts brand of tax rebellion. It has been organized by a coalition of consumer, labor, religious, urban and senior citizens' groups, and the proposed remedy has a distinctly populist flavor. Next Tuesday, Massachusetts voters will consider Question One, which would authorize classification of different kinds of property, increases taxes on business and give each homeowner

a $5,000 homestead exemption.

Liberal groups are watching closely to see whether the tax revolt can be commandeered to produce tax reform.

Elsewhere, tax reformers have suffered a dismal year.

Closing loopholes is definitely out of fashion. Politicians have stopped talking about the three-martini lunch. They're talking about cutting taxes. Since California's Jarvis amendment, which ended up producing more tax relief for businesses than consumers, tax reform groups have helplessly watched "their" issue of tax equity be transformed into a conservative crusade to starve big government into submission.

Question One in Massachusetts gives reform groups a chance to recoup. It pits a broadly based consumer coalition against a fairly narrow business-based Committee Against Property Tax Discrimination, in which the consumer side has nearly all of the troops and, surprisingly, most of the money. Both sides will spend more than a million dollars in a media blitz that is dwarfing the races for senator and governor in the campaign's final weeks.

More surprising, Question One stands a good chance to win. Supporters seem to have captured tax revolt fever in the Bay State, and have even captured Howard Jarvis' own ad agency, Butcher-Forde, to the annoyance of the right wing.

A Shambles of High Taxes

MASSACHUSETTS already has the highest property tax levels in the nation outside of Alaska and Hawaii, 64 percent higher than California's on the eve of Proposition 13. The Jarvis amendment limited property taxes to 1 percent of market value. Bostonians now pay close to 10 percent of market value. Their tax rate is an astronomical $252.90 per $1,000 of assessed valuation, and other localities are close behind.

Many residents, however, have been spared the worst by a casual and sometimes corrupt system of property valuation that keeps assessments at a fraction of true market value. But over the years, assessments have become a crazy quilt, ranging from as little as 10 percent of value in the Charlestown wards friendly to incumbent mayors to upwards of 60 percent in ghetto communities.

Historically, most assessors have valued businesses at closer to actual value on the widely accepted theory that income-producing property can pay more taxes than residences. But on Christmas Eve 1974, the Massachusetts Supreme Court threw this jerry-built system into chaos.

Responding to a suit by the town of Sudbury, the Court required all communities to assess all properties at 100 percent of actual value. As a result, business property would be taxed at the same rate as homes, shifting about $265 million in taxes now paid by business onto consumers.

Faced with this outcome, Massachusetts mayors, led by Boston's Kevin White, joined with several consumer groups to propose a constitutional amendment giving the legislature the power to set differential rates for homes, commercial and industrial property and vacant land. As required by state law, this "classification" amendment has passed two sessions of the legislature, and is now before the voters as Question One.

Backing Question One is a formidable coalition of state and local politicians rarely seen sharing the same platform, most Massachusetts trade unions, the Archdiocese of Boston and 215,000-member statewide consumer group, Mass Fair Share. Opposing it is the Committee Against Property Tax Discrimination, financed by the state's biggest businesses: Raytheon, New England Telephone, State Street Bank, Boston Edison, John Hancock, Gillette and a score of others.

"This is the classic populist campaign," says the director of Boston Fair Share, Miles Rapoport. "They have the core of Boston's business elite. We have everybody else. They don't even have bumper stickers."

The anti-One committee spokesman, Peter Harrington, concedes the point. "We don't have ground troops. This is a public information group. We have not tried to build a mass organization."

"If they win this one," contends Fair Share's Rapoport, "It will only prove that enough money can buy anything."

But the fact is that proponents of tax classification have most of the money as well as the troops. Last June, Mayor White persuaded the Boston City Council to appropriate nearly $1 million to promote the classification amendment. Opponents took White to court, but on Oct. 20, Justice William J. Brennan Jr. issued a stay pending full court review, allowing White to spend the money in the meantime. Labor is also putting about $100,000 into the campaign.

"They will outspend us 3 or 4 to 1 in the final week," says the business committee's Harrington. The committee is campaigning on the slogan, "Don't vote for anything but a tax cut." Opponents of Question One argue that, given continued inflation in government spending, the classification measure won't really lower taxes.

"This shifts taxes rather than providing real tax relief," according to Herbert Roth, the Waltham industrialist who founded the business committee. "We want to force government to cut spending."

"I'm Mad As Hell"

BUT OPPONENTS are in the awkward position of trying to beat something with nothing; no tax-cut proposal appears on the ballot this year other than an "advisory" question that failed to catch fire. Still, Harrington reasons, "If classification loses, the legislature will be forced to come up with something better."

There is little doubt that defeat of Question One would produce a California-style rebellion. Two weeks ago, the City of New Bedford moved its assessments closer toward 100 percent. A country and western disc-jockey opened up the phone lines to take listener complaints, casually suggesting that callers take their case to the mayor. The next day, in a scene reminiscent of the movie "Network," 4,000 did, wrecking the mayor's car and closing down City Hall.

Supporters of Question One were quick to pick up the theme. Their next full-page ad in the Boston papers borrowed "Network's" rallying cry. "I'm Mad As Hell And I'm Not Gonna Take It Any More," proclaimed the huge type. "You heard it in New Bedford . . . They want you to take a quarter of a billion dollar tax hike. Why not tell *them* to take a hike. Vote Yes on Question One."

Both sides, of course, have been railing against Them. For supporters, Them means big business, pictured in ads as a Chaplinesque machine menacing a modest home. To opponents ("Look what the big spenders are doing to our property tax now"), Them is irresponsible politicians. For Boston Mayor Kevin White, a slightly worn 11-year veteran very vulnerable to anti-incumbent sentiment in next year's reelection campaign, Them, mercifully, is somebody other than him.

White has been out in community meetings four and five nights a week, warning that uniform valuation would be a disaster for homeowners, and incidentally offering a slide show on his other accomplishments. Last Sunday, speaking to an overflow crowd at Faneuil Hall, White emotionally recalled the historic role of taxes in the American Revolution. "Their slogan was 'No Taxation Without Representation', he cried. "Ours is 'No Taxation Without Classification'. "

"Vintage Kevin," commented an organizer for Fair Share, which has temporarily buried the hatchet to work with White. "He wraps his self-interest in the public interest. You see through it, but you have to go along."

It is widely believed (and acknowledged by White aides) that the mayor is using Question One to tune up his own 1979 campaign apparatus. Three probable White opponents followed the mayor onto the Faneuil Hall platform, visibly uncomfortable, but backing the referendum nonetheless.

"Question One is mainly a ploy for Kevin White's reelection," says Herbert Roth, leader of the opposition. But be that as it may, the supporters of Question One are articulating tax revolt in Massachusetss more effectively than the opponents.

Contrasts With California

THE CONTRAST between Question One and Proposition 13 is striking.

• In California, tax reformers put together a hastily prepared reform package called Proposition Eight. There was a clear choice between reduction and reform. Reduction won. In Massachusetts, the reform proposal is the only one on the ballot.

• In California, Howard Jarvis had been organizing for years and enjoyed a real grass roots organization. In Massachusetts, the tax reduction committee has been in business less than six months. Reformers are well organized.

• In California, Jarvis's opponents were fragmented. The governor and the legislature could not agree on a tax reduction alternative until too late. The Massachusetts coalition behind Question One is almost unprecedented.

• The anti-Jarvis campaign in California had no credibility. With a $4-billion state surplus, opponents of Proposition 13 tried to convince skeptical voters that police and fire services would be the first to go.

• In California, Proposition 13 was a rollback measure, adopted after tax bills skyrocketed. The Massachusetts classification proposal is a defensive measure, intended to prevent assessments from rising.

Public opinion polls show Question One slightly ahead, but with a large vote still undecided. One poll taken last week shows a dead heat, but it indicates that many voters who plan to vote against Question One misunderstand the impact.

Opponents of Question One are trying to show that taxes are likely to rise even with the classification amendment, because of the absence of controls on government spending. "If the people are unsure, they won't vote on One, or they'll vote no, which is to our advantage," says Harrington. Leaders of the opposition committee also express concern that increased taxes on industry will worsen Massachusetts' business climate. But that theme is not publicized in the campaign. "People vote their self-interest," Harrington says. "We don't want to be seen as just business talking."

Supporters contend that business — especially downtown business — already enjoys too many tax concessions. In Boston, for example, very few office buildings have been built recently without massive tax abatement deals. "Business is for tax classification all right," says liberal State Assemblyman Barney Frank. "They just want it one building at a time."

National Implications

THE QUESTION ONE campaign, of course, has many features peculiar to Massachusetts. If tax classification loses, it will show that even under the most favorable circumstances a populist coalition was unable to take advantage of the tax revolt. But many national groups, particularly tax reform organizations and public employe unions, are hopeful it will succeed.

Robert Brandon, director of Ralph Nader's Tax Reform Research Group, says, "The same grievances that led to Proposition 13 can also produce progressive reform."

In fact, classifying property according to use for tax purposes is hardly a radical idea. Some 20 states currently use some version of classification. But in the year of the great tax revolt, tax classification stands as one plausible alternative to a Jarvis-type cut.

The other day in Boston, Howard Jarvis himself said he might support classification if there were no other alternative.

Despite the self-reinforcing publicity generated by Proposition 13 and its imitators, many states in recent years responded to tax inequities with redistributive remedies such as circuit-breakers, homestead exemptions and more progressive income taxes, rather than across-the-board cuts.

Depending on who gets to define the tax revolt, the future may bring tax reduction as well as tax reform. In Massachusetts, even if Question One carries, it is likely to be followed by tax cuts. Both candidates for governor support the classification referendum — and both also promise steep tax cuts. Polls taken on Question One show that both supporters and opponents think they are voting to reduce raxes.

"Turning Tax Rebellion Into Tax Reform" is reprinted by permission from the November 5, 1979, issue of *The Washington Post*.

CHAPTER 7

Circuit Breakers and Homestead Exemptions

Circuit breakers and homestead exemptions are both formulas to make the property tax less burdensome to homeowners. Without a circuit breaker or homestead exemption, the property tax is calculated exclusively on the value of property and the tax rate.

Since middle and low income people typically pay a higher portion of their total income for housing than the wealthy, the property tax is regressive. Circuit breakers — which introduce an income or ability to pay criterion into the property tax — and homestead exemptions can make it less regressive. They also can be used to stabilize property tax burdens for homeowners and renters and prevent or compensate for property tax shifts from business property onto residential property.

There is no single formula for a circuit breaker. It can operate on a sliding scale, or it can be drafted to provide relief to homeowners above a certain age, below a certain income, or when taxes reach a specified percentage of income. Generally, the state pays the circuit-breaker benefit to the homeowner, either directly or through a credit against the state income tax, so that local government is not penalized for having a high number of poor or elderly. In this manner, circuit breakers can help compensate poor communities as well as poor people for the inequitable distribution of wealth.

The main advantage of circuit breakers is that they target tax relief. The difficulty with some is that they target it so narrowly that you have to be very poor before you can qualify for benefits. Significantly, two states with broad-based circuit breakers, Oregon and Michigan, rejected Jarvis-style property tax limits in November, 1978.

Steve Gold's article in this chapter—**The Residential Circuitbreaker**—outlines the potential and the drawbacks of circuitbreakers. Gold discusses the central issues of eligibility and distribution of benefits, as well as the traditional critiques of the use of circuitbreakers. He concludes that homestead exemptions generally are not as progressive or cost-effective as circuit breakers.

The article by the Ohio AFL-CIO, **Circuitbreaker: Your Protection Against Property Tax Overload,** describes the circuitbreaker relief included in the Ohio Public Interest Campaign's Fair Tax Initiative. The Initiative would grant relief if property taxes exceed 2.5% of family or individual income. See chapter 25 for more on the Ohio Fair Tax Initiative.

Reassessing the Circuitbreaker describes the circuitbreaker proposed by Massachusetts Fair Share in its 1978 property tax reform campaign. The author Elizabeth Bass, points out some of the difficulties encountered in that campaign, making this a useful reference for other organizations as they consider options for tax relief and reform.

The final article, **Homestead Exemption Programs,** surveys existing state programs with an emphasis on eligibility requirements, equity effects, and fiscal consequences.

Homestead exemptions subtract a flat amount from the assessed value of the property. If a home is assessed at $20,000, a $5,000 exemption reduces the effective assessment to $15,000, and thereby cuts the tax by one-fourth. Everybody gets the same tax reduction from a homestead exemption, unlike a circuit breaker, but this is still much fairer than a Proposition 13 type cut, which gives much larger dollar reductions to high bracker taxpayers. California had a homestead exemption before Proposition 13, but its value was eroded by inflation. Ideally, homestead exemptions should be indexed to inflation. Another problem occurs when properties in some parts of the state are underassessed relative to others, since a flat exemption will give underassessed areas disproportionate benefits. In many states, older and poorer cities and neighborhoods are over-assessed relative to others. A flat homestead exemption will be of less value in these circumstances.

The Residential Circuitbreaker

by Steve Gold

A circuitbreaker may be defined as a form of property tax reduction in which relief depends on both income and property tax bills. Its advocates compare it to its electrical namesake—when there is an overload relative to income, the circuitbreaker shuts the property tax system off. It is potentially the most progressive form of property tax relief, offering the possibility of eliminating the tax's regressivity (or, as some would have it, increasing its progressivity). Although the circuitbreaker has spread rapidly in the past fifteen years, it is not without its drawbacks.

Description

A circuit breaker usually takes one of two forms—the threshold or the sliding scale. The Advisory Commission on Intergovernmental Relations (ACIR), a leading proponent of circuitbreakers, defines them as follows:

> Under the *threshold approach*, an "acceptable" tax burden is defined as some fixed percentage of household income (different percentages may be set for different income levels), and any tax above this portion of income is "excessive" and qualifies for relief. Under the *sliding-scale approach*, no threshold is defined. Rather a fixed percentage of property tax...is rebated for each eligible taxpayer within a given income class; the rebate percentage declines as income rises.[1]

Consider an example of each type. The Vermont threshold formula provides relief as follows, subject to a maximum benefit of $500 per household:

Income	Relief
Under $4,000	100% Property tax in excess of 4 percent of income
$4,000—7,999	100% Property tax in excess of 4½ percent of income
$8,000—11,999	100% Property tax in excess of 5 percent of income
$12,000—15,999	100% Property tax in excess of 5½ percent of income
$16,000—or over	100% Property tax in excess of 6 percent of income

Note: A more extensive version of this article appears in Property Tax Relief *by Steve Gold published by D.C. Heath Co.*

The Iowa sliding scale circuitbreaker for elderly households operated this way in 1979:[2]

Income	Relief
Under $2,000	100% of property tax
$2,000—2,999	95% of property tax
$3,000—3,999	85% of property tax
$4,000—4,999	70% of property tax
$5,000—5,999	55% of property tax
$6,000—6,999	40% of property tax
$7,000—7,999	30% of property tax
$8,000—8,999	25% of property tax
$9,000—9,999	20% of property tax

Thus, a family with income of $2,500 and a property bill of $400 would receive relief of $300 in Vermont ($400 minus 4% of $2,500) and $380 in Iowa. A tax bill of $600 and income of $8,500 would produce relief of $175 in Vermont ($600 minus 5% of $8,500) and $150 in Iowa. There would be no circuitbreaker relief in either state for a household whose income was $20,000 and property tax $1,000.

The circuitbreaker's benefits are usually paid through a refund check after a household has applied, although in a few cases the rebate is subtracted directly from the property tax bill.

History and Extent of Use

As of April, 1978, 28 states and the District of Columbia provided a circuitbreaker in some form.[3] This is an impressive tally considering that in 1970 there were just 6 circuitbreakers and that the first one was adopted in 1964.[4]

Circuitbreakers are common throughout the country, excepting the South. Eleven of the 22 states without circuitbreakers are in that region, four are in the Northeast, six in the West, and only one in the Midwest. Most of the non-circuitbreaker states have relatively low property taxes on homes. The four major exceptions are Massachusetts, New Jersey, Nebraska, and New Hampshire.[5] Only four other non-circuitbreaker states have above-average tax rates.

Programs differ considerably in their coverage, as indicated in Table 1, which summarizes major features of existing circuitbreakers. Most of them are only for elderly households, although nine have no age limit.

Table 1

Circuitbreaker Programs in 1977 and 1978

State	Income Ceiling	Average Benefit	Per Capita Cost	Percentage of Households Receiving Benefits (j)
All ages, homeowners and renters				
District of Columbia(a)	$20,000(b)	$220	$ 5.85	7
Kansas	13,500(c)	NA	NA	NA
Michigan	none	223	30.24	41
Minnesota	none	156	33.94	66
New York	12,000	NA	NA	NA
Oregon	16,000	148	31.20	60
Vermont	none	210	16.08	23
Wisconsin	9,300	206	10.31	15
All ages, homeowners; elderly renters				
Maryland	none	248	5.03	6

State	Income Ceiling	Average Benefit	Per Capita Cost	Percentage of Elderly Households Receiving Benefits (j)
Elderly, homeowners and renters				
California	20,000(d)	216	4.25	26
Colorado	8,300(e)	187	4.20	44
Connecticut	6,000	244	7.96	50
Illinois	10,000	250	8.85	55
Indiana	5,000	29	.16	8
Iowa	9,000(f)	115	3.34	35
Maine	6,000(g)	209	4.06	22
Missouri	7,500	125	1.46	14
Nevada	11,000	128	2.20	27
New Mexico	16,000	38	1.26	63
North Dakota	8,000	119	2.01	21
Pennsylvania	7,500	142	4.99	46
Rhode Island	5,000(h)	52	NA	NA
Utah	7,000	95	.75	16
West Virginia	5,000	14	.01	1
Elderly, homeowners only				
Arkansas	8,000	76	.36	5
Idaho	7,500	231	4.67	33
Ohio	10,000	135	4.26	47
Oklahoma	6,000	86	.13	2
South Dakota	7,375(i)	99	2.17	27

NOTES:

(a) Financial data for the District of Columbia is for 1978, while for other places it is for 1977.
(b) For elderly households; ceiling for nonelderly was $7,000 in 1978 and $20,000 in 1979.
(c) Nonelderly households only if they include a child under age 18.
(d) Gross income; net income ceiling is $12,000 for homeowners and $5,000 for renters.
(e) For married persons; ceiling for single persons is $7,300.
(f) Raised to $10,000 in 1979.
(g) For married persons; ceiling for single persons is $5,000.
(h) Raised to $7,000 in 1978.
(i) For married persons; ceiling for single persons is $4,625.
(j) These percentages are approximations based on number of households in the Spring of 1976 and program statistics in fiscal year 1977. Estimates for elderly programs do not consider that some programs include participation by nonelderly persons such as the blind or disabled.

SOURCES:

ACIR, *Significant Features of Fiscal Federalism,* 1978-79 Edition. Number of households is from U.S. Census Bureau, *Current Population Reports, Demographic, Social, and Economic Profile of States: Spring 1976* (p. 20, no. 334), (January 1979), p. 25.

Twenty-four states extend eligibility to both home-owners and renters; six are only for homeowners. (States which include renters make the assumption that some proportion of rent represents property tax passed on to the tenant by the landlord). The seven places with the broadest eligibility, covering home-owners and renters with no age limit, are the District of Columbia, Michigan, Minnesota, New York, Oregon, Vermont and Wisconsin.

There is a tendency for circuitbreakers to expand after they are introduced, particularly by increasing the ceiling on relief payments, raising percentages in sliding-scale programs, or boosting the maximum income for participation. In several states, coverage expanded by including renters (where originally only homeowners were eligible) or the nonelderly (where at first only the aged were covered).

Benefits range from moderate to meager. The highest average benefits are for elderly households in the District of Columbia ($285 in 1977). The benefits in the median state are $135 per recipient, and they fall as low as $14 in one state. However, average benefits can be deceptive measures of the impact of circuitbreakers since benefits are targeted to those eligible households which pay the highest property taxes in relation to their income. Although circuitbreakers are sometimes viewed as an income transfer program, they are rather small compared to such programs as Social Security, public assistance, and unemployment compensation.

The last column of Table 1, which shows the percent of households receiving circuitbreaker benefits, reflects both the structure of programs and the response to them. Many households do not benefit because their income is too high or property tax payment is too low. Others do not participate even though they are eligible because they are unaware of the program or for other reasons.

Nationally, the total cost of circuitbreaker programs more than doubled from 1974 to 1977 to $950 million, and the number of claimants increased 69 percent to 5,113,000, despite the fact that property tax revenue did not rise faster than income. This growth occurred because more states had programs, many states liberalized benefit schedules, and participation rates rose as knowledge of the programs' existence increased.

Design Issues

The circuitbreaker is one of the most complicated types of property tax relief, requiring decisions about a large number of issues. This complexity arises in part from the flexibility of the circuitbreaker, since it affords a wide range of choice with regard to who receives benefits and how much they receive.

The circuitbreaker can be designed to make the property tax proportional, progressive, or regressive; it may limit benefits to the very poor or to those of average means, or it may allow households with high income to participate; its benefits may be high or low; it can be limited to the aged or extended to all families, restricted to homeowners or extended to renters as well. It all depends on the objectives of the designers

and the available resources.

We shall first discuss eligibility, second the level and distribution of benefits, and finally technical issues such as the treatment of the family and the definition of income.

1. Eligibility

The issue of eligibility raises four major questions and several minor ones.

Income Ceiling

Most states place an upper bound on the income of households which may participate in the circuitbreaker, ranging from $5,000 to $20,000. The rationale for having an upper limit is to target relief to those believed to be in greatest need. Even states with no limit (Maryland, Michigan, Minnesota,[6] and Vermont) provide relatively little assistance to high-income households because of the way in which the circuitbreaker is designed and the tendency for residential property taxes to fall as a fraction of income as income rises. The issue boils down to a political judgment as to whether it is desirable to provide any assistance to households at middle or higher income levels with unusually large property tax bills. The cost to the state of providing relief for such persons is often not very large.

Some persons consider it very important to limit circuitbreaker benefits to the poor, but most states place the income maximum above the federal poverty line. This practice is very reasonable in view of the niggardliness of the federal definition of poverty, the fact that regressivity extends above the poverty line, and the blurriness of the distinction between the poor and the near-poor.

Age

As noted above, most circuitbreakers are limited to the elderly, with eligibility usually beginning at age 65, but sometimes at 60 or 62, and for widows and widowers even earlier. This practice is based upon the belief that the elderly should not be forced to move from their homes due to taxes. It is also consistent with the deeply ingrained notion that persons experiencing income distress are more deserving of governmental assistance if they are old than if they are not.

Even if the circuitbreaker is not limited to the elderly, older households receive a disproportionate share of benefits because the property tax claims a larger share of their income than it does for younger households, as Table 2 shows. A high percentage of the low income homeowners are elderly. Inclusion of renters has a much greater impact on total program cost if the nonelderly are eligible or if the program is not limited to households with low income.

Occupancy

The great majority of circuitbreakers (24 or 20) extend benefits to renters as well as homeowners. This practice is certainly appropriate, but the best means of doing so is in dispute. The method used in most states

Table 2

Real Estate Taxes as a Percentage of Family Income for Elderly and Non-Elderly Single-Family Homeowners, by Income Class: 1970

Family income –	Real estate tax as a percent of family income		Exhibit: Number of homeowners	
	Elderly (age 65 and over)	Non-Elderly (under 65)	Elderly Percent of total	Non-elderly Percent of total
Less than $2,000	15.8	18.9	74.5	25.5
$2,000-2,999	9.5	10.1	70.3	29.7
3,000-3,999	8.0	7.2	59.1	40.9
4,000-4,999	7.3	5.5	48.6	51.4
5,000-5,999	6.2	5.1	32.0	68.0
6,000-6,999	5.8	4.3	25.4	74.6
7,000-9,999	4.8	4.1	13.3	86.7
10,000-14,999	3.9	3.7	6.4	93.6
15,000-24,999	3.3	3.3	5.4	94.6
25,000 or more	2.7	2.9	9.8	90.2
All incomes	8.1[2]	4.1[2]	20.2	79.8

[1]Census definition of income (income from all sources). Income reported received in 1970.

[2]Arithmetic mean.

Source: U.S. Bureau of the Census, *Residential Finance Survey, 1970* (conducted in 1971), special tabulations prepared for the Advisory Commission on Intergovernmental Relations. Real estate tax data were compiled for properties acquired prior to 1970 and represent taxes-paid during 1970.

Table 3

Illustration of Benefits Under Sliding-Scale and Threshold Formulas

Income	Gross Property Tax	Net Property Tax[1]		Benefit[1]	
		Sliding-Scale[2]	Threshold[3]	Sliding-Scale	Threshold
$ 1500	$ 200	$ 10	$ 60	$190	$140
	600	30	60*	570	540*
	1000	50	60*	950	940*
5500	200	90	200	110	0
	600	270	247.50	330	352.50
	1000	450	247.50*	550	742.50*
9500	200	160	200	40	0
	600	480	475	120	125
	1000	800	475*	200	575*
13500	200	200	200	0	0
	600	600	600	0	0
	1000	1000	742.50	0	257.50

[1]Benefit = gross property tax—net property tax.

[2]The sliding-scale formula is that for the 1979 Iowa elderly circuit-breaker. Rates are shown on page 2 of this chapter.

[3]The threshold formula is that for the Vermont circuitbreaker. Rates are shown on page 1 of this chapter. The provision which limits the maximum benefit to $500 is ignored in this illustration.

*In the actual Vermont circuitbreaker, benefit would be lower and net property tax higher due to the $500 maximum benefit per household.

is to treat a fixed proportion of rent as if it represented property tax. The most common percentage employed is 20 percent, but it varies from 30 percent in Illinois to 6 percent in New Mexico. This procedure is very crude, since it fails to reflect variations in the proportion of rent which property tax actually constitutes as a result of differences in value-rent multipliers and local tax rates.[7] While improvements in this procedure are feasible, an arbitrary assumption about the extent to which the property tax is shifted to tenants would still be necessary.[8]

The treatment of rent has also been criticized because it usually provides renters with smaller benefits than homeowners. According to one estimate, in Wisconsin it would be necessary to treat 32.6% of rent as property tax to achieve equity between homeowners and renters. This criticism views the circuitbreaker as a housing subsidy rather than a tax relief measure.[9]

Definition of Household Unit

Most states define the recipient household as a one- or two-person family.[10] Conflicting criteria come into play here. For the sake of evenhandedness, it is desirable to include income from all persons living together except renters in determining tax rebates. But such a policy is difficult to police. Moreover, not all persons in a common living unit pool their incomes. It seems desirable to at least include all income of dependents. This issue is of much greater import for circuitbreakers not restricted by age since elderly households are less likely to have more than two members than younger households.

Other Eligibility Issues

There are a host of additional conditions of eligibility which may be imposed. Some states with elderly circuitbreakers extend them to the disabled or blind. On the other hand, students and public assistance recipients are sometimes expressly excluded. Maryland rules out anyone with more than $200,000 assets. Many states have a residency requirement.[11]

2. The Level and Distribution of Benefits

The circuitbreaker provides a rebate of a percentage of tax paid in excess of some proportion of income (the threshold level). The level and distribution of benefits depends upon the threshold percentage, the proportion of "excess taxes" rebated, the maximum amount of taxes to be considered, the maximum rebate which may be received, and the maximum income eligible to participate.[12]

3. Sliding Scale vs. Threshold Formula

The only difference between a sliding scale and a threshold circuitbreaker is that in the sliding scale the threshold percentage is zero and the rebate percentage declines as income rises. Table 3 shows how the structure of benefits differs under sliding scale and threshold formulas, using the Iowa and Vermont circuitbreakers as examples. The sliding scale gives relatively more relief to households at each income level with lower property taxes; the threshold gives relatively more relief to households at each income level with higher property taxes.

Persuasive arguments may be made on behalf of either formula. A defect of the sliding-scale approach is that it may leave some low-income families with high property tax burdens relative to their income while extending relief to other, higher-income families whose taxes are not excessive relative to their incomes. On the other hand, the sliding-scale guarantees that no one at a higher income level will receive benefits when someone at a lower level does not, thus providing greater vertical equity. In addition, while households at each income level with greater wealth generally receive greater benefits, this pattern is less pronounced for the sliding scale than for the threshold approach.

An important practical consideration is the amount of revenue available to pay for the circuitbreaker. The sliding scale approach is more costly because it gives relief from the first dollar of property tax paid while the threshold provides relief only on that portion of the property tax which is treated as "excessive".

4. Maximum Benefits

Every state uses some mechanism to limit the benefits which a household may receive. The simplest method is also the most commonly used—placing a ceiling on benefits directly. The next most common device is to limit the amount of property taxes eligible for reimbursement. The latter method tends to restrict benefits for higher income families more than a direct limit on benefits would.[13] However, the distinction is blurred because many states which limit benefits also lower the limit as income increases.

5. Co-Insurance

One effect of a circuitbreaker is to relieve local citizens of a portion of the cost of services financed by property taxation. Such an effect is not unique to the circuitbreaker, since deductibility of property taxes in determining income tax liability has the same impact. However, the circuitbreaker can potentially be much more powerful than deductibility.[14] If the proportion of excess taxes which is rebated is 100 percent, qualified citizens will not bear locally any of the cost of increased property taxes. This opens up the possibility that one negative side effect of a circuitbreaker is that local spending might expand more than it otherwise would, interfering with neutrality.

Most states, if they permit rebates of 100 percent of eligible taxes at all, limit this rate to the elderly and very low income households. Setting rebates below 100 percent is sometimes referred to as co-insurance. Another factor tending to limit the circuitbreaker's effect on voting behavior is the low limit on maximum benefits in most states.

There is some evidence that the behavior of some voters is affected by a circuitbreaker. The identical bond issue was first defeated and then passed in Troy, Michigan, with the initiation of that state's circuit-breaker occurring during the interim of one month between the votes.[15] A survey of Michigan school administrators found that most of them mentioned the circuitbreaker in their campaigns in support of tax measures.[16]

6. Other Design Issues

One other design issue is relatively uncontroversial. In nearly all states the circuitbreaker is financed at the state rather than the local level. This is appropriate for a program which is redistributive and state-mandated. However, this is not a particular advantage of the circuitbreaker, since it is common to many other forms of relief.

Three additional specific design issues are important: the definition of income, the treatment of net worth, and the treatment of family size. All involve serious tradeoffs among evaluative criteria—horizontal and vertical equity often conflict with administrative and compliance cost. Unfortunately, efforts to fine tune the circuitbreaker tend to increase its complexity. Simplicity often is the enemy of fairness.

From the point of view of horizontal equity, it is desirable to define income broadly, and most states do so. Many of the major types of income excluded from the income tax usually must be included in income for circuitbreaker purposes; examples include income from Social Security, public assistance, and interest on municipal bonds.[17]

A related issue is whether net worth should be taken into account as a measure of need. A major criticism of circuitbreakers is that wealthy people with low current income may be eligible.[18] While most writers agree that some recognition of new worth is desirable, it faces two practical difficulties: measures of wealth are difficult to verify, and the increased complexity of the application process may discourage households which do have real need. Defenders of omitting net worth also argue that even people with substantial net worth may have cash-flow difficulties, and that most wealth is in the hands of households whose incomes would disqualify them from circuitbreaker benefits.[19]

In practice, most states ignore assets. A 1975 survey found only eight states out of 24 which considered net worth in designing their programs. The authors praised Iowa's approach, in which 10 percent of net worth in excess of $35,000 was added to income for determining benefits.[20] Shortly thereafter, Iowa repealed this provision.

The final design issue is how family size should be treated. Although it would be desirable in the interest of fairness, most circuitbreakers do not differentiate between large and small households. A simple procedure would be to allow personal exemptions of $750 per person, as on the federal income tax. A more elaborate approach would establish different benefit schedules for varying family sizes.[21]

Evaluation

Most evaluations in the circuitbreaker literature are

friendly. The outstanding critic of the circuitbreaker approach is Henry Aaron.

One of Aaron's major attacks is that at a given income level the circuitbreaker provides greater relief as net worth increases. This is undoubtedly true and is a defect of the circuitbreaker.

In a similar vein, Aaron states that "many of the neediest households will not receive aid, while some households with substantial wealth will qualify for relief."[22] Here Aaron is on very weak ground. The first part of the statement may be true for a national circuitbreaker limited to the elderly which does not extend relief to renters, but it is not true for a state circuitbreaker which covers all age groups and includes renters. In a sliding scale circuitbreaker, all low income households receive benefits if they apply for relief; a threshold circuitbreaker might miss some low income households, but only if the threshold level is high, property tax rates are low, and the family does not spend much on housing. Many needy households in some states apparently do not receive aid, but this is because of poor publicity for programs, not the inherent nature of the circuitbreaker.

The second part of Aaron's statement quoted above points out that some wealthy households qualify for relief. The same can be said of every other type of property tax relief in use; the difference between the circuitbreaker and other programs is that it is much less true for the circuitbreaker. Most types of property tax relief provide disproportionate benefits to the rich. Circuitbreakers of the type presently in use favor those of relatively limited means primarily because eligibility tends to fall as income rises.

A related issue is the incidence of the property tax. According to Aaron, "The intellectual rationale for circuitbreakers rests on the alleged regressivity of the property tax." He describes the incidence theory currently influencing public officials as "an atavistic attachment to naive and obsolete theory in defiance of published theoretical advances that demolish the previous orthodoxy."[23] The two major advances to which he refers are the general equilibrium analysis of the property tax and the permanent income hypothesis.

Those who continue to regard the property tax as regressive are not necessarily "slaves of some defunct economist" whose legacy is "indefensible analysis."[24] Aaron's analysis was initially developed to analyze a national circuitbreaker; from that point of view, it is appropriate to use a general equilibrium model, which under certain assumptions leads to the conclusion that the property tax is borne by the owners of capital and is progressive. However, from a single state's position, a partial equilibrium analysis is more appropriate, and the excise tax effects which it incorporates may yield the conclusion that the property tax is regressive.[25]

The other major theoretical development referred to by Aaron is to view the incidence of the property tax in relation to permanent income rather than current annual income. Such a change definitely reduces the regressivity of the residential property tax and may make it proportional or progressive.[26] However, several economists have argued (and their sentiments are undoubtedly echoed by many noneconomists) that taxes have to be paid out of current income, so that past and especially future income are irrelevant. Even a family whose income is only temporarily depressed may be in sufficient distress to justify some temporary relief.

More than one writer has denied Aaron's assertion that the case for the circuitbreaker rests on the regressivity of the property tax. According to the ACIR,

> . . . there would be a need for property tax relief even if the tax were proportional—or even progressive if the absolute level of the tax worked a hardship on some persons. A reasonable analogy is the need for exemptions to shield subsistence-level income under an income tax that features sharply progressive rates.[27]

All of the discussion thus far concerns the allegation that the circuitbreaker aids the wrong households. A second major criticism is that the circuitbreaker provides disproportionate assistance in areas where local governments rely heavily on property taxation rather than other revenue sources.[28] Once again, this charge has more validity against a national relief program than one administered at the state level. There is much less variation in taxes used within states than among states.

A third criticism of circuitbreakers by Aaron is that they reduce the incentive for low income persons to raise their incomes: as income goes up, relief goes down. However, it can be shown that the marginal tax rates are usually so trivial that this is not a serious problem.[29]

Another problem, already alluded to in the section on design issues, is that a circuitbreaker may affect voting behavior, increasing the willingness to vote in favor of spending increases. This problem is most severe if there is a threshold formula with no limit on benefits and no co-insurance provision, but it can be greatly reduced by careful design of the circuitbreaker. There is little evidence that this is a serious problem in actual practice.

Two other criticisms are easily dismissed. One study criticizes circuitbreakers because they provide no incentive to reform the administration of the property tax.[30] The same is true of almost every other form of relief. Another argument is that the circuitbreaker encourages expansion of the property tax[31] and tends to retard the shift to sales and income taxes. First of all, this argument may be wrong, since sales or income taxes are the most likely source of revenue to pay for circuitbreaker relief. Second, it may be desirable to revive the property tax; many students of government finance regard this tax as vital to maintenance of local government autonomy.[32]

One major problem has not received sufficient public scrutiny. As it is actually administered, the horizontal equity of the circuitbreaker is far from what it should be, because many eligible households apparently fail to participate. Data on this problem is sketchy but suggestive. A 1974 ACIR survey estimated that the percent of eligible households which were in the program averaged 69 percent in states with elderly circuitbreakers and 82 percent in states with no age limit.[33] However, some of these rates are probably overestimates. Abt Associates, which has conducted the largest survey of circuitbreaker activity, found the data inadequate for estimation of participation rates but stressed the need for a well-organized outreach program to stimulate participation.[34] Fortunately, the participation rate does tend to rise as familiarity with the program increases, and outreach programs can be effective. But as long as many eligible households are not in the program, its reality falls siginficantly short of its potential.

General Evaluation of Circuitbreakers

In the overall evaluation of the circuitbreaker, perhaps the two most important factors are the urgency which is felt with regard to relieving taxes for households with relatively high property taxes in relation to their income and one's sense of political realities. The circuitbreaker is potentially the most progressive form of property tax relief. Its ability to target relief also is a great virtue in the eyes of many, but it is a wasted virtue to those who want across-the-board relief.

Political acceptability is a crucial consideration. Aaron admits that it tempts him, but instead he advocates deferral, a housing allowance, and comprehensive income maintenance, none of which have the apparent political momentum or appeal of the circuitbreaker.[35] Some circuitbreaker advocates concede that it is not their ideal solution but that it is much preferable to the practical alternatives.

In fact, the circuitbreaker's tendency to target relief on behalf of those with low and moderate income is a political liability in legislatures where the interests of the upper middle class and the wealthy are on the minds of many lawmakers. In Michigan, this problem was overcome by making the circuitbreaker part of a package which included business tax breaks and an increase of income tax exemptions which favored higher income groups.[36] The circuitbreaker considered by the 1977 California legislature was modified in order to confer greater benefits on middle class suburbanites, with 75% of its benefits for homeowners going to households with incomes between $10,000 and $42,500.[37]

In a general analysis, the circuitbreaker must be viewed as one form of relief for homeowners and renters in competition with the other types of relief. Two questions have to be confronted: how much relief should go to homeowners and renters as opposed to other property taxpayers? Is the circuitbreaker the most appropriate device for aiding homeowners and renters?

There is justification for providing relief to residential property rather than to all property under the conditions which have recently existed in many states. The proportion of taxes levied on residential property has tended to increase because home values have risen much faster than the values of business property. For example, in California single family homes increased from 32 percent to 43 percent of total net assessed value within five years, causing residential taxes to rise much faster than other property taxes.

Circuitbreakers and Homestead Exemptions

As a mechanism for residential property tax relief, the circuitbreaker must be compared with the homestead exemption or credit. Such exemptions, which are used in even more states than are circuit-breakers, exclude a specified amount of a home's assessed valuation from the tax base.

Many homestead exemptions are locally financed and offer no relief to renters. Such arrangements are inferior to the typical circuitbreaker, which is state-financed and covers both renters and homeowners. However, if a homestead exemption is financed by the state and is accompanied by a credit for renters, it deserves serious consideration as an alternative to the circuitbreaker.[38]

Vertical Equity. Homestead exemptions (or credits) tend to reduce the regressivity of the residential pro-perty tax (or increase its progressivity) because they constitute a larger proportion of income for low than high income households. They are generally not as progressive as the circuitbreakers presently in effect. Whether there is much difference in progressivity depends on housing patterns and on how each is designed.

Horizontal Equity. Even if a homestead exemption has the same incidence among income groups as a par-ticular circuitbreaker, there is a sharp contrast in benefits within each income group. The exemption provides relatively uniform benefits among home-owners in comparison to the circuitbreaker; as Aaron emphasized, the circuitbreaker bestows greater benefits on those with more valuable homes. While some regard this as an advantage of the homestead ex-emption, others come to the opposite conclusion on the ground that those with the highest taxes should receive more relief.

One advantage of the circuitbreaker is that it usual-ly covers renters as well as homeowners whereas the homestead exemption does not. This difference can be overcome, however, if a homestead program is coupled with a renter's credit.

Other Considerations. A homestead exemption has two other advantages: it is easier for the public to understand and comply with, so that low participation is not a problem; and it is administratively simpler, since income does not have to be verified. On the other hand, the threshold circuitbreaker is attractive in that it automatically cushions tax burdens when inflation

forces them up faster than income: with a threshold circuitbreaker, net taxes rise more slowly than gross taxes; with a homestead program, net taxes rise faster than gross taxes in percentage terms.

In some other respects, circuitbreakers and homestead programs are similar. Except for credits which are set at a flat rate, both credits and circuit-breakers provide greater benefits in jurisdictions where tax rates are relatively high. Likewise, both can be financed at the state level.

In coming to a final evaluation of the relative merits of homestead exemptions and circuitbreakers, one must distinguish between programs aimed at specific groups of households and programs intended for a broad coverage of residential property. The circuit-breaker can potentially fine tune relief for low income households with excessive tax burdens in relation to their income better than a homestead exemption or credit. It can also target relief to middle- and upper-income households with unusually high property taxes, if that is desired. Because funds to finance pro-perty tax relief are always limited, this tendency to concentrate relief on a limited number of households makes it possible to give them greater relief than would otherwise be possible. But as an instrument for general relief of residential property, the homestead exemption deserves serious consideration because of its simplicity. A crucial consideration in deciding be-tween them is the horizontal equity issue—whether one wants to give much more relief at each income level to those with high property taxes than to those with low property taxes.

In reality, there is no need to make an either/or decision. Many states have circuitbreakers alongside their homestead exemptions, thus enabling them to provide some benefits to everyone while giving extra relief to certain targeted groups of taxpayers. The in-terplay between the exemption and circuitbreaker often reduces significantly the net cost of the circuit-breaker.[39]

In conclusion, it must be emphasized that this analysis of the homestead exemption assumes that it is financed by the state and that it is accompanied by a credit for renters. Without these two features, the homestead exemption is decidedly inferior to the cir-cuitbreaker in terms of equity.

The answer to the question of which relief mechan-ism—the circuitbreaker or homestead exemption—is preferable and how it should be designed depends on priorities about who should get relief, whether rising tax rates or increasing assessments are the source of property tax "overloads," how much money is available for property tax relief, and what the politics of each situation dictates.

---

[1]ACIR, *Circuitbreakers*, pp. 3-4.
[2]This discussion ignores the fact that in Iowa the benefit of the homestead credit is subtracted from the circuitbreaker, so that the circuitbreaker provides less benefit than it would by itself.
[3]The descriptive statements in this chapter are based on Shannon and Tippett, unless otherwise noted. Their tally of circuitbreaker states is 30 plus the District of Columbia. However, they include Hawaii's program, which is a renter's credit for taxpayers with in-come under $20,000 and rent over $1,000 per year. Since benefits do

not vary as income changes, that program is not considered a cir-cuitbreaker in this study.
[4]Wisconsin was the first state to adopt a circuitbreaker. Credit for originating the idea is attributed to Harold Groves by Quindry and Cook (1969), p. 359.
[5]These states ranked first, second, fifth, and sixth (tie) in terms of 1975 effective tax rates on homes.
[6]Minnesota implicitly has an income ceiling of $36,000 because of the interaction with the homestead credit.

[7]California is the only state which does not treat an arbitrary percentage of rent as property tax. It uses a statewide statutory property tax equivalent for renters and makes relief a function of it and income.

[8]Grubb and Hoachlander, pp. 328-33.

[9]Cook, p. 181; see also Abt Associates.

[10]Abt Associates, *Final Report*, p. 97.

[11]Abt Associates, *A Compendium Report* is the broadest survey of circuitbreaker provisions; its information was gathered in 1974 and early 1975. It is the basis for statements in this section.

[12]If both the threshold percentage and the proportion of taxes rebated are constants and the threshold percentage is less than 100 percent, the resulting tax incidence will be regressive (assuming that the initial incidence of the property tax is regressive). If it is desired to make net burdens proportional or progressive, either the proportion of taxes rebated must decrease as income rises or the threshold percentage or the threshold must rise, as Grubb and Hoachlander show (p. 327).

[13]There are two reasons: First, the proportion of taxes rebated may drop as income increases and, second, high income people tend to have higher property taxes, which would increase their circuitbreaker benefits if there were no maximum.

[14]The net cost of deductible property taxes is found by multiplying the property tax by (1- marginal income tax rate). For example, the net cost of $100 property tax for someone in the 36 percent marginal tax bracket is $64.

[15]Abt Associates, *Final Report*, p. 52.

[16]Robert Kleine, personal correspondence.

[17]However, gifts, life insurance benefits, and relief in kind are usually excluded from the income measure. For details, see Abt Associates, *A Compendium Report*, p. 40. See also Bendick, p. 25.

[18]Aaron, *Who Pays?*, p. 76.

[19]See ACIR, p. 16 Abt Associates, A Compendium Report, pp. 47-51; and Bendick, p. 27.

[20]Abt Associates, *A Compendium Report*, p. 48.

[21]Bendick, pp. 25-26.

[22]Aaron, *What Do...Accomplish?*, p. 64.

[23]*Ibid.*, pp. 58-60.

[24]*Ibid.*, p. 53.

[25]See Charles E. McLure, "The 'New View' of the Property Tax: A Caveat", *National Tax Journal* (March, 1977), pp. 69-73. Aaron makes this same point on page 55 of *Who Pays?*, but 22 pages later he says, "Circuitbreaker relief for renters may be justified under the traditional view that the residential property tax is regressive, but makes little sense when one recognizes the property tax as a levy borne predominantly by owners of capital." A recent study by Allan Odden and Phillip E. Vincent concludes that even using the new view the property tax is regressive for most households; see their "The Regressivity of the Property Tax."

[26]Aaron, *Who Pays?*, pp. 27-32.

[27]ACIR, p. 16.

[28]Aaron, "What Do...?", p. 64.

[29]Grubb and Hoachlander, pp. 334-35; Aaron, "What Do...?", p. 65.

[30]Schroeder and Sjoquist, p. 6.

[31]*Ibid.*, p. 6; Aaron, "What Do...?", p. 64.

[32]James A. Maxwell and J. Richard Aronson, *Financing State and Local Governments*, 3rd ed. pp. 134-38; Bowman, p. 9.

[33]ACIR, p. 5.

[34]Abt Associates, *A Compendium Report*, pp. 60-67.

[35]Aaron, *Who Pays?*, pp. 78-79; Aaron, "What Does?", p. 64.

[36]Unpublished report by James Haughey, Gerald Miller, and Robert Kleine.

[37]See *Tax Backtalk*, October, 1977. *Tax Backtalk* is published by the California Tax Reform Association. Also, see Dean Tipps, "The Circuit Breaker" (California Tax Reform Association, 1977).

[38]The text discusses the most common type of homestead exemption, one in which a certain amount of a home's value is exempted from taxation. Much of the analysis also applies to a credit which is uniform for all homes. It does not apply to a credit used in a few states which rebates a certain percentage of the gross property tax.

[39]Thirteen states and the District of Columbia have both programs. Where the exemption is state-financed, it is usually subtracted from the circuitbreaker rebate which has been calculated according to the circuitbreaker formula.

CIRCUITBREAKER BIBLIOGRAPHY

AARON, Henry J. "What Do Circuit-Breaker Laws Accomplish?," in George E. Peterson, *Property Tax Reform*, pp. 53.64.

ABT ASSOCIATES. *Property Tax Relief Programs for the Elderly*. Three volumes: *A Compendium Report, An Evaluation, Final Report*.

ADVISORY COMMISSION ON INTERGOVERNMENTAL RELATIONS. *Property Tax Circuit-Breakers: Current Status and Policy Issues*.

BENDICK, Marc. "Designing Circuit Breaker Property Tax Relief," *National Tax Journal* (March, 1974), pp. 19-28.

COOK, Billy D. "The 'Circuit-Breaker' Approach for Granting Property Tax Relief with Special Emphasis on Wisconsin and Minnesota," in ACIR, *Financing Schools and Property Tax Relief*, pp. 175-87.

COOK, Billy D., QUINDRY, Kenneth E., and GROVES, Harold M., "Old Aged Homestead Relief—The Wisconsin Experience," *National Tax Journal* (September, 1966), pp. 319-24.

GOLD, Steven D. "A Note on the Design of Property Tax Circuitbreakers," *National Tax Journal* (December, 1976), pp. 477-81.

GRUBB, W. Norton and HOACHLANDER, E. Gaerth. "Circuit-breaker Schedules and Their Application in California," *Policy Analysis* (Summer, 1978), pp. 317-37.

HAUGHEY, James., MILLER, Gerald, and KLEINE, Robert. "The Michigan Property Tax Circuit Breaker: Design and Cyclical Sensitivity." Unpublished paper.

IRELAND, Thomas R. and Mitchell, William E. "A Public Choice Analysis of the Demand for Property Tax Circuit-breaker Legislation," *Public Finance Quarterly* (October, 1976), pp. 379-94.

QUINDRY, Kenneth E. "Residential Property Tax Relief for Senior Citizens in Maine and Vermont," in *Financing Schools and Property Tax Relief*, pp. 188-93.

QUINDRY, Kenneth E. and COOK, Billy D. "Humanization of the Property Tax for Low-Income Households," *National Tax Journal* (September, 1969), pp. 357-67.

SCHROEDER, Larry D. and Sjoquist, David L., "Property Tax Relief Through Circuit Breakers," *International Assessor* (May, 1977), pp. 2-6.

SHANNON, John. "The Property Tax: Reform or Relief?" in *Property Tax Reform*, pp. 25-52.

CIRCUITBREAKER: Your Protection Against Property Tax Overload

A circuit breaker, everyone knows, is that box in the basement you have to find with a flashlight when your kids forget the rules and plug the toaster, mixer and electric skillet into the same circuit with the coffee pot.

Well, there's a new kind of circuit breaker, and it doesn't have anything to do with electricity. This new kind of circuit breaker deals with property tax relief. It has been working in Wisconsin since 1963, Minnesota since 1967 and Washington, D.C. since 1969.

This circuit breaker cuts off property tax if it exceeds a certain percentage of income. It targets relief to those most in need, is based on actual property taxes paid—not assessed values—and does not apply to high-income families. Sound like a good deal? It may be on the way to Ohio, and you may have a chance to vote for it this November.

The Ohio Public Interest Campaign has submitted petitions to the Secretary of State's office calling for tax reform, including the circuit breaker feature. The issue, called the "Ohio Fair Tax Initiative" is tied up in the courts at the moment, but there is a good chance it will be on the ballot this November.

The Initiative would grant property tax relief to families and individuals if their property taxes exceed 2.5% of their income. The 2.5%, thus, is the circuit breaker—when property taxes exceed that figure the circuit breaker flips and property tax payers would receive a rebate or credit against state income taxes.

Renters, too, would be eligible for property tax relief through the circuit breaker mechanism by figuring 10% of their rent as property tax payment. An accompanying article explains how.

Those who make more than $30,000 a year would not be eligible for the circuit breaker property tax relief. It's estimated that 90% of families in Ohio earn less than $30,000 a year. Not all would be eligible, of course, but a computer analysis shows that close to 70% of homeowners and close to 65% of renters would benefit from a circuit breaker law.

A circuit breaker law could also be looked at as a property tax insurance policy. That is, if you are making a good income now and your property taxes aren't too high, you might not be eligible for relief. But, what happens if you lose your job, or are injured on the job, or for some other reason your income drops? Certainly, your property taxes won't decrease, but because your income is lower you probably would qualify for circuit breaker property tax relief.

It's estimated that a circuit breaker would bring $150 million in property tax relief to Ohioans.

And, it is not just residential property owners and renters who would benefit under the Ohio Fair Tax Initiative. The proposal is comprehensive and would grant tax relief to small businesses, increase the state income tax for Ohioans making more than $30,000 annually, increase taxes for huge profitable corporations, end future tax abatements, close other loopholes by which business and industry escape paying their fair share of taxes, require banks and savings and loans to pay state income taxes and eliminate the direct use sales tax exemption for manufacturers.

Under the Initiative, 87% of corporate taxpayers in Ohio would receive tax breaks or no increase in taxes. Small businesses making less than $25,000 would pay 3% income tax instead of the current 4%, and the next $25,000 would be taxed at 7% instead of the current 8%. Business income above $50,000 would be taxed at 10% instead of 8%.

Tax loopholes that allow businesses to pay an ever decreasing share of taxes would be closed. Under the proposal, personal property taxes firms pay on inventories and machinery would be frozen at 1978 levels. Tax abatement laws would be repealed and no new tax abatements could be granted to the likes of Nationwide Insurance, Sohio and City National Bank.

Another loophole that would close is that which allows banks and savings and loans to escape paying the state income tax. They, too, under the proposal, would pay their fair share of taxes.

Finally, elimination of the direct use sales tax exemption would mean that business and industry pay sales taxes just like individuals do when they buy consumer products.

Ending the exemption would bring in $300 million a year to the state, while an increase in the corporation income tax would add around $100 million. Increasing taxes on individuals earning more than $30,000 a year would bring in about $90 million extra annually to the state and extending the corporate income tax to banks and savings and loans would add close to $30 million. Repeal of the corporate income tax credit for new machinery would result in around $40 million increase in state revenues.

Once the state reimburses local governments for the loss of property tax revenues because of the circuit breaker feature, it is estimated the state would realize around $350 million a year in increased revenues, including $100 million in local revenues.

"Circuit-Breaker: Your Protection Against Property Tax Overload" is reprinted by permission from the February, 1979 issue of *Focus*, Ohio AFL-CIO.

Reassessing the Circuit Breaker

By Elizabeth Bass

In the hunt for progressive property tax relief, the circuit breaker is a popular weapon, its strength well known and much discussed.

When Massachusetts Fair Share undertook a circuit breaker campaign in 1978, they found that the measure carries its own weaknesses, in terms of both organizing and public policy. Some of these difficulties were expected; some were not. Some seemed peculiar to the Fair Share effort; some seemed intrinsic to the circuit breaker. Either way, Fair Share's experiences with the measure—and especially its problems with it—may be useful to other organizations as they consider options for tax relief and reform.

A circuit breaker is a way of progressively graduating the property tax by tying property taxes to income. To use the electrical metaphor that gave the measure its names, it is a way of protecting homeowners and tenants from property tax "overload." Circuit breakers set a ceiling on the percentage of income that can be taken in property taxes. Those who pay more than the ceiling get relief.

The attractions of Fair Share's plan were, in large part, common to all circuit breakers:

1) relief would be targeted, making a relatively small amount of money go further to help low and moderate income people.

2) relief would be concentrated in older cities and in their most deteriorated neighborhoods, since those areas tend to be overassessed.

3) all the relief would go to residential taxpayers.

4) tenants would not have to count on pass-throughs from landlords to get relief.

5) the relief would be direct, not subject to the sleight of hand that is widely perceived to occur when benefits have to filter through levels of government. Legislators, in turn, would have an easy time claiming credit for the relief.

6) By funding the relief from state revenues, part of the property tax burden would be shifted onto state taxes that are more broadbased and less regressive—in part, onto business.

7) the idea does not seem radical or unprecedented since many states have limited circuit breakers and a few have broad ones.

8) in Massachusetts, where voters have twice rejected graduating the flat income tax, the circuit breaker would be a back-door, second best approach to a graduated income tax.

Under Fair Share's circuit breaker, specifically, any household with an income (after personal state exemptions) of less than $30,000 would have gotten relief if it spent more than 8% of that income on property taxes. For tenants, 25% of rent would count as their property tax payment. The relief would have equalled 80% of the amount paid in excess of 8% of income. The maximum relief would be $500. Homeowners and tenants would have filed directly for rebates and received checks directly from the state. The program, estimated to cost about $150 million, would have been paid from out of the state surplus. In case of inadequate funding, people over 65 would have gotten their rebates first in full, with the rest of the money prorated to remaining eligible households.

If you've read the paragraph above, you already know the chief organizing problem with the circuit breaker: it tends to be complicated. Fair Share's bill was a good deal simpler than others that have been tried. But while it was relatively clean to explain in broad strokes, it got a lot muddier when the self-interested tenant or homeowner wanted to know, "How much, if anything, will *I* get?" There were a lot of questions: "Does Social Security count as income?" "What if I got an abatement last year?" What happens to my veterans' benefit?"

Eventually Fair Share drew up a fill-in-the-blanks worksheet to help people figure out their potential rebate. But a meeting that begins with people adding and subtracting—and some people concluding that they will get nothing—is not an ideal organizing situation.

One reason the circuit breaker must be somewhat complex is that it targets relief. That feature, an advantage from a public policy point of view, is itself a draw-

Elizabeth Bass is the editor of the Massachusetts Fair Share newspaper, Citizen Advocate. *(304 Boylston St., Boston, Mass. 02116). Bass has worked for Fair Share since 1976.*

back in organizing. On a single block, some families were eligible, their neighbors were not. Some of Fair Share's chapter areas had many fewer eligible families than others. The organization estimated that about 45% of the low and moderate income families in the state—the Fair Share constituency—would have gotten rebates. Organizers could not say to people, "You will get a rebate." Instead they had to say, "770,000 families will get rebates. You may be one of them, if..." And too many conditions followed that "if."

Another advantage of the circuit breaker—its directness—also posed problems. Fair Share had first planned to have the relief be a credit on the state income tax but changed that to direct rebate checks sent out in October, just before the election. This was done to sweeten the pot for legislators and to give the group a wonderful organizing tool (come to the meeting and file for your rebate.) It left Fair Share open, however, to charges that the bill would be an expensive "administrative nightmare" and that many eligible people would not know to file for the rebates. These objections were largely a convenient excuse for those who opposed the circuit breaker anyway. But they were plausible to many people.

There was also some feeling among some taxpayers that applying for a rebate was like asking for a handout. Perhaps tax credits, with their high finance, big business connotations, would have been less objectionable.

Fair Share also found that some liberal, good government types seemed repelled by the very idea of direct relief, as though it were intrinsically reactionary. One person from the League of Women Voters, for instance, said disparagingly, "People will just take the money and buy dresses and things." That kind of talk, of course, can be very good for organizing.

But there were some aspects to the circuit breaker that were more than just inconvenient.

Fair Share found the circuit breaker not well suited to giving relief to renters. The group estimated that nearly one-quarter of those getting rebates would be tenants. Yet their figures showed that at almost every income level, a substantially greater percentage of homeowners than tenants would be helped. For instance, 78% of single-family homeowners in the $6,700-$9,500 income range would have gotten rebates; only 52% of the tenants of that income would have been helped. 59% of the single-family homeowners making $13,000-$20,000 would have gotten rebates; no tenants of that income would have gotten anything.

That problem approaches the heart of the circuit breaker's weakness which is that, although it can easily be framed to have an overall progressive impact, it is not progressive in every case.

At any given income level, the circuit breaker favors those who spend a lot on housing, as opposed to those who spend a lot on medical care or food, for instance.

In addition, it is difficult to make the circuit breaker reliably help the poorest families. Fair Share's bill, for instance, clearly would have made the Massachusetts property tax system much less regressive than

it is now. Yet under its circuit breaker, a slightly greater percentage of families making $4,000-$13,000 would have gotten relief than those with incomes below $4,000. Some families with $4,000 income would have gotten nothing while some with $30,000 would have gotten a check in the mail.

Perhaps this is to say no more than that the circuit breaker does not bring perfect tax justice. Given the regressivity of the systems that it would change, that wouldn't be much of a problem. But the circuit breaker, by its nature, focuses attention on the question, "who deserves relief?" and claims to help those who need it most. This makes it more vulnerable to what could be called "assault by exception" in which the wildest hypothetical case is used to impugn the merit of the entire program.

This happened in Fair Share's case. Then-Gov. Dukakis repeatedly contended that the circuit breaker could give a rebate to a "swinging bachelor" living above his income in a waterfront condominium. That may have been true. But the implication, which Dukakis energetically encouraged, that the circuit breaker was therefore regressive, was not true at all.

Many of those who argued against the circuit breaker on those grounds meanwhile were working strenuously for the Governor's plan for a local aid increase. If that increase had been translated into property tax relief as promised, it would have cut taxes for the phone company and electric company in Boston alone by more than $2 million each, done nothing for tenants and delivered relief indiscriminately to rich and poor homeowners alike. A hypothetical $200 rebate for a "swinging bachelor" was intolerably regressive; a $2 million tax cut for the phone company was not. By its very indiscriminateness, the Governor's plan discouraged specific questions of equity.

Despite these problems, the circuit breaker was compelling to many people and the campaign was large and lively. Fair Share passed the measure through the House and Senate by wide margins—shockingly wide to the many State House observers who had treated it as a hopeless exercise four months before. The Governor vetoed the measure in the last days of the session. In line with a deal he had made with the legislative leadership, he refused to send his veto message back to the legislature so there was no chance for an override. The reps were off the hook.

This maneuver was unprecedented, possibly illegal and certainly a violation of Dukakis's open government, anti-bossism position. Yet the only people who seemed outraged by it were Fair Share members and one lone Boston Globe columnist.

That pointed up the killing weakness of the Fair Share circuit breaker—its political isolation. This isolation was caused more by circumstances specific to the campaign than to intrinsic problems with the circuit breaker.

The circuit breaker should have been attractive to a host of forces—social service advocates, liberal politicians, church groups and, most importantly, public employee unions—all of whom were being offered a progressive alternative to the right-wing tax and service cut efforts that were beginning in the state.

Yet even after Proposition 13 thundered to victory in June at the crucial point in Fair Share's campaign, the support was not there.

There were at least three reasons, all of them inter-related.

First, service providers and advocates did not feel they were under the gun. They did not seriously believe that they were threatened by the channels into which people's need for property tax relief might turn. In some cases, they did not even believe, in the face of all evidence, that this need was legitimate—and some of them probably still don't.

Second, Fair Share had not made a major effort to involve its potential allies in the planning of the circuit breaker. It is possible that they wouldn't have taken the organization or the problem seriously enough to become involved, but Fair Share didn't really try. By the time the circuit breaker was presented to potential allies, it was Fair Share's program and, as such, less likely to inspire a major committment from any other organization.

Probably most important, however, was that Fair Share did not provide an additional funding source for the circuit breaker, saying instead that it should be funded out of the state surplus. The Governor wanted to use this money for increased school aid and state assumption of court costs. Fair Share did not oppose or work against those programs, instead implying, more than arguing, that all three proposals could be partially funded. And, as things turned out, in its final form the circuit breaker was funded for only $50 million and would not have cut into the other plans.

Nonetheless, the circuitbreaker was seen by potential allies as being in direct competition with funding for public services. Even those who thought the rebate bill was a good idea had other priorities that outranked it. In addition, some feared that, once passed and popular, the circuit breaker would be expanded in future years—as Fair Share argued it should—and that that expansion would come at the expense of services. Some, of course, who voiced that objection publically were actually more concerned that future expansion might come at the expense of business.

When it first began considering a circuit breaker campaign in the spring of 1977 Fair Share considered trying to fund it through a sales tax on professional services. But in a pro-business climate, pro-tax cut atmosphere, Fair Share didn't feel able to raise taxes on business—especially not when there was a state surplus waiting. If Fair Share had won the circuit breaker, it almost surely would have attempted to get alternative funding sources in future years. But that was not part of the campaign. Given the lack or urgency that poten-

tial allies felt at the time (a feeling that has since changed) it is hard to tell whether including a new revenue source would have been enough to win their support for the circuit breaker and whether such a move would have, in net effect, made the circuit breaker campaign harder or easier. But it probably would have made Fair Share more comfortable with its own plan.

None of this should be taken to imply that the circuit breaker is a loser or even that it was necessarily a loser in Fair Share's case. In fact, when the organization begin looking at tax options for 1979 an expanded circuit breaker, along with a way to fund it, was one of the possibilities considered.

In fact, it seems clear that in some situations, the circuit breaker is the best measure around. If, for instance, there is a relatively small amount of money earmarked for tax relief and the major question is one of distribution, the progressive effects of the circuit breaker make it a highly attractive method to use.

In a broader campaign that emphasizes reform, rather than relief, the circuit breaker can be a valuable component, the piece offers immediate relief to a relatively small number of particularly hard-hit people. In such a campaign, the circuit breaker can be offered as relief for the few and insurance—against big tax increases or loss of income in the future—for the many.

This approach can probably work best if most people feel property taxes are a problem but are not yet a truly terrible personal burden.

Originally, Fair Share's circuit breaker was one of a dozen bills the organization introduced. The others dealt with tax exempt institutions, tax delinquents and assessing and abating processes. The circuit breaker was to be only one part of a package.

But in Massachusetts, where property taxes are the only source of local revenue and the average person pays nearly twice as much as the national average, this approach could not easily work. The need for relief was so great and so widespread that it caused the circuit breaker to take off as the most compelling part of Fair Share's program and, at the same time, highlighted the Fair Share circuit breaker's weaknesses as a way of delivering widespread relief.

This year, therefore, Fair Share is going with a coalition-backed relief and reform program that is more comprehensive than the circuit breaker. This $350 million plan guarantees at least a 10% cut for all residential taxpayers (with 20% cuts for the highest-taxed two-thirds of the state) and funding through a tax on professional services and on commercial bank assets.

But it was the circuit breaker campaign, for all its problems, that first gave Fair Share the standing to build a coalition that may have a shot at a broader program.

"Reassessing the Circuitbreaker" is reprinted by permission of Massachusetts Fair Share.

Homestead Exemption Programs

Homestead Exemption Programs

Despite the rising popularity of circuit breakers in recent years, the homestead exemption mechanism awards greater total benefits to more households nationwide than does the circuit breaker. Thirty-nine state-mandated homestead exemption programs in 23 states were identified in the first part of this Study; 27 of the 39 programs limit eligibility to the elderly and certain other groups such as the disabled and the blind.

Like the tax freeze and tax deferral mechanisms, homestead exemptions exclude renters from program coverage. Typically the homestead exemption functions by exempting from taxation a stipulated dollar amount of the assessed value of homes owned by eligible claimants. In practice, this amount varies from $1000 in Indiana to $20,000 in Hawaii. The value of benefits to an eligible claimant awarded under such a program are equal to the dollar amount of the exemption multiplied by the nominal tax rate used by the taxing jurisdiction.

Variations on this basic mechanism are found in some states. Montana, for example, reduces by 50% the assessed value of the homes of those who qualify for relief. In New Jersey, eligible homeowners are given a flat $160 reduction in the tax bill or the full amount of the tax, whichever is less. Washington varies the amount of exemption with personal income such that those with income $5000-$6000 are exempted only from 50% of all special levy taxes; those with incomes less than $4000 are exempted completely from special levy taxes and are given a $5000 reduction in assessed valuation for the purposes of regular property taxation.

A wide range of income and asset eligibility requirements can be applied to the homestead exemption mechanism to focus benefits on limited population groups. Twenty-three of the 39 programs currently in use incorporate household income ceilings to limit participation. Several also set maximum asset levels—in some cases limited to real property assets—to restrict eligibility further. Coverage can also be further curtailed by allowing stipulated exemptions only in determining specified types of property tax obligations. In some cases, just state property taxes, school district taxes, or municipal taxes can be reduced by the homestead exemption. While the mechanism allows this kind of flexibility in targeting relief to defined groups, serious drawbacks are apparent in its equity and fiscal consequences, and the magnitude of those drawbacks increase as the level of government sponsoring the program broadens in scope.

Equity Considerations

Given an equal tax rate within a local tax jurisdiction, relief under a program which reduces assessed value will be proportional to assessed value up to the maximum reduction allowed and disproportional thereafter (that is, the greater the assessed value of the home, the smaller the proportion of that value which will be relieved). Whether or not the equity effects across income categories will be similar depends upon the relationship between household income and assessed value of real property. Households with a high assessed value relative to income would benefit less from the program than households with a lower relative value. Since many elderly households are richer in property than in current income, such a program would benefit them relatively less than others with higher incomes and smaller property holdings. Within a jurisdiction, therefore, vertical equity is a function of the household income/home value relationship found among eligible households in the jurisdiction.

Among taxing jurisdictions the same forces bear on equity across income categories, but, in addition, horizontal equity problems will occur. These result, on the one hand, from variations in nominal tax rates among jurisdictions and, on the other, from significant intrajurisdictional variations in the ratio of assessed value to full market value of homes. Taken together, these two factors produce a wide range of effective tax rates among jurisdictions within states, interregionally, and nationwide.

The effects of these variations on the ability of the homestead exemption mechanism to deliver equitable amounts of relief to households within a given hypothetical state are illustrated in the following table.

EQUITY IMPLICATIONS OF A $5,000 HOMESTEAD EXEMPTION

Household Characteristics	Hypothetical Households			
	A	B	C	D
Household income	$15,000	$ 6,000	$15,000	$ 6,000
Full value of home	$20,000	$30,000	$20,000	$30,000
Assessment ratio	20%	25%	35%	50%
Nominal tax rate	3.5%	6.4%	7.1%	6.2%
Effective tax rate	.7%	1.6%	2.5%	3.1%
Tax before relief	$140	$480	$500	$930
Tax after relief	$105	$400	$375	$775
Value of relief	$ 35	$ 80	$125	$155
% tax relieved	25%	17%	25%	17%
Tax after relief/income	.007	.067	.019	.129

Households A, B, C, and D live in different areas of a state which provides a $5000 homestead exemption without income, assets, or age limitations. While state legislation requires all single-family homes to be assessed at 50% of their full market value, local variations in assessment practices result in actual assessment ratios ranging from a low of 20% to the statutory maximum of 50%. Each tax area has different revenue needs to finance varying levels of public services, and each has a different total value of property which it can tax to raise required revenues. The nominal tax rates set by each of the four jurisdictions reflect these inter-jurisdictional differences and vary accordingly.

Looking first at households A and B, it can be seen that relative to A, household B is income poor but has a more valuable home. Since this pattern is typical among the elderly, B will be designated as an elderly household; A, as nonelderly. The absolute value of B's benefits under the exemption is $80 while A's is only $35; however, in terms of the proportion of tax relieved, A fared much better with 25% than did B with 17%. But elderly household B still had to devote 6.7% of household income to property taxes after the exemption was applied, while A had to devote less than 1% of household income to the levy after homestead relief. Equity measured by a household's ability to pay property taxes is poorly served under these circumstances.

Horizontal equity is also abused under such a system. Households B and D—perhaps both elderly-headed households—live in different parts of the same state, have identical household incomes, and own houses of identical sales value. Both received benefits under the $5000 homestead exemption program but experience very different results from this relief. While B's relief is worth $75 less than D's ($155 – $80 = $75), B is faced with a remaining tax bill which consumes only 6.7% of his income while D must devote almost 13% of his income to pay property taxes remaining after homestead relief. For the four hypothetical households described here, tax liability after relief as a percentage of income is in the ratio of 1:3:10:18. Thus, the most burdened household must devote 18 times as much of its income to property taxes as does the least burdened.

Data on the range of actual effective property tax rates within states are difficult to obtain. The Census of Governments does, however, provide data showing comparisons of median effective property tax rates derived for selected cities within each region of the country. In 1971, for selected cities across the nation, median effective tax rates varied from 1% to over 4%.[1] The equity consequences illustrated in the foregoing example, therefore, could certainly be expected inter-regionally. It is quite plausible that they would also be experienced within some states.

Fiscal Policy Considerations

Within a local taxing jurisdiction, the fiscal consequences of a homestead exemption financed locally will be a function of the number of eligible households participating in the program and of the effective tax rate which prevails. The greater the number of participants, the greater the cost of the program and the greater the overall tax burdens that will have to be shifted to nonexempt properties to attain desired levels of revenue. Also, the higher the effective tax rate, the more each fixed dollar amount exemption will cost the jurisdiction. The majority of state-mandated homestead exemption programs currently in use are financed locally. It is not surprising, therefore, that while many local tax districts complain of the necessity of financing these programs, those with relatively higher tax rates feel most burdened because their cost is higher and proportional to the prevailing effective tax rate.

If financed at the state level, homestead programs may result in budget planning problems which arise from the state's inability to predict accurately the composite tax rates which will be set by each tax district annually. The overall configuration of local effective tax rates throughout a state will determine the ultimate cost of providing homestead exemption relief. The distribution of benefits to tax districts—via annual reimbursements to local governments—will direct relatively large amounts of money to these areas with higher than average effective tax rates. The result is that those areas which choose to tax residents most heavily (presumably to provide a higher level of public services than exist elsewhere) will receive more state aid in support of those services.

[1] **U.S. Department of Commerce.**

"Homestead Exemption Programs" is reprinted by permission from *Property Tax Relief Programs for the Elderly,* Abt Associates 1975.

IV

By Leonard Goldberg

Renters are in a difficult position in a tax system which offers many rewards to property ownership. Not only do renters bear the usual tax burdens which fall disproportionately on people with moderate incomes, they also receive none of the tax benefits of owning property. Nor, despite their position as property taxpayers, do they necessarily receive property tax relief when such relief is forthcoming. It is very easy to tax renters, but difficult to stop taxing them.

When you add in the expenditure side of the equation—that renters tend to be more dependent than homeowners on public services like public transportation, elderly services, public parks and recreation, and other public amenities which are not purchased privately—it becomes clear that current moves to drastically cut taxes and services have only one-way effects on renters. Their services are cut but their taxes stay the same. They are victims both of the tax system and the tax revolt.

Fortunately, renter tax problems are beginning to receive more attention. As the cost of homeownership rises and its feasibility recedes from many ordinary people, renters are starting to bring their problems to the attention of policy-makers. While the range of policy options developed so far has been limited, the options should increase as the political will to help renters becomes stronger.

The Tax Disadvantages of Renters

Renters as a group tend to have substantially lower incomes than homeowners, and therefore generally receive the same advantages and bear the same disadvantages that moderate income brings. They tend to bear the brunt of the regressivity of the sales tax, for example, and may benefit from low income credits or other progressive features of the income tax. Their primary disadvantage, of course, comes with the property-related features of our tax system.

The federal income tax, and state income taxes which follow the federal tax, have obvious and detrimental effects on renters. Federal and state taxes allow for deductions which are specifically related to the cost of owning property. Since renters by their nature do not own property, they are naturally not entitled to such deductions. Specifically, homeowners can itemize and deduct the interest payments on their loans, and the property tax payments which they pay on their homes. Interest payments can run into thousands of dollars, and property tax payments can be significant. The amount is significant enough that with few additions it will become beneficial for a homeowner to itemize. At middle levels of income, a renter without these deductions will probably not find it worthwhile to itemize deductions at all. In California, the difference which such property-related deductions can

make may easily amount to $1500 more in taxes for the renter at a $16,000 level of income. And since renters do not deduct, they will bear other costs disproportionately. The accompanying table, **Relative Income Tax Burdens of California Renters,** prepared by the California Commission on Government Reform, shows this somewhat differently. It demonstrates that renters as a whole pay disproportionate amounts of income tax at almost any level of income.

A final income tax disadvantage involves the treatment of property when it is sold. The appreciated value of a house is treated as a capital gain when it is sold, or is not taxed if the homeowner buys another house of equal or greater value. When an apartment appreciates in value, all the renter gets is higher rent.

Property-related deductions do accrue to the landlords, but they are simply reflected as business expenses and will have no downward pressure on the structure of rents. Rents will generally be determined by the structure of the housing market, and changes in the taxes paid by the landlord will probably have little effect on the renter. Herein lies the crux of the property tax problem for renters. It is generally conceded that renters pay the property tax indirectly through the rents, despite some recent claims to the contrary. The amount will vary depending on the size of the property tax, and may be as high as 25-30 per-

cent of the rent. A commonly used percentage when designing rebates for renters is 20 percent, which amounts to $600 per year on a rental of $250.

The renter is disadvantaged by the property tax structure in several ways. First, many states and localities have homeowners' property tax exemptions which do not accrue to landlords and would in any case not be passed on to renters. Second, increases in property tax from higher rates or assessment will be easily passed on to tenants, but decreases are not likely to lead to lower rents in a tight housing market. Third, property taxes are likely to be higher in the big cities, where renters predominate, than in outlying homeowner areas. Fourth, housing costs as a percentage of income tend to be higher for renters insofar as their incomes are lower than homeowners as a group, and therefore they will pay a higher percentage of their income in property taxes. The only place the renter may be at an advantage is in a slack housing market, where landlords cannot charge the full amount of the property tax to the renter or pass on increases in the property tax. However, in these days of housing shortages, slack housing markets are few and far between.

Providing Renter Relief

Since recent tax-cutting efforts have focused on the property tax, it is here where the most difficult prob-

lems arise with regard to the distribution of renter relief. How can renters share the benefits of property tax reduction, since such reduction is directed to owners, not to renters? Or, what other changes in tax law could be made to benefit renters directly, to give them some rough equivalence with homeowners? This problem arises not only with property tax slashing measures like Proposition 13, but also in cities which attempt to replace some portion of property taxes with other taxes or charges. The renters pay the new taxes or fees, but do not benefit from relief accorded the property owners.

In the absence of some form of rent control provisions which require the pass-through of any cost savings, it is very difficult to force landlords to pass through property tax reductions. And while property tax savings may lower the amount of rent which a landlord has to charge in order to maintain cash flow requirements, such a savings will be reflected in a greater capitalized value of the property. When the property is sold, it will be sold at a higher value which reflects its increased stream of future earnings as a result of the property tax savings. Thus the reductions will not benefit renters in any case, since the carrying costs on the building will be higher.

After the passage of Proposition 13 in California, legislation was introduced to require statewide rent rollbacks equal to 80 percent of the landlord's property tax savings, to be effective for a one-year period. While the legislation failed, similar measures were put on the ballot in several cities and passed. These measures were generally self-enforcing, and were based on the fact that the amount of savings was easily determinable by the tenant if the landlord disclosed false information. While these rollback measures are temporary, they have succeeded in some cases in requiring a sharing of property tax savings through temporary reductions in rent. However, without continued stabilization efforts, the tax savings could potentially be recaptured by the landlord.

A second means of improving renters relative tax position has been the attempt to "disaggregate" rent and taxes. Disaggregation involves dividing up the rent into its tax and nontax components, for the purpose of allowng the renter to deduct property taxes from state and federal income taxes. This approach is discussed by Peter Marcuse in **The McKinsey Report: Toward a New Deal for Renters**. In the summer of 1978 the state of New York adjusted legislation allowing the state's renters to deduct property taxes on their federal—but not their state—income taxes. **Bill Let's Renters Take Deductions**, from the Associated Press, reports on the bill's approval by the Assembly and Harrison Rainie's **Governor Signs $120 Million Renters' Tax Cut** reports its signature into law by Governor Carey. **Renters: No Break on Taxes**, by Kenneth R. Harney, reports that the I.R.S. later rejected this plan. A disaggregation proposal in California is contrasted unfavorably with legislation providing renters with refundable income tax credits in **Remembering California's Forgotten Taxpayers** by Jonathan Lewis

and Steven Spencer.

As Marcuse notes, disaggregation helps to eliminate some of the inequities between homeowners and renters. However, Lewis and Spencer point out that this policy only helps those renters who have incomes substantial enough to itemize deductions, and puts them at an even greater advantage than their moderate income counterparts in the absence of other relief mechanisms. There are other problems with this policy. A true disaggregation policy would also include interest payments on the mortgage which are also presumably paid by the tenant. Such a proposal, of course, would involve tenants too intimately with the financial arrangements of their housing and therefore would be strongly resisted by landlords. An additional political problem, of course, is the way such proposals divide renters—deductibility for the middle-class may weaken the general strength of organized renters pressuring for reforms. Third, property tax deductibility for renters perpetuates and strengthens the current use of the deductibility system which gives the most relief to the highest income taxpayers, when in fact other general reform alternatives may be more desirable.

A refundable renters credit may be the best way of distributing tax benefits to renters, though it too has its problems. The renters credit can either be flat rate or variable, and involves simply giving a credit on the income tax to those who are renters. Refundability is a key to the progressivity of this proposal. Renters must be able to receive a direct check from the state even if they have no tax liability, or if the size of the credit is greater than their liability. In such cases, the credit is intended in lieu of other tax relief, and the income tax becomes the vehicle to provide it.

The size of the renters credit will depend on the policy purposes it is intended to serve and, of course, the dollars available for tax relief. It may be designed to be the dollar equivalent of homestead exemptions, or the value of homeowner property tax and interest deductions, or the amount of property tax relief. Whatever the justification, it will be no larger than political will and available funding dictate.

A flat renters credit simply provides the same credit or payment to all renters. It will be progressive as long as it is refundable, since it will provide the same dollar amount relief to the taxpayer regardless of income. Use of the circuitbreaker for property tax relief is discussed in Chapter 7 above. It provides variable relief for renters based on the relationship between income and rent. Since lower income persons will pay a higher percentage of their incomes in rent, this approach is progressive among renters as well as generally among income levels.

A refundable renter credit has some difficulties from a policy standpoint. Determining the appropriate amount of relief involves a substantial amount of averaging, so that some renters may be hurt or benefitted disproportionately. Unrelated renters sharing a unit will cause either administrative or financial problems for the credit. If the renter credit is small (e.g., $50), each renter may reasonably

138

receive such a credit. But when the amount is larger (e.g., $150 or more), the credit will more logically be restricted to one per unit and divided up among individuals. The problem then becomes one of enforcement and administration, though it is arguably no more difficult to enforce than other provisions of the law which rely on the relative good faith of the taxpayer. A third problem is that property tax relief should in fact come from the landlords, rather than public funds as a renter credit provides. Finally, the renter credit can be captured by the landlord in the form of higher rent, leaving the renter no better off and the landlord receiving the credit.

In other words, as long as the property tax is paid by renters through their rents, it is difficult to make certain they receive relief without government intervention in the rental structure. Disaggregation could lead to modest reduction in property tax payments for some renters. But there are no guarantees that landlords will not recapture that amount, particularly since tenants have been paying a previously higher rent level. Thus, some form of rent control system may be necessary to target property tax relief to the renter, particularly in a tight housing market. The exception to this may be a slack rental market, as mentioned, or a property tax relief program targeted to owner-occupants only. In the latter case, renters should be benefitted by some form of compensating credit, since the landlord in fact has no savings to pass on.

In the final analysis, the renter problem stems from interrelated political problems. Renters tend to be of low income, and therefore of little political clout in a system responsive to the middle- and upper-middle classes. They tend, in may areas, to vote much less than their homeowning counterparts. They tend to be less organized, particularly on a state level where their needs may be the greatest. They often have the goal of home ownership, and therefore do not attempt to make their needs for tax equity felt. And they do not possess the cornerstone of our tax system—the property to which tax benefits so readily accrue. But they are currently organizing as never before, particularly in areas where the middle-class is beginning to feel the pinch of the housing shortage. Should this trend continue, politicians will start to take note of the inequities, and many of these problems will then be addressed.

Relative Income Tax Burden of California Renters

The following table gives the income tax distribution for California renters (at least those who filed and claimed a renter's credit) for 1976 compared with amounts for all taxable state income tax returns filed.

Taxable Returns
With Renter's Credit
1976 Income Year

Adjusted Gross Income Class	Returns With Credit	Total Taxable Returns	% of Total	Tax Assessed Returns With Credit	Tax Assessed All Returns	% of Total
Under $5,000	11,999	67,159	17.9	$ 234,466	$ 1,680,054	14.0
$5,000 - 10,000	594,088	997,262	59.6	73,165,038	111,617,586	65.5
10,000 - 15,000	704,918	1,439,608	49.0	180,093,358	308,044,496	58.5
15,000 - 20,000	344,300	1,083,447	31.8	165,928,121	407,798,673	40.7
20,000 - 25,000	148,014	741,170	20.0	108,775,692	427,636,740	25.4
25,000 - 30,000	54,825	442,195	12.4	60,806,117	376,464,302	16.2
30,000 - 40,000	41,157	370,908	11.1	66,254,787	496,492,816	13.3
40,000 - 50,000	7,826	114,661	6.8	21,270,627	257,705,422	8.3
50,000 - 100,000	8,390	117,260	7.2	39,253,875	509,618,730	7.7
Over 100,000	1,692	28,416	6.0	26,062,353	462,498,169	5.6
Total	1,917,209	5,402,086	35.5	$741,844,434	$3,359,556,988	22.1

This data shows that California renters as a taxpaying group account for a larger portion of the total state income tax than total returns filed at lower income levels up to around $50,000 in adjusted gross income and that thereafter a fairly proportional relationship is maintained. The largest discrepancy in taxes paid over returns filed (9 percent) occurs between $10,000 and $20,000.

This outcome can be explained by the inability of renters at lower income levels to do better than the standard deductions, absent deductions for property taxes and mortgage interest characteristic of homeowners, contrasted with those renters at much higher income levels who can claim other deductions (sales taxes, taxes on personal property, interest expenses, contributions, etc.) which exceed standard deduction amounts.

Source: **Principal Tax Burdens in California.** *Task Force Report II-2, Commission on Government Reform, October, 1978*

THE McKINSEY REPORT: TOWARD A NEW DEAL FOR RENTERS

By Peter Marcuse

New York City residents now pay at least $250 million more to Uncle Sam each year than the average national taxpayer, simply because the Federal tax system punishes people who rent homes and apartments and subsidizes people who own them. Nationally, the amount of the tax break given to home-owners has been estimated at $9.7 *billion* dollars a year—a tax inequity that, despite its scale, is so widespread in its application that even Senator McGovern flinched from challenging it in his tax reform proposals. This inequity comes about because of the deductibility of real estate taxes and mortgage interest to home-owners, and the exclusion from their taxable income of the proceeds of their investment in their homes. (How this works is explained in a minute.) The existence of the inequity is generally conceded by experts in the field of taxation, but its full magnitude is little appreciated by the average citizen-taxpayer.

With a large majority of its residents rent-paying tenants, New York City is the chief victim. If it simply had the same proportion of tenants as the national average, the reduction in New Yorkers' tax payments to the Federal Government would be over $250 million (see footnote, next page). If *all* renters got the same tax break as owners now get, the total tax savings to New York's tenants would then rise to $350 million.

And even this understates the inequity. Tenants are in general in a lower tax bracket than home-owners. In New York, for instance, their median income in 1970 was $7,200, compared with $11,200 for owners. Instead of equalizing treatment of tenants and owners by giving them both tax deductions (which helps the higher-income owners even more), tenants would benefit if *neither* were given the deduction. The increased Federal revenue thus gener-

ated would be enough to increase everyone's personal exemption on the order of some $240. This would be a much more progressive solution, for even if tenants got a tax break comparable to that of owners, it would be of considerably less value to them because of their lower income.

What is it in the Federal tax system that produces these staggering inequities? Simply this:

The Federal tax system permits a home-owner to deduct local real estate taxes and even the interest on his mortgage payment from his gross income when he prepares his Federal income tax return. The effect is to *lower* the net income on which he is taxed. Such a deduction is not inherently required by logic or justice; it simply arises out of a Congressional policy implicitly favoring home-ownership. From the taxpayer's point of view, real estate taxes and interest are simply personal expenses, much like clothing or fuel. The fact that a tax deduction happens to attach to a real estate tax payment or a mortgage interest payment is, for the individual, simply a gratuitous blessing. For the homeowner, it is as if 50 per cent (or whatever proportion his real estate taxes and interest come to) of his annual housing expense were automatically allowed as a deduction to him. A tenant is permitted no such deduction, although he indirectly pays the same items as part of his rent. The landlord, who does get the deduction, has it as a business expense, which is what it really is, to *him*.

To add insult to injury, not only is the home-owner allowed to deduct something that *is not* a business expense to him, he is also *not* taxed on what *is*, in effect, business income. If a businessman buys a house as an investment and makes a monthly profit of $100 on it, after deducting all expenses, taxes, and interest, he must pay an in-

come tax on the $100. But if he himself moves into the house, he escapes tax on the $100. This is called his "imputed net rent," and most calculations place the loss to the Federal treasury from non-taxation of imputed net rent as even larger than the loss from the deductibility of real estate taxes or mortgage interest.

These inequities have not gone entirely unchallenged. There are, in fact, several proposals afoot at least to ameliorate their results. One, in New York, is a bill introduced in the State Senate by Roy Goodman and William Conklin (SS 9795) that would shift the real estate tax from landlord to tenants, requiring (with some technical problems) a corresponding reduction in rent for the tenant. In the Congress, Representative Ed Koch has introduced a bill to amend the Federal Internal Revenue Code to permit the deduction by tenants of an amount equal to the tax their landlord pays. A third is the possibility, perhaps not even requiring supporting legislation, of drawing a legal instrument between landlord and tenant that shifts the legal liability for both interest and tax payment from landlord to tenant. It would, in effect, make the tenant the legal "owner" of his unit for the period of his occupancy, with the landlord repurchasing it at the termination of occupancy at such a price that the economic consequences of the real tenancy arrangement would be carried forward. (The Internal Revenue Service might look dubiously at such a document.)

One of the more elegant of the recent proposals dealing with the problem is one put forward by McKinsey and Com-

Most figures in this article are estimates from the limited data available, and rounded off on the conservative side. The McKinsey and Company figures cited here are based on their own calculations, based in some cases on original data and on calculations developed by them.

pany, the well-known consulting firm, in a short report prepared for the city's Bureau of the Budget. It is a plan that would benefit the tenant slightly but achieve a major bonus for the treasury of the City of New York—a not surprising objective, since McKinsey was hired by the City to examine its tax situation.

The plan starts with a variation on the Goodman-Conklin-Koch approach: drop the real-estate tax on landlords, assess the same tax instead against tenants, and then provide that the landlord shall collect it from the tenant and pay it to the city. The beauty of the idea is that the landlord and the city are in the same position as before, but the tenants have picked up a deduction for income tax purposes worth, McKinsey calculates, about $107 per year for a family of four with a $7,000 annual income in New York City; $231 a year for a $17,500 family; $480 to a $27,500 family—these are all *after-tax cash savings*, not before-tax. The larger the family—thus, generally, the higher its rent—the greater the in-pocket cash savings. For example, for a tenant earning $12,500 the savings are $108 for a one-person household, but $174 for a six-person household, if each pays a typical rent for an uncontrolled unit.

Now add one more wrinkle, since McKinsey is working for the City of New York, not the National Tenants Organization. Impose a city tax (McKinsey calls it a "recoupment" tax) on the savings that each tenant would realize on his Federal income tax. The simplest plan, of course, is to make the city recoupment tax directly proportional to the Federal tax savings; McKinsey estimates that if the city taxes 80 per cent of the savings, it would make $131.2 million a year on the plan!

A more beautiful way of increasing city tax revenues could not be imagined by the most beleaguered Mayor. The city passes a simple ordinance, which provides a direct and tangible benefit to a large group of its citizens, and it recoups part of that benefit by a new tax that is simple, reliable, and incontrovertibly fair. And it leaves everyone better off than he was before—with the (locally irrelevant) exception of the Federal Government.

There are, of course, some inelegant flies in this inspired ointment for sick cities, but they might be pulled out without too much difficulty. The idea

of directly taxing the actual amount of the Federal income tax savings received by each tenant was originally rejected by McKinsey as administratively unworkable and excessively slow in producing such tax revenue. As a realistic alternative, they suggested a recoupment tax fixed at a flat 6 per cent of all rental payments, exempting non-welfare families (why tax *them*, since the state and Federal government pay most of welfare families' rents?) with an annual gross income of under $6,000. This tax is administratively much easier to collect and results in nearly as much tax revenue for the city, estimated at $107 million for New York in 1971-1972. But such a flat tax could actually increase the total payments being made by some middle-income families in the $6,000-$15,000 income range. After some hesitation, McKinsey is finally recommending that the recoupment tax be directly on Federal income tax savings, thus ensuring the fairness of the tax, perhaps at 80 per cent. The city could overcome the delay—at a modest price—by selling tax anticipation notes, and McKinsey believes it has, or can, work out satisfactorily the administrative problems.

Some allocation formula has to be worked out for determining how much of the landlord's former real property taxes each tenant would pay in a multi-family building. McKinsey suggests making it proportional to the gross rent paid, certainly a simple method of handling the problem, if not necessarily the fairest. The city should not assume any increased burden of collection, or risk of noncollectibility, by shifting the tax from the landlord to the tenant; McKinsey suggests leaving the landlord secondarily liable for taxes. As a matter of fact, they whisper the suggestion that the landlord could be considered an agent or trustee for the state in collecting real property taxes from tenants, and be made criminally liable if he breached his trust by not remitting to the city taxes he had collected from tenants, thus strengthening rather than weakening existing enforcement procedures! The possible effect of such a procedure in slowing down the abandonment process is also hinted at.

The right to contest taxes would be given theoretically to a much larger number of people under the plan, and this could cause administrative problems. The report suggests that a 50 per cent consensus of tenants in a building

might be required before a real property tax appeal for that building could be initiated, but that once initiated, the costs and benefits would be shared equally among all tenants.

Some problems are not spelled out in McKinsey's report. There is some danger that landlords might take advantage of the imposition of the new tax to raise rents. The plan itself neither justifies nor impedes such a rent increase. As long as rent control in some form exists, increases presumably could not be justified, since there is no real additional cost to the landlord. Apart from rent control, whatever forces produce the existing rent structure would have to be relied upon to avoid any additional burden on tenants.

Other effects of the plan are not dealt with in the McKinsey report. Clearly, as among tenants, its immediate impact is regressive. The deduction made available to high-income taxpayers is greater than that to lower-income ones. Since the recoupment tax only takes a percentage of the savings, it too will be regressive.

On the other hand, the plan is progressive in three ways. First, it makes available to rent-payers some of the deduction benefits already available to home-owners. It thus reduces the heavily regressive features of the existing tax preferences for home-owners. Equally important, the plan really constitutes a form of unilateral revenue sharing between cities, now heavily dependent on regressive real property taxes, and the Federal Government, the major beneficiary of the more progressive income taxes. If we assume the Federal Government will raise tax rates enough to compensate for its loss, and the cities in turn will not raise real estate taxes, the net result would be a shift from a less to a more progressive tax. Finally, the distribution of the benefit will, for a change, favor those cities with a high level of multi-family occupancy—New York's is 87 per cent, compared with a national average of 27 per cent. The overwhelming odds are that cities with the largest numbers of poor will be the ones most benefited by the plan.

There is one final wrinkle to the McKinsey plan. If the recoupment tax is itself deductible on his income tax return, the benefit to the tenant and the possible level of recoupment might be even higher. In other words, taking the

New York City example, the city could, by the simple shift in the incidence of the real property tax, do the Federal Government out of $164 million saved by those benefiting from the plan. These beneficiaries would deduct $131.2 million of that total from their Federal tax, even further increasing the loss to the national treasury, and even further increasing the amount that the city could justifiably corral.

The plan might require a change in the Internal Revenue Code; the McKinsey report suggests that it would, although if the tax were properly formulated it should be held deductible under the Code's Section 164. Payments under California and Hawaii laws imposing real property taxes on lessees rather than owners of real property have been ruled deductible by the Service. The situations may be distinguished, and perhaps an advanced ruling should be required. Senators Goodman and Conklin were insecure enough on the point to make their bill contingent on a favorable ruling by the Internal Revenue Service.

Even if the Internal Revenue Code now permits the plan to become effective, the outrage of Congress at being so neatly hung by the logic of its own favoritism for home-owners might find expression: McKinsey's unilateral revenue-sharing scheme, then, would not be countenanced for long. A political battle might well be the result.

As far as the New York State income tax goes, the authors of the plan simply take it for granted that the Legislature would prohibit any cavalier deductions for state income tax purposes at the same time that it passed the enabling legislation needed to get the Federal deductions.

Other tax advantages of ownership over tenancy are not touched in the McKinsey plan. The owner-occupant can still deduct the interest paid on his mortgage, while the tenant receives no benefit from the interest his landlord pays. Even more, the exemption from tax of the imputed income on the homeowner's investment in his home remains untouched. And perhaps there should be a local recoupment tax on the homeowner's real estate tax deduction, too?

But there is a limit to the number of ills one can cure with one remedy.

The report does argue that the inner city may be assisted as a whole compared with the suburbs, although the relative attractiveness of co-operative and condominium ownership might also be diminished somewhat. The deductibility of real estate taxes has always been one of their advantages.

So, the McKinsey plan essentially has two quite separate components. The first is the simple extension to tenants, as well as to owners, of the deduction from income taxes for local real property taxes by having them pay real property taxes directly rather than as part of their rent. It is hard to argue with the logic of that suggestion. The second component, in the short run, appears equally logical. Having given a tremendous new benefit to a select group of taxpayers, the city should have the right to share in the benefits it has itself created for them. The McKinsey plan is one of the most aesthetically pleasing tax schemes that have come down the pipeline in a long time! It isn't often these days that city governments are able to beat the Feds financially and logically at their own game.

But all this still assumes that the deductibility of taxes and mortgage interest (and non-taxation of imputed rent) is here to stay for home-owners. If it is, New York City should certainly do what it can to equalize the situations for its tenants, and it can hardly be blamed for planning to share in their new benefit. But the argument for broader reform is compelling. The regressive nature of the home-owners' deduction has already been pointed out. The implicit subsidy the deductions confer upon higher-income taxpayers is in striking contrast to the sums paid out to subsidize lower-income families who cannot afford decent housing at market prices: $8.7 billion to the indirectly subsidized higher-income each year . . . as compared to a *total* Federal expenditure on *all* lower-income housing programs put together (including public housing; Sections 235 and 236 lower-income housing; rent supplements; rehabilitation, etc.) of substantially less than $3 billion. If Congress wants to put $11.7 billion into housing, there must be a more equitable, efficient, and accountable way to distribute the equivalent of 6 per cent of the Federal budget.

Finally, the long-term but less tangible costs of a tax system that grossly favors home-ownership may exceed even its short-term unfairness. Some 73 per cent of our housing is today single-family housing. It is this form of construction that has created the mushrooming suburbs of megalopolis, that has eaten up open space, accelerated inner city deterioration, forced miles upon miles of highway construction, rendered mass transit outdated, and accentuated segregation by race and by income. Yet single-family home-ownership is precisely what the tax laws foster, since 93 per cent of all owner-occupied units are one-family houses. As the distinguished Douglas Commission pointed out, it would be almost financial madness for an upper-income taxpayer to give up the home-owner benefits of the Internal Revenue Code in order to rent. The entire system of tax favoritism for home-ownership ought to be done away with.

"The McKinsey Report: Toward a New Deal for Renters" is reprinted by permission from the November, 1972 issue of *New York Magazine,* © 1972 by News Group Publications, Inc.

GOV SIGNS 120 M RENTERS' TAX CUT

In a move that could give renters in the state $120 million to $130 million in federal tax cuts, Gov. Carey signed a bill that permits renters to deduct from federal taxes the portion of their rent that goes to pay property taxes.

"This bill gives tenants the same real estate tax deduction privileges as home owners . . . and won't cost landlords one red cent," Carey declared as he approved the measure, with Assembly sponsor Mark Alan Siegel (D-Manhattan) and Assembly Speaker Stanley Steingut looking on.

Federal tax authorities must approve the measure for it to go into effect, however, and there was no word from Washington about which way it intended to go. New York is the first state to approve such a sweeping measure.

"Gov Signs 120M Renters' Tax Cut" is reprinted by permission from the July 7, 1978 issue of *The New York Daily News.*

Bill lets renters take deductions

ALBANY, N.Y. (AP) — Renters could get tens of millions of dollars in federal income-tax breaks by using some of the same deductions now available to people who own their homes, if a bill approved by the state Assembly ever becomes law.

But the bill faces an uncertain future in the Senate. And some legislators expressed doubt during the Assembly debate on Friday that the bill would achieve its intended purpose even if it won final approval.

The measure, sponsored by Assemblyman *Mark Siegel*, Manhattan, would attempt to let renters take a deduction for property taxes off their income for federal tax purposes, just as homeowners now may do.

Siegel estimated that this would bring renters at least an extra $120 million a year in reduced income taxes, and perhaps much more.

The bill, which cleared 114-3, was one of the 43 mostly minor bills the Assembly passed before winding up an unusual week in which it has been working in the Capitol without the accompaniment of the Senate.

Siegel's bill is aimed at getting renters some income-tax relief out of property taxes.

Under existing federal law, people who own their own homes can deduct from their income the full amount of local property taxes they pay.

Renters don't pay such taxes directly — the landlords do. But the landlords get the money for them out of the tenants' rent. And since the property taxes are generally not worth much as a deduction to the landlords, the idea behind the bill is to let the tenants get in on the deduction.

The way it would do that is to make all tenants technically liable for the property taxes on the premises they occupy, with the amounts figured on a proportion established by the amount of rent paid. The landlords would be made "agents" of the local taxing authority and responsible for collecting the taxes through the rent check.

Siegel asserted that through this legal reshuffling, tenants would be able to deduct the taxes from their income. For those who itemize deductions on their income tax, their federal income tax would be reduced by, say, 30 percent of the property taxes paid, if they are in the 30 percent bracket.

Since about $1.3 billion in local property taxes is now collected yearly from residential rental properties, the tax savings could be considerable, even though not all renters itemize and thus not all would benefit from the program.

During a brief debate some legislators protested that all the paperwork would cost so much that it would eat up the savings, but Siegel said "if you want $120 million you have to do with a little work."

Assemblyman *Harvey Strelzin*, D-Brooklyn, said that "this is a hare-brained idea. This will eventually justify a rent increase of some sort. I don't know how, but it will.

"Bill Lets Renters Take Deductions" is reprinted by permission of the Associated Press, June 2, 1978.

Renters: No Break On Taxes

By Kenneth R. Harney

The Treasury Department tipped its hand this week on the politically sensitive question of federal income tax relief for renters. The message was not favorable.

Treasury is faced with the prospect of losing billions of dollars of tax revenues if renters are encouraged by states—starting with New York—to take federal deductions for the property taxes paid on their units, and the department has served notice that it doesn't relish the idea.

In a meeting this week with mem-

the nation's HOUSING

bers of the New York State Legislature, Internal Revenue Service officials indicated that they will rule shortly against provisions of a law signed by New York Gov. Hugh Carey last year that would allow New York tenants to claim federal deductions on the portion of their rent that goes toward real estate taxes.

The legislators had come here to press for an affirmative revenue ruling from IRS, a ruling that is technically required before New York renters can begin taking property tax deductions with the confidence of avoiding later penalities.

The statute—which would affect taxes paid a year from now—has been regarded as a national model for dozens of other states eager to enact tax relief measures for apartment dwellers. The law requires rental property owners throughout New York to function, in effect, as tax-collecting agents for their local municipalities, and makes tenants liable for pro-rata shares of the property taxes on their buildings.

Tenants would continue to pay their regular rents, but a portion of each payment would be predefined—on the basis of square footage of the unit in relation to total rented space in the building—as being attributable to the local property tax. Landlords would report the property tax component as income, but would continue to deduct them as an expense item for federal tax purposes.

New York landlords would neither lose federal deductions nor gain them under the plan; only tenants would be aided.

A tenant in a building who pays $500 a month in rent—25 percent of which goes for property taxes—could deduct $1,500 under the state plan. If the tenant were in the 30 percent federal tax bracket, he or she would save $450 on federal taxes. Tenants in higher brackets would serve even more.

About $120 million would be cut from taxes owed by New Yorkers to the federal government in the first year alone, according to estimates prepared in Albany.

State proponents of the law believe the revised assignment of legal responsibilities creates a legitimate, definable property tax expense for renters that qualifies under existing IRS tests for deduction of local real property taxes. Leaders of the apartment construction industry, tenants organizations, elderly groups and others vigorously supported the New York law as a long-needed redressing of the imbalance between treatment of homeowners and renters under the federal tax code.

Financial help for renters is necessary, they argue, to put multifamily housing back on its feet and slow the wildfire conversion of apartments into condominiums in many urban areas. Homeowners routinely get to deduct local property taxes and mortgage interest; they saved $11 billion in federal taxes last year as a result. Renters, on the other hand, receive no such direct tax subsidies.

Legislators in a number of states support the concept, and moves have been under way in Michigan, Minnesota and California to duplicate the New York law.

The only obstacle to all this appears to be the Internal Revenue Service. It, after all, is the sole party that stands to lose money from renter tax relief. And if this week's meeting with the New York legislators was any guide, the IRS intends to squash the plan soon.

In a private meeting, IRS officials said they don't believe the New York statute creates a legally binding requirement on tenants to pay property taxes on the units they occupy. Therefore, they said, it doesn't create actual obligations for renters, and the deductions aren't to qualify for federal tax purposes.

According to a spokesman for New York State Sen. Roy M. Goodman, "IRS pulled the rug out from under our state law—or at least said it plans to do so." IRS expects to issue its formal ruling next month.

Goodman said he wasn't certain whether to challenge the stance of the officials by appealing directly to Treasury Department superiors, or to devise amendments to the New York law aimed at getting around IRS's rule.

National proponents of renter relief are likely to look now to Congress, where two bills that would essentially accomplish the same thing as the New York law were recently introduced.

Rep. Herbert Harris (D-Va.) has 53 co-sponsors for his bill, which would allow a tax credit equal to 25 percent of any tenant's proportional share of property taxes for his or her unit. The credit would be superior to a deduction for lower- and moderate-income taypayers, who tend to take the standard short-term deduction for federal tax purposes rather than itemize.

Rep. Robert K. Dornan (R-Calif.) has introduced a renter relief bill that goes two steps further: it would permit a credit for up to 30 percent of the proportionate share of property taxes and would make the credit refundable back to the 1978 tax year.

Both bills have been referred to the tax-writing House Ways and Means Committee. The Carter administration and the congressional Democratic leadership probably will oppose the measures in this budget-conscious year, but pro-tenant forces say they plan to push energetically for the bills later this session.

Kenneth R. Harney is executive editor of the Housing and Development Reporter, published weekly by BNA Inc.

"Renters: No Break on Taxes" is reprinted by permission from the April 21, 1979 issue of *The Washington Post*.

Remembering California's Forgotten Taxpayers

**BY JONATHAN LEWIS
and STEVEN SPENCER**

Sacramento is confronted with a pressing economic injustice: the lack of property-tax relief for renters. How the Legislature resolves this issue will tell us a great deal about its sense of fairness.

Two rival renter-relief measures are vying for legislative approval. One, backed by the California Tax Reform Assn., is Assembly Bill 81, introduced by Assemblyman Tom Bates (D-Oakland). The other is Assembly Bill 15, introduced by Assemblyman Mike Roos (D-Los Angeles).

The Bates bill would increase the *existing* state income-tax credit for renters from $37 to $300. Every renter in California would be entitled to receive this refundable credit.

(There are two other bills that would also increase the renters' credit. Both Sens. Bob Wilson (D-San Diego) and Milton Marks (R-San Francisco) have introduced legislation to raise the renters' credit to $137.)

Roos' competing measure would also raise the renters' credit, but only to $70 or, alternatively, it would permit renters who itemize their state returns to deduct a share of the property tax on the building in which they live.

But only 17% of the state's renters would benefit from the deductibility feature of the Roos plan. That is because renters, whose annual median income is $11,000, usually do not have enough income or deductions to make it economically reasonable to itemize their state or federal income-tax returns; most simply use the standard deduction. For the lucky few who can deduct property taxes, benefits under the Roos bill would be skewed toward wealthier renters. Consider two hypothetical Los Angeles tenants renting identical two-bedroom apartments, for which the federal Department of Housing and Urban Development has established a fair market value of $443 per month.

If property taxes represent 10% of rents, then both tenants might be paying $44.30 a month, or $531.60 a year, in property taxes.

But a renter in the 5% income-tax bracket would receive only $26.58 in relief; by contrast, a wealthier renter in the 11% bracket (the top state income-tax bracket), would receive benefits totaling $58.48. This is hardly a fair distribution of relief.

The deduction scheme hinges on the hope that the federal government will recognize the situation of renters and permit deductions on federal tax returns of renter property-tax payments.

However, there is no guarantee that Washington will adopt such a measure and, in fact, many tax experts think it highly improbable.

In addition, the renters'-deduction proposal would entail more paperwork for landlords, government officials and tenants; calculating each rental unit's share of the property tax could prove a nightmare for all concerned.

Another inequity created by the deduction scheme concerns very wealthy renters who spend lavish amounts on luxury rental units or who have more than one apartment. In such cases, the deductibility of property taxes would further widen the gap between the relief afforded average and more affluent renters.

Though 45%—or 3.6 million—of all California households are renter households, renters as a class are at the bottom of the economic ladder.

In fact, 44% of all renters in the state have incomes of less than $10,000 a year. By comparison, only 13% of California homeowners earn $10,000 or less annually. And only 13% of all renters in the state bring home $25,000 or more.

Among people earning less than $5,000 a year, renters outnumber homeowners 3 to 1. Most of these renters with very low incomes are elderly. One-third of all renters in the state cannot afford to pay more than $150 a month for all housing costs, including utilities.

But despite their low economic status, renters pay for property taxes through their rent. Before Proposition 13, economists estimated that 17% to 20% of every rent check went toward property taxes. Now, an estimated 10% of every rent payment goes toward property taxes.

Despite the campaign promises by landlords, apartment-house associations, real-estate interests and Howard Jarvis, few renters have seen any significant rent reduction as a result of Proposition 13. Indeed, one of the major causes of renewed legislative interest in renters' tax relief is the brazen attitude of landlords.

Legislators, renters and tax reformers have been galled by the real-estate industry's failure to pass on any significant amount of its average 57% property-tax savings. So far, only communities with rent control have been able to ease the tax burden for renters.

The Bates bill, if it becomes law, would end the glaring maldistribution of property-tax relief in California, and renters would no longer be the forgotten taxpayers.

"Remembering California's Forgotten Taxpayers" is reprinted by permission from the February 26, 1979 issue of *The Los Angeles Times,* © 1979, by the Times-Mirror Company.

V

American cities grow relentlessly. The social and economic consequences of this growth have been as far reaching as the explosive increase in land prices.

The rapid rise in the price of land has transformed the nature and dynamics of both urban and rural life. Two groups of people have borne much of the burden of this increase in land prices—the urban low income renters or homeowners, and the low and moderate income family farmer.

The rising price of land has been created by the rising demand of residential and commercial developers and speculators. They have been buying up houses and open land at an accelerating pace forcing the price up constantly. The wide open "market" for land and housing benefits only the speculators and developers.

State legislators and city councilpersons throughout the country have been looking for ways to prevent "speculators" from reaping all of the profits from the present situation.

Speculative profits from real estate investments have historically held a very uneasy place in economic thought. Even the ideologues of free enterprise, such as Adam Smith and John Stuart Mill, had serious doubts about private profits from increases in land values. Adam Smith believed the portion of rents attributable to the land—ground rents—were good targets for taxation because they accrue to the landlord without any work on his part. John Stuart Mill considered land gains as part of a large category of "unearned" income which he believed should be taxed at a higher rate than "earned" income.

The classical argument for taxing increases in land values has been on the basis of cause and effect. Proponents argue that land usually increases in value, not because of what the landowner does, but because of things that society does, such as the repair or extension of roads, the creation of mass transit systems, the building of a new school, or the construction of a bridge or interchange. Since the increase in land value is not due to the landowner, the increased value—or some portion of it—should accrue to the society that increased the value. This principle was the guiding one for Henry George, the 19th century political economist, who wanted to eliminate all taxes, save one on land.

The source of the current interest in land speculation comes primarily not from theory, but the actual problems created by real estate speculation and ac-

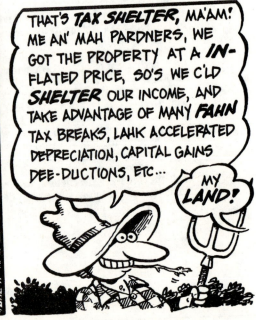

146

Taxes and Land Use

By Lee Webb

celerating land prices. As mentioned before, these problems have both an urban and rural dimension.

In a number of cities across the country, the renewed interest in urban housing on the part of young professionals has put enormous pressure on a limited housing supply. The result has been constantly accelerating prices, putting home ownership as well as rental housing out of the reach of all but the affluent. Speculators of all types move into this already difficult situation and make it much worse. They buy up scores of houses, make minor rehabilitation and sell them at much greater prices. These high housing prices are reflected in higher tax assessments for that property and surrounding property, putting an enormous financial burden on these middle and low income families which are trying to stay. In addition, the rapidly rising prices that speculators and developers must pay for multi-family units means that rents must rise after each new purchase in order to finance the longer mortgage.

In rural states, the speculative pressure on land prices comes from two sources. On the one hand in states such as Vermont, New Hampshire, Oregon, Montana and other "vacation" states, affluent city dwellers are buying up old farms or land for second homes or vacation retreats. They are able and willing to pay a much higher price for the farm than it is worth as a producing farm.

The consequence is that the farmland is lost from production. But equally important, the local tax asessor will increase the assessment of nearby farms and land to the level that the out-of-staters had paid for the first farm. The resulting higher property taxes put a heavier burden on still operating farms, slowly forcing them into debt and out of farming.

The land speculator accelerates this cycle. He often buys up farms, and then aggressively markets them— or pieces of them—to the affluent in the big cities. The speculators' profits are big and the process accelerates the loss of the family farms and farmland.

In other states, particularly those with very productive and profitable land such as Iowa, Kansas, California, Mississippi and others, the speculator is simply betting on and "touting" rapid increases in the price of farm land. Some farmers/speculators are less in the farming business than the buying and selling of farmland for short-term profit. The results are that land prices have gone through the roof, forcing taxes up on everyone else. The price of a farm has become so high that it is almost impossible for a

147

young man or woman to buy a farm and start farming anymore.

One of the first urban political leaders to understand this problem of land speculation and try to do something about it was Marion Barry, then a city Councilperson, and now Mayor of Washington, D.C. Barry in 1975 proposed a comprehensive anti-speculation measure that would tax rapid turnover of unimproved property at rates of up to 74%. It also required the licensing of all dealers in residential property.

In 1978 activists in cities in California took up the anti-land speculation fight in a big way. Californians had been hit by the incredibly rapid increase in home prices just as residents of Washington, D.C. Housing coalitions in Davis, San Francisco, Santa Cruz, Palo Alto, San Jose and other cities organized campaigns for anti-land speculation taxes. The passage of Proposition 13, however, stopped these efforts because it severely restricted cities' ability to enact new taxes. There is little doubt that urban land speculation efforts will accelerate as more and more cities begin to experience the explosive increase in housing prices first felt in Washington, D.C., and California.

Public officials and activists have reacted with equal vigor in rural states. State legislatures have devoted considerable energy restructuring their property tax systems to protect farmers and owners of open land from the effects of land speculation.

One of the most exciting and successful efforts to stop rural land speculation has been in Vermont. In 1973, the then new Governor of that state introduced and the legislature ultimately passed a law designed to stop the short term buying and selling of rural land. The Vermont Land Gains Tax, as it is called, included tax rates that were scaled so that the shorter the time that land was held before resale, and the greater the gain, the higher the tax rate would be. Similar bills were introduced in Montana, Oregon, California, Virginia and many other states—where the ideas are still germinating.

Many state legislatures have enacted some type of direct property tax relief for farmland. From the first such bill passed in Maryland in 1956, interest flowered so that now 42 of 50 states have some type of farmland tax relief. The major form of relief enacted has been so called "preferential assessment" which lowers the actual tax rate on all farm or open land by taxing it on its use value rather than market value.

However laudable the state legislatures' intentions have been in enacting "preferential assessment", nearly everyone who has studied these laws agrees that they do not work. At best these laws keep farmland out of development for a few years. At worst they subsidize the profits of developers and speculators by lowering the holding costs—by reducing taxes—of farmland they intend to develop. The other main problem is that such programs are not very efficient—to get tax relief to those farmers who need it most, the states must spend a great deal of money in benefits to many other landowners.

One of the most exciting new innovations aimed at giving tax relief to farmers is the "circuitbreaker". Two states—Michigan and Wisconsin—have already passed versions of this concept. It is modelled on the homeowner or senior citizen "circuitbreakers" which many states already have in effect. The basic principle is that the state will pay a share of the property taxes of a small farmer whose income is below a certain point. This type of relief is very targeted and efficient. Unlike preferential assessment the benefits do go to the people who need them the most.

CHAPTER 9

Protecting
Agricultural Land

Protecting agricultural land by new tax policies is becoming increasingly common in states and cities across the country. The type of tax legislation proposed varies enormously, as does the cost of the programs and the expected and actual beneficiaries.

The first article in this chapter, **Protecting Farm Land Through New Tax Policies,** surveys the history of using tax policy to protect farmland, and the major types of legislation which have been proposed or enacted. This article is taken from *New Directions in Farm, Land, and Food Policies,* and is strong evidence of the extraordinary range of possible new tax policies.

One of the most interesting and far-reaching proposed new tax policies is described in **The Progressive Land Tax** by Byron Dorgan, the North Dakota Tax Commissioner. Dorgan's proposal would require that large landowners would have to pay their property tax at a higher rate than small landowners. The proposal was designed to offset some of the disadvantages that small farmers face in competing with large ones. Regrettably, the bill based on the idea Dorgan described was defeated in the North Dakota

Legislature in 1978.

One of the biggest problems with most legislation which uses tax policies to protect farm land is targeting the tax relief to the land or the farmer who needs it. The most common form of tax relief to farm land is "preferential or use-value assessment". In those states with "use-value" assessment, farm or open land is taxed at a lower rate than other property. Benefits often go to all people who own such property, whether they are rich or poor, farmer or developer, whether they own a golf course or a pasture.

One of the most exciting new concepts is described in the third article, **Property Tax Relief for Farmers: New Use for Circuit Breakers.** The Advisory Commission on Intergovernmental Relations (ACIR) describes how the circuit breaker concept can be applied to "target" tax relief to those farmers who need it most. The article also details the weaknesses and problems of "use-value" assessment. In addition, it describes in detail the Michigan Farmland and Open Space Preservation Act of 1974 which established a circuit breaker program for farmers and owners of open land.

Protecting Farm Land Through New Tax Policies

By Lee Webb

State legislatures have been devoting considerable time to restructuring their property tax systems. These actual or proposed changes are aimed at two overlapping problems. One of the major problems is responding to the rapidly rising property tax burden of working farmers and another is the rising property taxes affecting all owners of open space, woodland, and farmland.

Many state legislatures have moved forward and have introduced direct tax relief for farmland. From the first farmland tax relief bill passed in Maryland in 1956, this approach has become increasingly popular. By the year 1969 a total of 22 states had similar laws, and as of 1976, 42 of the 50 states passed some significant form of farmland tax relief.

State farmland property tax relief varies enormously in a number of crucial public policy areas. All of the legislation has as its avowed purpose the modification of the property tax system to provide incentives for maintaining land for agricultural use. Many legislators are convinced that property taxes on farmland are much too high in relation to farm income. Tax reduction efforts also seem much more acceptable politically than state wide zoning or land use controls.

The states have chosen to modify their property tax systems by permitting that agricultural land be assessed at its use-value rather than its market-value. The use-value taxes are lower. The use-value of land is its value to produce food and fiber, while the market-value reflects its potential worth if developed as an industrial park, a golf course, a shopping center or home sites. Up until recently, most states required that assessments be based on market-value, thus forcing the farmer to pay much higher taxes, especially in counties where development pressures are increasing each year.

State legislatures have experimented with three basic types of systems for property tax relief through use-value assessments. The first is a simple "preferential assessment" in which agricultural land is assessed at its current use-value. No restrictions are placed on whose land is eligible and under what conditions. The second basic system is "deferred taxation" in which land is again assessed at its use-value, but if the land is later developed the tax relief provided must be paid back to the local or state government in some manner. Finally, the third system is the so-called "restrictive agreement" in which, in exchange for lower tax assessments, the government and the landowner sign a formal contract restricting the land to agricultural use for some designated period of time.

PREFERENTIAL ASSESSMENT

The nation's first farmland tax relief program is a good example of "preferential assessment." *The Maryland Preferential Assessment Law of 1956* makes all agricultural and open land eligible for assessment at use-value rather than market-value. Any landowner is eligible for the program, be they farmer, executive, or developer. A problem with this legislation is that there are no income limitations and also no requirements for payback if the land is eventually developed. Landowners, particularly near developing areas, can get large financial benefits from the program.

Criticism of the Maryland law has been growing. Developers, rather than working farmers, are getting the major financial benefits from the program. Developers are buying farmland they intend to develop, but while waiting for the market to rise, they graze a few cows or rent land out to local farmers and thus qualify for the lower assessment. Since there are no penalties if the land is later developed, the developer loses nothing from converting the agricultural land into a shopping center or suburban development.

DEFERRED TAXATION

Both the Massachusetts and the Pennsylvania laws meet some of the deficiencies of the Maryland law. Both are good examples of the system of "deferred taxation." *The Massachusetts Farmland Assessment Act of 1973* provides for taxation of both farmland and forestland at use-value. This is similar to the Maryland law. However, if the land is converted to uses other than agriculture, a conveyance tax is assessed on the sale price of the land. In addition, the seller of the land must pay "roll back" taxes equal to the difference between what the taxes would have been on the land at market-value and the actual taxes paid. The roll back taxes would cover the current and four preceding years.

The Pennsylvania Farmland and Forest Land Assessment Act of 1974 is similar to the Massachusetts bill. However, the roll back tax penalty is even more severe. If a landowner eventually develops land that had received lower taxes under this Act, he must pay the unpaid taxes for the current year and six previous years, plus 6% interest on those unpaid taxes. In addition, the roll back taxes become a lien on the property until paid.

RESTRICTIVE AGREEMENTS

The California Land Conservation Act of 1965, also known as the "Williamson Act," is an example of the "restrictive agreement" system. Basically, the act permits local governments to contract with landowners who agree to use their land only for agricultural purposes. In exchange, the landowners are taxed at use-value rather than market-value. The normal term of these contracts is ten years, renewable annually unless specifically cancelled by either party. If the landowner develops the land while the contract is in effect, he pays a substantial penalty. If he decides not to renew the 10 year contract, the assessment on his land gradually increases to market value.

On its surface the "Williamson Act" appears successful as contracts cover over 4.4 million acres of land or 40.4% of California's taxes. A recent study, however, revealed that the great majority of the land enjoying the lower taxes is far from the major cities and is not seriously threatened by development. Corporate farms and large land owners appear to have been the major beneficiaries of the law.

One of the major problems of all farmland tax relief programs has been the question of who ends up paying the taxes that farmers no longer will be paying. Most states' farm tax relief programs, in effect, turn over the operation and financing of these programs to local governments. By reducing property taxes on farmland or open space, counties or towns are in fact increasing property taxes on homeowners or on industrial or commercial property. The increased property tax payments by homeowners has been a major source of popular opposition to local government's implementation of farmland property tax relief proposals.

The Vermont Land Use-Value Taxation Act of 1978 takes the burden for financing farmland relief off the local homeowner. Under the Vermont law, local officials assess qualified farmland on use-value and market-value. The farmer pays taxes on use-value. The state of Vermont then reimburses the town for the difference between what the farmer actually pays and what the market value is. This interesting plan of shifting the burden of local farmland relief to a more progressive state tax structure may well become a viable model for other states.

CREATING AGRICULTURAL DISTRICTS

Superior to enacting property tax relief alone is to draft an overall program that includes farmland tax relief as one component. One of the best models is the *New York Agricultural District Act of 1971*. New York state farmers may petition their county government to create an "Agricultural District" as long as it includes more than 500 acres. If approved, the farmers only have to pay taxes on the use-value of the land. If the land is subsequently developed, the farmer must pay back taxes covering the previous five years.

The Agricultural District, however, gives the farmer a number of other benefits. Land within a District is strongly protected against eminent domain from any state agencies or departments. Certain local ordinances or regulations that might restrict farming are not applicable to land within agricultural districts. And farmers in the Districts do not have to pay any taxes for new public expenditures that would encourage development. The New York bill has served as a model for a proposed *Pennsylvania Agricultural District Act* which was introduced into the General Assembly in early 1978.

CAPITAL GAINS TAXES

States have also been willing to experiment with other elements of the tax structure to give tax relief to farmers. One of the most interesting innovations being watched closely by other states is the *Vermont Tax on Gains from the Sale or Exchange of Land*. Passed by the Legislature in

1973, the law's purpose is to reverse the trend of inflationary property values and to thereby slow down the increases in the farmer's property taxes caused by the significant, short term land speculation in Vermont.

Under the Vermont law, anyone buying and selling land within a period of six years must pay a capital gains tax on the profits from that sale. Individual homes and small lots of land are exempt. For example, if land is bought and then sold at a higher price within six months, the state tax is 70%. The rate of taxation declines annually, reaching zero at the end of six years. Speculators have protested that the law does not give them any incentive to buy and sell land for development.

The Vermont statute has encouraged legislators in a number of states to introduce similar bills. *The Montana Act Imposing an Additional Tax on the Capital Gains Realized in the Speculative Sale of Land* was introduced in 1975 by State Representative Ora Halversen. This bill also taxes capital gains from land purchases and sales starting at a high rate and declining to zero at the end of six years. However, the Montana bill provides even higher taxes in each category based on the percentage of profit the speculator made on each transaction. Legislators in other states have also introduced the *Virginia Land Gains Tax of 1976*; the *Oregon Tax on the Gains from the Sale or Exchange of Land in Oregon of 1975*; the *Washington Land Sales Excise Tax of 1975*; the *California Recreation Fund and Unearned Value Tax Act of 1972*; and the *Illinois Land Gains Tax of 1975*.

With the single exception of Vermont, no other state has a capital gains tax on land speculation aimed at protecting farmers. In this respect the United States is considerably behind other English speaking countries. Australia, New Zealand, Great Britain and Canada have used such taxes extensively to hold down speculation and thus keep rural land values from rising so rapidly. One of the most recent developments in this area was the passage by the Ontario Provincial Assembly of the *Ontario Land Speculation Act of 1974*.

PROGRESSIVE PROPERTY TAXES

Some states are also considering a "progressive" property tax. Under such a system, owners of large land holdings would be required to pay property taxes at a higher rate than owners of less land. At the encouragement of their respective Farmer's Unions, the states of Minnesota and North Dakota have been discussing what they call a "graduated" property tax. In North Dakota, Byron Dorgan, the elected State Tax Commissioner, is in the forefront of those discussions.

Another important area for innovation is in the overall structure of property tax rates. Most states have either constitutional prohibitions or statutes requiring that all property be assessed at the same percentage of value. Such prohibitions prevent counties, cities or towns from assessing commercial or industrial property at a higher rate than, say, residential or agricultural property.

Four states and the Canadian province of Alberta have "classification" property tax systems permitting the assessment of different types of property at different rates. The four states of Minnesota, Arizona, Alabama, and Tennessee are joined by two other states, Montana and West Virginia, which achieve the same effect by different means. In Arizona, for example, there are a number of different property tax classifications. Farm and residential property is assessed at 18%, commercial and industrial property at 25%, utility property at 40%, mining, railroad and airline property is at 60%, and producing oil and gas wells at 100%.

The obvious advantages of a sympathetic classification system have led a number of farm organizations and homeowners' associations to try to get their states to adopt classification systems. In Vermont, State Representative Norris Hoyt introduced the *Maximum Assessment of Agricultural, Forest and Open Land Act of 1975*. This bill would have required that all agricultural, forest, and open land would be assessed at 20% of fair market value, while all other property would be assessed at 50%. Massachusetts

Fair Share, a state-wide community organization, is strongly supporting a state referendum to allow the state to adopt some type of classification system to help residential homeowners and farmers.

ADDITIONAL TAX PROPOSALS

The states of Michigan and Wisconsin have tried another innovative method of using tax policy to assist farmers. Michigan has adopted a variation on the property tax "circuit-breaker" that had hitherto been used primarily to provide property tax relief to low-income and elderly homeowners. Under the Michigan law, a farmer is entitled to a credit on his income tax if his property taxes rise above 7% of his income. The other requirement to receive the tax credit is that the farmer enter into a ten year development rights contract ensuring that the land is not developed.

Wisconsin's *Farmland Preservation Act of 1977* is even more ambitious. State income tax credits are offered to farmers who are willing to participate in a detailed and extensive program aimed at preventing development of agricultural lands. The size of the income tax credit depends both on the household income of the farm family and the degree of their, and their county's, participation in the effort to protect agricultural land. More and more states will be intensively examining the Michigan and Wisconsin laws as possible models for legislation to protect farmland.

Finally, although no longer an active legislative proposal, the North Dakota Farmer's Union drafted a bill in the early 1970s which would help new farmers through their most difficult period of financial stress due to the enormous capital investment required to begin farming today. This program was modeled on a similar five year tax forgiveness given to new industries by most states.

Berry for the NEA

'We, in Washington, see prosperity just around the corner for the family farm. All you have to do is survive until the suburbs reach you, and you'll make a fortune in real estate!'

"Protecting Farm Land Through New Tax Policies" is reprinted from *New Directions in Farm, Land and Food Policies,* Conference on Alternative State and Local Policies, 1979.

The Progressive Land Tax: A Tax Incentive for the Family Farm

Byron L. Dorgan

INTRODUCTION

A mere mention of the "graduated land tax" will still make the blood boil in many North Dakota citizens who have participated in the sometimes bitter political debates on that subject in past decades. It was, according to some, a strategy for the preservation of family farms — and yet, to others, it was a radical scheme that would penalize farmers who were doing well.

The purpose of this paper is not to initiate a new heated political debate on that issue. However, a dialogue must begin somewhere on what to do about the continued disappearance of the family size farm, and this paper is offered as a vehicle to begin that discussion. To that end, the pages that follow contain an explanation of how the economy of an agricultural state suffers when family size farms decrease in number; a discussion of the disappearance of the family size farms in North Dakota; a review of the philosophy and history of using property tax incentives to assist in arresting the decline of the small family farm; a discussion of the progressive land tax concepts and how they have been used around the world; and some observations on the need for North Dakota to begin evaluating a progressive land tax system.

The Rural Life Style

Family farming is more than just a business. It is a way of life — a rural lifestyle. Adam Smith's description of old England as a nation of shopkeepers could be used to describe North Dakota's economy. Our towns and cities are made up primarily of small businesses, and the economy of these towns and cities is supported by and tied directly to an agricultural economy made up of thousands of family farm units that dot the prairies.

These family farm units support small towns and cities and together they create a rural lifestyle. For several decades, this lifestyle was considered dull and undesirable by many, and yet

Large Concentrations of Landholdings

However, in addition to the natural growth of the size of the average farm, there is evidence that the frequency distribution curve charting the size of farms has become skewed to the right with larger and larger concentrations of landholdings.

With more and more land being held in fewer and fewer hands, the average family size farm is having to compete with the awesome economic power of some landowners who perhaps have forty, eighty or even one hundred twenty quarter sections of land.

The sad fact is that family farmers always lose in that kind of competition because they don't wield the economic clout to bid for the next quarter of land to add to their existing unit if they are bidding against someone who already has a hundred twenty quarter sections of land.

The Census of Agriculture is conducted every five years, but it does not report landholdings in sufficiently detailed categories

to provide conclusive proof that the concentration of landholdings is serious. However, there is evidence from the Census of Agriculture that provides some clues about the shifting of landholdings. A review of the data from 1959, 1964, 1969 and 1974 shows the following about the number of farms in North Dakota and their acreage during specified years.

	1959	1964	1969	1974
Farms under 1000 acres	43,561	35,628	31,881	27,589
Farms 1000 - 1999 acres	9,278	10,635	11,343	11,332
Farms over 2000 acres	2,089	2,573	3,157	3,789
Total Farms in North Dakota	54,928	48,836	46,381	42,710[*4]

It can be seen that while the total number of farms in North Dakota has declined from almost 55,000 in 1959 to about 42,700 in 1974, a decrease of about 25%, the number of farms of over 2,000 acres has risen dramatically from less than 2,100 in 1959 to almost 3,800 in 1974, an increase of over 80%. At the same time, the number of farms in the 1,000 to 1,999 acre size range has increased by only 22%, from 9,278 to 11,332. In other words, it appears that the larger farms, those over 2,000 acres, are growing at a faster rate than those closer to the statewide average size of just over 1,000 acres.

PROVIDING AN ECONOMIC INCENTIVE FOR THE SMALL FAMILY FARM: A PROGRESSIVE LAND TAX APPROACH

While there are many factors influencing farming that are outside of the direct control of state government, the development of a property tax system that influences the growth of family farming is controlled by state government. Therefore, some argue that North Dakota should demonstrate, by the force of example, its commitment to the future of family farming by using this element of policy which is under our direct control to encourage the family farm unit.

Currently, the property tax, because it is a flat rate tax, offers no disincentive to large accumulations of land and no incentive to the family farm size unit. For example, under the present property tax system in North Dakota, if two farmers own property of identical value, but one owns ten times more land than the other, he or she pays ten times more in property taxes. The tax rate does not increase as the size of the farm unit increases. If, however, the large farming operation were subject to twelve times as much in taxes on ten times as much land, then there obviously would be a property tax disadvantage to accumulating more and more land.

In the United States our experience with progressive tax rates has been accomplished almost exclusively with the income tax, and not the property tax. A progressive tax in the income tax area is justified by the "ability to pay concept." There are some who argue that this same concept would not apply to the property tax because, although the possession of income directly reflects the ability to pay, the possession of property does not necessarily reflect the ability to pay. In some cases, that is a valid argument; however, there is certainly some relationship between the ability to purchase and accumulate large landholdings and the ability to pay taxes. In fact, the goal of a progressive property tax is to intercede in the decision by large landowners to use income gained from previous property owned to purchase more and more property.

Mechanics of a Progressive Land Tax

A graduated or progressive land tax would establish progressively higher tax rates on larger landholdings than on family sized farmland holdings. That way, the large farm operation not only would pay more tax than a small farm unit, but it would also pay a higher rate of tax.

A property tax system could provide tax discounts to the basic homestead unit while calling for progressively higher taxes on larger concentrations of land. In this manner, the system would not only provide a disincentive to the very large concentrations of land, but it would provide a direct incentive to the family size farm unit.

To illustrate how progressive land tax rates might apply, I have developed the following set of sample rates:

ILLUSTRATION OF HOW A PROGRESSIVE PROPERTY TAX RATE STRUCTURE MIGHT LOOK:

1. Up to $500,000 in fair market value of property, 98% of the standard rate for the county would apply.
2. From $500,000 to $1,000,000 in market value the tax would be the amount from No. 1 + the standard rate on everything over $500,000.
3. From $1,000,001 to $1,500,000 in market value, the tax would be the amount from No. 2 + 105% of the standard rate on everything over $1,000,000.
4. From $1,500,001 to $2,500,000 in market value, the tax would be the amount from No. 3 + 115% of the standard rate on everything over $1,500,000.
5. Over $2,500,000 in market value, the tax would be the amount from No. 4 + 130% of the standard rate on everything over $2,500,000.

[I have included the above example for illustration purposes only. The specific levels and rates for a progressive land tax would have to be studied at great length before enactment. A program, to be effective, must be flexible enough to allow reasonable expansion of family farm units without the threat of tax penalties, but it also must be tight enough to discourage the very large concentrations of land owned by one farming unit.]

In Theory, Progressive Tax Rates Reduce Land Prices

The economic argument for using a progressive property tax structure to encourage family size farming is that the higher property tax rate reduces the value of land, which reduces the price of land, making it more readily available for purchases by new or small farmers who otherwise could not afford to purchase the land. The large landholder is discouraged from adding that next quarter or section of land to his or her farm operation because the high tax rate makes the land less attractive as an investment. Theoretically, the price of land is reduced because "the capital value of an asset equals the discounted value of the expected net income stream."*6

Said another way, a progressive land tax should make land less expensive by changing the existing supply and demand relationship for land by serving as a disincentive for the large operator to bid on another expansion tract. As the large landowner's demand for more land diminishes, the supply and demand relationship for land is altered. When the normal supply demand relationship is altered by a progressive tax, land becomes more

available to family size farming units with less economic competition from the large landholders.

Of course, property taxes are not the only influences on land values. Many other factors may work to increase the value of all farm land at the same time the progressive property tax exerts some downward pressure on land prices.

Nonetheless, while a progressive property tax may fail to reduce the price of land in real terms, it may still succeed in its goal of discouraging larger accumulations of land by making persons who own those accumulations compete on more even terms for expansion tracts with the smaller farmers.

CONCLUSION — IT'S TIME FOR NORTH DAKOTA TO CONSIDER THE PROGRESSIVE LAND TAX

It is my opinion that North Dakota should begin a serious evaluation of the progressive land tax issue to determine whether such a tax system could be effective in aiding family farms in their struggle for existence. If that evaluation concluded that a progressive property tax system should be tried, then it should be initiated in a very slow and cautious manner in order to probe the capacity of that approach to assist family size farms.

To be acceptable, an experimental progressive land tax program would have to be implemented in a way that focuses only on those concentrations of land that are clearly threatening the family size farm units. For example, the individual who owns 110 quarters of land and is bidding on another quarter should find that a progressive land tax will offset the natural economic advantage he or she would otherwise have in acquiring that property when bidding against smaller farmers.

The question of what is a family sized farm would be one of the most difficult features of the progressive land tax legislation to determine. It is said that a big farm is always one quarter more than you own. The family size farm is not a monolithic term that can be applied to all farms in North Dakota. Different types of farming conducted in different locations of the state require different quantities of property in order to sustain a living for the farm family.

Most of us might agree that concentrations of land that approach 60, 80, or 100 quarter sections should be subjected to a marginally higher property tax than smaller farm units because of the natural economic advantage they already enjoy. However, when you move down the scale of ownership, the line is not as clear. I have not attempted in this paper to define the family farm, but I don't agree with those who say it can't be done.

Given some time, policy makers in the executive branch or the legislative branch could come up with a pretty good definition of what is a family size farm unit in North Dakota, using valuation as a criterion.

A progressive land tax would not prevent concentrations of landholdings from existing or even from becoming larger, but it would provide certain economic disincentives to offset the natural economic advantages that large landholders already have over the family farmers. I look at it as "evening things up."

"The Progressive Land Tax" is reprinted by permission from the Office of Byron L. Dorgan, North Dakota Tax Commissioner, 1978.

Property Tax Relief for Farmers: New Use for Circuit Breakers

IN BRIEF

Michigan has combined circuit-breaker property-tax relief with land-use legislation in an effort to aid over-burdened farmers and maintain open space.

At least 38 States now provide for some type of property tax relief for farmers; 27 of them tie it to maintaining open space; and 11 require contracts with penalties for violation.

Farmland and other open space in this nation has been dwindling as urban areas expand and land developers grind up the countryside for subdivisions, shopping centers, and industrial parks.

Farmers—on the average—pay a greater portion of their household incomes to the property tax collector than the population as a whole. In 1971, for example, property tax on farm property amounted to an estimated 7.6 percent of income while for the whole population, it was only 4.4 percent.

Thirty-eight States have some type of tax relief program for farmers. This year, Michigan adopted a plan that combines the circuit-breaker concept with tax relief for farmers and owners of open space land. It has several unique features:

- it is a State-financed program and thus does not require the nonfarm property in each local jurisdiction to underwrite tax relief for farmers;
- it ties aid to household income to avoid giving relief to those who are not heavily burdened relative to their incomes;
- it involves the State land use agency as an integral part of the program.

Background

The idea of property tax relief for farmers is not new—Maryland adopted a "preferential assessment" law in 1956. In the intervening 18 years, at least 37 other States have enacted as many as 43 programs—all under the heading of "differential assessment"—which generally fall into three categories: "preferential assessment," "deferred taxation," and "restrictive agreements." (See Table 1.)

Types of Differential Assessment

Preferential assessment implicitly is intended to grant property tax relief to farmers whose taxes have been pushed upward by pressures of urbanization. The local community underwrites the tax loss (unless State reimbursement is provided for); nothing is asked of the farmer in return. He is free to sell his

	Table 1		
States With Farm Property Tax Relief Programs			
States	Preferential Assessment	Deferred Taxation	Restrictive Agreements
ALABAMA		X	
ALASKA			
ARIZONA			
ARKANSAS	X		
CALIFORNIA			X
COLORADO	X		
CONNECTICUT		X	
DELAWARE	X		
FLORIDA	X		X
GEORGIA		X	X
HAWAII			
IDAHO		X	
ILLINOIS			
INDIANA	X		
IOWA	X		
KANSAS			
KENTUCKY		X	
LOUISIANA	X		
MAINE		X	X
MARYLAND		X	X
MASSACHUSETTS		X	
MICHIGAN			X
MINNESOTA		X	
MISSISSIPPI			
MISSOURI			
MONTANA		X	
NEBRASKA		X	
NEVADA		X	X
NEW HAMPSHIRE		X	
NEW JERSEY	X		
NEW MEXICO	X		
NEW YORK		X	X
NORTH CAROLINA		X	
NORTH DAKOTA	X		
OHIO		X	
OKLAHOMA		X	
OREGON			X
PENNSYLVANIA			X
RHODE ISLAND		X	
SOUTH CAROLINA			
SOUTH DAKOTA	X		
TENNESSEE			
TEXAS		X	
UTAH		X	
VERMONT			X
VIRGINIA		X	
WASHINGTON			X
WEST VIRGINIA			
WISCONSIN[2]			
WYOMING	X		
TOTAL	11	21	11

1. Circuit-breaker program includes agreement.
2. Circuit-breaker relief does not involve assessment process or contract process.

Source: Thomas F. Hady and Ann Gordon Sibold, U.S. Department of Agriculture.

land to developers, or to convert its use himself. Eleven States now have preferential assessment laws.

Deferred taxation on the other hand, requires that the farmer whose taxes are reduced while his land is used in agricultural pursuits pay back part or all of the reduction (the difference between the tax on full-value and on current-use value) when the land passes into non-agricultural use. Implicitly, this approach aruges that the increasing property wealth of the farmer whose land is appreciating in value is not to be ignored in determining ability to pay taxes, but that the tax on the increased value should not come due until the capital gain is realized. As in the case of preferential assessment, however, the farmer retains complete control over the decision of when to convert the land into non-agricultural use. Deferred taxation is provided for in 21 States.

Under *restrictive agreements* the community buys from the land owner the right to veto potential land-use changes for the duration of the contract (typically 10 years); the price paid by the community and received by the farmer is the difference between the property tax based on full-value assessment and that based on current-use assessment. Some restrictive-use contracts provide for recovery of the previously reduced tax amount and/or some other penalty if the farmer breaks the contract. The State of Washington, for example, provides for 10-year contracts and requires two years' notice of intention to have the land revert to conventional taxation (to terminate the contract). Upon termination, seven years' tax reduction is due, with interest. If the contract is broken without giving the required notice, the land owner must pay all the previous tax savings, plus a 20 percent penalty, plus interest. Eleven States now have contracts and agreements laws.

Some Drawbacks of Differential Assessment

In trying to achieve greater equity for farmers, differential assessment laws have complicated property tax administration by introducing the concept of "current-use" or "agricultural-use" valuation. These terms have no clear meaning. To try to restrict the benefits to "bona fide" farmers and keep land developers and speculators from cashing in, legislatures and tax administrators have to define, first, what constitutes farming or a farm, and then what the value of land is in farming.

Tests (restrictions) to be applied by property tax officials differ among States, but some examples are: use in agriculture for a minimum period of years prior to granting of tax relief; a minimum tract size of so many acres; a requirement that so much income (in absolute terms, dollars per acre, or as a percentage of household income) be derived from the property.

The income producing capacity of the property is a criterion for determining current-use value that is often prescribed. In some instances, actual income may be used for such calculations, but some States—to avoid rewarding inefficiency and penalizing efficiency—set forth methods for determining what income *would be* if certain farming practices were used, given the soil types, crops, and size of tract. In short, determining current-use value introduces considerable additional complexity to the assessor's job.

Restrictive agreements is the most complex of the three types of differential assessment to administer, but it is also the only one that makes any direct attempt to assure that land given a tax concession to relieve the tax pressures caused by development remains undeveloped. Reliance upon tax reduction almost certainly will not be effective in preserving farms and other open land because the taxes are small relative to the potential gains. It is not uncommon to hear of development pressures causing land values to rise to five or ten times the level associated with agricultural use. In contrast, property taxes typically are only two or three percent of the value of the property, and only a portion of this is waived as an inducement to keep the land from being developed. Even the larger penalties usually provided for in restrictive agreements law (vis-a-vis preferential assessment and deferred taxation) will often be quite small relative to the financial gains offered by development.

The Circuit-breaker Approach

The circuit-breaker aid avoids the latter of these drawbacks. It is a State program, so it does not reduce the local property tax base.

As its name implies, the circuit-breaker is designed to cut in when there is danger of an overload. Under most programs, when property tax reaches a percent of personal income considered an "overload," the household may apply for a credit against its State income tax. If its income tax liability is less than the amount of the overload—the frequent case—the family receives a rebate. The circuit-breaker is efficient in that it targets relief to those whose property tax burdens are greatest relative to income.

Thus, the local property tax base is unaffected. The relief is handled in a dignified manner—like any income tax deduction. And the program is relatively easy to administer.

The circuit-breaker was originated as a device to relieve low-income elderly homeowners whose property tax bill amounted to a percent of household income deemed excessive. Twenty-five States now have adopted such a measure. And five States—Michigan, New Mexico, Oregon, Vermont, and Wisconsin—have extended the program to the non-elderly as well as to renters. Of these, New Mexico places a relatively low limit on tax relief ($133), while the other four allow relief of $500 (except Oregon, where the ceiling is $490).

The Michigan Farm Circuit-Breaker

Michigan has one of the State circuit-breakers that extends to the non-elderly and to renters. On May 23, 1974, Governor William G. Milliken signed into law HB 4244, the Farmland and Open Space Preservation Act, to provide a circuit-breaker relief for farmers—and State-supported property tax relief for some owners of other open land—who contract with the State to maintain the land in its present use for at least ten years.

In signing the measure, Governor Milliken said, "The impact will be felt most immediately by those farmers living in areas of the Stte where real estate development is forcing land values up, but in a larger sense it will be felt all across the State and for generations to come as we reap the benefits of keeping food-producing land in operation."

Generally, here is how the Michigan Farmland and Open Space Preservation Act works:

The Farm Circuit-Breaker. Farmers receive a refundable tax credit for property taxes in excess of 7 percent of household income, which is defined as income from all sources (the same as under the State's general circuit-breaker act). By using the circuit-breaker rather than current-use assessment to determine immediate tax reduction, many administrative problems are avoided.

To obtain this relief credit, the farmer must enter into a development rights agreement to keep his farmland as farmland for at least ten years. The agreement—a detailed contract—must be approved by the local governing body and the State land use agency.

The State Tax Commission appraises the land. Then, the Department of Treasury administers the credit in connection with the income tax. The Treasury maintains records on the amount of credit granted each parcel of land, which it submits to the State land use agency when the contract expires.

If the contract is not renewed when the contractual period expires, the farmer must pay the State the total amount received under the program for the last seven years without interest or penalty.

The farmer may cancel the agreement prior to the expiration of the contractual period. If he obtains the approval of the State land use agency, he must pay the State the total amount he received under the program for the entire period of his participation plus interest at six percent per annum compounded.

If he does not obtain approval, however, the owner is subject to a civil penalty not to exceed twice the value of the land at the time the contract was made.

The farmer may sell the land without penalty if the buyer keeps it as farmland.

At any time, the State may cancel the agreement with the consent of the owner. In this case the farmer is relieved of any obligations to repay the State.

Open Space Land. Open space land is defined as any under-developed site designated under State law as:

- a historic site;
- riverfront ownership;
- undeveloped lands designated as environmental areas; and
- areas whose preservation would conserve natural or scenic resources including: the promotion of the conservation of soils, wet lands, and beaches; the enhancement of recreation opportunities; the preservation of historic sites; and idle potential farmland of at least 40 acres.

Instead of a circuit-breaker, on open space land separate values are determined for the development rights and for the land exclusive of the development rights. The owner pays property taxes only on the land. The State reimburses local government for the revenue forgone by not taxing the development rights.

The contract for open space property tax relief is submitted for approval to the local governing body. An unfavorable decision can be appealed to the State and the State legislature can authorize relief even after the local jurisdiction has ruled otherwise. The local government is reimbursed for revenue forgone, however, only if the agreement has been approved by the legislature. Thus, there is an incentive for local governments to reject open space tax reduction applications.

Planning. Planning and areawide coordination are important in the Michigan Act. Before approving an application, the local governing body is to notify the county planning commision or regional planning commission and the soil conservation district agency. If the county has jurisdiction it notifies the township board. If the land is within three miles of a city or one mile of a village the governing body of that city or village is to be notified. All these parties are allowed to submit comments before the local governing body makes its decision.

If the local governing body rejects the application, the owner may appeal to the State Land Use Agency, which exercises considerable authority over the administration of the act. The Land Use Agency also is empowered to promulgate rules for the administration of the act and functions as the State clearinghouse for the preservation of land. It is also directed to make recommendations to the legislature by January 1976 for a State plan for preserving these areas.

Wisconsin Farm Circuit-Breaker

Wisconsin is another State with a super circuit-breaker which extends to persons whose household income is less than $7,000 a year regardless of age or whether they own or rent their dwelling place. It also includes farms and other property up to 80 acres of land. (Other States' circuit-breakers typically restrict relief to farmers to the taxes on the dwelling and up to one acre of surrounding land.)

Conclusion

Property tax relief for farmers and the preservation of open space are two issues that remain in center stage for the States. Just since November 1973, five additional States acted on property tax relief for farmers. And others have proposals pending.

Traditional forms of property tax relief raise fiscal problems for the localities and pose questions of effectiveness for land use control. The circuit-breaker, combined with land use planning and zoning, regional coordination, and restrictive agreements with teeth, could be a solution.

For more information on property tax relief for farmers, see *State Programs for the Differential Assessment of Farms and Open Space Land* by Thomas F. Hady and Ann Gordon Sibold, Agricultural Economic Report No. 256 of the Economic Research Service, U.S. Department of Agriculture 20250. For more information on circuit-breakers and for copies of the Michigan legislation, write ACIR, 726 Jackson Place, N.W., Washington, D.C. 20575.

"Property Tax Relief for Farmers' New Use for Circuit-Breakers" is reprinted by permission from The Advisory Commission on Intergovernmental Relations, 1974.

CHAPTER 10

Taxing Urban Land Speculation

The skyrocketing price of land—one of the most important causes of the housing crisis— has stimulated many local campaigns aimed at stopping "land speculation". Such efforts have become very widespread in recent years.

The first article in this chapter, **Tax Reformers Go After Land Speculation,** by Lee Webb provides a general overview of recent organizing and legislative campaigns aimed at stopping land speculation. In all cases the mechanism is some type of tax on the profits from rapidly buying and selling land or housing.

The second article, **Myth and Facts About Real Estate Speculation in San Francisco,** was written by David Prowler as a leaflet for a campaign for an antispeculation tax in San Francisco. Although the leaflet was written about San Francisco, its description of the role of speculation in increasing housing costs and how a speculation tax would work will be useful in every community and city.

Restoring a City: Who Pays the Price, the third article, by Carol Richards and Jonathan Rowe, details both the problem of housing speculation in one city, Washington, D.C., and equally important, analyzes

the nature of the political debate and conflict around different versions of a proposed land speculation tax. The City Council of the District of Columbia ultimately did pass a land speculation tax.

Site Value Taxation May Be a Way To Stimulate Housing Construction and Rehabilitation, the final article in this chapter, is by Walter Rybeck. Although it is not about land speculation taxation, it makes an interesting argument for another useful innovation in the taxation of land—site-value taxation. Site-value taxation is a descendent of the ideas of Henry George, the 19th Century social reformer and economist. In a community with site-value taxation, only the property and not the improvements (homes, factories, office buildings, etc.) are taxed. Site-value proponents argue that the present tax system penalizes people who improve their property, and rewards people who speculate in open land as well as landlords who allow their buildings to deteriorate. A number of cities in Canada and Australia use site-value taxation and a number of cities in the United States have enacted it in a modified form.

Tax Reformers Go After Land Speculation

By Lee Webb

If you have been looking to buy a house in certain neighborhoods of many cities, the house will cost more than your wildest dreams. If you own your house, your assessment and taxes are rising faster than you can count. If you are a renter, part of your rent increase is going to pay the higher tax or your landlord.

Housing prices are rising very rapidly. In many neighborhoods, cities, and even in some states, like California, they are doubling every two years. In any other more "normal" areas, they are "only" rising 25 percent a year. Why the catastrophic increase in price? An important reason is simply that more people are willing to pay high prices to live in those certain areas. Other reasons, but less important, are the rising costs of labor, materials, and other factors that make up the price of a home. But another important source of the escalating prices for homes is *speculation*.

Speculators are different from most people. Most people buy a house to live in it. A speculator buys a house for the purpose of selling it. A "pure" speculator does not make any investments in his new property to improve or rehabilitate it.

In the past, housing policies both of cities and the federal government have seen speculation as a "positive" development and speculators as willing to "invest" in neighborhoods. Recently, however, housing advocacy groups, community organizations, and some state and city public officials have identified "speculation" not as a solution but a cause of the problem of high housing costs.

The City Council of Washington, DC, for instance, recently passed a tax on profits from short-term housing speculation. Sponsored by councilmember Marion Barry, a member of the Conference Steering Committee and presently a candidate for Mayor, the DC ordinance would force speculators to pay a high tax on profits from buying and selling housing within a short period, while profits from land or housing held over a long time would not be taxed.

California, however, is the site of the most rapidly rising housing prices, and it is also the site of most of the new anti-speculation measures. The San Francisco City Council is now debating a land speculation tax aimed at slowing down the increase in housing prices. It was prepared by the San Francisco Housing Coalition (944 Market St., Rm. 701, San Francisco, CA 94102). Unlike the Washington, DC, bill, which is primarily a tax on income, the proposed San Francisco ordinance is actually a progressive property transfer tax. The rate of the taxation varies according to how much the profit was on the buying and selling and how long the property was held. The City of Los Angeles is considering a similar progressive property transfer tax.

Another California city considering anti-speculation taxes is Santa Cruz. The Santa Cruz Housing Action Committee (1124 North Branciforte Ave., Santa Cruz, CA 95062) has written a bill entitled, "Real Property Documentary Transfer Tax," and has prepared extensive economic analysis of real estate speculation in that city to back up its support for the anti-speculation tax.

Speculators and the housing industry in California are attacking the proposed ordinances in California, claiming that cities lack the power to tax the profits from land speculation. The City of Davis, California, avoided this problem in the ordinance it passed over a year ago to slow down land speculation. It required that any person purchasing a home had to sign an affidavit promising that the purchaser was planning to live in the house and was not buying it for the purpose of selling.

The idea of using tax policy to slow land speculation comes from a variety of sources. Perhaps the most important is the 1973 Vermont statute, "Tax on Gains From the Sale or Exchange of Land." In an effort to slow down the rapid increase in the price of rural and agricultural land stimulated by the urban move to the rural areas, the Vermont General Assembly passed the nation's first land speculation tax. Similar bills have been introduced in Montana, Virginia, Oregon, and Washington, but have not passed. Although not joined by other states, Vermont's anti-speculation bill has served as a powerful example to housing and community groups in cities attempting to stop urban land speculation.

The California cities' interest in anti-speculation taxes has developed in the past year. Obviously, many other cities and states will consider anti-speculation taxes as a means to slow down the increase in land and housing prices.

The State and Local Tax Reform Project of the Conference has been collecting and analyzing information on anti-speculation taxes proposed across the country.

"Tax Reformers Go After Land Speculation" is reprinted from the July/August, 1978 issue of *Ways and Means*, Conference on Alternative State and Local Policies.

Myths and Facts About Real Estate Speculation in San Francisco

Myth:

The Realty Industry makes the claim that the proposed transfer tax will increase the cost of housing in two ways: first, by removing housing from the market, and second, by forcing sellers to tack the tax cost on to the price tag.

Fact:

The transfer tax will, in fact, slow down the spiralling costs of housing. The effect of the steep tax will be to discourage speculators from bidding up the cost of homes—they will put their money elsewhere. The true speculator will be unwilling to tie up his or her funds for the period of time necessary to avoid payment of the tax. Thus, the tax will affect the **demand** for housing (by speculators) much more than the supply. And the Housing Coalition's research clearly shows that rapid turnovers, of the type which the Board of Realtors contends will lower housing costs, correlate with **increasing** costs.

Any tax has two parts: the **base** (that which is taxed) and the **rate** (the percentage of the base which is paid in taxes). The Housing Coalition's Anti-Speculation Tax is written in such a way that it **cannot** be passed on to the homebuyer. First, because the tax is levied on the seller's profit, so maximizing the profit by sticking the tax on the buyer will simply enlarge the **base** and thus the tax. And second, the tax—which is 80% of net profit for a sale within one year of purchase—is too high to easily pass on. The Realtors are the first to point out that the market is not perfectly inelastic (that is, there are limits on what people will pay). A significant increase in cost does lead to a corresponding decrease in buyers. This, then, indicates that sellers have a price ceiling imposed by the market itself which prevents the "pass-on" of a steep tax.

Myth:

The tax will discourage home improvements.

Fact:

Any expenses which go toward non-cosmetic improvements of a home can be deducted dollar for dollar from the selling price. So a "rehabber" will not be penalized by the tax—particularly if the work takes enough time to put the property in a lower tax category.

Myth:

Sales are decreasing and a buyer's market is developing.

Fact:

Like most markets, the real estate market is cyclical in nature, so if it is true that speculators are decreasing their activity, they will return as the market cools off a bit. It may be that some speculators are hanging back at the moment, but this may be explained by their fear that the party will be ended by a transfer tax. The Housing Coalition's research shows that fully 40% of all properties sold in 1977 in San Francisco had been sold within the preceding five years. So any decrease in speculative activity would have to be pretty dramatic to stem the tide of increasing costs. Additionally, Bureau of Labor Statistics figures for housing costs in the San Francisco-Oakland area show huge leaps in costs every year—not the slowing or reversals to be found in a buyer's market.

Myth:

Housing cost increases are the result of inflation alone.

Fact:

The facts show otherwise. According to the Real Estate Research Council, the cost of a single family home rose an astounding 263.8% between 1967 and 1977. Meanwhile, the consumer price index rose "only" 180%.

Between 1971 and 1977, real personal incomes rose 16%. In those same six years, the Real Estate Research Council reports an increase in the cost of San Francisco housing of a whopping 147%. Inflation, overall, jumped 50% in that period.

The cost of properties which turned over more than once within the past year in San Francisco rose an average of 115% **per year.**

It is clear that housing cost increases, rather than resulting from inflation, are leading the trend.

Myth:

It is unfair to single out real estate speculators for excess profits tax.

Fact:

Speculation in housing is very different from speculation in other markets. Housing is probably your biggest expense, and it is a necessity. When prices in food items, clothing, art or textiles go up it is relatively easy to make do with less. But housing cost increases—particularly the large increases caused by speculation—are harder to absorb and the consequences are much worse. Housing speculation causes real hardship for **everybody**—renters and homeowners, poor and middle class, white and non-white. Housing is too important to allow the unearned profits of a few wheeler-dealers to price everybody else out of their homes.

Myth:

Housing cost increases are the result solely of foreign investors, environmentalists, bureaucrats, land costs, natural forces, or new households (pick one).

Fact:

All of the above **do** cause cost increases and the transfer tax will not mitigate their effects on prices. But speculators also cause rapid increases and the tax **will** discourage their involvement.

Myth:

People who **must** sell their homes will be penalized by the tax.

Fact:

If you hold on to your property for more than five years, the new tax will not apply to you. And if you must sell for good cause, the Appeals Board will exempt the sale from any tax liability.

Myth:

The Housing Coalition's proposed tax is illegal. It is confiscatory and a local income tax, prohibited by the Revenue and Taxation Code of the State of California.

Fact:

The tax is legal, according to the City Attorney. He says that the State **does** permit chartered cities to levy documentary transfer taxes, and that the tax is not confiscatory.

Article by: David Prowler

"Myths and Facts About Real Estate Speculation in San Francisco" is reprinted from *Public Policies for the 80's,* Conference on Alternative State and Local Policies, 1978.

Restoring a City: Who Pays the Price?

By Carol Richards and Jonathan Rowe

Block by block, private developers in Washington D.C. are converting decaying homes into elegant townhouses. Some see this restoration movement as a godsend, for it promises both to upgrade the city's housing stock and to expand the tax base. But there is another, less rosy side to the neighborhood rehabilitation: it has caused rampant speculation in residential property.

Housing prices, already among the nation's highest, have been driven even higher. And the overall effect is to force the city's poor out of neighborhoods they've lived in for years. Government urban renewal programs in the late 1950s and 1960s disrupted poor neighborhoods in much the same way. This time, however, there are no federal funds to relocate the homeless.

In a kind of reverse blockbusting, speculators comb neighborhoods on foot and by telephone just ahead of the restoration movement, making attractive cash offers to owners. If the owners refuse to sell, the more persistent speculators call in building inspectors who order expensive repairs on the old and dilapidated homes. Homes are bought and sold the same month, week, and even day for profits of up to 100

percent and more.

Often the speculators never even take title to the property but instead sell their purchase contract to a third party, a process called "flipping." (The term also is used to describe quick turnovers generally.) Between October 1972 and September 1974, 21 percent of all recorded sales of row and semidetached homes and flats in Washington involved two or more sales of the same property (80 percent within ten months of each other). Sixty-nine percent of these sales were in five neighborhoods. Moreover, many speculative transfers are not recorded.

Aside from the displacement caused by rehabilitation, the spiraling of home prices has its own dislocation effects. Tenants are sometimes evicted because they cannot afford the rent hikes that go hand in hand with the new landlord's high purchase price and increased property taxes. Since property tax assessments are based largely on sale prices of nearby properties, homeowners face tax increases whether or not their own properties have been improved; these higher taxes also are passed on to renters.

Some speculators turn the tax woes to their own advantage. At a city council hearing on property

tax assessments, a woman who lived on a street on which seven homes had been sold in two years testified that speculators had knocked on the doors of the remaining homeowners saying, "I understand your property taxes have gone up. Do you want to sell?"

Speculation is not new to the District of Columbia. Original District planner Pierre L'Enfant fought to keep land speculators from disrupting his plan for the orderly development of the city's neighborhoods. He was fired in the process. In this century, speculation and restoration started with Georgetown in the 1930s, went to Capitol Hill in the 1960s, and to Adams-Morgan, Mt. Pleasant, and other neighborhoods in the 1970s. In each case the pattern has been similar. In 1930, half of Georgetown's population was poor and black; now the neighborhood is rich and predominantly white. But it wasn't until the 1970s that community opposition in the District galvanized into resistance, or that the city itself had the power to do anything about speculation.

In 1974 Congress granted the District a measure of home rule, including its first elected government in 100 years. The 13-member elected city council has been faced with the problem of speculation and displacement of its constituents on the one hand, and the District's financial and housing problems on the other hand.

Washington has an acute housing shortage. The city's vacancy rate is less than 2 percent (anything under 5 percent is considered an "emergency" by HUD). In 1975, one estimate put the District's housing need at over 91,000 units. Much of the existing housing is in disrepair, with nearly half of the units over 35 years old. If these houses are not soon restored, they could be lost to the city forever.

Taxing flippers

On April 1, 1975, D.C. city council members David Clarke and Nadine Winter put a speculation bill before the council. Following the example of legislation in Vermont, Ontario, and New Zealand, they sought to curb speculation by taxing the profits of speculators. Their bill was a simple tax on short-term buying and selling of rowhouses with no deductions permitted for rehabilitation or other expenses. It was seen as a one-year stop-gap measure to allow the council time to develop a longer term solution.

Although the District is commonly perceived as merely a bland federal enclave, it is home for about three-quarters of a million people, who live in well-defined neighborhoods and who have a high degree of community consciousness. Clarke, a lawyer in his early thirties, was spurred to action by the speculation in his ward, which includes the Adams-Morgan neighborhood, one of the few racially mixed areas in the

city. Cosponsor Winter represents the heavily speculated Capitol Hill.

Because it was a tax bill, the speculation measure was referred to the council's Committee on Finance and Revenue, which is chaired by at-large council member Marion Barry. During the sixties, as head of the D.C. SNCC office and leader of the fleeting but feisty Free D.C. movement, Barry had been a chronic pain to the established powers, leading a boycott of the bus system and disrupting the Cherry Blossom Festival.

Now Barry is a leading D.C. Democrat and one of the home rule council's more influential members. Despite his radical image, the former chemistry instructor moves deliberately, particularly since he has been in the political arena. After careful — and to some, protracted — study, Barry and his staff decided that a more comprehensive approach to the speculation problem was necessary. What began as a six-page tax bill grew to eighty pages. The new measure not only taxed speculation, but required: licensing dealers in residential property; recording all transfers of residential property; registering vacant property; disclosing the seller's purchase price and costs to buyers of residential property. The bill also strengthened the tenant's right of first refusal under the District's rent control law by providing cash damages to tenants when their landlords fail to honor this right.

Barry, who says, "I like the tough ones," soon found himself in a crossfire gritty even by his own standards. On the one side were the District's real estate and financial interests, probably the largest private industry in town and a major supplier of campaign contributions in D.C. elections.

On the other side were community organizations from neighborhoods most directly affected by speculation.

The Adams-Morgan Organization (AMO), probably the most militant, had already picketed weekend showings of rehabilitated townhouses, had splattered paint on billboards announcing luxury condominium conversions, and had even prevented the rehabilitation of an entire block. The anti-speculation tax was the rallying point these groups had been waiting for. They were joined by their professional public interest allies such as Ralph Nader's Tax Reform Research Group. Included were some of Barry's early supporters, along with activists who in general feel entitled to a special claim on his loyalties and who have high expectations of his ability to produce change.

These organizations moved quickly to form a community-based speculation task force. The task force put out a pamphlet called "Our Neighborhoods for Sale" for citywide distribution, lobbied all the council members, and produced a draft antispeculation bill. Perhaps the crest of this activity was the council hearings in June 1975 when the coalition put on an impressive display of community support. Ministers, the teachers union, the Association of Black Social Workers, even the Afro-American Police Officers, all testified in favor of a tax on speculation. And a coalition-produced slide show on speculation upstaged the hearings.

The real estate industry was somewhat slower to react. Most directly affected by a speculation tax would be the "flippers" who buy and sell houses without improving them, and the "redevelopers" who buy old houses and repair them in varying degrees. (Often the same people do both.) The flippers and redevelopers were perhaps the last unorganized segment of the real estate industry. They are clever business operators whose office addresses are often tawdry mail drops in low-rent areas. They take pride in being "self-made" and genuinely feel that they are making a contribution to the city. "We're taking blights off the market," George Panagos, a long-time D.C. speculator and redeveloper, told the *Washington Post*.

In pre-home-rule days, these real estate operators had done as they pleased. Most lived in the suburbs and were little aware of the intensity of community feeling against them. The Clarke-Winter bill took them by surprise. Within a month of the bill's introduction, however, they had formed a $100-a-head Washington Residential Development Coalition (WRDC) and retained as lobbyist Chester Davenport, a politically connected black lawyer who was President Carter's transition man on housing and transportation and whose firm was the city's bond counsel. (The industry's contingency plan was to switch to a noted white litigator if the issue went to court.)

Choosing sides

The developing conflict raised issues beyond the immediate question of whether rehab should be encouraged. Political and even moral dilemmas arose as well. Foremost was the issue of race. In the District, "rehabilitation" is code for "black removal." When the *Post* real estate ads tout a neighborhood as "fast moving" and "up and coming," they mean that poor blacks are moving out and better-to-do whites (and some blacks) are moving in.

Questions of justice aside, black removal is politically ominous for the newly elected council members and mayor. The people being uprooted from their homes are their constituents. The young white townhouse owners who move in have different loyalties and little or no local memory.

The predicament is that not all of the District's 80 percent black population is poor. A solid middle class and pockets of affluence also exist. And at least some of the affluence stems from real estate. In the past, blacks had gained a measure of success in derivative activities such as brokering. As the market for homes in the city has heated up, they have begun to buy and rehab properties on their own behalf. As the newest entrants in the field, they are the most vulnerable. An antispeculation tax could knock them out, while merely inconveniencing the established white entrepreneurs whose deeper pockets, larger inventories, and firmer credit lines enable them to maneuver around it.

In addition, although most black renters and homeowners may resent the effects of speculation, at least some of the homeowners feel otherwise. They are delighted at the prospect of selling their home for a pocketful of cash or of having their neighborhoods upgraded while their own property appreciates in value.

As a result, stereotyped class and race roles have been confounded on this crux of self-interest. While poor blacks and their white activist allies come before the council demanding action against the speculators, the black entrepreneurs demand just as righteously to know how a black elected body can even consider taking away the piece of the

action they have laboriously, and against great odds, won.

Redeveloper Don Grey, an earnest young black with a large Afro, begins his testimony at council hearings with a reminder that he assisted Barry while the latter was head of SNCC. Beatrice Reed is the forceful president of the Washington Real Estate Brokers Association, an organization established by black brokers about 15 years ago in reaction to discrimination by the white-controlled Washington Board of Realtors. Reed makes speculation sound like black power. "We blacks will never rule this city," she tells a community forum in the auditorium of an old Baptist church near the 14th Street riot corridor, "until we *own* this city. That's what power is all about — *ownership*. What I do is helping my brothers and sisters to own their homes. And until we all do that, the whites will control us."

Long-time black residents in the audience had applauded and nodded in agreement as earlier speakers had torn into speculators. Now they applauded Reed too. Liberation means different things to different people and even to the same people at different times.

N ot all the black real estate entrepreneurs are happy about their role in the speculation controversy. Being portrayed — rightly or wrongly — as the antagonists of their own people is only one reason. Even more important is their relation to the white entrepreneurs. Although the newly organized WRDC is overwhelmingly white and suburban, its leaders pushed efforts to include blacks. Blacks have gone along primarily because their livelihoods are at stake. But they are sensitive to being used as showpieces by the white speculators. Finding themselves in that role is just the latest in the endless series of frustrations that have attended their efforts to earn a dollar in a way routinely accessible to whites.

The issue before the council became still more complex when the redevelopers' rebuttals made them appear less the phalanx of evil than they had first been portrayed. The expensively restored townhouses in the inner city neighborhoods had received most of the public attention, but the bread and butter of many D.C. rehabbers — especially the larger operators — were more modest improvements to properties farther from the urban core. A WRDC official testified at council hearings that of 1,500 units sold by its members the previous two years, the average price had been $24,500 and 90 percent of the purchasers had been black D.C. residents. According to the WRDC official, over 70 percent of the properties had been vacant at the time of acquisition. "I've sold two houses over $40,000 in the last two years," says WRDC president Jerry Lustine. "And most of my houses go to blacks."

Also, at least a few realtors and speculators were quietly attempting to help tenants themselves. Nathan Habib, a puckish, cagey man commonly labeled a "slumlord," has been selling off his properties to his tenants and "taking back the paper" (that is, financing them himself) without even requiring a down payment. In the Shaw area, a young broker named Richie Jones has been finding alternative housing in the community for tenants displaced by his transactions. He has also been trying to keep speculators out of the area by dealing directly with homebuyers. "We get better

rapport in the community by giving the homebuyers the real price" instead of a price jacked up by a speculator, he says.

While a few good apples cannot redeem a whole barrel, such examples tempered the good-guy, bad-guy melodrama that was important to the antispeculation cause. At the same time, the council's own posture was weakened on several counts. For one, it bears the cross of the D.C. government's own land acquisition activities, which have resulted in large-scale evictions and thousands of boarded-up houses concentrated in poor black neighborhoods throughout the city. "There are blocks and blocks of vacant land here and the government keeps buying more," says Joyce Chestnut of the Shaw Project Area Committee. "The speculation bill does nothing about government speculation, and the government is the biggest menace." This is perhaps the only point on which the industry and community groups agree. "It's criminal," says WRDC president Lustine. "The D.C. government should clean up its own house before picking on us."

These complications have left their mark on the bill, especially in its treatment of rehab. The original Clarke-Winter bill, by treating both flipping and rehab with equal severity, amounted to a straightforward one-year moratorium on redevelopment. Faced with heavy industry lobbying, the opposition of the mayor, and the reluctance of his fellow council members, Barry gradually modified this approach. First, he broadened the deductions for rehab expenses. Then he softened the tax rates on rehab. The emphasis shifted from stopping the redevelopment process to restraining excess profits and generating revenues to provide

low and moderate-income people with homeownership assistance. Finally, when his fellow Finance Committee members balked at even this modified approach, Barry had to scrap the tax on rehab entirely, along with some other provisions.

Competing causes

Even stripped down, the Barry bill is significant. His staff has found no other jurisdiction that requires the recording of all transfers of residential property (including contracts flipped to third parties) or that licenses dealers to the degree the bill does. And no urban area in the United States levies a tax on short-term buying and selling (without improvements) of residential property — let alone a tax in which rates go as high as 75 percent. The tenant's right of first refusal, and the disclosure of the seller's purchase and rehab costs to homebuyers are also trend-setting measures. Yet compared to what it set out to do, the bill is barely half a loaf in the eyes of its original supporters.

Will the bill, if passed, do anything about the displacement of tenants and low and moderate-income homeowners? The best answer now is, "Probably, to a degree." By curtailing flipping, it should deter the drastic price increases that impel the new landlords to raise rents, and that put houses out of reach of tenants and low and moderate-income persons generally. "I could have bought this place myself if they gave me a chance to buy it at the original price," said one black woman on a heavily speculated street on Capitol Hill. "But nobody offered it to me. And I sure can't pay what it's going for now."

In addition, by deterring flipping-induced price increases, the bill should restrain property tax assessment hikes, which will relieve the plights both of tenants who end up paying the tax in their rents, and of homeowners whose budgets are geared to property tax bills at prespeculation levels. A damper on flipping, moreover, should slow down the rehabilitation-displacement process somewhat, since it is the rapid churning over of properties that breaks them loose for redevelopers and creates a momentum that spreads through the neighborhood. It is nevertheless true that a property may be flipped several times without the tenants being evicted. Rehabilitation, however, means eviction. With rehab alive, evictions will continue.

Would a tax on rehab have stopped such displacement? The real estate industry argued that there are enough wealthy people looking for houses in the District to enable rehabbers simply to pass the tax along in higher prices. Alternatively, the larger speculators could hold houses off the market — perhaps keeping them vacant — for three years, after which time they would be clear of the tax. Then, after rehab, they could charge more to compensate themselves for the holding period. Either way, the real estate industry argued, the result would be a reduction in the number of rehabbed houses coming onto the market and a consequent increase in prices, making houses less, not more, available to low and moderate-income persons. Proponents of the tax argued differently, of course, and it is questionable whether the industry would have lobbied so intensely against the rehab tax if all that was at stake was higher prices for rehabbed houses.

The D.C. council was reluctant to tax rehab for a variety of rea-sons. The lengthy preparation of an ambitious bill gave opponents both time and openings for attack. Also, the council's principled stands on civil and human rights — a majority of council members were civil rights activists and tolerate few encroachments in that area — do not always translate into similarly progressive economic stands. But most important has been the lack of sustained grassroots pressure. The bill simply has not yet become a highly visible political issue.

The community speculation task force was really a committee of organization employees and leaders. Only one of these organizations — the Adams-Morgan Organization — was genuinely constituent based. The others were United-Fund-supported neighborhood houses and the like. Their proxies were in most cases valid, but they never established the ongoing community support that was necessary to turn on the heat.

As the issue dragged on, the task force wore down — a familiar malady, and fatal in this case. When people left, there was no mechanism for replacing them. The diffusion of the racial issue was also a serious blow. In addition, AMO was so offended by one provision in an early draft — an exemption for moderately priced rehabbed houses — that it went off in a corner and sulked, leaving the lobbying to the speculators. By the late fall of 1976, a week-long series on speculation in the *Washington Post* that would have prompted an angry demonstration at the District Building 18 months before provoked hardly a telephone call or letter to the council.

Among the leaders of the task force were several whites. The role of white activists in the black-majority District is uncertain, and especially so on the speculation issue. For one thing, it is difficult for white activists to invoke the same degree of outrage at black profit seekers as they do when the perpetrators are white. Then, too, white activists themselves play an inadvertent role in the speculation process. Many live in racially mixed, inner-city neighborhoods such as Adams-Morgan, where rents are relatively low and where speculation is booming. Their VWs and white faces calm the jitters of prospective home buyers apprehensive of such threatening surroundings, while their counter-cultural enterprises create an aura that speculators and realtors can exploit as a lure for affluent people on the search for urban chic. It is understandable that some blacks and Latinos perceive their white activist neighbors as accomplices in the very speculation process they are working to stop.

The positions of the two sides at this point compel a question. Should the antispeculation forces have started with a proposal more modest than a tax, which they could have won before their momentum waned? Some think Barry may have erred in expanding the original Clarke-Winter bill. "It would have been wise in retrospect to pass it" as originally introduced, Clarke said recently of his measure.

The industry has not been the only obstacle to the speculation bill. D.C. mayor Walter Washington, a cautious former housing administrator, has been cool to it from the beginning. "But what's wrong with speculation?" the mayor's city administrator Julian Dugas asked Barry with genuine bewilderment.

Despite these problems, the speculation issue is by no means dead. Barry intends to introduce his stripped-down bill early in 1977, and community groups, chastened by their setback, are regrouping. Whatever the outcome, a few lessons have emerged. The first concerns the limits of a progressive elected body. The D.C. council is probably as receptive to the idea of a speculation tax as any legislative body in the United States, but without solid constituent support it has hesitated to move. Also, the council members have felt intellectually insecure with the tax. It has not been made clear to them how the tax would remedy the displacement problem, nor what it would do to the real estate market generally, nor — and this is most important — what if anything would arise to take the place of the private speculative market. All sides agree that a tough speculation tax on rehab could doom the city to stagnation if positive housing programs were not wheeled quickly into place. Aside from some vague talk about cooperatives, these programs are nowhere in sight.

Looking nationally, there is a message to the Carter administration in the District's struggle.

During his campaign, Carter proposed a shift to rehabilitation as a source of housing for low and moderate-income city dwellers. Community workers in the District report that government-subsidized rehab programs have triggered the speculation and displacement processes in their neighborhoods. Without careful checks on such speculation, Carter's laudable approach could turn into a replay of urban renewal, with federally sponsored removal of poor and moderate-income people. And speculation could substantially drive up the cost to the taxpayers of any rehab programs.

Similarly, the speculation issue has flagged a hazard up the road for the antiredlining campaigns underway in many cities. Bank willingness to lend in a given neighborhood can add fuel to the speculative fires. Where conditions are right — a housing shortage combined with a growing demand for inner-city homes — a reversal of bank redlining policies could result in pressuring out the very residents the antiredlining drives have been trying to benefit.

What is most disjointing about the speculation controversy is the twisted face it has given to some cherished liberal causes. Investment in the inner city was supposed to be a good thing. It was supposed to be a good thing for well-to-do whites to leave the suburbs for the city. It was supposed to be a good thing to restore small-scale and often gracious rowhouses and brownstones in the inner cities, instead of demolishing them in favor of high-rise apartments or vacant lots. It was supposed to be a good thing for blacks to gain a piece of the action, as they have been doing in the District's active rehab market. Yet it was also supposed to be a good thing for poor people to develop pride in their neighborhoods, a sense of roots, and to improve their stature collectively from that basis. Urban renewal supposedly taught us the inhumanity of punishing people with displacement when their only crime was that they were not wealthy.

The clash of these competing causes has thus far left the poor the losers. If there is enough social and economic room under current arrangements to accommodate all of our good intentions in one small jurisdiction — the District of Columbia — the way to do so has not yet appeared.

"Restoring A City: Who Pays the Price?" is reprinted by permission from the Winter, 1977 issue of *Working Papers*.

Site Value Taxation May Be a Way to Stimulate Housing and Rehabilitation

By Walter Rybeck

If an enemy of society wanted to encourage blight and neighborhood instability and to drive business, residents, and tax base beyond the city limits, he might invent a system much like our present property tax. For example:

ITEM: Homeowner Jones installs central air conditioning. Neighbor Smith adds a rec room. As a direct result of these investments, their properties are assessed higher. Mr. Jones and Mr. Smith must pay more in property taxes, not only this year but for the life of these improvements.

ITEM: Neighbor Smart, across the street, lets his rented house run down. The roof sags; the yard is a mudhole; the paint is peeling. The assessor reduces the valuation of this eyesore and Mr. Smart's property taxes go down.

ITEM: Green Building Company erects a multi-family dwelling on a lot it owns, providing construction jobs, enhancing the neighborhood, and generating furniture business as well as creating housing opportunities. In return, the community requires the owner to pay property taxes that eventually will total from 50 to 100 percent of the cost of the building.

A tax that systematically penalizes those who put property to good social purpose while rewarding slumlords and land speculators clearly is not helping America attain its objectives of "a decent home and a suitable living environment" for every family, that elusive goal enunciated in the Housing Act of 1949.

Attention is now focussing on the disincentives of the property tax as one of the reasons that dozens of housing and development programs over the past decades have had limited success, at best. Site value taxation is increasingly being suggested as a corrective to those disincentives.

Under the site value tax, all new housing and existing housing is completely exempt from property taxes, as are all repairs and rehabilitation and all improvements on land for buildings of any kind. Abatements are not temporary on selected properties or blocks; rather, they are applied universally throughout the taxing jurisdiction. Site value taxation—or land value taxation—is, to some, a misleading term. Instead of immediately conveying the idea of *untaxing* housing and other structures, it sounds like a new tax, which it is not. What remains of the property tax after removal of the building tax is, of course, a tax on site values.

But current discussions of site value taxation do not concern themselves with terminology; they reach to bedrock issues. They have to do with the dynamics of urban growth; with how tax policies can be linked with other housing and land use policies; and with how the private sector can be brought into closer conformity with the public good.

Site Value Taxation in Washington, D.C.: Federal legislation of 1974 permits the city council of the District of Columbia to adopt site value taxation by imposing "different tax rates on land and on the improvements thereon." Former D. C. city council member Tedson J. Meyers, who played a major role in obtaining that option, said recently, "If the city were to make use of this legislation, I am convinced it would help bring back to life many of the abandoned, boarded-up housing shells in Washington. The property tax system now tells private housers, in effect, to squeeze out all they can while making the least possible investment. A site value tax would make these 'milking operations' less remunerative, shifting the profit advantage to those who offer more and better housing."

L. L. Ecker-Racz, one of the towering figures in local fiscal policy, suggested in the *Washington Post* this summer that Congress underwrite a site value tax experiment in the capital. "A meaningful test of how this kind of tax would work would benefit the whole nation," he wrote.

The District of Columbia's Finance and Revenue Department completed several valuable computer simulations of the burden shifts—who would gain and who would pay higher taxes—in a changeover to site value taxation. Dr. Margaret Reuss, chairperson of the economics department, University of the District of Columbia, summarized these burden shifts at a meeting of the Potomac Chapter of NAHRO in December 1976:

"Single-family homes would enjoy an average annual tax reduction of 11 percent citywide. Multi-family units would receive still larger reductions, 23 percent for elevator apartments and 39 percent for walk-up apartments. Lower-income neighborhoods would receive among the highest percentage decreases. This may seem surprising in view of the low value of their housing," Dr. Reuss explained, "but the decisive factor is the relationship of housing value to land value. In poorer parts of the community, such as Anacostia, the value of a house typically constitutes a very high proportion of total property value. In an affluent neighborhood, such as Georgetown, land values are remarkably high, absolutely and in proportion to building values, so many propertyowners would pay more taxes under site value taxation."

'Arithmetic' of Site Value Taxation: The computer simulations that produced the District of Columbia findings assume that as much revenue would be raised from taxing site values alone as had been raised from the traditional property tax. This required a bit of analysis and arithmetic.

First, it was determined that, of all taxable real estate, citywide, 60 percent of the assessed value represents building values and 40 percent represents land values. Thus, the current tax rate of 1.83 percent, which brings in roughly 150 million dollars of revenue, would be changed to a zero rate on buildings and a 4.5 percent rate on land values (1.83 percent times 100 percent equals 4.5 percent times 40 percent).

Any homeowner or propertyowner whose building values constitute more than the citywide average of 60 percent would receive a tax break under site value taxation. Buildings worth less than 60 percent of the total property value would pay more. Owners of vacant lots would feel the biggest initial pinch, with tax bills almost three times larger than previously.

These technical aspects are cited to suggest how any taxing jurisdiction can determine the first-year impacts of site value taxation. Obviously, because of different land-to-building ratios and different tax rates, the arithmetic differs somewhat from one place to another.

Experience to Date: No large city in the United States has adopted site value taxation. *Fairhope, Alabama*, has applied the principle since 1894 through a public corporation that collects land rent, using the fund to pay property taxes of the leaseholders and to finance public services. The community is flourishing, as is *Arden, Delaware*, another small enclave that has long exempted buildings from taxation.

Pittsburgh, since 1913 has had a differential property tax. Its tax rate on buildings is half the rate on land values. Local officials claimed this was a major reason that commercial development occurred in Pittsburgh during the depression years, when construction had come to a halt in most cities of similar size. But the differential rate applies only to the municipal portion of the property tax. The overlapping school districts and Allegheny County use the traditional uniform rate. As these school and county taxes increased, they reduced the overall land tax differential for Pittsburgh propertyowners from a two-to-one ratio to four-to-three—hardly enough to produce substantial changes in the local economic climate. Perhaps the main conclusion to draw from Pittsburgh is that this type of reform is feasible and politically palatable: such distinguished mayors as William N. McNair and David L. Lawrence vigorously supported the differential tax as an anti-speculation and pro-homeowner measure.

Harrisburg, Pennsylvania's Mayor Harold Swenson said the public was very unhappy, in 1974, with talk of increasing the property tax from 17 to 18 mills (i.e., an increase from a 1.7 percent tax to a 1.8 percent tax, or $1.70 to $1.80 per each $100 of assessed value). "I said we should keep the tax at 17 mills on buildings and raise it to 23 on land," Mayor Swenson recalls. "When David Lawrence was governor of Pennsylvania, he passed a law giving cities this kind of option. It was surprisingly easy to sell to council and to the public. I pointed out this was going to hit the parking lots because, except for little shacks, land value is all they've got. While the city raised its total revenue, most of our residential properties and substantial commercial properties actually got a small reduction."

In 1977, Harrisburg again raised the land value portion of its tax to 29 mills, dropping the building tax to 16. Next, Mayor Swenson said, he will try for 30 and 15. "You might ask, if two-to-one is good, why not go all the way on land values only? We want to be innovators, not radicals, so it's a question of how much you bite off at a time."

With the latest change, half of Harrisburg's 8000 propertyowners got a slight decrease in their tax bills. "Exceptions," according to the mayor, "were the most intense land users—such as City Towers, a modern highrise apartment building, that got pretty big tax decreases," he said. "City Towers' improvements are worth 17 times as much as its land, so you can see why the drop in building tax was good for it. Meanwhile, vacant land had a jump from 23 to 29 mills, about a 25 percent increase."

According to the mayor, propertyowners are more concerned with putting their land to higher use than previously: "One building owner had a lot next door that stood empty for years. As he watched the tax on that lot going up, this drove home that he should do something with it and he put up a building to match his other one. Ten years ago people with properties worth $100,000 watched them go down to $90,000 and $80,000 and even $60,000 but, in the last few years, we've turned that around with a 50 percent increase in land values. People realize you don't put cheap building on expensive land. The other day a big firm said it couldn't afford to put up a warehouse and we said, 'That's right, put it across the river and build your showrooms here in town.'"

Interestingly, Mayor Swenson says, with pride, "I've never owned a piece of property in my life. I'm a renter and always have been." After eight years as mayor, he is seeking his third four-year term. "It helps a great deal to understand ghetto economics and housing economics—but it also helps that nobody can say I have a private interest."

Salem, New Hampshire Campaign for 'SVT': All through the spring of 1977, Richard Noyes, editor of the *Salem Observer*, carried out an extensive campaign of editorials, news articles, and photo-journalism to drive home the point that Salem and other New Hampshire towns and cities "must tax homes, factories, office buildings, and other improvements much more lightly—and must tax land values much more heavily—if we are to hold onto the economic gains made during the past decade."

An increasingly serious housing gap sparked this campaign. "Housing at a reasonable price is no longer available but housing needs continue to grow," Mr. Noyes explained. "The costs of sites especially escalated to where they are now out of hand. An acre of land was bought in 1960 for $12,000 and sold in July 1977—with nothing but a rootbeer stand on it—for $250,000. State assessors calculate that land values statewide have risen about 18 percent, compounded annually, since 1970."

As elsewhere in the nation, Salem's housing gap, which used to affect mostly low-income families, has increasingly targeted on moderate-income people as well. Mr. Noyes analyzed the local situation: "Salem was a large, open town of 2000 people with gardens, fields and other empty space. As population expanded, many families cut loose their extra lands. Now we have 28,000 people and these sites are used up. The other owners, determined to keep their extra land out of use, make the market for space very tight."

The campaign has not yet persuaded a majority in Salem to support tax reform. "However," the editor said, "among both friends and enemies of site value taxation, there is fairly general agreement in our community on one thing—that it would force land on the market."

The *Observer* ran lists of properties of local people in different categories—selectmen, budget committee members, school board members, state legislators, apartment owners, veterans, and owners of businesses and industries—showing their 1976 property taxes; what the payments would have been with a site value tax;

An exasperated citizen finally asked in a letter to the editor: "Who will make up the difference for all of this savings?"

In response, the newspaper listed 59 owners whose property taxes would increase—some of them by 300 or 400 percent. The *Observer* reported that the biggest group comprised builder-developers holding vacant lots because "under our present system, that is the only way they can be sure of staying in business." The second largest group were big oil companies and their gas stations. A third classification included owners of summer homes, who use their valuable recreation sites a few weeks a year. Another major category comprised "absentee land speculators." Of the 59 sample properties, 44 were held by nonresidents of Salem.

Mr. Noyes would not predict how long it might take to persuade enough state legislators to give New Hampshire communities the option to untax buildings and to tax land more. "All I know is that this is the only way I can see to get at the housing shortage. The pressures for public revenue from other sources are also bound to continue until we collect more of the unearned increment of land values."

San Diego New Town Proposal: Owners of a nearly vacant 5000-acre tract within San Diego's corporate limits proposed a new community there to accommodate 40,000 people. City council balked at the costs involved but Councilman Floyd Morrow has been "agitating," as he says, for a development plan that would enable this North City West area to pay its own way. More specifically, he would require that all infrastructure—parks, police stations, schools, roads, utilities—be provided with revenues from taxes on land values alone.

"We could do this," said Mr. Morrow, "by making North City West a special assessment district. All the public facilities and amenities that make an area useful, accessible, and desirable will make land values rise. What could be fairer or more practical than to collect these rising land values to pay for the community's public services?"

Meanwhile, in midsummer, a council committee adopted a proposal to create a special tax abatement district in the Gas Lamp Quarters—a San Diego section dating back to the 1890-1910 era. Special state legislation would be required. Under the plan, land values would continue to be taxed but buildings would be tax exempt for owners who brought them into conformity with codes and conservation standards.

Yet strong support for continued taxation of buildings persists. "That's the reason," said Mr. Morrow, "that our central city is half vacant, that development grows in the county, where new public facilities have to be created, and that our redevelopment program has been floundering. As in many other cities, our approach is to invite in developers and then tax their new buildings heavily to pay off the cost of acquiring sites from land speculators. The incentives are totally backward. We give owners of redevelopable land an incentive to hold out as long as possible, to be the last on their block to sell, to get the highest possible price."

Iowa/Nebraska Study: During a three-year regional study embracing six counties—three in Iowa and three in Nebraska— a citizen task force, assisted by the Center for Applied Urban Research, University of Omaha, concentrated on special incentives to attract housing and business development. The major recommendation for attaining that objective was to pursue a study of site value taxation.

For the past three years, Gary E. Carlson, program coordinator for the Omaha housing and community development department, researched this issue and completed a detailed fiscal impact study of site value taxation for Omaha and Douglas County. He found that 36 percent of developed properties would enjoy tax decreases of 21 percent or greater and another 23 percent would get tax decreases of from 5 to 20 percent. In the case of apartments and single-family dwellings, 38 percent of the properties would get reductions of 21 percent or greater and 24 percent of them would get reductions of 5 to 20 percent under site value taxation.

"Such data," said Mr. Carlson, "are meaningful to the planning, housing, development, and land use professionals in our region who are trying to come to grips with undeveloped central cities and continued urbanization of outlying areas. They know we have to conserve scarce resources. They see much merit in a tax that would make it extremely difficult to hold on to high-value bare land but that would make it extremely profitable to build once improvements were tax exempt."

A constitutional amendment would be needed for this reform in Nebraska, Mr. Carlson said. "Possibly the biggest hurdle is that the citizens are gun shy—they've heard so many false promises on taxes in recent years."

International Experience: Australia and New Zealand have seen site value taxation catch on from one city to the next over the past century. Some 80 percent of New Zealand's local jurisdictions use the site value tax. The tax rates are generally low by United States standards and the effects, while salutary, are modest.

Sydney, Australia, on the other hand, has an effective tax rate of more than 5 percent in its central business district and the redevelopment stimulus has been dramatic. R. W. Archer, currently assistant secretary of the Australia Department of Environment, Housing and Community Development, reported that some 265 million dollars worth of new building was created in a highly compact area in little more than a decade. "The site value tax system," he said, "stimulates a more rapid and efficient redevelopment process by increasing the availability of sites for redevelopment and by encouraging the use of the most suitable sites first."

This compactness and constant private renewal of downtown Sydney is in contrast to the experience of Melbourne, a city of approximately the same size but with a property tax on buildings as well as on land. Melbourne's commercial development, Mr. Archer found, has been more scattered. Seemingly ripe redevelopment sites remain dormant with obsolete buildings and, compared with Sydney, a larger proportion of new structures are lowrise.

Site Value Taxation—One Tool Among Many: According to economists who have given most attention to the linkages between taxation, housing, and local development, such as Mason Gaffney of the University of California-Riverside, and Arthur P. Becker of the University of Wisconsin-Madison, the current property tax is a major obstacle to rational land use and wholesome urban growth patterns. This is not to say that site value taxation can single-handedly resolve city problems. It is being considered not as a replacement for planning and other regulating mechanisms but as a missing item that will make the existing kit of tools more effective. It offers a viable alternative to approaches—such as rent control—which employ police powers to try to manage market forces; site value taxation, by facilitating the generation of new housing to meet demand, would harness competitive forces to hold the lid on rents. This would make rent supplements and other direct housing subsidies go farther. In conjunction with public housing, site value taxation would reduce land acquisition costs, permitting units to be produced at lower unit costs.

Where constitutional or statutory constraints stand in the way of removing or reducing the tax rates on improvements, some jurisdictions are moving in that direction simply by living up to the law in respect to the standard property tax. Although local assessors are required to assess and tax both land and buildings according to market value, it is common practice to overassess buildings and underassess the land. The state of California and many localities have made impressive progress in correcting these abuses. The pro-development by-products of these assessment reforms, which have received considerable publicity in Southfield, Michigan, and Arlington County, Virginia, hint at the potency of the full site value tax reform. A dozen or so American cities are engaged in friendly competition to be first in line to reap the potential benefits.

"Site Value Taxation May Be a Way to Stimulate Housing Construction and Rehabilitation" is reprinted from *Public Policies for the 80's*, Conference on Alternative State and Local Policies, 1978.

VI

This section identifies some of the causes of property tax base inequities and proposes some remedies. A property "tax base" is simply the amount of taxable property from which taxes can be raised to finance essential public services.

If a community is growing and new property is being added to the tax rolls at the same or greater rate as expenses are increasing then the burden on the community's taxpayers either remains constant or may even decrease. However, in the case of most older urban areas the addition of property to the tax list is decreasing or increasing at a much slower rate than the escalating cost of government. In the latter situation, local government must either increase taxes, reduce services or both. At best, all three areas discussed—tax exempt property, school finance and tax base sharing—really represent some modest changes in a system of raising state and local revenues and distributing state revenues to the local level which in many ways has outlived its usefulness.

During the period of growth for urban areas, financing local government services was not a problem. The property tax base was expanding and the functions of local government to a large extent involved services to property. In recent years however, local governments have vastly expanded their responsibilities to include such service, as aging, juvenile,

handicapped, alcohol and drug treatment, sewage treatment, water purification, air quality control and other environmental programs. These new and costly programs are occuring at the same time the fiscal capacity of the cities is eroding.

The migration of the middle class to the suburbs has added further costs to the operation of the governments in the central cities. Local streets had to be built and maintained and police departments had to be expanded to accomodate the large flow of traffic in and out of the central city every day and a whole panoply of other services had to be provided. Fire protection and other services also had to be provided. The move to the suburbs by the middle class eroded the tax base and, at the same time, the changing nature of the available jobs from unskilled to skilled left the cities with a larger and larger proportion of the poor and the unemployed.

What did not change or is changing very slowly, are state and local tax raising and revenue distribution systems which were developed in earlier periods of expansion and prosperity. The older cities of our country do not have the resources to fund these ever increasing service requirements, nor has state and federal aid been sufficient to supplement the scarce resources of the cities. The cities, therefore, are faced with the impossible dilemma of cutting services or in-

172

Structural Inequities and Local Finance

By Gerald Kaufman

creasing taxes beyond the level that is tolerable or acceptable.

As these costs are increasing there is a shifting of the property tax burden to residential property throughout the country as residential property values are increasing at a faster rate than commercial and industrial property. Thus, it is the residential property taxpayers who are bearing an increasing share of these escalating costs.

Tax Exempt Property

At a time when the growth of taxable property of many older cities is not keeping pace with their expenses, many of these same cities are experiencing an increase in the amount of tax exempt property. While tax exempt property is disproportionately located in central cities, the benefits are enjoyed throughout the region. In many instances, tax exempt property such as museums, theaters, hospitals, and colleges are used predominantly by those living outside of the city.

Chapter 11 mentions several solutions for alleviating the problem of tax exempt properties. There are several others not mentioned. For instance, the zoning power can often be used to stop institutions from acquiring additional property. The municipality can refuse to issue demolition permits, building permits, curb cut permits or in many other ways harrass tax exempt organizations. Such actions ultimately may not be successful if challenged in court but they do force negotiations which can result in benefits to the affected city and its taxpayers. The city might negotiate for some service fees in lieu of taxes; an affirmative action hiring program; an agreement to use local contractors, purveyors and service providers; a reduced fee schedule for local residents; the institution of a service of particular importance to local residents; or any other concession that would meet local needs.

If real reform in this area is to be accomplished it is absolutely essential that local public opinion be aroused. This has the effect of putting pressure on local legislators and what is more important, pressure on the tax exempt organizations themselves. A reason that Connecticut enacted a payment in lieu of taxes (P.I.L.O.T.) program for private colleges and hospitals in 1978 is because the colleges and hospitals joined with the cities, business and citizen groups in an intensive lobbying effort. The schools and hospitals, acting through their state-wide organizations, were fearful that public opinion was turning against them and that their tax exemption might be eliminated altogether.

The whole issue of tax exemption also is likely to

be subjected to an increasing number of constitutional challenges in the courts on the grounds that one group of citizens, city dwellers, have to bear an undue burden as a result of state mandated tax exemption policies.

School Finance

There is a growing recognition by state governments, reinforced by several state supreme court decisions, that a system of funding public education which does not take into account the disparities between property-poor and property-rich school districts is inequitable, if not unconstitutional. The problem is that children living in property-poor towns do not have the same educational opportunities as children in wealthier districts. Since the same tax rate in a property-rich district will yield far higher revenues per student than it will in a property-poor district.

In response, states are developing education financing formulas that give such districts more aid so that their ability to fund education is more nearly equal to the wealthy school district.

As Allan Odden points out in Chapter 12, whether new school finance formulas actually reduce wealth-related disparities still remains to be seen. Moreover, there are several qualifications in regard to school finance equalization as a remedy for tax base inequities:

1. Increased State aid through an education finance equalization program might come at the expense of reduced State aid in other areas thereby resulting in no real benefits to property poor towns.

2. To the extent that education finance programs equalize per pupil expenditures throughout the State rather than equalizing property wealth differences from town to town the effect on tax base inequities might be minimal because inequities in the ability to finance other municipal services would still exist.

3. If a regressive tax is used to fund a school finance program, then the benefits received by lower income residents of property poor communities might be offset by the disproportionate share of the increased tax burden. In those circumstances they might be better off without the "benefits" of education finance equalization.

Regional Tax Base Sharing

Tax base sharing is a system of revenue sharing which has been implemented as an attempted solution to the balkanization of local tax bases which sets neighboring jurisdictions at each other's throats. In 1971, the seven counties in the Minneapolis-St. Paul metropolitan area agreed to share all additions to their commercial and industrial property tax bases. Whenever a new industry moved into the area, all the jurisdictions would benefit no matter where the plant located.

When one looks closely at tax base sharing both in theory and in practice, it is hard to find much support for its claimed benefits.

In Minneapolis-St. Paul the existence of tax base sharing has had little apparent success in lessening competition for development between communities. There has been some redistribution of tax base, thus narrowing slightly the gap between property-rich and property-poor towns. However, these inter-town property wealth disparities might have been lessened without tax base sharing and perhaps even to a greater extent. School finance equalization programs give aid to towns in an inverse proportion to their property wealth. To the extent that a municipality's tax base is increased by a tax sharing program its school finance allocation would be reduced. In the same manner there would be a decrease in other state and federal entitlements based on property wealth.

Politically the enactment of such a program is likely to relieve state government from the pressures both to aid communities receiving benefits from a tax base sharing program and to restructure the tax system.

The principle drawback to the adoption of tax base sharing is the uncertainty surrounding who the winners and losers will be. There are many reasons to believe that future development will occur increasingly in the cities and inner ring suburbs. It is more energy efficient to concentrate development in the urban area where there is already an infra-structure in place. Many states, with the encouragement of the federal government, are adopting plans of conservation and development to discourage sprawl and to provide incentives for urban development. If in fact development increasingly occurs in the central cities then tax base sharing would tend to provide benefits primarily to the suburbs.

Tax base sharing might be a useful tool as one part of a total state or regional development plan which controls growth in undeveloped areas.

Conclusion

The inability of many local governments to finance essential services because of static or dwindling tax bases cannot be solved solely by the reforms discussed in this section. At best, dealing with the problems of exempt properties, wealth related disparities in school finance and uneven growth within a metropolitan region will provide some short term relief.

Reform of state and local tax systems based on the principle of ability to pay is essential. All state aid to municipalities, not just education aid, should be distributed on the basis of need or wealth disparities. Presently the tax systems in most states are highly regressive. State aid to local governments is also highly regressive because wealthier communities often receive a disproportionate share of state aid programs.

While seeking to reform the overburdened property tax system we cannot forget that decaying central cities will continue their decline unless massive reinvestment takes place. That may be the silver that lines the energy crisis cloud.

CHAPTER 11

Exempt Property

The first article in this chapter, **Exempted America: Taxpayers Pay $15 Billion Extra Each Year,** by Associated Press writer Lee Mitgang, shows that property tax exemptions are a big pocketbook issue for U.S. taxpayers. The average family, Mitgang asserts, pays an extra $300 in property taxes each year because of all the real estate that is exempt. (If one includes other forms of exempt property such as intangibles, the price tag per family is even higher.)

There have been halting steps toward solving this problem. Some cities, such as Denver, Milwaukee, and Pittsburgh, require their tax exempt institutions to pay for part of their city services, while elsewhere universities such as Harvard and Northwestern make voluntary payments to their local governments.

Illustrating the immediate impact of exemptions on city finances, Mitgang quotes a city official in asserting that New York City could balance its budget if it could collect property taxes from just half of the forty percent of its real estate that is exempt. New York State has had a law since 1971 enabling local governments to charge tax exempt properties for services. However, the state legislature keeps postponing the effective date of this bill.

University of Connecticut Law Professor Richard Pomp has been working actively in his state to develop remedies for the burdens imposed by tax exempt property. In **Some Pay...Some Don't: Evaluating Property Tax Exemptions,** the chapter's second article, Mr. Pomp points out, among other things, how property tax exemptions can be abused. In the case cited, a church used land as a tax exempt "cemetery" while it held the tract for speculative profit. Among Mr. Pomp's proposed solutions are limits on the amount of land exempt institutions can hold, expiration dates for tax exemptions, and state reimbursement to cities for state-imposed exemptions.

Largely through Mr. Pomp's efforts, Connecticut adopted the last of these solutions. The final article, **Connecticut Adopts P.I.L.O.T. Legislation for Schools and Hospitals** by Lee Webb, discusses how that legislation came into being.

Exempted America:
Taxpayers Pay $15 Billion Each Year
Because Major Properties Are Going Untaxed

By Lee Mitgang
Associated Press

American taxpayers pay $15 billion a year in extra property taxes—about $300 a family—because a growing number of their neighbors pay none.

About one-third of America's real estate is tax-exempt. And that property is worth more than $800 billion, according to the Advisory Commission on Intergovernmental Relations.

Local governments determine how much property tax should be collected each year and then divide the burden among available property owners. What one property owner is excused from, someone else must pay.

Exemptions are granted for churches and non-profit cemeteries in all 50 states and the District. Also, 39 states exempt parsonages and university dorms, 34 exempt YMCAs and YMHAs, 31 exempt veteran organizations, 24 exempt fraternal organizations like the Elks and Eagles, and 10 states exempt labor and professional organizations—to name just a few groups that most commonly receive favored treatment.

Many states also give whole or partial exemptions to property-owning senior citizens, veterans and welfare recipients, hospitals and certain businesses and their inventories.

Tax-exempt property in the District, for instance, is currently assessed at $1.8 billion, the city assessment office says. If taxes were levied on that property, the District would take in $33.1 million in additional revenues, city assessors say. In addition to embassies, schools, churches and libraries and property belonging to the transit authority, organizations such as the National Geographic Society, the Brookings Institution, the American Legion, the National Council of Negro Women and the Medical Society have been granted tax-exempt status by Congress.

I don't think there's a public awareness of just how much property escapes taxation," says John Coleman, who sur-

veys exemptions every five years for the Census Bureau.

The reason people don't know, simply, is that less than half the states keep records on the amount of property that is untaxed. Even fewer keep annual accounts. The Census Bureau says it gets usable information from only 18 states and the District in its effort to track tax exemptions, and even those figures are considered very rough. An Associated Press survey of all 50 states was able to add only three states with partial statistics to that total.

The Census figures, combined with responses to the AP survey, showed tax-exempt rolls climbing rapidly everywhere—in many states even faster than the value of all real property. The problem is most acute in aging, highly taxed northeastern states, the survey showed.

A high percentage of tax-exempt property isn't necessarily a problem, nor is a low percentage a sign that trouble doesn't exist. Among the many variables: how much free service a city has to provide to the tax-free property and, on the other hand, how much economic activity the tax-exempt organization generates. Some examples:

Louisiana, Wyoming and Alaska contain vast amounts of federal land, which is constitutionally exempt from local taxes. But some federally owned facilities, such as military bases, often pay their own way by generating local employment. And the federal government disburses about $1 billion a year to local governments on land and buildings worth more than $450 billion.

Maine, North Dakota and Wyoming have high percentages of tax-exempt religious, charitable and educational property but also have relatively low tax burdens.

Denver, Milwaukee and Pittsburgh have arrangements with tax-exempt organizations providing for annual payments, service charges or special taxes that make

up for some of the lost taxes.

Some universities with vast tax-exempt real estate holdings, like Harvard in Cambridge, Mass., and Northwestern in Evanston, Ill., have agreed to make voluntary annual payments to local governments.

The trouble with tax exemptions really starts in cities or states that have high taxes and high concentrations of tax-exempt property.

An AP survey of some of the largest cities showed Los Angeles and Houston relatively free of problems, while older industrial cities like St. Louis, Philadelphia, Boston and—most of all—New York have seen relatively rapid growth of exemptions in recent years.

Tax-exempt property is most abundant in these urban areas—and thus may pose the biggest problems there—for several reasons. The poor, sick and elderly tend to live in cities, and thus many kinds of tax-exempt organizations like hospitals and veterans' organizations are also located in urban areas.

As service centers, large cities are the natural place for many tax-exempt organizations. Finally, some suburban communities have recognized the harm large amounts of tax-free property can do to their tax bases and have zoned them out.

"The big central cities in the Northeast are especially hard-hit. Over the years exemptions are granted, usually by state legislatures, and the city loses the revenues," ACIR's John Shannon says. And nowhere do the problems seem worse than in the nation's most taxed city, New York.

Marshall G. Kaplan, chairman of the New York City Tax Commission, says that 40 percent, or $25 billion worth of the city's property, escapes taxes each year. The figure has grown a rapid 8 percent in just the last two years.

Kaplan estimates this means $2.25 billion in extra taxes could be collected if no exemptions existed. If just half that amount of property were taxed, the debt-ridden city might be operating in the black:

In the past several months, the tax commission has lifted long-standing exemptions on private clubs, and is trying to crack down on hospitals, some of which own tax-exempt parking lots that charge commercial rates or own apartment buildings and permit doctors to carry on private practice in them.

However, attempts to close loopholes are frequently beaten back in court. And state legislatures generally find it politically easier to grant new exemptions than to remove old ones.

The first step in reforming the laws governing tax exemptions is to keep up-to-date records on who is not paying taxes. Most states don't.

Aside from the time and trouble of record-keeping, tax experts note that rocking the exemption boat—even with the simple act of keeping current assessments—is not something many state legislatures relish. Those who receive exemptions frequently command votes and dollars, including churches, universities, clubs, wealthy landholders or veterans' groups.

The Census Bureau's John Coleman, who compiles exemption records for the federal government every five years, has tried with little success to get local governments to keep up-to-date assessments of tax-free property and make them public.

"I don't sense any response at all. It's so sensitive they're intimidated, I suspect," he says.

New York State, which has one of the worst problems with growing tax-exempt rolls, provides a unique example of how timidly some state legislatures confront tax exemptions.

A law on the New York books since 1971 would allow local governments to impose service charges on tax-exempt institutions—including those of the state. But the legislature each year puts off the effective date of the law so that it has never taken effect.

"State legislatures have a habit of passing laws that don't take effect for two or three years. That way they get the glory of saying they are doing something about the problem, but then they keep putting off implementation," says Humphrey Tyler of the New York State Board of Equalization and Assessment.

Rarely do even the staunchest critics of exemptions advocate abolishing them altogether.

Tax-free organizations often perform services that government or profit-making organizations couldn't do as well. It has also been argued that the taxing power of government could be used to hinder the freedom of churches or universities.

And some places, particularly university towns or state capitals like Albany, N.Y., or Trenton, N.J., might be ghost towns if not for the jobs and revenues resulting from the presence of tax-exempt organizations.

But some tax officials remain deeply concerned about abuses, the virtual lack of current review, and the permanence of exemptions.

"Exempted America: Taxpayers Pay $15 Billion Extra Each Year Because Major Properties Are Going Untaxed" is reprinted from the February 4, 1978 issue of *The Washington Post,* by permission of The Associated Press.

Some Pay . . . Some Don't

Evaluating property tax exemptions

by Richard D. Pomp

The more I think about it the more I realize how little time I spend on taxable property. Take this weekend, for example. I spent a fair amount of time at the tax exempt State Library doing research on tax exempt property—not so much time, I might add, that I couldn't fit in some exercise at the tax exempt YMCA, or walk through the city's tax exempt parks, or visit a friend at the tax exempt Hartford Hospital, or drop in at the tax exempt museum. Later today, I will return to my tax exempt office at the university, park in a tax exempt lot, and eat at a tax exempt cafeteria.

All this good fortune ends when I return to a taxable home at the end of the day. But some taxpayers in New York have even managed to solve that problem, at least temporarily. For $20 the Universal Life Church will ordain you a minister through the mail. You might remember that the Church became famous during the Viet Nam War when ordination provided a divinity exemption from the draft. Now that the war is over the Church has found a new market by ordaining people who then claim that they're holding their homes as church property. For a modest $20 investment you can earn the right to argue with the assessor over whether or not your home is indeed a church.

The variety of exemptions is enormous: exemptions are granted for federal, state and municipal property, private colleges and universities, churches, hospitals, cemeteries, scientific, literary, historical, and charitable organizations. Exemptions are thus granted for the Daughters of the American Revolution, the Lions Club, the Boy Scouts, the Hartford Medical Society, various camps, agricultural associations, athletic associations and so forth. We have a saying in the income tax area that exemptions never die—they just multiply, and it would seem the same thing is true in the property tax area. In fact, it might be said that we actually have cradle to grave tax exemptions—we are born in tax exempt hospitals and are buried in tax exempt cemeteries.

Although the variety of exemptions is impressive, the largest proportion of tax exempt real property is found in the major cities. In the case of Hartford, the percentage of real property exempted from taxation is twice that found in the surrounding suburbs. While this is not surprising—since the cities are the administrative, cultural, medical, and educational centers for both their surrounding regions and the state—it also underscores the heart of the tax exempt problem: properties exempt from taxation provide regional and statewide benefits while the cost of such properties are disproportionately borne by the residents and businessess in the city. Indeed, as my weekend activities illustrate, I for one make ample use of tax exempt properties in Hartford but do not contribute in any direct way to the cost of these properties since I live outside the city.

The Dilemma: Draining the Tax Base

Let's be specific about what costs are imposed on the city by these tax exemptions. When land is removed from the taxable grand list because it is devoted to a tax exempt activity or purchased by a tax exempt organization, the city obviously loses the amount of property tax revenue that it previously collected. Nor does the city's cost in servicing that property necessarily decline. Tax exempt properties can consume a high level of local services in terms of fire and police protection, maintenance of the roads around the property, traffic control, sewer services, garbage collection, and so forth.

As the property tax base shrinks without a concomitant reduction in costs, the city is thrust into an untenable position. In order to make up the lost property tax revenue, either the tax rates on the remaining properties must be increased, or services must be reduced, or, more commonly, some combination of the two takes place. All this, at the same time that inflation is driving up the cost of maintaining even the existing level of services. An increase in property tax rates, coupled with a decline in the real level of services, only encourages individuals and businesses to leave the city and landlords to abandon marginal buildings.

As businesses and jobs leave the city, as buildings get abandoned, and as the more affluent residents migrate to the suburbs, the property tax base is eroded even further. Since the state has limited local governments to raising revenue only through the property tax, further erosion of this base touches off yet another cycle of raising the mill rate or cutting services.

This cycle has another and perhaps even more serious dimension to it. Because the more affluent and mobile individuals have migrated to the suburbs, the city is left with a disproportionate share of the state's poor and elderly. The cost of tax exempts thus falls on those least able to bear the additional costs, exacerbating the already regressive nature of the existing state and local tax system. Tax exempt property therefore raises a fundamental question of taxpayer equity: Is it fair to impose all of the burden of the state enacted real property exemption on the residents and businesses of the city, when the benefits and services generated by these properties (not to mention jobs provided for commuters), accrue to those living outside of the city?

Some numbers may help illustrate the problem. In Hartford, for example, the grand list actually declined from '75 to '76 while the value of tax exempt property actually increased. The tax revenue lost between '71 and '76 due to tax exempts (not including municipal property) has been estimated at $124 million. This is $124 million the city otherwise would have had, and which the city had to make up through an increase in property tax rates and a curtailment in services.

Approaching the Problem: Some Considerations

Obviously, any move involving that amount of revenue requires careful deliberation. In thinking about the subject of tax exempts, it is useful to break the problem down into three parts:

● whether the existing exemptions ought to be continued and if so, for which activities;

● which is the appropriate level of government to bear the costs of the exemptions; and

● what are alternative ways of subsidizing the activities of organizations that we wish to encourage, and generally what options are available to the state.

In approaching the first consideration, we have to keep in mind that once an exemption is provided by the law, taxpayers will restructure their transactions to bring themselves within the blessed exempt category. This is most clearly illustrated by the following example. A local Hartford church purchased 121 acres of vacant land in New Britain for $23,500. One body was buried there and the land was exempted as a cemetery. In 1966, when the land had appreciated to $607,000, the body was removed and the cemetery sold. Experiences of this sort are not unique to Connecticut; every state has its own parade of horribles. And we can only speculate on how many examples of abuse never surface.

Cleaning up the gray areas in the statute is of course desirable, but what is really necessary is a wholesale evaluation of the scope of existing exemptions. When tax rates were low, when the cities were thriving, we could live with broad, generous, wide reaching exemptions. We cannot today. If I were to reexamine the statute, I would grant an exemption only if the activity or service is one which the government would have to perform if a private entity did not, and only if the subsidy is required to provide the service at a price which all members of the public who ought to have access to the service are able to pay.

Thus, a strong candidate for exemption under my criterion would be the Red Cross, Salvation Army, a hospital that treated the indigent, or a library. A strong candidate for denial of an exemption might be a medical, dental, or bar association.

Assuming that *some* exemptions are in order, the next question is to decide which level of government should finance the costs of these exemptions. I've already suggested that many exempt properties provide general and diffused benefits to areas beyond their host jurisdiction. This fact is quite clearly seen in the case of state buildings such as the Capitol. This same lack of identity between the host jurisdiction and the tax exempt's constituency is true, at least to some degree, in other cases. A recent study found that less than half the patients treated in tax exempt hospitals in Bridgeport, Hartford, New Haven and New London actually lived in the host jurisdiction. The results were even more pronounced in the case of colleges and universities located in these cities.

Perhaps in the past there was more of an overlap between the jurisdiction in which the property was located and the jurisdiction in which the beneficiaries lived, but the growth of the suburbs and the increased mobility of individuals have produced a situation where many of the benefits and services generated by tax exempts are now provided to residents of other jurisdictions. In light of that situation, it's clear that the compensation for revenue loss should be provided by the *larger* jurisdiction benefitting from the exemptions.

Finally, assuming again that some special treatment is to be provided to certain organizations, what form should this take? The present treatment, an exemption from property taxes, is probably one of the least rational methods. Consider, for example, two organizations, X and Y. X is financially struggling and can afford only to rent office space; Y is well established, well endowed, and is known for its generous staff salaries and opulent headquarters located on highly desirable and expansive prime real estate. Has the state consciously chosen to ignore the struggling organization but grant benefits to the less needy organization? Has the state consciously chosen to increase its benefits on the basis of how much land and buildings Y owns?

To put it another way, if the state were to grant cash subsidies to organizations that are presently exempt, would it adopt a program that gave nothing to organizations so poor that they cannot afford to own real estate and instead, gave money on the basis of how much real property was owned? That is the effect of the existing law except that it is the *local* jurisdictions that are granting the cash subsidies by not collecting the property tax they otherwise would.

Because of these irrationalities, my own preference would be to replace the property tax exemptions with an explicit cash subsidy. (The exemption could be continued for religious organizations, since a cash subsidy would be unconstitutional.) If a system of cash grants were adopted, I have no doubts that the state would narrow the existing law, so as to channel money to only the neediest of qualifying organizations.

What's To Be Done: Some Options

I have no illusions about a wholesale change in the law and the following recommendations all assume that the general scheme of property tax exemptions will continue. Nonetheless, understanding the defects in the current approach is useful in identifying areas where a better balance can be reached among the interests of the tax exempts, the cities, and the state. There are a number of alternatives available, among them:

● **Requiring the permission of the local jurisdiction before any taxable property can be removed from the grand list.** This approach places the decision making power at the level of government which bears the cost of the exemption, and allows the localities to decide whether the *benefits* of the exemption really justify that *cost*.

● **Phasing in the exemption when taxable property is being removed from the grand list.** This option provides a cushion so that the jurisdiction does not suffer an abrupt decline in revenue in the year of purchase.

● **Setting a time period beyond which the exemption will be phased out.** A time limitation would enable new organizations to get started without the burden of the property tax but at the same time would assure that the host jurisdiction

is not burdened with a perpetual exemption. A sufficient time period will allow the organization to adequately plan for the eventual phasing out of the exemption.

● **Setting a limit on the number of acres qualifying for the exemption or a dollar limit on the amount of property which can be exempt.** These approaches attempt to balance the interests of the tax exempts against the revenue loss incurred by the host jurisdiction. Once some reasonable level of property ownership has been exempted, further expansion should not be at the expense of the local government. Meanwhile, an organization which owns property exceeding the ceiling indicates a certain level of wealth or ability to pay that does not justify any further exemption.

● **Imposing a user charge.** Although it may be deemed undesirable to subject tax exempt properties to the normal property tax, this option recognizes that these properties consume local services and at a minimum, should contribute something to the costs of local government.

A simple means of implementing a user charge approach is to estimate the percentage of the jurisdiction's total budget that is devoted to supplying services such as fire and police protection, traffic control, garbage collection, sewer services, and apply that percentage of the mill rate to the value of the tax exempt property. For instance, if 35% of the budget were estimated as being devoted to the provision of these services, and if the mill rate were 60, then the assessed value of tax exempts would be subject to a user charge of 21 mills (.35 x 60).

While it is obvious that many of the current tax exempts are fully capable financially of meeting the costs of user charges, it can be argued that others are not. To offset that problem, it would be possible to institute a system of user charge circuit breakers, which would provide relief based on need.

● **Requiring state payments to jurisdictions containing tax exempts.** This option recognizes that it is unfair for the host jurisdictions to bear the entire cost attributable the presence of tax exempts. Recently adopted in Connecticut, it extends the state's PILOT (Payments in Lieu of Taxes) program to *non*-state owned property, on the theory that the exemption from property tax, which is granted by the state, helps to implement state objectives and goals.

In order to channel funds where it is needed most, payments could be made only to jurisdictions having more than the statewide average of tax exempt property.

"Some Pay...Some Don't: Evaluating Property Tax Exemptions" is reprinted by permission from the September, 1978 issue of *People and Taxes,* Public Citizen Tax Reform Research Group.

Connecticut Adopts P.I.L.O.T. Legislation for Schools and Hospitals

By Lee Webb

In May 1978, Governor Grasso signed into law legislation requiring the state to reimburse cities and towns for twenty-five percent of the property taxes lost because of "private, non-profit institutions of higher education" and "general hospital facilities"— in effect, a payment in lieu of taxes (PILOT) program for schools and hospitals. $10 million dollars was appropriated for the 1979 fiscal year, of which Hartford will receive $1.9 million and New Haven $2.8 million.

Although unprecedented nationally, the new Connecticut law is still narrower than what many tax reformers had hoped. An earlier version of the legislation had provided for payments based on *all* nonprofit institutions, rather than just schools and hospitals. For most cities, the largest categories of tax-exempt property are schools, hospitals, and churches; thus, only the exclusion of churches in the final version of the legislation was of real significance.

Why were churches, which had been included in all earlier bills, excluded in the final version? Although some legislators may have thought otherwise, no constitutional problems appear to be raised by reimbursing a municipality for the presence of certain categories of nonprofit institutions, including churches. A more likely explanation is that some churches actively opposed their inclusion in the PILOT program. At first glance, their opposition seems surprising since the PILOT program would have no impact on them; indeed, by providing assistance to municipalities, the legislation helps to de-fuse other, more onerous alternatives, such as the institution of service charges. But the churches have long maintained that they impose no costs on a jurisdiction; to the contrary, they argued that their presence was only an asset. State assistance that was a function of the property owned by churches within a municipality would have compromised this position. The churches may well have worried about the long-term implications of compromising their position, should the PILOT program ever be phased out.

In addition to excluding churches, the law was also narrower in other respects. For example, the 25 percent reimbursement figure was less than what many reformers had wanted. Although no one had really expected a 100 percent reimbursement, a 35 percent figure seemed realistic since that is the amount used in determining the PILOT payments for state-owned property. It was also hoped that the legislation would channel payments only to those municipalities severely burdened by tax-exempt property, that is, the major urban areas. To accomplish this objective, one alternative discussed was to reimburse only those cities and towns housing more than the state-wide average of nonprofit institutions. Another alternative was to include only jurisdictions whose tax-exempt property exceeded a certain percentage of their total taxable property. In the end, however, in order to obtain sufficient legislative support, it was necessary to make *all* cities and towns eligible for PILOT payments.

Despite these legislative compromises, Connecticut's new law represents a significant philosophical breakthrough in the battle to gain recognition for the cost imposed on municipalities from state-mandated property tax exemptions. How is it that Connecticut, which has one of the most atavistic tax structures in the country, was able to enact one of the most progressive pieces of legislalation in the area of tax-exempt property? Most important, was that the cities, under the strong leadership of Hartford, had raised legislative consciousness by presenting their case for relief for a number of years. Sufficient time had passed for the seeds of a PILOT program to have germinated. Also, the cities had aggressively attempted to reform the existing law. Hartford, for example, consistently introduced bills that would have narrowed the definition of tax-exempt activities, that would have allowed municipalities to levy service charges, and that would have limited the expansion of the tax-exempt institutions. Moreover, Hartford was attempting to use its zoning powers to curtail the acquisition of taxable property by non-profit institutions.

These and similar attempts had placed the cities and tax-exempt institutions on a collision course. Through the efforts of some key Hartford politicians, however, this hostility was temporarily put aside as the city and the local institutions began a concerted effort to find a solution. Given some of the alternatives, the PILOT approach was a program that both sides could easily rally around, although the support of the tax exempts may not have been forthcoming had they not first been placed on the defensive by the cities. Also important was the role played by the Greater Hartford Chamber of Commerce, which helped to nurture the new-found dialogue between Hartford and the non-profits. The Chamber formed its own task force consisting of state and local legislators, representatives from the various tax-exempt organizations, as well as both business and individual taxpayers. Professor Richard D. Pomp of the University of Connecticut Law School served as a consultant to the task force. This group studied various proposals for dealing with the problem of tax-exempt property and ultimately endorsed a PILOT program. The support of the Chamber and the imprimatur of a respected and well-known academician lent considerable credibility to the cities in arguing their case before the legislature.

"Connecticut Adopts P.I.L.O.T. Legislation for Schools and Hospitals" is reprinted by permission from the Conference on Alternative State and Local Policies, 1979.

CHAPTER 12

Wealth Related
Disparities in School Finance

The landmark California Supreme Court case of *Serrano v. Priest* in the early 1970's started a wave of state court decisions requiring drastic overhaul in the way these states finance public education. State constitutional mandates and moral imperatives have kept this movement going despite a U.S. Supreme Court ruling (in *San Antonio vs. Rodriguez*) that the United States Constitution requires no such reform.

In the first article here, Dr. Allan Odden's **Public School Finance: Fine Tuning the System** gives an overview of the policy issues this movement has raised. Dr. Odden points out that at least twenty-five states have moved towards equalizing either per pupil expenditures or school property tax burdens between different localities. Despite this action, however, in most states there are communities which can spend more than three times per pupil than can their poorer counterparts. There have been fears that increased state funding of public schools would erode local control, but Dr. Odden asserts that this need not be so. He says that at least two states, California and Florida, deliberately decentralizd their schools when they enacted school funding reforms.

Following this general overview, **Money and Education: Where Did the $400 Million Go?** by Margaret Goertz looks closely at the school finance changes in one state, New Jersey, which were impelled by a State Supreme Court mandate. Ms. Goertz finds that these changes were not the reforms they were cracked up to be. Even though the state legislature upped the state aid ante by fifty per cent, the share of state funds going to poorer school districts actually decreased, while the spending gap between rich and poor districts widened. "The new law," Ms. Goertz concludes, "does not appear to adequately address the Court's concern with guaranteeing every child in the State a 'thorough and efficient' education."

Public School Finance: Fine-Tuning the System

by Allan Odden*

THE SET OF PUBLIC POLICY issues related to equitable and efficient financing of a state's elementary and secondary schools continues to dominate many state legislatures. Nearly all states, with the assistance of federal funds under Section 842 of the 1974 amendments to the Elementary and Secondary Education Act, are in the process of studying or evaluating their elementary-secondary education finance and tax structures. Since 1970, approximately 25 states have passed fundamental school finance reforms, with changes in education financing and related property tax reform constituting major elements in this resurgence. Courts, however, as indicated by the December 1977 decision of the California Supreme Court in the *Serrano* appeal and the March 1977 decision of the Connecticut Supreme Court in the *Horton* case, continue to apply pressure on states to develop fair and constitutionally permissible education finance systems.

Public elementary and secondary schools are still supported primarily by local property taxes. For 1976-77, it was estimated that local sources provided 48.3 percent of public school revenues, with state sources contributing 43.3 percent and the federal government 8.3 percent. These averages have remained fairly stable over the last 10 years. The proportions varied among the states, however, as indicated in the table on the

next page. Perhaps the most dramatic change over the past decade has been the increase in the state role, which rose by 4.2 percentage points.

For the 1976-77 school year, it was estimated that approximately $64 billion was spent for current operating purposes on public education for students in elementary and secondary schools. Current operating expenditures per pupil were estimated to average $1,564 across the country, an increase of 173 percent over the previous decade. As the table shows, however, per pupil expenditures in 1976-77 varied considerably across the states, ranging from a low of $1,095 to a high of $2,938. In addition, expenditures per pupil varied considerably within most states, with expenditure differences between high- and low-spending districts exceeding three-to-one ratios in most states.

Average teacher salaries in 1976-77 were estimated to be $13,830, an increase of 94 percent from the 1966-67 school year. After adjusting the salary figure by the consumer price index, however, the real gain in the purchasing power of the average teacher salary amounted to only 17.5 percent in the decade since the 1966-67 school year.

THE SHAPE OF SCHOOL FINANCE REFORM

Twenty-five states have enacted basic school finance reforms during the 1970s. The key feature of each new school aid program is a revised general aid equalization formula that distributes relatively more state aid to school districts poor in property wealth. Indeed,

*Dr. Odden is Director of the Education Finance Center, Education Commission of the States. A portion of this article will appear in the 1978-79 edition of *The Book of the States*, also published by the Council of State Governments.

California, Minnesota, Montana, and Utah have recapture clauses in their new programs under which the state collects excess property taxes raised in the wealthiest school districts and reallocates them to poorer districts.

Three different types of equalization formulas have been enacted:

(1) High-level foundation programs as found in Iowa, Minnesota, South Carolina, Tennessee, Utah, and Washington;

(2) Foundation programs augmented by guaranteed tax base or guaranteed yield programs for those districts that choose to spend above the foundation level, as found in California, Florida, Maine, Missouri, and South Dakota; and

(3) Guaranteed tax base, guaranteed yield, or percentage equalization programs that guarantee equal revenues for equal tax rates as found in Colorado, Illinois, Kansas, Michigan, New Jersey, Ohio, and Wisconsin.

Many states are phasing in these new programs over a three- to five-year period; thus, the full impact of the new finance structures will not occur until the programs are fully funded.

A second characteristic of the school finance reforms has been increased attention to student populations requiring special education, compensatory education, or bilingual-bicultural education services. The most dramatic increases in state aid have occurred in state special education appropriations; the billions of dollars states are spending for these services dwarfs, at this time, the $500 million federal role, although the federal role should rise when P.L. 94-142, the Education for All Handicapped Children Act, is fully funded. Florida, New Mexico, South Carolina, South Dakota, and Utah have linked the distribution of state special education aid to the general aid formula, by a pupil weighted formula, thus equalizing the flow of categorical aid in the same manner as general aid.

Nearly 20 states have enacted compensatory education programs for economically disadvantaged students. Illinois and Minnesota, moreover, recognize that it is concentration of poverty that produces the most severe educational disadvantage; these two states allocate greater dollar amounts per pupil as the concentration of poverty students increases in local school districts.

Bilingual programs are also rapidly being enacted in states with concentrations of students for whom English is not the first language.

California, Colorado, Massachusetts, New Mexico, New York, and Texas are states taking the lead in implementing these programs.

A third element in the new school aid bills is recognition of the fiscal plights of many central city school districts as well as the high costs incurred by school districts in poor and isolated rural areas. Michigan, in fact, recognizes the drain on the education budget of the demand for noneducation services by allocating additional state aid to school districts with noneducation tax rates that exceed the statewide average by more than 25 percent.

A fourth factor that describes the shape of newly enacted education finance structures is the increasing interest in and enactment of income factors. The new Missouri formula decreases the required tax rate for the foundation part of its formula for low-income districts and increases it for high-income districts. Kansas and Maryland measure local school district fiscal capacity by a combination of property wealth and taxable income. Connecticut and Rhode Island weigh the property wealth measure by a median family income ratio. California, Illinois, Michigan, Minnesota, Nebraska, Ohio, and Wisconsin are studying the role of income and possible ways of modifying their aid programs with income factors.

A fifth new element of school finance reform is the increasing interest in cost-of-education adjustments. Florida adjusts its state aid allocations by a cost-of-living factor, but that adjustment has been criticized because cost-of-living differences are not the same as cost-of-education differences. Missouri is completing a two-year study of cost-of-education differences and California has begun a major study which will produce cost-of-education indices for each local school district.

A final element in the revised school aid program is the increasing use of tax and expenditure controls to stabilize property tax rates and prevent education expenditures from increasing too rapidly. Although the expenditure controls in some states have become outdated with the nation's high rate of inflation and actually impede the progress of low-spending districts in "catching up" with high-spending districts, the use of expenditure controls and tax limits continues both in school aid formulas as well as in programs for other state and local services.

In addition to these characteristics of the new state aid distribution mechanisms, property tax relief and reform have accompanied school finance changes. Arizona, Colorado, Kansas, North Dakota, and Wisconsin are states whose school finance programs reduced absolutely the property tax burden. Equalizing property wealth school aid formulas makes the property tax burden more equitable on a school district basis both by decreasing tax rates in poor school districts and by providing equal revenue for equal tax rates. Many states have also enacted state-financed circuit-breakers for property tax relief that limit property tax payments as a percent of income for low-income families and individuals, thus creating a property tax structure that is equitable for both school districts and individuals. Minnesota, Michigan, and Wisconsin are states that have expanded their circuit-breaker programs in the wake of school finance reform to protect all low-income households, especially those in wealthy school districts, from property tax overburdens.

As mentioned earlier, another hallmark of school finance reform has been a large increase in the state fiscal role. For the 18 states that enacted new school aid bills prior to 1975, the state role increased from 39 to 51 percent, a rise of 12 percentage points. In most cases, this increase occurred without increases in state sales or income tax rates, but Minnesota revised both corporate and individual income tax rates as part of its 1971 reform and New Jersey enacted an income tax to fund its new program.

It is important to note, moreover, that an increase in state financing of elementary and secondary schools can occur without an increase in state administrative control over the schools. In both California and Florida, for example, the school aid changes have been accompanied by governance changes that not only encourage but in some cases require decentralization of both budget and administrative control below the district level to the school site level.

MAJOR POLICY ISSUES IN SCHOOL FINANCE REFORM

School finance reform is not a one-time event. Most states continue to adjust and refine their school aid formulas. As this process evolves, states must keep in mind that there are two different definitions of equity in school finance that require different state policies and produce different fiscal results.

One equity standard requires that expenditures per pupil be equal across all school districts in a state. The expenditure figure should be adjusted for differences in pupil need and education costs across districts. This standard is focused on students. It is concerned with the expenditure per pupil gaps between the high- and low-spending school districts. Meeting this equity standard will produce equal education resources for students in all school districts and requires expenditure per pupil gaps to be minimized.

The second equity standard, called fiscal neutrality, requires only that expenditure per pupil differences not be related to differences in local school district property wealth. The focus of this equity standard is on taxpayers. The objective of the standard is to eliminate the relationship between local wealth and expenditure levels and to make the ability to raise education revenues from state and local sources equal across all school districts. The fiscal neutrality standard allows for expenditure per pupil differences among school districts. In states that have enacted new formulas designed to create fiscally neutral structures, moreover, expenditure per pupil differences have not been reduced, although the relationship between the expenditure differences and local wealth have been eliminated.

Whatever standard of equity or equalization a state adopts, there are three different aspects of equalization that a comprehensive state aid formula must address: wealth equalization, pupil need equalization, and cost equalization. With respect to wealth equalization, recent studies show that not only is the total amount of property wealth per pupil important, but also that the composition of the property tax base affects school district decisions. Given equal total amounts of property wealth, school districts with larger percentages of nonresidential property have higher tax rates and higher expenditure levels. Moreover, the composition of even the nonresidential component of the tax base — in terms of commercial, industrial, and agricultural property — also differentially influences school district tax and expenditure levels.

In addition to property wealth and its composition, however, is the effect of household income on school finance. Studies are also demonstrating that, irrespective of whether schools levy income taxes, the income of school districts is an important fiscal variable in school district decisions on tax rate and expenditure levels, with higher-income districts, other things being equal, levying higher tax rates and enjoying higher expenditures per pupil.

With respect to pupil need equalization, the first element is whether the state has comprehensive and fully funded programs to assist local school districts in providing education services for the special needs of handicapped students, economically disadvantaged students, bilingual students, and gifted and talented students, as well as state assistance for transportation services and for school facilities. However, the major emerging issue is the degree to which the allocation of state as well as federal aid for these programs complements or detracts from the equalization thrust of the general aid formula. Most state allocation mechanisms for categorical programs allocate aid on the basis of identified need only, without regard for the fiscal ability of a school district to share in covering the costs. Again, however, studies are beginning to show that high-wealth, high-expenditure school districts are able, for example, to identify relatively greater percentages of students needing special education services and thus to qualify for greater amounts of state aid. This can result in an unequalized distribution of categorical state aid.

The last equalization issue relates to cost equalization. Cost-of-living adjustments, as well as adjustments based on teacher education and experience factors, are crude cost adjustments, at best, and in some instances can cause greater amounts of aid to flow to the high-income, high-wealth school districts. Cost-of-education differences that are converted into district cost-of-education indices and then applied to the calculation of state aid can be used to adjust state aid distributions to account for the varying purchasing power of the education dollar. The plans developed in California, Michigan, and Missouri are examples of ways these cost indices have been developed and used.

In addition to the three topics included under equalization objectives are four special topics in education finance not to be overlooked in developing equitable finance structures for elementary and secondary students. The first is the impact of a school finance structure on fiscally pressed urban areas. Central city school districts across the country have declining or stagnant property tax bases and a student population that is increasing in its minority, poverty, and handicapped composition. School finance structures that do not recognize these factors, that do not fully fund comprehensive programs for special student needs, and that do not consider poverty concentration as a factor in the allocation of state aid will continue the fiscal squeeze on central city school districts. The responses of legislatures in California and Michigan to the unique school finance problems of urban school districts could serve as models for other states in this regard.

Second is the impact of school finance reforms on minority and low-income students in general. School aid formulas based on property wealth alone may adversely affect the gains made by low-income minorities in property wealthy urban areas. Likewise, urban-oriented school aid programs may inadvertently overlook the extra education needs of minorities and low-income students in poor rural areas. The flight of white students from many school districts and the potential underfunding of the predominantly minority student body that remains needs increased attention. The state role in financing and delivering education services to Indian students in public schools is an issue that is rapidly emerging in many states and is an issue that merits close scrutiny by state education policymakers.

Third is research assessing the impacts of school finance reforms that have been enacted in this decade. New school aid programs must be analyzed for their fiscal effects of producing fiscally neutral structures or reducing expenditure per pupil gaps; for their programmatic effects in terms of what the new dollars buy, how the new resources are used, what kinds of new education programs are developed, and what types of students are benefited; and for their student outcome effects in terms of how school finance reforms affect student achievement.

FEDERAL ROLE ADDRESSED

Finally, two topics related to the federal role in elementary-secondary education finance need to be reassessed. First, federal and state programs targeted on the same student populations—for example, handicapped and low-income students—must be made more compatible, both in their fiscal designs and in their programmatic and regulatory requirements. As the federal Elementary and Secondary Education Act of 1965 becomes reauthorized and as refinements are made in the federal Education for All Handicapped Children

Act, the commonalities of federal and state programs must be recognized, mechanisms for comingling state and federal funds must be developed, and a new state-federal partnership must be created that shifts the accountability concerns away from the current concentration on fiscal controls to student-based programmatic and education planning.

Second, the time may be ripe to raise anew the policy issues related to a federal program of general education aid. Education expenditures per pupil as well as state fiscal capacity, in terms of per capita income, differ by factors of two-to-one across the states. In short, education opportunities are not equal among the states and perhaps only the federal government can address these inequities.

A federal role in interstate equalization is clearly a program that would be implemented at some future date; nevertheless, work should begin now to describe and assess the degree of inequity within and among the states and to develop policy alternatives for a federal program of general aid for the time when such a new federal education policy initiative could be a reality.

ESTIMATED REVENUE RECEIPTS, PUBLIC SCHOOLS, 1976-77; STATE AND LOCAL TAX COLLECTION AS A PERCENTAGE OF PERSONAL INCOME, 1975; AND ESTIMATED EXPENDITURES FOR PUBLIC ELEMENTARY AND SECONDARY SCHOOLS, 1976-77*

State or other jurisdiction	Total receipts (in thousands of dollars)	Receipts by source (percent)			Total state and local tax collections as a percentage of personal income	Total current expenditures (in thousands of dollars)	Per pupil in ADA	Capital outlay (in thousands of dollars)	Total current expenditures, capital outlay, and interest (in thousands of dollars)
		Federal	State	Local					
Total	$73,882,867	8.3	43.3	48.3	11.4	$63,865,988	$1,564	$6,067,122	$74,075,722
Alabama	899,833	15.7	63.0	21.3	9.1	825,786	1,163	71,780	912,406
Alaska	302,920	16.5	66.4	17.0	8.7	252,129	2,938	42,000	308,629
Arizona	788,146	10.3	45.7	44.0	11.4	660,840	1,446	103,653	788,146
Arkansas	513,085	16.3	51.1	32.6	9.1	462,079	1,112	41,625	517,757
California	8,512,547	10.5	37.4	52.1	12.6	6,825,005	1,595	580,000	8,114,784
Colorado	968,200	6.7	39.2	54.1	10.6	820,000	1,556	150,000	1,001,500
Connecticut	1,213,075	4.8	30.3	64.9	10.7	1,124,762	1,888	25,000	1,189,762
Delaware	239,000	9.2	68.2	22.6	10.8	209,000	1,866	13,000	232,000
Florida	2,144,774	10.1	52.3	37.6	9.6	2,067,173	1,483	220,000	2,341,173
Georgia	1,329,820	11.3	60.5	28.1	10.0	1,147,465	1,144	44,600	1,240,165
Hawaii	283,250	11.3	85.0	3.7	12.7	209,381	1,275	35,000	258,981
Idaho	259,720	10.3	48.8	41.0	9.7	219,231	1,158	62,400	288,974
Illinois	4,224,800	7.7	47.4	45.0	11.2	3,670,015	1,876	625,342	4,616,331
Indiana	1,657,297	5.9	42.2	51.9	10.6	1,365,000	1,307	160,000	1,606,000
Iowa	1,224,014	3.7	40.8	55.5	11.2	903,037	1,669	132,635	1,052,575
Kansas	700,737	7.8	44.4	47.8	10.4	636,620	1,555	66,690	744,395
Kentucky	881,640	12.2	58.4	29.3	9.9	696,300	1,095	45,000	772,500
Louisiana	957,500	17.5	55.9	26.5	11.3	852,800	1,123	73,000	956,000
Maine	318,600	8.2	45.4	46.5	13.0	300,000	1,333	18,000	338,300
Maryland	...	...	...	...	...	1,466,390	1,889	155,096	1,664,241
Massachusetts	2,213,000	3.9	22.0	74.1	13.3	1,879,280	1,683	100,000	2,157,990
Michigan	3,352,271	7.7	36.2	56.1	11.5	3,042,545	1,589	333,269	3,557,159
Minnesota	1,542,000	5.4	54.7	39.9	12.8	1,341,533	1,646	210,000	1,712,533
Mississippi	543,000	21.2	55.2	23.6	11.2	548,565	1,148	28,100	583,365
Missouri	1,343,768	7.5	36.4	56.1	10.0	1,106,623	1,300	93,000	1,246,623
Montana	294,500	5.4	60.6	34.0	11.8	281,755	1,730	10,000	295,355
Nebraska	467,736	8.8	22.7	68.5	10.3	451,713	1,534	9,928	476,850
Nevada	211,000	5.2	37.4	57.3	12.3	184,000	1,423	17,000	212,600
New Hampshire	255,241	5.1	8.6	86.3	9.8	203,373	1,261	13,451	223,232
New Jersey	2,910,000	4.1	38.9	57.0	10.9	2,714,000	2,104	130,000	2,957,000
New Mexico	406,567	16.9	67.2	15.9	11.7	363,018	1,342	70,210	445,628
New York	7,956,000	4.3	39.1	56.6	15.5	6,995,800	2,333	360,000	7,824,200
North Carolina	1,699,609	14.6	66.0	19.4	9.9	1,323,928	1,210	175,000	1,738,623
North Dakota	190,000	8.7	46.3	45.0	9.3	173,240	1,399	16,000	195,740
Ohio	3,201,416	6.1	39.8	54.1	9.0	2,903,000	1,403	300,000	3,363,000
Oklahoma	797,000	11.3	52.7	36.0	9.4	705,000	1,261	70,000	792,000
Oregon	806,000	5.5	28.8	65.8	10.8	680,000	1,600	95,000	792,000
Pennsylvania	4,401,556	8.7	46.5	44.8	11.3	3,379,400	1,862	219,000	4,415,300
Rhode Island	326,025	7.2	35.7	57.1	11.3	236,000	1,499	16,250	274,700
South Carolina	760,456	15.1	55.2	29.6	9.8	661,476	1,104	90,000	784,476
South Dakota	195,600	12.1	14.3	73.6	11.1	178,122	1,280	27,567	210,059
Tennessee	1,012,523	12.2	48.8	39.0	9.3	952,524	1,146	135,035	1,143,529
Texas	3,890,520	10.4	48.1	41.5	9.4	2,959,736	1,154	378,400	3,502,136
Utah	448,081	7.1	52.7	40.1	10.5	365,706	1,242	96,245	484,543
Vermont	169,440	6.6	26.9	66.6	14.6	144,329	1,440	11,500	165,710
Virginia	1,552,050	10.2	28.8	61.0	9.6	1,416,064	1,395	107,131	1,608,637
Washington	1,281,956	7.7	65.1	27.2	10.9	1,225,388	1,694	70,640	1,338,549
West Virginia	526,711	11.2	59.6	29.2	10.3	437,025	1,194	79,116	527,054
Wisconsin	1,683,064	4.4	34.5	61.2	13.3	1,519,103	1,926	94,725	1,659,759
Wyoming	181,500	5.7	30.4	63.9	10.9	146,000	1,765	44,900	196,700
Dist. of Col.	246,053	18.1	...	81.9	10.3	234,719	2,060	834	246,053

*Source: National Education Association, *Estimates of School Statistics*, 1976-77, and *Rankings of the States*, 1976.

"Public School Finance: Fine Tuning the System" is reprinted by permission from the Winter, 1978 issue of *State Government*.

Money and Education: Where Did the $400 Million Go? The Impact of the New Jersey Public School Education Act of 1975

By Margaret Goertz

In 1970, Kenneth Robinson and his parents sued the State of New Jersey, charging that the way in which the public schools were funded denied a "thorough" education to students who lived in poor school districts. Although New Jersey is an affluent state that spends a great deal of money on educating its children, they argued the distribution of that money is uneven. In 1971-72, Jersey City was spending $897 per pupil on education while its neighbors in Secaucus were spending $1184. Yet its citizens were being taxes at a rate of $2.82 per $100 of equalized valuation while Secaucus taxpayers paid a rate of only $1.10. Similar contrasts appeared in every county in the State: Trenton-Princeton; Newark-Millburn; Hampton-Tewksbury; South Bound Brook-Bedminster, and so on.

The ensuing legal and legislative battles brought about a landmark court decision, *Robinson v. Cahill*; a modified state school finance formula in The Public School Education Act of 1975; and a commitment by the State to increase its share of educational expenditures by $400 million, beginning in the 1976-77 school year. But did these decisions change the inequitable patterns linking wealth, school expenditures and tax rates documented in the legal briefs? Has increased state funding of education given students in the schools of Jersey City and other poor districts of the State, rural and suburban as well as urban, the educational resources necessary to insure a "thorough and efficient" education?

Findings: What the New Law Does

We asked three major questions in this research; what we found is grouped under these concerns:

Who received the $400 million of new state aid?

68% of the $400 million went to districts of moderate wealth—those with $30,000 to $70,000 valuation per pupil. 12% flowed to poor districts with less than $30,000 valuation per pupil. The outcome? Although poor districts, which include four of New Jersey's six major cities, received $300 per pupil more in state aid, their share of the state aid pot decreased. In 1975-76 they had received 33% of total state aid. They received 24% of the total in 1977-78—a loss to the poor districts of nine percent under the new law.

The basic distribution pattern for aid was unchanged. High-wealth districts, through minimum aid, transportation aid and special education aid—all of which are not "equalized" to correct for disparities in property wealth—received more than $300 per pupil in aid. Differences in aid payments to low and high-wealth districts were not substantially larger in 1977-78 than they had been under the old law.

As Figure 1 suggests, state funds are distributed today in the same way they were under the old law.

Were the new funds used to increase school expenditures or to provide property tax relief?

Districts with low wealth (less than $30,000 valuation per pupil) and with high wealth (more than $110,000 per pupil) increased their per pupil expenditures at a rate slightly below the State average for the two-year period (22%). However, the poorer districts lowered their tax rates to a significantly greater degree (26%) than the statewide averages of 16%. The "budget caps" constrained the ability of poor districts to increase their expenditures at a faster rate, and forced them to *substitute* state aid for locally-raised education revenues. Even under the "caps," though, high-wealth districts increased their spending $400 per pupil between 1975 and 1977. Yet expenditures by poor districts grew by only $300 per pupil in the same period.

Did the new law succeed in making New Jersey's school finance system measurably fairer?

The new plan had no impact on disparities among districts in per pupil expenditure. In fact, the dollar gap between districts spending at the low 5th percentile and districts spending at the high 95th percentile widened in the period. The expenditure level of the lowest spending districts increased from 73% to 76% of the State average, while the expenditure level of districts with a history of high expenditures dropped only from 136% to 135% of the statewide average.

Concurrently the gap in tax rates began to narrow. High tax rate districts dropped their rates from 150% to 139% of the statewide average, while low taxing districts remained at about 40% of the statewide average.

Although the new system significantly increased the flow of state dollars to compensatory and bilingual education in districts with severe educational need, these districts still spent considerably less per weighted pupil[1] than did wealthier districts with lower educational need in 1977-78.

As Figure 2 suggests, the broad outcome of the new law in operation has been almost negligible. District wealth is still the major factor in determining the level of educational expenditures in New Jersey.

[1] Weighted Pupils represent the sum of the number of students enrolled in a district and the additional cost factors applied to students with special educational needs.

Issues for the Future: What Policymakers Should Consider

The new school finance law in New Jersey is no more equalizing than the old one, despite a 50% increase in state aid dollars. Why?

The distribution pattern remains unchanged. High-wealth districts continue to receive more than $300 per pupil in types of aid which are not "wealth-equalized." The new law revised aid payments to high- and low-wealth districts, but these revisions were not large enough to offset the substantial disparities in wealth across New Jersey, nor to correct the mismatch between the location of resources and the location of severest needs.

Struggling under heavy tax burdens and state mandated "budget caps," the low-wealth districts applied part of their increased state aid to tax relief. If all of the new state aid had been devoted to raising educational spending, expenditure disparities among districts could have been narrowed.

Rapid increases in property valuations on the upper end of the property wealth scale widened disparities among districts over the two-year period we studied. Therefore, an ever-increasing amount of state aid will be required to compensate for wealth-based differences in spending.

Further study must examine whether certain of these results are inevitable under a Guaranteed Tax Base formula, which the new law represents.

Policymakers and the public should also be concerned that the "caps" placed on school expenditures failed to hold down expenditures of high-spending school districts. What has been the impact of "caps" on districts poor in property?

Another issue raised by the brief history of New Jersey's new school finance law is that of implementing compensatory education funding. Devised under special categories and set up to reflect both poverty and student achievement in their distribution, these funds produced $30 per pupil for New Jersey's wealthy districts in the two-year period. Is this method the most effective way of distributing compensatory education aid?

In short, while The Public School Education Act of 1975 was designed to create a more equitable system of school finance in New Jersey, the realities of this reform were substantially different. The new law, with the resulting disparities in expenditures and tax rates, does not appear to adequately address the Court's concern with guaranteeing every child in the State a "thorough and efficient" education.

How Were the New Funds Used?

School districts in New Jersey could choose to use increased school aid to increase educational expenditures and/or cut property tax rates for schools. Due to a combination of local choice and the constraints of "budget caps," most districts applied only part of their "new" state aid to increasing expenditures; the remainder was used to decrease their reliance on local property taxes to pay for public elementary and secondary education.

When we look at districts classified by wealth we see that *low-wealth districts increased their current expenditures slightly less than the State average increase, while making substantially larger reductions in their property tax rates.* Districts with less than $30,000 valuation per pupil, on the average, increased current expenditures 20.8% and decreased tax rates 26.1% from 1975 to 1977; districts with greater than $110,000 valuation per pupil increased current expenditures an average of 20% while dropping their equalized tax rate an average of 7.1%.

In sum, although the State substantially increased its contribution to funding education, *the beneficiaries were not the students of poor districts.* Rather than leading to substantial increases in the education budgets of low-wealth districts, *the new school finance program provided the greatest benefit to taxpayers of low- and moderate-wealth communities.*

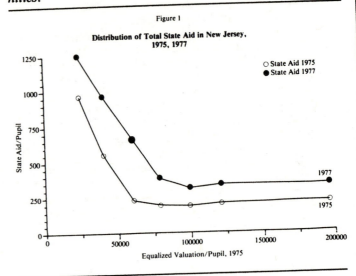

Figure 1

Distribution of Total State Aid in New Jersey, 1975, 1977

○ State Aid 1975
● State Aid 1977

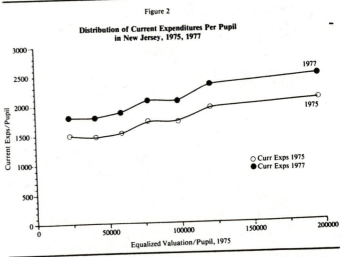

Figure 2

Distribution of Current Expenditures Per Pupil in New Jersey, 1975, 1977

○ Curr Exps 1975
● Curr Exps 1977

"Money and Education: Where Did the $400 Million Go? The Impact of the New Jersey Public School Education Act of 1975" is reprinted by permission from the Educational Testing Service, Princeton, N.J.

CHAPTER 13

Metropolitan Tax Base Sharing

The warfare between states and localities to attract new industry is a running sore in American public finance which has eroded the ability of public officials to distribute tax burdens fairly.

The following article, entitled **Minnesota Helps Its Metropolis Share the Tax Base** by Peter Nye, describes one of the most imaginative and promising responses to this problem, the "Fiscal Disparities" or tax base sharing program devised in Minnesota early in this decade for the seven county Minneapolis-St. Paul region. Under this program, the communities in the region share 40% of all the increases to their commercial and industrial property tax base. In other words, no matter where new industries locate in the region, every community gets a share of the new tax revenue.

The author catalogues the advantages of the program. A main one, of course, is that it "works to right the lopsided bonanza of winner-take-all urban development." Furthermore, the act reduces somewhat the enthusiasm of bedroom suburbs for zoning out poor people, because the shared tax base is allocated partly according to population. At the same time, tax base sharing preserves local control because tax base, and not tax revenue, is shared. Each community decides for itself how heavily to tax its share of the pool.

The article also explores the complex politics of tax base sharing, and summarizes its impact to date. Of forty-one localities, eighteen have gained tax base and twenty-three have lost. The gainers included the older central cities of Minneapolis and St. Paul, while the losers tended to be bedroom suburbs. One problem, Mr. Nye notes, is that some assessors tend to underassess their commercial and industrial property, thus keeping value out of the common pool.

Minnesota Helps Its Metropolis Share the Tax Base

Minnesota's innovative tax base sharing program is like a game, one observer says, where everybody puts something in and everybody takes something back. Some take back more than they contribute, others less. In the three years now that the program has been in effect, it has redistributed several hundred million dollars in communities in the greater St. Paul-Minneapolis area to help overcome the disequilibrium among different taxing jurisdictions.

Officially it is called the Minnesota Fiscal Disparities Act of 1971. Colloquially, is known as tax base sharing. Actually, what it does is compare each jurisdiction's current year's taxes to its 1971 taxes, and if there has been any commercial or industrial tax growth, 40 percent of that growth goes into an area-wide pool for distribution according to a formula based on population and relative municipal indigence. Each taxing jurisdiction keeps the remaining 60 percent. The adjusted tax base of each community is then its tax base from 1971, plus 60 percent of its growth and its assigned distribution from the regional pool.

Its philosophy is based in part on spreading the property value for each person around to help finance municipal services in each of the approximately 300 taxing jurisdictions in the 3,000-square-mile area. It affects a locality's capacity to raise revenue, without raising any revenue itself.

Tax base sharing is a regional approach to help finance a multitude of local governments whose wealth varies widely. At the same time it preserves local decision making. It's a player's game, not a winner's, for it works to right the lopsided bonanza of winner-take-all urban development. It softens the self-perpetuating pattern in which new development continues to enter a community that has lower property taxes.

The distribution formula is complex, but essentially it is based on population and is adjusted to include property valuation compared to the metropolitan aver-age per person. Under the adjustment, if a community is below the metropolitan average, its government receives a larger share; if a community has property valuation above the metropolitan average, it receives a smaller share.

The tax base sharing program in the North Star State is the only one of its kind in the country (New Jersey has a modified version within the Hackensack Meadowlands District, but this is part of a master redevelopment plan and thus considered to be a special case), and it attracts increasing attention nationally. Three state legislatures—Maryland, Michigan, and Virginia—have rejected tax base sharing bills, and other states—California, Pennsylvania, Washington—and the province of Alberta in Canada are looking into tax base sharing with the Minnesota program as a model. HUD is examining tax base sharing as a possible federal link between public finance and economic development for cities.

Residential growth is exempt, and revenue from it goes to the governments where the buildings are located.

In updating tax bases, numerous elements are taken into consideration such as new construction, buildings torn down, and revaluation (values increasing through inflation or depreciating by becoming obsolete). This helps share the profits as well as absorb the burden of decline.

"As the years approach infinity, we

TWIN CITIES METROPOLITAN AREA
Political Boundaries, 1975

approach [pooling] 40 percent of the total commercial and industrial property in the area," said Paul Gilje, associate director of the Citizens League, a non-profit organization based in Minneapolis that identifies regional and state problems and offers solutions. From 1975 to 1977 (with 1977 taxes payable in 1978), the tax base pool has increased from about 5 percent to approximately 9 percent of the total assessed commercial and industrial valuation. "Of course, we only approach 40 percent. We would only get there if a city had no commercial or industrial business there in 1971 and acquired some later."

Supporters say the beauty of tax base sharing is that each locality continues to make its own policy decisions for levying property taxes within its jurisdiction. There is a broader tax base to work with, regardless of the existence of 7 counties, 135 municipalities, 60 townships, and nearly 100 special districts for schools, libraries, and parks in the St. Paul-Minneapolis area. All these approximately 300 taxing jurisdictions retain their autonomy, and no metropolitan agency is created. It helps homogenize the regional tax base to some degree and makes a contribution to the communities that are stagnating or declining economically.

"What it does is help carry a central city that is faced with declining revenues through transition," said Ted Kolderie, director of the Citizens League. It gives to the Twin Cities a percentage of the money to be distributed that is in proportion to their share of the area population. St. Paul gets about 16 percent of the money, Minneapolis about 20 percent.

Tax base sharing, Kolderie and other supporters say, helps even out those peaks and valleys of the economic cycle. For example, a suburban municipality that has a number of subdivisions being built has high costs before major commercial and industrial facilities are attracted to the community. Later, the mature municipality has to contend with high costs for the replacement of streets, bridges, schools, and other facilities before it can restore the momentum to its commercial and industrial redevelopment. The latter is what tax base sharing supporters say is happening to the Twin Cities of St. Paul-Minneapolis.

One social advantage of tax base shar-

ing is that it helps break down economic barriers between center cities and their suburbs. Tax base sharing reduces incentives for fiscal zoning, a practice some suburbs use to keep out certain kinds of development that would lower the area property tax base. Some communities have excluded low- and moderate-income housing with the protest that such housing won't provide sufficient tax returns for the services residents require.

Under tax base sharing, however, the more people in a community, the greater the local share of the region's commercial and industrial base growth. In addition, under HUD Secretary Patricia Harris's administration, more communities would be eligible for community development (CD) block grant funds. Secretary Harris has said repeatedly that HUD assistance to communities is contingent upon their taking in low- and moderate-income housing.

Another social advantage is better land use. Jim Solem, director of local and urban affairs at the state planning agency in St. Paul, said that with tax base sharing, communities can be more selective about businesses that enter their community. "In the case of a chemical factory, for example, I think people step back and see whether the factory will cause environmental problems," he said. "That may result in the community deciding to turn down a chemical company's offer to move in."

Tax base sharing also diminishes the rivalry between communities to woo businesses away from one another, particularly in cases of suburbs competing against suburbs. Instead, they can compete together for firms from elsewhere in the nation. With the trend in recent years toward larger and larger shopping centers that offer greater arrays of merchandise and professional services, observers say, there will tend to be fewer shopping centers. The commercial and industrial tax benefits will be more intense but will go to fewer communities. Under tax base sharing local competition can give way to a more rational land use.

What helps make tax base sharing work in the Twin Cities metropolitan area is a concentration of about half of the state's 3.9 million people, which gives a compact commercial, industrial, and labor base to draw from. The Twin

Cities enjoyed a head start over other cities in the area. They had the older industries, Minnesota Mining and Manufacturing Co. in St. Paul and Pillsbury Co. in Minneapolis. But these and other industries since have decentralized and moved out of the state, leaving mainly their headquarters offices behind. For the most part the commercial and industrial base is widely scattered around the metropolitan area. Today the region's economy is centered on *services and management* businesses which cover a wide range of activities such as corporate management, banking (the Ninth Federal Reserve District Bank was established in Minneapolis in 1917), and data processing. The area's work force has more than doubled between 1950 and 1976, from 450,000 to 925,000.

St. Paul and Minneapolis adjoin, with St. Paul to the east. Their centers are about 10 miles apart. They have unusually homogeneous populations, a factor that reduces conflicts of interest and helps groups reach a consensus more smoothly on a regional basis. The area's population is overwhelmingly white (97 percent). Most of them come from German, Scandinavian, English, and Irish descent. They form a solid middle class that retains its work ethic and has a strong sense of self-reliance. They show their hardiness by enduring (some say prevailing) in the coldest major metropolitan area in the country, which averages a daily low in January of two degrees Fahrenheit.

There are, however, sufficient differences to foster a notorious rivalry between the two cities. St. Paul is located on the Mississippi River at the mouth of the Minnesota River and was settled as a steamboat terminus on the Mississippi in the 1820s. It still is a big shipping and railroad center in addition to being the state capital. St. Paul's 310,000 population is mostly Catholic.

Minneapolis was settled a few years later along the Mississippi. Population expanded when railroads were laid westward to attract more people across the Northwest frontier. In 1880 the population of Minneapolis surpassed St. Paul. The 434,000 people in Minneapolis are mostly Protestant, and the city has a more diversified economy than has St. Paul.

John McLean, a former Minnesotan

turned Washington, D.C., civil servant, once neatly characterized the difference between the two cities. "Minneapolis," he said, "looks to Boston for its model. St. Paul looks to Chicago."

The area has a history of thinking and acting meaningfully about metropolitan problems. To go back a bit, the groundwork for acting on metropolitan issues was laid when the Minnesota legislature created the Metropolitan Planning Commission (MPC) in 1957 to identify metropolitan problems and suggest solutions. The MPC, made up of local elected officials and members appointed by the governor, was in operation for 10 years. One of the most important issues it tackled was the problem of providing adequate sanitary sewer facilities. The issues of location of treatment plants, how to finance them, and what kinds of systems to have had languished unresolved before the legislature for 10 years.

Out of the MPC and the issue of sanitary sewer facilities grew the successor to MPC, the Metropolitan Council, created by the legislature in 1967 and empowered with real authority to effect solutions—something the MPC, an advisory group, lacked. The Metropolitan Council is made up of 16 members appointed by the governor and confirmed by the state senate.

This new agency was mandated by the legislature in 1967 to return to the next legislative session, in 1969, with detailed recommendations about the sewer treatment problems of greater St. Paul-Minneapolis.

The issue of fiscal disparities among the local government units became more pronounced when local officials examined how different local governments would finance the required services for the proposed sewage treatment plants. The ratio of disparities ranged as broadly as 12 to 1 in valuations for each person living in the different taxing jurisdictions.

Jim Solem, the state planner, contends that construction of a power plant in Oak Park Heights precipitated tax base sharing as a means of resolving the differences between local fiscal disparities and public policies. People took sides on whether to construct a power plant in Oak Park Heights or preserve the surrounding verdant St. Croix valley,

which separates Minnesota from Wisconsin, east of the Twin Cities. Residents of Washington County, which embraces the valley, would gain in their tax base. They said if people in the metropolitan area wanted the valley to be maintained as a park for its aesthetic value, then the whole metropolitan area should pay the costs of Washington County's local government.

At the same time this debate was going on, State Representative Charles R. Weaver, chairman of the House Fiscal Affairs Subcommittee of the House Committee on Metropolitan and Urban Affairs, was looking for a system that

Charles Weaver

would give part of commercial and industrial developments to areas lacking development. Weaver represented Anoka, a middle-income residential suburb in Anoka County on the northern metropolitan rim.

The forward-thinking Citizens League picked up on the search. Each year the league's board selects six local-oriented political issues which a committee studies for six to nine months, followed by another three to four months of debate until the committee members reach a conclusion. Funds for the league come from its approximately 3,200 dues-paying members and grants from another 500 foundations, business groups, and other organizations.

One proposal the league was considering was creation of a metropolitan taxing district that would impose a uniform tax on all property and distribute the revenues back to local governments.

What finally clinched tax base sharing as politically acceptable and financially practical was a suggestion advanced by a member of the league's Fiscal Disparities Committee, F. Warren Preeshl. In December, 1968, when the committee was debating alternative solutions for giving local governments access to the tax resources of the entire metropolitan area, Preeshl, a municipal bond consultant, released a three-page memorandum that suggested sharing 40 percent of the growth in the assessed commercial and industrial tax base.

"It was important to leave people with what they had," he said in a recent interview in Minneapolis. "Only 40 percent of the growth is shared. That is less than half. The community still retains more than half of the growth."

Preeshl, a soft-spoken man who smokes a pipe and wears a close-cropped white beard, has been in the local municipal bond business since 1950. He says through his work he has helped finance the first and second tiers of suburbs and beyond. The problem of fiscal disparities was an intellectual one in which he could bring his knowledge of bond structures and taxation into play.

"We capture just the commercial and industrial growth," he continued. "Apartments and other residences are excluded from this because they have kids. That tax base is important to the school districts and shouldn't be shared with anybody. But commerce and industry are attracted to where people are, and you need to tax that."

Representative Weaver took sugges-

Lyle Olsen

tions, including Preeshl's, from an outline the league drew up and drafted a bill in April, 1969, to carry out tax base sharing. The bill was warmly received and passed the House overwhelmingly, 115-14, but the 120-day session ran out before the Senate could hold a hearing on it.

Weaver reintroduced the bill, by then called the Weaver Bill, in the 1971 legislative session. In the two intervening years, however, the state government went through some profound changes that changed the atmosphere for the proposed bill.

One was the election of Wendell Anderson in 1970 as the new governor. Anderson was a member of the Democratic Farmer Labor party, the state's equivalent to the Democratic party. (In 1944 the Minnesota Democratic party merged with the larger Farmer Labor party to form the DFL, as it is called; the Republican party is known as the Independent Republicans of Minnesota.) Part of Anderson's gubernatorial campaign was devoted to property tax reform. In the three years prior to the campaign, property taxes had increased steadily by an average of 20 percent annually and showed signs of climbing even more steeply. Controversy around property tax reform helped gain visibility for the issue that Anderson was identified with. Anderson was then carefully grooming a promising political career. He had served two two-year terms as state representative from east St. Paul and two four-year terms in the state senate. When he was elected governor, he was 37, then youngest governor in the nation. (Reelected as governor in 1974, he resigned shortly after the 1976 presidential election and was appointed by his

successor, Gov. Rudy Perpich, on December 30, 1976, to complete Walter Mondale's term as junior U.S. senator from Minnesota.) Anderson provided state leadership for the Weaver Bill by endorsing it.

Another change that was a boost to the Weaver Bill was an influx of DFL legislators. The Republicans lost many seats in the 1970 elections but they still managed, just barely, to control both houses. In the 1971 session, Republicans controlled the House by five votes (70 to 65), the Senate by only one vote (34 to 33).

But obstacles arose in the two-year interim. More legislators were getting pressure to oppose the Weaver Bill. Communities that anticipated they would lose tax base figured they were better off growing alone. In addition, city assessors cast doubts about how the bill could be administered.

Another obstacle was that some rural legislators, especially senators, who lived outside the seven-county metropolitan area saw the Weaver Bill as a means for replacing local control with regional government. Once the state legislature passed tax base sharing for the seven counties, some senators reasoned, it could be expanded to apply to the entire state.

"My argument all through this debate was that this was the only way to save local government," Weaver said in a recent interview. "We live in a complex society that is more and more interdependent. I said tax base sharing was a way of helping communities cut down on such wide fiscal disparities. It definitely cuts down on local competition to attract new businesses."

Many of the rural representatives

Wendell R. Anderson

from beyond the metropolitan area supported Weaver, whose community wasn't readily identified as one chiefly of urban interests. Partisanship favored the Weaver Bill because the DFLers endorsed it while the Republicans had no caucus position and, subsequently, were split.

When the Weaver Bill was back on the legislative floor in 1971, the House passed it a second time by a vote of 83-39, a substantial margin but without the popularity it enjoyed the first time. Rural opposition was more apparent in the senate. But Senator Wayne G. Popham, who authored the bill in the senate, skillfully garnered sufficient support; the bill squeaked by with a three-vote margin, 34-31. Once it passed the legislature in July during an extended session, Governor Anderson signed it.

No sooner had the ink dried on the new law than the village of Burnsville, a booming suburb south of Minneapolis (its population swelled by 50 percent from 1970 to 1973—from 20,000 to 30,000), started preparing a lawsuit to contest the new law's constitutionality. When plans were under way in late 1972 to put tax base sharing into use, Burnsville, located in Dakota County, filed suit in the Dakota County District Court.

The Dakota District Court ruled in early 1973 that the law was unconstitutional. In handing down the decision, Judge Robert Breunig said tax base sharing "fails to pass the test of constitutional uniformity requiring that the burden of a tax must fall equally and impartially upon all persons and projects subject to it." While the decision was on appeal to the Minnesota Supreme Court, the district court declined to permit tax base sharing to be carried out.

In September, 1974, the Minnesota Supreme Court reversed the lower court's decision and upheld the constitutionality of the law by a vote of 4-3, with two judges not participating. The majority opinion, written by Justice James Otis, pointed to the principles established in the U.S. Supreme Court case of the *San Antonio Independent School District* v. *Rodriguez*, in which the U.S. Supreme Court ruled in March, 1973, that solutions for pupil expenditure disparities among districts "must come from the lawmakers and from the democratic pressures of those who elect them." Justice Otis said tax base sharing was an innovative and bold vehicle to balance "the benefits and burdens of taxation."

An appeal by Burnsville to the U.S. Supreme Court in 1975 was turned down because the case lacked a substantial federal question.

By the time the law made it through the legal wrangle in the fall of 1974, there was a total of $137 million for distribution. The sum represented a three-year accumulation of the total assessed valuation in the seven-county area.

Most of the taxing jurisdictions that gained were the older communities: St. Paul and Minneapolis and the first ring of suburbs. The Twin Cities received the largest share—together they got 36 percent of the area-wide pool. St. Paul gained a net of $20.3 million while Minneapolis gained a net of $29.6 million. Most of the net losers (contributing more commercial and industrial valuation to the metropolitan pool than they received back) were developing suburbs located between the first-ring suburbs and the rural areas.

Inver Grove Heights, south of St. Paul, lost the most tax base for each person. This year, with 1976 taxes payable in 1977, Inver Grove Heights will lose a net of $4.5 million.

The community that gained the most for each person was not either of the big center cities but Stillwater, located northeast of St. Paul on the St. Croix River. It is an economically stagnating community that is mostly residential and has had nearly no commercial or industrial growth since the late 1940s.

Before the sharing formula was applied, the 41 communities that had populations of more than 10,000 had a range of commercial-industrial valuation in 1976 from $221 to $2,503 for each person, according to figures released by the Metropolitan Council. Today the disparity has narrowed somewhat to a range of $319 to $2,193.

Other figures show that 18 of the 41 communities gained net revenues as a result of tax base sharing, and 23 lost. Communities that gained improved their

valuation range for each person from $221 to $1,379 before sharing to a narrower range of $319 to $1,395. Before tax base sharing the median valuation (middle figure in the range for the area's property valuation tax base) was $482; after sharing it was $505. Among the communities that had a net loss, valuations for each person ranged from $370 to $2,503 before sharing and shrank to a range of $354 to $2,196 after sharing. Before sharing, the median valuation was $1,369 for each person; after sharing it was $1,151.

The amount of tax base to be shared has grown from $137 million in 1975. In 1976 the tax base sharing total amounted to $187 million.

One state revenue official, who declined to be identified, said tax base sharing was a program in which the state doesn't really get involved. "It's the cities and counties that are involved," he said. Its value to the state is that it relieves the state from having to generate another revenue-raising program.

The state treasurer collects tax base sharing revenues from the county treasurers and returns to the county treasurers their respective county distribution. The county treasurer in turn distributes the money to every taxing jurisdiction in the county, such as watershed districts, schools districts, and the county itself.

From the counties' viewpoint, tax base sharing has created a great deal of controversy but relatively little money. Each of the seven counties covers a wide area that also includes a fairly equal commercial and industrial spread; the tax base contribution and redistribution nets little change compared to total county revenues.

Another state official who also declined to be identified said the tax base sharing program would be substantially greater if there were a major electric generating plant in any one of the seven counties. "What we are sharing is the corner drug store," he said and shrugged. "That may sound like an oversimplification, but that's what it comes down to. If there were at least one electric generating plant worth more than $1 billion in the seven-county area, the value that would be shared would be worth talking about."

There are three major electric generating plants for the area, each located outside the seven-county tax base sharing jurisdiction. Two nuclear power plants are in Red Wing and Monticello, and a coal fire electric plant is in Becker.

A variety of officials of different opinions about tax base sharing agree that it has done what it was intended to do—reduce long-range differences in the commercial and industrial valuation for each person among metropolitan communities.

The revenues from tax base sharing are much less than those generated by the Fair School Financing Law, a school aid formula passed in 1971, shortly after the Fiscal Disparities Act. Under the school aid formula, there is a standard mill levy rate applied to all school districts across the state toward the state-established expenditure for each pupil. The state then makes up the difference between what the levy rate is and the education costs for each pupil. In some communities, where there is low valuation, the state pays as much as 90 percent of each student's education costs. School aid revenues come from the state income tax.

"This simply swamps the effects of tax base sharing," Preeshl said. "It has 10 to 20 times the effect of tax base sharing."

With tax base sharing diminished by the school aid, critics of tax base sharing claim there already are sufficient funding means to provide financially disadvantaged communities with the money they need.

"The Fiscal Disparities Act is like putting out a forest fire with a squirt gun," said leading critic Lyle Olson, director of Staff Services, which over-

F. Warren Preeshl

sees the assessment activities for Bloomington, a suburb in Hennepin County, south of Minneapolis. "The money that cities get is peanuts compared to the funds coming from the state, county, and federal governments."

He said a recent state-wide survey of federal, state, and county aid per person in 1975 shows Minneapolis and St. Paul were the two Minnesota cities receiving the most revenue per person. Minneapolis's share worked out to an average of $162 per person, St. Paul $128. Olson said tax base sharing money was considerably less; Minneapolis receiving $4 per person and St. Paul $7.

Bloomington has expanded its commercial and industrial base greatly in the last 15 years although its 79,000 population has decreased 3.4 percent since 1970. Its officials don't feel happy about giving any of its burgeoning tax base away. Since tax base sharing was put into action, Bloomington has lost a net of $13 million, Olson said.

"We agree with the intent of the Fiscal Disparities Act, but we oppose the way it's being done," he said. "Basically we question whether the state legislature has the power to pass a law that in effect will levy taxes in one city to help pay the expenses or reduce taxes in another city. That is precisely what happens."

Olson and other critics of tax base sharing say that it indirectly raises residential taxes by way of reducing the commercial and industrial base, which is less base for the community to draw from.

In another flourishing suburb, Shakopee, about 30 miles southwest of St. Paul, City Assessor LeRoy Houser is incensed over what tax base sharing means to Shakopee. This city of 10,000 people (compared to 6,900 in 1970) has been contributing more than it has been getting back. "It is really a horror story. If you were to try tax base sharing outside the state of Minnesota, they would tar and feather you."

During an interview in his office he pulled out a long horizontal sheet of figures for 1975. "The owner of a house with a market value of $30,000 would pay $759.16 if it weren't for tax base sharing. But the net tax with tax base sharing is $841.28. That's a difference of $82.12. A parent could buy two or three pairs of trousers and a pair of shoes for one of their kids with that money."

Houser said the increased real estate taxes following the application of tax base sharing has brought a steep upsurge in the number of homeowners suing the city over property taxes. "Last year I had to go to court for more than 300 lawsuits," he said. "Before tax base sharing, there weren't any of these lawsuits."

A state law passed this year makes it illegal to underassess the value of property. Under the Improper Assessment Penalty Law, Shakopee could lose up to $50,000 in state aid for underassessing the value of property, Houser said.

Underassessment has been a thorny problem with tax base sharing, particularly in Ramsey, Dakota, and Scott Counties, where property has long been underassessed. Shakopee is in Scott County, which values property the lowest (67.7 percent) compared to its actual value, according to 1975 figures from the Minnesota Department of Revenue. (Highest is Hennepin County at 90 percent.)

But proponents of tax base sharing contend it has greater long-term benefits since it stabilizes the regional tax base, thus encouraging businesses to remain and expand rather than move away.

One such supporter is Dr. Katharine C. Lyall, former professor of political economy at Johns Hopkins University and now a deputy assistant secretary for economic affairs at HUD. Lyall researched tax base sharing for a bill submitted before the Maryland House of Representatives each year from 1973 to 1975. She said a survey of business leaders showed tax base sharing would greatly cut down incentives for communities to apply irregular tax rates in order to make their community more attractive to new businesses.

"To a degree, the business people don't care about paying taxes," she said. "They have to pay taxes anyway. But business leaders don't like it when they pay a higher tax rate than another business in the taxing jurisdiction. Tax base sharing further narrows the taxing differential among communities."

Critics of tax base sharing say the drive to attract new businesses is greatly diminished since the community gains scarcely more than half of the growth—it took time and effort to get.

Supporters respond that 60 percent of new growth is better than 100 percent of nothing. Moreover, supporters say, local jurisdictions have good reasons to attract new businesses. The most important is to boost local employment. Another is to help provide businesses and services for the local population.

Critics also report there are more businesses springing up outside the metropolitan area since the Fiscal Disparities Act went into effect. They say the businesses illustrate that tax base sharing discourages drawing new businesses.

However, Eugene Knaff, economist and planner for the Metropolitan Council, said those businesses tend to be labor-intensive, with jobs that don't match skills inside the metropolitan area.

It is still too early to get hard evidence to show whether tax base sharing has a tangible effect on where businesses locate in relation to the tax base sharing area. But examination of the base assessed values on which taxes are levied shows at least thus far commercial and industrial growth hasn't been hampered. In 1971, the assessed base value was $1,693,383,307. During the next two years figures weren't developed because the case was under litigation. But the 1974 figures showed there had been consistent improvement, with the base rising to $2,037,641,209. The next two years showed further growth: $2,121,867,695 in 1975, and $2,192,346,130 in 1976.

Tax base sharing is headed once again for the courts. The town of Shakopee is getting a lawsuit ready to contest its constitutionality. Lawyer Rod Krass, who is handling the case for Shakopee, said, "Our central argument is basically in the application, not the concept, of the Fiscal Disparities Act. We are saying if you look at how it works, it is unfair to the citizens of Shakopee."

A motion already has been denied by the state for a summary judgment, which means the case will be tried on a different point than the first time it was settled. The case is expected to be tried in the Scott County District Court early next year. With the decision rests the future of the only regional approach in the country for resolving local fiscal disparities.

"Minnesota Helps Its Metropolis Share The Tax Base" is reprinted by permission from *Nations Cities* The National League of Cities.

VII

Consider the cases of the fictional Henry K. Rockefeller and Joe Schmo.

Among the vast holdings of Mr. Rockefeller are shares of stock he purchased fifteen years ago for $15,000. These shares are now worth $65,000. The same year that Rockefeller made his stock market move, Joe Schmo, an appliance repairman, scraped together the downpayment for a $15,000 home. This home, still the only substantial property Joe Schmo possesses, is now worth the same amount as Rockefeller's stock, $65,000.

How do we treat Rockefeller's and Schmo's property at tax time? One might think that a house being an essential, and with Schmo living close to the bone to begin with, we would give Schmo a little break. In fact we do just the opposite. Mr. Rockefeller's stock property is exempt from property taxes, while Schmo's house is subject to taxes which go up every time the house increases in value.

What makes this even more galling for Schmo is that for most of these fifteen years he has "owned" just a small percentage of the house on which he is paying taxes. Actually, the bank owned most of it, as he slowly paid off his mortgage. The property tax, however, falls entirely on Schmo as though the bank had no piece of the action.

It doesn't take a Ph.D. in philosophy to see the in-justice. Single-family homes—in fact real estate generally—comprise just a fraction of the property in the U.S. Yet this real estate bears practically the entire property tax burden. Originally, the property tax covered *all* kinds of property. How can we justify dumping the whole load onto homeowners and other real estate owners the way we do today?

Predictably, there are numerous theories. It is argued, for example, that since Rockefeller pays tax on the dividends he receives from the stock, it would be unfair to tax the value of his stock too. This theory doesn't cut too much mustard with Schmo. To keep up with his outrageous electric bills he has begun renting his back bedroom to a local college student, and this rent, like Rockefeller's dividends, is treated as income for tax purposes. Schmo, in short, pays tax on both his property's value and on the income he receives from the property. Why shouldn't Rockefeller do the same?

Another theory is that returning stocks to the property tax would "discourage" people like Rockefeller from buying stocks. "What is Rockefeller going to do with his money, hide it in the refrigerator?" Schmo asks. "And hey, why doesn't anyone ever worry about all these property taxes discouraging *me* from buying a *house*?"

Enlisting more kinds of property to help

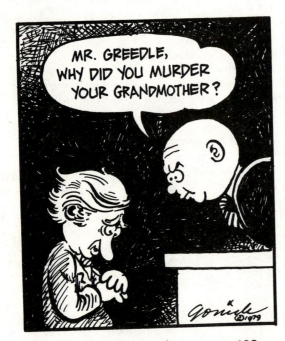

MR. GREEDLE, WHY DID YOU MURDER YOUR GRANDMOTHER?

YOUR HONOR, SHE HAD AMASSED A COLLECTION OF STOCKS, BONDS, PERSIAN RUGS, RARE WINES, BUTTERFLIES, AND MINKS. SINCE, FOR SOME IDIOTIC REASON, THE STATE DOESN'T *TAX* THESE FORMS OF PROPERTY, THE OLD GIRL GREW IMMENSELY *RICH!*

Alternative Strategies for Taxing Wealth

By Jonathan Rowe

homeowners carry the property tax burden would make most people's load a little lighter. Property taxes on intangibles could raise large amounts of revenue at very low rates. They could, moreover, make the tax system more fair. The gradual shift of the property tax burden onto homeowners has mirrored the shift of the income tax from a tax on all income to a tax mainly on wages. Bringing paper property back into the property tax base would help reverse this tax burden shift and would help meet homeowner demands for tax relief without decimating public services.

Taxing Inherited Wealth

"The earth belongs to the living," declared Thomas Jefferson. "The portion occupied by an individual ceases to be his when (he) himself ceases to be, and reverts to the society."

Given this important strain in our political tradition, along with our worries about taxes stifling the productive enterprises of the living, it is a puzzle why the property of the departed—i.e. estates—has languished as a forgotten outpost of tax policy, while taxes on the living have mounted.

Estate and inheritance taxes have never amounted to much in the U.S., and their role has diminished continually. Back in 1922, these taxes provided 4.4%

of federal and 8.6% of state and local revenues. By 1976 the amounts were 1.75% and 1.7% respectively.

Why do we tax living people heavily and tax so lightly what they leave when they pass from the scene? It would seem more just and practical to do the reverse, to allow people to enjoy the fruits of their efforts while they are living, and to claim society's share when the individual's—and his or her spouse's—enjoyment of these fruits has ended. If there must be taxes—and surely there must be some—then death seems the least painful time to levy them.

Other Advantages

Consider these other advantages of taxing estates as opposed to taxing the activities and property of the living.

1. Some critics argue that income taxes "discourage" people from working and investing. It can hardly be argued that estate taxes will discourage people from dying.

2. Estates, often in the form of trusts, tend to be managed and invested very conservatively. They tend to be invested only in the largest, most established "blue chip" firms instead of in new firms and innovative technologies. This worsens the problems of monopoly power and technological lag. Estate taxes

would free up this capital for investment in new firms and in the riskier, innovative technologies which are desperately needed.

3. Estate taxes tend to put each member of each generation at the same starting line, and thus promote the ideal that individuals should succeed according to individual merit, and not because of inherited advantages or disadvantages. They can prevent large concentrations of wealth and power in particular families.

4. Jefferson maintained that the third generation of wealthy families is usually idle, incompetent, and inclined to use its inherited wealth foolishly. Estate taxes tend to preclude this problem.

5. Enforcement of estate taxes is relatively easy, because there is always a final accounting of estates for the benefit of the heirs.

It is possible to argue that estate taxes discourage people from working hard to accumulate large estates. This raises a host of questions, such as whether rich individuals continue to work mainly to make more income, or whether it truly is desirable for people who have accumulated enough for their family's needs, and more, to persist in acquisitiveness. Suffice it to say here that most people don't even have a chance to compile a large estate, and that "life" taxes weigh far more heavily upon them than "estate" taxes would weigh upon the departed. Even if estate taxes were some sort of "disincentive" they would certainly be less so than life taxes such as property and income taxes. And perhaps the "disincentive" of estate taxes would not be all that bad. If wealthy people were to spend their later years in benevolent activities instead of in octogenarian profit-maximizing pursuits, then everyone might benefit.

As the article by L.L. Ecker-Racz in Chapter 15 notes, there is disagreement over whether these taxes should be levied on the entire estate, or whether they should be levied separately on the inheritance of each heir. This question, though important, is secondary to that of reviving this type of tax *in some form*. For this reason, in this introduction, the term "estate tax" has been used generically for the various kinds of taxes on the transfer of property at death.

Widows and Family

People often feel skittish about estate taxes because they worry about the impacts upon widows, family farms, and small businesses. "Why shouldn't a person be able to leave his or her spouse enough to live comfortably, or enough for the children's or grandchildren's education?" people ask. "And is it right that estate taxes should force cash-poor heirs to sell a family farm or business to a conglomerate to raise the cash to pay the taxes?"

These are legitimate concerns which estate tax policy should respect. Forcing the sale of family farms and businesses to conglomerates is completely contrary to the Jeffersonian ideals which estate taxes are supposed to promote (as is forcing the sale of inner-city rowhouses to real estate speculators.)

Enabling people to make provision for their spouse and children is both fair and does little violence to any compelling ideal which would dictate otherwise. Perhaps most important, if estate taxes threaten spouses, family farms, and the like, then political support is apt to be spotty. Exemptions and credits can take care of these problems, which Congress and some states already have addressed to some degree.

A particular injustice is the way estate tax laws sometimes discriminate against women. These laws sometimes do not treat property held jointly by husband and wife as the fruits of a partnership. To the contrary, the surviving spouse must prove an actual contribution to the cost of the assets in question, in order for that portion of the value to be left out of the taxable estate. In traditional marriage, in which the husband is the breadwinner, it is easy for the husband to prove his contribution, and exceedingly difficult for the wife to prove hers. To the extent this vicious test is eliminated, and marriage is deemed to be an economic partnership, estate taxes would hold less threat for wives when their spouses pass from the scene.

Corporations: Major Blind Spot

There remains a major estate tax blind spot—corporations. Unlike people, the largest corporations rarely die. They keep accumulating and accumulating and accumulating, from one generation to the next. Nothing stops them. Corporations thus acquire more and more power, while individuals, less.

It can be argued that corporate stock shares are included in estates, and that for this reason estate taxes on individuals tend to disperse stock ownership and thus the control of corporations. This assertion is naive. Even if estate taxes did effectively disperse the shareholder power of families such as the Rockefellers, Mellons and Fords, such dispersal does nothing to slow the accumulating power of the corporation itself. To the contrary, if anything, dispersal of shareholder power in large corporations merely shifts more power to corporate managements.

The solution to this problem would be a landmark innovation in public policy. Corporations are not "natural" beings. They are creatures of human law. They "live" as long as human law says they live. Currently, human law says they can live forever. That need not be so. Many business privileges conferred by law—such as licenses—have time limits. Corporations over a certain size likewise could have time limits. Every so many years—70, for example—large corporations could be required to "divest" (i.e. sell off) their assets above a certain value. This would clear the economic decks for new entrepreneurs with new and better ideas. It would encourage competition and innovation. It could diminish the overwhelming political power of large corporations. And it could take some of the load off of the cumbersome and ineffective antitrust laws, which are all we have for keeping large corporations within civilized limits.

200

A Lesson From the Past

Another way of restraining the power of large corporations—specifically, their power over the states and communities in which they reside—can be drawn from estate tax history. Early in this century, a few states, notably Florida and Nevada, began eliminating their estate taxes in order to attract wealthy senior citizens, much as today states are enacting tax abatements to entice large corporations. Congress stepped in to curb this earlier interstate tax warfare by, in effect, putting a floor under estate taxes. By allowing a credit for state estate taxes against up to 80% of the federal tax, Congress in essence said that no matter where a person had resided when he or she died, at least a certain amount of estate tax would be paid. The only question was whether it all went to the federal government, or whether the state claimed its share. State estate tax "breaks" beyond a certain point would not save the taxpayer any money. They would simply hand over to the federal government revenues which the state itself could have claimed.

This same device could pull the rug out from the efforts of large corporations to play the states off against each other to get the best tax "deal." A federal credit for state corporate taxes would guarantee that corporations paid at least a minimum of state taxes no matter where they located. It would call a partial truce in the self-defeating war between the states to attract large corporations through tax reductions and abatements. It would free state legislators from tax policy paralysis brought on by fear of driving out their corporate taxpayers. It would even slow somewhat the migration of U.S. factories to low wage dictatorships abroad by extending to U.S. plants a tax advantage—the federal tax credit—already enjoyed by such facilities owned by U.S. corporations but located in foreign countries.

CHAPTER 14

Intangible Property

"Intangible" property is, literally, property you cannot touch. In practice, the term includes "paper" property such as stocks and bonds which are valuable not because of what they are made of, but because of what they represent.

The first article, **Taxing Wealth—A New Source of Government Revenue** by Jonathan Rowe, asks why we single out homes for the full brunt of property taxation, when a home is the most essential form of property and for most people, the only substantial property they will ever own. Why not take a little of the burden off of homes and put it onto intangible property? The article points out that the ownership of wealth in the U.S. is much more concentrated in a few hands than is income, making general wealth taxes more in keeping with our democratic ideals. Furthermore, the exemption for intangible property is one of the reasons that the tax burden has been shifting from wealthy corporations and individuals to middle and low income homeowners.

The article refutes the common objections to intangibles taxes, such as the antiquated argument that they cannot be enforced. At very low rates, the article points out, the tax could raise enough revenue to cut homeowner property taxes substantially. And since these taxes are deductible for federal income tax purposes, they amount to do-it-yourself revenue sharing with the federal government.

The second article, by lawyer/accountant Leonard Greenberg, **Tax Intangibles for Homeowner Relief,** shows these arguments percolating into the political arena. Mr. Greenberg, a member of a special tax study committee in Rockland County, N.Y., observes that a modest tax on intangibles could have reduced homeowner taxes in New York State by almost 14%. Such a tax would not be an additional income tax, Mr. Greenberg writes, but would instead impose a tax on the ownership of a class of property that unfairly escapes property taxation.

TAXING WEALTH –

A New Source of Government Revenue

by Jonathan Rowe

The District of Columbia City Council recently held public hearings on property taxes.

"I just can't understand why the D.C. government singles out real estate for property taxes" one taxpayer said. "Consider all the kinds of property in the District: stocks, bonds, paintings, sculpture, antiques—property that belongs almost entirely to rich people. And yet what kind of property do we tax? Homes! The first and often the only substantial property that most people own; and unlike the other kinds of property, a life essential."

This is a very good question. Why do we single out homes and other real estate for property taxes while virtually ignoring the other forms of property.

At last count, well over half the total assets in the U.S. were paper, or "intangible" property—stocks, bonds, and the like. Half of this "intangible property" is accounts receiveable, corporate "goodwill", and other property that would be very difficult to assess and tax. But the other half consists of income-producing stocks and bond which are easily located. With a few exceptions, such intangibles are exempted from state and local property tax. It is ironic that reformers regularly vent their outrage at tax exempt property such as that owned by churches, without complaining about the exemption of intangibles which are worth two to four times as much.

Privately held stocks and bonds belong largely to rich people. The distribution of income in America appears positively egalitarian compared to the distribution of wealth. The top one-fifth of all U.S. families have about 43 percent of the total income but about 80 percent of the total wealth. The top .008 percent of families have about as many assets as the bottom one-half. Looking at corporate stock alone, the top one percent of the population holds about 70 percent of the total. There are reasons, such as chronic under-reporting of dividend income, to believe that even these figures understate the concentration of stock ownership and wealth.

Compare the ownership of stock, which is mainly excluded from property taxes, with the ownership of real estate, which is taxed very heavily. Only 30 percent of the nation's real estate wealth is held by individuals with gross incomes over $60,000, while 88 percent of the corporate stock is so held.

The immediate question is not whether people should be that rich, nor whether America should tolerate such a skewed pattern of wealth ownership. The question is where the money is going to come from to pay for state and local governments.

Moderate income people are being taxed to the limit. During roughly the past twenty years, the overall tax burden on the typical moderate income family

has increased at over twice the rate as the tax burden on upper-income families. Part of the reason is that the intangible property from which such upper-income families derive a large share of their affluence is treated with favor at tax time. Apart from the light treatment under property taxes, such provisions as the following express the tax system's benevolence towards people of wealth:

● The first $100 of corporate dividends are excluded from income, for federal income tax purposes.

● Capital gains are not taxed to the owner until the gain is "realized" at sale.

● Even then, capital gains—gains from the sale of property—are taxed at one-half the rates that working people pay on their salaries and wages.

● When a wealthy person dies, the gain that accrued between the time that person bought the property in question, and the time the person died, goes completely untaxed.

It is the rich who benefit from such income tax favors, as the following table shows:

1974 FEDERAL INCOME TAX

	Average Benefit From		
Income Class	$100 dividend Exclusion	Capital Gains	Untaxed Capital Gains at Death
$15,000-$20,000	$ 4.67	$28.61	$6.49
$100,000 and over	$81.25	$194,321.25	$1,125.00

In theory, estate and inheritance taxes pick up the intangible property that slips through the property and income taxes. And the seemingly-high estate and inheritance tax rates reinforce this notion. The reality is something else. Liberal exemptions and exclusions make estate and inheritance taxes the most underused in our entire tax system. They provide only about one-half of one percent of total state and local revenues. The federal and state taxes together take only 5 percent of the nation's wealth from each generation. This is less than the sales tax rate that people in many states pay for necessities such as food and clothing. In a recent year, estate and inheritance taxes amounted to about two-tenths of one percent of the nation's net worth.

The undiminished concentration of wealth among the richest families alone attests to the slight impact of estate and inheritance taxes.

The conclusion is this: Wealth, especially wealth in

the form of intangible property, is taxed lightly. The people who own the bulk of it are the richest in the nation, and hence the most able to pay taxes. In short, as other tax wells run dry, we have here a potential revenue source to which state and local governments can turn, as several already have.

There are additional reasons that states and localities should begin to shift their property tax burdens from real estate to other forms of wealth:

The current favoring of intangible property discourages investments in real estate and encourages investment in stocks and bonds. Consider: Rhode Island gets little if any tax benefit if one of its residents buys 1000 shares of General Motors preferred stock that the company will use to finance a new plant in Alabama. But Rhode Island does get greater tax revenues if this same person invests instead in local real estate. Shifting part of the property tax burden from real estate to paper property could encourage local real estate investment and, thus, local economic development. The present practice distorts the investor's decision.

Intangible property taxes amount to do-it-yourself revenue sharing with the federal government. Property taxes are deductible for federal income tax purposes. Since most owners of stocks and bonds are in the higher income tax brackets, this deduction will compensate them for up to 50 percent and even more of the intangible property tax they pay to their state. In other words, the federal treasury picks up as much as half the tab or more for the intangible property taxes which a state or local government levies against its wealthiest taxpayers.

There is so much intangible property that it would yield substantial revenues even at very low rates. High rates could persuade wealthy individuals to move to a different state to avoid the tax. With low rates, the incentives to move would be reduced.

A very modest tax on income-producing intangible property, levied at one-fifth the rate applied to real estate, would yield close to ten billion dollars nationally, about one-sixth of the nation's current property tax collections. Such a levy could reduce existing real property tax rates by up to 30 percent. For administrative convenience, asset value might be measured by the income produced rather than by current market value. Commercial real estate is commonly assessed for real property tax purposes according to the income it produced for the owners, so there is ample precedent for this income-based approach.

Two main arguments commonly raised against intangible property taxes are: First, that such taxes cannot be administered; and second that they amount to "double taxation". Let us take these arguments in turn.

There was a time when owners of stocks, bonds, and other intangibles could easily hide this property from local tax assessors. And they regularly did so. But in their difficulties with intangible property these local assessors were in good company. The Internal Revenue Service was similarly vexed by enforcing the income tax laws against owners of stocks and bonds. As recently as 1960, the U.S. Treasury estimated that 11 percent of the dividend income and 34 percent of the interest income was going unreported. Tax loss to

the Treasury: $3.7 billion per year.

In response to such disclosures, Congress passed laws requiring corporations to report each year their dividend and interest payments to U.S. taxpayers. Internal Revenue Service can now cross-check these corporate reports against individual tax returns.

Congress has also passed laws enabling states to match their own tax returns against the federal returns filed by the same taxpayer. Almost all the states have entered into data sharing agreements with the U.S. Treasury. These "Federal Match" programs, as the tax administrators call them, are the keystones of the enforcement programs of the states which effectively tax intangible property. The match programs make intangible property taxes on income-yielding intangibles no more difficult to enforce than state income taxes.

State enforcement of these taxes is essential however. Every state that successfully taxes intangibles administers the tax at the state level.

The federal match program is just one of the ways states can make sure that taxes on intangible property are paid. Both Ohio and Florida require every corporation doing business in the state to report each year all the dividends and interest paid to their residents. Florida takes the additional step of requiring all in-state stock brokers to report all their transactions on behalf of Florida residents.

Another way to catch intangibles-tax avoiders is to look carefully at the property transmitted through estates. Michigan formerly held up the settlement of estates until any back intangibles taxes were paid in full, with penalties and interest.

The double taxation argument goes like this: In theory, a share of stock in the Ford Motor Company simply represents the physical assets of the corporation. These assets, presumably, are already subject to real property taxes. When the stock certificate also is taxed, the same property is, in effect, being taxed twice.

This double taxation argument has more logic than reality. Much industrial real estate and machinery is *not* taxed. Michigan, for example, exempts machinery used in the manufacture of automobiles. Increasing numbers of states are exempting all industrial machinery. Some states exempt new manufacturing facilities completely for a number of years.

On top of this, a good deal of the value of a corporation—value reflected by the stock—consists not of real estate or equipment, but of intangibles such as copyrights and patent rights, trademarks, "goodwill", and the like.

The amount of double taxation that would occur in practice would appear to be minor. Lester Snyder of the University of Connecticut Law School has estimated that taxing corporate stock would result in at most about 20 percent double taxation.

The U.S. Supreme Court has found nothing wrong with double taxation. More important, it occurs in our tax system all the time. Workers are taxed when they earn their wages and again when they spend them. Owners of real estate are taxed both on the value of their property and the income it yields. The owners of corporate securities have no special claim.

Nevertheless, some states allow a set-off against intangibles taxes for property taxes paid in the state. More on this point appears below.

The early property tax laws were broad based, and attempted to include wealth of every form. Assessors in New Plymouth Colony were bidden in 1643 to assess all residents "according to their estates or faculties, that is, according to (their) goods, lands, improved faculties, and personal abilities." Such colonial levies were called "faculties" taxes rather than property taxes, because they reflected a desire to take the individual's total taxpaying ability into account. Even professions were considered a form of property, or "faculty" and were assessed and taxed accordingly. Attorneys in Connecticut were taxed on their practices, the "least practitioners" at 50 pounds and others "in proportion to their practice."

In the nineteenth century a wave of economic democracy resulted in "uniformity" provisions in many state constitutions. These provisions required that *all* property be assessed and taxed alike. Underfunded local assessors with primitive enforcement tools were not up to the job of assessing intangibles, however, and gradually collection of this portion of the property tax became a national scandal. It was paid only by the dumb and the unwary.

Despite the ensuing trend toward repeal of the intangibles tax laws, these have endured to a greater extent than most people are aware. Fewer than half the states have legally exempted intangibles; and of these, only New York has done so by constitutional amendment. In the other twenty three states, a mere act of state legislature could restore intangibles to the tax base.

The remaining states tax intangibles as follows:

● Seventeen states still include intangibles in their general property taxes.

Eleven states levy special property taxes on intangibles.

● Three states levy or have recently levied special taxes on the income from intangible property.

● Two states include in their general income taxes higher rates on unearned income than on wages and salaries.

The seventeen states which still include intangibles in their general property taxes are those in which administration is generally the weakest. In some of these, such as Alabama and Arkansas, the tax has been virtually ignored. A major reason for the weak administration is that the task is still entrusted to local assessors.

The laws remain on the books, however, waiting for alert taxpayers to take notice. In Arkansas, farmers angry over their rising assessments sued their local assessor for failing to assess intangibles, and won a court order compelling him to fulfill this duty. Arkansas Community Organizations for Reform Now (ACORN) promptly produced a list of large financial institutions that were failing to pay about $73 million in intangible property taxes. (Under a state law entitling citizens to 10 percent of any unpaid taxes they report to authorities, ACORN claimed $7.3 million of that amount. At this writing it has not received the money.)

Arkansas' financial interests boosted a drive to amend the state constitution to enable the legislature to give intangibles special treatment, including complete exemption. The voters approved the amendment, largely because the financial interests frightened them with warnings that an intangible tax would confiscate their small savings accounts. The legislature has yet to act on its new authority, however; and there the matter rests.

The states which have enacted special intangible property taxes generally administer the taxes at the state level, and overall have done a better job than those still relying on local assessors. Florida and Ohio are often singled out as leaders in an admittedly spotty field.

Florida levies a one-tenth of one percent tax on the value of intangible property with the first $20,000 per taxpayer exempt. The tax yielded $95 million in 1973-74. Florida's experience points dramatically to the importance of state administration. When administration was shifted from county assessors to the state Department of Revenue in 1972, the revenues from the tax *doubled*.

Ohio has dual tax on intangibles. Income-producing investments—such as stocks and bonds—are taxed at 5 percent of their yield. Other intangibles are taxed according to their value, at rates around two-tenths of one percent. The business portion is administered by the state, while county assessors still administer the tax on individuals. Total receipts have been over $150 million.

The Illinois capital stock tax on domestic corporations is a most intriguing concept. The tax is levied on the difference between the company's total value, and the value of its property assessed for local property tax purposes. Not only does the tax thus reach intangibles such as corporate "goodwill"; in addition, it picks up any underassessment of real estate, machinery and equipment.

The Illinois tax was to be administered by the state. But certain interests, such as manufacturers, retailers, mining concerns, and newspapers, won the right to be assessed by local assessors. The State Department of Local Government Affairs does respectably on its portion of the tax, but administration at the county level makes Cook County voting practices appear models of probity by comparison. Item: the state's attorney has been settling corporate tax liabilities for two-cents on the dollar. Even the staid Commerce Clearing House State Tax Reporter, (a lawyer's tax information service) editorializes on local administration of the Illinois Capital Stock Tax. "The effectiveness of capital stock assessments depends on the experience, perserverence, and public support of local assessors," CCH delicately puts it.

The two states which levy special income taxes on intangibles, New Hampshire and Tennessee, have no broad-based income tax. New Hampshire taxes 4.5 percent of dividends and interest, excluding the first $600. Tennessee taxes this income at 6 percent. The rate is 4 percent, however, on dividends from stock in any corporation that pays property taxes in Tennessee, if at least 74 percent of all the corporations's property is in the state. This is one way to reduce any double taxation, but at the same time it favors companies which are investing their money within the state.

Two states with broad-based income taxes subject income from intangibles to special high rates. Colorado levies a 2 percent surtax on such income, while Massachusetts taxes it at 9 percent compared with a 5 percent rate on wages and salaries.

The latest entrants in the field of intangible property taxation have been Connecticut and New Jersey. Each enacted the tax in part to avert broad-based income taxes, which they have avoided largely to remain tax-havens for highly-salaried executives who work in New York. When New Jersey finally adopted an income tax last year, it eliminated its tax on intangibles.

The Connecticut tax, though assessed on the income yielded by intangibles, was conceived to compensate for the exclusion of this property from the general property tax. Since its enactment in 1969, it has taken some political bounces. Originally, it applied only to capital gains. In 1971 a Democratic administration added dividends. In 1973, a Republican administration took dividends out. In 1975, when Democrat Ella Grasso became Governor, dividends were put back in.

Interest has been excluded all along, apparently so that ordinary wage earners with small savings accounts would not feel threatened. Recall that opponents of intangibles taxes in Arkansas prevailed in a constitutional initiative by telling the public that the tax would jeopardize their small savings accounts. Formerly the Connecticut tax was a flat 7 percent. This year, however, the rates have been scaled, from 1 percent to 9 percent, depending on the taxpayers adjusted gross income. The dividends of all persons with adjusted gross incomes under $20,000 are exempted, and the capital gains of such persons are exempted if they come to $100 or less. Last year the tax produced $50 million—$14-million from capital gains and $36 million from dividends.

New Jersey's tax cut a broader swath than the Connecticut version, including not just dividends and capital gains, but other forms of "unearned income" such as interest and royalties. However, individuals making under $15,000 (and couples making under $30,000) were exempted. The rates ranged from 1.5 percent to 8 percent, depending on the taxpayer's adjusted gross income. The tax raised approximately $30 million in the year before it was repealed.

"Taxing Wealth—A New Source of Government Revenue" is reprinted by permission from the August, 1977 issue of *Public Interest Economics*.

Tax Intangibles for Homeowner Relief

By Leonard Greenberg

The property tax, the mainstay of public education financing in New York, is generally acknowledged to be a regressive tax. *The Wall Street Journal* described its regressive nature as follows in a front-page article on July 3, 1967:

> "Tax specialists generally applaud such switches to broader-based forms of taxation. Property taxes are considered among the most 'regressive' of all taxes. They hit a low-income property owner much harder than they hit a wealthy property owner, because a poor man's mortgaged home represents nearly all of his assets. A wealthy man's assets usually are in the form of securities or other 'intangible' investments that often are taxed at rates far lower than property tax levels..."

In New York it's even more regressive because intangibles escape property taxation entirely and the New York State Constitution irrationally prevents the State Legislature from even considering the most obvious way of making it more equitable. How and why it happened in a progressive state like New York can be explained, but what is inexplicable is the lack of any concerted effort over the years to change it.

From its beginnings in the early 1600's, the direct tax on property in New York was justified on the theory that a person's possessions were a good indication of ability to pay. Originally the tax covered only land, houses and livestock, but as new forms of property evolved, the scope of the tax was expanded. Although intangible assets such as stocks, bonds and savings accounts became worth far more than land and buildings, tax administrators continued to rely on real property.

Over the years many attempts have been made to cure the defects in local assessment of property, but to no avail. In fact, in 1938 the voters approved a measure which not only did not remedy any defects in the property tax system, but, rather, insured that reform would be quite difficult to attain in the future. It sounds unbelievable today, but it actually happened.

Constitution Forbids Tax on Intangibles

In 1938, New York held a constitutional convention which considered hundreds of proposals. With no fanfare whatsoever, a provision was slipped into a package containing eight articles and forty-nine main topics, which was submitted to the voters as one of nine amendments and approved. The provision in question, consisting of one sentence, today appears in Article XVI, Section 3. It forbids the direct taxation of intangible personal property and only permits the income produced by intangibles to be taxed as part of a general income tax. New York is the only state in the Union with such a prohibition.

As a result, the Legislature can't even consider a property tax on stocks, bonds and savings accounts although it was perfectly legal in New York for over 300 years and is widely used elsewhere in the United States. Why?

The rationale appears in the official *Record* of the 1938 convention. The committee chairman proposing the amendment said:

> "In order to avert any possible experimental return to outmoded, useless taxing methods with respect to intangibles..." (page 798).

> "...we have tried and other states have tried...and have utterly failed. The reason we went away from the personal property tax was on account of the impossibility of taxing intangible personal property the same as real estate...We don't want to get back, we want to close the door on that obsolete method of taxation..." (page 1170).

In summary, the rationale was the difficulty or impossibility *in 1938* of valuation and ownership determination. That may have been true in 1938, but that was B.C. *Before computers.* The development of data processing, the present sophistication of our systems of federal and state income taxation and the increased cooperation between them absolutely destroys the rationale that led to the adoption of the amendment and destroys any reason for its further existence.

This was recognized in 1967 when a special committee of The Association of the Bar of the City of New York recommended repeal of the provision, saying in its report:

"...Not only is the feasibility of such taxation more likely in the years to come, but it is increasingly apparent that the real property tax...neither meets a reasonable test of progressivity nor does it spread the tax burden in a rationally justifiable manner..."

The recommendation was not adopted, and in November the voters rejected all the proposed amendments approved by the 1967 constitutional convention.

In a study conducted by the highly-respected Public Citizen Tax Reform Research Group, which was published in *People and Taxes* in September 1976, taxation was proposed of certain intangibles owned by resident individuals and by executors and trustees on their behalf. The study estimated that an 8% tax on dividends, interest, capital gains and royalties reported by such persons, after allowing for a 10% reduction to cover exemptions for small property owners, could produce over 1.1 billion dollars annually in New York, enough to have reduced all property taxes statewide by almost 14% in 1976.

It should be stressed that such a tax is not an additional income tax. It is a tax on the ownership of a class of property that today unfairly excapes the property tax in New York. Its purpose is to eliminate an unwarranted and unfair distinction between two forms of wealth and in so doing to provide some relief to overburdened homeowners and tenants who bear the brunt of the real property tax. Such a tax is presently in force in Colorado, Michigan and Ohio.

Repeal Ban on Intangibles Tax

The property tax produces more revenue than any other local or state tax and it's easy to administer. It's been with us for over 300 years and it isn't going to just disappear. However, if we are ever going to have *real* property tax reform in New York, the outmoded, irrational and unfair ban on the taxation of intangibles must be repealed. I also propose that New York undertake immediately a detailed study on intangibles taxation for the purpose of providing statewide relief to homeowners and tenants from the burden of the real property tax. *Real* property tax reform demands no less!

CHAPTER 15

Inheritance, Estate and Gift Taxes

From different perspectives, the two articles in this chapter call for revival and reform of estate taxes.

The first is a chapter from the *Politics and Economics of State and Local Finance,* entitled **Inheritance and Estate Taxes** by Lazlo Ecker-Racz, one of the nation's most respected students of this subject. Declaring that "inheritance and estate taxes are among our oldest and also our most neglected taxes," Mr. Ecker-Racz proceeds to show that they are both consistent with our traditional ideals, and practical. One advantage he cites is that these taxes have "little if any deterrent effect upon working and saving." Another is that they fill in one of the biggest gaps in the federal income tax laws—the exemption for increases in value of property such as stocks and bonds.

For reasons the author sets forth, state estate taxes are the tail on the donkey of the federal tax, so that reform must begin in Washington. Congress, however, has shown little interest, for which Mr. Ecker-Racz offers an intriguing explanation. The leadership of the Congressional tax-writing Committees have been wary of estate tax reform, he writes, because "they tend to be men of advanced years as a result of the seniority principle."

In the second article, **Death and Taxes—The American Estate Tax: A Death Penalty,** North Dakota State Tax Commissioner Byron Dorgan calls the estate tax an "antirevolution" tax because it can prevent the concentrations of wealth and power which give rise to violent revolutions. The tax, however, has not been functioning as it should, in part because it has been catching small farmers and businesses in its net. The reason, Mr. Dorgan says, is that despite inflation, the exemption levels and rate tables had not been revised since the nineteen forties. Mr. Dorgan calls for revising these provisions to lift the burden from those who were not intended to bear it. He also calls for ending the way the tax can discriminate against women.

(Note: Since Mr. Dorgan's article first appeared, Congress has enacted partial remedies for both of these problems.)

Inheritance and Estate Taxes

By Dr. L.L. Ecker-Racz

Inheritance and estate taxes are among our oldest and also our most neglected taxes, neglected alike by legislators, administrators, and the public. Sales, income, property, and some of the other taxes figure almost daily in public discussions; but literally years can pass without a single press reference to the taxes on inherited wealth.

Although the present federal estate tax is over fifty years old, Congress has looked at this tax (even perfunctorily) only once during the last quarter century. At that time (1948) it reduced it substantially by legislating the marital deduction to exempt up to half of any estate so long as it is left to the surviving spouse. This tax also has suffered neglect at the state level, where death taxes have been in existence for a century. Even in recent years, when virtually every state has had to enact several major revenue measures, one would be hard pressed to find two or three states where inheritance taxes received more than cursory mention.

The neglect of these taxes ought to be corrected. In a nation with the world's largest accumulation of private wealth, and where the number of millionaires grows by the score year after year, taxes on inherited wealth are capable of making a substantial revenue contribution—particularly at a time when the tax burdens on low- and middle-income groups are being pushed steadily to higher levels.

THEY APPEAR IN DIFFERENT FORMS

Most of us have no personal acquaintance with these taxes, so it might be well to begin with an explanation of two or three terms.

The family of taxes that focus on inherited wealth is known as the property transfer tax system. It includes, in addition to the estate tax and the inheritance tax, the gift tax.

The estate tax is levied on the right to bequeath property at death. It applies to the decedent's total estate, after a variety of exemptions (or subtractions) and is imposed at graduated rates. The estate tax is used by the federal government and by some of the states. The federal govern-ment allows a $60,000 exemption and taxes the remainder of the net estate, after various allowable subtractions, at rates ranging from 3 percent on the first $5,000 to 77 percent on the portion of an estate in excess of $10,000,000.

The predominant state tax on inherited wealth is the inheritance tax which, unlike the estate tax, is levied on the beneficiaries of the estate on their privilege to inherit property. Each heir is treated as a separate tax-payer. Each is allowed a separate exemption, and the size of the exemption varies, as do the applicable tax rates, with the relationship of the heir to the decedent. Generally, the closer that relationship (spouse, child, or parent), the higher the exemption and the lower the tax rate. A widow may be taxed at rates ranging from 1 percent to 5 percent after a $25,000 exemption, while an unrelated friend may be allowed no exemption and be taxed at rates ranging from 5 to 30 percent.

States also use estate taxes, but these do not lend themselves to ready generalization. The simplest of these state taxes is known as the "pick-up" tax. Because the federal government allows a limited amount of state taxes as an offset against its estate tax, a handful of states follows the simple route of levying an estate tax "equal to the maximum" allowable offset against the federal tax. In other words, these states pick up the offset and nothing more. Other states rely principally on inheritance taxes and then add a supplemental "catchall" pick-up tax just in case, in some situation, their regular tax falls short of the maximum allowable offset. Since inheritance taxes, particularly in the lower brackets, generally exceed the allowable offset, these catchall estate taxes come into play mostly on large estates.

The two taxes—estate and inheritance—are also known as death taxes.

The third tax in the property transfer tax system is the gift tax. It was invented to prevent avoidance of the first two by transferring property before death. Without a gift tax, estate taxes could be avoided by gifts before death. The federal gift tax is the liability of the person who makes the gift, and for this purpose a running record is kept of all gifts he makes during his lifetime and provision is made for various exemptions. The tax rates are approximately two-thirds of the estate tax rates (2¼ percent to 57¾ percent). This encourages distribution before death, and caters to the view that children should be afforded an opportunity to acquire experience in handling wealth.

To exclude small gifts, the taxpayer and his spouse are each permitted to disregard the first $3,000 given to any individual during each year without limit on the number of different individuals. In other words, a couple can give, free of tax, $6,000 each year to each of their relatives and friends and repeat this yearly throughout their lifetime. In addition, each is allowed a one-time $30,000 exemption. To the extent that their gifts exceed the yearly and the "one-time" exemption, the amount of gifts is cumulated, a tax is computed under a graduated tax rate schedule, and a credit is allowed for gift taxes that would be payable at current tax rates on prior years' gifts. The difference is the federal tax payable on the current year's gifts.

Only thirteen states make use of the gift tax. The others ignore it because it would not produce appreciable amounts of revenue and is difficult to enforce. Assets, particularly stocks and bonds, are often kept outside the state and beyond the view of the state tax administrators.

THEY ARE UNIVERSAL AND OLD TAXES

Death taxes are in use virtually the world over. They enjoy support because they apply only where there is taxpaying ability and, unlike most other taxes, have little if any deterrent effect on working and saving.

To most of us, wealth symbolizes taxpaying ability—perhaps even more so than income. We think of income as a flow that fluctuates from year to year and may stop at any time. Wealth handled with care can last into perpetuity and produce income all the while. This is the reason that taxing wealth squares with taxpaying ability, and the reason why some countries, such as Sweden, Denmark, and Germany, tax wealth annually much as we tax income. In a sense, these wealth taxes are adjuncts to the income tax.

The case for taxing inherited wealth is especially strong in the United States because it helps to compensate for the imperfections of the income tax, such as the fact that sizable increases in wealth are not taken into account in determining taxable income. An increase in the value of securities or real estate is recognized for income tax purposes only after the gain is realized through sale; and even then the capital gain is taxed only at half or less of the tax rate applicable to wages, salaries, or most other income sources. Moreover, those who can avoid "realizing" their gains by holding on to their appreciated assets until they die, instead of selling them, can escape the tax permanently. Once the appreciated stock or real estate is in the hands of the heirs it is treated for tax purposes as if the heirs had paid for it what it was worth on the day they inherited. Thus, in a sense, the taxation of inherited wealth can be said to supplement the ability-to-pay mission of the income tax.

Death taxes are quite old. Some states began using them over a century ago, but they remained neglected until after the turn of this century when public interest and the concentration of wealth associated with "robber barons" focused legislative attention on them. They were on the statute books of all but six states by the time of the introduction of the present federal estate tax in 1916.

The federal government had made use of death taxes even earlier than in 1916 (first in 1798) but only for short periods at a time to help finance war emergencies. The tax enacted in 1916 was part of the World War I tax program. Its enactment was allegedly on a temporary basis and over the objections of the states which considered death taxes their province. After the war, the sentiment in Congress and the administration was to repeal this tax, and legislation to this effect was actively considered.

STATES NEED FEDERAL HELP TO ENFORCE THEM

The processing of the legislation to repeal the wartime federal estate tax happened to coincide with the emergence of interstate tax competition for wealthy residents. Some states were actually advertising in national journals that they would give immunity from death taxes to those who settled within their borders. Two amended their constitutions to guarantee freedom from death taxes. State leadership was quick to recognize that interstate tax competition, if left unchecked, would destroy death taxation for them all.

Heeding the plea of state leaders, Congress agreed to substitute tax reduction and a federal tax credit (a new kind of tax reduction) for repeal of the federal estate tax. Specifically, it permitted 80 percent of the reduced federal estate tax liability to be offset, dollar for dollar, with receipts for death taxes paid to states. The import of the credit was that it put a floor under state taxes. It became a matter of indifference to people of wealth that a state reduced its tax below the federal credit; for if the tax was not payable to the state, it had to be paid to the federal government. Most people prefer that the taxes they pay remain in their home state.

This arrangement, if continued, would have split the death tax revenue in the ratio of 80 percent for the states and 20 percent for the national government. But the arrangement did not survive. During the next fifteen years Congress increased the federal estate tax several times by reducing exemptions and raising rates, but retained all the new revenue for the federal government by allowing no state taxes to be credited against the increases.

Another factor that contributed to the reduction in the states' relative share of death tax revenues was the enactment of a permanent federal gift tax in 1932. Since there are substantial tax savings by putting property transfers through the gift tax rather than the estate tax mill, the gift tax encourages property distributions during life and correspondingly reduces the size of estates subject to taxation at death, when state taxes apply. The federal government allows no credit for gift taxes to the thirteen states which use them.

These developments—allowing no credit for state taxes against the increases in the federal estate tax and against the gift tax—have cut the states' relative share in the revenues from these taxes to about one-fifth. The credit still provides a floor under state taxes and to this extent prevents interstate tax competition. It does not, however, prevent wide variations in state liabilities above the credit. Moreover, the prospect that some day Congress will get around to revising the credit arrangement to give the states a more adequate share of the revenues has provided opponents with a ready-made argument against increases in state death taxes.

INTEREST IN THEM IS LACKING

Collection statistics reflect the reluctance of the states and federal government to fully exploit the revenue possibilities of the property transfer tax system. In 1967, when America's tax collections at all levels of government exceeded $176 billion, the contribution of all property transfer taxes —those occasioned by death as well as those on gifts—aggregated less than $3.8 billion. That was actually a banner year for these taxes. Rising property values and the accelerating accumulation of private fortunes more than doubled these tax yields between 1950 and 1960, and nearly doubled them again after 1960. The states' share in the $3.8 billion aggregate was $800 million.

Although most of those who have thought about it are agreed that the contribution of these taxes to the American revenue system can and should be increased substantially, there is no consensus on what the states can do about it. Their freedom is circumscribed by the dominating position of the federal tax. The relative state and federal roles in death taxation has been an issue for years; and though repeatedly urged to do so (most recently by the Advisory Commission on Intergovernmental Relations) neither Congress nor the Administration has as yet focused on it.

There is no telling when Congress can turn its attention to updating federal-state death tax relationships. In times of war, legislatures avoid increasing estate taxes because it would be unfair to penalize those who chance to die during the wartime emergency. In times of peace they disdain consideration of them because, as they are wont to say, these taxes pose complex issues which can be explored only when adequate time is available.

The reluctance to tap this potential source of revenue appears to be associated in an unarticulated way with the view that those astute enough to make a fortune should be rewarded and certainly not penalized. Another factor is the sensitivity of the leadership of legislative tax committees to death tax considerations, since they tend to be men of advanced years as a result of the seniority principle. In the meantime, states are foregoing revenue they could use to meet pressing needs. Although handicapped by the uncertainty about the direction of future federal action, they have some freedom to act on those aspects of the problem where the direction of congressional action is relatively clear or in which Congress has relatively little interest. Clearly, then, states would not be well advised to try to influence the way in which people of wealth arrange their property dispositions because, in this respect, the much larger federal tax is in control.

THE ESTATE TAX IS PREFERABLE

The rearrangement of federal-state tax relationships is likely to involve the issue of inheritance vs. estate taxes. As noted, a few states rely on the estate tax; but most use inheritance taxes, and rely on the estate tax solely for the purpose of absorbing any part of the federal credit that might otherwise be lost. After imposing its separate inheritance taxes, the state adds up the inheritance tax pieces emanating from each estate. If the sum of the several inheritance taxes falls short of the total allowable as a credit against the federal tax for taxes paid to states, it imposes a so-called "pick-up" estate tax to claim the difference.

It should be kept in mind that so long as the taxes imposed by the state qualify for purposes of the federal credit, the state adds nothing to the aggregate tax liability of the estate. However, it does preempt for the state an amount that, in the absence of the state tax, would have to be paid to the U. S. Treasury.

From the viewpoint of ability-to-pay and tax fairness, the inheritance tax has more initial appeal than the estate tax because there is no necessary relationship between the size of an estate and the respective shares of its several heirs. However, the use of "pick-up" taxes by the states generally means that the estate's aggregate burden will tend to be the same under either system. In other words, any differentiation in rates and exemptions based on the relationship between decedent and his heirs tends to be neutralized because the aggregate state tax is ultimately raised (especially for large estates) to the level of the federal credit.

In addition, the inheritance tax ignores the criterion of taxpaying ability in the sense that any one heir may be a beneficiary under a number of wills but is taxed as if he received only one inheritance. Some have proposed a new kind of tax—the accessions tax—to compensate for this weakness of the inheritance tax.

The accessions tax applies gift tax mechanics to the inheritance tax. When a person received a bequest he would add it to the total of gifts and bequests he had previously received, and compute the tax on the total at current tax rates. He would take a credit against this liability for the taxes that would be payable at current rates on the gifts and bequests previously received. The difference would be the tax due and payable on the last inheritance. Although conceptually attractive, because it comes closer to taxing on the basis of ability-to-pay than other types of death taxes, the accessions tax has not progressed much beyond the discussion stage. Japan adopted it in 1950 on the recommendation of an American tax expert, Carl Shoup, but withdrew it three years later pleading administrative difficulty.

The overwhelming argument for state adoption of the estate tax is that the federal government uses it. If the states did likewise, the compliance burdens of taxpayers and the enforcement tasks of state tax administrators would be eased. States, moreover, could make more effective use of audit and related information available from federal Internal Revenue records. Furthermore, the inheritance tax raises more difficult valuation problems, particularly if life estate and remainders are involved. Consider the problems involved in fixing the present value of the share of a cousin's life interest in an estate which is to be activated only when the decedent's widow and two children die. What is involved here is estimating the cousin's age at the time the widow and both children will have died, and then estimating the cousin's life expectancy at that age. This would provide the basis of appraising the probable (actuarial) value of his future share of the estate at the time of the donor's death.

The chief virtue of the inheritance tax—that it recognizes the closeness or remoteness of the relationship between heir and decedent—can be approached also through the estate tax. This can be accomplished by making the size of the estate tax exemption depend on the relationship of the heirs to the decedent, as is presently done in New York. In effect, each heir is allotted an exemption based on his or her relationship to the decedent; but the sum of these exemptions is limited to some stated amount, say $60,000. In this way an estate left entirely to a spouse or a child is given a larger exemption than one going to a cousin, and one shared by a spouse and a cousin is given a larger exemption than one left entirely to one or the other.

The amounts that states collect from these taxes represent little more than 1 percent of state and local tax collections. The federal government's estate and gift revenues represent about 2½ percent of its tax collections.

We do not have any firm figures on the value of American private wealth. Even on very conservative assumptions, it probably exceeds $2,500 billion. If we assume that this property passes from one generation to the next once every thirty years, the amount involved in yearly transfers is about $80 billion. In other words, the $4 billion death tax collections of the federal and state governments take on the average about 5 percent of private wealth once in a generation. This is very modest compared with other countries' practices, and is a reflection of America's aversion to penalizing those who inherit wealth or have made a financial success of their lives.

There are several ways in which the states might increase their revenue from the property transfer tax system without waiting for the long overdue revision of the federal estate tax with its important implications for state tax policy.

Logically, the states might concentrate more attention on the smaller and middle-sized estates. On the grounds of administrative convenience, the federal exemption for estates tends to be relatively high—$60,000. This frees small estates from federal taxation, and results in relatively low tax burdens on medium-size estates. However, the number of small and moderate-size estates is vast and potentially capable of producing important amounts of revenue.

Although America is noted for its great private fortunes, most of the private wealth is held in relatively modest amounts. Increased state reliance on this portion of the tax base would have several advantages in addition to the added revenue. It would improve the stability of state revenues, because small and medium-size estates are numerous and their number is relatively stable. The present instability of death tax revenues is due to the irregularity and the relative revenue significance of the large estates. The smaller nonindustrialized states, in any event, have only a few if any wealthy residents.

Most states appear to be concerned with the effect of death taxes on their attractiveness for new residents. They choose to disregard the fact that tax considerations are minimal for people with relatively modest estates. In any event, most people are not likely to select their state of residence out of consideration for potential death taxes if only because man tends to proceed on the assumption that death will somehow continue to pass him by. Notice the number of people of advanced age who die without having made a will.

To the extent that estate and gift tax considerations influence the way people dispose of their wealth, federal law with its sharply graduated rates is controlling. The relatively low rates of state taxes mean that these taxes are not particularly influential in how people dispose of their property. A case in point is the unlimited exemption of bequests to educational, charitable, and religious organizations. Federal law grants these exemptions on the theory that these organizations merit public encouragement because they perform socially desirable services, of which at least a part would otherwise be performed at public expense.

The federal exemption exerts a strong pressure in favor of such bequests, particularly for large estates. When the otherwise applicable estate tax rate would be 60 or 70 percent, the charitable bequest is made largely at federal expense even if the donor credits no value to his role as a benefactor. If the bequest were not made, and the property remained in the owner's estate, then on his death 60 or 70 percent of it would pass to the government in estate taxes. In other words, if the bequest were not made, only 30 or 40 percent of the amount involved would actually accrue to the heirs, and they would forego also such benefits—possibly substantial, if intangible—as may redound to them by virtue of their parent's public generosity. Little wonder that the tax-exempt foundation is today a vast national institution, and is growing. In these circumstances, it is doubtful that the presence or absence of a comparable state exemption of bequests from the generally prevailing moderate state tax rates would have any material influence on the size of charitable bequests.

State governments hard pressed for revenue might understandably reach the conclusion that they could make more effective use of the added dollars, from the viewpoint of the public welfare, than the charitable foundation and, accordingly, limit the exemptions they grant to bequests to nonprofit organizations. However, there is no evidence that their thoughts are moving in this direction.

Gift taxes, on the other hand, hold little revenue promise for the states. They would not influence the amount of giving before death (since here federal provisions are controlling) and could not give the gift tax effective enforcement. About the only argument in favor of state use of gift taxes is the possibility that it might improve the states' case for an increased federal estate tax credit—when and if Congress actively turns to consideration of the tax credit question.

"Inheritance and Estate Taxes" is reprinted by permission from *The Politics and Economics of State and Local Finance,* © 1970, Prentice-Hall, Inc., Englewood Cliffs, N.J.

The American Estate Tax: A Death Penalty

by Byron L. Dorgan

THE AMERICAN PUBLIC has begun sending loud messages to the United States Congress and the State Legislatures that there desperately needs to be some changes made in our estate or death tax laws. The American public is right. The estate tax is weary with age and no longer relates successfully to today's economy with its exemptions and rates. That is the major reason the U.S. Congress is considering proposed changes to the estate tax law. Political observers predict that this is the year the changes might happen.

ANTIREVOLUTION TAX

Some years ago when I was studying economics, and more specifically the field of taxation, I perceived that the estate or death tax system in this country was part of a grand plan in the American system to redistribute wealth. Idealistically, I thought the estate tax was an "antirevolution tax." Basic history lessons tell us that many other societies in the world have invariably had to experience violent revolutions in order to redistribute wealth when that wealth became concentrated in the hands of a few. It

appeared the United States, through a system of taxing transfers of estates, was engaging in a method of redistributing concentrations of wealth peacefully through our tax system. Philosophically, that has made a lot of sense.

In 1935, President Franklin D. Roosevelt emphasized the relationship of the federal estate tax system to this concept of redistribution of wealth. According to Roosevelt:

> The desire to provide security for one's self and one's family is natural and wholesome but it is adequately served by a reasonable inheritance. Great accumulations of wealth cannot be justified on the basis of personal and family security. In the last analysis such accumulations amount to a perpetuation of great and undesirable concentration of control in a relatively few individuals over the employment and welfare of many, many others. Such inherited economic power is as inconsistent with the ideals of this generation as inherited political power was inconsistent with the ideals of the generation which established our government.

Notwithstanding these reflective thoughts expressed by President Roosevelt, the redistribution of wealth effect was only a by-product of the major reason for the initial imposition of estate taxes. In fact, estate taxes historically have been imposed and increased in order to finance war efforts by this country.

HISTORY

For example, in 1862 the first estate tax was enacted in order to help defray the cost of the Civil War. In 1870, however, a distinguished member of the U.S. House Ways and Means Committee named "Pig Iron" Kelley led the charge to abolish the estate tax. Actually, he proposed to abolish the Internal Revenue Service completely, but had to accept the death of the estate tax as a consolation prize. For the next 28 years the United States government had no federal estate tax. In 1898 another House Ways and Means Committee member, Representative Dingley, proposed an estate tax ranging to 15 percent to help finance the Spanish American War. Since 1916 the present estate tax has been part of the federal taxation system. In 1917, the estate tax rates were raised to a maximum of 25 percent to help finance World War I.

There have been a lot of minor changes in between, but in 1941 during World War II the estate tax rates were fixed from 3 percent to 77 percent and in 1942 the estate exemption was raised to $60,000. That is essentially the same estate tax that the American public now lives and dies with in 1976.

As we can see, history casts only a small shadow on the "redistribution of wealth" ideal. Nevertheless, while the estate tax has been primarily a revenue measure during times of national crises, the tax is still well grounded philosophically and can operate as a pressure relief valve to redistribute wealth through an orderly process in our society.

The fundamental problem of the estate tax in 1976 is that it's antiquated. It does not reflect today's economic realities. If the image of the estate tax was bruised yesterday because its revenue financed wars, its image is far more damaged today because we are tampering with the fundamental importance of estate taxation as a means to redistribute concentrations of great wealth. In practice the estate tax has become increasingly traumatic to the family of modest means.

We need an estate tax in this country that will prevent the transmission from generation to generation of vast fortunes by will, inheritance, or gift because such a transmission of concentrated wealth seems inconsistent with the ideals of the American people. At the same time, however, we do not want an estate tax to behave as a punitive tax that destroys the average family's ability to retain a small family farm or business. We do not want an estate tax that destroys the continuity of the economic unit owned by persons of modest means who would like to pass that heritage to either their spouse or lineal descendants.

CHANGING TIMES

Times change, and so should tax laws. Unless tax laws change with the times, that which is transcendentally true can become existentially false. A good example of this principle is the $60,000 basic exemption in the federal estate tax system. In 1942 that exemption would have allowed the transfer of a farm with well over 1,000 acres without any estate tax obligation. At that time, the size of the average farm in this country was far below 1,000 acres. Today, for example, in North Dakota the size of the average family farm is slightly over 1,000 acres and yet at today's prices the transfer of that family farming unit can and does incur a substantial estate tax obligation. The same principle is true with the moderately successful small business or, in the wage earner's case, a home and lifetime accumulation of savings or assets. In 1942 all of these could be passed on to the spouse or to a lineal descendant without estate tax liability. However, because the tax law has not changed with the times and because we have had unprecedented economic changes, particularly inflationary price level changes, now the average family farm cannot be transferred without a substantial estate tax obligation. Nor can a small business or a moderate accumulation of assets by a wage earner be transferred without an estate tax obligation.

We need to increase the estate tax exemption in our federal estate tax system in order to reflect today's economic standards. A $200,000 basic estate tax exemption that has been widely proposed is proper for all estates of farmers, businessmen, and wage earners. This would not be any substantial departure from past policy, since it would approximate and be relative to the estate tax enacted in this country in the 1940s.

In addition to increasing the basic exemption, we must study and change the estate tax rates, particularly in the low- and middle-sized estates. The rate structure, like the exemption, must change with the times or it too will effect an unplanned change in the incidence of taxation.

For example, if in 1942 a family estate had a taxable estate tax base of $30,000, that family would have paid $3,000 in estate tax or an effective taxable estate tax rate of 10 percent. If, as a result of price level increases and the decline of purchasing power of the dollar due to prolonged periods of inflation, the head of that same family would have a taxable estate of $100,000 today, then the estate tax would be $20,700 or 21 percent of the taxable estate. Although the average family unit has the same purchasing power relative to all other families in our society, it is now paying an estate tax that is several times higher than the estate tax paid by the average family 30 years ago. While the real money value of the estate might have remained approximately the same, inflation has pushed the inflated market value of the estate upward over time and pushed that estate into a higher tax bracket. This is a hypothetical case used to illustrate the effects of inflation on the incidence of the estate tax itself. A football analogy seems most appropriate here. The dollar, much like the football, is moving in value. The down markers (in this case the estate tax rates) must be moved also in order to maintain an accurate measurement at any given point in time.

CHANGING THE WIDOW TAX

Even if we raise the basic exemption and lower the tax rates, the estate tax will not have received a complete overhaul unless its reform includes recognition of a surviving widow's contribution to the family estate. The present estate tax law discriminates against women in cases where property is owned jointly by husband and wife, as it implies that a housewife makes no monetary contribution to the accumulation of a family's estate. For example, upon the death of one spouse, the law dictates that the surviving spouse must pay a death tax on the full estate (if owned jointly) unless it can be proved that he or she contributed in actual dollars to the building of that estate. A widower can easily prove contribution because he has probably earned a wage all of his adult life. Unfortunately, a widowed housewife cannot prove contribution so easily. She is not paid a salary and, consequently, the law assumes that her contribution to the estate is without value.

We live in a decade when law after law is being changed to recognize a woman's self-worth. The estate tax law must change as well, to recognize and assume that a woman contributes to the building of an estate on an equal basis with her husband. Specifically, when property is owned jointly by a husband and wife, and the estate is passed on to the surviving spouse, one half of that estate must be automatically exempt from taxation on the presumption that the surviving spouse, whether male or female, whether wage earner or housewife, has contributed to one half of the entire estate. Any further deduction, such as the marital deduction, should be considered after this automatic division of property.

REFORM NECESSARY

As Tax Commissioner of North Dakota, I believe my State epitomizes the urgent need for estate tax reform. North Dakota is one of the most rural States in America. It is also a State with a relatively high per capita income (we rank 15th in the Nation) and our economy, while very healthy, resembles Adam Smith's description of early England, when he pictorialized the intermingling of small agricultural units amid a nation of shopkeepers. We have about 42,000 farms in North Dakota that support a large number of small towns and a lot of small merchants. We have a law in North Dakota prohibiting corporate farming and therefore the farms in North Dakota are family owned and operated and still maintain a base of support for small towns which are the hubs of economic activity for rural living. There are not many large estates that show massive accumulations of wealth in North Dakota. Most estates reflect the accumulation of the assets of a small farm, small business, or a wage earner's investments over a lifetime. In 1942 most of these accumulations would have been allowed to pass to descendants without economic interruption. Because the estate tax law has not kept pace with changing times, these estates and the economic units they represent are now being interrupted by an estate tax.

Philosophically, most Americans support the notion that an estate tax or inheritance tax could and should be used to fragment the immense collection of wealth over long periods of time in this country. However, the estate tax should not interrupt the continuity of the individual family units that make up our type of economy and should not impede the ability of average Americans to pass a modest accumulation of assets to their heirs without burdensome estate taxes.

"Death and Taxes, The American Estate Tax: A Death Penalty" is reprinted by permission from the Spring, 1976 issue of *State Government*.

VIII

Despite their first place status as a producer of state tax collections (sales taxes alone account for 31 percent of total collections) and their inherent regressivity, sales taxes have generated relatively little concern among state and local tax reformers. This is true largely for four reasons:

- The same characteristic which makes it an obvious target for scrutiny by tax reformers—its prodigious generating power—is also an attractive feature to persons who wish to avoid making cuts in state and local spending programs.
- With respect to the problem of vertical equity (the notion generally used to justify ability to pay taxation), many of the tax reform battles have been won as legislators have increasingly come to recognize that the regressivity of general consumption taxes can be minimized or even eliminated by adopting either over-the-counter or "blanket" exemptions for certain items (usually food and medicine) or tax credits which can be geared to sales tax burdens and taken on state income tax returns.
- Taxing individuals in their roles as con-

sumers is, for some jurisdictions, an effective way to "export" part of the taxing authority's tax base to non-residents. This argument may be particularly significant for persons in those jurisdictions who feel that non-residents directly or indirectly generate substantial but unreimbursed public service costs related to police protection, traffic congestion, health maintenance, and/or environmental degradation.

- Consumption taxes of a user or beneficiary nature conform well to the criterion of benefits received—i.e., the criterion which holds that people who derive the benefits of a service should also be the ones who pay the taxes to finance that service.

Despite these attractive features, however, consumption taxes—particularly the general sales tax—have several structural defects. Examples include the relatively minor problems of some states failure to tax rentals of tangible personal property to collection problems, especially those associated with street vendor operations. Not so minor, due to their prevalence and the amounts of tax dollars involved,

218

Taxing Consumption

are the equity and neutrality issues associated with the definition of the size of the general sales tax base. Here two issues deserve particular attention—namely, the tax credit *vs.* the over-the-counter food exemption approaches to eliminating the regressivity of consumer type levies, and the extension of sales taxation to services, including professional services.

Food: Credit vs. Exemptions

Few tax issues seem to be as controversial, and as subject to misunderstanding, as the choice between over-the-counter sales tax exemption *vs.* an income tax credit for sales taxes paid. Under the exemption (employed in 22 states), that part of the sales tax which normally is charged to the consumer is simply not collected at the time of purchase. With the credit (now used by seven states) the sales tax is applied to food and non-food items alike, but then part or all of the sales tax on the food portion is returned at the end of the year in the form of a lump sum reduction in income taxes.

The primary justification for each approach is to reduce the regressivity of the sales tax. And both methods are generally successful. The exemption tends to make the sales tax proportional over most income classes. However, it still permits sales tax regressivity at the very low income levels.

The credit also achieves the anti-regressivity effect—if it is used by those for whom it is intended. It is this caveat—that the credit may be theoretically attractive but practically less appealing because of low participation rates—which has become a major argument against the replacement of the credit for the exemption. However, experience in credit states such as New Mexico has demonstrated that if a government makes a serious effort to educate its low income residents as to the availability and advantage of a credit, a high rate of compliance will result.

Once this compliance problem is solved, and it can be, the credit is superior to the exemption in nearly every respect. Unlike the exemption which accrues to consumers regardless of their personal or economic status, the credit can be targeted to resident taxpayers on the basis of income level, age, and/or family size. As a result, it can be designed to achieve the same antiregressivity goal as the exemption but at a substantially lower revenue loss to the state. Furthermore, the credit accomplishes its equity goal with a minimum of administrative problems (e.g., defining ''food'' vs. ''non-food'' items).

Services

The extension of sales taxes to all services is a more complex issue. Nevertheless, the arguments for such base broadening are persuasive. These arguments include lessening the regressivity of the sales tax (since consumption of most services is concentrated in the high income groups), minimizing the distortion of private consumer decisions in favor of tax exempt as against taxable purchases, the facilitation of tax administration as a result of the ability of the auditor to avoid the extensive examination of vendors who sell both taxable goods and exempt services.

This sales tax broadening may, however, present some difficult policy tradeoffs to states which have interjurisdictional competition along their borders. Two issues are of particular concern. First, problems of tax enforcement and administration would be created because some service forms (especially professionals) can avoid the tax rather easily by establishing out-of-state offices for billing and other internal administrative purposes, and yet maintain "branch" offices in the neighboring state. Second, a unilateral base broadening would tend to encourage some "footloose' businesses to locate just across a state line. Again, the professional firms provide the best example. Despite these problems, however, it does not necessarily follow that the best policy is one of complete exemption. Ideally an "optimal" (but politically difficult) sales tax structure requires that sales taxes should be levied at "high" rates on those goods and services which exhibit a relatively price inelastic demand (the quantity of the product demanded is relatively unresponsive to small price changes); and that those products with relatively price elastic demands are candidates for "lower" (but not necessarily a zero rate) rates of taxation.

User Fees

Currently user fees and charges account for about 15 percent of total state and local revenues. During the fifties and sixties user fees were among the fastest growing of state and local revenue sources. Although that growth has leveled off somewhat during this decade, we are once again entering an era when the user charge will be getting increased policy attention. This follows largely from the fact that as tax limitation laws and constitutional amendments are adopted, local governments will have to turn to non-property tax sources of revenues if they are to maintain spending at levels sufficient to guarantee maintenance of the existing (pre-limitation) scope and quality of public services.

Since the property tax is the mainstay of local tax revenues (81.5 percent in 1976), the localities have only two other general revenue avenues: lobby the states and Congress for more intergovernmental aid for, and thus, takeover of, local functions, and/or attempt to use local non-property tax revenue sources more intensively. Clearly the user charge is important among these non-property tax sources.

At first glance, user fees are pretty straightforward. The idea is to extend the *quid-pro-quo* of the market sector to the public sector. Ideally, the fee or charge for a government service is to be set at a level so that the user of the service pays just enough to cover its cost of production. Such a system could be truly efficient as well as meet the benefit received criterion for distribution of the tax burden.

Practical difficulties with user fees do, however, abound. These difficulties range from the problems of both defining (e.g., marginal, average, or total costs?) and estimating how the "cost-of-services" will be measured to determining those types of government services for which the user charge solution is appropriate from both an efficiency and an equity point of view.

CHAPTER 16

Sales and Use Tax

As was noted in this Section's introduction, the two most debated issues on sales taxation concern, first, the "best" mechanism for reducing the regressivity of the general sales tax and, second, whether professional services ought to be included in the tax base. The policy importance of these topics is reflected in the first three articles in this chapter. First, Diane Fuchs in **A Look at the Sales Tax** presents an excellent overview of both issues, including a discussion of the pros and cons of the exemption vs. credit anti-regressivity approaches. The second article, **Retail Sales and Use Tax**, from the District of Columbia Tax Revision Commission report, examines the same topics within a "real world" context of having a citizens commission make policy choices as to the desirability of both the credit—exemption choice and the extension of the D.C. sales tax to its large force of attorneys, consultants, and other professionals.

It is interesting to note that when the D.C. Commissioners cast their votes on these issues they tended to "vote their own pocketbooks." Thus, faced with the choice between (a) fully taxing food and providing a credit *vs.* (b) exempting food, the credit was supported by persons associated with labor unions, consumer interests, and community development agencies. The food exemption, however, was supported by those largely identified with organizations representing high income persons. A similar vote line-up on the extension of the sales tax to services resulted in failure to tax the professionals. However, in this second case the anti-professional tax was due to concern as to whether the tax could be administered in addition to any "pocketbook" view.

Exempting Necessities from the Sales Tax: The Arkansas Case, by Larry Ginsburg, examines the recent Arkansas experience with the food tax debate and discusses a "real world" voter choice. Here the issue was whether, by initiative, Arkansas should end its sales tax on food and medicine. The credit as an alternative to an exemption was not considered. Of particular interest for readers of this volume is Mr. Ginsburg's discussion of the political organizing efforts of ACORN (Association of Community Organizations for Reform Now), an Arkansas tax activist group. Once again the vote was generally along "class lines," the poor areas being pro-exemption, but losing the issue to the wealthier areas in the state. One should note, however, that unlike for the D.C.

vote, the Arkansas initiative would have meant a revenue loss to the state budget. Given that circumstance, then, it may be that the vote was not all that "anti-poor." That judgement could not be made until one sees how the sales tax revenue loss might have been "financed" (e.g., cuts in welfare or health?, higher taxes on real estate?) if the exemption had passed.

The last article in this chapter,**Louisiana's Advance Sales Tax Law** by J. Eugene Martin and Donald C. Dawson, focuses on Lousiana's "advance" method of sales tax collection. The procedure is a simple one, and is an adaptation of the collection method which has been long in use by European Economic Community countries with their value added tax (VAT). For example under a VAT, a manufacturer (or wholesaler) collects the tax on his sales and then pays the government this amount minus any VAT paid on his own purchases—with the tax on both sides being easily traced for audit purposes by invoices. The retail business "customer" of the wholesaler or manufacturer then has an interest in seeing to it that the amount of tax charged by the seller is correct since he, in turn, will use that amount as a credit against any of his taxes due when they are collected at the sale to the final consumer. It is a neat self-policing mechanism, particularly when it is levied at all stages of the production process—from extractive industries to retail sale. Multiple taxation is avoided since the "advance" tax paid is subtracted from taxes subsequently collected at a successive stage of the process. Some slippage may occur, however, at the last stage—the retail level. This is true simply because the final consumer does not file any sales (or VAT) return to the government, thereby eliminating the self-policing aspect.

Louisiana's "advance" system is a limited version of the VAT since it applies its tax, the sales tax, only at the last wholesale transaction. However, because it is limited to just the wholesale-retail transaction, the last stage slippage problem still exists and thus its self-policing effect is also limited. On the other hand, by using the wholesaler as an intermediary for collection, one would expect that unlike other retail sales tax jurisdictions, Louisiana would automatically have some built-in benchmarks of market activity by which to judge (audit) the retailer. Accordingly, the Lousiana method is worth a closer look by tax reform advocates.

A Look at the Sales Tax

by Diane Fuchs

In 1976 the average American family paid $642.35 in sales taxes—more than was spent on all other state taxes combined, and more than twice that paid in state income taxes. Yet, when an Advisory Commission on Intergovernmental Relations (ACIR) survey that year asked, "Suppose your state government must raise taxes substantially, which tax do you think would be the best way to do it?" 45% of those polled opted for the sales tax.

The sales tax's popularity can be explained by its semi-hidden nature. Sales taxes are collected incrementally, at what appears to most to be low rates. The full impact is not felt immediately and consumers view the tax as relatively painless.

For legislators and state politicians, it is seen as an excellent, stable, and ready source of state revenue. In 1976 general and special state sales taxes yielded $47.4 billion nationally.

Consumers tend to maintain a certain level of taxable expenditure even when their income drops. Therefore, legislators can rely on the tax to raise consistant revenues year after year even when the general economy flounders. Also, a small penny increase in the tax can often yield millions in additional state revenues.

Description

While the income tax is a levy on earnings at their source, the sales tax, as a levy on consumption, reaches part of the disposition of that income. Today, all but five states impose a sales tax, with rates ranging from 2% in Oklahoma to 7% in Connecticut. While it is primarily the states which assess this tax, it is not unknown at the local level. At least half of the states have local jurisdictions which impose sales taxes in addition to the state level tax.

There are two basic kinds of sales tax. The general sales tax covers a broad range of items (generally, all personal tangible property and other consumer goods), and taxes them at the same rate. On the other hand, selective sales taxes are aimed at particular items like cigarettes, liquor, and gasoline, which are often taxed at rates

different from the general sales tax rate.

Most states which have enacted general sales taxes also have a "fishnet" tax known as a use tax. It is a levy on items purchased outside the state for use in the state—items that would otherwise escape the sales tax.

The rationale for a sales tax is that consumption is an appropriate basis on which to distribute a substantial part of the state tax load. But while the vast bulk of the sales of tangible personal property is taxed, many states fail to tax services, or tax only a few—most often utility services and motel and hotel services. Only a handful of states tax the fuller range of services including such things as drycleaning, repair services of all kinds, amusement,

advertising, and architects' and lawyers' fees, although expenditures of these kinds are increasing each year as a percentage of consumer spending.

Regressivity

Despite its relative popularity, few experts dispute that the sales tax is one which takes the most from those least able to sustain the burden. It is not a tax based on the ability to pay, as is—theoretically—the income tax. Rather it is a fixed tax on items which must be bought by all consumers, no matter what their income.

High-income people tend to spend larger portions of their income on non-taxable items than do low- and middle-income

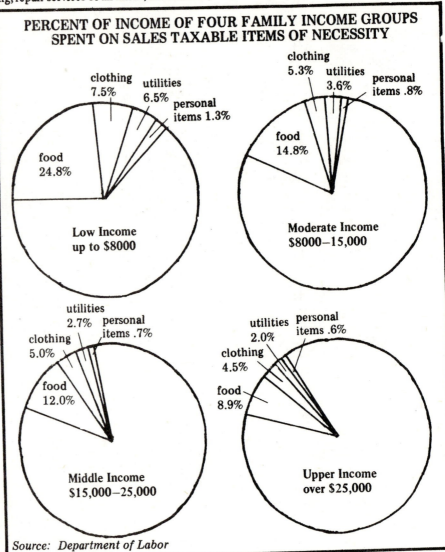

PERCENT OF INCOME OF FOUR FAMILY INCOME GROUPS SPENT ON SALES TAXABLE ITEMS OF NECESSITY

Low Income up to $8000 — food 24.8%, clothing 7.5%, utilities 6.5%, personal items 1.3%

Moderate Income $8000–15,000 — food 14.8%, clothing 5.3%, utilities 3.6%, personal items .8%

Middle Income $15,000–25,000 — food 12.0%, clothing 5.0%, utilities 2.7%, personal items .7%

Upper Income over $25,000 — food 8.9%, clothing 4.5%, utilities 2.0%, personal items .6%

Source: Department of Labor

individuals. Wealthier people put some of their income into investments and savings; poorer people do not have this option. Wealthy families also spend more of their income on personal services, while lower income families spend a greater proportion of their income on necessities such as food, medicine, and utilities (see chart).

Since the sales tax is applied by flat rate on consumer goods, taxing necessity items hurts poor and middle-income families more than wealthy families.

Measures to Offset Regressivity

Ways to deal with the regressivity of the tax range from some reformers' quixotic pleas for repeal of the tax altogether to keeping the tax and greatly expanding its base to include many more services—especially those most frequently used by people in the upper income brackets.

Some of the most popular alternative means of redressing the regressivity of the tax have been enacting income tax credits or passing exemptions for necessity items like food and drugs.

The number of states enacting credits and exemptions has been increasing in the past 10 years. Six states, following New Mexico's example, now provide credits against income tax liability for sales taxes paid. Similar to property tax "circuit breaker" formulas, most target the credit relief to low and modest income families.

Twenty-two sales tax states and the District of Columbia now exempt groceries from the tax. Most recently, citizens in Washington state passed an initiative to exempt food. Exemptions for medicine and related necessities have been enacted in 35 states and the District of Columbia.

Exempting items from the tax base, though, results in significant losses of revenue to the state. In Washington, for instance, elimination of the tax on food is estimated to cost the state $200 million annually. The District of Columbia, which did not exempt food until 1976, sustained a loss of almost $6 million after the passage of the exemption. Such losses have to be recovered in other ways—usually by raising tax rates or cutting back on state-provided services.

Another relief mechanism which would cause less revenue loss is the provision of a credit for sales taxes on income tax returns. This measure would sustain revenues and provide relief by targeting the low income families and providing them with a credit to compensate for the sales tax paid.

Still, reformers point out that giving an income tax credit to compensate for the regressivity of the sales tax acknowledges that the tax ought to be based on ability to pay. It would make more sense, then, to simply use or expand the income tax, which has the potential for the greatest equity.

Opponents of the credit solution also argue that it is administratively cumbersome and further complicates the income tax. In those four states that have no income tax, but do have a sales tax, such as Connecticut, the mechanism of a credit would be difficult to administer.

Finally, the problem with all such credit systems tied to the income tax return is that those to whom the relief is aimed, due to their low incomes, often do not file returns, and thus fail to receive the rebates due them.

One of the more promising reforms is expanding the sales tax base to include those services used primarily by the wealthy and the big corporations. Only a few states, though, have begun to include a wider range of services. New York City recently began to impose sales and use taxes on credit rating, adjustment and collection services, as well as protective and detective services and interior cleaning and maintenance. Wisconsin has just extended its tax to computer software.

In the District of Columbia, where about half of all services are exempt, it has been estimated that sales revenues would be increased by $25 million, or 15%, if all services were taxed. Because consumption of most services is concentrated among high income groups, the bulk of the additional revenue would be provided by high-income consumers. These revenues could be used to cut overall sales tax rates.

Extending the sales tax base to cover services provided by businesses and professionals could also help ameliorate the pessimistic fiscal prospects of the center cities. Cities have been experiencing a decline in their manufacturing sectors, and raising revenue from this sector through the property tax is becoming increasingly less productive. Taxing the growing service sector could help to fill this revenue gap.

Apart from its regressivity, the sales tax has caused administrators much concern. In *The Abuse of Power: The Permanent Government and the Fall of New York*, Jack Newfield and Paul DuBrui report that the city of New York alone is losing $200 million a year in taxes collected by merchants but never turned over to the tax collector.

Large-scale businesses are some of the most serious sales tax evaders. Albert Stoessel, former president of the Iowa Petroleum Association, estimated that his state loses $50 million a year in uncollected diesel fuel taxes mainly because it is a hard area to enforce.

States have taken a number of steps to improve the situation. Texas has initiated an ambitious program which will bring state auditors to each business to insure that they have registered with the state. This requires a huge staff which is often not available to tax administration officials.

Louisiana took innovative steps in 1964 which have paid off well. The system requires prepayment of the tax to the state before the goods are sold at retail level. Under the program, wholesalers remit to the state the tax collected from the retailer. Wholesalers and retailers are encouraged to register and report all sales fully by a compensation based on a percentage of the tax collected and reported. The adoption of this program in 1965 increased collections in that year by $8 million.

Lastly, another major problem with the tax is the degree to which states lose revenue as a result of a federal act which exempts from state sales tax all purchases at military PX's and commissaries. The ACIR estimates that over $266 million in combined sales and cigarette tax revenues is lost to the states each year because of the Buck Act provisions.

"A Look at the Sales Tax" is reprinted by permission from the January, 1978, issue of *People and Taxes*, Public Citizens Tax Reform Research Group.

RETAIL SALES AND USE TAX

A SALES TAX is a tax on part of the disposition of income (consumption, not savings) rather than a tax at the source of income. A sales tax can be either general or selective in its application. A general sales tax would apply to a broadly defined, though not totally comprehensive, consumption base. A selective sales tax would only be applied to an individual consumption good. Selective and general sales taxes can be and often are used simultaneously.

A general sales tax will not be comprehensive because some items are excluded as a result of

1.) the administrative difficulty of including some consumption goods, *e.g.*, imputed rent,
2.) decisions by policy-makers to attempt to reduce the perceived regressivity of the tax, *e.g.*, excluding food purchased for home consumption, or
3.) attempts by policy-makers to encourage the consumption of goods thought to be socially desirable, *e.g.*, prescription drugs.

Selective sales taxes are applied to particular products in an effort to

1). provide a substitute for service charges, *e.g.*, a gasoline tax,
2.) improving the progressivity of a general sales tax, *e.g.*, taxing restaurant meals at differential rates,
3.) discourage consumption of products considered immoral or unhealthy, *e.g.*, cigarette or alcoholic beverage taxes, or
4.) to export part of the tax burden to those outside the jurisdiction, *e.g.*, tax on transient accomodations.

The sales tax may be calculated as a percentage of the sales price, in which case it is referred to as an *ad valorem* tax. Alternatively, the tax may be a fixed amount per unit of product, in which case it is referred to as a *unit* tax. The first is a tax on the value of sales while the second is a tax on the quantity.

EFFICIENCY

The basic question is *"To what extent does one observe a change in consumption by both District and suburban residents due to differential sales tax rates, both between commodities and jurisdictions?"* It is generally argued that imposition of a sales tax by one jurisdiction in a region will create incentives for individuals to purchase exempt goods more and taxable goods in non-taxing or low taxing jurisdictions. The potential result is a decrease in sales in the taxing jurisdiction and redistribution of sales toward establishments concentrating in tax exempt goods.

These changes in consumption patterns are a result of the *substitution* and *income* effects of tax induced changes in relative prices. First, imposition of a sales tax increases the price of taxed goods, thereby reducing the consumer's disposable income, and thus the quantities of *all* goods that consumers purchase. The aggregate effect is to decrease sales. Since some goods are now taxed, a portion of the consumer's income must be allocated to paying the tax, thereby reducing the amount of income available to purchase goods and services.

Second, assuming that the incidence of the sales tax is at least partially on consumers, the imposition of the tax on only some commodities will induce consumers to substitute, to some degree, exempt goods for taxable goods.

Finally, if some jurisdictions in a region do not tax a commodity as heavily as other competing jurisdictions, consumers are induced to transfer, to some degree, their purchases from the higher to the lower tax jurisdiction. For a central city, with a higher tax rate than the surrounding suburbs, the result of the city/suburb substitution depends on the ease with which individuals are able to substitute purchases outside the jurisdiction for purchases inside the city. Consequently, the substitution incentive will be greater:

1.) the higher the net tax price,
2.) the greater the tax rate differential,
3.) the greater the relative importance of the product in the basket of goods purchased by the consumer, and
4.) the less expensive are transportation costs. [1]

The transportation cost issue has an added dimension, the possibility of multipurpose trips. Commuters from the suburbs to the city for work purposes view transportation cost as fixed. They do not face additional transportation costs to shop in the District, since they are already there. Therefore, they would be less sensitive to small disadvantageous tax rate differentials in the District than individuals who make special trips to shop in the District.

Estimating the degree to which non-taxed goods substituted for taxed goods depends on 1.) whether the non-taxed good satisfies the same needs as the taxed good, and 2.) whether the consumer's demand for the taxed good is sensitive to price changes. For example, a tax on food increases the food price which results in some reduction in food purchases. Since food is essential—demand is not too sensitive to price—one would probably observe a change in the type of food purchases rather than an absolute decline in food consumption, *e.g.*, substitute vegetables and grains for meat.

A portion of the reduced food demand reflects the income effect of instituting the tax and can easily be remedied with an appropriate credit through the personal income tax system. Additionally, one would expect outside-the-home consumption of food to be increased because the new tax on food purchases changes relative prices. But it must be remembered that restaurant meals are subject to an even higher sales tax than the general rate which in this hypothetical example would apply to food purchased for home consumption. One would expect, however, that this substitution would be minimal in the case of food and, for that matter, most other tax exempt commodities.

A recent study [2] of the District of Columbia general sales tax revenue collections concludes that

1.) rate differentials between the central city and its surrounding jurisdictions are *not* a significant factor in explaining variations in general sales tax collections in the District. However, this does not say that we can reject the idea that changes in the general sales rate do *not* cause consumers to change the location of purchases in aggregate, and

2.) a one point increase in the sales tax rate, from 5 to 6 percent (a 20 percent increase), is expected to provide about an 18 percent increase in sales tax revenues.

These empirical results were verified even when allowance was made for changes in the sales tax base and the opening of major new shopping centers in suburban jurisdictions. Regarding this last point, it should be emphasized that adjustments were only made for the year in which the shopping center opened, so this does *not* imply that there is no long-term effect on sales tax revenues as both consumers and retailers relocate.

The study also investigated the special case of taxing food purchased for home consumption. The general conclusions were that

1.) sales tax rate differentials on food do cause changes in where consumers buy food, and

2.) by untaxing food, the District might have increased food sales in the District by as much as 14 percent.

3.) a 2 percent tax on food in FY 1977 was esti-

Table 12-1

Effective Sales Tax Rates By Income Class Under Alternative Sales Tax Structures

AGI Class	Existing Structure	Food Taxed at 5 Percent	Proposed Credit[1]
Less than $ 3,000	3.95%	6.05%	2.33%
$ 3,000- 3,999	2.35	3.58	1.87
4,000- 4,999	1.94	3.05	1.58
5,000- 5,999	1.90	2.83	2.00
6,000- 6,999	1.76	2.57	1.83
7,000- 7,999	1.76	2.53	1.86
8,000- 9,999	1.60	2.30	1.68
10,000-11,999	1.48	2.10	1.82
12,000-14,999	1.47	2.04	2.04
15,000-19,999	1.40	2.04	2.04
20,000-24,999	1.33	1.90	1.90
25,000 and above	1.00	1.78	1.78
	1.00	1.28	1.28

Source: Staff computations, based on U.S. Department of Labor, Bureau of Labor Statistics. *Consumer Expenditure Survey Series: Interview Survey, 1972 and 1973.* Washington, D.C., 1976.
[1]This proposal assumes all food is taxed at the 5 percent rate and the following sales tax credit is in effect,
A $40 credit per dependent for family AGI of $3,000 or less
A $30 credit per dependent for family AGI of $3,000 - 4,999
A $20 credit per dependent for family AGI of $5,000 - 9,999
A $10 credit per dependent for family AGI of $10,000 - 11,999
A $ 0 credit per dependent for family AGI of $12,000 and above
The estimated revenue loss from the credit is $10.5 million, resulting in a net revenue gain of approximately $6 - 7 million.

mated to raise approximately $7 million in additional revenue. This is contrasted to the approximately $12 million which would be raised if the general sales tax rate were increased to 6 percent.

EQUITY

Vertical Equity

The traditional criticism of the sales tax from an equity point of view is that the distribution of the tax burden between income classes, measured by the percentage of income paid as tax, is regressive. If the tax burden is expressed as a percentage of consumption, rather than income, the "regressivity" is substantially reduced. However, the apparent proportionality of the tax when the base is consumption is misleading. Low-income families generally have consumption expenditures which exceed their income, thereby reducing the percentage of the base being paid in sales taxes, given the level of taxes paid. On the other hand, high income families generally have consumption expenditures substantially less than their incomes because of savings, thereby increasing the percentage of the base being paid in sales taxes. Thus, for a given level of taxes, the distribution may appear to be highly or slightly regressive depending on the base to which one compares the tax liability.

If the desired social policy is to reduce the regressivity of the sales tax, there are three different approaches which can be considered:

1.) exempt certain consumption goods which are preceived to be income inelastic, such as food,
2.) tax all goods, but provide an income tax credit to offset the desired portion of the sales tax liability for lower income families, or
3.) expand the sales tax base to include all services—especially those generally considered to face income elastic demands, such as accountants, all amusements, and lawyers.

In evaluating alternative strategies for redressing the distributional inequities of the sales tax, these three alternative approaches should not be considered as being mutually exclusive.

Using preliminary data from the U.S. Department of Labor Consumer Expenditure Surveys for 1972 and 1973, it was possible to make estimates of effective sales tax rates of alternative sales tax structures in the District. Specifically, equal yield[3] effective rates were estimated for the current structure (5% general rate,

6% rate on alcoholic beverages and the 8% rate on restaurant meals) and the current structure plus a 5% tax on food for home consumption with and without an income tax credit. As expected, the results, as shown in *Table 12-I*, indicate that

1.) the District of Columbia sales tax is regressive over all income levels,
2.) the structure with food taxed at 5 percent and the credit is less regressive than the current structure with food exempt from taxation,
3.) for every income class over $5,000 the rate is higher when food is taxed and a credit allowed than when food is exempt, and
4.) under the proposed credit the sales tax burden is essentially proportional for all income classes, with those families with incomes below $5,000 benefitting the most.

CREDITS VS. EXEMPTIONS: Income tax credits and commodity exemptions are the most popular alternative means of improving the equity of the general sales tax. As indicated, the District's general sales tax is regressively distributed across all income classes. However, the District's general tax rate is not excessive compared to the national standard. Of the 47 states which have general sales taxes, 22 have combined state-local rates which are equal to or exceed the 5 percent rate in the District.[4] Thus, the concern with providing sales tax relief in the District rests primarily with the distribution (regressivity) rather than the level of the tax.

Under the exemption approach, the 5 percent District of Columbia sales tax is eliminated on purchases for food, prescription drugs and laundry and dry cleaning at the time one purchases exempt items. The sales tax credit is given to consumers 'all at once' at the end of the year in the form of a reduced personal income tax liability. Most states using the credit approach restrict the credit to low-income groups and permit a tax rebate if the amount of the credit exceeds a person's income tax liability.

In effect, a tax credit directly increases one's disposable income but eliminates special tax induced relative price changes. In contrast, a commodity exemption alters relative prices (which increases disposable income somewhat) and thus provides an incentive to consume more of the exempt good which now becomes relatively cheaper. In this sense, credits and exemptions are not substitutes.

How does any jurisdiction evaluate the relative desirability of over-the-counter exemptions vis-a-vis a tax credit approach? The policy answer should be based on how well these alternatives satisfy the criteria for a 'good' tax system.[5]

Revenue Productivity: A tax provision is an 'efficient' revenue device if it achieves its goals at a minimum revenue loss (least cost) to the government treasury. If that the goal is to reduce the regressivity of the sales tax for low-income groups, then the credit is preferable to the exemption. To put it another way, for equally progressive tax structures, less revenue will be collected if an exemption is used instead of a tax credit.

Whether the credit will reduce the absolute effective rate (tax burden) for all income class is, of course, a function of the amount of the credits. For example, if the District eliminated the current over-the-counter sales tax exemptions and adopted the (variable vanishing) credit schedule which permitted

```
A $40 credit per dependent for family AGI of $3,000 or less
A $30 credit per dependent for family AGI of $3,000 - 4,999
A $20 credit per dependent for family AGI of $5,000 - 9,999
A $10 credit per dependent for family AGI of $10,000 - 11,999
A $0 credit per dependent for family AGI of $12,000 and above
```

then, according to the data in *Table 12-1*, the District sales tax would:

1.) be transformed from an overall regressive tax to one which is essentially proportional;

2.) produce net added revenues of approximately $7 million, and

3.) result in lower effective rates (vis-a vis the current sales tax structure) for all income groups below $5,000.

An across-the-board exemption could achieve these goals only at a much higher cost to the District in terms of foregone revenues because the relief is not targeted to the District's low-income residents.

Neutrality: Neutrality in taxation requires that persons in the same economic circumstances (in this case, defined as 'equal incomes' despite the caveats regarding the income measure as noted below) should be treated equally. With an exemption, however, two persons alike in every respect including total consumption patterns, but with differences in tastes will pay different amounts in sales tax—a violation of the 'equal treatment of equal (income)' rule. [6]

Further, since consumption varies by family size and rural vs. urban characteristics, food, drug, and dry cleaning expenditures (the exempt items in the District) become a very crude measure for designing tax relief. In contrast, a credit permits persons to 'apply' the sales tax reduction to whatever one wishes—be it movies or mushrooms, athletic events or aspirins—and is flexible enough to have statutory adjustments made for family and age differences.

Compliance: Unlike the credit, the exemption creates more paper work for retailers since separate records are required for taxable vs. tax exempt sales.

Taxpayer Ease: The over-the-counter exemption requires practically no consumer effort—the tax relief is given at the check-out-counter. The credit, however, requires the consumer to fill out an income tax form. And unless the tax department is careful, that can become a cumbersome process. But, it need not be! This complexity can become an especially severe problem for consumers if the City Council were to attempt to define 'income for credit qualification' different from (as D.C. does for its property tax credit) the commonly used concept (as adopted on the District of Columbia income tax) of Adjusted Gross Income.

Several states which have used a consumer credit approach, however, have greatly simplified the credit procedure. Only one line on the income tax form needs to be filled out in order to use the credit.

BASE BROADENING: A third, less popular, approach to decreasing the undesirable effects of the general sales tax's regressivity would be to truly make it a 'general' sales tax, including in the tax base all services rendered, including those of a professional, technical or scientific nature.

Expanding the base to include all services would increase sales tax revenues substantially—about $25 million in the District since about half of all services are exempt from taxation. [7] In addition, since the consumption of most of these services is concentrated in high-income groups, the sales tax's regressivity would be significantly reduced since most additional revenue would come from the high-income groups.

Besides the concern with the sales tax's regressivity, the extension of the sales tax base to include all services may be desirable because it responds to one of the fundamental revenue raising problems confronting central cities—a changing economic base. The service sector is the fastest and often only growing sector in most central cities. Because of current local government revenue structures, the growth of the service sector and the continued decline of the manufacturing sector have serious implications for the natural overall revenue growth of central cities. Expanding the sales tax base to include all services is one short term means of addressing the pessimistic revenue prospects of central cities.

In addition, arguments supporting the inclusion of all services in the retail sales tax base include:

1.) A narrower base tends to distort private consumer decisions (a violation of the neutrality principle in taxation) in favor of tax exempt purchases and against taxable goods.

2.) Expenditures on services constitute consumer expenditures just as do purchases of goods. There is no significant difference from the standpoint of satisfaction of wants.

3.) A broader base enables lower rates on other business firms.

4.) Broad taxation of services reduces sales tax regressivity since expenditures on services as a whole rise as income increases.

5.) The 'intermediate' sales issue is not relevant since the District does not provide for a retail sales exemption for other kinds of goods (and some services) sold to business firms (*e.g.*, a department store's display shelves are taxable when purchased under the sales/use tax law).

6.) Inclusion of services facilitates administration of some aspect of taxes. For example, registered vendors may have both taxable sales and exempt services.

As is true for nearly any tax change, expanding the sales tax base to include all services involves difficult public policy tradeoffs. First, some problems of tax enforcement and administration would be created. Some service firms (especially the professionals) could avoid the tax rather easily by establishing suburban offices for billing and internal administrative purposes, and yet maintain 'branch' offices in the District. That would require District revenue officials to make cumbersome case-by-case determinations of what part of a given firm's total income or receipts were actually attributable to District sources, and thus, subject to taxation.

Second, certain service businesses are not taxed in Maryland or Virginia (although both states are hard pressed for financial resources and might follow the District's lead in this area). Unilateral base broadening would tend to encourage these 'footloose' businsses to locate just outside of the District. Again, the professional firms provide the best example—particularly those firms which deal largely with the Federal Government.

In these special cases, practical fiscal expediency suggests that sales tax base broadening to fully tax all services may be unwise and self defeating. But, even if one recognizes that these locational and administrative problems exist, it does not necessarily follow that the best economic policy is complete tax exemption for these specific services. Indeed, economists argue that a theoretically 'optimal' sales tax structure requires that sales taxes should be levied at 'high' rates on those goods and services which exhibit a

relatively price inelastic demand. Those products with relatively price elastic demands are candidates for 'lower' (but not necessarily a zero rate) rates of taxation.

Therefore, just as is the case under the current sales tax, some services should be taxed at lower rates than others, *i.e.*, those services which face the most competitive market conditions should be taxed at the lowest rate. However, there is no a priori assumption that that rate should necessarily be a zero rate.

EXPORTING: The discussion so far has assumed that District residents make all purchases in the District. This is a simplification which ignores the extent to which sales taxes can be 'exported' to non-residents through their District purchases.

Tax exporting does not greatly influence vertical equity—*i.e.*, the relative degree of regressivity of the *absolute* burden actually borne by District residents. It has been estimated[5] that 47 percent of the District's sales tax is paid by District residents; 25 percent by tourists; 12 percent by residents of the metropolitan area; and 16 percent by businesses. While these empirical results should be interpreted with caution, it is clear that a substantial portion of the District's general sales tax is exported to non-residents.

Horizontal Equity

This alternative equity criterion applied to a broad-based sales tax asks whether families with equal incomes pay equal amounts of sales tax. Families in the same income class will pay different amounts of sales tax if a.) total consumption varies between equal income families, or if b.) the consumption of taxable goods varies within income classes. One important economic reason why both conditions should be true is that current consumption depends on lifetime income rather than current income only. One usually expects this effect to be very important at the lower income levels. For example, one can compare the consumption of two relatively low-income families, one a retired couple, the other a young married couple. The young couple may be consuming much more than the older couple on the expectation of higher future incomes.

A serious question can be raised about the appropriateness of using observed annual (even estimated permanent) income to gauge the degree of horizontal (vertical) equity. Individuals cannot only vary their consumption of particular goods, but they can also vary their consumption of leisure (non-work). The more leisure one opts for, the less income he will generate. Thus, the fact that some people are observed to have low income levels may, in part, reflect their choice for more leisure and less work.[9] Thus, because two individuals have identical incomes does not necessarily imply that they are of equal circumstances. The result is that the percent of income paid in taxes—whether permanent or current—is not an ideal index of equality.

Since disaggregate data on individual expenditure patterns *within* income classes is not available, no estimates are made of the horizontal equity of the District's sales tax. But a concern over horizontal equity would argue for a broad-based general sales tax. Therefore, if the objective is to provide sales tax relief, the credit approach will further the attainment of horizontal equity to a much greater extent than the exemption approach.

FOOTNOTES

[1]Thus, the completion of Metro will make it less costly to travel to and shop at Rosslyn and White Flint Mall.

[2]Ronald C. Fisher, "The Sales Tax in the District of Columbia Revenue System, "a paper prepared for the District of Columbia Tax Revision Commission, 1977.

[3]The equal yield concept does not apply to the case of the sales tax with clarity. For example, in comparing the difference between the current structure plus a tax on food to the current structure without a food tax, one can generate an equal yield by increasing the general rate, the alcoholic beverage rate or the restaurant meal rate. The resulting effective rates for each income class will differ—possibly

substantially—depending on how the equal yield adjustment is made. The 2 percent tax on food is estimated to be $820,000. The net revenue is $6.4 million—a 9 percent increase. Thus, for comparisons on an equal yield basis, the *general rate* is assumed to be 5.5 percent.

[4]*Significant Features of Fiscal Federalism, 1976-77*, U.S. Advisory Commission on Intergovernmental Relations, Washington, D.C., 1977, Table 96. Since this data represent the situation as of July 1, 1976, it does not reflect the recent increase in Maryland's general sales tax rate to 5 percent. There are 21 states which exempt food from sales taxation, while six states have some form of income tax credit.

[5]Some economists do not see these as 'alternatives' as represented. Fisher, for example, argues that the credit is a device to make the income tax more progressive, and can be used along with the exemptions. In contrast, see Emil M. Sunley, Jr. and Gail R. Wilensky, "The District of Columbia Individual Income Tax," a paper prepared for the District of Columbia Tax Revision Commission. In this study, Sunley and Wilsensky take the traditional view—and the one adopted here—that as a policy matter these two approaches are alternatives of one another.

[6]The credit still violates 'equal treatment' rule within income classes. See Sunley and Wilensky, "District of Columbia Income," p.22

[7]Staff estimates, based on data from *1972 Census of Business, Selected Services,* and *County Business Patterns* for 1972 and 1974.

[8]Ronald C. Fisher, "The Sales Tax," p. 45.

[9]David F. Bradford and Harvey Rosen, "The Optimal Taxation of Commodities and Income," *American Economic Review*, May 1976, pp. 94-101.

Exempting Necessities from the Sales Tax: The Arkansas Case

By Larry Ginsburg

When a delegation of ACORN (Association of Community Organizations for Reform Now) members delivered boxes of petitions signed by 110,000 Arkansas residents to end the sales tax on food and medicine to the Secretary of State, they knew this would be one of the most important campaigns in ACORN's nine year history. In the words of an Arkansas ACORN Executive Board member, a victory will "provide us with the momentum, the reputation, and the power to organize this whole state." The effort to repeal the sales tax on food and medicine was ACORN's first statewide initiative and a major step on the part of Arkansas's low and moderate income people to organize in their own interests, and thereby, to exercise control over their government. Although there were still six months until the November election, everyone understood that it would be an uphill battle all the way.

The Issue

The sales tax on food and medicine was a particularly important issue for low and moderate income citizens in Arkansas. Although taxes in Arkansas are relatively low (Arkansas ranked 33rd of the fifty states in taxes paid per $1000 of income), the 3% sales tax placed an unfair burden on the low and moderate income citizens of the state. While families earning between $25,000 and $50,000 annually spend about 1.8% of their income on sales tax, people earning $6,000 to $8,000 spend almost twice that much— 3.5%. Repealing the tax on food and medicine would save Arkansas residents between $100 and $150 a year, or an extra one to two weeks worth of groceries annually.

Although the actual dollars and cents savings which Arkansas residents would reap from the repeal of the sales tax was a critical issue in its own right, equally important was the emotional impact evoked by a tax on necessities of life. The drive and intensity behind the campaign came from this public feeling that a tax on necessities was basically unfair. This perception of injustice provided much of the public support for the issue, probably even more than the statistical inequities that analysis of the tax regressivity revealed.

The sales tax campaign consisted of two parts: 1) collecting enough signatures to qualify the constitutional amendment for the ballot and 2) working to win at the ballot box. The strategy in both phases was grounded in the basic tenets of the ACORN organizing model—maximum membership involvement, extensive door to door convassing, basic grassroots organizing. The strategy enabled ACORN to draw on its local affiliates which are organized as neighborhood based community groups, all affiliated with the state organization. From these neighborhood groups, ACORN could mount a campaign from the ground up, consolidating its strength where it counts in a ballot issue— with the voters, and especially with those voters who would be most likely to support this issue—the low and moderate income citizens.

Collecting Signatures

The campaign to collect signatures to qualify the constitutional amendment for the ballot began in September, 1977. ACORN offices in eight regions of the state began the push to collect the needed 72,000 signatures. (Although 72,000 valid signatures were required to get the initiative on the ballot, ACORN estimated that over 100,000 were necessary to insure that 72,000 of them would be valid.) This involved getting members out to county fairs, shopping centers, football games—anywhere there were large numbers of people. ACORN had tremendous success at collecting signatures at the polls during the primary and runoff elections. Not only was there a steady stream of people, these polling places had the advantage of attracting only registered voters which meant that almost all the signatures collected were valid.

Larry Ginsburg is Research Director of the Association of Community Organizations for Reform Now (ACORN).

ACORN also made an effort to involve other organizations in gathering signatures—labor unions, churches, community action agencies, and other special interest groups.

Intensive effort at collecting signatures did not begin until late April, 1978, which was cutting it a little too close for comfort. Though the going was rough in the beginning, by the end of the drive in June, ACORN staff, membership, and supporting organizations were bringing in 500 signatures a day. When the June 7 deadline rolled around, ACORN had more than enough signatures to qualify for the ballot.

Election Strategy

The plan for the election campaign was in many ways similar to the strategy for collecting signatures. The essential ingredient was a high level of membership involvement in the grassroots organizing effort, since money to carry on a sophisticated media campaign or a direct mail fundraising and publicity campaign was obviously not forthcoming. The outcome of the election would be determined by ACORN's ability to mobilize its own membership, leadership, staff and supporting allied organizations.

Support was raised for the issue in a number of ways: 1) activities in the local ACORN neighborhood organizations, 2) lining up endorsements, 3) setting up a citizen's committee to give speaking engagements around the state and 4) working with other organizations.

ACORN's neighborhood base lent itself well to the organizing effort. At the local group meetings, ACORN members spread the word about the sales tax campaign to their neighbors and friends, enlisted their aid in flyering, fundraising, and door to door canvassing drives, and urged them to bring others into the fight.

A second emphasis in the campaign was lining up endorsements for the amendment, and making sure that these endorsements were followed up by active support in the campaign. For this, labor unions, senior citizens groups, churches, League of Women Voters, any and all organizations that would support the effort were contacted and encouraged to involve their members in supporting Amendment 59.

A key component of ACORN's campaign was an active citizens committee. Committee members traveled around the state on speaking tours addressing groups like senior citizens, Democratic party committees, civic clubs, etc. They also held press conferences to publicize the issue.

The committee was made up of people from a variety of different organizations. The committee included Winston Bryant, the Secretary of State, who spoke to over 50 different groups; Bill Becker, President of the State AFL-CIO; Jim Lynch, Chief Deputy to the Pulaski County Judge (a position comparable to the Mayor); Mike Watts, an accountant and university professor; and Father Biltz of the Catholic Diocese.

These speaking engagements were invaluable for making contacts around the state and tying in supporters.

A large number of groups supported Amendment 59. Groups from local chapters of the American Association of Retired People to the State AFL-CIO to the Republican Party all raised money for the tax repeal, printed information for their membership in newsletters and bulletins, and spoke in favor of the amendment at their group meetings.

Powerful opposition to the campaign came from key state legislators, the Chamber of Commerce, the education establishment, and the new Democratic Gubernatorial candidate. Behind the scenes in the fight were the key political forces in the state—bankers, business leaders, and old guard politicians.

The major opposition argument was straightforward—if the tax is repealed from food and medicine, the state will not have the revenue to maintain the level of services that were currently provided. The choice, they said, was simple. Either new taxes would have to be imposed, or services would be cut. Not only did these organizations fear the possibility of higher taxes on business, but viewed the election as a test of ACORN strength, and reacted to defeat ACORN.

The fear of higher taxes was fueled by the very popular winner of the Democratic gubernatorial primary who came out against the amendment. His position was that until the revenue replacement was secured, no taxes should be removed. The argument was specious. A different interpretation of the facts points to an entirely different reality.

ACORN, some state legislators, the Secretary of State, and other supporters of the issue realized that the revenues in the state of Arkansas over the past five years had grown by about 15%. The sales tax on food and medicine amounted to only 5% of the revenues that the state collected. With experts anticipating continued growth, the decreased revenues could easily be absorbed.

The measure, which would have cost the state about $50 million a year, was almost exactly the current surplus in the state treasury. By the time the act would take effect, the surpluses would have exceeded $80 million. The tax would return the surplus to the people.

For years, the Arkansas Tax Revision Commission, which was created by the Arkansas Legislature, had been recommending changes in the tax structure which would have supplied the needed revenue. Some of these recommendations were:

1) an in-house audit for the state income tax—this would increase revenues by up to $7.5 million annually by finding non-residents who should have paid taxes in Arkansas but didn't.
2) eliminate exemptions to out of state companies whose subsidiaries did business in Arkansas but paid no taxes—this could increase revenues by $3 million annually.
3) applying the sales tax to professional services like

lawyers' fees and business services, and subjecting advertising services to the sales tax—this would increase revenues by $14.4 million dollars a year.

ACORN supported these changes. Not only would they provide much of the needed revenue, but they would be taxes that would not be imposed on low and moderate income people who couldn't afford it. ACORN felt that the eight months from the passage of the act to the time it would take effect would allow ample time for the state legislators to find equitable ways to replace the revenue.

Money, Media, and Momentum

Many factors worked against ACORN in the campaign. The degree to which they were within ACORN's control varied tremendously. Unfortunately, many of the more influential forces which shaped the campaign were factors over which ACORN had little control. The most important of these was money.

From the outset, finances were going to be a problem, and they continued to be throughout the campaign. Only one person was hired full-time to work on the campaign. Most of the work would be done by volunteers, members and staff. ACORN members and staff realized that the campaign would have to be conducted on a very limited budget. This in itself would not have been disastrous, but when compared to the opposition's bottomless well of financial support, the meager ACORN resources could not have been expected to go far. ACORN's lack of money gave the opposition a tremendous advantage—the ability to set the tone of the campaign. This was done primarily through an extensive television campaign. ACORN, of course, was unable to afford any television time. Although the equal time provisions offered some exposure, what may have been time was certainly not equal.

The tone that the business community was able to set for the campaign was one of fear—fear of changes generally, and fear of the new taxes that would have to be imposed if Amendment 59 passed. The message was that there was no free lunch—either services would have to be cut or new taxes levied. The TV message emphasized that higher taxes were on their way as soon as the ink dried on the new amendment.

Endorsements played an important part in this campaign in an unexpected way. The endorsements that ACORN received were from traditional allies— the state AFL-CIO, senior citizens groups, churches and independent labor unions. These were obtained early in the campaign and were the important endorsements that ACORN expected to get and needed to win. The surprise, and a weakness in the campaign, was with the endorsements that ACORN did not line up early, and did not get. These organizations who came out in opposition of the amendment were the mid-level organizations, city councils, school boards, etc. This hurt not because these endorsements were not secured, but because the wave of anti-amendment

groups which surfaced late in the campaign created a bandwagon effect that was difficult to halt. Each day, to the delight of the statewide press, another several groups came out against the amendment, adding to the growing list of anti 59 organizations. Many of these were very minor groups like the Arkansas Gem Dealers Association whose input in the political process is normally negligible. But the cumulative effect of each of these groups coming out against the amendment was devastating.

The Vote

The repeal of the sales tax on food and medicine, Amendment 59, lost on December 7th by 56% to 44%. The amendment carried in only 20 of the 75 Arkansas counties.

The issue of the sales tax on food and medicine had a definite class appeal. In poor areas, among senior citizens and minorities, the amendment did much better than it did in the wealthier areas. Another interesting aspect of the voting analysis was that there was almost no distinction in voting patterns between areas in which ACORN organized and non-ACORN areas. There was not the polarization of opinion for or against ACORN, something that had happened in ACORN's lifeline utility rate campaign in 1976. Here the vote was clearly divided along class lines. With the television saturation, this class appeal was somewhat blurred and weakened sufficiently so the initiative failed, but not so much that the pattern was not distinguishable.

Although the voters did not perceive the initiative as an ACORN issue, this was not true of the top political establishment in the state. As mentioned earlier, most of the state's prominent politicians was the amendment as a test of ACORN's strength, and almost unanimously opposed it. Because they feared ACORN, even the moderate and liberal politicians opposed the issue in order to contain ACORN. This was partly due to the political strength and popularity of the incoming governor; but it also reflected the controversy surrounding ACORN as an organization.

In a period when tax cutting proposals and spending limitations were being adopted all over the country, the results were somewhat surprising. Some analysts felt that the Proposition 13 sentiment worked against ACORN. Because the media was so effective, the prevalent opinion was that a vote against Amendment 59 would actually keep taxes down. This was ironic because the initial press interest in the campaign focused on the opposite theme—this was Arkansas' chance to join the tax revolt.

But the politicians couldn't completely ignore the campaign, or the enormous support among low and moderate income citizens of the idea that necessities should not be taxed. In January, 1979, the Speaker of the Arkansas House introduced a bill to exempt medicine from the sales tax. It passed unanimously. This was a direct result of ACORN's campaign.

FOOD AND MEDICINES
FOR PIGS AND CHICKENS
ARE NOT TAXED

WHY TAX FOOD
AND MEDICINE FOR PEOPLE?

Amendment 59 will end the sales tax on food and medicine.

Amendment 59 will save the average family $100 a year.

VOTE <u>FOR</u>
AMENDMENT 59
ON NOVEMBER 7

Citizens Committee To Fight Unfair Taxes
Winston Bryant, Chairman

"Exempting Necessities from the Sales Tax: The Arkansas Case" is reprinted by permission from the Association of Community Organizations for Reform Now, 1979.

Louisiana's Advance Sales Tax Law: History, Application and Current Status

J. Eugene Martin and Donald L. Dawson, Louisiana Department of Revenue

The ultimate effect of sales tax law, Louisiana's or anyone else's, is regressive. Low income families pay out a larger percentage of their earnings in sales taxes than do higher income families. The general sales tax is a relative newcomer in modern tax systems and, because of its regressive nature, has usually been introduced in times of fiscal emergency. On the other hand, it has commonly provided satisfactory revenues within a very short time after its enactment or increase. The sales tax has survived to this day, not because it is a particularly fair tax, but because in matters of practical taxation, fiscal adequacy is stronger than other considerations.

Another reason the sales tax has survived is that the consumer only pays out a small amount of money at the time. It hurts less, or at least the consumer notices the hurt less than he would miss the same amount of money paid out as a lump sum.

Bearing this in mind, we tax administrators have a serious obligation to the taxpaying public and ourselves to ensure the dollars they pay to retailers in good faith toward the operation of state government actually winds up in the state treasury. Every taxpayer in Louisana or any other taxing jurisdiction has a right to know that his government is doing everything possible to make sure that takes place.

Inaccurate reporting gives dishonest businessmen and honest businessmen who make mistakes, a distinct profit advantage over their more honest or more knowledgeable competitors. It enables some businessmen to keep money that does not belong to them, and when it is done deliberately, it amounts to nothing less than theft.

The traditional answers to the problems of accurate and maximal sales tax collection are familiar to you as they were in 1964 to Louisiana tax administrators and public officials. We employed auditors, and still do, but there weren't enough to deal with the thousands who did not fully understand and account for the tax. Many would total their receipts for the month, take two percent of that, and remit it to the state. Under that system, the amount charged as sales tax was not necessarily the amount that was being remitted to the state. Many retailers, especially the owners of small businesses, failed to keep accurate records, or in some cases no records at all. We also have the perennial problem of persons collecting the tax but failing to remit it to the state. There were and are many excuses: lack of knowledge, lack of bookkeeping facilities, and lack of time, but whatever the reason, the result was the same. Money was being collected from citizens which never made it to the state treasury. Our auditing staff was overworked and made all too small a dent in the problem.

In 1964, officials of the Louisana Department of Revenue devised a law designed to minimize these problems. It was a law designed to put to work the self-interest of businessmen. In a special session of the Louisana Legislature in November, 1964, the Advance Sales Tax Law was adopted. The law, under which wholesalers were to collect sales tax from retailers, was originally limited to about 20% of the state's wholesalers. This included those dealing in food, soft drinks and other beverages, cosmetics, tobacco products, automotive parts and petroleum products. It was felt at the time that our greatest non-compliance problems lay in those areas. In the regular legislative session of 1965, a bill was adopted which required the collection of advance sales tax from all wholesalers. Both of these acts were strongly backed by the administration then in office.

How the Law Works

Dealer Registration

Prior to the time a dealer, as defined by law, commences to do business in Louisiana, sales and use tax registration is required. The registration form to be submitted by the dealer requires the name and address of the business, the date of commencement, a description of the type of business to be conducted, and other relevant information.

When the registration form is received by the Department of Revenue, it is reviewed and assigned a sales and use tax number. If the registrant is a retail dealer who sells primarily to consumers, a retail sales tax number is assigned to the dealer. A certificate showing the name, address and sales tax number is mailed to the dealer. If the dealer is deemed to be a wholesale dealer (any person who sells to other dealers, who in turn sells to consumers), a wholesale sales tax number is assigned to the dealer, and a certificatee showing the name, address and sales tax number is issued to the dealer.

After the enactment of the advance sales tax law, manufacturers, wholesalers, jobbers, suppliers and brokers who sold their wares to retail dealers were required to register with the Department of Revenue for sales tax purposes and to collect an advance sales tax from the retail dealers. This category of registrants is required to file a return with the Department of Revenue each month showing total gross sales and the amount of sales tax collected. As compensation for doing this, the wholesaler may deduct one and one-half percent (1 ½ %) of the tax as vendor's compensation when remitting the tax to the Department of

Revenue. Vendor's compensation is payment to the dealer for record-keeping.

The retail dealer, who purchases wares from a wholesaler, keeps a record of the advance sales tax paid to the wholesaler each month. The retailer is also required to keep a record of all sales made to ultimate consumers, and the amount of sales tax collected from them. At the end of each month, the retailer files a sales tax return with the Department of Revenue whereby he reports the total gross sales made and the total tax collected or due from these sales. As compensation for doing this, the retailer may also deduct one and one-half percent (1½%) of the tax due as vendor's compensation when remitting the tax to the Department of Revenue. Before remitting the tax due, however, the retailer deducts one hundred percent (100%) of the advance sales tax previously paid to wholesalers; thus, only the net amount of tax due is remitted to the Department of Revenue. The retail dealer is required to collect the same amount of sales tax from the consumer as required before the enactment of the advance sales tax law.

Examples of How Advance Sales Tax Works

As stated previously, under the Advance Sales Tax Law, every dealer doing business in Louisiana is required to register with the Department of Revenue in order to receive a sales tax registration number. The number issued to the dealer determines whether or not the dealer can purchase wares for resale without paying advance sales tax.

When registrants make purchases for resale, the supplier will ask for a sales tax number. If the number contains a "W", all purchases may be made without payment of the advance sales tax. The determination of whether or not a dealer can purchase wares for resale without paying advance sales tax is determined by the Department of Revenue only at the time of registration.

This Law was not passed merely to achieve a new standard of fairness to the state's taxpayers. It was passed during a time of fiscal stress for Louisiana and its intent was to furnish additional money for the operation of state government. When the Bill was passed in 1964, it was estimated that sales tax collections would increase by 7.5 million dollars. The actual increase was 12 million dollars. The 1965 bill increasing the number of businesses paying the advance sales tax was estimated to increase collections by 8 million dollars, which it did. The implementation of the two bills caused an increase of collections of 13.5 percent after allowing for normal growth factors. The total effect of both bills was 20 million dollars for the state treasury in the 1965-66 fiscal year. Obviously, many dealers had not been reporting properly—many others had not been reporting at all. No change was made during this period of the rate of the tax or in the application of the tax—only in the collection procedure.

Current Status

When Louisiana's Advance Sales Tax Law was created, the officials of the Department of Revenue knew that unanticipated problems and objections to the system would arise.

On the positive side, the enactment of the law has assisted the Department of Revenue in the collection of sales tax, and provided a better method of accounting and checking for accuracy. It has increased collections with no change in the obligation of the ultimate taxpayer and with no change in the number of persons needed to administer the law. With the imposition of the collection of the sales tax at the wholesale level, the major portion of the tax is collected and remitted by the wholesale dealer or distributor who is generally better equipped for accounting purposes and more knowledgeable than the small retail dealer. The implementation of the advance tax system has resulted in a reduction of delinquent accounts because the retailer has a smaller amount of tax to remit to the Department of Revenue. It will also result in improved processing as we are now able to register more taxpayers on a quarterly filing basis rather than monthly.

At the same time, a number of objections began to be raised concerning the system. Some of the objections which were raised are without basis and others were compensated for by specific provisions of the law:

Objection No. 1—Payment of the advance sales tax is unfair to retailers since, on a cash flow basis, it results in a reduction in the amount of funds available for inventory investment.

Answer—This is not true since money which is collected for sales tax purpose is held for as much as one month by the retailer until it becomes time to remit the tax to the Department of Revenue. In the past, the retailer had the use of these funds for one month. The advance sales tax law merely equalizes the situation.

Objection No. 2—Wholesalers who also sell at retail would be competing with other retailers on an unfair basis, since they would not be subject to the payment of advance sales taxes in many cases.

Answer—This is not a true picture of the situation. Sales tax, since it is paid by the ultimate consumer at the rate prescribed by law, should have no effect on competition.

Objection No. 3—The bookkeeping required by this law is burdensome and unjust, especially since wholesalers should have nothing to do with the collection of sales tax.

Answer—A vendor's compensation at the rate of one and one-half percent (1½%) of the amount collected goes to the wholesalers. This amount has been judged adequate by most of the parties involved.

Objection No. 4—Retailers will buy outside of the state and thereby avoid the payment of advance sales tax. This will affect the total economy of the state.

Answer—We register out-of-state suppliers where there is jurisdiction. If they do not collect the tax, they face legal action. Since use tax applies in the case of goods bought for use inside of the boundaries of the state, the end result is the same.

Objection No.5—The payment of advance sales tax actually amounts to double taxation.

Answer—A credit is allowed to the retailer for all taxes which are paid to wholesalers, therefore, there is no double taxation involved.

Objection No. 6—Who is actually the ultimate consumer of the goods and services on which sales taxes are paid?

Answer—This is a legitimate problem, but it is a problem whether or not there is an advance sales system.

In the collection of advance sales taxes, there are some legitimate problems which are foreseeable and need to be dealt with. First, many retailers, and this is especially true in Louisiana, cannot deduct the advance sales tax because they do not collect the tax at the retail level, i.e., sales in interstate commerce, sales for offshore use, or sales to businesses which have special exemptions. Another problem is that of the classification of mixed businesses. Where should the line be drawn between a wholesale business and a retail business, or between business furnishing taxable or non-taxable merchandise? Many materials which are sold at the wholesale level are sold to other wholesalers, or are sold for further processing. This creates administrative as well as tax appeal and court problems. Another problem with the collection of the advance sales tax is political. People want special considerations which will furnish them an edge over competition. In Louisiana, wholesaler exemption numbers have been issued. These numbers permit wholesalers to dispense with the collection of advanced sales tax in certain situations. It should be pointed out that those exemptions are not designed to exempt the wholesaler from the payment of any tax on materials not purchased for resale. In the past, these numbers were issued to a number of businesses, primarily those involved in contractor supply, which had no right to them under the Law. Now, those with exemptions have come to include 9,000 businesses of 72,000 registered in Louisiana.

Sales tax collections increased dramatically with the enactment of the Advanced Sales Tax Provision. A thirteen and one-half percent (13½%) improvement is very significant where no change is made as far as the consumer is concerned. The law, with all the objections that have been raised, and all of its problems, has been a good one.

"Louisiana's Advance Sales Tax Law" is reprinted by permission from the Louisiana Department of Revenue.

CHAPTER 17

User Charges

The idea of a benefit charge has long been a battleground for the efficiency vs. equity concerns in evaluating a tax system. **User Charge Financing**, the first article in this chapter, is a reprint of a 1974 report by the U.S. Advisory Commission on Intergovernmental Relations which lays out the debate quite clearly. On the pro-side user fees discourage waste, are easily collected, and, if not applied to services having general community-wide benefit, are quite consistent with principles of equity or "fairness" in taxation.

But, there are a couple of problems with the use of fees—problems which are likely to become more severe as user fees are used more intensively in order to either generate additional state/local revenues or replace other tax sources which can no longer be relied upon. The Proposition 13 case, which is discussed by Jonathan Lewis in the second article entitled **Proposition 13 Forces Shift to User Fees**, provides the classic example of this replacement situation. What has happened there is that as the fee approach has been used more intensively, their structural defects have become so apparent as to make some of the charges intolerable. In their attempts to raise sufficient revenues in order to maintain the existing scope and quality of their program structure, local jurisdictions have levied fees for some services for which they have little experience in pricing and/or which have deprived low income persons from even using selected public facilities.

The California situation illustrates the need to recognize that although user fees do have several attractive features, they can, like any tax, be abused. In this regard two critical questions must be asked of any fee proposal: Will the charge eliminate some persons from using services which have community wide benefits? And, is the charge necessary in order for the government to keep offering the particular service? If the answer to the second is yes (if its "no," a zero or reduced fee may be warranted) then the first concern becomes paramount and some adjustments are necessary, probably through special price discrimination devices (some creativity is needed!) in order to insure that low income persons are not excluded. Clearly the solution is ultimately political.

Development Charges by Donald Hagman addresses two other forms of beneficiary charge—extractions designed to capture some of the windfall gains which, as a result of community generated growth accrue to private interests, and special impact taxes levied in order to cover certain costs of private development. The Hagman excerpts here are brief descriptive summaries. The reader interested in further exploring this topic should examine both the source for this article and the recent and most comprehensive discussion on such topics by Hagman and Misczynski, eds., in *Windfalls for Wipeouts* (1978, American Planning Association, Chicago).

User Charge Financing

In a market economy, prices serve the dual roles of determining what goods and services will be produced and of rationing the available goods and services among competing bidders. Pure user charges (prices paid for goods and services) potentially serve the same role in the public sector that prices serve in the private sector. Four characteristics of the service or facility to be priced must be examined in deciding whether to levy a user charge for a particular service or facility.

Behavior Modification

One purpose of user charges is to ration what is available in limited supply, influence people to alter behavior drawing on public resources, and restrain the level of consumption to the desired level. Charging the user or beneficiary of a service (or more precisely, the person whose actions motivated the expenditure) compels the individual to take account of the costs that his actions impose on the system. In some cases, use will be very sensitive to the price charged. In the case of some services, however, the amount of use is likely to be the same whether the service is unpriced or priced at full cost.

Indeed, some methods of pricing offer little incentive to alter behavior. When flat charges are imposed, the user pays the same amount regardless of how much he uses the service. For example, if a $3 per month charge is levied on each house for garbage removal or water supply, the occupants have little reason to be careful or moderate in their use of water or their production of trash. If the water charge is levied on the basis of the size of the lot rather than the quantity of water used, then homeowners will not have an incentive to reduce the quantity of water used but will have an incentive to reduce the size of the lot. This is the desirable arrangement if, as Vickrey asserts, cost depends principally upon the length of the pipe that must be laid to reach the user.[1]

Nature of Benefits

In many cases, the very reason for government performance of a function is that the price directed, market economy is inappropriate. Sometimes users are too general or diffuse to be identified, as in trying to assess the beneficiaries of a particular police patrol. Even when immediate users are identified (those persons being immunized against a disease in the case of public health), the ultimate beneficiaries, who were the real reason for public performance of this function, may be someone else and thus too diffuse to be billed. The public at large might benefit in either of two ways: because it is protected from an epidemic and because it derives satisfaction from knowing that the persons immunized are protected. Charging the person to be immunized may make him less willing and thus reduce the benefits to the ultimate beneficiaries.

Administrability

Even when a system of identifying and collecting from users can in concept be created, the actual cost may be high. The waste resulting from employing toll collectors, meter readers, inspectors or other enforcers may outweigh the waste that results from allowing unlimited use of the service or facility. Although general taxes also entail collection costs, an increase in taxes does not entail a substantial increase in collection costs. Creation of a new user charge does. As Adam Smith stated:

> Every tax (or other source of governmental revenue) ought to be so contrived as both to take out and to keep out of the pockets of the people as little as possible, over and above what it brings into the public treasury of the state. A tax may either take out or keep out of the pockets of the people a great deal more than it brings into the public treasury, in the four following ways. First, the levying of it may require a great number of officers, whose salaries may eat up the greater part of the produce of the tax. . . .[2]

On the other hand, an increase in a user charge also does not entail an increase in collection costs. Thus, while administrative considerations may argue for foregoing a possible user charge and thus financing from general revenue, such considerations do not argue for light use of the charge.

Equity

Objections to user charges are frequently made on the grounds that user charges place a disproportionate burden on lower income people. As a general proposition, however, the claim of regressivity is not intuititively obvious or meaningful. For some goods and services, with pricing policies based on exact usage, lower income persons would pay a larger percentage of income than higher income persons; for other goods and services the higher income persons will pay a larger percentage. In this respect, goods and services for which user charges might be imposed are not different from other, privately provided goods. Furthermore, horizontal equity argues that if one person uses a good or service and another equally well off person does not, only the actual user should pay for the service.

As actual pricing practice deviates from exact usage pricing, however, the charges take on an arbitrary character. The extreme case is a charge imposed on all potential users which is the same regardless of the amount of actual use, such as a $3 per month charge per house for water or sewage or trash removal. Such charges are virtually taxes but would generally be subject to criticism as highly regressive if labeled as taxes.

User charges do have the potential for restoring equity in the case of two groups who may use city services but do not pay taxes: tax exempt organizations and non-residents.

Summary of Criteria

John Due summarizes the criteria for evaluating particular use charges.[3]

> The case for charging most or all of the costs against the users is strongest if —
>
> A. Substantial waste of the service will result if it is provided free of charge.
> B. The benefits are primarily individual in character rather than benefiting the community as a whole.
> C. The prices for the services can be collected easily.
> D. The method does not result in burdens on individuals which are considered to be contrary to accepted principles of equity.
>
> In contrast, the case for providing the services free of charge and covering their costs from taxation is strong if —
>
> A. The services are of such nature that little waste will occur if they are made available without charge.
> B. The benefits accrue in part to the community as a whole, so that the charging of a price will result in unnecessary restriction of use of the service.
> C. Costs of collection of prices are high.

D. The pattern of distribution of burden which would result from charging for the services is one which would be regarded as inequitable.

Frequently, however, the choice is not simply between user charges and taxes, but between (for example) a charge capable of influencing behavior and a charge that can be administered cheaply. Johnson, in his examination of sewer charges, examined several possible types of charges with respect to the above and other criteria. The results showed that whatever charge ranked especially high on one criterion, ranked quite low on another.[4]

Efficient Pricing

Some discussions of user charges assume that user charges would cover the full cost of the service and thus obviate the need to finance that function from taxes. Other authorities question this conclusion.

Frequently, the production and use of a good affects beneficially or adversely someone other than the buyer and seller of the good. Such 'effects are called externalities. The existence of such external benefits is said to indicate that total benefits exceed total cost and thus that provision should be increased through a partial subsidy.

Many public services require facilities such as roads, airfields, bridges, and sewage plants with a large fixed (initial) cost and a relatively low variable (and thus marginal) cost. The existence of fixed costs is frequently said to require charging a price that is not high enough to recover the cost of the facility. The following is a persuasive presentation of this point of view:

Consider, for example, the ''production'' of bridge crossings. Assume, to take an extreme instance, that once the bridge in question is built, all wear and tear is a function of time rather than use, i.e., that there are no additional costs associated with extra crossings. (The bridge is never so full as to give rise to crowding.) The marginal cost to society, in terms of scarce resources, of an additional crossing is zero. It follows — the proposition is mathematically demonstrable, as well as, in this case, intuitively obvious — that the efficient ration price for a crossing is precisely zero. A positive price such as would discourage even a single crossing would cause allocation to be inefficient; there would remain unexploited a costless crossing which could make someone better off without hurting anyone else. Yet it is equally evident that charging a price of zero for crossings will hardly raise sufficient revenue to cover the cost of building the bridge.

To a sophisticated businessman used to running a decentralized multidivision firm all this would not come as too much of a surprise. Not every process in a well run firm should be expected to cover its cost in terms of the right set of internal accounting prices. Total profit is the deciding criterion, and it may be worthwhile for a firm to build a private bridge between its two installations on opposite sides of a river yet charge a zero accounting price for its use by the various decentralized manufacturing and administrative divisions. (Zero would certainly be the right price if a positive accounting price discouraged the use of the bridge while extra use involved no extra cost.) The bridge considered as a separate activity would make accounting losses, yet total company profits would be increased.[5]

Even if the bridge crossings (to continue the above example) were not costless, the same reasoning indicates that the proper charge for a bridge crossing is the associated increment in total cost, and charging by that rule would raise less than the full cost of the bridge. To do otherwise would be to deny use of the bridge to someone willing to pay the entire cost associated with his crossing.

This conclusion that such deficits should be allowed is not unchallenged. Economic analysis generally holds that if all goods are priced at marginal cost, then buyers will seek to purchase and suppliers will provide that combination of goods most desired by everyone. Financing a deficit on the bridge requires taxes, and taxes on other goods will raise their price above marginal cost. Thus efficiency requires balancing the effect of pricing the publicly provided good above its marginal cost against forcing the price of all other goods above their own marginal costs.

Although each user should pay only for the

cost of what he consumes, jointly all users should bear the total cost themselves. As a matter of equity, in general, non-users should not have to pay part of the cost. As a matter of efficiency, the market test acts as a check against inefficient projects.

The policy of pricing at marginal cost and financing the deficit from general revenues is often misapplied. If the capacity of the facility will never be fully utilized (i.e., more persons can use the facility at the same time) and if building a less expensive facility with a smaller capacity is impossible then the argument for marginal cost pricing may be applicable. On the other hand, if the capacity is fully utilized at nearly all times, then the additional cost of the larger capacity is one of the costs of providing service to the additional person and efficiency requires that he be charged accordingly. If the capacity is fully utilized on some occasions (peak periods, e.g., "rush hours") and not at others, then there should be two prices: (a) a peak period price high enough to cover the capital costs (the cost of providing the capacity) and the actual operating costs related to the use by the peak period group; (b) a non-peak period price covering only the actual operating costs related to the use by the non-peak period users.

Intergovernmental Constraints

Local governments do not have complete freedom in the selection of user charges. First the state may prohibit certain user charges. Second, the Federal government and most states allow personal deductions for certain major taxes levied by local government but not for user charges and certain use related taxes. This creates a bias in favor of general taxation rather than user charges. Third, Federal revenue sharing and some state programs base aid upon fiscal effort, defined in terms of taxes collected but excluding user charges.

Federal Income Tax Deductions

Since the deductibility of a local tax has the effect of reducing how much the taxpayer actually gives up as a result of a given local tax, this creates a bias against the use of user charges and special assessments. A person who must pay $100 for water, sewage, and fire protection would rather pay it as a property tax than as a set of user charges since paying it as a property tax will allow him a partially offsetting reduction in income tax. The deductibility of the gasoline tax and registra-

tion fees based on the value of the vehicle creates a bias against tolls, zone and time passes for use of city streets, and metered use of roads (as well as against license fees levied at a flat rate or upon vehicle characteristics such as weight or engine size).

The bias does not affect all segments of the public. For businesses, both charges and taxes are deductible as an income related expense. More than 60 percent of the income tax filers used the standard deduction and thus cannot deduct taxes and would not be able to deduct user charges.

If the deductibility of taxes and user charges were extended beyond its present scope, the taxpayer would have to keep records for all the various taxes and charges in order to know how much to claim and would have to retain the appropriate receipts for three years to defend himself against IRS challenge. Alternatively, IRS could prepare appropriate tables as is now done for the gasoline and sales taxes. If such tables are to account for local taxes and charges, a separate table would have to be prepared for each jurisdiction in the country — a formidable task.

One possible compromise is to allow the deduction of specific charges and fees related to the place of residence, provided that they are listed on the property tax bill. Such a provision could include any special charges for fire protection, sewers, and garbage. A decision would have to be made about water, gas, and electricity because these services are publicly provided in some places and privately in others. (Water is generally public; gas and electricity are generally private.) Indeed, some people are already deducting user charges billed simultaneously with the tax bill, from failure to read carefully either the local tax bill or the Federal income tax guide.

State Income Tax Deductions

For the same reasons, the state income taxes also create a bias against user charges. Whereas states have the freedom to permit or deny whatever deductions they choose, for the convenience of both taxpayers and state tax collectors, states tend to copy the Federal tax.

Furthermore, the state income tax deduction is of considerably less significance since the state rates are much lower than the Federal rates. The lowest rate in the Federal income tax is 14 percent. Only Delaware and Vermont have any rate higher than 14 percent and that rate does not apply until income exceeds $75,000 and $44,000, respectively.

Federal Revenue Sharing

The *State and Local Fiscal Assistance Act of 1972* (revenue sharing) bases the allotments to units of local government in part upon the amount of tax revenue raised by that unit from its own sources. Taxes for this purpose means "compulsory contributions enacted . . . for public purposes . . ., as such contributions are determined by the Bureau of the Census for general statistical purposes." (Employee and employer assessments and contributions to finance retirement and social insurance systems are specifically excluded.) The term taxes does include some licenses such as for motor vehicles, animal, building, and marriage. It does not include charges for use of airport facilities, or hospitals, parking meter receipts, sewage charges, or taxes on property based on some measure other than value such as area or front footage. Also excluded from taxes are proceeds from publicly owned utilities (including water and electricity) and government owned liquor stores.

State Financial Assistance Programs

A number of states have some program of financial assistance to units of local government in which the amount of aid received from the state depends upon the amount of tax revenue raised by the local government. By excluding user charges, these programs also work to bias local governments against user charges.

State Legal Requirements

Sometimes user charges cannot be levied because state law prohibits their use or at least does not specifically authorize it. The prohibition against tuition at public schools is the strongest example of where such a prohibition exists and is generally approved. Also some states specifically forbid supplementary charges for specific items such as books, laboratory and gymnasium equipment, and lockers.

Licenses and fees are generally restricted in amount to what is needed to cover the costs of regulation, except where broader powers have been granted to the local government imposing the charge.[6]

Charging for water, sewage, and garbage would seem to present little difficulty. Charges for road use and fire protection would most likely be regarded as taxes and thus would not be easily imposed without state authorization. For example,

even if an excise tax on gasoline were a feasible form of imposing a service charge on road users, most cities could not use it without enabling legislation.

Parking meters are an example of the complex nature of the legality of particular user charges. Parking meter ordinances have sometimes been adjudged invalid because they were instituted as revenue producing rather than regulatory measures. The fee collected is subject to limitations of reasonableness and equality, but may be sufficient to defray the cost of installation, maintenance and supervision of the meters. However, it cannot be in effect a tax for general revenue, except when the city is specifically authorized to levy such a tax.[7] The following quotation indicates more of the complexity:

Indeed, the view has been taken that the fee which may be charged by the use of parking meters is not necessarily limited to the approximate cost of purchase, maintenance and policing of the meters. Nor is the regulation of parking through parking meters invalidated by an incidental increase in the city's receipts. The parking fee collected through such meters may be fixed at a point where some parking will be discouraged without violating the limitation of reasonableness and equality. Excess revenue from parking meters may be expended to maintain and improve streets and highways, including streets on which the meters are not located. Or the excess revenue may be used to acquire, construct, improve, maintain and manage parking areas."[8]

Project Grant Requirements

Sometimes a Federal grant program requires or encourages the use of user charges. The *Federal Water Project Recreation Act of 1965* specifies that non-Federal agencies must bear 50 percent of the separable costs allocated to recreation, fish and wildlife investment in Federal water projects and all of the operation, maintenance, and replacement costs thereafter. The non-Federal share can be borne in two ways: (1) payment or provision of land or facilities for the project; or (2) repayment with interest within 50 years, provided that the source of payment be limited to entrance fees and user charges. This amounts to a loan under the condition that user charges be used in the future.[9] The *Federal Water Pollution*

Control Act Amendments of 1972[10] provides for grants for the construction of waste treatment plants but requires that the applicant adopt a system of charges to assure that each recipient of waste treatment services pay its proportionate share of the costs of operation and maintenance (including replacement) and make provision for the payment by industrial users of the portion of construction costs allocable to the treatment of industrial wastes.

On the other hand, sometimes a Federal law forbids user charges. Prior to 1973, several airports had imposed boarding fees, generally of $1 per passenger. Challenged in several lawsuits as interference in interstate commerce, the charges were upheld by the Supreme Court.[11] Congress reacted by including a provision in the *Airport Development Acceleration Act of 1973*[12] prohibiting taxes, fees, head charges, and other charges, directly or indirectly levied on persons traveling in air commerce, on the carriage of persons, on the sale of air transportation, and on the gross receipts thus derived. (The law does not prohibit property, income, franchise, or sales taxes, nor does it prohibit rental charges, landing fees, and other service charges levied on aircraft *operators*.)

Implementation Problems

Once a decision has been made to raise more revenue from user charges, many choices still remain to be made: Which department? Which activity? Which fee? How large an increase? Making such decisions generally requires detailed knowledge of the department and service involved or the wholehearted cooperation of the department. One might expect departments that are repeatedly requesting additional funding to point out possible sources of funds, but the opposite seems to be the case. In his study of Oakland, California, Meltsner found the departments generally reluctant and unresponsive when the city managers undertook a study of charges. Some departments did not know what their costs actually were. Some departments did not know why they charge fees.

In Oakland individual departments varied to the extent that they tried to collect fees. The building inspectors recovered 90 percent of costs through charges for permits and inspections in a normal construction year, but when construction slumped revenue declined also while costs continued. The director of the municipal auditorium was con-

sidered by Meltsner as the most commercial official on the city payroll. As a matter of professional pride he would have liked to break even, and felt that charities, patriotic organizations and conventions should not be given special rates. However, for him "to break even" meant to cover about 60 percent of operating costs. The recreation department in general wished to provide free services for youth and children. However, the department did try to recover costs on sailing and golf and actually made a profit from one golf course.

The other approach to setting fees, i.e., having non-employees of the department who are very familiar with its operations (e.g., budget analysts) determine the fees and charges, was not explicitly discussed by Meltsner. But the evidence which he accumulated shows little prospect of this approach succeeding. The budget analysts were generally unfamiliar with the details of the department's operations. Departmental requests were cut on the basis of rules of thumb rather than on any concrete knowledge of the proposed expenditure. Such people are unlikely to be successful in determining when a charge should be imposed or increased.[13]

FOOTNOTES

[1]William Vickrey, "General and Specific Financing of Urban Services," *Public Expenditure Decisions in the Urban Community* (Howard Schaller, ed.), 1963.

[2]Adam Smith, *The Wealth of Nations*, p. 778.

[3]John Due, *Government Finance*, 1959.

[4]James A. Johnson, "Distribution of the Burden of Sewer User Charges Under Various Charge Formulas," *National Tax Journal* December 1969, pp. 472-485.

[5]Francis M. Bator, *The Question of Government Spending*, 1960, pp. 93-95.

[6]Eugene McQuillin, *The Law of Municipal Corporations*, Third Edition, Callaghan and Co., Chicago, 1950, Sec. 26.15 ff.

[7]*Ibid*, Sec. 26.167, 26.168, 30.58.

[8]*Ibid*, Sec. 26.168.

[9]Public Law 89-72, as summarized by Jerome W. Milliman, "Beneficiary Charges — Toward a Unified Theory," *Public Prices for Public Products*, pp. 41-42.

[10]Public Law 93-44.

[11]*Chicago Home Rule Commission Report and Recommendations*, 1972, pp. 429-433.

[12]Public Law 93-44.

[13]Arnold Meltsner, *The Politics of City Revenue*, University of California Press, Berkeley, 1971, pp. 71-85, 177-184.

"User Charge Financing" is reprinted by permission from the Advisory Commission on Intergovernmental Relations, *Local Revenue Diversification*, 1974.

Proposition 13 Forces Shift to User Fees

by Jonathan Lewis

In the wake of Proposition 13 cutbacks, some California cities are going begging. Communities which have traditionally been identified as havens for the wealthy and elite are asking their residents for donations.

Hillsborough, Piedmont and San Marino are three California cities which have passed the hat. San Marino provides a typical example.

The *L.A. Times* reports that in 1978 San Marino's Save Our Services (SOS) had 40 volunteers calling city residents asking for donations to make up a $1.5 million Propositon 13 loss in revenue. The campaigners are asking for 15 percent of each resident's Proposition 13 tax savings.

At least $500,000 from 1100 donors had been raised as of the first of this year. Typical home values in San Marino exceed $100,000, which means an average savings of $2000 per household due to Proposition 13. Seventy-five percent of the San Marinoites voted for Propositon 13.

Other cities—without such wealthy and generous residents—have turned to service charges, user fees, admission taxes and other pay-as-you-go taxes. Altogether, 43 percent of California's cities and 74 percent of the counties have turned to these taxes.

One example of the impact of fees is what happened to the L.A. Museum of Art. The Museum instituted an admission fee and daily attendance dropped from 1400 people to 370 people. The museum's $1.50 fee kept away the people who most used the museum in the first place, students and senior citizens. On the one day a month that admission is free, attendance soars.

Historically, one major reason for the impositon of user fees has been to change public behavior. A good example is bridge fares. Tolls are not only used to pay for building the bridge. Society also hopes that drivers will decide that it is more economical to utilize public transportation—thereby cutting down on smog, traffic congestion, and the drain on gasoline supplies.

However, the use of fees to change behavior works a particular hardship on the poor and middle-income taxpayer. Except for fees which are levied at extraordinarily high rates, most user fees are only insignificant nuisances to wealthier taxpayers. In effect, user fees designed to change public behavior hit the poorer citizens, and permit richer Californians to "buy" themselves out of any responsibility for the socially or ecologically harmful activity.

A second rationale for user fees and charges is that government services should be on a pay-as-you-go system. Unfortunately, some recipients of governmental services are less able to pay for basic services than others.

Garbage collection is a good example. A flat rate for garbage collection is easier for a wealthier garbage-maker to pay than for a poorer garbage-maker. Both need the service. In fact, society demands that garbage be collected so that it isn't dumped in the streets, alleys and parks. Such dumping was the custom during the Feudal Ages and still happens in the poorer sections of many large cities.

Of course, most governmental programs benefit the community as a whole. Education, air and water quality, police and fire protection, senior citizen programs, streets and more are all important to the quality of life of the entire population. None of us want to live in cities where the streets are dirty and in disrepair, the educatonal level is near illiteracy, people beg in the streets, parks don't exist, and so on.

Pay-as-you-go taxes are attractive because, as Professor George Break said, "the best tax is the one somebody else pays." However, it is worth separating user fees for luxuries from charges for essential services. A special charge, or admission tax, or user fee for a yacht harbor is one thing. A user fee on a necessary service, such as garbage collection or water and utility hookups, amounts to a tax.

As a tax, user fees must be viewed with great caution since they are not ability to pay taxes.

"Prop. 13 Forces Shift to User Fees" is reprinted by permission from *The Taxes Ranger,* California Tax Reform Association, 1979.

Development Charges

Donald G. Hagman

Exactions on Development Permission

Landowner Jones comes before the city planning commission to ask for permission to develop his parcel. The planners agree, on the condition that Jones build the streets and sidewalks for his development, install the sewers, give the city some land to widen an arterial street, and agree to hold open some land for a school site. Those conditions are exactions on development permission. They may be imposed at the time of the subdivision, as in the example, or at the time of application for a rezoning, a conditional use permit, a building permit, or annexation. Exactions are now a primary means the public uses to provide infrastructure associated with new development.

Exactions ar a kind of windfall recapture device. If the costs of the infrastructure in newly developing or redeveloping areas are paid by the existing community, either the landowner, or the consumer of the developed property will have or share a windfall.

The United States Experience

Until the Great Depression, cities provided most infrastructure, sometimes recapturing part of its cost by special assessments. In the depression, defaults on assessment backed bonds were widespread, and the assessment approach fell into relative disrepute.

After World War ll, cities began to require that developers provide some of the infrastructure themselves. Usually though, requirements were imposed at the time of subdivision of the land, since subdivision required local government approval. Gradually more and more of the infrastructure responsibilities associated with new development were shifted to the developer.

The next step was the exaction of fees in lieu of the infrastructure. In lieu fees made it possible to charge even small subdivisions for their pro rata share of the cost of some infrastructure that was either offsite or oversized in relation to a particular development.

Local governments then began applying the exaction technique at other leverage points, such as zoning, building permits, and annexation.

Authority to impose exactions comes from the police power of the state. The states may enable local governments to impose exactions by statute or by delegating general regulatory power over them. Home rule may also be a source of power. Statutes sometimes specify the exactions permitted; sometimes permissable exactions are inferred on the basis that the power to regulate land development includes the power to require permits and that permits in turn can be conditioned in a variety of ways, including required compliance with exactions.

There are probably many exactions which are in excess of regulatory authority delegated to local governments by the state. Developers comply as the cost of doing business, recognizing that the courts are slow and costly, and the a Pyrrhic legal victory may be followed by harassment by an aroused local government either with respect to the litigated development itself or with future projects.

When developers do litigate onerous exactions, they sometimes win, often on constitutional grounds. The police power and associated exactions can only be imposed constitutionally if a public purpose is served and if the exactions are reasonable. A regulation is unreasonable if it is arbitrary, is discriminatory, is confiscatory or constitutes a taking. An arbitrary exaction is one where there is no rational connection between the exaction and its expressed purpose. A discriminatory exaction is one where similarly circumstanced developers are treated differently, thus violating equal protection principles. If property subject to exactions is reduced too much in value, a court might find it to be confiscated or taken in contravention of constitutional provisions which preclude the taking of private property without just compensation.

Exactions which only benefit the land being developed are uniformly upheld as valid. A curb is an example of a public facility of little benefit other than to the parcel of land to which it is adjacent.

At the other extreme, suppose as a condition of obtaining development permission for single family homes, a developer of five acres was required to buy 20 acres and build a new regional high school costing $20 million. Here the benefits are general and only a small portion of them are captured by the five acre development.

Local governments have tended to move over the years from exactions of strictly local benefit to those of general benefit. Developer groups have fought every inch of the way, leading to a considerable amount of litigation. The state of the litigation along the continuum varies from state to state, but in some states, so long as the land being developed is worth no less with the exaction than it was without the development permission, the exaction is valid.

Impact Taxes

Impact taxes are a sequel to development exactions. Exactions have been used pricipally to provide infrastructure on the site of a development. But other public facilities and services will eventually be needed to serve that development. These include such things as sewage trunk lines and treatment plants, schools, public libraries and other buildings and fire and police service. To lessen the financial burden of providing those facilities, communities invented the impact tax. They imposed a charge, as for example

$500 per dwelling unit, on new construction. In theory, the money is used to pay for facilities as described above.

Like exactions, impact taxes are a kind of windfall recapture device. If the public provided these off site facilities for free, the landowner, developer, or home buyer would reap a kind of windfall. The impact tax helps recapture that windfall.

Legal Challenges

Impact taxes do not enjoy the same legal acceptance as exactions. A number have been invalidated by the courts.

Some impact taxes have been held invalid because the city imposing them did not have statutory authority to do so. Impact taxes have been invalidated on that ground in Arizona, Michigan and New Jersey.

The Utah Supreme Court invalidated an impact tax in the form of a $100 building permit fee on grounds that it placed a disproportionate burden of the cost of city government on new households. This was held to violate the constitutional guarantee of equal protection.

The Florida Supreme Court recently invalidated a charge for the privilege of connecting to the sewer and water systems of the City of Dunedin. The court suggested that such a charge would be all right if (1) the charge did not exceed the proportionate share of the facility properly pro rated to the new development, (2) a capital facility expansion was reasonably required, and (3) the funds collected were earmarked for the required expansion.

A Nevada statute allows an impact tax based on a philosophy somewhat like Florida's. Nevada communities may impose a residential construction tax if the money is used only to fund acquisition or servicing of public park and playground land.

The loosest impact tax state is California. If skillfully drafted, an impact tax in California need not be tied in any way to servicing the contributing development. The leading court test came from the City of Newark, which imposed a per dwelling unit charge on developers, calling it a business license tax. The court not only upheld the charge as a legitimate use of the city's taxing powers, but did not bother to look into the way the money was spent.

Conclusion

Who should pay for the public costs associated with new development is a current controversial question. Cities are increasingly using impact taxes as one way of feeling their way toward an answer to this question. In that role, impact taxes may have a legitimate place. They may be appropriate as more general windfall recapture devices.

"Development Charges" is reprinted by permission from *Financing State and Local Government: Trends, Policies, and Law,* © 1977, by the American Law Institute.

IX

By Dean Tipps

The personal income tax is the third largest source of state and local revenues, ranking behind the property tax and the sales tax. However, it also is the fastest growing, yielding $30.9 billion in 1977 compared to $3.2 billion in 1962—an increase of 869%.

Theoretically, progressive personal income taxes are the fairest means of taxation (excepting, of course, a comprehensive progressive wealth tax). In practice, however, state income taxes often depart from the ideal. Their rate structures frequently lack progressivity, and what progessivity they do have is eroded by inflation. They also are riddled with special exclusions, exemptions, credits, and deductions — often patterned after similar loopholes in federal law — which disproportionately benefit the wealthiest taxpayers. Thus, while states have moved toward greater reliance on personal income taxes, they have moved far less rapidly to make their personal income taxes fairer by adopting progressive rate structures and closing loopholes.

Progressive income tax rates increase as the taxpayer's income increases. The top rate does not apply to the taxpayer's entire income. Instead, the graduated rates apply in turn to succeeding chunks of income: the first $5,000 may be taxed at one rate, the next $1,000 at a higher rate, and so on.

The purpose of progressive tax rates is to adjust tax burdens on an ability to pay basis. One way they do this is by asking wealthy taxpayers to contribute more to the support of government than poor taxpayers. Another way they accomplish this is by adjusting tax burdens up and down to reflect changes in the earning power of individuals and families over the course of their lives. Except for the wealthiest of taxpayers, most families find that their income fluctuates over their lifetimes. Retirement, unemployment, disability, the death of a husband or wife, and divorce are examples of some of the major life-cycle crises which affect families' ability to pay taxes. The progressive income tax acknowledges such changes in economic circumstances by increasing the tax burden as a family's income rises and reducing its tax liability when its income declines. The homeowner property tax is a good example of a tax which ignores such variations. The property tax is determined by the market value of a family's home and the tax rate. If these increase, so does the family's property tax bill, regardless of any changes in its economic circumstances.

Most states have income taxes with at least nominally progressive rates. However, several states — including Illinois, Massachusetts, Michigan, and Pennsylvania — continue to employ a single flat rate. Other states have tax rate schedules which are progressive at the low or moderate end of the income spectrum but in effect apply flat rates to higher incomes. In California, for example, the top bracket of 11% starts at $31,000 taxable income on a joint return. Thus, income gains for families with incomes

248

The Income Tax—A Progressive Alternative **18**

below $31,000 are taxed at progressively higher rates, while for families with incomes already above $31,000 any increase in income is taxed at the same 11% rate. Thirteen states have progressive tax rates which "top out" at $10,000 income or less, while only five states have progressive rates which extend beyond $50,000.

The first article in this chapter, **Rating a Rate,** by Allen D. Manvel, demonstrates one of the principal advantages of enacting steeply progressive income tax rates at the state level: in addition to conforming to the ability to pay principle, they also are heavily subsidized by the federal government. Since state income taxes are deductible on federal income tax returns, a large share of state income tax burdens can be passed onto the federal government by wealthy taxpayers. By deducting state income taxes, they reduce their federal tax bill. And the more money they make, the higher their federal marginal tax rate and the greater the share of their state tax bill that is "paid for" by the federal government. This is one federal revenue-sharing program which the states can legislate for themselves simply by enacting steeply progressive tax rates. Ironically, the state of Delaware, which is the subject of Mr. Manvel's analysis, subsequently bowed to pressures from the Chamber of Commerce and other wealthy interests by reducing its maximum income tax rate from 19.8% to 13.5%.

Four Advantages of Progressive Income Taxes by Mssrs. Taylor, Peppard, and Willits summarizes the principal advantages of progressive income taxes. One feature of progressive tax rates which they call attention to is their flexibility when it comes time to increase taxes. While flat rate income taxes tend to "lock in" across-the-board tax increases, graduated income taxes provide two additional options which allow tax increases to be targeted to specific income groups: adjusting the size of one or more tax brackets to produce more revenues or adding additional high income brackets.

Inflation and Progressive Income Taxes

One tax issue of growing importance is the impact of inflation on graduated income taxes. This complex issue is summarized by the Advisory Commission on Intergovernmental Relations in **Income Taxes and Inflation** for both federal and state income taxes. For state governments, the question of income tax "indexing" — that is, the annual adjustment of tax brackets, standard deductions, low income exemptions, and other features of the income tax to offset the effects of inflation — poses a basic trade-off between the revenue needs of state government and the tax policy advantages of indexing.

One effect of indexing is to eliminate the automatic revenue windfalls which accrue to government when

incomes increase because inflation pushes taxpayers into higher tax brackets even though they are no better off than they were before. When tax brackets are indexed, inflation based additions to income continues to be taxed, yielding revenues to offset the impact of inflation on government, but they are no longer taxed at progressively higher rates. "Graduation" into a higher tax bracket is limited to increases in real income or in legislated tax rates.

Offsetting the revenue consequences of indexing are four principal advantages. First, indexing preserves the progressivity of progressive income taxes. Since for most state income taxes the highest marginal tax rates kick in at relatively modest income levels (unlike the federal income tax), inflationary income increases tend to push more and more taxpayers into the top bracket, converting a progressive income tax into one that is increasingly proportional as more and more income is taxed on a flat rate basis.

A second advantage of indexing is that the limited progressivity of tax brackets in the states (in contrast to the federal income tax) means that low and middle income taxpayers benefit most directly from indexing since they are the taxpayers most directly affected by graduated tax rates.

A third advantage stems from the second. From an organizing standpoint, indexing may help build a constituency for making income taxes more progressive by removing the fear of moderate income taxpayers that inflation will eventually push them into the highest tax bracket even though they enjoy no real increase in purchasing power. In fact, one way to offset the revenue consequences of indexing is to add additional high income tax brackets at the same time.

A fourth advantage of indexing is that it gradually reduces the tax burden of taxpayers whose incomes are fixed or fail to keep pace with inflation.

Income Tax Loopholes

The effect of all tax preferences, exemptions, deductions, and credits is to create a gap between the "nominal" tax rates listed in tax tables and the actual or "effective" tax rates paid by the taxpayer, whether measured by the rate of taxation on the last dollar of income or by the percentage of all income actually paid in taxes.

This loophole-generated gap between nominal and effective tax rates undermines the fairness of income taxes in two ways. First, since wealthy taxpayers generally receive greater benefits from such tax loopholes than ordinary taxpayers, they tend to undermine the basic progressivity of the income tax. Second, they compromise the fairness of the income tax by allowing two taxpayers with the same income to bear substantially different tax burdens simply because one was able to take advantage of more loopholes than the other. As noted in Chapter 8, renters tend to pay higher income taxes than homeowners with equivalent incomes simply becaue state (and federal) income tax laws provide major tax subsidies to homeowners that are not enjoyed by renters (for example, deduction of home mortgage interest and property taxes). Another example is the preferential treatment of income from capital gains.

Martin Helmke analyzes the capital gains loophole in **Capital Gains Benefits Favor Rich** and shows how preferential taxation of capital gains benefits the wealthy at the expense of wage earners.

In the following article, **Improving the California Personal Income Tax**, Martin Huff outlines a set of reforms which would create a model income tax combining simplicity and equity. One approach to simplifying state income tax law which Mr. Huff quite rightly rejects is the notion of federal conformity — that is, the notion that state income tax law should mimic the federal system. Duplicating federal loopholes erodes tax equity, costs the state revenues, reduces deductions of state taxes on federal income taxes, and shifts control over state tax policy from state capitols to Congress and the interests in Washington which influence federal tax policy. Mr. Huff also notes that "When taxpayers' actions are motivated by federal law, similar state provisions reward those actions with windfall gains." Instead of conforming to loophole-riddled federal law, he argues that simplicity and equity should be wedded by treating all income as income, minimizing tax loopholes, and adopting progressive tax rates.

The California Tax Reform Association responded to Mr. Huff's plea for a fairer income tax with the Tax Simplicity Act which Mr. Huff describes in his *Los Angeles Times* article, **Tangled Tax Law Strangles Californians.** As the accompanying advertisement from the *Sacramento Bee* states, the Tax Simplicity Act shows taxpayers they need not vote to lower their services in order to redress the inequities of a tax system that has shifted more and more of the tax burden onto the average citizen.

Other Issues

State income taxes can be useful vehicles for relieving the burden of other taxes. The benefits of property tax circuitbreaker programs can be given to homeowners and renters in the form of refundable income tax credits. Several state income taxes provide tax credits designed to offset the regressivity of the sales tax. In **The Low–Income Comprehensive Tax Rebate**, Charles D. Turpin describes a comprehensive refundable tax credit program established in New Mexico which is intended to offset the overall regressivity of the state's combined state and local tax burden. One major problem common to all tax credit programs is the gap between the number of people eligible for a credit and the number who actually apply. Mr. Turpin notes that New Mexico was able to significantly increase participation in its program by undertaking a major outreach effort.

The final article explores a different issue: the local income tax. Local income taxes represent a largely untapped resource for diversifying local tax bases and reducing local government dependence on the property tax. The New York State Temporary Commission on State and Local Finances study entitled **The Possibility of a Local Income Tax in New York State** concludes its review of the issues surrounding implementation of local income taxes by recommending that they are best levied as optional supplements to state income taxes.

RATING A RATE

by Allen D. Manvel

In any controversy over taxes, hyperbole is the name of the game.

During recent weeks, a parade of witnesses before the House Ways and Means Committee has forecast a disastrous impact on business from the Administration's proposed tax reforms. The restaurant and amusement industries, it is claimed, could not survive an end of present expense-account abuses. Nor could U.S. firms with operations abroad afford to continue them if their American overseas employees had to pay taxes at anything like the rates that apply to Americans here at home. And so on.

As Jimmy Carter probably recalls from his Georgia background, hyperbole also has a place in the discussion of state tax problems. A recent example is provided by the board chairman of the DuPont

Company, Irving S. Shapiro, who has been at odds with the Republican governor of Delaware, Pierre S. du Pont, about that state's revenue needs. In a statement given front page treatment by the Wall Street Journal, Shapiro said: "If a friend of mine in industry calls up and says, 'Irv, we've had a presentation that says we ought to build a plant in Delaware, what do you say?' I couldn't in good conscience invite a fellow chief executive to come to Delaware and subject himself to a 19.8% [state individual income] tax rate."

That 19.8 percent figure does sound pretty drastic, and Shapiro could cite it, correctly, as the highest marginal rate of state income taxation in the nation. In fact, most income-taxing states apply schedules that do not go above a maximum rate of ten percent. Unlike Delaware, however, most income-taxing states also impose general

Calculated Rates of State Income Tax
for "Typical" High-Income Taxpayers in Delaware

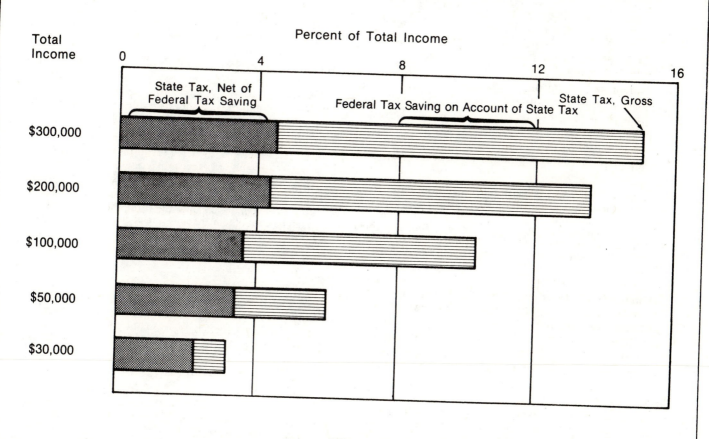

sales taxes, and in most of them, as well, property tax rates are far higher than in Delaware. Any business executive seriously interested in comparative economics of industry location would surely want to consider the total tax climate, and not just the level of state individual income taxation.

But even looking only at the Delaware state income tax, one finds that the 19.8 percent figure gives a grossly misleading impression. As illustrated by the accompanying chart, the actual burden imposed by the Delaware tax upon taxpayers receiving up to $300,000 a year is likely to be less than five percent of their total income. There are three reasons for the striking contrast between these two sets of "tax rate" figures: (1) The high percentage cited by Shapiro is the rate that applies only to taxable income in excess of $100,000; even for taxpayers well above that level, much income is taxed at lower rates, ranging upwards from 1.6 percent; (2) The high percentage also refers only to taxable income, while the "less than five percent" rate relates tax liability to total income, including allowable deductions and exemptions; and (3) For high-income taxpayers, a very large fraction of state tax liability is offset by a reduction in Federal income tax, due to the deductibility provisions of the Federal law.

For example, as the chart illustrates, a "typical" Delaware taxpayer at the $300,000-income level (with a spouse and two dependents) might expect to pay $45,000 or 15 percent of his income as state income tax. But with his Federal tax liability reduced through deductions by $31,600 (or 10.5 percent of income) the net cost of the state tax would be only $13,400, or 4.5 percent of his income. In similar fashion, the Federal tax offset is found to reduce the cost of the state income tax by more than half for taxpayers at the $100,000- and $200,000- income levels, and to reduce it materially also for taxpayers earning $30,000 and $50,000 a year.

Figures underlying the chart, and related data, are as follows:

"Typical" high income Delaware taxpayers

		A	B	C	D	E
a.	Total income	$30,000	$50,000	$100,000	$200,000	$300,000
b.	Assumed deductions for state income tax[1]	3,600	5,600	10,600	20,600	30,600
c.	Exemptions for state income tax[2]	2,400	2,400	2,400	2,400	2,400
d.	Taxable income for state tax (a minus b and c)	24,000	42,000	87,000	177,000	267,000
e.	State tax (rate schedule applied to line d)	938	3,000	9,886	27,277	45,097
f.	Assumed deductions for Federal tax (b plus e less footnote 1 amount)	3,938	8,000	19,886	47,277	75,097
g.	Exemptions for Federal tax[2]	3,000	3,000	3,000	3,000	3,000
h.	Taxable income for Federal tax (a minus f and g)	23,062	39,000	77,114	149,723	221,903
i.	Federal tax saving due to deductibility of state income tax	300	1,359	5,742	18,309	31,568
j.	State tax rate, gross (e/a)	3.13%	6.00%	9.89%	13.64%	15.03%
k.	Federal tax saving as % of income (i/a)	1.00%	2.72%	5.74%	9.15%	10.52%
l.	Net state tax burden (j minus k)	2.13%	3.28%	4.15%	4.49%	4.51%

Source: Tax amounts calculated from rate schedules for Delaware state income tax as shown in Advisory Commission on Intergovernmental Relations, Significant Features of Fiscal Federalism, 1976, Vol. II, tables 106 and 107, and rate schedules for Federal income tax as shown in Department of the Treasury, The President's 1978 Tax Program (January 21, 1978), table 11.
[1]The $600 maximum allowed for deduction of Federal income tax, plus ten percent of total income, a relationship which appears reasonable for deductions other than state income tax in the light of 1975 U.S. Statistics of Income.
[2]Assuming a joint return for a taxpayer with two dependents.

"Rating a Rate" is reprinted by permission from the April 24, 1978, issue of *Tax Notes,* Taxation with Representation Fund.

Four Advantages of Progressive Income Taxes

by

Milton Taylor
Donald Peppard
Richard Willits

There are four advantages in using graduated income tax rates at the state level as compared to flat rates. First, a graduated tax is more equitable because it is more closely related to ability to pay. This means that, as income rises, taxpayers pay proportionately larger percentages of their income in taxes under a system of graduated rates than would be paid under a flat-rate structure. Second, a graduated tax is more responsive to changes in personal income than is a flat-rate tax. As personal income in Michigan rises, taxpayers move into higher tax brackets and pay more of their incomes in taxes. Therefore, a given increase in income will yield a larger increase in revenue under a graduated rate structure than under the type of income tax currently in use.

The third advantage is that a graduated income tax allows the state to shift a larger burden of the tax to the federal government. This results because state income tax payments are deductible from federal taxable income. Since a graduated tax places more of the burden of the tax on wealthy taxpayers in high federal income tax brackets, these taxpayers obtain larger deductions and pay less to the federal government. Thus, the federal level assumes more of the burden of state income taxes.

The fourth advantage of graduated rates is that they are more easily adjusted in order to avoid increasing the tax burden on low-income taxpayers in the event that additional state revenue is needed. Rates may be changed so that all of the increase in tax revenue is derived from taxpayers above, say, $15,000 in income, or some other arbitrary level of income. An increase in the flat-rate, by comparison, would increase everyone's tax burden.

"Four Advantages of Progressive Income Taxes" is reprinted from *The Easy Case for Progressive Income Taxation in Michigan,* by Milton Taylor, Donald Peppard and Richard Willits, 1977. The authors were associated with the Economics Department of the University of Michigan.

Income Taxes and Inflation

A SUMMARY OF FINDINGS OF THE REPORT

The major findings of this report are as follows:

FISCAL ACCOUNTABILITY

- *Inflation interacts with any progressive individual income tax to generate increases in tax revenue more than proportionate to the rate of inflation. These increases occur with practically no public debate or disclosure of the fact.* Although progressive income taxes also exhibit elasticity with respect to real income growth, that property is inherent in a progressive tax and can be considered intended. Since recent inflation rates and those projected for the immediate future are well above the historical average, the automatic increase in aggregate, effective, personal income tax rates due to inflation is a significantly new and different issue.

TAX EQUITY

- *Among the different taxpayers, the inflation induced increases in personal income taxes without legislated tax cuts are arbitrary.* They depend on differences among taxpayers as to family size, level of gross income, type of income received, and the degree to which the various dollar limitations in the tax code affect tax liabilities.

- *Inflation is especially hard on low-income families and all families with many dependents because it erodes the value of personal exemptions, the low-income allowance, the maximum limit of the standard deduction and per capita credits.* After one year of 7 percent inflation, the value (in constant dollars) of a $750 personal exemption falls to $701, the $1,600 low income allowance falls to $1,495, the $2,600 maximum standard deduction for married persons falls to $2,430. The income tax impact of the decline in the real value of personal exemptions increases with family size. The relative increase in tax liability because of the effect of inflation on all these variables will be greater for lower income taxpayers (with the exception that those with very low income may still owe no tax even after inflation erodes the value of these tax features).

- *On the average, increases in tax liabilities due to the inflation erosion of income tax brackets will be greater for taxpayers in the upper income range where brackets are narrow and the rise in tax rates between brackets is fastest.* For the Federal personal income tax, this occurs in the $28,000 to $200,000 income range.

- *The middle-income taxpayers, those with income between $10,000 and $15,000, incur the smallest decline in real, after-tax purchasing power due to the inflation-income tax interplay.* This occurs because the exemption-credit-deduction effect diminishes in importance faster than the bracket effect grows in importance.

- *On balance, the four major tax cuts enacted since 1960 have introduced a greater element of progressivity into the income tax structure than would have been the case under an indexed system.* This inference can be drawn from the fact that classes of taxpayers below $25,000 generally have lower 1975 effective tax rates than they would have had if the 1960 law had been indexed and no other changes had been made. Taxpayers with incomes above $200,000 also had lower 1975 effective tax rates than they would have had under an indexed system.

- *Both the magnitude and the differential impacts of the inflation-induced individual tax increases, in the absence of indexation and enacted tax cuts, can be substantial.* For example, after five years of 7 percent inflation, the inflation-induced tax increase in the fifth year is $352 for an average family with constant real income of $6,000, $602 for a real income of $15,000, and $1,743 for a real income of $30,000. From another viewpoint, the decreases in real disposable income over this five-year period for families with these real incomes are: $6,000 income—a $449 or 7.4 percent decrease in disposal income, $15,000 income—a $420 or a 3.1 percent decrease, and $30,000 income—a $1,235 or 4.9 percent decline.

PUBLIC SECTOR GROWTH

- Assuming annual 6 percent inflation, annual 6 percent real income growth, and no discretionary tax code changes from 1976 on:

- *The inflation-induced real increase in personal income tax revenue for a hypothetical "average state" (under the above assumptions and assuming a state personal income tax elasticity equalling 1.65) would be about $15 million or 3 percent of income tax after one year and about $140 million or 14 percent of income tax after five years.* Again, these are the amounts of the automatic increase in income tax that would be eliminated by tax indexation. Any given state's situation will vary from this projection depending on its income tax elasticity, the nominal amount of income tax revenue, and the state's reliance on the income tax in its total revenue picture.

- *Since few local governments utilize progressive personal income taxes, the inflation impact is not significant at the local level.* Important exceptions to this generality are: local jurisdictions in Maryland where the local individual income tax is a percent of the state income tax; New York City which has a progressive individual income tax and allows personal exemptions specified in fixed dollars; and the District of Columbia which has a progressive individual income tax.

- *Most states have not cut their income tax rates so as to reduce the inflation impact on their revenues.* From 1966 to 1973, state discretionary action in the aggregate served to increase income taxes beyond the impact of income growth and inflation. Since 1973, most states have not raised their rates but have relied on inflation's impact on their revenue to maintain their public service levels.

- *Using the economic projection of the Congressional Budget Office—average annual total income growth of 10 percent including about a 6 percent average annual inflation rate—the average annual increases in aggregate state income tax revenue will be about 13 percent from 1977 to 1980 with indexation; and about 16.5 percent without indexation.* In contrast, actual aggregate state individual income tax revenue increased at an average annual rate of about 15.5 percent from 1971 to 1975.

INTERGOVERNMENTAL FISCAL EFFECTS

Without Indexation

In the absence of indexation, the interaction of substantial inflation with progressive income taxes is likely to produce the following intergovernmental fiscal effects:

- *Of the revenue systems of the three levels of government, the Federal sector has the greatest capacity to automatically realize the revenues which accrue as inflation generates nominal increases on various tax bases.* The Federal government makes relatively intensive use of the progressive personal income tax. Federal collections account for about 85 percent of all individual income taxes.

- *State governments have the second greatest ability to realize inflation-generated tax revenues.* States rely more heavily on progressive personal income taxation than do local jurisdictions.

- *On the expenditure side, local governments tend to be more "inflation prone" than the other sectors (Federal, state, private) of the economy.* Local government services are relatively most labor intensive (e.g., teaching, health).

- *The 16 states which permit their residents to deduct their Federal income tax liability in computing the state income tax will experience, during an inflation, a lower growth of revenues than would otherwise occur.* As inflation induces Federal personal income tax increases that are proportionately greater than inflation, these higher liabilities will erode these states' income tax base.

- *States which "piggyback" their state income tax on the Federal income tax (state tax liability is computed as a set percentage of Federal liability) are likely to find a roller-coaster effect on their income tax revenues.* Their tax collections will automatically rise with inflation due to the inflation responsiveness of the Federal income tax. If Congress follows past practice, however, (as is plausible) and enacts tax cuts to offset the inflation-generated, real income tax increases, the piggyback states will experience declines in their tax revenues (for a given tax rate). At the very least, the "piggyback" states will experience uncertainty of revenues with inflation.

- *Most state and local governments will be in too weak a fiscal position to enact tax reductions during the next few years.* State and local governments do not, in general, have highly inflation-responsive tax structures. Some state governments and many local governments have been forced to restrict or even reduce the quality and scope of their services in the last few years. Unlike the Federal government, they cannot engage in extended deficit financing to bridge their current expenditure-revenue gap. Accordingly, in the next two-three years, new state and local expenditures may be needed just to maintain past (e.g., 1972) program service levels.

- *The inflation-personal income tax interaction will slightly reduce the net resident burden of state and local taxes.* This interesting and beneficial twist for state-local jurisdictions results from the fact that the major state and local taxes are deductible when a taxpayer itemizes deductions on his or her Federal income tax. The reduced "cost" of state-local taxes thus occurs as inflation pushes taxpayers into higher Federal tax rate brackets and, as a result, increases the dollar value of the state-local tax deduction.

With Federal Indexation

With the indexation of the Federal individual income tax, the following intergovernmental effects are likely to occur:

- *State and local governments would find that their residents experience a rise in the net burden of state-local taxes relative to what otherwise would occur because of the reduction in the dollar value of the state-local tax deduction on the Federal income tax return.* Federal tax indexation would permit taxpayers with constant real incomes to avoid being moved into higher tax rate brackets where the dollar value of the state-local tax deduction on the Federal tax return is slightly increased.

- *States which permit the deductibility of Federal tax liability against their state income taxes would experience a slight increase in the revenue productivity of their taxes as Federal tax liabilities have the automatic "inflation tax" component eliminated.*

- *Piggyback income tax states would, just as the Federal government, lose the revenues once generated by the "inflation tax."* Federal indexation might reduce to some extent, the fiscal uncertainty these states now experience as a consequence of the possible periodic Congressional reductions in the Federal personal income tax.

State Indexation (In Addition to the Federal)

If the states as well as the Federal government index the individual income tax, the following fiscal effects are likely to occur:

- *In general, state income tax indexation could be expected to increase state-local fiscal tensions.* Because state governments have limited ability to incur deficits to finance current expenditure-revenue gaps and because their long-run budget situation *is at best one of balance or slight surplus,* indexation at the state level would mean either reduction in the rate of expenditure growth and/or the likelihood of **more tax increases than would be the case in the absence of indexation.**

- *The degree of fiscal stress due to indexation would vary among states depending on the extent to which they rely on progressive personal income taxation. In general, jurisdictions which have a high reliance on the personal income tax would experience the most fiscal strain due to indexation.* But some states which have rapidly growing economic bases (e.g., the "energy rich" states) may well be able to afford indexation and still be able to increase the scope and quality of their public services or cut taxes.

- *To the extent that indexation would reduce the fiscal flexibility of certain states, local governments in these states would also experience financial strain if the states become more reluctant to increase state to local aid (e.g., for property tax relief) and/or take over certain local fiscal responsibilities (e.g., school financing).* Over the last 20 years, state aid as a percent of local general revenue has risen from 42 to 60 percent.

OTHER INDEXATION ISSUES

- *Indexation is not likely to alter the built-in, economic stabilizing influence of the Federal individual income tax.* The response of income taxes to changes in real national income would remain under indexation. Any indexation impact on the built-in stabilizer would depend somewhat on how the index is determined.

- *If unions or individuals bargain for wage levels high enough to maintain real after-tax purchasing power, then indexation would reduce pressure for wage increases.* Indeed, the severe inflation (about 15% per year) in Australia has prompted the labor unions in that country to "bargain" for real wage increases by urging income tax indexation as a means to protect automatically at least part of wage gains negotiated at the bargaining table.

STATE RECOMMENDATIONS

The policy implications of state income tax indexation differ from the Federal in two important respects. First, state governments face budgetary constraints and economic pressures which are fundamentally different from the national government (e.g., limits on deficit financing, special vulnerability of expenditures to inflation).

Second, statements about the effects of indexation on state income taxes are less subject to generalization due to the fact that there are 30 different broad-based, state income taxes with varying degrees of progressivity and relative quantitative importance.

FULL DISCLOSURE AND ANNUAL INDEXATION OF STATE INDIVIDUAL INCOME TAX

The Commission recognizes that inflation induces increases in real income tax revenue and introduces distortions in interpersonal tax equity. The Commission is persuaded that taxpayers may not readily perceive the automatic, real tax increase that occurs from the inflation-personal income tax interplay. Therefore, the Commission recommends, in the interest of complete public information, that governors have an estimate made of the amount of the inflation-induced state personal income tax increase and publicize the estimate for each tax year.

While a full disclosure policy is a desirable first step, the Commission also believes that effective personal income tax rates should be increased only by overt state legislative action and should not be an automatic consequence of inflation. The Commission recommends, therefore, that all states give early and favorable consideration to annual indexation of exemptions, deductions, per capita tax credits, and tax rate brackets. The Commission believes that the need for this remedial action is especially apparent for those states that combine a highly progressive, income tax rate structure with heavy reliance on the tax.

The same major considerations—fiscal accountability, tax equity, public sector growth—that prompted the Advisory Commission to recommend the indexation of the Federal income tax also support indexation of the state personal income tax.

Over the last 15 or 20 years, many states have moved strongly to make balanced use of various revenue sources including particularly the personal income tax. Thirty-nine states now use progressive individual income taxes that provide, on average, a substantial portion of own-source state revenue. As a result, state revenue systems now generally enjoy higher elasticity—that is stronger growth responsiveness—than ever before. There is little doubt that the inflation-induced real increases in income tax revenue encouraged the states to make greater use of income taxes. Now that these progressive, state personal income taxes are established, however, further automatic real increases *due to inflation* should not be tolerated.

With indexation, the distortions in interpersonal tax equity that are introduced by inflation interacting with progressive state income taxes would be largely eliminated. Furthermore, states would still enjoy substantial, income tax elasticity from the income tax response to real economic growth. Indeed, the evidence suggests that, with indexation, aggregate state personal income tax collections can increase over the next four years at about 13 percent annually. This is only 2.5 percentage points less than the actual annual revenue growth between 1971 and 1975—a period of significant legislative action to raise taxes.

Although state individual income tax collections approximate only 20 percent of Federal collections from this source, this average obscures the heavy reliance certain states make of this tax instrument. While Ohio and Louisiana income tax yields are only about 7 percent of the Federal, Minnesota and Wisconsin income tax yields are 41 and 38 percent, respectively, of Federal collections. In states where a highly progressive rate structure is combined with heavy reliance on the income tax, the impact of inflation on the state's income tax collections can be substantial.

"Income Taxes and Inflation" is reprinted by permission from the Advisory Commission on Intergovernmental Relations, *Inflation and Federal and State Income Taxes*, 1976.

CALIFORNIA TAX RESEARCH REPORT

Capital Gains Benefits Favor Rich

By Martin Helmke
Fiscal Consultant, Sacramento

The most glaring loophole in the California income tax law is the privileged treatment of income from capital gains. This provision, akin to that offered by the federal income tax, is designed to reward those who sell stock, real estate, or other assets for a profit.

The state grants the subsidy by pretending that a portion of the gain was not received by the taxpayer. For example, suppose that an individual had purchased 1000 shares of stock for $50 per share and then sold it five years later for $100 per share.

The gain from the sale would be $50,000, but the California tax law generously forgives one-half of the gain ($25,000). If the taxpayer is in the maximum tax bracket he saves 11 percent of $25,000 or $2,750 in California tax (not to mention a savings of $12,000 to $15,000 in federal tax).

Privileged Income

Income from the sale of capital assets is the only type of income to be treated in this privileged manner. Wages and salaries are fully taxable, as are income from a taxpayer's business (most small unincorporated businesses fall into this category) or savings account.

Capital gains typically are received by those with high incomes. Thus, as Table 1 shows, the wealthy receive the lion's share of this subsidy.

Of the approximately $100 million in tax benefits, the top 31,000 taxpayers receive $44 million, an average of $1,420 per privileged taxpayer. In fact, the 8,000 taxpayers with incomes over $100,000 (the top one-tenth of one percent of California Taxpayers) receive $28 million in capital gains subsidy, an average of $3,500 each.

Table 2 shows how much tax is paid, on the average, on $10,000 of income from different types of income. As is clearly seen, capital gains are taxed far less heavily than other types of income. In fact, capital gains are taxed only slightly more than wages, on the average, even though capital gains are generally received by the wealthy, who, according to the tax schedules, should be paying a much higher tax.

Pros & Cons

There are several reasons often given for allowing the capital gains provision to remain on the books. First, it is argued that the subsidy is necessary in order to encourage individuals to put their money into new, and perhaps risky, ventures. Without the subsidy, it is argued, the present "capital shortage" will become even worse.

However, it has never been shown that the capital gains subsidy actually induces people to invest, rather than spend their money. It has been demonstrated that individuals may tend to switch from one form of investment to another in order to take advantage of the subsidy.

TABLE I
WHO BENEFITS FROM THE CAPITOL GAINS SUBSIDY?

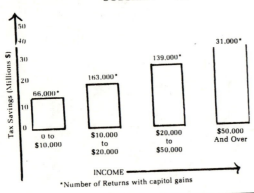

INCOME ————▶
*Number of Returns with capitol gains

TABLE 2

AVERAGE TAX ON $10,000 OF INCOME BY TYPE OF INCOME

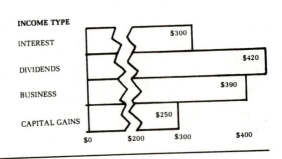

And it is becoming increasingly apparent that certain types of investment, such as land speculation, should be discouraged rather than subsidized. It does not seem logical for the people of California, through their tax structure, to absorb blindly a substantial volume of speculative risk, when the ventures invested in are often counter to sound public policy.

Second, proponents of the capital gains subsidy contend that some adjustment should be made for rising prices over the years. "After all," they say, "Most of my capital gains are just the result of inflation."

But wage earners must pay the price of inflation every year. The only difference is in the timing of earnings — inflation affects both to the same degree over time.

Comparison

Third, capital gains recipients argue that because of the progressive nature of the tax structure, it would be unfair to make them pay in just one year a tax based on a gain which accumulated over several years. For example, Table 3 shows the situation of two taxpayers, the first earning $30,000 per year from a business, and the second receiving $20,000 per year from dividends plus $50,000 in the last year in capital gains.

Both individuals receive the same total income over the five-year period. But without the capital gains provision the second taxpayer, the investor, would have paid $1,400 more in state tax than did the second taxpayer, the businessman, just because the $50,000 was received in one year rather than spread over five years.

Present law, however, permits taxpayers to average their incomes over five years. So here again the capital gains subsidy is unnecessary. The capital gains, in the above example, overcompensates by giving the investor a $1,350 tax break.

It is clear, then, that the sole function of the capital gains provision is to subsidize the wealthy recipient of capital gains. And, since all subsidies must be paid for, the lower and middle income taxpayer is left to pay the bill through higher tax rates.

TABLE 3

LUMP SUM EFFECT OF CAPITAL GAINS

Taxpayer A		Taxpayer B		
Income	Tax	Income	Tax Under Present Law	Tax Without Subsidy
$ 30,000	$1,159	$ 20,000	$ 424	$ 424
30,000	1,159	20,000	424	424
30,000	1159	20,000	424	424
30,000	1,159	20,000	424	424
30,000	1,159	70,000	2,749	5,499
$150,000	$5,795	$150,000	$4,445	$7,195

"Capital Gains Benefits Favor Rich" is reprinted by permission from the July, 1976 issue of *Tax Back Talk*, The California Tax Reform Association.

IMPROVING THE CALIFORNIA PERSONAL INCOME TAX

Martin Huff

California's Personal Income Tax Law is confusing, difficult to administer, and unfair.

In part, this results from the state's policy of selective, but substantial, conformity to the U.S. Internal Revenue Code. Like the federal code, state law has become a patchwork of exclusions, deductions, exemptions, credits, and special rates.

What can we do to reform our state law? Ideally, we should forsake the federal model, scrap our present law and design a new one. Realistically, we are limited to working within the framework of existing law, to make it simpler and more equitable.

The first step is to outline the key features of a sound law.

- It should be understandable in concept and operation.

- It should be as simple as economic realities will permit.

- Revisions should be measured against overall fairness, taxpayer understanding, and relative ease of administration.

- Where there is a conflict between fairness to a particular sector and overall fairness, the latter should prevail.

The second step is to set forth some fundamental tenets.

- There is a need for progressivity, i.e., a scale of increasing marginal tax rates as income increases ("ability to pay").

- Income is income. This statement of the obvious strikes at one of the most critical defects

in the present system, i.e., the notion that some kinds of income should be excluded from the tax base.

- Those advocating loopholes (preferences) should be required to support their case with objective factual information.

The third step is to dispel two myths. One myth is that blind conformity to federal exclusions, deductions, and exemptions is desirable. In reality, conformity can mean inequity. The dollar benefits of special tax breaks are distributed unevenly among taxpayers. The result is that a disproportionate share of the tax burden is shifted to middle-income taxpayers.

Furthermore, conformity usually means complexity. The greater the number of special provisions, the more difficult it becomes for taxpayers to understand and comply with the law and for administrators to interpret and enforce it.

The second myth is that state tax law can be used to bolster the economy or change society. It is true that federal tax law, with its high rates, may affect taxpayers' economic decisions. But California's personal income tax rates of 1 to 11 percent are too low to induce taxpayers to alter their choices. When taxpayers' actions are motivated by federal law, similar state provisions reward those actions with windfall gains.

Taking these factors into consideration, there are six reforms that would make the present law both simpler and more equitable.

First, eliminate preferential treatment of capital gains. The capital gains provisions contribute the most to the complexity of our tax laws. They are also unfair: they favor investment over labor. The person with investment income can exclude as much as 50 per cent of the gain from tax. The person with only salary income, however, is taxed on every dollar earned. The amount of tax

should be a function of ability to pay, which is based on the amount of income, not its source.

Second, include transfer payments in taxable income, excluding that portion previously taxed to the recipient. The "ability to pay" of a person with a $20,000 income, part of which is from unemployment insurance, welfare or social security, is the same as that of a person with $20,000 income entirely from wages.

Third, eliminate deductions and credits for homeownership, rental, and other normal personal expenditures. Activities subsidized through special deductions and credits range from homeownership to the purchase of solar energy devices. All may be desirable from an economic or social standpoint, but state personal income tax law is not a good tool for economic or social engineering. Its purpose should be to generate revenue for needed services. Taxable income should be reduced only by the cost of producing income or the costs of uncontrollable, catastrophic events which drastically reduce ability to pay.

Fourth, substitute tax credits for deductions. Deductions favor high income taxpayers, whereas credits benefit taxpayers equally.

Fifth, liberalize the income averaging provisions. We extract a higher tax from persons whose income fluctuates greatly from year to year. This inequity should be minimized.

And finally, increase the breadth and number of tax brackets. If special tax breaks are eliminated, needed revenues can be generated at lower rates. Taxpayers would not move so rapidly into higher tax rates.

Adoption of the above suggestions would result in a more understandable and more equitable California Personal Income Tax Law.

Editor's Note: This is the seventh in a series of 15 articles exploring California tax issues. In this article, Martin Huff, executive officer of the California State Franchise Tax Board, lists features of a sound personal income tax law, uses them to evaluate California's present system, and suggests specific improvements. This series is co-sponsored by Courses by Newspaper, a project of University Extension, University of California, San Diego, and the California Tax Reform Association Foundation. It is funded by the California Council for the Humanities in Public Policy.

"Improving the California Personal Income Tax" is reprinted by permission from *Taxation: A California Perspective*, California Tax Reform Association, 1978.

Tangled Tax Law Strangles Californians: State's Personal-Income Levy, Patterned After U.S. Code, Is Confusing and Unfair

By MARTIN HUFF

Californians are the victims of a tax system that they don't understand and that works against their economic interest. The state's personal-income-tax law is confusing, difficult to administer and unfair. Patterned after the federal code, it has become a patchwork of exclusions, deductions, exemptions, credits and special rates. Long, complicated forms and incomprehensible regulations confuse and frustrate the taxpayer. Worst of all, the bank and corporation tax burden is increasingly being shifted onto the individual.

I speak from 16 years' experience in attempting to administer the state's income-tax laws as the head of the State Franchise Tax Board. When California adopted the personal income tax in the depth of the Depression, there was some justification for patterning the law after its federal counterpart. However, the reason disappeared altogether with the enactment of the 1969 Federal Tax Reform Act—sometimes jocularly referred to as the Attorneys' and Accountants' Relief Act. It's been a continuous downhill slide ever since.

It's time to get back to fundamentals. We need a personal-income-tax law that is understandable in concept and in operation, as simple as economic realities will allow, revised only to increase its fairness or ease of administration, and devoid of loopholes and special treatment.

Two myths about income tax must be dispelled. One is that total conformity by the state to federal exclusions, deductions and exemptions would result in equity; the truth is that total conformity would shift a larger share of the tax burden to middle-income taxpayers.

The second myth is that the state personal-income-tax law can effectively bolster the economy or effect social change. Federal law, with its high rates, affects taxpayer behavior through special breaks. If California were to adopt similar provisions, the result would be a windfall for the taxpayer who takes advantage of the federal break, and a heavier burden for everyone else.

What, specifically, should be the fundamental principles of a fair tax? Most important, the rate structure should reflect one's ability to pay. One of the most serious defects in the current system is the special treatment, or exemption, of some kinds of income. Beyond that, those proposing loopholes should be required to support their cases with objective factual information.

The following are changes that would result in a more understandable and equitable state income-tax law:

—Preferential treatment of capital-gains income should be eliminated. These provisions contribute the most to the complexity of the tax laws, and unfairly favor investment over labor. An individual who has investment income can exclude as much as 50% of the gain from taxation; someone with only salary income is taxed on every dollar earned. Thus, we are rewarding the investor at the expense of the wage-earner. The amount of tax should be a function of the ability to pay, which is determined by the *amount* and not the *source* of income.

—Deductions and credits for home ownership, rental and other normal personal expenditures should be eliminated. Special deductions and credits subsidize a wide variety of activities ranging from home ownership to the purchase of solar-energy devices. While these may be highly desirable from an economic or social standpoint, the California personal-income-tax law is not a proper tool for economic or social engineering. Once imbedded in law, this type of provision is virtually impossible to dislodge, regardless of whether it has outlived its usefulness.

A comprehensive tax-reform and -relief initiative is slated for the November ballot. Known as the Tax Simplicity Act, it is the most extensive proposed reform of California's personal income tax since its inception.

The principal sponsor of the measure is the California Tax Reform Assn., a 3,500-member citizens' group.

The act would simplify the personal income tax by eliminating most exemptions, credits and deductions, thereby balancing the tax burden more equitably among individual taxpayers and between individual taxpayers and corporations.

The Tax Simplicity Act would replace the confusing, lengthy tax return with a simpler one-page form; it would eliminate unwarranted tax hiding places and would permit all Californians to compute their taxes easily. In addition, the act would exempt from taxation the first $10,000 of income for single people and the first $20,000 of income for couples.

The new top 12% bracket would start at $25,400 for single people and $50,800 for married couples. Most taxpayers would be in significantly lower tax-rate brackets than they are now.

Deductions for business expenses, alimony, charitable contributions, return of capital and deferred-compensation plans would continue as under current law. The dependent credit would be raised to $25 (from $9), and the credits that are permitted for taxes previously paid or paid to other states would be continued. The bank and corporation tax rate would be increased to 12%, and $200 million worth of corporate tax breaks would be eliminated.

The act would cause a dual tax shift. First, $950 million in taxes from corporations would be utilized for income-tax relief for individuals. Second, 7 million California income taxpayers who are now overtaxed would realize a tax decrease.

All income would be taxable, with the exception of government transfer payments (Social Security, welfare, Medicaid, etc.), employer contributions to pension and health-benefit plans, life-insurance proceeds, gifts and inheritances, amounts received for injuries or sickness or from accident or health-insurance plans, and reasonable employee fringe benefits.

It's time to bring greater fairness and more understandability to California's income-tax system; the Tax Simplicity Act would be a significant first step in the right direction. ☐

Martin Huff, currently the president of the California Tax Reform Assn., served as the executive officer of the State Franchise Tax Board from 1963 to 1979.

"Tangled Tax Law Strangles Californians..." is reprinted by permission from the *Los Angeles Times*, February 11, 1980.

ATTENTION TAXPAYERS!

Howard Jarvis' Proposition 9 is a tax scheme for the rich. 40% of the tax relief that Proposition 9 provides will go to the wealthiest 4% of California's taxpayers. But, as usual, middle-income taxpayers' services will be the first to be cut if we let Jarvis' plan become law.

THE TAX SIMPLICITY ACT CUTS YOUR TAXES WITHOUT CUTTING YOUR SERVICES

Look for yourself:

	Tax Simplicity Act	Proposition 9
Closes Tax loopholes	YES	no
Saves governmental services	YES	no
Eliminates taxes on $20,000 of income for couples	YES	no
Eliminates taxes on $10,000 of income for single people	YES	no
Increases corporate taxes	YES	no
Simplifies the tax form	YES	no
Prohibits new tax loopholes	YES	YES
Inflation-proofs the tax rates	YES	no
Increases the children's tax credit	YES	

Compare your tax relief:

Family of three, $30,000 annual income:	
Tax Simplicity Act tax cut	Proposition 9 tax cut
—$440	—$353

Single person, $15,000 annual income:	
Tax Simplicity Act tax cut	Proposition 9 tax cut
—$285	—$241

FIGHT PROPOSITION NINE'S TAXPAYER RIPOFF AND HELP THE TAX SIMPLICITY ACT

Call the
California Tax Reform Association
(916) 446-0145

Paid for by the California Tax Reform Association, 1228½ H Street, Sacramento CA 95814 (916) 446-0145, Treasurer: David Nagler.

Yes! I want to get involved!
☐ I want to be a campaign volunteer
☐ Enclosed is a campaign donation

Name

Address

City   Zip

Phone

CLIP OUT AND MAIL TO: California Tax Reform Association 1228½ H Street   Sacramento, CA 95814

Advertisement sponsored by the California Tax Reform Association appearing in the *Sacramento Bee*, February 22, 1980.

THE LOW-INCOME COMPREHENSIVE TAX REBATE: NEW MEXICO'S BROAD-BASED TAX RELIEF PROGRAM

by Charles D. Turpen, Director of Tax Research

NATIONAL RECOGNITION FOR NEW MEXICO'S PROGRAM

The Low-Income Comprehensive Tax Rebate (LICTR) is recognized as one of the best approaches to tax relief for low-income families. A 1975 report by the U.S. Advisory Commission on Intergovernmental Relations states:

"Programs like the New Mexico LICTC [LICTR],[1] if properly funded and administered, are potentially the most powerful tools yet tried for providing broad-based relief to low- and moderate-income families . . ."[2]

Another 1975 report, sponsored by the U.S. Department of Housing and Urban Development, states:

"The mechanism [of the LICTR] is a flexible one and offers attractive administrative advantages . . . Because the comprehensive credit condenses many of the other tax credits currently being used by the states to reduce regressivity (property tax, renters, food tax and sales tax credits) into a single, efficient, easily administered credit formula, it has great promise for both New Mexico and other governments that select this approach."[2]

Inquiries continue to be received concerning the program, and a number of states appear to be moving toward this comprehensive approach to tax relief.

HOW THE LICTR WORKS

The LICTR, which began in tax year 1972, has been designed to lessen the overall regressivity of the state and local tax system in the lower end of the income scale.[3] The intent of the credit is to give back part of the total taxes paid by low-income, resident families during the taxable year, so that no family below the "poverty level" (as defined by the U.S. Department of Commerce) will pay a greater share of its income to taxes than a family at the "poverty level." Although it is a partial reimbursement for taxes of all types, including sales taxes, property taxes, etc., the LICTR is treated as an income tax rebate for administrative convenience. The rebate is obtained by completing a special section on the personal income tax form; the amount of the rebate is determined on a table by the number of allowable exemptions and by the claimant's "Modified Gross Income." (Modified Gross Income, MGI, means all income undiminished by losses, and from whatever source derived.) The LICTR table and special instructions are incorporated in the personal income tax instructions.

PURPOSE OF THE LICTR

The Low-Income Comprehensive Tax Rebate is very definitely not "just another giveaway!" The overall state and local tax system is indeed regressive — the average low-income family does pay a greater share (percentage) of its income to state and local taxes than does the high-income family! The regressivity of our tax system is largely a result of heavy dependence upon gross receipts and other sales taxes as well as property tax; that dependence is a problem in all states, stemming from the heavy use of income taxes at the federal level which inhibits greater use of income taxes by states. The inequity of regressive state and local taxes is a very real problem which few, if any, would care to debate. Suggested solutions to the problem are much more debatable!

Other states have exempted food and medicines from sales tax, a costly approach because all families, both high and low-income families, have their absolute tax burden reduced. Such exemptions create substantial administrative difficulties for government, and require additional accounting complexity by businesses. "Circuit Breaker" tax relief has been used in other states to reduce the property tax burden of the elderly; but that approach may greatly damage the tax base in a local jurisdiction with a high concentration of aged persons or low-income families. It also makes more complex a tax which is generally accepted as the most difficult tax to administer in an equitable and efficient manner. The foregoing comments are not intended to argue that such

tax relief is "bad" or unnecessary! Rather, the intent is to point out that the LICTR program is a much superior mechanism to offset the regressivity problem!

Thus, an important responsibility of the Bureau of Revenue is to inform and convince the general public that the LICTR is not "just another giveaway." Rather, it is a superior approach to offsetting a very real, and to a degree unavoidable, defect of state and local tax systems. That responsibility is a continuing one if successive generations of citizens and their legislative representatives are to be kept informed, and if the LICTR is to be adjusted periodically to reflect the effects of inflation and further changes in our tax system.

CUMULATIVE IMPACT OF THE LICTR:

Adding up the total number of claims processed for taxable years 1972 through 1975, it is clear that the program is doing a great deal to offset the regressive impact of our state and local tax structure on low-income families and

TABLE I
AMOUNT OF LICTR ($ millions) PROCESSED FOR:

Processed In Fiscal Year	CY 1972	CY 1973	CY 1974	CY 1975	4-Year Total
61st (1972-73)	$ 1.20*	—	—	—	$ 1.20
62nd (1973-74)	.15*	$ 1.65	—	—	1.80
63rd (1974-75)	.15*	.22	$ 2.53	—	2.90
64th (1975-76)	.05*	.13*	.18	$ 5.37	5.73
4-FY TOTAL	$ 1.55*	$ 2.00	$ 2.71	$ 5.37	$11.63

* — An asterisk in this and the next three tables denotes an estimate based upon samples and upon information from later year returns. Other figures on the tables are derived directly from computer listings by taxable (calendar) year.

TABLE II
NUMBER OF LICTR RETURNS PROCESSED FOR:

Processed In Fiscal Year	CY 1972	CY 1973	CY 1974	CY 1975	4-Year Total
61st (1972-73)	29,000*	—	—	—	29,000
62nd (1973-74)	3,600*	34,628	—	—	38,228
63rd (1974-75)	3,600*	4,189	44,835	—	52,624
64th (1975-76)	1,300*	2,700*	3,181	61,865	69,046
4-FY TOTAL	37,500	41,517	48,016	61,865	188,898

individuals. Through the end of June, 1976, nearly 189,000 claims were processed for a total rebate of over $11.6 million. If our projections for the 1976 LICTR are near the mark, the cumulative LICTR will have grown (by the end of June, 1977) to over one quarter of a million claims totalling roughly $18.0 million.

THE NEED FOR AN OUTREACH PROGRAM

Legislative changes are not the only factors causing the LICTR to grow. A great deal has been accomplished through the Bureau of Revenue's outreach programs, in cooperation with other government agencies, private volunteer groups and the voluntary assistance of individual citizens.[5]

Why has a special outreach program been necessary? Probably the most important factor contributing to public unawareness of the LICTR program is the fact that the majority of claimants would not otherwise be required to file a personal income tax (PIT) return. As a result, such "non-filers" must be reached (the first time) by means other than additions to the PIT form and instructions. Eligible families have been informed through mailings in both Spanish and English, through radio, television and press announcements, and through programs of personal assistance in completing the relevant portions of the PIT form.

Each year the outreach efforts have become more extensive and better organized both within and without the Bureau. Voluntary assistance — personal contact — has been expanded and emphasized as perhaps the most productive aspect of outreach. An LICTR outreach coordinator was hired to expand both Bureau and volunteer efforts for the 1974 LICTR and again for the 1975 program. An auditor from the Santa Fe District Office, Mr. Mac Fresquez, is in charge of coordinating the outreach program for the 1976 LICTR, currently in process.

An important dividend of such efforts has been the added public awareness achieved through efforts of LICTR claimants themselves. Once an eligible family receives its first rebate and understands the program, it will probably apply again the following year, and it may publicize the program to other families in similar circumstances.

One hundred percent compliance by all eligible families is not to be expected, but efforts continue to maximize the amount of

rebate disbursed, within the Bureau's overall budgetary and personnel constraints. It should be noted that some eligible claimants, located on the fringes of the LICTR table due to their relative MGI and their number of exemptions, may just not bother to file a return (if they would not otherwise need to file) in order to receive six or eight dollars. The Bureau does not anticipate that one hundred percent of such potential claims will ever be filed, no matter how extensive outreach efforts may be.

It is important to reemphasize, however, that the compliance for any particular taxable year continues to improve over time, since claimants may file for past years as well as for a current year rebate. As a result of "late" claims for the LICTR, rebate returns in the 64th FY totaled 69,046; the split by tax year was 61,865 for 1975, 3,181 for 1974, 2,700 for 1973, and about 1,300 for 1972.

However, the ability to file "late" is limited as follows: (a) for CY 1972, 1973 and 1974, limited by the 3-year statute of limitations; (b) for CY 1975 and thereafter, limited to the end of the second calendar year following the calendar year to which the rebate is applicable (the result of an amendment by the 1975 Legislature). Thus, for example, claims for the 1972 LICTR were accepted until the end of 1976; claims for the 1975 LICTR will be accepted until the end of 1977.

DETAILS OF THE 1975 LICTR

As a wrap up to this discussion, the following tables provide a detailed look at the characteristics of the recipients of the 1975 LICTR, processed in the 64th FY. (Similar details for the 1972, 1973 and 1974 LICTR have been published in Bureau of Revenue annual reports.)

Better than one-third of the rebate claims for 1975 were made by families or individuals whose major source of income was wages and salaries — the "working poor." One-third of the claims showed social security as the major source of income. The balance of claims showed their major income from public assistance, unemployment compensation, annuities, gifts, etc. Over the first four years of the program, the relative shares of claims by social security and public assistance recipients have grown, while the share of wage and salary workers has declined. Such a shift in the proportions of claimants appears to confirm that more and more of those persons, who would not otherwise need to file a PIT return, have been informed about the LICTR by the outreach programs and by word-of-mouth.

One group of potential claimants, of special interest to the LICTR Program, is the population of elderly New Mexicans. The number of returns claiming exemptions for persons age 65 and over increased from 10,175 for the 1973 LICTR to 19,770 for the 1975 LICTR.

TABLE V

1975 LICTR Returns By Major Source Of Income**

Major Source	Returns Processed	
Of MGI	Number	Percent
Wages & Salaries	22,820	36.9
Social Security	20,780	33.6
Public Assistance	11,214	18.1
Other	7,051	11.4
ALL SOURCES	61,865	100.0

**—Statistics based upon a research sample of 2,744 returns — sample designed by Public Finance Research Program, U.N.M.

TABLE VI

1975 LICTR Returns From The Aged**

Number of Persons Age 65 And Over	Number of Returns	Average MGI	Rebate
One	14,101	$2,434	$ 73
Two	5,669	4,215	212
TOTAL	19,770	$2,944	$113

**—Statistics based upon research sample.

The results of a sample survey indicate that rebates went to 25,439 aged persons in claims (numbering 19,770) showing one or two additional LICTR exemptions for the aged. The 1970 Census (the most recent detailed information available) showed 24,699 aged persons with incomes below the "poverty level," as then defined. We have no precise data available to estimate the number of the aged in poverty in 1975 — certainly that number has grown. Nevertheless, it appears safe to suggest that

the great majority of eligible claimants age 65 and over are receiving the LICTR — a great deal of credit goes to senior citizens groups that have worked hard to insure the success of the program. It is interesting to note that nearly 32 percent of all claims for the 1975 LICTR were from aged claimants; those claims represented over $2.2 million in rebates.

The final table, VII, is a summary of 1975 LICTR returns by number of exemptions and modified gross income of claimants. One-fourth of all returns claimed only one exemption. Roughly 26 percent claimed three exemptions and nearly 21 percent claimed six or more exemptions; of course, in both of these cases, the proportions have been inflated because of the frequency of returns claiming triple exemptions for aged persons.

The returns may also be categorized according to their frequency by MGI class. About 20 percent of all claimants declared modified gross incomes between $1,500 and $2,000, while another 18 percent were between $2,000 and $2,500. In terms of cumulative percentages of claimants, a little less than 60 percent reported $2,500 MGI or less. Nearly 84 percent reported $4,000 MGI or less, while better than 95 percent reported $6,000 MGI or less.

THE FUTURE OF THE LICTR

The New Mexico Low-Income Comprehensive Tax Rebate is a successful, operational mechanism which should continue to be used to channel tax relief to low-income families in order to offset the inherently regressive nature of the state and local tax system. In order to carry out this function, the LICTR must be reviewed and revised periodically to account for the effects of inflation, changing income and consumption patterns, and changes in the definition of the poverty level.

ENDNOTES

1 — The Bureau of Revenue formerly referred to the program as a tax "credit," but has changed the name to tax "rebate" to distinguish it from another "credit" mentioned on the personal income tax return, and to emphasize the state's effort to "rebate" tax already paid.

2 — These quotations are taken from a special research report on the 1975 LICTR, prepared by Dr. Jerry Boyle, Public Finance Research Program, University of New Mexico — dated September 1, 1976. Many of the statistics in this article are derived from that report. The other statistical sources are computer listings from the Bureau's own personal income tax files.

3 — Dr. Jerry Boyle, Public Finance Research Program, University of New Mexico, was responsible for the original research and design of the LICTR. The best technical explanation of the LICTR is found in his article published in the December, 1974, issue of the **National Tax Journal**: "A Comprehensive Tax Credit For Achieving Proportionality In State And Local Tax Structures."

4 — Estimating the universe of eligible claimants is hazardous at best; the job is made more difficult because the target moves through time in response to changes in population, age distribution, income, inflation and the LICTR table itself. The most recent estimates, by a research group at the University of New Mexico, are as follows:

CY 1972 — 63,000 families and individuals
CY 1973 — 63,000 families and individuals
CY 1974 — 75,000 families and individuals
CY 1975 — 91,000 families and individuals

5 — Official statements of gratitude to these volunteer groups and individuals have been made by the Bureau on numerous occasions in public testimony and in press releases. The Legislature formally recognized the vital importance of the voluntary outreach programs with the passage of House Joint Memorial 6 in the 1975 Legislative Session. Persons interested in finding out more about the outreach programs are encouraged to contact the Bureau of Revenue.

TABLE VII
LOW-INCOME COMPREHENSIVE TAX REBATE RETURNS, 1975
BY MODIFIED GROSS INCOME CLASS AND NUMBER OF EXEMPTIONS**

Modified Gross Income Over	But Not Over	1	2	3	4	5	6 or More	Total Number of Returns
$ 0	$ 500	2,493	227	392	62	21	21	3,216
500	1,000	2,268	453	392	165	62	103	3,443
1,000	1,500	3,030	990	1,566	639	124	103	6,452
1,500	2,000	4,721	1,690	4,618	804	288	289	12,410
2,000	2,500	2,846	1,134	4,556	1,381	618	763	11,298
2,500	3,000	0	1,196	1,773	1,072	803	1,752	6,596
3,000	3,500	0	0	1,649	928	454	1,752	4,783
3,500	4,000	0	0	1,237	845	268	1,196	3,546
4,000	4,500	0	0	0	1,113	371	1,464	2,948
4,500	5,000	0	0	0	804	330	866	2,000
5,000	5,500	0	0	0	0	289	927	1,216
5,500	6,000	0	0	0	0	309	886	1,195
6,000	6,500	0	0	0	0	0	845	845
6,500	7,000	0	0	0	0	0	639	639
7,000	7,500	0	0	0	0	0	783	783
7,500	8,000	0	0	0	0	0	495	495
TOTALS		15,358	5,690	16,183	7,813	3,937	12,884	61,865

EXHIBITS:

	1	2	3	4	5	6 or More	Total
Average Modified Gross Income	$1,375	$1,830	$2,193	$2,987	$3,361	$4,418	$2,595
Average Rebate	$41	$46	$59	$76	$116	$200	$87

**— Statistics based upon research sample.

"The Low-Income Comprehensive Tax Rebate: New Mexico's Broad-Based Tax Relief Program" is reprinted by permission from the March, 1977, issue of *Revenues Review*.

The Possibility of a Local Income Tax in New York State

THE TRADITIONAL METHOD of financing local governments has been the real property tax. However, since the Depression there has been a significant trend in New York State (among others) toward authorization of various non-property taxes for use by municipalities. This trend has developed largely due to questions regarding the equity of the property tax, its burden on low and middle income residents and its revenue raising ability.

In New York State, this trend toward non-property oriented taxes has brought about a decreasing reliance on real property taxes as the major source of local government revenues. In 1962 over 61 percent of all locally-raised revenues of upstate counties, cities, towns and villages was derived from the real property tax. By 1972 the property tax accounted for only 50% of these revenues.[1] This increased reliance on non-property taxes has produced growing criticism of them regarding their adequacy and equity.

Dissatisfaction with the real property tax and the various non-property taxes has led many local officials to advocate the authorization of a local income tax. This would enable local governments to tap the most progressive and equitable of all State taxes and would provide a high degree of flexibility. In 1973 the Temporary State Commission on the Powers of Local Government (the Wagner Commission) recommended that "...enabling legislation should be enacted which would give counties the option of imposing a county income tax."[2]

More recently, the Temporary State Commission on Constitutional Tax Limitations (the Bergen Commission) recommended in its final report that Buffalo, Rochester, Yonkers and Syracuse and the city school districts in cities of less than 125,000 (or the counties in which such municipalities are located) be authorized "...to impose a local income tax on residents and a franchise tax on corporations in the form of a surcharge on the State income and franchise taxes..."[3] Given the Commission's goal of providing a "solution" to the *Hurd v. City of Buffalo* decision, (41 A.D. 2d, aff'd. 34 N.Y. 2d 628, 1974) the proceeds of the tax (along with those of a proposed State real property tax) would not exceed the retirement and social security contributions of a municipality.

Authorization of a local income tax should be made only after a comprehensive review of all facets of local government finance. This Commission, in its one year of study, has been able to analyze only a small part of the local fiscal structure, primarily in relation to State revenue sharing, state mandates to local governments and the real property tax. This report is an analysis in response to increasing calls for a local income tax. Its purpose is to serve as a basis for further consideration and study.

Locally-Administered Taxes

Local income taxes have been imposed by over 3,500 units of local government in the United States, and are generally of two types: locally administered taxes and local supplements to State taxes. Each is discussed and compared below.[4] There are three basic types of locally-administered taxes. The first, commonly referred to as payroll tax, is levied at a flat rate on all earned income (wages, salaries, commissions, etc.) originating in the jurisdiction whether received by residents or non-residents. This type of tax is authorized by five states: Alabama, Kentucky, Ohio, Pennsylvania and Missouri. Except in the latter case, the rate is determined by the localities, subject to a maximum rate.

Michigan authorizes a locally-administered tax on earned as well as unearned income (dividends, interest, capital gains). The mandatory rate is one percent on residents and one-half of one percent with tax credit provisions for non-residents.

The third variation of this type of tax has been adopted by New York City and combines a broad base (earned and unearned income) with a graduated rate structure. The base of this tax for residents is similar to that of the State income tax; while the rate is graduated from 0.7 percent on taxable income under $1,000 to 3.5 percent on taxable income over $30,000. The flat non-resident rate is 0.45 percent for the self-employed and 0.65 percent for others, applied to incomes less a decreasing exemption.

Optional Local Supplements to State Income Taxes

There are three general characteristics of this type of local income tax, which is of relatively recent origin. First, *imposition of the tax should be optional*. A mandatory supplement is more logically considered a shared tax.

Also, a mandatory tax at some stated minimum level would lessen tax competition but not eliminate it. Since even the levy of a real property tax is a local option, there seems little legal justification for imposing a mandatory local income tax. However, if the goal of instituting a local income tax is to lessen, or for some minor jurisdictions perhaps eliminate the property tax, a mandatory local tax on income is one method of achieving such a goal.

A local supplement must, by definition, be administered by the State. Substantively, State administration would assure equitable enforcement and the exploitation of economies of scale. Also, State administration would establish a uniform base for all localities, using either the State taxable income or the State tax liability. (These criteria generally are met by the most prevalent local supplement, the general sales tax.)

Two states presently authorize local supplements to their income taxes. Maryland has a mandatory state-administered supplement of 20 percent of the state tax liability, with authorization to increase the rate to 50 percent. The law provides for a formula-based direct payment to incorporated municipalities in each county.

Indiana's local supplement plan is entirely optional. Since the authorization was enacted in 1973, approximately one-third of the counties in the state, and over 300 small municipalities have adopted the local supplement. The base of the local tax is state taxable income, and localities are authorized to enact rates of 0.5 percent to 2 percent on Indiana residents and 0.5 percent on others. In the case of commuters, the jurisdiction of residence takes precedence over that of employment.

While both the Wagner and the Bergen Commissions recommended a local supplement arrangement, the locally-administered tax is in far more common use nationwide.

Local Income Tax Policy Options

The generally-accepted criteria which may be used to appraise fiscal policy options are adequacy, equity, efficiency, predictability and responsibility.

Adequacy, or revenue sufficiency, implies a reasonable rate of revenue growth over time, as personal income rises. From the point of view of absolute adequacy of yield, there is little basis for preferring one of the options over the other since each could be designed to provide virtually any level of financing desired. However, the adequacy of the income elasticity of the revenue yield would depend on the elasticity of the revenue source involved. On this account, a considerable advantage would have to be ascribed to a supplement arrangement tied to the State personal income tax, as it would provide the highest possible income elasticity of yield. Moreover, a flat-rate local supplement based on State income tax liability (as in Maryland) would have a higher

income elasticity than a flat-rate supplement based on State taxable income (as in Indiana).

In terms of equity, if the option to impose the income tax were equally available to all units of a jurisdictional class (county governments), then there would be no grounds for preferring one option over the other. The incidence of the tax among individuals in unequal economic circumstances would depend on the design of the tax, and there is no objective basis for preferring one over the other. While each option could be structured to be non-capricious, the local supplement presumably would be more easily so structured.

Concerning minimization of administrative costs, the preference must be assigned to tax supplements, given the clear economies of scale associated with State administration. Locally-administered taxes are less efficient because of the costs involved in duplicating administration. As is done in Maryland, the State could debit each recipient municipalities' share to finance the operating costs of the program. This could be done on a prorated basis, using (for example) the number of returns or the total tax liability.

For many reasons, it is difficult, even under the best of circumstances, to project the yields of taxes. However, some degree of confidence is warranted for projections of State income tax yields, due to the close relationship between yields and personal income, and the ready availability of personal income projections for local areas (down to the county level). This suggests that a modest preference for predictability should be accorded supplements to the State income tax.

Both the tax supplement and the locally-administered tax alternatives could be structured to provide the same degree of local fiscal responsibility since the enactment would rest with the local governing body. To fully satisfy this criterion, the tax should be entirely optional.

On balance, as both the Wagner and the Bergen Commissions concluded, supplement arrangements emerge as decidedly superior to locally-administered taxes, primarily in terms of revenue adequacy and efficiency. Therefore, if it were determined that local governments should be authorized to tap personal income as a direct revenue source, the more desirable method would be through an optional supplement to the New York State personal income tax. Several critical issues must be resolved such as eligibility to impose the tax, distribution to other units of government, the tax base, and rates and the treatment of non-residents.

"The Possibility of a Local Income Tax in New York State" is reprinted by permission from the *New York Temporary State Commission on State and Local Finance*, Vol. 5, 1975.

Probably more than any issue in public finance, business taxation polarizes the public. High property taxes may be unpopular, but few would advocate their repeal. Income taxes are sometimes a burden (and often a hassle as April 15 approaches), but the progressive income tax continues to have broad support among the American people.

But business taxes, whether in the form of corporate income taxes, property taxes, or special excise or severance taxes, draw continuing and vociferous opposition from the business community. At the same time, they draw often enthusiastic support from the majority of individual taxpayers. In some ways, this is not surprising. It is a political truism that the only popular taxes are taxes on someone else. For the overwhelming majority of Americans, taxes on business *are* taxes on someone else.

In the context of the "tax revolt"—the increased opposition by ordinary citizens to rising taxes—business taxes can play an important role. For the state or locality that wants to maintain public services but decides to give in to business pleas for lower taxes, the affect is clear: taxes on homeowners and workers will go up, aggravating the "tax revolt." On the other hand, higher business taxes can fund tax relief for individual taxpayers while public services are maintained. A number of the more successful progressive responses to the "tax revolt"—for exam-

ple, the 1978 fight for a classified property tax in Massachusetts—have taken this approach.

From a political point of view, raising taxes on business has generally been a staple of progressive candidates. Businesses, particularly big businesses, whatever their other political influence, don't vote. Homeowners and workers do. Over the years, it has not been unusual to see candidates for state and local office basing their campaigns *primarily* on proposals to increase business taxes. In 1970, Reuben Askew made enactment of a corporate income tax *the* major plank in his platform in his successful campaign for governor of Florida. Even California Governor Jerry Brown, now identified with across-the-board tax cutting, felt it politically wise, when he first ran for governor in 1974, to call for closing tax loopholes for the oil companies.

Often, the economics of business taxation are as, or more, attractive as the politics. The great debate among economists is who pays business taxes. The corporations argue that only people pay taxes. When a state or locality imposes a tax on a business, they argue, the tax is either passed *forward* to its customers (in higher prices) or passed *backwards* to its stockholders (in lower dividends), or employees (in the form of lower wages). If companies just pass on taxes, corporate lobbyists argue, why not just tax people directly? Why pretend to be taxing business?

Taxing Business

By James Rosapepe

The answer, according to supporters of business taxation, is that in deciding how it wants to tax business, government can decide who it wants the tax passed on to. For example, a severance tax on coal mined in Wyoming but sold primarily in the East will, if the tax is passed on to consumers, bring tax revenue to Wyoming from people on the other side of the continent. Or a corporate income tax imposed by Ohio on the major auto companies will, if it is primarily passed back to the companies' stockholders, raise money primarily from higher income people. An excise tax imposed by central cities on services like parking lots but paid primarily by suburban commuters can shift the tax burden from the residents of the inner city to those of more affluent surrounding suburbs.

Moreover, businesses as economic institutions, not just as collections of people, make use of government services. Well-maintained county roads, for example, are necessities for successful suburban shopping centers just as much as are skilled workers or lines of credit. Paying taxes to build and repair the roads is not much different than paying workers wages or banks interest. Each of them is a cost of doing business.

Particularly at the state and local level, business taxation can provide an ideal vehicle for shifting the tax burden off of local working people. There, of course, lies the political obstacle to business taxation. Despite their easy assertion that they don't pay business taxes anyway, business leaders are quick to oppose any efforts to increase business taxes. Indeed, particularly in the industrial states of the Midwest and the Northeast, big business interests have gone on the offensive against taxation.

Fortunately, they have not been totally successful. In the last several years, for example, a number of Western states have enacted tough severance taxes on mineral mining companies. West Virginia has levied a special tax on electricity produced for export out of state. Massachusetts voters adopted a classified property tax system, permitting heavier taxation of business than residential property. And many states have beefed up their enforcement of business tax laws already on the books.

For public-minded officials at the state and local level seeking revenue to pay for improved public services or for tax relief for ordinary citizens, business taxation will and should remain a major target. From an economic point of view, the money is there. From a political point of view, so is the public support.

CHAPTER 19

The Economic Impact of State and Local Business Taxes

As part of its continuing fight to reduce business taxes, the corporate community has, in the last several years, made the issue of the "business climate" a dominant one in many states. **Battling for Business**, Jerry Jacob's article in *People and Taxes*, points out that, "Since 1973, twelve states have enacted legislation enabling selected localities to create business property tax reductions or exemptions of up to twenty years." He continued, "Forty states now offer some form of tax break on corporate income or property taxes for new or expanded business developments."

The theory behind these business tax breaks is that, by lowering taxes on corporate taxpayers, the "business climate" will be improved. As a result, the argument goes, more companies will want to invest or expand in the state that grants the exemptions.

Unfortunately, for states and localities that pin their hopes for economic development on such policies, the evidence that these policies work is not great.

Business Lures Useless, Nader Says is a report by Larry Kramer on a recent study of business tax incentives by Ralph Nader's Public Interest Research Group which concluded such incentives had little or no effect on where businesses locate. Instead, Nader claims they "made the rich richer and the poor poorer. Rich taxpayers and big corporations get reduced taxes. The difference is made up by the little guy, the small taxpayer and homeowner who has to pay higher taxes to make up for the taxes not paid by the plant across the meadows."

In their exhaustive survey of the literature on business tax incentives, **The Political Economy of States Job-Creation Business Incentives**, economists Bennett Harrison and Sandra Kanter reached the same conclusion. They point out that, "The average U.S. business paid only 4.4 percent of its income to state and local governments." Hardly a big part of location decisions. Moreover, they note, "Because the states are continually matching one another's incentive packages, the de facto differential subsidies from one place to another are smaller still." They conclude, "There is neither theoretical nor empirical support for the belief that interstate business incentive differentials make an important difference to the decisions of firms with respect to relocation, expansion, or start-up of new facilities."

In recent years, one of the most popular ways to reduce business taxes at the state or local level has been the property tax abatement. Among the most aggressive challengers of tax abatements have been two state-wide citizen groups, Massachusetts Fair Share and the Ohio Public Interest Campaign. OPIC has blocked a number of proposed tax abatements in Cleveland. The chapter concludes with, **Tax Abatement: The Big Giveaway**, an article from the Ohio AFL-CIO *Focus*. It notes that, "Tax abatements occur over a period of time and the tax burden shift from business to wage earner is gradual. But as taxpayers revolt and refuse to pay higher taxes, services deteriorate and the people and business both suffer."

Battling For Business

by Jerry Jacobs

It may not be another civil war yet, but there *is* a war of sorts being waged between the states today, one that is costing taxpayers millions of dollars every year. The war propaganda itself is expensive: magazine advertisements alone cost some $7 million last year, and that cost has gone up 40% this year.

The war is the competition between states (or between localities) for industry. It is being fought increasingly by offering tax breaks as incentives for businesses to expand or to relocate—and it is a threat not only to the tax bases of states and localities, but to the whole idea of tax fairness.

War Cries

One of the most frequently-heard maxims in Congress, in state legislatures and city councils these days is also one of the least supportable: "Tax breaks for business mean jobs and prosperity." This notion is being forwarded by business lobbyists and unfortunately is being bought wholesale by states and cities, who are now offering what the *Wall Street Journal* has described as a "candy store of incentive programs" in the hopes of attracting business investment.

Most observers agree that the interstate competition for business has never been more heated, with even typically staid journals describing the situation in the most dramatic terms. According to *Business Week*, "traditional competition among regions, states and municipalities for industry and jobs appears to be escalating into fierce—perhaps ruinous—warfare." State economic development officials uniformly acknowledge the current escalation, while often admitting that neighboring states are their chief targets. *The New York Times*, referring to this cutthroat behavior, remarks that "regional cooperation is one thing, but when it comes to competition for the dollars, it's every state for itself."

The competition is flourishing on both state and local levels. Municipal property tax abatement programs have spread rapidly this decade, as mayors strive to alleviate the persistently high levels of unemployment by any means available. Since 1973, 12 states have enacted legislation enabling selected localities to grant business property tax reductions or exemptions of up to 20 years. Alabama, for one, allows major cities to grant 15-year property tax exemptions on downtown commercial and industrial facilities, which pay tax only on the pre-improvement property value.

And state corporate tax relief has grown in step with local abatement trends. Since 1973, 10 states have instituted investment tax credits on state corporate income taxes. Forty states now offer some form of tax break on corporate income or property taxes for new or expanded business developments.

States and localities proclaim their business incentive programs in brash advertising campaigns aimed at corporate investors: "TEXAS is Number One for Business"; "If it's profits you want, NEW JERSEY'S got it." Wisconsin puts out a 12-page spread emphasizing statistics and analysis, whereas Rhode Island's colorful 20-page ad seeks to establish the state's claim as New England's tax haven.

The industrial promotion is not restricted to depressed areas. Campaigns are also underway in prosperous places like Virginia's Fairfax County, whose business promotion budget was recently tripled to $700,000. Ads for booming sunbelt cities such as Tampa and Atlanta run regularly in *Fortune* magazine.

The Other Costs

Tax relief for business costs cities and states in more than just promotional fees. In just over a year, New York City has exempted $461 million in properties from nearly $44 million in taxes. St. Louis has exempted nearly $1 billion worth of real estate—equal to half of the city's property value—including a property tax abatement for the First National Bank of St. Louis, estimated to cost the city $17 million alone. Michigan's incentives may cost $50 million in state revenues and $30 million in local revenues annually if continued into the 1980's.

And All For What?

If the whole costly tax competition campaign is aimed at expanding industry, it's important to see whether the tax incentives are accomplishing that goal. In fact, these incentives are singularly *ineffective* in increasing overall business construction. At best they *redirect* investment that would otherwise have located elsewhere. As economist William Morgan puts it, "From the national point of view, none of these tax incentives makes any sense at all. . . .You're not creating any new industry, just moving it someplace different."

But governors are more interested in the narrower question: Whether tax cuts are effective in helping the state economy, even if it means siphoning off business from other areas. Even on this score, the evidence overwhelmingly indicates that tax incentives are ineffective. Taxes are at best a marginal factor in a firm's location decisions. Markets, transportation and labor costs are typically the decisive considerations for new investment decisions.

Even the lucky beneficiaries admit that the tax breaks really have little to do with relocation decisions. Last year county officials offered a new sodium bicarbonate plant a 12-year property tax break for moving to Senaca County, Ohio. The corporation's controller was quoted in the *Wall Street Journal* as saying: "The tax abatement was a nice kicker at the end, but we chose Ohio mainly because of its strategic location for distribution and market growth."

Who's Fooling Whom?

But it appears that somewhere along the line there must have been a mix-up: an Ohio economic development official still maintains that the tax abatement was "the keystone of the deal" to get the corporation to settle there.

This discrepancy points out one of the most serious problems with the tax competition battle: the fact that state and local officials are feeling *pressured* to grant tax rewards to business—often for doing what they would do anyway. And the problem is self-perpetuating—as more and more states offer the tax incentives, the businesses can come to expect them as a matter of course, and the tax competition becomes even fiercer.

The Real Wages of the War

The overall result of the growing tax competition is alarming: business' share of state and local taxes, which was shrinking gradually in the 1950's and 1960's, is now on a very rapid decline.

Ironically, too, the tax breaks are being offered to the very businesses who don't need them—the largest and most powerful. As the president of a company which puts out a trade publication *Industrial Development* notes, while the offerings of tax incentives grow, "they're being used more by blue chip and Fortune 500 companies."

In the meantime, it is the smaller businesses and individuals who pay more taxes as the tax burden shifts. According to North Dakota Tax Commissioner Byron Dorgan, (see interview, p. 6) "You'll never see a welder, or a barber, or a punchpress operator who's thinking of moving to Buffalo or to Cleveland saying 'Well, let's see. What kind of tax deal are you going to give me first?' "

"Battling for Business" is reprinted by permission from the September, 1978 issue of *People and Taxes*, Public Citizens Tax Reform Research Group.

Business Lures Useless, Nader Says

By Larry Kramer
Washington Post Staff Writer

States are wasting billions of dollars to attract businesses by offering them incentives that actually have little or no effect on where those businesses ultimately locate, according to a new report by Ralph Nader's Public Interest Research Group.

The report shows that the tax breaks and subsidies offered by the 50 states are so similar that corporate officers admit openly that those issues are not even considered when their companies plan moves.

States and localities are increasingly offering more attractive financial lures to corporations, Nader said in a press conference at which he released the report yesterday, and they frequently even compete with neighboring states.

But, he said, the money is going predominantly to the nation's largest corporations—who, he said, need the handouts the least.

"Well over half of the $18 billion in industrial development and pollution control bonds (tax-free bonds that can be issued by the benefited corporation) issued during the 1960s and 1970s was issued to a few giant corporations, those with over 5,000 employes and gross sales in excess of $1 billion," said report author Jerry Jacobs, who was with Nader at the press conference.

"States are bidding against each other for the right to enrich these big businesses," Nader said. "It's a war of all against all and nobody wins except the companies."

Although some states were innovative in first offering the incentives, he said, "They have all come up to speed and are offering essentially the same thing now."

The report noted that the U.S. Treasury will lose $21.1 billion over the next dacede in taxes because the companies involved are being allowed to issue tax-free bonds.

The tax incentives offered "serve to make the rich richer and the poor poorer," Nader said. "Rich taxpayers (who can buy the tax-free bonds, which are usually sold in large denominations) and big corporations get reduced taxes. The difference is made up by the little guy, the small taxpayer and homeowner who has to pay higher taxes to make up for the taxes not paid by the plant across the meadows."

Jacobs said the corporate executives he interviewed said they all "decide first where they want their plant to be, and then look for the subsidies they can get," thus defeating the purpose of offering incentives.

Robert Gulian, financial officer for Union Carbide Corp., when asked if pollution control bonds had enabled his company to initiate any projects, is quoted in the report as saying, "No. I can say very positively that has not been the case. We always identify the project first and then go to the municipality."

Still, he noted, Union Carbide has never been turned down in a request for a tax-free pollution control bond.

"Business Lures Useless, Nader Says" is reprinted by permission from the August 2, 1979 issue of *The Washington Post*.

The Political Economy of States' Job-Creation Business Incentives

Bennett Harrison and Sandra Kanter

Nearly every state government in the country uses tax credits, subsidized loans, and other instruments to induce private investors to expand or construct new facilities within its borders. A theoretical analysis of such policies, in the context of a realistic picture of the contemporary structure of American industry, indicates no reason to expect that tax or related cost-side incentives will—by themselves—generate new investment (if any segment of the business community *is* likely to be responsive, it would be those firms paying the lowest wages and employing the fewest workers). A review of the empirical literature strongly supports the argument against such incentives. Finally, a political-economical analysis of business incentive policies leads the authors to conclude that these costly subsidies constitute a form of "welfare grant" to the business sector, especially in declining areas of the country.

Almost without exception, state government officials across the country advocate the use of incentives to the business sector to stimulate additional production of goods and services, and the additional derived demand for labor. This is popularly known as job-creation.

These policies include tax credits and "forgivenesses," the provision of capital raised by the flotation of tax exempt bonds, low-interest loans, and state guarantees of loans or mortgages written by private sector lenders. Nearly every state in the union provides some mix of these business incentives. One way or the other, all are designed to reduce firms' (fixed or operating) "costs of doing business" in that state relative to other states. It is hoped that this will induce expansions or new investments and a consequent growth in employment. In the declining areas of the northeastern "frost-belt," such incentives are being advocated as a policy for retaining existing enterprises which might otherwise move away or shut down altogether.

The most benign explanation for the widespread popularity of these policies is that state officials gen-uinely believe in the efficacy of business incentives. A perusal of statehouse hearings and staff reports on the various pieces of legislation makes this understandable, for no aspect of economic policy has been more poorly argued and documented, yet so uniformly (and warmly) supported by special interest lobbyists. If "everyone" believes that business incentives are a good thing, and there is virtually no articulated criticism accessible to politicians, then perhaps it is no wonder

Bennett Harrison is associate professor of economics and urban studies in the Department of Urban Studies and Planning at MIT where he teaches economic development, employment planning, and political economy. He also participates in the development of progressive economic legislation at the state level and is the author of five books.

Sandra Kanter is assistant professor of economics at the University of Massachusetts, Boston, and director of the Community Economics Learning Center, an experimental, federally funded University of Massachusetts program which trains community activists in political economy. She was formerly staff director of the Joint Committee on Commerce and Labor in the Massachusetts legislature.

that the prescription is believed. Besides, it sounds perfectly plausible: if one state reduces the relative costs of doing business, vis-à-vis other states, surely firms will find it a more attractive environment for doing business.

It is the contention here that these business incentives do not produce new output or jobs, but that they do have real costs in the form of foregone tax revenues which have valuable alternative uses. It is also possible that some of these incentives raise the price that state governments and less privileged private investors have to pay for borrowing capital from the private sector. Because they cost taxpayers money, but do not produce much (if any) new employment, these business incentives constitute a regressive redistribution of income from workers-consumers-taxpayers to the corporate sector. The objective of this article is to articulate and to statistically document, in so far as possible, the case against business incentives as an effective state economic development policy.

If the position is correct, then the implications are straightforward: repeal the existing legislation, pass national laws that make it harder for states to deploy these "weapons," and commit the resulting public savings to direct investment in the production of socially useful goods and services, with the consequent creation of new jobs at decent pay.

The next section describes the range of tax and other business incentive policies currently in use. This is followed by a theoretical exploration of the expected operation and impacts of state job-creation business aids, focusing on tax incentives. Next is presented a review and evaluation of the existing empirical work on the subject, describing actual outcomes. A concluding section offers some political-economic explanations for why such a thoroughly unproven policy as this continues to be so widely endorsed.

Business incentives that states are using

State business incentives can be categorized in one of three ways. First are state laws which permit cities, towns, counties, or the state itself to reduce business tax obligations. The tax concessions can be either in the form of an exemption from corporate, personal, income, or realty taxes or in the form of an outright tax credit.

The second category of incentives is the subsidization of business loans. There are three general types. The most popular seem to be those which are proffered by privately sponsored, usually tax exempt development credit corporations. They are set up to lend private monies to firms allegedly unable to find conventional (unsubsidized) financing. In addition, a number of states lend monies directly to firms for the purchase of equipment and machinery. A few states also have programs to guarantee private loans

to industry for plant expansion or other new development.

The third type of state business incentive relates to projects undertaken by the state or other jurisdiction to encourage industrial growth. Most often, this means the public financing of industrial parks to house new industry. The financing is usually accomplished by floating public bonds, of which there are two kinds. Revenue bonds are paid solely from the proceeds of the project and do not become the obligation of any government. General obligation bonds are guaranteed by the full faith and credit of the state or municipality.

The industrial development bonds are the most widely used of all the tools. Forty-eight states have laws permitting industrial revenue bonds to be issued. Twenty-one also guarantee the repayment of their bonds.

Loan programs are also widespread. Thirty-four states now have privately sponsored development credit corporations. Seventeen states or their civil subdivisions lend money directly to business for building construction and for the purchase of machinery and equipment. Thirteen states have programs which guarantee business loans and mortgages.

Finally, most states have at least one type of business tax exemption or credit. There are a number of versions. A few examples illustrate the range of possibilities. Twenty-one states, for instance, exempt a part of the corporate income tax. Thirty-one states exempt or delay tax payments on land, capital improvement, and machinery. Last, but not least, thirty-seven states exempt manufacturers' inventories from taxes, while nine grant tax exemptions to encourage research and development (*Industrial Development* 1978).

What should be expected from business incentives

Popular—and legislative—discussions about business incentives to create jobs are invariably couched in simplistic and highly general terms, e.g. "cut *taxes* and get *businesses* to create new *jobs*." But which taxes (and by what amounts)? What kinds of businesses? And which sorts of jobs? Is the policy targeted at firms considering expansion at a given location, at plant relocation, or at new start-ups altogether? Presumably, the levels of activity of profit-making firms (the constituency for this type of legislation) depend not only on the costs of doing business, but also on the existence and certainty of markets for the output of those firms. What sorts of biases are introduced by the assumption—implicit in all incentive programs—that changes in relative costs, with no changes in potential sales, are sufficient to induce changes in output and employment? These are just some of the theoretical complexities that are usually left out of the popular discussions of this subject.

With such a maze of variables with which to contend, how shall this analysis proceed? Organization into two parts seems useful. First to be considered are the differences between short-run (plant activity-increasing) and long-run (plant expansion or relocation) policies. Then the examination will turn to some general problems with business incentives that seem to apply in both the short- and the long-run. In all that follows, the concentration will be on tax incentives and loan interest subsidies; these have emerged as the principal "hard" policy instruments of the Carter administration's urban revitalization program.

Short-run job creation through increasing levels of plant utilization

To the economist, the short run is that planning period during which physical plant is taken as given. What is variable (at least to some extent) is the level of activity at which that plant (or office or hamburger stand) is operated. In particular, how much labor is being employed, in combination with other resources, to produce output? And—more to the immediate point—how is the managerial decision to increase or decrease employment in that plant affected by changes in costs, especially tax and interest costs?

Even in pure theory, the answer depends crucially on whether the firm under study is in a competitive or an oligopolistic industry. T-shirt factories and barber shops behave differently than automobile manufacturers and large department stores. If the industry is reasonably competitive, then firms are forced by the existence of their competitors to sell their output at the going price, regardless of their costs of production. Under such conditions, they will try to produce and sell as much as possible, subject to the constraints of given physical capacity, access to finance capital, etc. Any reduction in costs—whether the costs relate to capital or to labor—will induce at least some change in the output-employment decision.[1] This is apparently the image of decision making in the firm that the advocates of job-creating incentives have in mind.

The history of capitalism is a history of the continual transformation of the economy from a system in which at least some aspects of competition were prevalent to one dominated by large corporations, possessing great economic and political power. Nearly every one of those assumptions underlying the textbook theory of competition no longer holds—and many of them (such as virtually frictionless labor mobility) *never* held in the real world. Not even among "small" firms are these conditions always satisfied (although size is one important measure of the extent of potential economic and political power). For example, many family firms hire and fire workers, remain open or closed for more or less of the year, and decide whether or not to get out of business and reinvest their capital elsewhere according to considerations that go beyond pecuniary profit, such as a strong family tradition of association with the product or location.

Firms in industries characterized by a relatively smaller number of producers are called oligopolists. Their main characteristic is some degree of market power, defined as the ability to set prices as well as output levels, in their search for profits and market shares. The thing which permits this price-making power is the real or manufactured differentiation of their product-service from one another, whether by virtue of style differences (Chevy Novas vs. Plymouth Satellites) or locational monopolies (the electric company in New York City cannot compete with the one in Boston). The greater the extent to which price increases do not drive an oligopolist's customers away from it and to a competitor, the greater the extent of that market power.[2] Firms with substantial market power can protect their profit margins, when costs increase, by passing at least part of these increases along to their customers in the form of higher prices (they may also pass them along at a markup, thereby gaining a windfall profit). And when costs fall, at least part of those savings get captured in the form of windfall profits, because they need *not* be entirely passed along to customers as lower product (or service) prices.

It follows that declining costs will have a relatively smaller impact on the output and employment decisions of an oligopolist than on a competitor. At best, with flexible technology—the ability to recombine labor and capital in varying amounts, more or less continuously—the additional quantity of labor needed will be small (and may, of course, not match the skills of that segment of the labor force which the state government wants to [re-]employ). If the technology is less flexible, whether because labor is hired at discrete periods or on fixed-duration contracts, or because additional amounts of labor cannot be added continuously to a given machine in a corner of the plant, then the incentive may well produce no extra employment at all.

In recent years, a literature has developed on the rules of thumb and other institutional procedures by which oligopolists make output and employment decisions when faced with uncertainty about prices and other market conditions and given the need to manage complex labor relations (Doeringer and Piore 1971, Hamilton 1974, Sherer 1970). This literature stresses the importance of threshold effects: unless price, cost, and other conditions change by more than some minimum amount in a given period of time, the firm will probably choose to ignore those changes, since the very act of adjusting to them would have real costs.

If firms of any type can capture larger shares of their respective markets—if they think they can sell more output—then of course they will consider increasing the level of utilization of their existing capacity (and if that is still insufficient, they may expand that capacity, i.e., build additional plant). But at the state level, neither tax nor other business incentives can significantly stimulate the demand for goods and services (although *consumer* income or property tax deductions or credits may do so). That is why federal expenditure and tax policies are the principal determinants of economic growth in any region, certainly in the short-run.

In principle, it is true that there might be some level of business incentive so great that the resulting cost reduction would—at least over time—induce a significant increase in output and employment within at least some private firms. But (and this point will be developed later) the larger the incentives, the greater the foregone revenue which could otherwise have been used to finance, e.g., state social services, repayment of interest on the state's bonded debt, or property tax relief. There are, therefore, political limits to the feasible magnitude of the business incentives. It is quite possible that the range of operational incentives—between some floor set by the behavioral rules of thumb used by oligopolistic decision makers, and a ceiling set by the politically unacceptable opportunity costs of the foregone tax revenue—is too narrow to make this an effective policy instrument for job creation.

Finally, it must be asked what kinds of jobs get created if and when some firms do respond to the introduction of, say, tax incentives by increasing output and employment. According to the "dual labor market" literature and its antecedents, the jobs in those industries which most closely approximate the competitive ideal type will in general pay lower wages, offer worse (and less amply capitalized) working conditions, provide less stable (full-year and/or full-week) employment, and make it more difficult for labor to organize in order to protect its class interests (Harrison and Hill 1978). Yet the theoretical analysis leads to the expectation that it is precisely these competitive firms which are most likely to respond to an incremental job-creation incentive, if anyone does. Thus, business incentives appear to be policy instruments which —if they work at all—are most likely to stimulate increased capacity utilization in the sector of the economy with the least desirable jobs, while providing windfall profits to the segment of the business community that needs them least.

Long-run job creation: investment in new start-ups or plant expansions

Economic theory probably has met with its least amount of predictive success in trying to understand the dynamics of the investment decision. The same rules of thumb and threshold effects mentioned earlier operate in the long run as well, and are perhaps even more common in a realm of such great uncertainty. Peter Bearse, formerly executive director of the Council of Economic Advisers to the governor of New Jersey, discusses the role of such indivisibilities in the decision-making process:

The decision to move or build a plant is subject to thresholds and long gestation periods. Marginal adjustments in the cost of debt finance or in certain tax rates do not stand a chance of affecting a major decision unless a firm is at or near a threshold; and even then, several other factors are also operative. . . . It is a question of probabilities—the odds that a given policy can have an intended effect. I claim that the concept of an adaptive, sequential decision-making process subject to thresholds makes the efficacy of current policies look very dubious (1976, pp. 44–45).

Another earlier conclusion obtains here as well. Almost anything that a government can do to reduce a firm's uncertainty about sales is likely to have as great an impact on the private decision to invest (build or expand the plant) as any other kind of public action—including the granting of incentives. Indeed, an even stronger statement can be made: since uncertainty is usually greater with respect to expected revenues than costs, exclusively cost-side policies are certain to be insufficient to induce investment activity that would not have taken place anyway, in the absence of the incentive.

Orthodox theory is silent on the question of who has access to capital for investment in the first place. Most treatments seem to assume that capital is spatially ubiquitous (for a price), so that if it *pays* an investor to borrow the capital in order to build or expand his or her facilities (because the expected rate of return is higher than that available from other applications of the funds), the borrowing-investing will in fact take place (Strazheim 1971). There is strong evidence that debt capital does flow efficiently (via modern communications systems) to those uses that provide reliable private pecuniary returns. But this doesn't mean that *anyone* can borrow. For example, blacks, women, entrepreneurs working in low-income communities, and nonprofit developers have an especially difficult time getting capital at *any* price.

Moreover, development turns in part on the debt-to-equity capital mix. Businesses lacking sufficient equity (or "front-end") capital—the kind that requires the borrower to pay the lender (usually the stockholder) a share of the profits if *and when* there are any profits—face high probabilities of failure (or of inability to grow), because of their indebtedness (the interest on a loan must usually begin to be paid back immediately, whether there are profits or not). Equity capital seems to be in especially short supply now; those who control its allocation are especially risk adverse, and minorities and community groups have particular difficulty in gaining equal access to it (Daniels 1974).

Even with debt financing, there may be elements of market failure. It is the smallest firms, with the poorest track records, and the least powerful small investors or groups, perhaps with no track record at all, who find it most difficult to borrow. Large firms with good credit ratings have less trouble raising their own capital, whether externally or through their own retained earnings. But if the investigating-lending of private banks (or of state economic development authorities) is conditioned upon the credit worthiness of the borrower, then the normal operation of the capital markets will work to channel ever more financial resources to the oligopolists, exacerbating the relative scarcity of finance capital for the more competitive segment of the market. This can only reinforce the intersectoral inequalities.

The upshot of all this is that firms in concentrated industries do not need tax and interest rate incentives as much as firms in the more competitive industries. But if the latter face relatively greater uncertainty about costs as well as future revenues, then they are less likely to invest, i.e., to take advantage of state business incentives. Thus, it appears likely that state business incentives will end up as windfall profits to oligopolists, generating little or no investment that was not already planned by those who got the subsidies.

Long-run job creation: plant relocation

From the speeches of elected and appointed officials, and the terminology used by newspaper editorial writers, it would seem that the way in which most people expect new jobs to be created in a state economy over time is through the relocation into the state of plants that had been closed down elsewhere, or through the decision of multiplant (maybe even multinational) firms to build their next new plant in the state.

Beyond the factors already discussed, actual physical relocation involves some additional considerations. There is also a new policy instrument involved: industrial recruiting. States hire advertising agencies or management consultants to place ads and "hustle up" new business. Visiting company representatives are wined and dined, and shown around the state. All of this costs money—sometimes a great deal of it.

Starting up a new business has its own fixed costs. But relocating a plant from one site (let alone state) to another may be even more expensive, since the old plant must be scrapped or sold, possibly at a loss. This alone should imply reluctance by firms to undertake such relocations.

Although the hypothesis has not been well researched, it seems plausible that a significant amount of plant relocation out of the United States altogether is the result of absorption of what were previously locally owned businesses into multinational corporations or conglomerates that choose locations on the basis of international comparative costs, federal tax

policies, and overseas political conditions. Obviously there is little that an American state government can (or should want to) do to emulate, say, the repressive labor policies of South Korea or Taiwan.

Interregional (long-distance) and intraregional relocations involve very different kinds of decisions. Firms select regions by broad, qualitative criteria such as the availability of basic resources, adequate transportation access, and (although it is seldom put so bluntly) a politically passive labor force. Once a region (e.g., a state) has been selected, the choice of a particular location *within* that region may turn on interjurisdictional variations in costs and site amenities. However, tax differentials appear, from recent research, not to be particularly important at this level, either (Schmenner 1978).

Economists have discovered that some long-distance moves are made in clusters. For example, if a firm in industry x moves from location A to location B, and if x and industry y are agglomerated (meaning that there are technological or market processes that link them together, such as a unit-cost-saving tendency to share similar kinds of labor or infrastructure), then one or another firm in industry y may move to B, too. On the other hand, if x does *not* move, then y may not be movable either, no matter how large the business incentive offered by region B, or how intensive the recruiting effort (Bergsman, Greenston, and Healy 1972).

A game-theoretic analysis of the interstate plant relocation process suggests that expensive recruitment and incentive policies may be quite irrational. Improving one's business environment (say, by building industrial parks, cleaning up the rivers, or training the labor force) makes sense for a state, except perhaps to the extent that there is a net overbuilding of industrial park—or shopping center—capacity, something which may well have occurred in the U.S. (We can't tell for sure, since the two recessions since 1970 have obscured the structural effect by reducing demand.) To the extent that other states try to compete by similar policies within their own boundaries, everyone benefits. But a "recruited" plant relocation is piracy, and the state that was "ripped off" will probably try to retaliate. The net effect turns on the fact that for each recruitable plant, this competition among the states is a zero-sum game. Only one prize can be won, while there are many players. According to Chiang, "Such a game therefore can only *redistribute*, but never *create*, the object of payoff" (1974, p. 743). All states incur costs: certainly the costs of engaging in recruiting, but perhaps also the foregone tax revenues if firms that would have immigrated anyway claim eligibility for relocation tax incentives. But only one player can win; $n-1$ must lose. It follows that, for each player, the expected net payoff must *at best* be very small, and is almost certainly negative. Perhaps the reason why the players (i.e., the government officials who legislate and administer these policies) seem so positive about them is that they are incorrectly focusing on the potential benefits but ignoring the probable losses.

There is another aspect of the phenomenon of plant relocation which suggests that states may sometimes be better off without those new plants—however they are induced to come. If the company brings part or all of its labor force with it, the new families will place an increasing burden on the social services, housing, and labor markets of the receiving state. And the net effect on the local unemployment rate will obviously be smaller than was envisioned when the legislature passed the recruiting or tax incentive measures in the first place. Perhaps only the skilled labor force is relocated, in which case the only local job creation occurs in the unskilled, low-wage segment of the labor market. Only recently have state and local planners begun to look carefully at the expected impact of new plants on environmental quality and maintenance costs; under many circumstances these, too, could more than offset the job-creation and tax benefits accruing to the state from industrial recruiting.

Three crucial overriding issues

Whether the new jobs are to be created through increased utilization of existing plant, through new investment in local start-ups or plant expansions, or through actual physical plant relocations, and whether it is competitive or oligopolistic industries that are the explicit or implicit targets of job-creation tax incentive policies, there are three crucial overriding issues that have not been discussed so far in this article. Consideration of them will complete the theoretical analysis of the problem.

Apparent vs. actual corporate savings. Whenever a company's state income taxes go down, its federal taxable income rises, thereby increasing its federal tax liability. For the less powerful firms in the corporate sector, this means that actual additions to net revenue will generally amount to only about half of the state incentive. Even for the most powerful corporations with access to federal tax "loopholes," the net gain in profits will average only about 70–75 percent of what the state policy makers had intended.

Budget substitution, or maintenance of effort. Employment and training planners have, for several years, administered federal grants to state and local governments (for public service job creation) and to private corporations (for wage subsidies for the "hard-core unemployment"). There is evidence that grant recipients sometimes use the transferred funds to finance activities they would have undertaken anyway, in the absence of the grant, with local (or internal) resources. The federal grants partly substitute for, rather than fully complement, those local resources. The result is that the net job-creation impact is less than the gross or intended impact (Hammermesh, forthcoming, Harrison 1972, Wiseman 1976).

State business incentives may encounter the same problem. It is difficult to prove that a firm taking (say) a tax credit would not have acted as it did, even in the absence of the incentive. Perhaps states could protect themselves by targeting grants, loans, or tax credits exclusively to new projects, created expressly for the purposes defined by the grant or credit legislation, or by using performance contracts combined with trend analysis on each recipient's presubsidy behavior.

The opportunity costs of the tax incentives. Finally, it is important to confront the popular belief that—apart from the administrative expenses (which are generally small)—these various business incentives are essentially costless. In fact, tax incentives which do not lead to new jobs force the state to forego tax revenue, the revenue which would have been collected in the absence of the policy. Those foregone revenues have other productive uses, and it is the goods and services which those foregone revenues *could* have purchased that constitute the real (social or opportunity) cost of the incentives (Surrey 1970a, 1970b). How many ways can a state spend its money? On housing, health, transportation, its own job creation via public employment—or in the form of personal income or property tax relief. Planners need to closely examine the goods and services that are foregone as a consequence of the implementation of business tax incentives.

Both the additional job-creating investment activity of private firms and the additional spending by state government will have multiplier effects within the state (averaging about $1.25 to $1.50 of total additional income for each $1 of new spending[3]). But if the contention is correct that tax incentives do not induce firms to undertake investment activity that they would not have undertaken in the absence of the incentives, while the foregone revenues could have financed new state spending, then the net multiplier effect of these state tax incentives would be negative; a $1 tax incentive removes 25¢ to 50¢ from the economy. Even if firms do undertake at least some new investment in connection with the incentives, both the timing and the mix (by sector, location, race, sex, and skill composition of the extra labor demanded) are sure to vary between private investment and public spending. Good economic planning requires a much closer examination of these differences than anyone has ever undertaken, to see what kinds of jobs the state tax incentives create, even when they *are* "working."

What business incentives have actually produced: a review of the evidence

Since the 1950s, government agencies and independent researchers have attempted to measure the relative impact of business incentives on industrial location of expansion. By contrast, not until recently have serious attempts been made to measure the opportunity costs of such incentives, and then only in one state. Measures also are needed of the size of the business cost items which these incentives are designed to reduce; are they large enough to matter? And how many plants actually *do* move from one state to another over time?

Although the number of published studies and reports on the subject turns out to be substantial, the quality of the material is very poor (the last comprehensive literature review is by Due in 1961). Inadequate attention has been paid to statistically controlling for differences in regional conditions, points in the business cycle, or financial condition of the companies involved in the various incentives programs. The benefit-cost type studies invariably commit the basic fallacy of comparing before-the-program and after-the-program conditions and attributing changed conditions to the program, when in fact what is called for is a comparison of conditions *with* and *without* the program.

If the findings from these various studies were sharply at odds with one another about the effectiveness of state business incentives, then it would probably be impossible to draw even weak conclusions because of the inability to say with any assurance which studies were better than others, or to compare different studies. But that turns out not to be a problem. With a very few exceptions, the empirical literature fails to reveal significant plant relocation or expansion resulting from (or even correlated with) differentials in state business incentives.

Survey research on the impact of business incentives

Many surveys have been conducted of firms either expanding their facilities in a particular location or region, or moving into that area. Those employers asked to volunteer the factors that "mattered" in their decision seldom mentioned such things as state and local taxes or the availability of subsidized credit. When taxes (or credits) were specified by the interviewer, the proportion of respondents checking them off usually rose to between 5 and 15 percent. But when the latter surveys went on to ask the respondent to indicate whether these factors were "critical" or not, few considered them as such. In most cases access to markets, labor costs, and the availability of physical space were the paramount locational considerations. One of the earliest such surveys was conducted in 1950 by the Survey Research Center of the University of Michigan (1950). Only 9 percent of the 188 plants moving into Michigan had managers who felt that state's tax benefits were an "important consideration" in the move. A Regional Plan Association study of firms moving plants out of New York City between

1947 and 1955 concluded that only 15 percent of the moves were related to interregional tax differentials (Campbell 1958).[4] One particularly careful study was conducted at the Stanford Research Institute in 1964 by Robert Spiegelman. He analyzed the locational behavior of one of the more footloose industries: precision instrument manufacturing. More than half of the forty-five firms in the study considered interregional tax differentials "relevant," but only one called them "the most important factor." Only 13 percent of the firms in a mid-1960s survey of industrial migration into Texas considered taxes to be one determinant of their decision (McMillan 1965).

A national mail survey conducted by the U.S. Department of Commerce in 1972, covering 2,900 companies in high-growth industries across the country, revealed that fully 78 percent considered tax incentives or "holidays" to be "relevant" to their locational decisions. But only 8 percent rated such incentives as "critical" (U.S. Department of Commerce 1975).[5]

There is, of course, no way of knowing who answers these mail questionnaires. Is it a public relations staffer in the company? A lower level manager saying what he or she thinks is going on (or what should be going on)? In 1974, in order to make company responses more precise, personal in-depth interviews were conducted in two New England states, Massachusetts and Connecticut. Executives of fifteen Massachusetts companies were sampled by two legislative staffers from the pool of companies that had applied for and received state job-creation tax credits, fourteen of them for alleged expansion in excess of normal growth and one for relocation into the commonwealth. Every interview yielded the same result: the company took actions according to its own plans, *then* learned about the existence of the tax credits and applied for them (often at the explicit urging of the state bureaucrats in charge of the program).[6]

Another set of interviews with Connecticut business persons participating in that state's incentive programs produced identical results (Dumont 1975). In these cases, at least, the causality is unmistakable: the availability of the incentives did not induce business behavior that would not have occurred otherwise. Instead, the incentives functioned as a windfall for the companies—at the expense of the taxpayers.

Correlations of interstate business tax differentials with interstate growth (or unemployment) rates

One way to deal with the inherently subjective nature of the survey approach—"Mr. Businessman, do taxes matter to you?" "Of course they do"—is to compare states with high and low business taxes, to see whether or not they vary systematically in the growth of jobs. In this literature, the results so far have been uniformly negative.

C. C. Bloom (1955) correlated growth in manufacturing employment with per capita state and local tax collections among all the states, for the periods 1939–53 and 1947–53. In neither case was there a statistically significant relationship. The first of the multiple equation state econometric models, describing the growth of the Michigan economy between 1947 and 1953, showed no significant relationship between state and local taxes and employment growth over time (Thompson and Mattila 1959). A nonprofit citizens organization, the Pennsylvania Economy League, rank ordered eleven states in 1971 according to the burden of state and local taxation on ten specific industries. There is no systematic correlation between this rank-ordering and the state unemployment rates; in fact, the lowest unemployment state (Indiana) was consistently found to be among the very *highest* tax burden states for most of the industries (Harrison 1974). Finally, a 300-equation econometric model of the Massachusetts economy, describing the period 1950 to 1972, has been constructed by George Treysz, Anne Friedlaender, and Richard Tresch. For fifteen of the sixteen major industries studied, there was no statistically significant relationship between quarter-to-quarter changes in Massachusetts's share of national employment and changes in the ratio of Massachusetts business taxes to the average for all states (Treysz, Friedlaender, and Tresch 1976).

Opportunity costs of business incentives

The tax revenues that governments must forego when tax related subsidies or credits ("tax expenditures") are legislated could have been used to purchase goods and services, thus putting people to work. Some quantitative estimates have been made of these costs.

Surrey estimates that in fiscal year 1968 the federal income tax deduction of the interest on state and municipal bonds cost the U.S. treasury about $1.8 billion (1970a). More recent figures calculated by the U.S. Office of Management and Budget for FY 1976 show that foregone federal revenues amounted to nearly $4.8 billion that year, with three-fourths of that accruing to corporations and only one-quarter to private individuals (U.S. Senate 1976).

In 1975, at the request of state Senator William Bulger, the then Massachusetts Commissioner of Taxation Nicholas Metaxas prepared an estimate of the annual revenue loss associated with that state's comprehensive business subsidy package known as Mass Incentives. The commissioner estimated that a 3 percent tax credit for the purchase of buildings and machinery cost the commonwealth $18 million in foregone revenue. A rollback on tangible property taxes cost another $25 million. Two different tax credits for payroll employment expansion cost about $12 million.

The elimination of sales taxes on the purchase of materials, fuel and machinery resulted in a state treasury loss of about $25 million. The commissioner was not able to estimate the cost of the four remaining subsidies in the Mass Incentives package. They include provisions exempting corporate personal property from local taxation, limiting corporate taxes to a percentage of business activity conducted in the state, providing for a carryover of a tax loss for five years, and permitting a firm that leased a plant from a publicly owned development corporation to receive a 3 percent investment credit.

The commonwealth thus sustained a loss of about $80 million in foregone revenues through the implementation of six out of ten tax incentives in fiscal year 1974. It is the estimate here that calculations performed for the other four incentives, especially the local personal property tax exemption, might well have brought the cost to over $100 million per annum.

A related problem has to do with the nature of the market for municipal bonds, whose tax free status makes them a widely used development tool. In recent years, commercial banks have come to hold almost two-thirds of all state and local industrial development bonds. Banks are very unstable customers; they tend to purchase tax exempt bonds when money is easy and they have met their obligations of a legally required reserve and satisfied the loan needs of their customers. When money becomes tight, banks will often raise net free reserves by selling or at least reducing the proportion of state and local securities held by them. State and local governments wishing to finance their capital projects in periods when banks are reducing their portfolio of state and local bonds have two choices: they can either offer to pay high interest rates on the bonds to attract other investors or, where possible, finance their project with short-term notes. But financing with short-term notes requires paying frequent and substantial underwriting charges which, when added to the already high interest rates, increases the taxpayers' burden. In addition, such short-term notes are only a temporary solution to a serious economic problem and are not themselves marketable when banks' free reserves are extremely limited.

Relative scale of the base against which the incentives are applied

Most of the business incentives studied, whatever their particular thrust (labor subsidies, investment credits, etc.), transfer the subsidy by reducing a company's tax burden. How important *are* state and local taxes as a percentage of the typical firm's cost of doing business? If this ratio is very small, then the application of even a large rate of subsidy to such a small base is unlikely to yield significant savings to most firms.

In the empirical literature, state and local taxes are consistently estimated at from 0.5 to 3 percent of value added and from 2 to 5 percent of sales (none of the studies measures taxes in relation to business *costs* per se). A 1954 study in New York showed state and local taxes to be 1 percent of value added (Campbell 1958). A study of the Washington State economy in 1963 found taxes as a percent of value added to range from 0.93 percent in the food industry to a high of 2.73 percent in fabricated metals (Washington State 1963). Recently the Federal Reserve Bank of Boston estimated that the average U.S. business paid 4.4 percent of its income to state and local governments (Eisenmenger et al. 1975).[7] Since corporate and unincorporated business income averages about one-eighth of value added, this translates into an average ratio of state and local taxes to value added of about six-tenths of one percent.

Perhaps even more important is the 1961 finding of J. A. Stockfish for the California Economic Development Agency that state and local taxes as a percentage of stockholders' equity varied among selected industries over seventeen states within a very narrow range: 3.9 percent (fabricated metals) to 6.4 percent (apparel).

Remember that a major objective of these various incentives is to impact relocation: to attract companies planning to make a *physical move* from one state to another (or, more generally, to open a branch in a new location). Evidence now exists that the incidence of such relocations or branchings is actually very small in the U.S.—whatever the causes. Between December, 1969, and December, 1972, according to an MIT-Harvard Joint Center for Urban Studies report using Dun and Bradstreet credit rating data on all manufacturing and most nonmanufacturing firms in the country, only about 0.3 percent of the jobs added to the economy and only about 0.2 percent of the jobs lost to the economy were in branch plants that made interstate moves, i.e. that appeared in or disappeared from a state during the period. In no state was the share of net job change in "moving" plants ever greater than 0.5 percent (Allaman and Birch 1975). This was, of course, a recessionary period, and forthcoming data through 1973 may show increased movement of plants. Nevertheless, the first empirical estimate of the size of the "game" which so many state officials have been trying to capture should give any analyst some food for thought.[8]

A note on national tax incentives

It has been shown that business taxes constitute a small percentage of total costs, and that the incentive rates applied to this small base are also very low, of political necessity. Finally, because the states are continually matching one another's incentive packages,

the de facto differential subsidies from one place to another are smaller still. It is not surprising, therefore, to find the empirical support for state tax (and related business development) incentives so weak.

But the evidence for *national* investment tax credits is mixed, as well. In a series of papers, economists associated with the Brookings Institution evaluated the impact of the 1962 federal investment tax credit, designed to stimulate the business sector's demand for capital goods and, therefore, the demand for labor. Half of the studies concluded that the credit worked. But half concluded that it did not affect output and employment at all (Fromm 1969). The U.S. Congressional Budget Office estimates that a $1 billion national corporate and personal income tax cut would—over the twenty-four months following its inception—create fewer jobs, have a smaller impact on the unemployment rate, and return fewer savings to the federal treasury (in the form of obviated welfare and unemployment compensation payments) than any alternative job-creation policy also costing $1 billion (public service employment, countercyclical revenue sharing, accelerated public works, or increased across-the-board government purchases) (Congressional Budget Office 1975). Most recently, in an analysis of both national and interregional investment incentives, two economists at the Federal Reserve Bank of Boston conclude that both tax credits and subsidized interest rates on loans are likely to be less efficacious than even accelerated depreciation allowances (Kopcke and Syron 1978). This is especially interesting in light of the publication in March of President Carter's long awaited urban policy, which places great weight on tax credits and subsidized business loans.

Conclusions and speculations

This research indicates that neither conventional economic theory nor the (admittedly limited) empirical evidence provide much support for the popular belief that states can significantly affect industrial expansion, relocation, or start-ups with the kind of incremental incentives they have been using. Yet the policies continue to be used—even when officials admit that they are unlikely to create jobs. What can explain this apparent inconsistency? Is it just a stubbornly irrational attachment to an outworn conventional wisdom? Or does the ubiquity of these business incentives suggest that they have some definite function after all, one which conventional economic analysis cannot grasp?

Although work on this question has just begun, there are indications that political-economic analysis does indeed suggest some systematic explanations for the existence of state business incentive policies. This concluding section presents a sketch of these explanations.

The short-run struggle over taxes and profits

The continuing struggle between capitalists and workers over access to and control over capital—and therefore over the distribution of the national income—is the central concern of radical political economists. That struggle is taking place in every institution of American life. It should not surprise anyone that it occurs as well at the statehouse.

In order to reproduce the system, governments must tax the business sector to help finance the production and delivery of public goods and services, many of which effectively redistribute real income from capitalists to workers. Not surprisingly, capitalists are constantly trying to resist this redistribution and to reverse it wherever possible. To assist them in this process, business firms employ paid lobbyists (as, of course, do the organized labor and consumer groups as well). But firms can also count on the assistance of many of the officials of the government agencies administering the many programs that affect business, and the legislators who vote upon them.[9] Where direct reductions in business taxes are politically unattainable, argues James Dumont, capitalists and their friends at court will seek the same redistribution to profits by the "back door" (1975). Tax and capital subsidies that do not actually compel companies to do anything differently serve this purpose admirably. The manifest function of state business incentives may be to create jobs, but the latent function is to increase profits at the expense of workers-consumers.

Some capitalists are remarkably frank about this. One representative of Jobs for Massachusetts, a prominent business lobbying group, told Dumont that he would prefer an outright cut in the state's corporate income tax rate, but since the former was hard to obtain, "tax incentives will have to do." Another lobbyist, who led the successful struggle for passage of the Massachusetts $500 job creation tax credit, admitted that his organization fully intended the credit to be a gift to companies, to compensate for the state's high tax rates.

Long-run economic growth and the shift to the "sunbelt"

The day-to-day struggles described above are taking place within a broader historical frame. Capitalist economic growth is by nature assymetric and unbalanced, following a process which has been described as "uneven development."[10] When capital (or systems of physical capital, like neighborhoods and even whole regions) becomes less profitable to employ, those who control the process of production begin to abandon it, in a kind of industrial emulation of the profligate slash-and-burn agriculture practiced by some traditional cultures. Those who are left behind are increasingly thrown upon the mercy of the public sector, to be supported by the taxpayers.

Bearse argues that uneven development explains much of the secular decline in the economic fortunes of the older industrial belt of the U.S. As markets, capital, and even new research and development shift their locus from the older region (with New York City as its political center) to the "newer" South and Southwest (with Texas as the potential new capital), the older places undergo secular deterioration. There is some evidence that the business incentives are in fact most readily available in these older areas. But—seen in this larger historical context—the idea of restoring the older areas' "comparative advantage" seems ludicrous. Besides, the new region can still afford to forego, e.g., high taxes, given the relatively lower standard of living that is consistent with its reproduction at this stage of its development. As public cost of reproduction rises over time, taxes and other costs of doing business will rise in the South and the West, too. But there is no reason to think that firms will then turn around and repopulate New England. Capitalist economic development is simply not that easily reversible. A more likely forecast would be for increased exporting of capital and jobs out of the country altogether.

This shifting of the center of economic activity away from the Northeast and North Central parts of the country (a shift which goes a long way in explaining the fiscal crisis of the older cities and states) has been supported and consciously promoted by the federal government, ever since the end of World War II. Public investments in infrastructure, military production contracts, and new bank charters have all been awarded increasingly to southern and southeastern capitalists, often at the expense of capitalists in the older regions (especially New York). In this context, state incentives to business in lagging areas have some of the character of welfare grants, serving at best to ease the pain associated with what for many business operations is becoming chronic poverty.

Conclusion: development and dependency

The conventional theory of local economic development is centered around the concept of the industry producing for export, thereby employing local workers and purchasing locally produced goods and (especially) services. Who owns and controls that exporting activity, and especially whether that ownership-control is "absentee," is pretty much ignored by this conventional wisdom. Because the payoff to capturing (or growing) such export base activity is believed to be so high, states and local governments engage in a ferocious competition for the thousand or so new plants built in this country each year. Among the major weapons in the arsenal of these protagonists are the business incentives studied in this article.

The conclusion was reached that there is neither

theoretical nor empirical support for the belief that interstate business incentive differentials make an important difference to the decisions of firms with respect to relocation, expansion, or start-up of new facilities. In this last part of the article, speculation was raised about some political-historical explanations of the continued deployment of what seem to be such ineffective instruments of policy. It remains to make the argument that, even if the incentive approach were successful, it would be misplaced.

The kind of economic development based upon the implantation of "foreign" capital into a state or other political community produces the same kind of dependency and unbalanced economic growth here in the rich United States as it has always done in the poor Third World. New plants that are controlled by outsiders impose enormous infrastructure costs on a community, import much of their labor (especially at the level of the "good jobs"), often house their highest-paid workers outside the taxing jurisdiction where the plant is situated, and then—after all the effort expanded to get them in the first place—often move away again to some other place when the local inducements run out.[11]

But, writes development planner Barry Stein:

There is an alternative. The true aim of economic development must be the self-renewing community based on the creation of a capability for continuing local action and a degree of self-reliance. This emphatically doesn't mean . . . self-sufficiency; that is both inappropriate and impossible in practice. . . . This approach to local development differs from more conventional ones in three ways. First, it creates an ongoing institutional capacity within the community to act on its own behalf, rather than to be "acted on." Second, criteria for evaluating alternative development options are related to increasing the community's retention and breadth of distribution of benefits created, and its control over its own affairs, rather than to increasing per capita income, employment per se, etc. Third, economic activities are oriented as much as is feasible toward replacement of imported goods and services by locally-produced ones (1974, p.86).

It is the planning and financing of such community based enterprises—owned wholly by local governments or in partnership with socially controlled private businesses—which should be getting the lion's share of the resources generated by state and local (and federal) taxes.[12] The present applications of such resources are—the evidence seems convincing—going largely to windfall profits for the business sector. Surely, that is at best a waste of scarce resources, and at worst a politically inequitable approach to the problem of regional economic development in the United States.

Notes

1. In economics textbook jargon, the marginal cost curve shifts to the right (downward), indicating that profits would now be maximized at a higher level of production—and therefore at a higher level of employment.
2. That is, the more "inelastic" the firm's product demand curve, with respect to price, the greater the firm's oligopoly power.
3. This is consistent with both an econometric estimate recently published by George Treysz, Anne Friedlaender, and Richard Tresch (1976), and with the fact that a state multiplier must be smaller than the corresponding *national* multiplier since the former economy is more open (has greater leakage from the flow of internal spending) than the latter economy. The U.S. eighteen to twenty-four month income multiplier is generally thought by most econometric model builders to be about 2.0.
4. A more recent study of firms moving facilities out of New York State, conducted for the Legislative Commission on Expenditure Review in 1974, shows a much greater sensitivity to taxes as a cost of doing business, with half of the respondents indicating taxes to be one factor in their relocation decision. But there is no way to be certain that taxes—or any other particular factor—really mattered (or were the critical factor that tipped the balance). It is possible that managers mention taxes either because discussion of taxes is in the air—certainly the case in New York in recent years—or because it is hoped that such mentions will induce states to lower business taxes—a self-fulfilling prophecy which does indeed occur in many places.
5. Research done on the state of Massachusetts by Margaret Dewar, a doctoral candidate in urban studies at MIT, reveals that another common incentive, the industrial revenue bond, has little impact on business location decisions. Personal interviews with fourteen business executives from firms that had used the bonds revealed that a lack of space or other type of inefficiency in an existing plant was the most important reason behind the decision to move or expand. Only three of the fourteen managers who were questioned voluntarily cited revenue bonds as influencing the choice of a site within a region.
6. The results of the interviews are contained in a memo written by David Knisely and Jeffrey Simon to Massachusetts State senators Allan R. McKinnon and William Bulger in 1975.
7. This estimate for 1973 breaks down into 0.9 percent going to pay corporate income taxes, 1.9 percent for property taxes, 0.8 percent for unemployment compensation contributions, and 0.8 percent for "other business taxes."
8. Of course, these kinds of measures, while accurately counting actual openings and closings of branch plants in any period, do not give a dynamic picture of the long-term *process* of investment or disinvestment. The latter in particular has become increasingly interesting to planners, especially in the northern industrial belt. Disinvestment—the failure to replace depreciating physical capital, gradually reducing the productive capacity of a plant (or public structure or movie theater)—may continue for many years before the firm actually shuts the place down.
9. Bearse (1976) observes that some capitalists are better organized than others to engage in this struggle. Thus "it should be no surprise to anyone that development programs are biased towards established industry, larger firms, low-risk debt finance and manufacturing. Any stroll through state legislative chambers will show that these are the better organized, articulate political interests" (p.39).

10. Friedrich Engels, for example, described the process of growth in a capitalistic society as a vicious circle with "overproduction, glutting of the market, crises every ten years" (Engels 1935). Other authors, including Joseph Schumpeter and Gunnar Myrdal, have considered the spatial consequences behind one aspect of this vicious circle. Schumpeter observes, "if the industry of a country is financed by another country and if a wave of prosperity sweeps over the latter, which offers capital more profitable than it has found hitherto in the former country, then there will exist a tendency to withdraw capital from its previous investments. If this happens quickly and inconsiderately it can result in a crisis in the first country. . . . Obviously this can happen . . . also between different parts of one country . . . "(1934, p.221). Also see Myrdal (1957), especially chapter 3, "The Drift towards Regional Economic Inequalities in a Country." A more recent analysis of regional uneven development in capitalist economies is Holland (1976).

11. Two useful essays on dependency theory are Amin (1977) and Fusfeld (1973).

12. For a review of some North American experiments with local public enterprise, see Case, Goldberg, and Shearer (1976).

References

Allaman, Peter M., and Birch, David L. 1975. *Components of employment change for metropolitan and rural areas in the U.S. by industry group: 1970-1972.* Cambridge, Mass.: Joint Center for Urban Studies of MIT and Harvard.

Amin, Samir. 1977. *Unequal development.* New York: Monthly Review Press.

Bearse, Peter. 1976. Government as innovator: a new paradigm for state economic development policy. *New England Journal of Business and Economics* 2, 2: 34-54.

Bergin, Thomas, and Eagan, William. 1961. Economic growth and community facilities. *Municipal Finance* 133, 47: 146-49.

Bergsman, Joel; Greenston, Peter; and Healy, Robert. 1972. The agglomeration process in urban growth. *Urban Studies* 9, 3: 263-88.

Bloom, C. C. 1955. *State and local tax differentials.* Iowa City: State University of Iowa.

Campbell, A. K. 1958. Taxes and industrial location within the New York metropolitan region. *National Tax Journal* 10, 4: 195-218.

———. 1969. Taxation and industrial location. In *Comparative total tax loads of selected manufacturers,* ed. D. Soule. Lexington: University of Kentucky.

Case, John; Goldberg, Leonard; and Shearer, Derek. 1976. State business. *Working Papers for a New Society* spring: 67-75.

Chiang, Alpha. 1974. *Fundamental methods of mathematical economics.* New York: McGraw-Hill.

Congressional Budget Office. 1975. *Temporary measures to stimulate employment: an evaluation of some alternatives.* Washington, D.C.: U.S. Government Printing Office.

Daniels, Belden. 1974. *There is no equity.* Cambridge, Mass.: Center for Community Economic Development.

Doeringer, Peter B., and Piore, Michael J. 1971. *Internal labor markets and manpower analysis.* Lexington, Mass.: D.C. Heath.

Due, John. 1961. Studies of state-local tax influences in location of industry. *National Tax Journal* 2, 3: 163-73.

Dumont, James. 1975. State economic development: Massachusetts and Connecticut. Senior honors thesis in public administration. Mimeographed. Harvard University.

Eisenmenger, Robert; Munnell, Alicia; Poskanzer, Joan; Syron, Richard; and Weiss, Steven. 1975. *Options for fiscal structure reform in Massachusetts.* Research Report no. 57. Boston: Federal Reserve Bank of Boston.

Engels, Friedrich. 1935 edition. *Socialism: utopian and scientific.* New York: International Publishers.

Fromm, Gary, ed. 1969. *Tax incentives and capital spending.* Washington, D.C.: The Brookings Institution.

Fusfeld, Daniel. 1973. *The basic economics of the urban racial crisis.* Chicago: Holt, Rinehart and Winston.

Hamilton, F. E. Ian, ed. 1974. *Spatial perspectives on industrial organization and decision-making.* New York: John Wiley.

Hammermesh, Daniel. Forthcoming. Subsidized job creation in the private sector. In *Job-creation,* ed. John Palmer. Washington, D.C.: The Brookings Institution.

Harrison, Bennett. 1972. *Education, training, and the urban ghetto.* Baltimore: Johns Hopkins University Press.

———. 1974. *The economic development of Massachusetts.* Boston: Joint Committee on Commerce and Labor, Massachusetts Legislature.

Harrison, Bennett, and Hill, Edward. 1978. The changing structure of jobs in older and younger cities. In *Central city economic development,* ed. Benjamin Chinitz. Binghamton: Center for Social Analysis, State University of New York.

Holland, Stuart. 1976. *Capital versus the regions.* London: St. Martins. *Industrial Development.* 1978. 147, 1.

Kopcke, Richard W., and Syron, Richard F. 1978. Tax incentives: their impact on investment decisions and their cost to the treasury. *New England Economic Review* Jan.-Feb.: 19-32.

McMillan, Thomas. 1965. Why manufacturers choose plant locations. *Land Economics* 41, 1: 239-46.

Myrdal, Gunnar. 1957. *Economic theory and underdeveloped regions.* London: Duckworth and Co.

Schmenner, Roger. 1978. Industrial location and urban public management. In *Urban growth and development,* ed. Arthur P. Solomon. Cambridge, Mass.: Joint Center for Urban Studies of MIT and Harvard.

Schumpeter, Joseph. 1934. *The theory of economic development.* Cambridge, Mass.: Harvard University Press.

Sherer, F. M. 1970. *Industrial market structure and economic performance.* Chicago: Rand McNally.

Spiegelman, Robert. 1964. Location characteristics in footloose industries. *Land Economics* 40, 1: 79-86.

Stein, Barry. 1974. *Size, efficiency, and community enterprise.* Cambridge, Mass.: Center for Community Economic Development.

Stockfish, J. A. 1961. *A study of California's tax treatment of manufacturing industry.* Sacramento: California Economic Development Agency.

Strazheim, Mahlon. 1971. An introduction and overview of regional money capital markets. In *Essays in regional economics,* eds. John F. Kain and John R. Meyer. Cambridge, Mass.: Harvard University Press.

Surrey, Stanley. 1970a. Tax incentives as a device for implementing government policy. *Harvard Law Review* 83, 4: 705-38.

———. 1970b. Federal income tax reforms: replacing tax expenditures with direct government assistance. *Harvard Law Review* 84, 2: 352-408.

Survey Research Center. 1950. *Industrial mobility in Michigan.* Ann Arbor: University of Michigan.

Thompson, Wilbur, R., and Mattila, John. 1959. *State industrial development.* Detroit: Wayne State University Press.

Treysz, George; Friedlaender, Anne; and Tresch, Richard. 1976. An overview of a quarterly econometric model of Massachusetts and its fiscal structure. *New England Journal of Business and Economics* 1, 1: 57-72.

U.S., Department of Commerce. 1975. *Industrial location determinants.* Washington, D.C.: U.S. Government Printing Office.

U.S., Senate, Committee on the Budget. 1976. *Tax expenditures.* Washington, D.C.: U.S. Government Printing Office.

"The Political Economy of States' Job-Creation Business Incentives" is reprinted by permission of the *Journal of the American Institute of Planners,* October, 1978.

The BIG Giveaway
TAX ABATEMENT

Ohio taxpayers are being nickeled and dimed to death in the name of industrial development. And, it's going to get worse unless the Ohio Legislature and Governor Rhodes put a halt to this charade that allows business to avoid taxes with no questions asked.

Tax abatement (or tax incentives, which are the same thing) is of particular concern to local and state officials and school leaders who are hard-pressed to maintain vital services. In the case of schools, of course, we're seeing Ohio primary and secondary education systems shut down because of no money.

For several reasons, many people, when they hear the words "tax abatement," equate it with industrial and business development in Ohio. Nothing could be further from the truth. In actuality, study after study and tax expert after tax expert have demonstrated that tax abatement and business development have little or nothing to do with one another.

In fact, tax abatement can have the opposite effect: If enough services are cut or eliminated and schools close because of lack of industrial and business tax revenues, the very reasons that business decides to re-locate or expand to a certain area will disappear.

Businessmen and industrialists themselves will testify that they want their new plants and offices in areas where vital public services — the most important being education — are kept at a high level. With tax abatement, it is difficult to stretch fewer dollars to keep police and fire protection, lighting and other essential city services operating.

There are several forms of tax abatement, but the two which have attracted the most attention are the so-called "impacted cities act" and reduction in business personal property taxes.

The first allows city councils to declare certain areas "blighted" and forgive businesses that construct buildings in the areas any increased property taxes. The reduced tax liabilities are granted for up to 20 years.

Remember late last year when Cleveland couldn't pay its teachers because it had run out of money? The same year saw Cleveland City Council grant three businesses nearly $21 million in tax abatement. These tax losses will be spread over a number of years, but annual losses will average well over $1 million.

When Nationwide Insurance built its new world headquarters across the street from its old office building in Columbus, few people were surprised. It was a logical place to build it, and had been planned for years. Yet, giant Nationwide received tax abatement amounting to $20 million over 20 years for constructing a building. Columbus, without passage of a levy, predicts their schools will close this fall.

Dayton has used tax abatement more than any other Ohio city. Yet, it's certain that Dayton Power and Light Co. would not have moved its headquarters from Dayton, or that Mead Corp. would not have thought of uprooting its employes from that city if tax abatement had not been granted. Yet, these two profitable firms and five others have received tax abatement totaling $20 million.

A trend has started in Ohio cities. Nothing is being built in prime downtown locations unless tax abatements are granted. But, downtown is where the high cost of services are incurred. So, instead of business paying, residents get stuck with the bill of providing downtown services for rich corporations.

A second form of "tax abatement" is the recent legislation reducing personal property taxes for business. But, this was not "tax abatement," it was an outright tax cut since these reduced taxes are permanent.

The personal property tax, which yields about a third of local property taxes, can be an unfair tax since businesses have to pay even if they are operating at a loss. The Ohio AFL-CIO supports repeal of this form of tax, but only if business agrees to replace it with another tax so local communities do not suffer.

Business, however, has not shown any willingness to substitute a fairer tax for the personal property tax. They only want to reduce the personal property tax and shift their tax burden to other taxpayers.

So, in the name of attracting new industry Gov. Rhodes and the Legislature have given a further reduction in the personal property tax, with no requirement that this form of "tax abatement" be tied to jobs. Passage of H.B. 828 in 1977 will cost the state $60 million annually since it will have to make up the tax loss to local government.

If tax abatement, as preached by Gov. Rhodes, is carried to its logical conclusion, states will continue to offer more and more incentives to attract business — at your expense, of course. Already, as a result of H.B. 828, Chrysler Corp. is threatening to move one of its Michigan plants to Ohio if that state doesn't come up with a set of more and better tax breaks.

United Auto Worker President Douglas Fraser has called this ploy "industrial blackmail."

If states compete for business with tax breaks, the "bottom line" will become ZERO for business taxes in all states. Tax abatements occur over a period of time and the tax burden shift from business to wage earners is gradual. But as taxpayers revolt and refuse to pay higher taxes, services deteriorate and the people and business both suffer — something business leaders in Ohio ought to think about before going back to the Legislature for more tax breaks.

"Tax Abatement: The Big Giveaway" is reprinted by permission from the March, 1978, issue of *Focus,* Ohio AFL-CIO.

CHAPTER 20

Taxing Corporate Profits

Taxing corporate profits sounds a lot easier in the legislature when tax laws are written than it is when tax auditors have to pour over a corporation's records. **A Tussle over Taxes: Business v. States** by Linda Hudak cites example after example of cases where complex accounting maneuvers have allowed large corporations to escape state corporate tax laws. Only with great technical skills and a political commitment to make sure that big business pays its fair share can state and local governments hope to solve this problem.

One solution to the corporate tax shell game is vividly described in Larry Gonick's **How the Corporation Dodged Its Taxes—an Unjust-so Story,** published here for the first time. Because giant corporations, often with hundreds of subsidiaries across the country and around the world, have been able to hide profits from state tax collectors, many states are moving towards what is called the "unitary" method.

"In this method," the cartoon explains, "state auditors completely ignore a company's tangle of subsidiaries and treat the whole business as a single unit." Thus, a myriad of complex accounting techniques for avoiding taxes become impossible.

In testimony submitted to the Missouri Legislature, Jonathan Rowe, then with the Multi-State Tax Commission, makes the case against what are called "weighted factor formulas", in a **Statement for Missouri Legislature Concerning Bill To Establish Uniform Rules for Corporations Reporting Income to Missouri.** In recent years a number of states, particularly in the northeast, have adopted such policies (similar to tax abatements) designed to attract business to their states. As Rowe points out, instead of really benefitting the states, such gimmicks reduce business taxes throughout the country, without giving individual states any particular advantage.

An alternative to taxing corporate profits that is gaining favor with big business is the "value added" tax. Much like a sales tax, a VAT generally is less progressive than other options. **VAT: It's Broccoli, My Dear,** an article from *Tax Notes* by Charles Kingson, offers a critique of a proposal by Senator Russell Long for a federal VAT which can be applied equally to the states. In response to the observation that the VAT is "painless," Mr. Kingson quotes an Italian who observed that "Painless means that the rich manage to have the poor pay the taxes without the poor noticing it." Michigan is the first state to adopt a VAT-style tax. It is evaluated by Allen Schenk in **The Michigan Single Business Tax: A State Value Added Tax?** Replacing taxes levied on corporate income, on the privilege of doing business, on inventory and intangibles, the Michigan SBT, according to Mr. Schenk, shifted the burden from incorporated to unincorporated businesses, from highly profitable to less profitable businesses, and from owners of property to employers of labor.

A Tussle Over Taxes: Business vs. the States

By Linda Hudak

IN 1972 ALASKA'S Cook Inlet oil fields produced more than $16 million in profits. No fewer than 34 oil companies were scurrying from the Arctic Circle to the Yukon, drilling, extracting crude oil, laying pipeline and staking claim to a portion of Alaska's vast oil wealth. Yet only two of the companies paid any income taxes to the state that year.

"We decided it was time for, some reforms," recalls Sterling Gallagher, Alaska's revenue commissioner. So Alaska hit the companies where it hurts — in their accounting techniques.

It required use of a method known as "unitary" accounting, which holds that if a multistate or multinational company operates as a single economic entity, with all of its operations contributing to income, then it is taxed as such. The technique, therefore, divides a company's total income among all the states and countries where it does business, and each then can tax its share of the total. Among other things, this prevents companies from switching income earned in one state or country to others with lower tax rates or no income tax at all.

That did the trick. By the following year, 32 oil companies suddenly were paying income taxes to Alaska.

"They certainly weren't overjoyed," Gallagher says, "but they knew they owed us the money, and they paid." Today, he estimates, this accounting reform is producing $10 million a year more for Alaska than would have come in under the old "separate" accounting method, which looks at only the income companies report as directly earned by their operations in a state.

The Alaska experience is just one example of a growing determination in many states to prevent businesses from eluding taxes. In some cases this means crackdowns on illegal tax evaders, in others accounting reforms to curb legal tax avoidance, in still others both.

Almost every state could be collecting substantially more revenue from businesses, according to the Multistate Tax Commission, a 19-state compact created in 1967 to conduct joint audits of large corporations and otherwise crack down on business taxes. While corporations paid $6.6 billion in state income taxes in 1975, the commission estimates that an additional $1 billion to $3 billion went uncollected. Separately, up to 5 percent of state and local sales taxes may illegally elude collection each year, according to University of Illinois tax authority John Due — a loss of up to $1 billion a year.

Hudak is a former legislative director for a national consumer group and has worked on energy legislation for the state of Wisconsin.

Texas, for example, began going after illegal tax evasion in 1973 after a legislative investigation had revealed 70,000 sales tax delinquencies totaling more than $60 million over the preceding decade. The report had found that taxpayers "presently do not feel in jeopardy for failure to file and pay."

A new state comptroller, Bob Bullock, wasted no time in changing their minds. Shortly after taking office, he embarked on a series of well-publicized tax raids, personally closing delinquent businesses and seizing their property to put it up for sale at public auction.

The comptroller kicked off the campaign with a Wild West-style raid on a San Antonio liquor store whose proprietor owed $405,000 in back taxes. Flanked by television reporters and gesturing at a waiting U-Haul truck, Bullock strode into the store and demanded either the taxes or the bottles of booze. The owner pulled out his wallet and drawled, "I don't have the cash." At that reply, state revenue agents seized 20 van loads of liquor and carted them away. Nearly 600 businesses were closed during the three-month campaign.

"The raids were real attention-getters and drastically increased voluntary compliance with the sales tax," according to Bill Collier, an aide to the Texas comptroller, "In Houston, a man came up to Bullock and gave him a check for a $15,000 delinquency that hadn't even shown up on the computer."

With these operations under his belt, Bullock convinced the legislature that investing in tax enforcement made good economic sense. The legislature more than doubled his 1976-77 budget to $70.3 million in return for a pledge to collect an additional $100 million in tax revenue above the increase anticipated from growth and inflation.

To meet this goal Bullock increased his staff to 420 auditors, computerized numerous clerical operations and leased a plane to fly his staff around the country to audit out-of-state corporations. As a result, he topped his quota by more than $10 million. Sales tax collected from out-of-state corporations alone jumped from $15 million in 1974 to $80.2 million in 1977. The state is currently getting a return of $10 for every $1 spent on audit and enforcement activities.

Other states have strengthened enforcement in quieter ways. Virginia, for example, began a corporate audit program in 1973 with 10 auditors. Despite this small staff, it was able to collect $1.7 million in additional revenue that first year, according to William West, supervisor of corporate income taxes. In 1976 the audit program had identified and collected $5.5 million in back taxes.

The Delaware Dispute

IN DELAWARE, for example, the state has collected no income tax since 1971 from the Getty Oil subsidiary that operates a refinery there. Although the parent Getty corporation earns about a quarter of a billion dollars a year worldwide, it has reported no taxable income for the past seven years for the operations of its only East Coast refinery, in Delaware City.

A number of observers suspect that the company has been engaging in such a transfer-pricing manipulation, called "downstreaming" in the oil industry, in which a company's foreign producing and transporting subsidiaries overcharge the same company's U.S. refinery for crude oil.

In the view of Thomas Field, a former Treasury Department tax attorney who is currently director of Tax Analysts and Advocates, a Washington-based public interest group, "For each dollar that goes out of Delaware through downstreaming, the state loses about 7 cents and the federal government loses about 44 cents. It would be a fair inference that Delaware and the United States have financed Getty's North Sea operations."

In an interview with Delaware Today magazine, however, Tom Clarke, tax manager of Getty's Delaware subsidiary, said that Getty was not "downstreaming" and stated that the company has paid standard rates for its crude oil and tanker services.

The state made no major move to find a way of taxing Getty until early 1975, when Delaware public school teachers and custodians were demanding a wage increase and the state was faced with a budget crunch. In an attempt to extract additional tax revenue from Getty, then-Gov. Sherman Tribbett proposed a 3-mill-per-gallon "through-put" tax on crude oil shipped to the Getty refinery. The legislature embraced the idea so enthusiastically that they more than tripled the tax rate before passing the measure. But their enthusiasm was short-lived.

Within hours, according to some reports, Getty officials threatened to shut down their Delaware operations if the tax was implemented. Getty employes went to the capitol to lobby for their jobs. Several weeks later the governor vetoed the tax measure he had initiated.

After this incident, the state resumed its attempts to obtain audit information on the Getty refinery operations. The IRS signed an agreement with the state promising to provide copies of federal audits of Getty. Thus far, however, the IRS has not been able to supply any audits which are current enough to be of use to the state, according to John Sullivan, Delaware's revenue commissioner.

"We can't do anything until we obtain more recent audit information, and this won't be available until the IRS settles the unresolved questions in its current audits," he says. The state doesn't have the resources to conduct its own audit of Getty.

Ted Keller, head of the Delaware Citizens Coalition for Tax Reform, believes that the state should have been collecting between $5.8 million and $7.2 million annually in income taxes from Getty. Keller believes that if Delaware required unitary apportionment, it would have collected most of this revenue. Sullivan, however, doesn't think it's that easy. "Perhaps that's right," he said, "but we really

don't know; there's not enough information to make that determination."

How prevalent is the oil company practice of downstreaming its profits? No one knows for sure, but there seem to be a number of examples.

Georgia, for instance, is currently involved in a dispute with an unidentified oil company over allegedly downstreaming its Georgia income. The company itself brought the case to the attention of revenue officials when it claimed an $80,000 tax refund despite its position as a major gas retailer in the state. Officials were suspicious and, according to Tom Harrold, Georgia's deputy commissioner for revenue, a subsequent audit revealed that the company was downstreaming its Georgia income by assigning all its profits to Texas, a state which does not tax income from producing oil wells.

The Georgia audit concluded that rather than the state owing the company a refund, the company owed the state $1.3 million in back taxes. The company offerred to settle for $600,000, according to Harrold, but the state refused and the parties are still negotiating. If Georgia law authorized the use of unitary opportionment, Harrold says, "it would greatly strengthen our arsenal" of legal tools.

It has certainly strengthened the tools of the Multistate Tax Commission, which has proved exceedingly profitable for its members. Its dollar return on investment for the years 1973-77 was 12 to 1, and for 1977 alone the ratio was 31 to 1. Some states have enjoyed enormous dollar returns, including Kansas, with 55 to 1, and Idaho, with 34 to 1.

A Pair of Challenges

THE RISE of the commission is only one sign of the continuing struggle between the business community and a group of states with aggressive tax-enforcement programs. Thus far the states have won most of the major confrontations, including a recently decided battle involving a suit filed in 1972 by U.S. Steel, Procter & Gamble, ITT and other corporations challenging the constitutionality of the commission. A number of large companies had refused to give the commission access to their financial records until the suit was resolved.

The litigation dragged on for six years, but the Supreme Court finally settled the question last February when it ruled in favor of the 19-state compact.

"The climate changed dramatically after the Supreme Court decision," according to Gene Corrigan, the commission's executive director. "Business leaders now have to admit our legitimacy." U.S. Steel's Bodfish concurs: "This is now the law of the land, and we accept it."

Another major business challenge came in a recent legislative battle over a provision in the proposed U.S.-British tax treaty. It would have barred the states from using the unitary approach with British-based multinationals and probably would have led to demands for similar treatment by businesses based in other nations.

"Resorting to the treaty process to achieve the unitary restriction was a stroke of strategic genius for the corporations," according to Jonathan Rowe, deputy director of the multistate commission. "The Treasury was able to bargain away state revenue without sacrificing a dime of its own, he explained; furthermore, a treaty, once ratified, would be more difficult to amend than legislation.

The states received no warning that the tax issue had been included in the treaty negotiations, and they were furious. "What really made us angry," says Georgia's Harrold, "was that the Treasury tried to negotiate a state issue without getting any state input or even letting us know it was being discussed."

States felt that after tackling the corporate audit problem on their own and developing an innovative solution, the Treasury was now telling them to go back to a technique that had proved ineffective.

Out-of-State Headquarters

THE FIRST YEARS of enforcement and audit operations usually show the most dramatic revenue increases; it's often a matter of just dropping by to pick up the check. But tax collectors are soon faced with more sophisticated problems.

When Byron Dorgan was appointed tax commissioner of North Dakota in 1969, he discovered that more than 20 percent of the corporations doing business in the state were not even registered to pay taxes. "It was easy at first to send an auditor to the corner gas station or the mom and pop store in Grand Forks," Dorgan explains. "But we soon recognized that there was a more serious problem. North Dakota — and most other states — had never bothered to send auditors to headquarters of the big corporations in Chicago or New York."

When the state finally set up an out-of-state corporate audit program, the number of companies filing returns in the state almost doubled. By 1977 the state had collected an additional $20 million in income tax revenue, which was used to reduce its sales tax and add to the state surplus. The state's annual dollar return on its tax enforcement investment has been 35 to 1.

One of North Dakota's most successful cases involved AT&T's manufacturing arm, Western Electric. The company, which received a federal contract to design and install equipment at the Safeguard anti-ballistic missile base near Grand Forks, had refused to pay sales tax on its purchases, claiming that it was acting as an agent of the federal government and was therefore exempt. The state challenged the exemption, but when the case went to court, the federal government formally joined with Western Electric. It appeared that the state had been outmaneuvered.

But Dorgan turned the tables by unearthing a long-forgotten 1955 Pentagon document stating that companies could not avoid state taxes because they were acting under federal contracts. Western Electric ended up paying more than $4 million.

Auditing Cargill, the multinational grain company, presented North Dakota officials with different challenges. In a brief filed in federal court, state auditors detailed numerous frustrating trips to Cargill's Minnesota headquarters several hundred miles away. Typically, they said, they were told that the company hadn't had the time to put together requested information or that documents couldn't

be located. Once, they testified, Cargill's state tax administrator threatened to throw them out of his office, a charge he denied.

The state's difficulty in auditing multistate companies led Dorgan to active involvement in the Multistate Tax Commission and its joint audits. The joint audits are designed, for one thing, to prevent corporations from using conflicting reporting practices with different states to escape taxation.

One case currently in litigation, for example, involves Montgomery Ward & Co. and the interest income it received from loans to its parent company, Marcor, and to its subsidiaries. Arkansas officials have charged in court papers that Ward's had been reporting to the state that this was non-business income taxable only in its home state of Illinois, but reporting it to Illinois as ordinary business income which is apportionable among all the states — including Arkansas — where the corporation does business. Montgomery Ward officials disagree with the contention that they were reporting different things to different states and explain that a special provision in Illinois law permits these reporting procedures. Arkansas' complaint is that because of the lack of uniformity in reporting practices, some corporate income is slipping through the cracks and is not taxed by any state.

Unitary Accounting

A MAJOR POINT of difference between the states and the corporations is the unitary accounting procedure used in the multistate commission's audits, as opposed to the separate accounting method favored by the Internal Revenue Service.

California, which has taken pride in developing its own expertise on tax matters rather than depending on the IRS, was the first state to initiate wide use of the unitary technique. The method has proved especially helpful in collecting taxes from the motion picture industry.

Members of the film industry have been known to avoid taxes in the following way: A film is produced for, say, $10 million and earns that sum or less in U.S. sales. The company reports no earnings. Then, when the film is distributed overseas, the owners claim that all the profits are earned abroad and therefore are not subject to state taxation.

The unitary approach, which uses a formula involving a company's total property, payroll and sales to determine how much a state may tax, ends this practice for the film industry and many others doing business in California.

The state estimates that use of the unitary approach has boosted its revenues by about $100 million annually. It is currently litigating a number of cases under the unitary method, including a $4.3 million claim against U.S. Steel, a $12.6 million case against Mobil Oil and a $26.4 million dispute with Gulf Oil.

Unitary accounting is not much in favor among businesses, particularly multinational corporations. James Bodfish, general manager of taxes for U.S. Steel, for example, contends that by using a company's worldwide income as a base for tax assessments, the unitary method allows states to tax foreign operations "for which they provide no services."

But proponents of the unitary method maintain that this misses the point, that the method is designed to prevent companies from shifting high-tax U.S. income to foreign subsidiaries taxed at lower rates, if they are taxed at all.

This is often accomplished by having a foreign subsidiary overcharge its own domestic subsidiary in transactions between the two. Under the separate accounting method, it is exceedingly difficult for auditors to detect such transactions, requiring them to sift through a gargantuan number of invoices and to determine the market prices of such items as patented production processes and new drugs.

The Treasury's own studies had concluded that the separate accounting method "would strain the administrative capability of many states," and that, in fact, it fails 40 percent of the time the IRS itself tries to use it.

Some states contended that use of the unitary method has certain advantages for businesses. "The unitary method is inherently fairer," explains Jim Hamilton, assistant chief counsel of California's Franchise Tax Board, "because it is based on one set of principles that are applied to all businesses, while separate accounting subjects each case to individual negotiations and unpredictable settlements."

The multinationals argued that the separate accounting method was the international norm. "So are hunger and poverty," retorted the multistate commission's Rowe, "but that doesn't make them U.S. policy objectives."

With Sen. Frank Church (D-Idaho) leading the fight, a coalition of liberals and states' rights conservatives convinced the Senate to strike the state taxation restriction from the treaty.

Although use of the unitary method has produced a bonanza for some states, there is no consensus on using it because, as one southeastern state official explains, "the unitary concept is a volatile political issue — it's considered antibusiness. We're trying to attract companies to our state, and even though the unitary method might bring us more revenue, there's no way we'd require its use."

No one contends that corporations should pay more than their fair share of taxes. The controversy centers on changing state tax laws to prohibit tax avoidance techniques which are currently legal and to require more effective methods of enforcing laws already on the books. As Thomas Field of Tax Analysts and Advocates remarks, corporations "are entitled to rip off the state until the state stops them. If there is any ethical problem, it is the problem of the people who are letting them get away with it."

"A Tussle Over Taxes: Business *vs*. The States" is reprinted by permission from the August 13, 1978, issue of *The Washington Post*.

HOW THE CORPORATION DODGED ITS TAXES

AN UNJUST-SO STORY

I DON'T JUST SIT ON MY HANDS!

IT PLEADS POVERTY!!

ONCE UPON A TIME, THERE WAS A COMPANY CALLED THE AMALGAMATED GIGANTIC CORPORATION. AMALGAMATED GIGANTIC, OR "ALGI" FOR SHORT, HAD SUBSIDIARIES DOING BUSINESS IN MOST STATES OF THE UNION, CANADA, MEXICO, BRITAIN, FRANCE, GERMANY, IRAN, VENEZUELA, THE CAYMAN ISLANDS, AND MANY OTHER PLACES TOO NUMEROUS TO MENTION!!

BUT TAX OFFICIALS IN ONE WESTERN STATE COULDN'T HELP BUT NOTICE SOMETHING *STRANGE* ABOUT ALGI : ALTHOUGH IT MAINTAINED 17 FACTORIES, 21 REFINERIES, 51 WAREHOUSES, AND 1318 RETAIL OUTLETS IN THE STATE, THE CORPULENT CORPORATION NEVER PAID A CENT IN STATE INCOME TAX! HOW COULD THIS BE ?

TRANSFER PRICING

THE REASON WAS A SIMPLE TRICK CALLED "TRANFER PRICING", BY WHICH ALGI'S SUBSIDIARIES SOLD PRODUCTS TO EACH OTHER AT PRICES ESPECIALLY RIGGED TO AVOID TAXES. HERE'S HOW IT WORKED IN ALGI'S WORLDWIDE WIDGET TRADE:

FIRST, ALGI'S SUBSIDIARY IN OUTER MOLDAVIA BOUGHT WIDGETS FOR $3 EACH AND SOLD THEM, ALSO FOR $3, TO THE ALGI UNIT IN HONDORICO, A COUNTRY WITH NO CORPORATE INCOME TAX.

ALGI OF HONDORICO MARKED UP THE WIDGETS TO $6— TAKING AN UNTAXED PROFIT OF $3 APIECE—AND SOLD THEM TO THE ALGI SUBSIDIARY IN OUR LARGE WESTERN STATE. THERE THE WIDGETS RETAIL FOR $5 EACH, A "LOSS" OF $1.

SNIF POOR ME!!

BY SELLING $3 WIDGETS FOR $5, AMALGAMATED GIGANTIC MADE AN OVERALL PROFIT OF $2 PER WIDGET, BUT WITH CAREFULLY CHOSEN "TRANSFER PRICES", THE COMPANY TOOK ALL THE PROFIT IN TAX-FREE HONDORICO, WHILE SHOWING A LOSS IN THE WESTERN STATE!

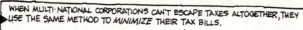

WHEN MULTI-NATIONAL CORPORATIONS CAN'T ESCAPE TAXES ALTOGETHER, THEY USE THE SAME METHOD TO *MINIMIZE* THEIR TAX BILLS.

OIL COMPANIES, FOR EXAMPLE, GENERALLY TAKE MOST OF THEIR PROFIT "AT THE WELLHEAD" IN ORDER TO TAKE ADVANTAGE OF BREAKS LIKE THE OIL DEPLETION ALLOWANCE OR THE FOREIGN TAX CREDIT. THE SAME GAME ALSO WORKS AT THE INTERSTATE LEVEL, WHERE COMPANIES TRY TO TAKE AS MUCH PROFIT AS POSSIBLE IN STATES WITHOUT AN INCOME TAX.

BESIDES TRANSFER PRICING, ALGI HAS OTHER WAYS OF SHIFTING PROFITS AMONG SUBSIDIARIES, LIKE HAVING ONE UNIT "BORROW" MONEY FROM ANOTHER, THEN DEDUCT THE INTEREST PAYMENTS FROM TAXABLE INCOME.

BY CONTRAST, SMALL BUSINESSES, WITHOUT STRINGS OF SUBSIDIARIES, CAN'T USE THESE TRICKS AND MUST PAY TAXES ON WHAT THEY ACTUALLY EARN.

OF COURSE, NOT EVERYONE CAN KEEP ONE END OVER THE STATE LINE!!

THE ARM'S LENGTH METHOD IS THE

APPROACH CURRENTLY USED BY THE INTERNAL REVENUE SERVICE IN ITS ATTEMPTS TO PREVENT TRANSFER-PRICING ABUSE. THE I.R.S. EXAMINES *ALL* TRANSACTIONS AMONG A CORPORATION'S SUBSIDIARIES, AND READJUSTS PRICES TO THOSE WHICH WOULD BE PAID "AT ARM'S LENGTH," I.E., ON THE FREE MARKET BETWEEN UNRELATED COMPANIES.
   THIS METHOD HAS TWO MAIN FLAWS:

   1) IT REQUIRES AN ARMY OF EXPERT AUDITORS AND ECONOMISTS, WHICH MOST STATES CAN'T AFFORD.

   2) IT JUST *DOESN'T WORK.* IN MANY CASES (40%, BY I.R.S. ESTIMATE), A "FREE MARKET" PRICE *DOESN'T EXIST,* BECAUSE A FREE MARKET DOESN'T EXIST. THE OIL INDUSTRY IS A PRIME EXAMPLE.

ARM'S LENGTH? DEPENDS ON WHICH ARM!

③

① AS WE HAVE SEEN, MULTI-NATIONALS' "FOREIGN INCOME" IS OFTEN THE RESULT OF FUND-JUGGLING AMONG SUBSIDIARIES.

IT'S UNCONSTITUTIONAL FOR THE STATES TO TAX INCOME THAT'S REALLY FOREIGN, AND THE SUPREME COURT HAS HELD *REPEATEDLY* THAT THE UNITARY METHOD DOES NOT VIOLATE THIS PROHIBITION.

OF COURSE, ALL THIS DODGING IS VERY TAXING!" HEH HEH

② THE UNITARY METHOD IS IMMENSELY SIMPLER THAN THE ARM'S-LENGTH SYSTEM CURRENTLY IN USE. COMPANIES SAY THAT THEY WOULD BE FORCED TO PROVIDE INFORMATION THEY DON'T HAVE. IN FACT, THE PROBLEM IS OVER-BLOWN AND THE DATA EASILY COLLECTED.

THE UNITARY METHOD ACTUALLY FORCES COMPANIES TO PROVIDE DATA WHICH ACCURATELY REFLECT THEIR OPERATIONS!

YIKE!

③ THERE IS NO EVIDENCE TO SUGGEST THAT THE UNITARY METHOD DISCOURAGES FOREIGN INVESTMENT. IN FACT, IT CAN BE ARGUED THAT THE REVERSE IS TRUE. THAT IS, WITHOUT THE UNITARY METHOD, CAPITAL IS ENCOURAGED TO LEAVE THE COUNTRY, SETTLE IN A NICE TAX HAVEN, AND MERELY MARKET GOODS HERE, TAKING THE PROFITS OUT OF REACH OF STATE AND FEDERAL REVENUE COLLECTORS. THIS MEANS A LOSS OF TAX REVENUE AND A LOSS OF JOBS.

IN OTHER WORDS, WHAT HAPPENS EVERY DAY!

⑤

THE UNITARY METHOD

TO OVERCOME THE PROBLEMS OF FIGURING "ARM'S-LENGTH" PRICES, SOME STATES HAVE BEEN MOVING TOWARD A NEW AND SIMPLER METHOD OF AUDITING CORPORATE TAX RETURNS: THE 'UNITARY' OR "WHOLE BUSINESS" METHOD. IN THIS METHOD, STATE AUDITORS COMPLETELY IGNORE A COMPANY'S TANGLE OF SUBSIDIARIES AND TREAT THE WHOLE BUSINESS AS A SINGLE UNIT. USING AN ESTABLISHED FORMULA, THE STATE DIVIDES THE CORPORATION'S WORLD-WIDE INCOME AMONG ALL THE STATES AND COUNTRIES WHERE IT DEALS, ACCORDING TO WHAT PROPORTION OF THE COMPANY'S BUSINESS IS DONE IN EACH PLACE. THE FORMULA, CALLED THE 3-FACTOR FORMULA, IS BASED ON SALES, PAYROLL, AND CAPITAL.

THUS, IF 1/20 OF ALGI'S OVERALL SALES, PAYROLL, AND CAPITAL ARE IN MY STATE, WE CAN TAX 1/20 OF ALGI'S OVERALL INCOME!

AND HOW DOES ALGI FEEL ABOUT THE UNITARY METHOD?

VERY BAD!!

THE MULTI-NATIONALS (AND THE U.S. TREASURY) HAVE ADVANCED THREE ARGUMENTS AGAINST THE UNITARY METHOD. ACCORDING TO THEM:

1) IT IMPROPERLY TAXES FOREIGN INCOME.

2) IT IS ADMINISTRATIVELY CUMBERSOME.

3) IT DISCOURAGES FOREIGN INVESTMENT IN THE U.S.

NONE OF THESE STATEMENTS HOLDS UP WHEN EXAMINED "AT ARM'S LENGTH."

④

THE MULTI-NATIONALS DON'T ONLY ARGUE THE MATTER. JUST ABOUT EVERY LEGISLATIVE SESSION, THEIR LOBBYISTS PERSUADE SOME MEMBER OF CONGRESS TO PROPOSE A LIMITATION OR BAN ON THE UNITARY METHOD.

RECENTLY, ALGI'S FRIENDS AT THE U.S. TREASURY NEGOTIATED WITH GREAT BRITAIN A TREATY WHICH WOULD FORBID USE OF THE UNITARY METHOD ON ANY CORPORATION BASED IN THE UNITED KINGDOM.

ALTHOUGH EXEMPTING ONLY BRITISH COMPANIES, THIS WAS CLEARLY A FIRST STEP TOWARD A TOTAL BAN, SINCE IT ALLOWS OTHER MULTI-NATIONALS TO ARGUE FOR EQUAL TREATMENT.

A COALITION OF FARM STATE, STATES' RIGHTS, AND LIBERAL SENATORS DEFEATED THIS SCHEME. BUT THE MULTI-NATIONALS AREN'T GIVING UP.

DON'T YOU SEE, SENATOR, THE UNITARY METHOD IMPROPERLY TAXES FOREIGN INCOME, IS ADMINISTRATIVELY CUMBERSOME, AND DISCOURAGES FURRY VESTS!

HM?

PSSPSSPSS

ER-MAKE THAT FOREIGN INVESTMENT!!

U.S. TREASURY

NOW THEY'RE LOBBYING CONGRESS FOR A TOTAL BAN ON THE UNITARY METHOD, *PLUS* THEY WANT A TOTAL BAN ON STATE TAX-ATION OF DIVIDENDS FROM FOREIGN SUBSIDIARIES.

PSSPSSPSS

⑥

"How the Corporation Dodged Its Taxes" is reprinted by permission from Larry Gonick, freelance cartoonist, 247 Missouri Street, San Francisco, California.

AND WHAT IF THE UNITARY METHOD WERE BANNED?

THE OBVIOUS IMPACT WOULD BE LOST REVENUE—POSSIBLY BILLIONS OF DOLLARS. THE ACTUAL AMOUNT IS IMPOSSIBLE TO CALCULATE, BECAUSE THE STATES ARE JUST BEGINNING TO TURN TO THE UNITARY METHOD. CALIFORNIA TAX OFFICIALS, WHO PIONEERED THE UNITARY METHOD, ESTIMATE THAT A BAN WOULD COST THEIR STATE SOME

$500 MILLION

AND THAT MEANS MORE TAXES FOR THE REST OF US!

EVERY YEAR—AND THAT'S JUST ONE STATE!!

BEYOND THE REVENUE LOSS, HOWEVER, THERE IS MORE AT STAKE:

① WILL TAX OFFICIALS BE ALLOWED TO EXAMINE THE MULTI-NATIONALS' OPERATIONS?

② WILL ALL TAXPAYERS BE TREATED EQUALLY?

SMALL BUSINESSES DON'T HAVE FOREIGN AFFILIATES WHERE THEY CAN STASH THEIR PROFITS, AND AT TAX TIME THEY HAVE TO PAY UP. THE UNITARY METHOD IS DESIGNED TO SUBJECT BIG COMPANIES TO THE SAME SCRUTINY AS SMALL. BANNING IT WOULD PERPETUATE TWO CLASSES OF TAXPAYER—THE LITTLE GUYS, WHO HAVE NO PLACE TO HIDE AT TAX TIME, AND THE BIG ONES WHO DO.

IT'S TIME TO PIN ALGI DOWN!!

END

Statement for Missouri Legislature Concerning Bill to Establish Uniform Rules for Corporations Reporting Income to Missouri

Jonathan Rowe
Deputy Director, Multistate Tax Commission

You have asked for my comments on a pending bill concerning the ground rules by which multistate corporations divide their income for tax purposes among the different states in which they operate.

The bill would eliminate the option currently extended to multistate taxpayers to use the erratic and unusual single-factor formula based on sales only. The effect would be to require the use of the now-optional three-factor formula (property, payroll and sales) which is overwhelmingly favored among income tax states.

The division of income issue is probably the most important, and most controversial, in the whole area of state corporate income taxation. It also is an issue fraught with hidden dangers for the states.

It is neither my role nor my desire to attempt to tell the Missouri Legislature what to think about this issue. However, from my vantage point here in Washington, D.C., and from my involvement in this matter in numerous states, I would comment that there may be some implications of the choice before the legislature on which I may be able to shed some light.

In brief, the danger is that the states, by adopting erratic taxing formulas from which they expect to derive small marginal gains, will invite federal restrictions which will leave them much worse off than if they had adhered voluntarily to more uniform procedures.

Perhaps I should state the problem in simple terms. When a business crosses state borders, there must be rules for determining how much of the income of that business is taxable in each of the states in which it operates. Each state adopts its own rules. If these rules are not consistent with each other, if they do not mesh, then difficulties can arise. Most commonly, substantial income of selected multistate taxpayers falls through the cracks and is reported nowhere. On the other side of the coin, some corporate income may be subject to tax in theory (though not necessarily taxed) in more than one state.

Inconsistencies in the attribution rules of different states also can impose extra compliance costs upon taxpayers, and extra enforcement costs upon state tax officials. Perhaps most importnat, such inconsistencies have prompted demands by corporate taxpayers that Congress enact severe taxing power limitations upon the states, taking away from the states much more than they could gain from the disparate approaches some states have adopted.

The most common approach is a formula, called the three-factor formula because it is based on the three primary indicators of business activity: property, payroll and sales. The three-factor formula, now used in the vast majority of the states with corporate income taxes, says in effect, "It is impossible to tell precisely how much of a corporation's income is attributable to each state in which it operates, and so we will use the three indicators of business activity as a workable measure. If one-twentieth of a particular taxpayer's property, payroll and sales are present in our state, then one-twentieth of this taxpayer's income will be deemed taxable here also."

The three-factor formula is not perfect. However, it is the best approximation yet devised. The only alternative to a formula approach is to go to the books of the taxpayer and try to disentangle its activities in one state from its activities in other states. Applied to a large multistate taxpayer, this so-called "separate accounting" method is a Herculean task. It is the accounting equivalent of trying to determine how much the effectiveness of Bob Gibson's fastball was due to his wrist, elbow, shoulder, back, chest and legs, respectively. Even given an unlimited tax enforcement budget and an army of auditors, it is doubtful that this "separate accounting" method could work effectively.

The three-factor formula, or any other formula, does **not** determine how much tax a firm pays in Missouri or in any other state. This is a key point that many people overlook. The formula merely determines how much of the firm's income is **available** to the state to tax. The tax rates, and the credits and deductions in the state law are what decide how much or how little tax a firm actually pays.

I will return to this point shortly.

A few states, Missouri among them, have departed from the standard three-factor formula. Currently, Missouri offers multistate businesses the option of attributing their income on the basis of their sales alone, without regard to where their property and payroll are located. In other words, if one-twentieth of the firm's sales are made in Missouri, then one-twentieth of its income would be deemed taxable in Missouri. This erratic "single-factor" formula is of special benefit to those firms which make a large proportion of their sales outside the state. Other businesses use the standard three-factor formula also offered under Missouri law.

The proposal under consideration would eliminate the dual computation system and would subject all multistate taxpayers to the same, uniform three-factor formula.

The justification for the single-factor option is that

it allegedly boosts economic development by favoring firms which produce in Missouri but sell a large portion of these products outside the state. This result would arise, in theory, because the sales factor would in effect throw much of the firm's taxable income out of the state's taxing jurisdiction. If other states do not adopt interlocking formulas which claim the income which Missouri's formula tosses out to them (an important "if"), then a tax reduction for these firms results.

There appears to be no doubt that the single-factor formula option reduces the income which some firms report to Missouri. This recognition, however, merely begs a host of questions which are the substance of this controversy. Some of these questions are:

1. How much economic development, if any, actually arises from this reduction in taxable income reported to Missouri by some firms? Does the tax break merely reward some firms for doing what they would have done anyway, or for doing nothing?
2. Are there less expensive, and more equitable and effective ways, to achieve the desired economic development effects?
3. Are the benefits of this tax reduction really targeted to those firms most likely to use this bonus to expand their operations in the state? Do the benefits to go older, established, low-growth sectors at the expense of newer, high-growth sectors for which other measures would be more effective?
4. Are Missouri firms that make most of their sales in the state put at a disadvantage by this tax break available to firms making most of their sales out-of-state?
5. Might other states enact measures to nullify any advantage the single-factor formula bestows upon Missouri? Could they nullify this advantage by adopting formulas which in effect claim the income which the single-factor formula throws out at them?
6. Are there ways that Missouri could bestow tax reductions upon some or all firms without inviting taxing power restrictions imposed by the federal government?

I know of no study which adequately addresses all of these questions, for Missouri or any other state. Variations in state apportionment formulas usually have ridden the crests of emotionalism, fear, and unsubstantiated allegation. Nevertheless, it is possible to offer a few observations.

It is recognized generally that state taxes have very little effect on corporate decisions as to where to locate. The Fantus Company, an internationally known business location consulting firm, asserted in a recent report to the New Jersey Manufacturers Insurance Company that "(t)ypically, corporate income taxes are not the critical screening factor in location decisions. This is especially true of multiplant companies (with facilities in a number of states) where allocation of income often involves complex computations based on total corporate accounts."

The availability of trained labor, and its cost, is one of several factors considerably more important than state corporate income taxes. Ironically, corporate tax reductions can shift the state tax load onto workers, giving rise to demands for higher wages so that workers can maintain their purchasing power. Nationally, over the past twenty years, the portion of state revenues arising from income taxes on individuals has tripled, while the portion arising from corporations has remained constant. This tax shift, and the higher wage demands it has inspired, has had a yet-unchartered effect upon economic development and the business climate generally in the industrial states.

It is important to remember that state corporate income taxes are deductible from federal taxable income. For a large multistate business, the federal government is picking up close to one-half of the business' state tax load. This is one of the reasons that state taxes are not crucial in most business location decisions. It also implies that, in part, state corporate income taxes really are part of an indirect federal revenue sharing program with the states.

Recently the New Jersey Department of Revenue completed a thorough study of a proposal that that state adopt a "double weighted" sales factor which would be similar in effect to Missouri's single-factor option. The report concluded that "(d)ouble weighting of the sales factor would result in a substantial reduction in corporate taxes for a small number of corporations ... Although it has been claimed that the change would generate increased corporate activity and increased corporate taxes, there is no evidence to that effect."

The "Summary of Findings" from that New Jersey report follows:

Summary of Findings

As an Inducement to Industry

1. The probability is slight that location decisions will be favorably influenced by a double weighting of sales in the allocation factor.
2. Some location decisions will be adversely influenced by a change in allocation factors.
3. The lighter weight given to property and payroll in the proposed allocation factor are insufficient to counterbalance the relatively high costs of labor and property in this State.
4. There is no evidence to indicate that the proposed formula will expand the Corporate Tax Base.
5. Our research indicates that industry prefers uniformity of allocation among states, and views a change from standard allocation formula as an annoyance.

Impact Upon State Revenue

1. Increased administrative costs would be expected to result from increased audit activity.
2. The revenue effect is substantial. Calculations for all allocating corporations for the 1975 income year (1976 collections) indicate a reduction of $16.1 million in net income tax for 3,937

corporations. Application of the same optional allocation formula to net worth would reduce the corporation tax by another $3.2 million—bringing the total tax reduction to $19.3 million before adjustment for prepayment losses during the first year.

Approximately 81% of the calculated corporation tax reduction would apply to 200 large multistate corporations. Some examples are included.

Growth in corporation income, net worth and tax since 1975 suggests tax reductions higher than the $19.3 million calculated for that year.

The juggling of apportionment formulas for state corporate income taxes seems to fall within this general rule. Overall, such taxes comprise only about 1% of business expenses. The tax savings provided by variations in the apportionment formula, such as Missouri's single-factor option, therefore would amount to only a fraction of that one percent. Such a relatively minor savings would seem relatively unimportant compared to such important factors as labor and utility costs, highways and transportation, and the like.

This does not mean that any state can afford to ignore its business climate. It does suggest that state corporate income taxes are only one small part of a state's business climate, and that variations in the apportionment formula are merely one small part of that one small part. Seen in this context, the disadvantages of such variations seem all the more important.

One obvious disadvantage of a single factor option is that it injects an element of roulette into the state's tax system. Depending upon the happenstance of the mix of a firm's in-state and out-of-state property, payroll and sales, the firm either wins or loses. A multistate firm with many sales out of state can gain a tax advantage over an in-state firm making most of its sales within the state. The multistate firm may continue to enjoy the single-factor bonus even though its current plant expansions are focussed not in Missouri but in other states or nations. This is neither tax justice nor effective targeting of economic development resources.

In addition, even if the single-factor formula were effective in promoting economic development, how long it could continue to be so is questionable.

Historically, any cutting edge which such inducements might have had, has been blunted by the "lowest common denominator effect." Once one state adopts them, businesses in neighboring states pressure their legislatures to follow suit. The end result is lower revenues in all the states concerned, and no competitive advantage for any of them.

Most important is the response brewing here in Washington to diverse state apportionment formulas such as Missouri's single-factor formula.

For at least ten years large multistate taxpayers have been insisting upon federal legislation to impose severe taxing power restrictions upon the states. I work in this area every day and in my view the possibility of such legislation is gaining. The states themselves are largely responsible because they have allowed themselves to be lured into a legislative draw play. One by one, the states are lobbied to enact erratic apportionment formulas and rules. The same taxpayers who have lobbied the states for such discrepancies go to Washington and demand federal legislation on the grounds that the states themselves have not achieved consistency in this area. The taxing power restrictions which they are demanding, moreover, would have serious and far-reaching detrimental effects on state revenues.

It is true that Missouri's single factor formula is optional, and that the state offers taxpayers the option of the standard three-factor formula. My conversations with Senators and their staffs have indicated, however, that such fine distinctions are often lost upon busy legislators who have much more on their minds than the apportionment formulas provided under state income tax laws. Furthermore, the very existence of the controversial option introduces uncertainty and complexity which themselves are not good for the business climate. The Fantus Co., wrote concerning New Jersey that "Uncertainty concerning the tax outlook in the State has also hindered development in the past." The U.S. Chamber of Commerce has called for uniformity in the rules for dividing corporate income among the states.

The pressure for federal restrictions is increasing. The staff of Senate Finance Committee Chairman Russell Long is now exploring the issue. For Missouri to eliminate its dual system and stand firmly with the uniform formula would be a message to Washington that the states can and will clean up their own house. To hold back from this step could play into the hands of the advocates of federal restrictions.

Reluctance to give up the dual formula system is totally unnecessary, because there are so many other ways to achieve the same result. The tax rate can be cut. Credits and deductions can be adjusted. Such devices do no violence to the system for dividing a corporation's income among the states and thus do not invite the federal involvement that the diverse apportionment formulas arouse.

It is my opinion, therefore, that it would be in the best interests of Missouri to dispense with the single-factor formula. You would be establishing the standard three-factor formula as the sole means by which to attribute income to your state for corporate income tax purposes; and you would be joining the vast majority of income tax states in doing so.

"Statement for Missouri Legislature Concerning Bill to Establish Uniform Rules for Corporations Reporting Income to Missouri" is reprinted by permission from the Multistate Tax Commission, February 16, 1979.

VAT: IT'S BROCCOLI,

DEAR

by Charles I. Kingson

Charles I. Kingson is an attorney with a New York City law firm. He was formerly a member of the staff of the Treasury's Office of International Tax Counsel.

In this article, Kingson critiques Senator Russell B. Long's recent proposal to substitute a value added tax (VAT) for the social security tax, and for a portion of the existing income tax.

Readers of Tax Notes may also be interested in another article by Mr. Kingson on VAT. It appeared in the Cornell Law Review for January 1973 (Vol. 58, No. 2) under the title "Value Added Tax versus Broader Income Base: Tax Reform for the Rich or the Not So Rich."

Mother: It's broccoli, dear.
Child: I say it's spinach, and to hell with it.
New Yorker cartoon.

To criticize VAT for being regressive is like criticizing Tom Thumb for being short: that's what each is. In evaluating VAT, therefore, the relevant issue is not whether it is wholly or marginally regressive. Rather, there are two questions: one, is VAT desirable *because of* or *despite* its regressiveness; and two, if VAT is "better," with what is it being compared?

Russell Long says he supports VAT despite its regressiveness; and what Senator Long supports, the Treasury studies. In a talk last November at Tulane, the Senator gave his reasons:

1. "We should abandon the use of the income tax as a device to effect a major redistribution of wealth."
2. "[T]he only way that a value added tax can be sold [is] that the social security tax will be repealed and the income tax will be drastically reduced."
3. "The principal disadvantage is that a VAT is regressive, compared to the individual income tax. But it is less regressive than the social security tax it would replace."
4. "[A] combination of a graduated income tax . . . along with a value added tax can be *every bit as progressive as the American people want it to be.*" Emphasis added)

Since there was no suggestion that a device other than the income tax should effect redistribution of wealth, a reasonable interpretation of those remarks is:

1. Redistribution of wealth has gone too far.
2. The obvious and dramatic employment tax increases make it necessary to find a politically less painful way to finance social security.

3. VAT can be sold politically as a replacement for social security and in part for progressive taxation.
4. Americans don't want too progressive a tax system.

That redistribution of wealth has gone too far and that Americans don't want too progressive a tax system do not sound like the concerns of a man who embraces VAT despite — rather than because of — regressiveness. Moreover, Senator Long's remarks answer the second question in two ways: VAT is better than both employment taxes *and* high income tax rates. This blurs separate issues.

Replacing employment taxes by VAT might not, as compared with present law, significantly change progressivity. Replacing high income tax rates by VAT definitely would, and Senator Long refrained from saying it would not. Thus, support for VAT will depend on a fundamental confusion. Middle-income Americans will support VAT over employment taxes, because they *think* they would pay less. Upper-income Americans will support VAT over high income tax rates, because they *know* they would pay less. An uneasy alliance, with each group trying to slip the old rubber peach to somebody else.

Tax Compliance and VAT

Our choice of VAT over income tax would be a luxury. For many European countries, it was a necessity: they resorted to VAT because their citizens commonly evaded income tax. I suggest that this European attitude toward the income tax arose in part because of a perception that the rich could escape it, and that the income tax itself was therefore corrupt.[1] How well the French rich fought progressive taxation was once summed up by a government expert: "The selfishness of the possessing classes is not reducible. We have to adapt to it."[2]

By contrast, Americans' acceptance of and compliance with the tax laws are astonishing national assets. Implicit in people's bragging about their tax shelters is the assumption that others pay their full share. This

---

[1] A similar uproar in the United States resulting from the disclosure that 600 millionaires had not paid any income tax, led to the largely cosmetic minimum tax.
[2] See Shirer, *The Collapse of the French Republic*, p. 156.

To most people, fairness equates somewhat with ability to pay; and VAT would gamble with that belief.

acceptance and compliance persist despite the fact that under present law earned income is the worst kind of income to have, unless one earns more than $50,000. They persist because of belief that the law, as well as the people administering it, are fundamentally fair. To the extent that the belief evaporates, voters could turn to solutions like Proposition 13. To most people, fairness equates somewhat with ability to pay; and VAT would gamble with that belief.

The gamble is that not seeing VAT will, to most people, mean not paying VAT. Other justifications, like encouraging the poor to save, convince only the unpoor. Higher prices plus income tax refunds could in fact encourage more down payments on consumer goods, rather than more saving. Besides, if you want to encourage the poor to save, a good beginning might be to pay them a fair rate of return.

Capital Formation and the Poor

Most important to VAT, however, is the idea that this country has redistributed too much to the poor, and that what we need is capital formation. (Proponents of capital formation would generally achieve this by more regressive taxation, but regressive taxation is an awkward banner to march under.) I am not an economist, but let me give some fairly recent statistics, which I discovered when President Nixon's aides were suggesting VAT to save us from property taxes:

- two percent of the population gets more than 40 percent of corporate dividends, but accounts for less than six percent of consumer expenditures;
- the Tax Reform Act of 1969 reduced the average tax burden on the poor — federal, state and local — from 28 to 26 percent of income; and
- the original low-income allowance was predicated on a need (at 1966 prices) for $1.50 a day to cover all nonfood expenses.

Three Factors Support VAT Push

At bottom, the appeal of VAT — its hidden and regressive character — stems from three factors. One is America's shrinking economic position. Generosity toward the poor rests to a great extent on prosperity. In less fortunate times, people become inclined to look out for themselves; and those best able to do so are those most affected by progressive taxation.

Two, the Carter Administration talked tax reform to a country weary of tax reform. The push to eliminate the capital gains preference reflected fidelity to an implied campaign promise that few cared about, and it resulted only in greater preference for capital gain. How much progressive taxation is on the defensive is reflected in the Administration's program, which has shrunk to opposing repeal of a reform (carryover basis) enacted before it took office.

Three, social security taxes now perceptibly hurt middle income people, particularly where husband and wife both work. Insistence that the system be self-

financing represents a fear that, unless the tax is sufficiently visible, political pressure for increased benefits cannot be offset by political distaste for increasing taxes. At the same time, it softens distaste for a regressive tax by associating it with a popular expenditure. VAT combines association with social security payments with the appeal of invisibility. From an economic standpoint, however, the result would be the same if the tax were associated with defense spending or welfare payments.[3]

The link is therefore political rather than financial. It is significant that Senator Long is willing to finance social security from general revenues, so long as those revenues are less progressive than the present income tax.[4] This continues the recent trend away from progressiveness, embodied in the reduction of capital gains and estate taxes and the increases in employment taxes. So far, successful tax protest has been confined to the state level; and it may be that VAT will not change that fact.

The Race for VAT Preferences

But VAT is not as easy to enact in detail as it is to support in concept. No matter what the credits, it is doubtful whether payments for cancer surgery, home purchases or college tuition will be subject to the tax; and it is far from certain that the rate on purchases of newspapers will be the same as that on diamond bracelets. The race for preference will continue in new arenas.[5]

To forestall possible protest, Senator Long suggested at Tulane a constitutional amendment freezing the maximum rate of income tax at, say, 33 percent. Politically, however, it has so far not been feasible to reduce the top rates on individuals from 70 to 50 percent, despite the negligible additional revenue collected. A little over a year ago, in a tribute to the late Laurence N. Woodworth, Senator Long spoke eloquently of the income tax law as a series of carefully constructed compromises among people of strongly held views. Now he is willing to throw much of the system up for grabs, with all the compromises to be worked out again and tax rates to become a constitutional issue.

Painless Taxation?

The effort, if successful, would produce what Senator Long describes as relatively painless taxation. The best definition of painless taxation was by an Italian, who contrasted the high tax on consumer goods with the ineffective income tax in Italy: "Painless means that the rich manage to have the poor pay the taxes without the poor noticing it."[6]

It's quite a gamble — that they won't notice it. After a taste of VAT, a lot of taxpayers might conclude that it's not broccoli after all.

"VAT: It's Broccoli, Dear" is reprinted by permission from the March 12, 1979 issue of *Tax Notes*, Taxation With Representation Fund.

[3]The unreality of allocating specific taxes to specific expenditures is shown by the Revenue Act of 1971, which repealed the federal excise tax on cars. In order to continue highway construction without having to justify expenditures from general revenues, the Act allocated funds from the alcohol tax to highway trust funds. The only logic to this is that highways benefit drinkers.

[4]The recent cut in individual income tax rates to compensate for the rise in employment tax rates in effect financed social security from general revenues.

[5]A credit cannot distinguish between the spending patterns of, say, a 65-year-old couple and a newly married couple furnishing a home.

[6]*The Schoolboys of Barbania, Letter to a Teacher.*

THE MICHIGAN SINGLE BUSINESS

TAX: A STATE VALUE

ADDED TAX?

by Alan Schenk

Alan Schenk is a professor of law at Wayne State University Law School in Detroit, Michigan. He is the author of "Value Added Tax in the United Kingdom," Commerce Clearing House, 1976, and other scholarly publications.

In this article, Professor Schenk describes and critiques the Michigan Single Business Tax, which has frequently been described in the press as a variety of value added tax. Schenk first discusses the legislative background of the Single Business Tax, and then describes the ways in which it differs from the various forms of value added tax. He concludes that the Michigan tax has been made excessively complicated by concessions granted in response to lobbying pressures at the time of its enactment, and thereafter.

On January 1, 1976, the State of Michigan once again became an innovator in the field of state taxation. On that date, the Single Business Tax Act (P.A. 228 (1975)) replaced a series of taxes formerly levied on Michigan businesses.[1] As its name implies, it imposes a single tax on business activity in Michigan.[2]

Michigan's pioneering efforts with the Single Business Tax (SBT) was but another example of the state's tax experimentation. In 1953, Michigan was the first state to enact a modified form of a value-added tax—the Business Activities Tax (BAT). The BAT, however, was short-lived. Due to increased state revenue needs, in 1967, it was replaced by a corporate income tax. The revenue capacity of the corporate tax fluctuated with the swings in the economic cycle in Michigan. As a state dependent on the health of the auto industry, these swings were dramatic. It thus is not surprising that the governor and the legislature were anxious to develop a more dependable revenue structure for the state.

Legislative Background

Four factors prompted the legislature to seriously consider the SBT and the business community to support it:

1. The Michigan-based auto companies were building many new production facilities in the Sunbelt rather than in Michigan. Other corporations were threatening to leave the state unless Michigan's tax climate improved. The exodus was creating political problems in the state.

2. In 1975, the state projected a $200 million cash flow deficit for 1976. This deficit had to be covered by increasing taxes or changing the payment schedule for some state taxes. The quarterly reporting for the SBT, to substitute for the semi-annual reporting for the corporate income tax, would remedy some of the cash flow problems. Deferring the effective date of the repeal of the franchise taxes provided needed revenue.

3. The existing tax structure made some state revenue dependent on corporate profits and vulnerable to economic swings in the auto industry.

4. In 1974, Michigan administratively applied the "unitary tax concept" to international companies doing business in Michigan. Applying the unitary tax concept, the department of revenue attributed to Michigan a portion of the worldwide income of international companies doing business in the state. Corporations adversely affected by the "unitary tax concept" favored abolition of Michigan's corporate income tax.

At the recommendation of Governor William Milliken and the urging of some large industrial corporations operating in Michigan, the legislature therefore decided to alter and simplify Michigan's tax structure. The governor proposed a single tax on business and, after legislative tinkering with the proposal, the SBT was enacted.

The SBT Tax Base

The SBT cannot readily be identified as an income tax, a gross receipts tax, or a property tax. Some have described it as a value added tax. In order to establish its appropriate classification, the tax base must be analyzed. With some exceptions, a 2.35% SBT is imposed on the "adjusted tax base" of every person with business activity allocated or apportioned to Michigan. Persons engaged in taxable business activity in Michigan are subject to the SBT, regardless of the legal form used to conduct their

---

Michigan's single business tax is an example of what a value added tax should not be.

---

[1] The Michigan Single Business Tax is the subject of a symposium issue of the Wayne Law Review: 22 Wayne L. Rev. No. 4 (July, 1976).

[2] Michigan also imposes a real property tax on business property, a sales tax to be collected and remitted by retail businesses, and a personal income tax on owners of unincorporated businesses.

business. Thus, the tax is imposed on production and service industries conducted by an individual, partnership, trust, corporation, financial institution, or other groups or combinations.

The major components of the tax base are:
- Compensation paid to employees,
- Business income, and
- Adjustments for the acquisition of capital goods.

Compensation accounts for approximately three-quarters[3] of the total SBT base. Compensation is broadly defined to include such items as payments for salary, fringe benefits, and workmen's compensation, employer contributions to pension and profit sharing plans and employer payments for social security and unemployment compensation taxes. Compensation does not include payments to independent contractors.

It should be clear from the Michigan experience that lobby pressures to inject statutory preferences and exceptions . . . complicate taxpayer compliance and administrative enforcement . . . .

The "business income" component in the SBT base is based on federal taxable income from business, but it then must be adjusted. The major adjustment is for compensation described above. Income taxes, royalties and certain interest expense deducted for federal tax purposes is added to the SBT base, while dividend, interest and royalty income included for federal tax purposes, is deducted. In addition, capital losses reduce the SBT base in the year incurred without regard to federal tax limitations on such losses. Business losses are deductible (subject to adjustments) and unused losses can be carried forward. Other statutory adjustments to federal taxable income also are required.

The taxpayer receives an SBT deduction for a portion of, or the total cost of acquiring capital goods. The entire deduction is allowed in the year of purchase. Depreciation on these goods, deducted for federal tax purposes, must be added back to the SBT base.

The SBT is imposed only on business activity allocated or apportioned to Michigan. Except for transportation services, the taxpayer's total tax base is allocated to Michigan if its entire business activity is in Michigan. For all other taxpayers, a three-factor sales, property and payroll formula apportions business activity to Michigan.

A basic $40,000 exemption removes some small businesses from the SBT rolls. An additional $12,000 per partner exemption (not exceeding $48,000), for certain partners of partnerships and shareholders of subchapter S and professional corporations, removes others from the scope of the SBT. These exemptions are phased-out as business income increases above the exemption level. Other exemptions are provided for commercial farming activities, nonprofit cooperative housing, and certain insurance activities. For practical political and administrative reasons, casual sales not in the ordinary

course of business are tax exempt; thus, a sale of a personal residence is not taxed.

Special Interest Pressures Affect Base

Lobbying pressures resulted in the addition of "special interest" adjustments to the basic tax base. For example, at its election the taxpayer's tax base may be limited to 50% of its modified gross receipts. Alternatively, a labor intensive business may elect to reduce its tax base if its "compensation" exceeds 63% of its total tax base. With this election, the compensation component of the tax base is capped at the 63% amount.[4] Almost one-half of the SBT taxpayers use this 63% circuit breaker election.

In addition, retail food stores not electing the above caps based on gross receipts or compensation may elect an "industry" special deduction based on high compensation costs. A similar tax concession is provided for firms providing private security or building maintenance services if a large proportion of their tax base is compensation costs. A tax preference also is granted to rental housing investments when the taxpayer's interest expense and depreciation amount to 70% or more of the adjusted tax base.

There are special tax credits available to some taxpayers. These tax credits benefit small businesses, unincorporated businesses and Subchapter S corporations.

SBT Compared with Varied Forms of VAT

If the SBT is a value added tax (VAT), it could be compared most closely with a consumption style, additive method VAT based on the origin principle. A VAT is a tax imposed on the value added to taxable goods and services at each stage of production and distribution. If it is applied uniformly at all stages, it raises the same tax revenue as a single-stage retail sales tax imposed at the same rate.

The legislative desire to accommodate businesses . . . led to statutory complexity which masks the basic nature of the tax.

The SBT uses an additive rather than a credit-subtractive method of computing the tax base. The credit-subtractive method VAT currently is used in the Common Market and some other West European countries. Under the credit-subtractive method, at each stage the VAT base equals the difference between (1) the tax chargeable on the taxpayer's sales of goods and services and (2) the VAT charged on its purchases. In contrast, under an additive method VAT, the VAT base at each stage is computed by adding the factors of production by which the taxpayer adds value to its goods and services. The factors of production included in an additive method VAT base commonly are:
- Compensation payments,
- Profit,
- Interest expense on borrowed funds, and
- Rent expense on leased property.

For example, assume that in one tax period a manufacturer purchased goods for $50,000 on which it

---

[3] *See* Kasischke, Computation of the Michigan Single Business Tax: Theory and Mechanics, 22 Wayne L. Rev. 1072 (1976).

[4] This special deduction cannot exceed 35 percent of the adjusted tax base.

paid a 2% VAT of $1,000. In addition, the manufacturer had compensation expense of $30,000, rent expense of $5,000, interest expense of $2,000, and profit of $8,000. The manufacturer's net VAT liability under either a 2% additive or credit-subtractive method VAT would be $900, computed as shown in Tables 1 and 2.

Table 1

ADDITIVE METHOD OF COMPUTING VAT LIABILITY

Factors of Production	Rates and Amounts
Compensation	$30,000
Rent Expense	5,000
Interest Expense	2,000
Profit	8,000
Total Tax Base	45,000
2% VAT Rate	2%
Net Tax Due	$ 900

Table 2

CREDIT-SUBTRACTIVE METHOD OF COMPUTING VAT LIABILITY

Item	Rates and Amounts
Selling price of goods	$95,000*
2% VAT rate	2%
Tax on Sales	$ 1,900
less VAT on purchases of $50,000 (exclusive of VAT)	1,000
Net Tax Due	$ 900

*The $95,000 sales price is based on the $45,000 factors of production plus the assumed $50,000 tax-exclusive cost of purchases. Since under the credit-subtractive method, the taxpayer receives a credit for VAT paid on purchases, this cost should not enter the pricing structure for goods sold.

The SBT liability is based on the factors included in the tax base (mainly compensation and business income) rather than based on the level of sales and purchases. Thus, while the SBT modifies the traditional "factors of production" included in an additive method VAT base, it does resemble the additive method VAT.

Treatment of Imports and Exports

A VAT's jurisdictional rules govern the tax treatment of imports and exports. Under the destination principle VAT used in Europe, the tax ultimately burdens goods consumed in the taxing country, regardless of where they were produced.[5] Exports are tax exempt and imports are taxed. In contrast, under an origin principle VAT, the tax is a burden on goods and services produced or rendered in the taxing country, regardless of where those goods and services are finally consumed. An origin principle VAT is not imposed on imports nor is it rebated on exports. The

---

[5]The EEC-version VAT generally exempts the import as well as export of services.

three-factor SBT apportionment formula is consistent with an origin principle tax.

Treatment of Capital Investments

Depending upon how investments in capital goods are treated, a VAT can be characterized as a gross national product (GNP), national income or consumption style VAT. If the SBT is a VAT, it more closely resembles a consumption style VAT.

Under the GNP-VAT, the taxpayer's tax liability is not affected by the purchase of capital goods. The purchaser bears the VAT component in the cost of capital acquisitions. Under the National Income VAT, the taxpayer recovers the VAT component in capital goods by deducting the cost of such goods (reducing the profit component of the VAT base) over the asset's estimated useful life. The depreciation deduction for income tax purposes provides the most convenient method of recovering this cost. Under the consumption VAT (the Common Market style VAT), at the time of purchase, the taxpayer recovers the tax component in the cost of capital acquisitions by reducing its tax base by the amount of such purchases.

The SBT basically incorporates the consumption principle by granting an SBT deduction for a portion of the cost of tangible depreciable personal property and for the full cost of depreciable real property physically located in Michigan. When assets eligible for this capital acquisition deduction are sold, the statute requires adjustments in the SBT base.

With enactment of the SBT, the tax burden shifted ... from incorporated to unincorporated businesses and from production and distribution to personal service enterprises.

In principle, the SBT resembles the economic concept of a value added tax because (1) the major components of the tax base are wages and profit and (2) the tax is levied on economic value added to goods and services at each stage of production and distribution. It attempts to avoid the cascade effect of a gross receipts or turnover tax by eliminating from the tax base the cost of purchases and the cost of services provided by independent contractors. Nevertheless, the legislative desire to accommodate businesses adversely affected by the switch to the SBT (small businesses, service enterprises and labor intensive businesses) led to statutory complexity which masks the basic nature of the tax.

How the SBT Altered the Tax Burden

The Michigan SBT replaced mainly taxes levied on corporate income, on the privilege of doing business, on inventory and on intangibles. Of these taxes, the corporate income tax was the major revenue raiser. With the enactment of the SBT, the tax burden shifted to some extent from incorporated to unincorporated businesses and from production and distribution to personal service enterprises. The professions, other than those conducted as taxpaying corporations, were not burdened by the former taxes, but now are subject to the SBT. Within the corporate sector, generally, the highly profitable businesses will pay less total state tax under the SBT, while unprofitable or marginally profitable businesses will pay higher taxes.

With the switch to the SBT, the state has shifted some of the overall tax burden from the ownership of property to the employment of labor, because the property taxes on business inventory and intangibles were eliminated, and because compensation represents a large portion of the SBT base. In addition, the SBT grants a tax deduction for the purchase of capital goods. Formerly, Michigan taxed the manufacture and sale of goods more heavily than the rendition of services. The new state tax structure, with the addition of the SBT, taxes goods and services more uniformly. Since labor accounts for a large part of the tax base, SBT revenue depends in part upon the level of employment in the state.

Highly profitable businesses will pay less total state tax under the SBT, while unprofitable or marginally profitable businesses will pay higher taxes.

The SBT is a tax initially imposed on business, but—as a cost of doing business—the tax ordinarily will be shifted to the buyer in the form of higher prices for goods and services. The incidence of the SBT depends in part on the taxpayer's industry and on the taxpayer's competitive position within the industry. For example, some companies in the automobile industry may be able to shift SBT costs more readily than companies in the highly competitive electronics industry. Within the automobile industry, General Motors is better able to shift tax costs like the SBT than can American Motors.

The Value of an SBT Preference

A tax concession under the SBT is more valuable than a tax preference granted under one of the replaced state taxes. Formerly, taxpayers benefiting from a tax concession under one tax still were subject to the other state taxes levied on business. Except for liability under the state sales tax, personal income tax and real property tax, generally a taxpayer receiving an exemption under the SBT is not contributing to state revenue. A tax concession to an industry (e.g., agriculture) or a group (e.g., private security firms) shifts the tax burden either (a) to taxpayers subject to the SBT or (b) to persons subject to the state personal income or other taxes.

Special Effects of the SBT

The SBT may adversely affect labor intensive businesses that are vulnerable to downturns in the economy, because it imposes tax on firms with large wage costs and minimal or no profit for the year. Compared with the corporate income tax, the SBT also may adversely affect the competitive position of marginal or inefficient businesses.

For example, when competitors set their prices based on a predetermined after-tax return, the corporate income tax increases the price and gives the marginal producer who does not pay the corporate tax some price flexibility. The switch from the corporate income tax to the SBT eliminates this spread for the marginal producer.

Conclusion

The recent national interest in Michigan's Single Business Tax is prompted by Senator Russell B. Long's and Representative Al Ullman's discussion of a possible federal value added tax. If Congress considers a VAT, it should be clear from the Michigan experience that lobby pressures to inject statutory preferences and exceptions obfuscate the true character of the tax, alter the tax burden, and complicate taxpayer compliance and administrative enforcement and collection of the tax. Michigan's SBT is an example of what a value added tax should not be.

"The Michigan Single Business Tax: A State Value Added Tax?" is reprinted by permission from the April 9, 1979 issue of *Tax Notes*, Taxation With Representation Fund.

CHAPTER 21

Severance Taxes

For resource states trying to pay for the cost of development and to protect themselves against the day when resources run out, severance taxes have become an increasingly important source of revenue. Generally levied as an excise on coal, oil, natural gas, timber, or other resources, these taxes brought the state, less than $700 million in 1979. By 1976, that total had risen to over $2 billion.

Digging for Dollars by Kay Christensen outlines what some states have done in recent years to increase the effectiveness of severance taxation. "Although the distribution of severance tax revenue varies from state to state," Ms. Christensen reports, "most legislatures have apportioned part of these collections to areas affected by the mining, alternate energy research, roads, reclamation and repair of environmental damage and schools."

Noting that "nearly 90 percent of the coal mined in North Dakota in the future will be mined in order to produce energy for persons living outside of this state," **Taxing Coal,** by State Tax Commissioner Byron L. Dorgan, explains why his state has recently enacted a heavy severance tax on coal. These taxes "are simply a logical extension of the philosophy of government financing that we have embraced in this region of the country for decades—it's called a 'pay as you go' philosophy," Dorgan argues.

A number of states have not yet embraced the policy of severance taxation. For example, West Virginia relies primarily on property taxes to reach the value of the extensive mineral wealth it contains. But as Lincoln Citizens for Tax Reform points out in **Lincoln County, W. Va.,** property taxation often just doesn't do the job. For example, in Lincoln County, West Virginia where the citizen group operates, corporations control 96 percent of the mineral rights, but pay only 14 percent of the property taxes. "Columbia Gas' mineral holdings are assessed on the average at only $4.33 an acre!" their pamphlet points out. "Do you think Columbia Gas would be willing to sell you an acre of its gas rights for $4.33?" The citizens' group has urged the local assessor, the county commissioners, and the state tax commissioner to raise the assessment on these mineral properties.

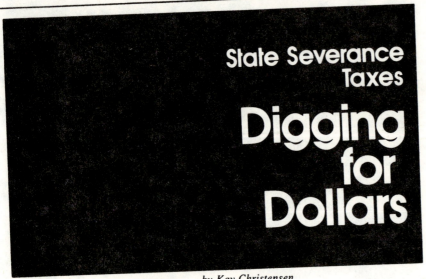

State Severance Taxes

Digging for Dollars

by Kay Christensen

Coal, oil and natural gas aren't limited to providing heat for the furnace and gasoline for the car. These valuable natural resources also put money in the bank for many state treasuries.

Severance taxes, levies placed on minerals and other resources extracted from the land, brought in $2.03 billion to the states in fiscal year 1976, according to Commerce Clearinghouse, Inc. That's almost triple the $686 million garnered in 1970.

In Louisiana, where oil and natural gas deposits abound, severance taxes accounted for $548 million in 1975, representing 34 percent of the state's revenue. Kentucky, whose economy depends upon coal production, collected $91 million in the 1975-76 fiscal year.

Many legislators in the past were fearful severance taxes would deter mining development. But these figures reflect the increasing receptiveness of state legislatures to look to severance taxes as a source of revenue.

During the 1977 session, the Republican-dominated Colorado Legislature passed its first severance tax on coal, 60-cents per ton if strip mined. Gov. Dick Lamm, a Democrat who complained the tax was too low and that the bill was written by industry lobbyists, let it become law without his signature.

While the nation's energy shortage has brought increased attention to the value of minerals, proponents of severance taxes still maintain the original rationale for the levy.

"You are severing from the ground an irreplaceable resource forever lost for future generations," says Sen. Joe Schieffelin, co-sponsor of the Colorado bill. "You should replace that resource with another resource, that is, money."

But Schieffelin admitted the energy crunch offered a second justification for the tax on natural resources. "The development of energy is going to have an impact on local governments," he said, noting that Colorado's bill sets aside a portion of revenues to help cities and counties provide essential services to mining towns. Some of these small communities become "boom towns" when their population swells due to mining activity, creating scores of social problems that can range from sewage treatment to crime control. For each person moving into an energy development area, Gov. Lamm estimates it costs local governments $4,000 to provide essential social services.

Although the distribution of severance tax revenues varies from state to state, most legislatures have apportioned part of these collections to areas affected by the mining, alternate energy research, roads, reclamation and repair of environmental damage and schools. In Montana, nearly $10 million went to its mining centers in Rosebud, Big Horn and Treasure Counties during the past two years to meet their local needs. Revenues from the coal severance tax in Wyoming are administered by the Farm Loan Board, which assists impacted communities in financing public water, sewer, highway, road or street projects.

The first state to impose a severance tax was Michigan in 1846. Today, states levy the charge on a broad range of natural resources, including lumber, uranium, sand, limestone, clay, butane, salt, marble and gravel.

U.S. Sen. Lee Metcalf (D-Mont.), worried about competitive disadvantages for mines located in heavily-taxed states, is sponsoring legislation calling for a national severance tax on coal and oil shale.

States would retain their current tax load, but the difference between the state level and the higher national rate would go to the federal government. Ultimately, it would encourage states to raise their severance taxes to match the national level so they could have a 100 percent return on their money.

"The states have a right to receive revenues for the severance of their non-renewable resources," Metcalf said. "These are treasures which can never be replaced. The states should receive revenues to assist the impacted communities and to provide for a future when these resources no longer exist."

Robert Stauffer, general counsel to the National Coal Association, believes any additional tax would be passed onto the consumer. "The industry would have to eat some of it, but not all," he said.

Highest Tax

The highest tax on coal can be found in Montana where lignite, a fuel with low heat quality, is subject to a 20 percent tax if extracted by surface mining, while coal with greater heating potential (more than 7,000 BTUs) is taxed at 30 percent of its value. To encourage natural gas production, however, the legislature this year granted a tax break to new natural gas producers.

The Wyoming Legislature enacted two laws in 1977 which boost the overall severance tax on coal to 10.1 percent. Sen. John Ostlund, chairman of the Mines, Minerals and Industrial Development Committee, noted that 1½ percent of the new tax is earmarked for badly-needed water projects. "There has been a feeling that we need to develop some water projects in the state," Ostlund explained. "So we decided to use revenues gained from a non-renewable source to develop a renewable resource."

In North Dakota, a new severance tax calls for a 65-cent charge per ton of coal extracted, but the rate automatically climbs one cent for every point increase in the wholesale price index. In Arkansas, an additional tax of one-half cent per barrel of oil became law this year.

Not all states, however, rely on severance taxes to collect revenues from the development of natural resources. Pennsylvania and Illinois use the ad valorem tax as their primary source of mining revenue, based on the mine's assessed value and the local millage rate. Other states impose a gross production tax, calculated on the dollar value of the product extracted, while others offer a net production tax that allows companies to deduct their expenses.

"State Severance Taxes: Digging for Dollars" is reprinted by permission from the September/October, 1977 issue of *State Legislatures*.

Taxing Coal

THE COAL INDUSTRY MEETS ITS MATCH

Byron L. Dorgan
North Dakota Tax Commissioner
11-4-77

THE PHILOSOPHICAL BASIS FOR A COAL SEVERANCE TAX

We frequently hear the charge that North Dakotans and Montanans have enacted a new and special coal severance tax to extort as much money as is possible from the urban areas to the east.

The facts, however, do not support that charge, In fact, the coal severance taxes enacted or under consideration in the Northern Great Plains states are simply a logical extension of the philosophy of government financing that we have embraced in this region of the country for decades—it's called a "pay as you go" philosophy.

THE GENERAL FRAMEWORK OF STATE AND LOCAL TAXATION

Conventional Taxes To Cover Routine Costs

The tax structures of state and local governments in most areas of the United States represent a balanced system of consumption, income, and wealth taxes to finance normal and routine government expenditures. Generally, this type of tax structure responds to normal increases in industrial activity without any new adjustments.

Industry-Specific Taxes to Offset Extra-Ordinary Costs.

There are, however, areas where governmental units must spend money to cover costs that are not normal and routine governmental expenditures. That is—they are not costs brought about by the needs and activities of the society as a whole, but rather by a specific, easily defined group within the society. In order to cover these kinds of costs, governments generally institute a special levy on those responsible for the cost. They must "pay their own way."

"Industry-specific" taxes are not unusual. Motor fuels excise taxes, electric generating production taxes, and oil and gas gross production taxes are just some examples of industry-specific taxes. Such taxes have not been limited to the financing of current day to day operating costs of government. In the case of mineral taxation, it has been long recognized that the extraction and consumption of a nonrenewable resource is a "one time harvest." Therefore,

the tax on resources must respond not only to today's development impact costs but also to the need for special financial resources for use by future generations who will not have a comparable resource at their disposal. Because of this, North Dakota, Montana and most other states in the union levy some kind of production taxes on the extraction of natural resources such as oil, gas, iron ore, copper, coal, etc.

MASSIVE COAL DEVELOPMENT DICTATES TAX LAW CHANGES

In the past, even the small amount of coal development in Montana and North Dakota and the costs related to it were financed without difficulty by the existing tax structures.

These past developments were relatively small compared to today's coal development projects. They were widely separated, and constructed during different time periods. As a result, the "costs" associated with the influx of a relatively small number of additional workers did not represent any abnormal level of economic activity that required a special tax adjustment for financing purposes.

The plans for intensive coal development in our states pose quite different problems for our tax structures. The "costs" associated with this level of development cannot be handled by our conventional taxes alone. Within the framework of a tax system that has already contained some industry-specific taxes, the Northern Great Plains states faced with sudden, massive coal development have had to enact some new and innovative tax laws that respond to three needs:

1. **The need to replace or complement traditional taxes, particularly the property tax, in the financing of ordinary costs that are basic to any kind of increased industrial development — those for schools, roads, health care, law enforcement, recreation, etc.;**
2. **The need to implement some kind of "industry-specific" tax that would place a dollar value on some of the previously unacknowledged costs that are extra-ordinary and unique to coal development;**
3. **The need to extablish a form of compensation for the cost to future generations of losing a non-renewable resource.**

SEVERANCE TAX COVERS ALL THREE AREAS OF NEED

As it happens, we have devised one new tax that responds to all three of these needs — the severance tax on coal. In order to adequately relate just how the severance tax responds to these three needs, it is first necessary to detail some of the severance tax programs. I will discuss the North Dakota tax because I am more familiar with it, but it would be fair for the reader to assume that the concepts and considerations which background Montana's tax are similar.

North Dakota currently has a 66¢ per ton coal severance tax (the equivalent of about 20% of market value) that increases one cent per ton for every one-point increase in the wholesale price index. That 66¢ a ton coal severance tax is distributed as follows: 30% to the State general fund, 35% to a State Coal Impact Office (which serves as a clearinghouse for the financing of regional impact costs arising from large scale coal development), 20% to the counties in which the coal is mined, and 15% to a "State trust fund."

Ordinary Costs

The financing of ordinary impact costs is accomplished by the distribution of the severance tax to the State general fund, the Coal Impact Office, and the coal-producing counties. First, the 30% that goes to the State general fund replaces a sales tax that the State used to levy on the retail sale of coal prior to enacting a coal severance tax. Therefore, at least this 30% portion of the coal severance tax is a sales tax with a name change.

Second, the 35% of the severance tax allocated to the Coal Impact Office and the 20% allocated directly to the coal-producing counties represent 55% of the coal severance tax collections. That 55% goes to local government as a replacement for the ad valorem property tax which would normally have been collected. Traditionally, the property tax would be the mechanism used to pay for increased costs of schools, law enforcement, roads, recreation, health, welfare, etc., which accompany industrial expansion.

In the case of coal development, the sheer size of the impact in the Northern Great Plains and in North Dakota, in particular, coupled with the need for front-end impact money, rendered the property tax ineffective in meeting the increased costs resulting from rapid and massive influx of people and investment. The thousands of workers and families coming to our state to work on this development will account for dramatic increases in population. If you consider the normal impact costs resulting from one 1000 megawatt electric generating plant costing over $500 million and then project an overlapping schedule for the development of at least three additional 440 megawatt plants and a one billion dollar gasification plant, you would have some idea of the kind of people and property investment that faces at least one of the Northern Great Plains states — North Dakota.

Therefore, as a result of the inability of the traditional property tax to cope with this type of development, part of the severance tax is really a replacement for the property tax. The 20% of the severance tax sent back to the coal-producing counties and the 35% that goes into the Coal Impact Office represent the replaced property tax that can be used to finance regional impact resulting from coal development.

"Taxing Coal" is reprinted by permission from *The Coal Industry Meets Its Match in the West,* Byron L. Dorgan, North Dakota State Tax Commissioner, 1977.

"Extraordinary" or "Unique Costs"

I have illustrated that 85% of the "special" severance tax on coal is a replacement of other traditional elements of our tax structure. That leaves 15%, or only about 10¢ per ton of our existing severance tax to pay for the extraordinary or unique costs that are associated with coal development and to provide some compensation for the loss of a non-renewable resource. This is the only portion of the severance tax that could be considered a new or additional special tax.

The three areas of costs that are unique to coal development projects of this magnitude are (a) the costs of environmental risks, (b) social costs, and (c) boom-bust cycle costs.

Cost of Environmental Risks

A discussion of details of these risks and costs has been set out in Appendix A. However, it is sufficient here to point out that in the area of environmental risks, complete land reclamation is still a scientific uncertainty in our climate. Some risk to human health and vegetation because of air pollution from coal processing is a certainty, and the disturbances to water aquifers and potential changes in rainfall patterns is still the subject of scientific debate.

Social Costs

The social costs to a people and a way of life are almost impossible to quantify; but, again, substantial research documents the dramatic and, in many cases, unwanted social changes that will be foisted on the people in our states. To ignore the human costs here would be wrong.

Boom-Bust Cycle Costs

The boom-bust cycle costs are those that are most often ignored in developments such as these. It is estimated that the coal development projects will have a 30 to 40 year life, and the experience all around the country has been that when the last dragline stops, the economic shock to a region catches its citizens in a financial squeeze. Part of the costs of a project is the cost of stopping it and what it does to the economics that had to be built to accommodate it in the first place — again, a difficult cost to predict, but one which cannot be ignored.

Loss of a Non-renewable Resource — A "One-Time Harvest"

Nearly 90% of the coal mined in North Dakota in the future will be mined in order to produce energy for persons living outside of this state. Montana's situation is very similar. Once this coal has been mined and burned and the product of it has been sent to regional and national users, that resource is lost forever to the Northern Great Plains states. Both North Dakota and Montana have earmarked portions of their severance taxes to go to an "endowment fund" or a "trust fund" which will be a resource available to future generations who will be trying to cope with the same type of energy problems that we are coping with in the 1970's but who will no longer have available to them the natural resource that we are now exploiting. The mining of coal is truly a one-time harvest; and the failure to provide an alternate available resource, in this case a trust or endowment fund, has been due to lack of planning in past years and in other regions of the country. The Northern Great Plains states are attempting to avoid that, and that is why they have set aside a small portion of the new severance tax revenues for use by future generations.

Lincoln County, W. Va.

The following is an excerpt from a pamphlet, prepared by Lincoln Citizens for Tax Reform. It not only illustrates once again how and why the people of Appalachia have lost control of their own resources, but in this instance, what can be done at a grass-roots level to organize against out-of-state energy corporations.

Q. *Who owns Lincoln County?*

A. Columbia Gas. In mineral wealth, expecially oil and gas, Lincoln County is one of the wealthiest counties in West Virginia. Whoever owns and controls this mineral wealth owns and controls the county. Of the 279,704 acres of minerals in Lincoln County, Columbia Gas owns 218,794 acres, or 78 percent of all the minerals in the county. All together, Columbia Gas and ten other corporations own 96 percent of all the minerals in Lincoln County.

Q. *How much property tax does Columbia Gas pay on its mineral holdings in Lincoln County?*

A. Only 12 cents an acre! Because of such low taxes paid by Columbia Gas — and other corporations — on their mineral holdings in Lincoln County, the rest of us have to pay 86 percent of the property tax levied in Lincoln County. Columbia Gas and the ten other corporations who own 96 percent of the mineral wealth in the county pay only 14 percent of the county's property tax levy.

Q. *Why is Lincoln County lowest among all counties in West Virginia in the amount of property tax revenues collected for school purposes?*

A. Because Columbia Gas, Armco Steel, and the other corporations who between them own 267,196 acres of minerals assessed and taxed in Lincoln County pay an average of only 14 cents an acre in property taxes on their mineral wealth.

Q. *Why is Lincoln County 49th (out of 55 counties in our state) in the amount of money it makes availabie each year to educate each one of its students?*

A. Because Columbia Gas and the other corporations who own Lincoln County do not pay fair property taxes on their mineral wealth. Armco Steel, for example, which owns 12,991 acres of minerals in Lincoln County, pays only ten cents an acre in property taxes on this mineral wealth.

In contrast to the $895 Lincoln County makes available each year for the education of each of its students, Boone County makes available $1,050; Putnam County, $1,075; Cabell County, $1,100; Kanawha County, $1,120; Grant County, $1,428. Throughout West Virginia, the average county expenditure each year per student is $1,036.

Q. *If the absentee-owner corporations in Lincoln County are not paying fair property taxes, who is supporting the county school system?*

A. We are. Each tax-paying resident of Lincoln County has to make up for what the corporations don't pay. In addition, much of our other tax money goes into the West Virginia State General Fund, which continually assumes an increasingly larger burden of the Lincoln County school budget. In this way, we taxpayers subsidize the corporations who operate in Lincoln County (and· take their profits outside the county)!

Q. *Why have we taxpayers been asked to tax ourselves an additional $3,125,000 to help finance the Lincoln County school system?*

A. Because Lincoln County authorites refuse to assess and tax fully and justly Columbia Gas, Armco Steel, Pennzoil, and the other corporations who own Lincoln County. An example of the unfair and unjust assessment and taxation policy in Lincoln County is the following situation in Duval District. A 154-acre (fee holding, that is, including both surface and mineral rights) plot of land owned by Pennzoil on Sugartree Creek, in the area of the rich Griffithsville Oil Field, is assessed at only $10.06 an acre, and taxed at only 24 cents an acre; a privately-owned 54-acre (also a fee holding) farm, on the other hand, on Panther's Creek is assessed at $28.98 an acre, and taxed at 35 cents an acre. In Lincoln County, the farmer is assessed and taxed more heavily than the multi-billion dollar corporation!

If the mineral wealth of the corporations which own Lincoln County were assessed and taxed fairly and justly, there would be no need for school bonds. There would be increased — and regular — revenues made available each year for the education of our children.

School bonds are short-term attempts to bail out our school system by increasing the taxes of the ordinary taxpayer; tax reform is a lasting solution for our ailing schools, at the expense, not of the ordinary taxpayer, but of the wealthy corporations who own and control our county.

Q. *Is it possible to tax these corporations fully and justly?*

A. Yes. The Boone County Assessor, Robert Totten, between the years of 1966 and 1972, raised assessments on mineral property owned by corporations in Boone County from $5 an acre to $105 an acre. (The Lincoln County Assessor, Dennis Browning, on the other hand, assesses the mineral property owned by corporations in Lincoln County at only $5.06 an acre, on the average. Columbia Gas' mineral holdings are assessed, on the average, at only $4.33 an acre! Do you think Columbia Gas would be willing to sell you an acre of its gas rights for $4.33?)

A recent re-assessment of mineral property in Wyoming County brought in an additional $750,000 to the county, over 70 percent of which each year will be available to support and improve the county's school system.

A reassessment of mineral property in Harrison County increased the assessed value of property in the county from $2,000,000 to $52,000,000. The resulting property tax revenue provides the county's school system each year with additional thousands of dollars, with no extra burden on the ordinary land and home owner.

Q. *Who is responsible for assessing and taxing property in Lincoln County?*

A. Lincoln County Assessor: Dennis Browning; Lincoln County Commissioners: Louis Abraham, Jack Stowers, Buster Stowers; West Virginia State Tax Commissioner: David Hardesty.

County Assessor: According to West Virginia Tax Code (ch. 11, art. 3, sec. 2): "All property shall be assessed annually ... at its true and actual value; that is to say, at the price for which such property would sell if voluntarily offered for sale by the owner thereof." The valuation and assessment period is July 1st to January 30th annually.

County Commissioners: The County Court must meet as a board of review and equalization not later than February 1st each year. If the court finds that property has not been assessed at its true and actual value, it has the power to change the valuation.

State Tax Commissioner: According to West Virginia Tax Code, (ch. 11, art. 1, sec 2): "...it shall be the duty of the commissioner to ... inspect the work of ... assessors ... and require such action as will tend to produce full and just assessments throughout the state...."

Q. *Who else is responsible?*

A. We are ... to see that the county assessor and commissioners, elected and paid by us, do their job; that is, work for us, and not for the corporations — whose headquarters are situated outside of Lincoln County, and, in the case of Columbia Gas, Pennzoil, Armco Steel, Ashland Oil, and Bethlehem Steel, outside West Virginia.

The county assessor and commissioners will work for us only if we make them work for us.

Minerals Owned and Taxes Paid by Corporations in Lincoln County, West Virginia

Corporation	Mineral Acres	Assessed Value	Assessed Value/Acre	Taxes	Taxes Per Acre
Columbia Gas	*218,794	$ 946,570	$ 4.33	$25,595.08	$0.12
Armco Steel	12,991	$ 49,500	$ 3.81	$ 1,338.48	$0.10
Horse Creek					
Land and Mining	11,250	$ 118,315	$10.52	$ 3,193.18	$0.28
Sweetland Land	8,060	$ 75,315	$ 9.34	$ 2,004.66	$0.25
Southeastern Gas	7,072	$ 70,720	$10.00	$ 1,912.26	$0.27
Courtney Corp.	2,482	$ 27,925	$11.25	$ 755.10	$0.30
Big Ugly Coal	3,196	$ 36,025	$11.27	$ 974.12	$0.30
Mohler Lumber	†(3,184)				
Ashland Oil	1,361	13,600	$ 9.99	$ 367.74	$0.27
Bethlehem Steel	1,052	$ 4,675	$ 5.06	•$36,551.36	$0.27
Arabo	196	$ 4,675	$ 4.98	$ 126.40	$0.13
TOTALS	267,196	$1,353,160	$ 5.06	•$36,551.36	$0.14

*Columbia Gas owns an additional 70,881 utility acres in Lincoln County, which are assessed and taxed (at a rate of $5.01 per acre) by the West Virginia State Board of Public Works. Most of the tax revenue returns to Lincoln County.

Value placed on property by Assessor for purposes of taxation.

†Mohler Lumber owns 3,184 acres in fee (that is, both surface and mineral rights) in Lincoln County.

•These corporations pay an additional $10,491.10 in property taxes on their ownership of surface and fee (fee equals ownership of both surface and mineral rights) property in Lincoln County. They therefore pay a total of $47,042.46 in property taxes for state, county, school, and municipal purposes for the fiscal year of 1976-1977 was $329,750.40. the combined amount of property taxes paid by these corporations is only 14% of the county's total property taxes.

"Lincoln County, W. VA." is reprinted by permission from *The Elements*, Public Resource Center, April, 1978.

XI

If there is one thing to be learned from Proposition 13, it is that taxation and spending decisions must be made accountable to the public and not simply to the few special interests who effectively manage to gain access to the decision making process. Proposition 13 is a clear manifestation of both the public's frustration over their distance from the formulation of the economic policies affecting their lives, as well as over the failure of politicians, bureaucrats, professionals, and corporate officials to be responsive to their needs.

Disgusted and afraid, citizens first in California, and then in a number of other states, used the initiative process to vent their anger. They seized simple measures, the only solutions they were offered, and limited not only taxes, spending and the services available to them, but also tried to limit the power of those who were not being sufficiently accountable.

The irony of course is that along with the inflexible fiscal constraints placed on politicians, the voters made themselves and their governments more, not less susceptible to the will of a small minority. By incorporating provisions requiring extraordinary (two thirds) majorities to override the limits, or to raise new revenues, most of these measures give an effective veto power to the minority. In addition, the various limits and rollbacks recently passed fail to provide the means necessary to make legislators and administrators more responsive. They simply place them in straight jackets, imposing inflexible formulas which limit their options by reducing the revenues or the amount that can be spent.

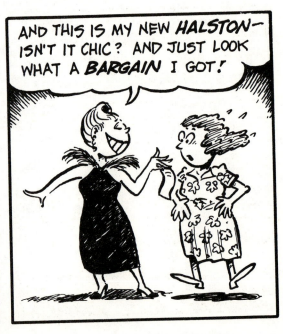

The Limits of Tax and Spending Limitations

By Diane Fuchs

Although it is still too early to evaluate the overall impact of limitation measures, they have tended to shift a greater percentage of the tax burden away from the business sector; to shift responsibility for funding local programs to higher levels of government; to reduce the amount and quality of services provided by the public sector; and to affect the surrounding economy by reducing investment in the public facilities needed to service economic expansion and by increasing public sector unemployment.

In addition, limitations on spending, whether they are tied to a flat percentage or to the rate of population growth, may have another particularly significant impact on economic growth. Once a jurisdiction reaches its limit, the services required by new development will require redistributing resources away from existing businness and residences for the benefit of the new development. The zero-sum nature of the equation may seriously discourage growth beyond the established spending limitation.

Unfortunately, the Richter scale tremors of Proposition 13 in California obscured from public view a number of promising measures passed earlier in the 1970's to encourage, if not require, accountability to the public on taxation and spending matters. Because these measures are relatively new and have been implemented in only a handful of states, they have not gained public recognition or understanding. Most notable among them is the tax expenditure budget pioneered in California, and the full disclosure (or truth in taxation) law first passed in Florida.

Tax expenditure budgets provide legislators and citizens with line by line estimates of the cost of indirect expenditures. These are revenues that are lost through tax forgiveness provisions in state law.

While preparation of tax expenditure budgets provides important information for the public and for tax policy makers, it does not insure that legislatures review these "expenditures" regularly and act upon them accordingly. To make tax expenditure budgets effective accountability tools, review of the "expenditures" by sunset or some other oversight mechanism is essential.

Truth in taxation laws mainly concern local property taxation levels. They are designed to prohibit local officials from quietly reaping the benefits of inflation's impact on property values. These laws require local officials to determine what rate applied to the current year's assessment base would produce the same amount of revenue as in the previous year or in the previous year after an adjustment for inflation. If they wish to exceed this rate, local officials must publicize their intention and additionally, may be required to vote upon an increase.

As Bob Kuttner mentions in his introduction to Section III, truth in taxation laws may have some drawbacks because they are usually applied to all revenue generated by the property tax not just to revenue derived from the residential sector. If, within a jurisdiction, increases in assessments tend to be concentrated on the homeowner side of the tax base and there is no provision for split tax rates, the tax rate rollbacks mandated by truth in taxation laws may end up reducing business property taxes at the expense of homeowners.

CHAPTER 22

Tax Expenditure Reform

Every time a legislature passes a measure providing an income tax deduction, a property tax abatement, or a sales tax exemption, to name just a few, it is making an expenditure of public funds just as if it had voted to give a direct grant or subsidy to the beneficiary of the measure. For, just like direct expenditures, the indirect tax expenditure costs money. The former require a cash outlay, while the latter represent an amount of tax revenue that is "spent" simply by not being collected.

Unfortunately, the two types of expenditures are seldom treated equivalently in terms of the scrutiny given to them either before or after passage. Few legislators, not to mention the public, are ever aware of exactly how much the indirect tax expenditures cost, nor are they required to review these spending items on a regular basis to see whether or not they are accomplishing their purpose.

The tax expenditure budget is a mechanism designed to enable legislators and the public to evaluate the effectiveness of indirect expenditures and to measure them against their cost. However, without sunset provisions or other oversight mechanisms, the tax expenditure budget is purely informational. By requiring that indirect expenditures be reviewed as line items along with the regular budget, citizens and legislators can, for example, compare the cost-effectiveness of an employment tax credit with a direct expenditure for a public employment program—something that could not be done if the actual dollar cost of the former were not known.

The excerpt **Tax Expenditures,** taken from the California Governor's Budget for 1779-1980 describes the policy behind this practice which was pioneered in California and now followed by the Federal government and two other states. It also demonstrates that indirect expenditures are as significant dollar-wise as direct expenditures. There are well over 200 of them and they cost the State of California more than $6.6 billion a year or 36% of state revenues.

Ironically, requiring the preparation of tax expenditure budgets will become especially imporant in this era of tax and spending limitation fever. As pointed out by Russell Lidman in **Limits May Encourage Tax Expenditures**, a statutory limitation on state revenue growth which will be on Washington's November 1979 ballot may actually encourage tax expenditures. Tax expenditures become "costless" in the face of a restrictive limit and therefore may become attractive to legislators and other fiscal policy makers seeking a way around the limitation.

Both articles in this chapter indirectly raise the point that for the tax and spending system to be made accountable to the public, tax expenditures must be subjected to the same degree of public, legislative, and executive oversight as are actual expenditures. Tax expenditure budgets are a necessary first step toward achieving such oversight.

Tax Expenditures

By Governor Edmund G. Brown

It has only been in the last 10 years that attention has been given to tax expenditures. The California Legislature recognized by enactment of Chapter 1762 in 1971 that the State budget did not provide a complete accounting of total expenditures. Chapter 575, Statutes of 1976, requires the Department of Finance to prepare a tax expenditure report to be included in the Governor's Budget for each fiscal year beginning in an odd-numbered year. At the federal level, the Congressional Budget Act of 1974 required that tax expenditures be a part of the budget, beginning in fiscal year 1976.

In recent years the public has become increasingly concerned about the level of public spending, as evidenced by the current tax limitation movement. However, there is little public awareness of the magnitude and purpose of tax expenditures, which are essentially equivalent to direct expenditures. This report estimates that California tax expenditures exceed $6.6 billion. In addition there are $2.7 billion of local property and sales tax expenditures. To put these figures into perspective, State tax expenditures are equal to 36 percent of State revenues and property tax expenditures represent more than 40 percent of local property taxes.

Tax expenditures are revenue losses resulting from provisions of the tax laws that provide special or selective tax relief to certain categories of taxpayers. Such revenue losses are called tax expenditures because they are very much like payments made by government except that they are made through a reduction in taxes rather than through the legislative appropriation process. For example, if a person in the ten-percent state income tax bracket contributes $1,000 to charity, then the State income tax is reduced by $100. Under the current procedure, the taxpayer chooses the recipient of the contribution. Instead of allowing this deduction, the State could collect the $100 in tax and then spend the $100 for a program of its own choosing—e.g., tax relief.

Tax expenditures provide relief in the following manner:

1. Special exclusions, exemptions and deductions, which reduce the amount of taxable income and therefore result in a lower amount of tax. For example, excluding municipal bond interest from the income tax, exempting the sales of candy from the sales tax, or allowing a deduction for bad debts in the bank and corporation tax.
2. Preferential rates, which reduce taxes by providing a lower tax rate on similar activities. For example, the one-half of one percent insurance tax rate that is applied to premiums on annuities whereas the rate on all other premiums is 2.35 percent.
3. Special credits, which are subtracted from the actual taxes due. For example, the income tax credit allowed for solar energy devices.
4. Deferral of tax, which generally results from allowing, in the current year, deductions that are properly attributable to a future year. For example, accelerated depreciation.

The tax relief provided by tax expenditures is generally available to any taxpayer who meets the requirement of the tax law. It is similar to an expenditure item in the budget. However, with tax expenditures the amount expended is usually not subject to any annual review or limit.

Levels of Tax Expenditures

Tax expenditures frequently have been enacted to: (1) enhance the business climate, such as the 50 percent exemption of inventories from the property tax; (2) provide tax relief, such as exempting low-income persons from income taxes; (3) provide equal treatment for certain kinds of property, such as taxing sport fishing boats in the same manner as commercial fishing boats; (4) provide a relatively low tax rate to allow an infant industry to flourish, such as the one-cent per gallon tax on wine; (5) expand an exemption already granted, such as extending the food exemption to candy; or (6) conform with federal law, such as the retirement credit for the elderly.

Unlike legislative appropriations, a tax expenditure is usually not reviewed unless (1) it has received unfavorable publicity, as with the oil depletion allowance; (2) the Federal law has been changed; or (3) the law enacting the tax expenditure has a provision that causes the tax expenditure to expire on a given date or event.

According to the study on tax expenditures prepared for the Commission on Government Reform, there are over 200 identifiable tax expenditures in the California State and local structure. We estimate that these tax expenditures will total $9.3 billion in 1979–80, or approximately one-third of all tax receipts.

Tax expenditure estimates cannot be simply added together to form totals for functional areas or a grand total. In some cases, the revenue gain resulting from the deletion of two tax expenditure items would be greater than the sum of the individual estimates. For example, if interest income from State and local government securities were made taxable and capital gains were taxed at ordinary rates, many individuals would be pushed into higher tax brackets than if just one of these sources of income became fully taxable; the combined effect on revenue would be greater than the sum of the two separate estimates.

In other cases, the revenue gain from the deletion of two items would be smaller than the sum of the individual estimates. If the deductibility of mortgage interest payments and homeowner property taxes were both repealed, and the standard deduction unchanged, many individuals who now itemize their deductions for income tax purposes would opt for the standard deduction, thus limiting the revenue gain. In general, elimination of multiple items that are personal deductions would increase revenues by less than the simple sum of the revenue gains from eliminating each item measured separately, since many taxpayers would switch to the standard deduction. Conversely, elimination of multiple items that are exclusions from adjusted gross income would increase revenues by more than the sum of the individual gains as taxpayers

would be pushed into higher tax brackets. Where tax expenditures for both individuals and corporations result from the same tax code provision, the two estimates may appropriately be added together.

The Legislature should review all existing tax expenditures in order to identify the beneficiary, and to determine if the original objectives are still deserving of the subsidy. It should be recognized that tax expenditures are subsidies granted to a special category of taxpayers and are financed by all other taxpayers. If all personal income tax expenditures were repealed, then the resultant revenue gain would allow personal income tax rates to be reduced by more than half. If all property tax exemptions were repealed, property taxes could be reduced by at least 40 percent.

A summary of the levels of identifiable tax expenditures by major tax is shown in the following table.

IDENTIFIABLE TAX EXPENDITURES
1979–80

	(In Millions)
State tax expenditures:	
Personal income taxes	$3,838
Retail sales and use taxes	1,835
Inheritance Tax	660
Bank and corporation tax	152
Motor vehicle fuel taxes	80
Insurance tax	40
Horse racing	5
Total State tax expenditures	$6,610
Local tax expenditures:	
Property tax	$2,144
Sales tax	514
Total local tax expenditures	$2,658
TOTAL	$9,268

Property Tax

The passage of Proposition 13, which reduced local tax revenue by approximately $7 billion in 1978–79, makes the study of property tax expenditures particularly appropriate at this time. Proposition 13 reduced receipts of this tax by over 50 percent, and this reduction should be considered by the Legislature in the evaluation of existing property tax expenditures. In light of the low property tax rates and local funding needs, the legislature may want to determine if some of them are still appropriate.

The property tax is an ad valorem tax based

on the assessed value of property as of March 1 and is the largest source of revenue for local government in California. Property is defined as property capable of ownership whether real, personal, tangible or intangible. The State Board of Equalization assesses property owned by public utilities and sets standards by which local governments assess all other property. The tax liability is determined by applying the one-percent tax rate prescribed by Section 1A, Article XIII-A, plus the rate needed to pay interest and redemption charges of any indebtedness approved by the voters before June 7, 1978 to the base year value adjusted annually by an inflation rate not to exceed 2%.

Originally, property taxation was based on the assumption that a physical stock of wealth was the most equitable measure of ability to pay a tax. However, as the economic system developed, other measures of ability to pay, such as income, expenditures, and intangible assets (stocks, bonds, etc.) became more important. At the same time, the establishment of long-term mortgages and installment purchases (allowing other than the very wealthy to own property) made ownership of tangible property a less precise measure of ability to pay. Many exclusions, exemptions, and preferential rates have been adopted to reflect these changes.

The Constitution provides that all real property exemptions must be made by constitutional, rather than statutory, amendment. The following highlights some constitutional changes that illustrate this.

In 1894, fruit and nut trees under four years of age, and grapevines under three years old were exempted. Church property was first explicitly exempted in 1900. Insurance companies' personal property was exempted when they were placed under an in-lieu tax structure in 1910. The taxation of intangibles under the general property tax was abandoned when the Constitution was amended in 1924 to give the Legislature authority to "provide for the taxation of intangibles in a manner, at a rate, or in proportion to value different from other property." In 1944, the "welfare exemption" was added to the Constitution. This provision allows the Legislature to fully or partially exempt property used for religious, hospital or charitable purposes if it is

owned and operated by a nonprofit organization. Legislation enacted in 1945 expanded the exemption to include property used for scientific purposes. Today the exemption is extensively used, and has been interpreted by the courts to cover a variety of uses.

Recent constitutional changes have concentrated on providing for a value standard other than full cash value rather than directly exempting items from the base. In 1960, 1966, and 1972, the State adopted provisions which restrict the factors to be used in assessing the value of golf courses, open-space lands, and owner-occupied single-family dwellings. In contrast, a 1968 constitutional amendment was adopted which granted homeowners an exemption of up to $750 of their assessed value. In 1972, the people extended the homeowner's exemption to $1,750 of assessed value.

In June 1978, the voters, in adopting Proposition 13, placed a limit on the tax rate that could be used and restricted the amount of increase by which the assessed value of a property could increase unless a change of ownership occurred. In November 1978, Proposition 13 was amended to allow real property reconstructed after a disaster, as declared by the Governor, not to be considered as newly constructed for property tax purposes if the fair market value of such property, as reconstructed, is comparable to its fair market value prior to reconstruction. The Legislature also excluded certain transactions from the definition of a change in ownership, such as interspousal transfers.

The following have been identified as property tax expenditures.

PROPERTY TAX EXPENDITURES

	1979–80 Cost
Government-owned property.	$656,000,000
Household furnishings	400,000,000
The homeowners' exemption of $7,000 of full value	354,000,000
Business inventories (50 percent exempt) reported on business property statement	238,000,000
Bonds (and intangibles).	200,000,000
Property used exclusively for religious, hospital, scientific, or charitable purposes	79,000,000
Property used exclusively for public schools.	66,000,000
Open-space property.	50,000,000
Church property	31,000,000
Colleges.	23,000,000
Computer software	10,000,000
Livestock.	6,000,000
Student organization personal property	5,700,000

Ground time exemption for air carriers.	3,550,000
Aircraft owned by U.S., State and political subdivision or foreign government.	3,000,000
Vessels, over 50 tons, or vessels used exclusively in commercial fishing.	3,000,000
Disabled veterans' residence exemption of $60,000 of full value.	2,660,000
Aircraft being repaired.	2,000,000
Baled cotton.	2,000,000
Racehorses, foals.	2,000,000
Movie film.	1,500,000
California Academy of Sciences, School of Mechanical Arts, Huntington Library and Art Gallery, and the Cogswell Polytechnic College.	1,000,000
Cemeteries	1,000,000
Fruit, nut trees under four years, and grapevines under three years of age or held for planting.	1,000,000
Growing crops, including turf grass.	1,000,000
Vessels, $400 market value or less.	1,000,000
Veteran's exemption on property in the amount of $1,000 for a single veteran who owns property valued at less than $5,000 or for a married veteran with property less than $10,000.	379,000
Veterans' organizations property.	20,000
Wine and brandy.	15,000
Business records.	7,000
Blind vending stand operator, does not apply to cafeterias. Exempts first $1,500 of inventory.	N/A
Blood and human body parts.	N/A
Civil Air Patrol, personal property only.	N/A
Documented vessels.	N/A
Goods in interstate or foreign commerce.	N/A
Historic property.	N/A
Livestock, raised by nonprofit youth organization	N/A
Personal property owned or leased by educational TV and FM stations.	N/A
Property brought to this State for exhibition at a fair or exposition	N/A
Property used for free public libraries and free museums is exempt.	N/A
Seed potatoes held for planting.	N/A
Timber.	N/A
Vessels under construction.	N/A
Works of art made available for display in a publicly-owned gallery or museum	N/A
Total	$2,143,831,000

Considerations

Since tax expenditures are subsidies provided to certain categories of taxpayers by all the taxpayers, it is desirable that the public should obtain a benefit from the recipient wherever reasonable. Simply stated, a public subsidy should result in a public benefit. This principle was incorporated last year by Chapter 1019 which exempted from the sales tax works of art purchased by museums, provided the museum allows the public free admission to all or part of its exhibits for a stipulated period of time. Thus, the public, in providing the sales tax exemption, may view that property without charge in exchange for the exemption. A similar provision is contained in the property tax law which provides that property used exclusively for the preservation of native plants or animals, or open-space lands used solely for the recreation and enjoyment of scenic beauty, is exempt from property tax provided it is open to the public. In this context, consideration might be given to the requirement that the beneficiary of a charitable bequest be located in this State in order to obtain a reduction in State taxes.

Some tax expenditures in the property tax which could be considered for amendment to provide a public benefit are:

Exempt works of art from the property tax if displayed without an admission charge in California.

Allow some free admission to exhibits brought into the State as a condition of exemption.

Require all hospitals to maintain and staff emergency facilities as a condition of receiving the tax exemption.

Require tax exempt schools and colleges to make available, under reasonable conditions, some of their facilities such as meeting rooms for community organizations or library access to local residents.

Disallow property tax exemptions to organizations, other than religious or ethnic, that practice discrimination against a segment of the population such as the handicapped or elderly.

Consideration might also be given by the Legislature to imposing a fee on all exempt improved property to pay for some of the services provided to that property. This fee could be based on the amount of exempt square footage or other nonvaluation measure, and could be applied against State property as well as other property.

Sunset Provisions

Programs that include a termination date are said to contain a "sunset provision." Sunset provisions are usually enacted to give the Legislature time for study and to determine if it is desirable to continue the program. Frequently a bill will receive the necessary votes for passage only after a time limit is added to the measure.

Much has been written about putting time limits on certain tax expenditure provisions so that the program could be evaluated. We believe that this review process should be realistic and follow an accepted schedule. The sunset concept calls for a termination of the program unless it is affirmatively reenacted. The purpose of this requirement is to compel a review of each program. Part of the review process should contain a requirement that the matter be heard by a legislative interim committee. The studies that have been made for the Legislature in conjunction with sunset provisions have been prepared by the Office of the Legislative Analyst. Quite frequently the data required to prepare an analysis of the economic impact and cost of a particular exemption are unavailable and the resultant study is inconclusive. In the absence of any information, the Legislature has frequently reenacted the exemption without another sunset provision rather than direct a definitive study. We recommend that every study should include a firm recommendation as to continuation or curtailment of the program.

Another approach to putting a time limit on tax expenditure provisions might be to put a dollar limit on it. For example, Chapter 1082, Statutes of 1977, which provided the solar energy tax credit, is scheduled to expire after the 1980 income year. At the time that this bill was considered, it was estimated that it would result in a $90 million revenue loss during the life of the bill. The Legislature could have terminated the credit in the year that it would be concluded that the $90 million cost would have been reached. This would have the advantage of putting an absolute limit on the amount of cost the State would be willing to assume for a particular program. If it were believed, as in this case, that it would take a $90 million subsidy to get this industry started, then it should not matter whether the $90 million cost occurs in one year or in ten years.

State Tax Expenditures

The following table summarizes the 1979-80 cost of state tax expenditures which have been identified. Estimates were made on each tax expenditure individually and no allowance was made for their interaction. A variety of data sources were used in order to prepare estimates of these costs.

Estimated Annual Cost
(In millions)

Sales and Use Tax	State	Local
Food		
To be consumed at home	$800	$224
Candy	45	13
Vending machines—33% provision	12	3
Gas, electricity, and water	525	147
Vessels and aircraft	200	56
Cargo and returnable containers	110	31
Prescription medicines	75	21
Newspapers and periodicals	26	8
Leases of motion pictures	20	6
Option to pay on cost rather than rental receipts	13	4
Sales by charitable organizations	2	0.5
Master tapes	2	0.5
Vending machine operators	2	0.5
Monetized bullion	1	–
Optometrists and podiatrists	1	–
Hot food sold to airlines	1	–
Total	$1,835	$514.5

Costs not available—Sales to U.S. government, sales to banks, common carriers, out-of-state contractors, printing materials, certain meals, property loaned to educational institutions and occasional sales.

Bank and Corporation Tax

	State
Exploration and development expenses	$40
Accelerated depreciation	35
Research and experimental expenses	20
Exempt corporations (from minimum tax only)	13
Charitable contributions	10
Solar energy devices	10
Depreciation of low-income rental housing	6
Exemption from preference tax	6
Percentage depletion	5
Bad debt reserves	4
Certain agriculture costs	2
Pollution equipment	1
Total	$152

Costs not available—Cooperatives, lessee improvements; foreign sea or air carriers; periodical circulation expenses; deferral or organization expenses; certain dividends; real estate investment trusts; consolidated filing; installment sales; trademark expenses; life insurance proceeds.

Personal Income Tax

	State
Interest expense	$735
Personal and dependent credit	450
Property, sales, and vehicle taxes	370
Capital gains exclusion	350
Charitable contributions	215
Trade & business expense, union dues and miscellaneous	195
Employer contributions to pension plans	190
Medical expenses	130
Head of household status	115
Employer contributions to health plans	115
Employee business expense	97
Standard deduction	90
Income averaging	75
Social Security Income	58
Capital gains on death	50
Interest on government bonds	44
Expensing of certain agricultural costs	38
Compensation for injuries or sickness	30
Low income credit	30
Exclusion of $100,000 of gain from sale of home	25
Individual retirement accounts & self employed retirement accounts	24
Casualty losses	19
Accelerated depreciation	16
Taxes paid to another state	15
Solar energy device/credits	15
Professional corporations	12
Meals & lodging furnished by employer	9
Moving expense	8
Scholarships & fellowships	5
Exploration & development costs	4
Percentage depletion	3
Timber valuation for capital gains	3
Military pay exclusion	3
Total	$3,538

Additional items for which costs are not available or are of less significance include: small business first-year depreciation; periodical circulation expenses; research and experimental expenses; trademark expenses; exemption from preference tax; pollution equipment; rental value of parsonages; depreciation of child care facilities; child support and alimony; payments; sale of residence; certain deferred compensation; depreciation of low-income rental housing; political contributions; income splitting for surviving spouse; and employee death benefits.

Horseracing Tax

	State
Preferential rates	3
Preferential breakage treatment	2
Total	5

Gift Tax

Cost not available—Preferential rates to class A and B beneficiaries (those related to donor); community property; charitable contributions; specific exemptions; annual exemption; intangible property.

Inheritance Tax

	State
Preferential rates: class A and B beneficiaries	$315
Specific exemptions	235
Charitable contributions	100
Life insurance exclusion	10
Total	$660

Cost not available—Public pensions; armed services; war risk insurance; nonresident intangible property; open-space land valuation; powers of appointment.

Insurance Tax

	State
Nonprofit hospital service plans	$27
Pensions and profit-sharing	12
Fraternal benefit societies	1
Total	$40

Alcoholic Beverage Taxes

Cost not available—Industrial spirits and wine; distilled spirits used in food products; sales to government agencies for scientific uses.

Motor Vehicle Fuel Taxes

	State
Aircraft uses, primarily commercial	$45
Sales to military	35
Total	$80

Cost not available—Rapid transit systems.

Motor Vehicle Fees

Cost not available—Government vehicles; local passenger common carriers; privately owned schoolbuses.

"Tax Expenditures" is reprinted from *Governor's Budget for 1979-1980*, Gov. Edmund G. Brown, January, 1979.

Limits May Encourage Tax Expenditures

By Russell Lidman

Many of those who favor limits are concerned about the size of government and especially about some of the consequences of government intervention in the economy. Supporters of limits view them as a way of restraining the size and scope of government.

This view is based on an incomplete picture of government. We cannot judge the significance of a government only by the amount which it collects and spends. Governments have long recognized that they can attempt to influence the behavior of households and business through means other than the funding of programs of one kind or another.

Governments, for example, can attempt to accomplish goals through creating incentives within their tax systems. In some cases, incentives are created by raising tax rates, in others by lowering them. There are numerous examples of taxes whose principal justification is related to their incentive as opposed to revenue effects. High liquor and tobacco taxes, for example, are most often justified on the grounds that they create a disincentive to indulge in drinking and smoking. The federal government permits the deduction of mortgage interest payments in calculating taxable income and in so doing creates an incentive for home ownership. When the federal government wishes to stimulate the amount of investment in new capital by business, often such measures as tax credits and accelerated depreciation are considered. Recently, state officials have implemented a measure which permits business to postpone certain of their sales tax obligations on new construction on the grounds that this delay, through providing an incentive for additional business investment, creates additional employment.

Tax Expenditures

The creation of incentives through the reduction of tax rates or liabilities is termed tax expenditures. In many cases, the purposes of these tax expenditures are clear and they are not especially controversial. Increasing concern has been expressed about the potential and actual abuses of the tax expenditure route to accomplishing public ends.

One facet of tax expenditures has been singled out as especially worrisome. That is that tax expenditures are not subject to the same degree of legislative or executive oversight as are actual expenditures and can continue in existence long after they have accomplished, or failed in, the purposes for which they were designed. Public officials are held accountable for the

"Limits May Encourage Expenditures" is reprinted by permission from *An Analysis of Initiative 62*, by Russell M. Lidman. Lidman is on the Economics Faculty of the Evergreen State College, Olympia, Washington. Lidman was supported by the National Science Foundation's Public Science Resident Program when this paper was prepared. The conclusions are those of the author and not those of the funding source or any other organization.

funds which they spend. The legislative budget making process probably has the most direct responsibility for this task and it receives additional support from executive agencies, such as the Office of Financial Management, and the State Auditor. Authorization for the expenditure of state funds must be renewed at least every other year when the biennial budget is considered.

Tax expenditures, in comparison, are subject to considerably less stringent monitoring. Most tax expenditures, at either the federal or state level, do not expire at any particular time and are not automatically brought up for reveiw. The revenue which would be collected in the absence of a tax expenditure does not, in most cases, pass through a public treasury and is therefore not accounted for as it would be if it were in an agency's budget. It shoud be emphasized that in a most significant respect, a dollar spent by a government is similar to a dollar not collected in taxes. The dollar actually spent is raised by taxes; the dollar in taxes not collected is replaced by taxes collected from a different source. Expenditures and tax expenditures are horses of a different color, but they have been treated as if they were entirely different animals.

Tax Limitations

Limit measures have ignored tax expenditures by focusing entirely on the revenue which is collected and spent. Worse still, limits can potentially create an incentive for governments to rely on tax expenditures. Consider a situation where a limit has been enacted and a government wishes to undertake some activity which would push the budget beyond its limit. Assume that this activity is not of sufficiently high priority to displace items already included within the budget. This activity is not necessarily precluded by the limit measure if a suitable tax expenditure can be designed and it receives the necessary legislative and executive support.

Tax expenditures can obviously not be used to subsidize all types of activities. It is necessary, at a minimum, that the group of individuals who are to benefit from the tax expenditure are paying or would be paying taxes in its absence and that they are sufficiently unique to be identified in the tax law.

Tax expenditures are 'costless' to a government faced by a restrictive limit. Financial incentives for certain activities can be 'funded' through appropriately designed tax relief and the cost of these incentives are not recorded on any budget document. In the face of a limit, we would expect tax expenditures to be relied upon to an increasing degree. Since not all groups have the characteristics necessary to receive this kind of expenditure, we cannot expect that the direct benefits of tax expenditures will be widely shared.

CHAPTER 23

Truth in Taxing/ Full Disclosure

Full disclosure is a system of property tax accountability which prevents local officials from quietly reaping the windfall revenue benefits caused by the natural working of inflation upon property values without ever increasing tax rates. It requires officials to calculate a rate that would produce the same revenue as was produced in the previous year or the previous year adjusted for inflation. If officials intend to raise the tax rate above this amount, they must notify the public and vote to do so.

Full disclosure or truth-in-taxation laws focus public scrutiny on the fiscal decision-making process. Because these laws require public participation in tax and spending decisions prior to increasing revenues, the accountability of politicians to the public is enhanced, and the quality of decision-making may be improved. The tax limitation approach, on the other hand, actually diminishes public scrutiny by focusing attention on the limit instead of the spending decisions made within it, by leaving legislators and the public few choices and little to scrutinize once the collection of revenues reaches the threshold limit, and by encouraging hidden spending through tax expenditures and other devices.

Full disclosure laws have been implemented in five states and the District of Columbia. **Full Disclosure of Property Tax Increases** by the Advisory Commission on Intergovernmental Relations describes how they work and what they are designed to accomplish. To date, as is related in Jane Bryant Quinn's article **Property Tax Issue Really Nothing New**, most of these measures have not been in effect long enough to evaluate their effectiveness in promoting official fiscal responsibility and accountability to the public.

Full Disclosure of Property Tax Increases[1] Truth in Taxation

Legislation vesting responsibility with local governing bodies for determining property tax rates and levies is necessary when details concerning local taxing powers, and restrictions thereon, are removed from constitutions. Based on the California *Government Code* (Division 4, art. 3, sec. 43090-43096) provides such authority.

The following legislation suggests:

1) establishing a "full disclosure" policy regarding the effect of rate and base changes on local revenues, and

2) providing for the imposition of temporary limitations on local government expenditures or tax levies.

Under a democratic system, justice and fair play demand that citizens have an opportunity to be informed about the fiscal affairs of their government and to express their views on major fiscal decisions.

The Advisory Commission on Intergovernmental Relations believes that one of the specific elements that should be disclosed to the public is the effect changes in the rate and base of local taxes, fees, and charges have on local revenue. Such a policy is particularly applicable to ad valorem taxation, where an increase in taxable property value *can automatically increase tax revenues without any specific or visible action by the governing body.* A "full disclosure" or "constant yield" requirement would force the governing body to make specific revenue raising decisions with full awareness by the taxpaying public, and would bring within the scope of such decisions, and the attendant public awareness the growth of assessments as well as rate-fixing.

One way to assure such disclosure is enactment of state legislation designed to encourage public discussion of local tax decisions before proposed tax and spending plans become final. Such legislation,

popularly termed "truth in taxation," relies on strengthening the control inherent in public awareness of the political process, rather than on imposing explicit tax or spending limits.

Under a full disclosure procedure, applicable, for example, to the property tax, the local assessor each year must announce a certified tax rate which, when applied to the assessment base, will provide the same amount of property tax revenue as was obtained in the previous year. This certified rate then becomes the highest tax rate the taxing jurisdiction is authorized to impose unless it advertises its intention to raise the level of property taxation and holds a hearing to obtain public reaction.

To illustrate the procedure, let us assume that the taxable assessed value for a certain taxing district is $10 million currently and the tax levy is $100,000 based on a rate of 10 mills, or $1 per $100 of assessed value. The assessor adds $1 million to the assessment roll for the upcoming year ($500,000 in re-evaluation; $500,000 in new construction). Thus, the total taxable value of the jurisdiction for the upcoming year will be $11 million, a 10% increase in the tax base.

In those circumstances the jurisdiction would net a 10% increase in property tax revenues without changing its tax rate. Under a full disclosure or constant yield procedure, the assessor would be required to calculate a tax rate (9.1 mills) which, when applied to the new assessed value ($11 million) would produce $100,000, the same revenue as is currently obtained.

To allow for some automatic growth in the local budget, however, the law might allow subtraction of new construction from the full amount of the new assessment roll. Thus, the assessor would determine the certified rate by dividing $100,000 (the current levy) by the total assessed value less new construction, or $10,500,000. The certified rate would be 9.5 mills, a half mill lower than the current rate.

If the local taxing district chose to accept the new, lower rate of 9.5 mills, the total levy would $104,-500, a 4.5% increase. Any taxpayer whose assessed value increased by 5% or less would experience no

---

[1]Derived from Advisory Commission on Intergovernmental Relations, *State Constitutional and Statutory Restrictions or Local Taxing Powers*, A-14, Washington, DC, U.S. Government Printing Office, October 1962; and *State Limitations on Local Taxes and Expenditures*, A-64, Washington, DC, U.S. Government Printing Office, February 1977. The Commission recommends the initiation of a process to warn citizens of pending tax rate and levy changes and to provide an opportunity for the expression of public sentiment on any important tax changes.

tax increase whatever because the new rate is 5% lower than the current rate.

If the 5% increase in the total tax levy appeared to be inadequate for the needs of the taxing jurisdiction, its officials could increase the revenue by exceeding the certified rate as long as the higher rate had been advertised, a public hearing held, and the local governing body had then voted to approve the higher rate.

The full disclosure approach, as described here, serves two purposes. First, it provides citizens with the information and opportunity they need to express themselves on proposed expenditure and tax increases. Secondly, it fixes political responsibility for any property tax increase where it belongs, on the local governing body, rather than on the local assessor or any state officials who have the administrative task of determining the assessed value.

The distinction between property tax levy limits and full disclosure laws is in the method provided for exceeding the limit. In the case of levy limits, laws usually provide that the voters must approve at a referendum any property tax levy greater than that allowed by the limit. With the full disclosure procedure, the final judgment to exceed the established millage rate rests with the local governing body. Under full disclosure, when assessments rise, property tax rates are automatically reduced pending tax rate action by elected officials.

Six jurisdictions have applied the full disclosure procedure to the property tax: Florida (1971); Montana (1974); the District of Columbia (1975); Hawaii (1976); Virginia (1976); and Maryland (1977). The full disclosure sections of the suggested legislation are based on the laws of Florida, Montana, and Virginia (Chap. 70-368; *Property Taxpayers Information Act*, Chap. 386, *Laws of 1974*; and Chap. 622, *Acts of Assembly*, 1975, respectively).

"Full Disclosure of Property Tax Increases—Truth in Taxation" is reprinted by permission from *State Constitutional and Statutory Restrictions on Local Taxing Powers,* Advisory Commission on Intergovernmental Relations, 1978.

Property Tax Issue Really Nothing New

JANE BRYANT QUINN

California's Proposition 13 may be the most drastic strike at property taxes ever to come along, but it's far from the first attempt to reduce levies and control government spending. Since 1970, some 17 states have passed various measures to limit local taxes.

Most provide for restrictions on property tax rates, or limit the total amount of money the tax is allowed to raise. The trouble with the former — as Californians and others know all too well — is that when assessments rise, so do taxes — even though the tax rate remains the same. The trouble with the latter is that it imposes arbitrary spending limits that may not be suitable for all communities all the time.

The method of property-tax reform favored by the Advisory Commission on Intergovernmental Relations is the one called "truth-in-taxation," as pioneered by the state of Florida. According to Florida state representative Carl Ogden, who fathered the law, it works like this:

Every year, the tax appraisers reassess homes in light of current market values, which generally are higher than the year before. The tax rate is then reduced, so as to generate no additional revenue from the reassessment. The only "fudge factor" is new construction, which can be taxed outside the normal rolls for the first year.

If last year's revenues plus the fudge factor aren't enough for this year's public expenditures, the taxing unit — for example, the city council — has to put the following quarter-page ad into the local newspaper of largest circulation: "The City Council proposes to increase your property taxes. Hearings will be held on (such-and-such a date)."

Lest you overlook the ad, it must be surrounded by a thick black border.

If after the public hearing, the council goes ahead and raises taxes, another black-bordered, quarter-page ad must be placed: "The City Council has voted to raise your property taxes. Hearings will be held (no such-and-such date)." After the second set of hearings, there's another vote. Only then can taxes actually be increased.

"Public officials call the ad The Death Notice," Ogden says with a laugh. "I'd say that no more than 5 percent of the municipalities have had the nerve to run the ad" since 1975, when this version of the law was passed. (An earlier version allowed so much data in the ads — tables and charts and budget breakdowns — that no one read or understood them.)

The idea behind this approach is to avoid tying local governments into arbitrary spending limits. Instead, officials are forced to be candid about who's raising taxes, and why. Says Ogden: "If the gov-

This bears out an ACIR study of local spending limits, published last year. Where limits exist, the commission found, there's a 6 to 8 percent lower level of expenditure per capita at the local level.

ernment can sell a tax increase to the people, to cover inflation or specific city projects, fine. If it can't, that's tough luck."

Washington, D.C. has this sort of full-disclosure law, but it's not effective, says John Shannon of ACIR, because there's no requirement to place a death notice. The assessor reports on what tax rates should be, in order to avoid revenue increases, but it's often overlooked by the public.

Hawaii embarked on Florida-style truth-in-taxation two years ago and reports some success in holding down spending. In Virginia and Maryland, the law is too new to have had much effect.

Rep. Ogden concedes that Florida communities have had other sources of revenue, to replace lost property taxes. There has been some additional money from state revenue-sharing; many municipalities have increased taxes on utilities; and there has been enough new construction to make the "fudge factor" a good source of cash. The state, in 1975, picked up the cost of the local court system — an important saving. Also, communities have become adept at ferreting out special-project funds — for example, federal aid for sewer projects.

Tax and expenditure limitations are an outgrowth of the public's frustrated demand for lower taxes and more fiscal accountability. As tools to accomplish this, limitation measures are generally inflexible and overly simplistic.

Constitutional measures are more flexible than statutory ones because of the greater difficulty involved in amending the former. Spending lids are generally considered more rigid than tax lids because the latter usually fall on revenue from a single source such as the property tax, leaving open other ways to raise revenue. Spending lids, on the other hand, prohibit any expenditures beyond a certain percentage amount, no matter whether there is a sizable surplus or whether revenues can be raised from other sources.

In addition there are technical considerations raised by limitation measures. For example, tax and spending lids are usually tied to percentage thresholds which cannot be exceeded except under certain circumstances. These circumstances usually require the approval of an extraordinary (two thirds) majority. Most percentage thresholds are tied to indicators of inflation such as the consumer price index or measures of economic growth such as personal income. Others are set at some flat percentage that remains fixed as long as the measure is in effect, regardless of the level of inflation or rate of economic growth.

Of the threshold formulas, those tied to inflation are considered more flexible than flat percentages and those tied to projected growth in personal income are preferable to those based on the CPI. The CPI reflects the cost of consumer goods, not the cost of providing public services. Nor does it reflect a sensitivity to population growth and the increased demand for services which accompanies economic

CHAPTER 24

Tax and Expenditure Limitations

growth. The personal income formula tends to address these two concerns although, like the CPI indicator, it will create serious hardship when the business cycle enters into a recession. During periods of slow growth or economic decline, there will likely be a greater demand for human services such as unemployment compensation and health care, but a lower CPI or a lower level of personal income growth will translate into reduced allowable growth rates for expenditures or revenues.

The Great Tax Limits Debate by Diane Fuchs describes the history and shortcomings of limitations. It points out that many have been around since the 1870's and are nothing new, as well as arguing that they are not tools of reform but rather quite the opposite. They hinder the process of making the tax structure more equitable by obscuring the equity issues and focusing attention on the "quick-fix" of an across-the-board reduction that gives equal cuts to all regardless of whether or not they are currently paying their fair share. As a result, they often reinforce rather than remedy the tax shifts from business onto individual taxpayers which are the root cause of the tax revolt in California and elsewhere.

The table **An "Impressionistic" Evaluation**, prepared by the Advisory Commission on Intergovernmental Relations classifies the various types of limitation measures according to the severity and degree of inflexibility of the restraint, their effect on representative government and the philosophy behind the measure.

State Tax and Spending Limitations, by the AFSCME Public Policy Department, describes the various problems with implementing the different types of limitations. Limits on taxation may produce a greater dependence on other more regressive revenue sources, like the sales tax and certain user fees; curtailment of public services, especially human services; and a distortion in state-local relationships.

Only New Jersey and, most recently, Massachusetts impose limits on overall municipal spending although some states do impose limits on local school spending. **New Jersey's 5% Cap on Municipal Budgets** by Sanford Jacobs describes the practical implications of such caps and points out the bind in which it places local officials. Their budgets are composed of a large percentage of fixed expenses such as pension and insurance costs which cannot be cut back. As a result, other budget items like fire protection and garbage collection must suffer.

The final article, **After Jarvis: Tough Questions for Fiscal Policymakers** by John Shannon and Carol Weissert, sums up their concerns about political accountability and how to make the fiscal system more accountable while retaining a maximum degree of flexibility. One course of action recommended by the authors is increased use of full disclosure laws. They also warn states against imposing fiscal restraints on localities without allowing local government to raise new sources of revenue or without providing increased state aid.

Lastly, their article recognizes the property tax as the focal point for the tax revolt and sets out several elements of reform which, if followed, should in the long run reduce the irritations frequently associated with the property tax by making it fairer and better administered. Several of these elements, such as a state-financed circuit breaker program have been incorporated in the progressive alternatives that have been sponsored by groups in Ohio, Massachusetts, and Illinois. One option not mentioned by the authors that can be an important tool in responding to the tax revolt is property classification.

The Great Tax Limits Debate

By Diane Fuchs

Likening state limitations on local taxing powers to Chinese foot-binding, an economist at the turn of the century set the tone for the current debate over how far, if at all, states should go to limit the authority of localities to prepare budgets, raise revenues, and make expenditures.

Recent rapid rises in local property taxes and local expenditures have made such limitations appear more and more attractive, but they must be carefully analyzed to determine their potential effects. While in fact *some* well-conceived limitations may be necessary and helpful in the short run, leaders of a current "tax revolt" movement are captivating the media with proposals for the most extreme types of limitations.

Background

Property tax rate limits originated as a means to curb rising local government expenditures during the panic of 1870 when tax rates were skyrocketing, and graft and inefficiency were rampant in many large cities. Limitations became a means of protection from the then loose spending practices of local governments and the severe debts they incurred.

The 1930s saw another upsurge in limitations, and many of the existing ones were originally established to curtail rising burdens during the Great Depression.

Forty-six states now have some form or another of property tax limitations—all but Connecticut, Maryland, Massachusetts, and New Hampshire.

Current Relief Measures

Recently state legislators have again been faced with taxpayers' demand for property tax relief, and are responding through a variety of steps. One such measure provides for full or partial state funding of previously local functions, such as welfare and public education. In addition, state legislatures and courts are moving to establish uniform and fair property assessment practices. This has often involved major increases in real property assessments to bring them into line with statutory and constitutional requirements.

To insure that the relief measures actually benefit those intended—the local property taxpayers—states have imposed property tax and expenditure limits on localities. They argue that without the expenditure controls localities receiving extra aid could easily use it to fund new programs rather than to reduce property tax liabilities. Without property tax controls, localities could create undue taxpayer hardships by applying former tax rates to the new state-mandated assessment increases.

The leaders of the property tax "revolts," though, are trying to justify even broader limitations, basing their proposals on the belief that local government is wasteful and inefficient, and need not provide services at taxpayer expense. They also assert that real estate should bear only a limited burden of the cost of local government, in order, some of them say, to make localities more attractive to business and industry.

Those like the Advisory Commission on Intergovernmental Relations (ACIR), who generally oppose state limitations, recognize that there is a potential for conflict between local government officials in favor of local fiscal flexibility and state officials wanting certain property tax relief and political accountability. The ACIR maintains that limits are not really effective in controlling expenditures or in providing property tax relief, and finds them tolerable only if states adequately compensate localities for the revenue loss limits bring about.

Types of Limits

Rate limits: The most common and oldest type of control on local fiscal activity—found in 36 states—is the limitation on the local property tax *rate.* This limit sets the maximum rate that may be applied against the assessed value of property. When a jurisdiction's tax rate has reached the rate ceiling, its property tax revenue can increase only as a result of an increase in assessed value. If assessed valuations are rising rapidly, these rate limits have little effect, since taxes may rise enormously even though tax rates drop.

Limits on assessment increases: State tax laws can limit the statewide increase of assessments for all or only for certain types of property. Provisions in such limits are often made to allow for a certain percentage increase each year. Limits only on assessments do little to limit revenue growth—the key is the interaction between assessment limits and tax rate limits. If assessments are permitted to rise, for example, just 6% a year, and tax rates not at all, property tax revenue growth will be severely limited. Thus, this combined limitation can operate as an indirect form of budget control. But if rates are not also controlled, higher rates can be applied by the local taxing authority to limited or frozen assessments to obtain more revenue.

Levy limits: A levy limit establishes the maximum revenue that can be raised by a jurisdiction through the property tax. The maximum is usually expressed as an allowed annual percentage increase over the prior year's or some other designated year's property tax levy. If the assessed value of the jurisdiction increases substantially, as a result of increases in property values, the property tax rate may have to be reduced to produce the controlled levy amount. This type of control is stricter than limits on tax rates or assessment levels alone because it will be binding even when assessments are rising rapidly.

At least 12 states have adopted some form of levy control—California, Indiana, Iowa, Kansas, Minnesota, Ohio, Washington, Wisconsin, Arizona, Colorado, Oregon and New Jersey. In those states voter approval is required in order to collect levies above the set limit.

Expenditure or total revenue limits: This measure places a ceiling on the amount a particular jurisdiction can either appropriate or spend during a year, and is most often expressed in terms of a maximum allowed percentage increase in annual operating expenses. Expenditure lids are most prevalent in the school finance reform area. For example, when New Jersey enacted an income tax last year to help finance public education, it earmarked funds for property tax relief and put lids on municipal spending and the county tax levy rather than on final appropriations.

Full tax disclosure laws: Full disclosure is the term applied to a fairly new form of control that is growing in popularity. It does not rely on explicit tax or spending lids, rather, it prohibits automatic, often unnoticed increases in property tax levies resulting from inflation's impact on property values. Under full disclosure, a property tax rate is established that will provide a levy equal to the previous year's when applied to some percentage of the current year's tax base. Thus, where the current year's tax base is higher than the previous year's by a significant percentage, the new rate may be lower than the rate for the previous year. In order to increase the levy, the local governing board must advertise its intent to set a higher rate, and hold public hearings.

The full disclosure approach is intended to serve two purposes: to impose public influence on local government expenditure increases, and to direct political responsibility for any property tax increase to local governments and away from local assessors or state offficials.

Full disclosure laws exist in Florida, Hawaii, Montana, Virginia, and Washington, D.C.

Problems

Merely limiting property tax rates, assessments, levies and expenditures can not replace either well-targeted tax relief or much needed property tax reform. In the process of promising equal across-the-board tax relief to all taxpayers (rather than to those most in need), the limits tend to gloss over basic important problems with the property tax system, such as:

● One-third of all real property—government, church, and educational—is exempt from the property tax. In some cities like Newark and Boston, one-half of the property is exempt, meaning that the remaining property, mostly residential, bears twice the tax burden.

● Existing property tax systems are being used to promote "public policy"—as in the currently popular practice of giving businesses tax breaks to attract them to a locality—creating unfair tax advantages to businesses over individuals, and increasing individuals' burden.

Besides ignoring these problems, limits pose potential new problems. Limiting local expenditures, for instance, could create extreme fiscal hardships and give local officials the convenient excuse to cut out necessary (but sometimes politically unpopular) local services like welfare or medical assistance for the poor, or cut back on public employment and salaries.

Taken to an extreme, limits on property tax rates and assessments can virtually obliterate the tax, shifting local control to the state level, and creating increased dependence on statewide taxes like the often overburdened income tax, or the regressive sales tax.

"The Great Tax Limits Debate" is reprinted by permission from the April, 1978 issue of *People and Taxes*, Public Citizen Tax Reform Research Group.

An "Impressionistic" Evaluation of Several Ways to Slow Down State and Local Spending

	STRENGTHENED FISCAL ACCOUNTABILITY		EXPENDITURE LIDS		TAX ROLLBACKS AND TAX LIDS (Proposition 13) California
	Fiscal Constraints	Full Disclosure-Type Lids	Fairly Tight Lids	Tight Lids	
EXAMPLES	1. Indexation of state personal income tax to prevent unlegislated tax rate increases caused by inflation (Colorado, Arizona, and California).*(S) 2. State reimbursement to local governments for certain expenditure mandates (California and Tennessee).*(S) *Policy recommended by ACIR.	1. Tennessee plan--state spending growth not to exceed growth in the economy; with a majority vote of both houses limitation can be exceeded under a full disclosure procedure. (C) Texas Proposal. 2. Florida's truth in property taxation plan-- with a majority vote local representatives can raise property taxes under a full disclosure procedure (Hawaii, Maryland, and Virginia). (S) Texas Proposal.	Hawaiian proposal--growth in state expenditure not to exceed the growth in the economy; require two-thirds vote of both houses to raise limit under a full disclosure procedure. (C) The Arizona proposal is similar to the Hawaiian plan.	Colorado proposal--state and local expenditures not to exceed the increase in cost of living (adjusted to population change); requires approval of a majority of voters to raise spending limit. (C)	A Proposition 13-type plan that calls for: 1. major rollback in local property taxes 2. partial assessment freeze 3. a two-thirds vote of qualified electors required to raise local taxes 4. a two-thirds vote of both houses required to raise state taxes. (C) Proposed--Oregon, Idaho, Nevada, & Michigan
EXPENDITURE EFFECT	MILD TO MODERATE CONSTRAINT--depending in large part on willingness of elected officials to accept political responsibility for higher expenditures and taxes.		MILD TO FAIRLY SEVERE CONSTRAINT--relatively moderate limit but fairly difficult to exceed.	SEVERE CONSTRAINT--tight limit and very difficult to exceed.	VERY SEVERE CONSTRAINT-- unless state funds are sufficient to cushion the shock of local property tax rollback-- increased local dependency on state government.
REPRESENTATIVE GOVERNMENT EFFECT	Strengthens representative government by turning a brighter spotlight on tax and expenditure decisions.		Tends to undercut representative government by granting to legislative minority the right to veto major expenditure increases.	Undercuts representative government by granting to the general electorate the power to approve expenditure increases.	Undercuts both representative government and majority rule.
FISCAL FLEXIBILITY EFFECT	No substantial impairment--state and local officials can increase tax and spending levels as high as they deem appropriate but they are required under this approach to accept full political responsibility.		Some impairment of expenditure flexibility. Public sector cannot grow faster than the economy.	Substantial impairment of expenditure flexibility. Public sector will shrink in relation to the economy.	Severe impairment on tax side and thereby reduces expenditure options. The partial assessment freeze also portends serious property tax inequities over time.
PHILOSOPHY	Representative government can work well when elected officials are held accountable by an informed citizenry--brighter spotlights not fiscal handcuffs.		A majority of elected officials cannot be expected to act prudently--require special expenditure constraints.		Elected officials cannot be trusted to act prudently--cut taxes and make it difficult for them to obtain replacement revenue.

(C) Constitutional
(S) Statutory

"An Impressionistic Evaluation of Several Ways to Slow Down State and Local Spending" is reprinted by permission of John Shannon, Advisory Commission on Intergovernmental Relations, September, 1978.

State Tax and Spending Limitations

California's Proposition 13 touched off a wave of interest in the use of tax and/or spending limitations to restrain the growth of government. The following outline summarizes the more popular forms that have appeared and discusses some of the dangers inherent in these proposals.

I. Limits on Taxes

A. These are designed to keep the *tax burden* constant over time.

B. The most popular form requires that state *taxes* remain a constant percentage of state personal income.
- this kind of proposal is currently pending in Massachusetts and Washington.

Problems

1. May result in greater dependence on user fees and charges or other forms of *non-tax* revenue.
   - These are *regressive* levies—disproportionately hurting the low and middle citizen.
2. May inhibit the ability of the state to issue bonds (at least those that are backed by the state's ability to raise revenue).
3. Severely curtails the ability of the state to finance and/or expand public services.
   - This is especially detrimental in states with relatively underdeveloped public sectors.
4. Distorts the state-local relationship.
   - New state initiatives, such as increased aid to education or other local functions, would be virtually impossible to fund.
5. Inhibits the ability of the state to undertake meaningful *tax reform*.
   - In the past, excess tax revenues have often been used to increase the progressivity of a state's tax system, e.g., implementation of a circuit-breaker mechanism to provide property tax relief.
6. May increase the competition for a limited supply of funds—which may result in some service cutbacks.
   - Some spending is uncontrollable—e.g., pensions, contractual obligations, debt service. Revenues must be allocated to these needs first—leaving limited resources for other needs.

II. Limits on Spending

A. Expenditure limitations purport to "hold down the size of government."

B. In general, a spending limitation will tie increases in state spending to increases in an economic indicator, such as personal income.
- Hawaii, Tennessee and New Jersey all have this kind of limitation. This form is also under consideration in other states, including Minnesota and Wisconsin.

Problems

1. Severely limits the flexibility of government.
   - The economic indicator chosen may not accurately reflect either the *demand* for public services or the *costs* of providing such services.
2. Does not adequately consider the cyclical nature of state spending.
   - During a recession, personal income may increase only slightly, while welfare and other public aid expenditures will skyrocket.
   - A limitation on spending will not adequately provide for such developments.
3. Problems arise if some revenue sources are cut back or cut off.
   - e.g., federal aid declines coupled with spending limits have created an irrational situation in New Jersey. Jurisdictions are *not* allowed to make up for lost federal aid because of their spending ceilings—this has forced service cuts and even some layoffs.
4. Other problems exist that are similar to those associated with tax limitations, such as:
   - inhibiting the ability of the state to increase aid to local governments, to finance tax reform or to expand public services.
   - also, there are technical problems with choosing the economic indicator.

Note: There are an infinite number of variations of these limitations—each with its own special problems, each meriting close study.

Conclusion: Limitations on state taxes or spending are relatively new developments—so far, we have had no experience with these propositions during economic upturns and downturns. However, because these are artificial constraints on government, it is quite clear that they would severely limit the efficient delivery of public services. This is especially true in relatively slow growth states. The northeast and central areas of the country which are experiencing very slow personal income growth would be especially hamstrung by these limitations.

"State Tax and Spending Limitations" is reprinted by permission of the Public Policy Department, AFSCME , 1978.

New Jersey's 5% Cap On Municipal Budgets

By Sanford L. Jacobs

Fire trucks in Trenton respond to alarms with only three men aboard. Priceless shade trees in Montclair aren't being maintained. There's talk of widespread labor unrest across the state.

Municipal officials in New Jersey blame such problems on the financial shackles the state put on municipal spending. Reacting to taxpayer unrest, the legislature in 1976 enacted "caps" on state and local budgets.

They set the loosest cap on the state budget. (No surprise there.) So far, it hasn't come close to hindering state spending. But county, school and municipal officials were handcuffed. For the most part, they can expand their budgets by no more than 5 percent a year.

The spending limit of course was enacted to provide relief for property taxpayers.

Thus, New Jersey took a tack earlier and different than California where Proposition 13 cut tax levies directly. Restricting the ability of state and local governments to levy taxes as California did seems too severe to be a better prescription for relieving taxpayers. Which means there's a lot of interest in New Jersey's spending limit; nearly a third of the states have some form of state or local budget or tax limitation measure on the ballot this fall.

"We get calls from all over asking us how to do it the right way," says John E. Laezza, the enthusiastic head of the state's local government services division which polices the municipal cap.

Five percent isn't much with inflation running more than that. Prices are rising closer to 10 percent and it would be a rare employee, whether on a private or government payroll, who would accept 5 percent as a fair wage increase. So being able to increase spending by "only" 5 percent a year really has meaning for New Jersey's municipal officials.

"It means I'm in the wringer," laments Betty Evans, one of five elected members of the Montclair town commission, and the commissioner in charge of revenue and finance, a position that assures, she feels pressure caused by the 5 percent cap. "There is pressure to spend because everything is more expensive and our employees want more pay because they need to

live," Evans says. The 5 percent limit means there isn't enough to cover all the demands on the town budget. So Evans and her colleagues and officials like them elsewhere in the state have to decide how to dole out what they have.

Deciding how to spend what you have to spend is a normal budget process. But for public officials with the power to levy taxes to cover spending at the jot of a pen, being subject to a severe spending limit is a new experience. Before the cap, most local officials budgeted by the seats of their pants. About the only restraint was what their instincts told them they could get away with. Election years found them seized by fits of fiscal austerity. Now a measure of austerity is imposed on them every year.

Too much austerity, municipal officials say. The 5 percent cap has squeezed town budgets a little tighter each year. Next year the squeeze will be too much, the New Jersey Mayors Assn. figures: it wants the state to grant some relief immediately. If relief isn't granted towns won't be able to give their employees raises next year, and there will be a rash of strikes, the association says. Specifically, the mayors group wants to exempt from the cap such expenses as insurance, utility and pension cost increases. Towns can't do much about these expenses, officials argue.

Pension and insurance increases anticipated next year worry Montclair comptroller William H. Fraser. He expects these two expenses will consume much of the $495,000 the cap allows Montclair's budget to rise next year. He figures there will be about $108,000 of the permissible cap increase remaining after covering pension and insurance increases. However, Montclair will lose $100,000 of federal aid in 1979, so that will have to be covered, too. After that, only $8329.47 of the cap increase will remain to apply to the rest of the budget, Fraser calculates.

Obviously, $8329.47 can't begin to cover pay raises and other increases in the town's $13.6 million budget. So, 1979 shapes up as a fiscal nightmare for Montclair officials. "It will be hell," predicts Evans. She and her colleagues already have had a taste of the peculiar hell the cap puts elected officials through. It has forced them to shrink

the municipal payroll curtail maintenance and often act like disciples of Scrooge himself.

Because of the cap there are fewer workers in city hall, on the garbage-collection force and in the police and fire departments. Promotions, which mean higher salaries, have been slowed; vacancies are left unfilled. And the town has been forced to say "no" to social service agencies. The Child Guidance Center, which aids families with problem children, was cut to $4000 this year from $8000 a year ago. A drug abuse agency got $5000 from Montclair a year ago, but nothing this year.

Heightened competition for federal funds has made it hard for local social service agencies to get money from Uncle Sam, Fraser says. "When they don't get enough from Washington, they look to us. But we can't help them anymore."

Some accounting tricks get around the cap. It doesn't apply to capital outlays. So items that used to appear on the operating budget are shifted to the capital budget if they can be. Only items with a five-year life qualify as capital items. Montclair used this trick with garbage trucks. It used to buy a truck a year as a pay-as-you-go method to maintain its fleet. That way the town could avoid being hit by a big expense one year to replace a lot of trucks. That made them a capital purchase outside the cap. Bonds weren't actually sold; surplus funds were used. Each year part of the outlay appears as a deferred expense on the budget.

But such maneuvers won't let spending rise enough next year, and if Fraser's dire expectations are realized services in Montclair probably will be severely curtailed. Such curtailments loom across the state for towns squeezed between inflation and the spending limit. "Trying to operate against a 5 percent cap with 8 percent inflation won't work," insists Trenton's Mayor Arthur T. Holland.

Trenton, capital city of New Jersey, is an example of what happens to a city in need of money. To be sure, its problems predate the cap. Like other big cities, Trenton deteriorated as prosperous taxpayers fled to the suburbs, pulling with them many of the retail and commercial taxpayers who served them in the city. The cap just makes it tougher for Trenton. "We would be spending more if it weren't for the cap," Holland asserts.

As it is, Trenton's fire trucks run with three men. Its detective bureau recently lost five investigators and the police traffic unit was shrunk to 12 from 30 due to the cap. "We can't put radar units out at night," Holland says. The city also greatly reduced park maintenance. "The parks show it," he says.

Montclair had to cut maintenance, too. It used to trim shade trees, which give its streets charm, every three years. That was too costly and went to every 10 years. Now, "if a tree falls down we'll take care of it," Evans says. Scheduled street resurfacing also has been abandoned. Maintenance usually is the first thing to be cut because the effects don't show at first. But neglect can be costly too.

New York City lies only 16 miles east of Montclair and is a reminder of what neglecting municipal assets like streets, bridges and parks can mean. New York neglected these assets so long

that the city can't afford the astronomical cost to restore them. That could happen in New Jersey.

In any event, the cap provides some tax relief. The first year it took hold, 1977, property taxes statewide shrank 2.6 percent, or $88.5 million. That dip reversed a trend of steady increases of about 10 percent a year in years immediately before the cap. A state income tax went into effect in 1977 also. The state shares income tax proceeds with local school districts. For many districts that has made the cap easier to live with. But for others it hasn't because the school-budget cap was designed to force rich districts to cut spending and to encourage poor districts to increase theirs. The richer districts complain that the paltry budget increases they are permitted each year force them to slowly degrade the quality of education in their schools. State officials say it forces equality of education across the state.

In the meantime, towns aren't getting big doses of state and federal aid like the schools. One thing that can

help them with the cap is new construction. Tax revenue increases from new construction don't count against the spending limit. Thus, growing towns aren't affected by the 5 percent spending limit as much as mature communities with no land for additional construction.

The cap discriminates against communities such as Montclair that can't grow, officials complain. But favoring growth is an old practice in this country. Federal tax laws offer bigger incentives to build anew than for holding on to the old. Only recently have federal policy makers begun to consider the effects this discrimination has on troubled older inner cities.

It would be a bitter irony if efforts at the tax relief in New Jersey, whose motto is "Liberty and Prosperity," were responsible for beginning the deterioration of fine old suburban communities that have no room for growth. As complaining taxpayers elsewhere contemplate shackling elected officials with spending limits, let them beware.

After Jarvis: Tough Questions for Fiscal Policymakers

by John Shannon
and Carol S. Weissert

Shock waves of increasing intensity have jolted the state-local finance sector during the last four years. If their severity could be measured on a scale of 1-to-10, then the 1975 New York City crisis might register a Richter-type reading of 5, the 1974-76 recession about 8, and the 1978 passage of Proposition 13—an amendment to the California constitution sometimes called the "California tax revolt"—almost 10.

While the first two shocks—the New York City crisis and the recession—strengthened the hands of the fiscal conservatives, the California tax revolt has put into effect a four-point action program for sharply cutting back state and local government taxes. As of July 1, 1978, the California constitution provides that:

☐ No property can be taxed at more than 1% of its estimated 1975-76 market value.

☐ No property tax assessment can be increased in any one year by more than 2% unless that property is sold, at which time it can be reassessed on the basis of its market value.

☐ No local tax can be increased or a new tax imposed without the approval of two-thirds of the qualified voters.

☐ No additional state taxes can be imposed unless approved by at least two-thirds of the total membership of both houses of the legislature.

Proposition 13—also called Jarvis-Gann for its key sponsors—has become a banner to many, a red flag to others. This fascination with Proposition 13 can be attributed to extensive press coverage, dire predictions of doom from many officials, the especially binding nature of the amendment, and the fact that California is the most populous and, in many cases, our most trend-setting state. Immediately following the vote, "experts" and commentators wasted little time in evaluating, criticizing, and predicting the "meaning" of Jarvis-Gann. Yet it is the policymakers—particularly at the state and local levels—who will determine the meaning and who must respond to Jarvis and Jarvis-type actions. To do this, they must deal with these hard questions.

Does the Jarvis approach for controlling the growth of public spending represent the wave of the future?

Although a wave of Jarvis-type limits is rolling across many states—three states now have similar measures on the November ballot and several states have called, or plan to call, special legislative sessions to consider post-Jarvis action—there are several mitigating circumstances which render the California situation highly unusual, if not unique. Foremost among these was a $5.5 billion state surplus to cushion the initial shock of the local property tax rollback. This extraordinary surplus, together with a well above average property tax burden, a high and rising combined state-local tax burden, a strong populist tradition, and an unusually rapid growth in residential property values in Southern California all combined to give explosive support for Proposition 13. California Assembly Speaker Leo McCarthy attributes a major part of the vote to one additional cause—one not unique to California—"an anti-government feeling—part of a tide of skepticism and cynicism."

While huge local property tax rollbacks or partial assessment freezes appear unlikely in most other states, the strong support for Proposition 13 will certainly hurry history along on three fronts where some states had already been making great strides prior to the California vote.

☐ *More Restrictions on Local Tax and Spending Powers.* Since 1970 at least 14 states have placed restrictions on the power of local officials to raise property taxes.

☐ *More Restrictions on State Tax and Spending Powers.* Since 1976, New Jersey, Michigan, Colorado, Tennessee, and now, California, have taken various restrictive actions to check the growth of state spending. (See page 10.)

☐ *Greater Support for Home Owner Property Tax Relief.* Proposals calling for expanded circuit-breakers, split rolls, larger homestead exemptions, and tax deferrals will compete even more intensively for state legislative support.

Is it possible to moderate state expenditure growth rates without placing fiscal shackles on state legislative bodies?

Two considerations give this question an urgency that cannot be denied. First, there is clear evidence that an increasing number of citizens no longer want the state-local sector to keep growing at a faster clip than the growth in their own income. Ever since World War II, all systems have been "go" for the Nation's largest growth industry.

The Growth of the State-Local Sector, 1948-77
(State-Local Expenditures and Taxes as a Percent of State Personal Income)

Fiscal Year	State-Local Direct General Expenditures		State-Local Tax Revenue	Exhibit: State-Local Employees per 10,000 Population
	Total	From Own Funds (excluding federal aid)		
1948	9.32%	8.34%	7.03%	240[1]
1958	12.93	11.53	8.85	298
1968	16.38	13.64	10.81	396
1976	20.32	15.90	12.47	475
1977 est.	20.75	16.05[2]	12.87	485

Based on population including armed forces overseas.
This 1976-77 slight increase varies from an earlier ACIR finding of a slight decrease in the relation of state and local spending to gross national product. This tabulation used census data, fiscal year, and personal income. The earlier analysis used national income accounts, calendar year, and gross national product.

Source: ACIR staff computations based on U.S. Bureau of the Census, Governments Division, various reports, and staff estimates.

Second, there is also evidence to suggest that a part of this growth rate can be traced to imperfections in our system for holding elected officials clearly accountable for the growth in taxes and expenditures—imperfections that become more serious during inflation in these ways:

☐ *Unlegislated Tax Rate Increases.* Inflation subtly pushes taxpayers into higher federal and state income tax brackets.

☐ *The Diffusion and Misdirection of Political Responsibility for Higher Local Property Taxes.* Is the taxpayer to blame the assessor, the school board, the city council, or the county board for his tax increase?

☐ *Diffusion and Misdirection of Political Responsibility for New Spending Programs.* In many instances, Congress takes the political credit for enacting a new program (such as the *Safe Drinking Water Act*) while mandating the additional expenditure requirements on states and localities. Similarly, state legislatures often mandate new services or the upgrading of the wages and pension benefits of local employees and force the added expenditure requirements on local governments. There is also the frequent case in which one legislature will take political credit for the enactment of a new program but leave to the next legislature the task of funding it.

In order to remove these imperfections from the political marketplace, the political accountability of elected officials must be strengthened. By so doing, expenditure growth rates can be slowed down without doing violence to the concepts of representative government, majority rule, and fiscal flexibility. Examples of this strengthened accountability approach can be found on both the tax and expenditure sides of the fiscal equation.

A good example of strengthening political accountability for expenditure decisions is the 1978 Tennessee constitutional amendment that restricts state spending to the growth in the state economy. The state legislature can exceed this limit by a simple majority vote, provided it follows a full disclosure procedure. This amendment also directed the state legislature (a) to at least partially reimburse local governments for state expenditure mandates, and (b) to fully fund the first-year cost of all new state programs. In effect, then, it directs the state legislature to put its money where its mouth is.

The State of Colorado strengthened political accountability when it indexed the personal income tax this year so as to prevent inflation from pushing taxpayers into higher tax brackets. Similarly, Arizona passed a law indexing its deductions, credits, and exemptions. The ACIR has recommended this action on the grounds that higher income tax rates should result from overt state legislative action rather than as the silent consequence of inflation.

Admittedly, these various means for focusing a sharper spotlight on tax and expenditure decisions will come under attack from the hard line fiscal conservatives as very "weak tea." Underpinning their objections is the firm conviction that elected representatives can no longer say "no" to all the various pressure groups—that their backbones must be stiffened by replacing a simple majority requirement with a constitutional provision that calls for two-thirds majority approval as the prerequisite for either the enactment of new taxes or a decision to raise expenditures significantly. In effect, this hard line approach gives the conservative minority a veto power over all major tax or expenditure decisions. It, of course, completely undercuts the concepts of representative government, majority rule, and fiscal flexibility—the Jarvis prescription.

A policy of strengthening political accountability will also come under fire from the left side of the political spectrum. Liberals are apt to oppose some of these policies on the grounds that they represent a foot in the door for the fiscal conservatives. Many liberals believe that the public sector is still undernourished, particularly in those program areas that are of most concern to the poor and minority groups. Thus, in their judgment, tax and expenditure questions should be resolved in favor of meeting these urgent public needs—not in figuring out new ways to slow down the growth in state and local government.

Confronted with these conflicting demands and philosophies, many policymakers will opt for the middle course—that of slowing down expenditure growth rates by strengthening the political accountability of elected officials.

When is a state justified in imposing a tight, permanent, lid on local property tax authorities?

In the judgment of the Advisory Commission, the state is justified in adopting a permanent, tight lid policy *only* if the state is willing to provide adequate financial leeway to local governments. The tighter the lid, the more persuasive is the case for a new source of local revenue. Adequate flexibility could take the form of a major new source of tax revenue for local governments or the enactment of a substantial state program of unconditional aid to localities.

Without this compensatory action, the trend toward fiscal centralization will become even more dramatic. This centralizing tendency was clearly underscored by recent ACIR findings that while state lids on local levies reduced property tax levels, this effect was offset by higher state taxes.

Can state policymakers prevent locally elected officials from reaping inflation "windfalls" from rapidly rising property tax assessments without imposing arbitrary and tight tax or spending lids on localities?

This issue becomes especially acute during periods of inflation when property values generally and residential property values in particular rise at a faster clip than the income of the property owner.

In many cases, local legislative bodies do not cut back their property tax rates roughly commensurate with a substantial hike in the tax assessment base and the assessor—not the local legislative body—is mistakenly blamed for the resultant increase in the property tax load.

Florida has resolved this property tax windfall issue without imposing restrictive lids through the adoption of a "truth-in-taxation" procedure. The author of this pioneering legislation, State Representative Carl Ogden, recently described the full disclosure procedure:

Every year, the tax appraisers reassess homes in light of current market values, which generally are higher than the year before. The tax rate is then reduced, so as to generate no additional revenue

Recent State Restrictions on State Tax-Spending Powers

State	Type of Restriction and Year of Enactment		Remarks
	Constitutional	Statutory	
Colorado		1977	Allows a 7% increase in general fund spending with an additional 4% to reserve fund. Amounts over 11% refunded to taxpayers.
		1978	Indexation of the state personal income tax to prevent inflation from pushing taxpayers into higher tax brackets.
Michigan		1977	Budget stabilization fund provided. Percent in excess of 2% of adjusted personal income multiplied by previous year general purpose revenue to determine amount to be deposited in budget stabilization fund. Withdrawals are provided if there is a decrease in adjusted personal income.
New Jersey		1976	Spending increase limited to increase in the state personal income (federal series). Increase of between 9% and 10% for this year.
Tennessee	1978		Spending increase limited to growth in the economy. Increase approximately 11% this year. Provisions for full or shared costs for mandated programs to local governments.
California	1978		Proposition 13 (Jarvis-Gann), by constitutional revision, provides that any changes in state taxes enacted for the purpose of increasing revenues must be imposed by an act passed by not less than two-thirds of all members elected to each of the two houses of the legislature, except that no new ad valorem taxes on real property or sales or transaction taxes on the sales of real property may be imposed.

Source: ACIR staff compilation, 7/10/78.

from the reassessment. The only "fudge factor" is new construction, which can be taxed outside the normal rolls for the first year.

If last year's revenues plus the fudge factor aren't enough for this year's public expenditures, the taxing unit—for example, the city council—has to put [a] . . . quarter-page ad into the local newspaper of largest circulation: 'The City Council proposes to increase your property taxes. Hearings will be held on (such-and-such a date).'

Lest you overlook the ad, it must be surrounded by thick black border.

If after the public hearing, the council goes ahead and raises taxes, another black-bordered, quarter-page ad must be placed: 'The City Council has voted to raise your property taxes. Hearings will be held (on such-and-such a date).' After the second set of hearings, there's another vote. Only then can taxes actually be increased.[1]

While such a procedure may appear restrictive to many local officials, it nevertheless permits them to raise rates as high as they want by a simple majority vote. In effect, local officials have as much fiscal leeway as they want to exercise—provided they're willing to accept full responsibility for their decision to raise taxes.

What is the best instrument to provide property tax relief to home owners?

In the judgment of the Advisory Commission, a state-financed circuit-breaker gets the nod. Three considerations support this judgment.

First, the circuit-breaker can provide tax relief to those who need it most at a lower cost than a homestead exemption. If the objective is to relieve residential property taxes that are unduly burdensome, the relief should go to those households that are carrying above average property tax loads in relation to their income—the circuit-breaker can do just that.

Second, in contrast to homestead exemptions, renters as well as home owners can be given relief under circuit-breakers. On the assumption that landlords pass on a substantial share of their property taxes to renters in the form of higher rents, the majority of circuit-breaker states designate some percentage of rent as a property tax equivalent which enter the circuit-breaker calculation in exactly the same manner as owners' tax payments.

Third, the circuit-breaker is less likely to encounter legal obstacles than the homestead exemptions or other proposals that tax business property more heavily than residential property, such as the "split roll." Because of the uniformity provisions, a constitutional amendment appears to be a prerequisite for homestead exemptions or split roll proposals in many states. By contrast, because the circuit-breaker can grant relief from residential property taxes without adjusting either tax assessments or tax liability, the courts have consistently held that the circuit-breaker does not violate state constitutional provisions. By the same token, spokesmen for industrial and commercial property owners usually

[1]*The Washington Post*, June 19, 1978, p. D10.

find the circuit-breaker the least objectionable method of providing preferential treatment for homeowners.

Our latest survey indicates that, in 1977, 30 states paid out almost $1 billion in circuit-breaker relief to five million householders—a 112% increase when compared to circuit-breaker payments made three years earlier.

Costs and Participation Rates of State Property Tax Circuit-Breaker Programs: Fiscal Years 1974 and 1977				
Year	Total Cost of programs (in thousands)	Number of Claimants	Average Cost Per Claimant	Cost Per Capita
1974 (21 states)	$446,970	3,020,755	$147.97	$4.41
1977 (29 states) +D.C.	949,561	5,112,738	185.72	6.90
Percent Increase	112.4%	69.3%	25.5%	56.5%

Does it make political and economic sense to retain the property tax as a major source of local revenue in an inflation-ridden economy?

Despite obvious defects and poor public image, the property tax has significant political and fiscal virtues. First, it is the one major revenue source directly available to local government and therefore serves as the traditional defense against fiscal centralization. Second, it is the one tax in general use that can recapture for the community the property value partially created by that community. Third, its high visibility makes it a force that can work in favor of greater public accountability.

Beyond these three considerations there is the inescapable element of fiscal realism—the Nation's local governments will not quickly come up with an acceptable substitute for this powerful $65 billion revenue producer. Prudent public policy, therefore, would dictate the adoption of measures designed to reduce the irritant content of this levy.

What is the ACIR prescription for keeping the irritant content of the local property tax at tolerable levels—particularly during periods of inflation?

The danger of a California-type property tax blowout can be minimized if a state adopts a "five-ply" protection plan. While each of the "plys" or elements is important on its own, all must be combined to provide maximum protection against inflation-produced stresses on the property tax. These elements include:
1. A uniform system for administering the property tax marked by:
   ☐ market value appraisal of all taxable property;
   ☐ professional appraisers;
   ☐ either strong state supervision of local assessors or state administration of the tax assessment system; and
   ☐ the preparation and disclosure of assessment ratio findings to enable taxpayers to judge the fairness of their assessments.

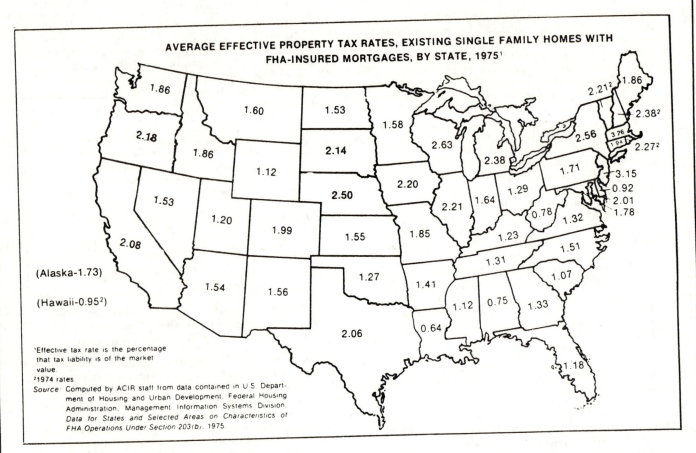

AVERAGE EFFECTIVE PROPERTY TAX RATES, EXISTING SINGLE FAMILY HOMES WITH FHA-INSURED MORTGAGES, BY STATE, 1975[1]

(Alaska-1.73)

(Hawaii-0.95[2])

[1]Effective tax rate is the percentage that tax liability is of the market value.
[2]1974 rates.

Source: Computed by ACIR staff from data contained in U.S. Department of Housing and Urban Development, Federal Housing Administration, Management Information Systems Division, *Data for States and Selected Areas on Characteristics of FHA Operations Under Section 203(b), 1975.*

2. A "truth in property taxation" process along the lines of the Florida plan that will enable taxpayers to fix political responsibility for higher property taxes.
3. A state-financed circuit-breaker system to shield home owners and renters with low and fixed income from property tax overload situations.
4. An intergovernmental "fair play" policy. When the state mandates additional expenditure responsibilities on local government, it should be prepared to help finance the added expenditure burden. When a state mandates a partial or complete exemption from the local property tax (such as a homestead exemption), it should reimburse the localities for the revenue loss.
5. A tax utilization philosophy that rests on the premise that a good property tax is a moderate property tax. As with any other tax, the heavier it becomes, the less obvious are its virtues and the more glaring are its defects. A moderate property tax should fall in the 1% to 1.5% of market value range. Beyond 1.5% of the market value, the amber warning light turns on, beyond 2% the red danger light flashes. If a state assumes the full cost of welfare and Medicaid and at least 65% of the cost of local schools, it

will probably be able to hold local property tax levels below 2% of market value (see map).[2]

There is room for guarded optimism about the prospects for this five-point program for remedial property tax action. Legislatures in many states may find it far more acceptable than the radical surgery alternative prescribed by Doctors Jarvis and Gann. If this turns out to be the case, then Proposition 13 Day—June 6, 1978—will also become a red letter day in the long and troubled history of the property tax.

---

[2]These recommendations and background supporting them are contained in these ACIR publications: *The Role of the States in Strengthening the Property Tax* (A-17), reissued in 1976; *State Limitations on Local Taxes and Expenditures* (A-64), 1977; *Property Tax Circuit-Breakers: Current Status and Policy Issues* (M-87), 1975; *State Mandating of Local Expenditures,* forthcoming ACIR report; and *The States and Intergovernmental Aid* (A-59), 1977. In addition, ACIR had drafted model state legislation in each of the first four areas.

John Shannon is Assistant Director for Taxation and Finance and Carol S. Weissert is Information Officer for the Advisory Commission on Intergovernmental Relations.

"After Jarvis: Tough Questions for Fiscal Policymakers" is reprinted by permission from the Summer, 1978 issue of *Intergovernmental Perspective,* Advisory Commission on Intergovernmental Relations.

XII

By Dean Tipps

Activists around the country, many of whom had worked for years on tax reform issues, were taken by surprise by the right's capacity to capture the tax revolt after Proposition 13. Finding themselves in a defensive posture, they quickly realized they could not fight limitations by simply arguing that such measures were unfair or caused by hardship. Rather, a different approach is needed, one that involves comprehensive programs providing concrete and credible tax relief to wage earners, retirees and others living on low or fixed incomes.

In these and other states, coalitions of citizen organizations, public interest groups, labor unions, and progressive officials have formed and have proposed by initiative or in legislatures impressive numbers of comprehensive tax reform packages. A significant component of these programs has been identifying responsible sources of additional revenue to finance them through progressive tax reforms, while assuring that public services will not be cut. Many of these packages are partially financed by

plugging corporate tax loopholes. This allows the existing tax burden to be shifted away from middle and low income taxpayers and back on to the largest corporations...corporations which often avoid not only political and economic accountability, but also payment of their share for the many benefits and services provided to them by state and local governments.

Leadership of the tax revolt can be claimed only if we — and not just the right wing — define the issues and provide the solutions. The two articles in this section and the respective campaign flyers which follow each, describe the attitude, strategy, and approach taken by many who are confident that they can turn the tax revolt on its head.

The Massachusetts Fair Share Tax Campaign by Elizabeth Bass outlines the Fair Share strategy for framing the property tax campaign in Massachusetts. The focal point of its campaign has been who pays and who doesn't. The solutions it proposes provide low and middle income wage earners with tax relief by asking wealthy individual and corporate "tax evaders and avoiders" to pay up.

CHAPTER 25

David Osborn's **Renegade Tax Reform: Turning Prop 13 on its Head** describes the Ohio Public Interest Campaign's analysis of the tax revolt. Like Fair Share, OPIC views the revolt as one against the unfairness of the distribution of the tax burden, rather than against minorities, the poor, or government spending per se. Progressive reforms proposed not only in Ohio, but also in Massachusetts and elsewhere meet this analysis head on by providing tax relief to low and middle income wage earners. Rather than scapegoating the poor, minorities, or public officials, these programs point the finger at the real culprits, the corporations and their insatiable appetite for avoiding taxes, as well as at those politicians who feed the corporations and their wealthy shareholders while watching schools, the cities, and the poor starve.

In short, the progressive approach is a positive one. The unfair tax burden oppressing individuals can be rectified if the large corporations and wealthy pay their fair share. **The Ohio Fair Tax Initiative,** for example, provides property tax circuit breaker relief to middle and low-income households by plugging corporate loopholes such as property tax exemptions for personal property and real property tax abatements for new or expanded industrial and commercial buildings.

The best and most innovative programs will get nowhere unless part of the campaign strategy includes developing a broad base of support. The success to date of campaigns in places like Massachusetts, Ohio, and Illinois, has occurred only because citizen groups, labor unions, consumers, and many others have chosen to work together to provide the public education and the political clout needed to succeed.

Spurred by these examples, others in all parts of the country are starting to propose programs, form alliances and take on the empty rhetoric of the right. To provide real relief to those who need it the most is the challenge of the tax revolt. It is a progressive challenge, creating the opportunity to achieve a fairer tax system and a government held accountable not to corporate lobbyists and their political action committees, but to the people.

The Massachusetts Fair Share Tax Campaign

By Elizabeth Bass

Right wing tax cutting fever has many organizations anxious to find ways of dealing progressively with tax issues. Massachusetts Fair Share's property tax campaign, in its length and variety, provides some interesting examples of what can be done.

The property tax in Massachusetts is the only local tax. So property taxes are very high: per person, state residents pay almost twice as much in property taxes as the national average, and Boston residents pay almost three times as much. Property taxes have been rising by an average 11% annually over the last decade. And they are highly regressive. An average Boston family making $10,500 a year pays 14.1% of its income in property taxes and 19.3% of its income in all state and local taxes combined. For a family making $55,000 a year, the corresponding figures are 3.7% and 10.7%.

Perhaps the harshness of the Bay State situation made it easier to see the potential for right wing populist tax movements in Massachusetts than in other parts of the country. Whatever the reason, Fair Share realized relatively early in its life that its own constituency of low and moderate income families, particularly blue collar workers, could become a prime target for right wing organizing on the issue. This gave a sense of urgency as Fair Share tried to build and position itself so that it could help channel the very legitimate desire for relief into progressive means of reform.

Fair Share's work has consistently focused on two questions—who pays? and who benefits? The group has struggled to undercut the right-wing fiction that a tax cut is a tax cut is a tax cut—whether it goes to the First National Bank or the triple decker tenant. To do this, it has aimed its campaigns primarily at big business in its civic role as tax evader and avoider. It has defined the problem not as one of welfare fraud or overpaid bureaucrats, but of unfair distribution of the tax burden. Fair Share has argued that, while there is

surely some government waste, significant tax relief for low and moderate income families can only come through progressive reform—otherwise it is just a shell game in which those who need help end up subsidizing tax relief for wealthy individuals and corporations through higher taxes of other types or through the loss of jobs and services.

Fair Share's campaigns have moved from local efforts to citywide fights to statewide legislative and ballot fights. Except at the start, these campaigns have gone on simultaneously, with efforts—increasingly successful as the right-wing threat has become larger—to build coalitions at every level. The local fights bring in members, build chapters, develop leaders and teach valuable lessons about power relationships and tax inequity. The statewide campaigns build the reputation of the organization and provide a larger vision that can begin to address members' needs and use their growing talents.

As a result, Fair Share today is seen both as a group of angry local homeowners and tenants, fighting municipal corruption and corporate wrong-doing in their own city, and as an organization with the potential and range to influence state policy.

In 1975, the Dorchester Community Action Council became the Dorchester chapter of Fair Share. DCAC had been running an abatement campaign for homeowners in its overassessed area; if it had remained simply a neighborhood group it probably would have made a major issue of unfair assessments within the city of Boston. But Fair Share had chapters in places that were assessed lower than Dorchester. Treating the tax issue as a neighborhood problem would have pitted low and moderate income homeowners in one neighborhood against their counterparts in others who were not much, if any, better off.

Instead, Boston Fair Share looked to develop issues that united homeowners and tenants against common corporate enemies. They framed these issues defensively under the heading "close the loopholes." Six areas were identified: overassessments (the homeowner abatement campaign was continued); big corporate tax delinquents; tax exempt institutions; preconstruction tax breaks between the city and developers; large corporate abatements and other

Elizabeth Bass is the editor of the Massachusetts Fair Share monthly newspaper, **Citizen Advocate** *(304 Boylston St., Boston, Mass. 02116). Bass has worked for Fair Share since 1976.*

"incentives"; and tax exempt, profit-making property at the airport. When a $56 tax hike came down in August, 1976—raising the Boston tax rate to $252 per thousand—the campaign was ready to go.

This campaign had several strengths.

First, it was framed in a way that played up the unfairness involved and spurred moral outrage. When people found out that Jimmy's Harborside Restaurant, a politicians' hang-out where working people can't afford to eat, owed $60,000 in taxes, they were plain mad. Jimmy's, a symbolic though small delinquent, was the target of the campaign's first action—a brown bag lunch outside the restaurant led to speedy payment.

Second, the campaign was multi-faceted. If one part stalled for a while, there was always another angle to move on. As it happened, the campaign has focused largely on big tax delinquents since Fair Share won a ruling in May, 1977, that made public the list of Boston delinquents. But if that break had not come through, the organization would simply have moved harder against Harvard or the pre-construction agreements.

The Boston campaign—and the local campaigns in other cities that were modeled on it—were heavy on actions. When the back tax rolls were released, the press picked up on the celebrities named, including the Archdiocese, F. Lee Bailey and a deputy mayor. But Fair Share drew up a "Dirty Dozen Plus Two" list of particularly egregious corporate holdouts and sent out "citizens' tax bills" demanding payment within a week. New England Life paid up its $110,000 a half-hour before the deadline and let Fair Share know about it through a letter hand-delivered to the office. Several others also complied. The holdouts were targeted at repeated demonstrations.

At the same time, Fair Share went after airlines that owed the city more than $10 million. The airlines were within their legal rights—as Fair Share pointed out—since they were paying half their tax bill while appealing their taxes. Fair Share argued, however, that they had a responsibility to a city in which taxes—and airline profits—were high and services were threatened. The organization concentrated its efforts on Eastern Airlines, which was the largest non-payer and had a well-publicized president who occasionally showed up in town. There were several demonstrations at the airport, including one in which Fair Share members passed out "free ride" tickets because "Eastern's been taking a free ride on us for years." When Transportation Secretary Brock Adams came for a visit, Fair Share "deputized" him to help collect the back taxes. In the spring of 1977, the airlines paid up.

The organization also found ways to reach out to allies and other constituencies through its tax work and to make clear that the corporations were delinquent in more than taxes. When Worcester and Dorchester chapters were targeting the delinquent owner of a major nursing home chain, they joined with union workers seeking decent contracts in the homes. After Boston landlords were granted a rent increase to cover the tax hike, Fair Share identified the delinquents among them and, using the rent control law, won

several hundred thousand dollars in rent rebates. This tied in with a successful fight by a Fair Share-led coalition to save rent control in the city.

The campaign naturally targeted some of the city's most resented institutions, such as the airport and Harvard University, and some of its most powerful, such as banks and insurance companies. It made clear that the people who got big tax breaks were tax delinquents, were redliners, were rent gougers, were utility company trustees . . . and so on. The financial institutions' credibility on tax issues was undermined in the eyes of Fair Share members—sure, they're tax cutters, people said, they've been cutting their own taxes, at our expense, for years.

The Boston campaign wedded a direct self-interest "come and get it" campaign—abatements—with more complicated issues of public policy, such as the treatment of tax exempt institutions. Fair Share organizers are of mixed opinion about the abatement drives, which are still being run, although on a much smaller scale. Some feel they met a pressing need, brought many people in, and provided the underpinnings for citywide action. Others feel that they were extraneous to Fair Share's tax work, encouraged people to think of Fair Share as a service organization and turned into a drain as the organization was called on to follow through on appeals over a period of years. Whatever the verdict, the abatement campaigns were done only in Boston.

In other cities, campaigns focused on delinquents, underassessment of commercial property, non-collection of personal property taxes on business equipment and related issues.

By the summer of 1977 hot fights were still going on in chapter cities. But it was becoming obvious to people that their local efforts could never significantly cut their tax bills. They were also beginning to weary of beating their heads against local assessing departments. At the same time, a Jarvis-like outfit called Citizens for Limited Taxation was rumbling louder than before. Fair Share believed it had built a base for statewide action and could begin to affect the outcome of the public debate on taxes that was beginning in earnest at the statewide level.

With that in mind, Fair Share's leadership began formulating a strategy that would carry the organization, not completely unscathed, through the next 18 months. The plan was to bring together the chapters' loopholes campaigns into a set of demands on the state tax commissioner. These demands boiled down to him pressuring and, in some cases, superceding local tax officials to do what Fair Share wanted.

From the state tax commissioner, Fair Share would move into a legislative campaign with powerful allies to win assessing reforms, the closing of loopholes and direct relief through a circuitbreaker. Fresh from a victory at the State House, Fair Share and its allies would wage a strong campaign to pass the classification amendment on the ballot in November, 1978.

The fight over classification already had organizers' mouths watering. It was an amendment to head off a $265 million property tax shift from business on-to residential taxpayers that would otherwise occur from court-ordered 100% revaluation. Fair Share rightly saw this as a classic defensive fight with great power to unify virtually everyone except big business. For business, beating classification meant more than a tax windfall; it meant setting up frightened home-owners for any tax-cutting scheme, no matter how regressive.

The organization began moving on the tax commissioner. Its demands, designed to meet the needs of individual chapter campaigns, were numerous and complex. It is unlikely that they excited anyone who was not already involved. Meanwhile, Fair Share passed up the issue of state tax delinquency which, in the hands of the Boston Globe and a Republican candidate-to-be for governor, turned into a major scandal. Fair Share added a demand or two to its list, but it was the Globe that forced the tax commissioner from office. The campaign seemed so strongly focused on property taxes, that it was hard for it to shift its vision.

But the tax commissioner had always been seen as only a way station. Fair Share moved, as planned, into the legislature with a three-part program: a $150 million circuitbreaker; 11 bills to close loopholes, clean up assessing practices and open up local abatement procedures to public view; and classification. The group did not, however, build the coalition it had hoped for.

Even by late winter, 1978, only six months before the victory of Proposition 13, human service advocates and public employees were not feeling the chill wind on their necks—or in their guts. They did not seriously believe they were in trouble. Nor had Fair Share tried to involve its potential allies in the formulation of the circuit breaker the previous summer and fall. It is perfectly possible that they would not have taken the organization or the tax relief problem seriously enough to sign on. But Fair Share didn't really try.

Moreover, Fair Share proposed no revenue source, other than the state surplus, to fund the circuit breaker. It might have done differently if it had been working with allies from the start. But faced with the choice of trying to raise business taxes or trying to get a piece of the money that was already there, the organization chose what seemed to be the easier way. This put the circuit breaker in competition with other priorities of potential allies, especially then-Gov. Dukakis's plan for increased school aid and state assumption of court costs, which would mean public jobs on the local level. By the time the circuit breaker got to the Governor's desk, it was funded for only $50 million and could have been done without cutting into other programs. But by then Fair Share's potential allies were skeptical about, if not opposed to, the circuit breaker.

Originally, Fair Share had given equal weight to the circuitbreaker and its loopholes bills. The idea was that if the circuit breaker seemed doomed early, as State House observers had predicted, Fair Share could concentrate on the loopholes measures and still come away with something. But the circuit breaker was clearly the most compelling part of the package and

even before it had shown objective signs of survival the organization was concentrating heavily upon it. At Fair Share's taxpayers' rally on April Fool's Day, for instance, equal time was given to the three parts of the plan. But the theme of the rally was "we won't be fooled again—this time we want guaranteed tax relief"—the circuit breaker. By the end of the session, relatively few Fair Share members realized that some of their loopholes measures had become law. They came away feeling strong—and angry—solely on the basis of the circuit breaker's fate.

The legislative campaign was big, vigorous and constant. There were local meetings with state legislators, mass appearances at the State House, constant attendance at committee meetings, and lobbying that turned into vigils with members twice spending all night in the House gallery. There were also many talk show appearances and press conferences. For the first time, Fair Share's at-large or non-chapter members were involved in considerable numbers, lobbying by mail, phone and in person. The campaign was tied into actions against local tax targets and into the beginnings of the classification campaign.

Fair Share found that the circuit breaker was harder to organize around than expected. It was complicated to explain and did not offer relief to everyone—or even a clear majority—in Fair Share neighborhoods. (For a more detailed discussion of the circuitbreaker, see the article on drawbacks of the circuit breaker.)

Nonetheless, Fair Share surprised the experts by passing its rebate bill, as it was commonly called, through the House and Senate with wide margins. But the group learned late in the game that there was a deal. The legislative leaders would let their members vote as they wished on the bill. But Gov. Dukakis would veto it and refuse to transmit his veto message back to the legislators so they would have to decide whether or not to vote to override.

Although Fair Share could and did move 1,200 people against the Governor to ask that he sign the bill, it was playing from weakness. It had not worked on the governor until late in the campaign and had not seriously thought about how to deal with a veto. The pick-pocket veto, as Fair Share called it, went through as planned. Although it was unprecedented and possibly illegal, nobody outside the organization was outraged. The fact that the deal had been made was, in a sense, a tribute to Fair Share's perceived power. The fact that it could work so easily was a reflection of the group's political isolation on the bill.

Fair Share was determined not to let itself be isolated again. By the time the circuit breaker died, the group was well into the work of building a strong and unusually broad coalition to pass classification. In this, the credibility it had built through its near-win on the circuit breaker was important. Fair Share hoped that once this coalition had tasted victory it could be held together to fight for progressive tax relief and reform in 1979. It is far from certain whether Fair Share would have undertaken another major legislative tax fight alone.

The Taxbraker

A bill pending before the state legislature sponsored by dozens of citizens' and labor organizations.

Campaign for Tax Cuts, Jobs & Services

Guarantees property tax rollback:

The TAXBRAKER guarantees home-owners in the highest taxed areas (2/3 of the state) a 20% rollback. It also guarantees at least a 10% cut on all other residential property and provides individual tenants with a share of the relief. It's the only program that guarantees property tax relief this year.

CITY OF
Property Tax Bill
Fall-1978
$2,000

CITY OF
Taxbraker Bill
Fall-1979
$1,600
20% Tax Rollback

Protects jobs & services:

The TAXBRAKER is the only tax relief program that preserves our basic public services and prevents thousands of layoffs in the public and private sectors. TAXBRAKER will protect our neighborhoods and the local services we depend on.

Makes taxes fair:

The TAXBRAKER makes the tax system fairer by closing huge tax loopholes. TAXBRAKER makes corporations pay their fair share in order to ease the burden on the ordinary family. By closing tax loopholes, TAXBRAKER insures that we can get property tax relief without destroying jobs and services.

read on!

9

As it turned out, it didn't have to—thanks to a great deal of time and effort lavished on the care and feeding of the coalition by staff and top tax leadership. The Vote Yes on One Committee, as it was called, ended up including every major public and private union, including the state AFL-CIO, the Mass. Mayors Association, the Mass. League of Cities and Towns, senior, veterans, church, environmental and anti-poverty groups.

While coalition members concentrated on getting the "vote yes" message to their constituency, Fair Share ran an action campaign as well, targeting savings banks (don't contribute to the opposition) as well as the big guns of the other side—commercial banks, utilities, insurance companies, retail chains.

In its chapter cities except Boston, where the mayor tended to dominate the issue in the public perception, Fair Share led the coalition campaigns. Working together over a period of months, Fair Share leaders and staff built valuable relationships with other coalition members, especially unions.

After classification won by a 2-1 margin (with 13-1 votes or better in several cities), Fair Share began a slow and painstaking process of evolving a property tax program that its members understood and endorsed from the ground up and that other coalition members could stand behind. The organization saw it as crucial that its allies feel they "own" the package. The organization had three basic policy criteria: significant relief for low and moderate income tenants and homeowners; no loss in jobs or services; no increase in taxes working people pay. In addition, Fair Share strove to come up with a plan that would provide more direct relief than any of the right-wing alternatives against which it would be competing. The organization thought it important to show—both for short-term success and long-term education—that a progressive plan could out-tax-cut the tax cutters.

The sensitive planning process and the work of holding together major portions of the coalition was made easier by the election of Edward J. King, whose gubernatorial campaign had featured pledges to "crack down on welfare fraud"—in astronomical amounts—and a transparently false and endlessly repeated promise to cut property taxes by $500 million. In his inaugural speech, King promised "no increase in human suffering"—not the most ambitious pledge ever heard from a Democrat. If Proposition 13 was a warning from the west, then King, the big business populist, was the wolf at the door.

The coalition, now calling itself the Campaign for Tax Cuts, Jobs and Services, came up with a package that would cut residential tax rates by 20% in the highest taxed two-thirds of the state and by a minimum of 10% everywhere else, with a mandatory pass-through for tenants of 50% in smaller buildings and 80% in buildings of eight units or more. It would cut industrial tax rates by 10% and freeze commercial tax rates.

This would be funded by a 7.5% excise tax on professional services raising $340 million and a one-eighth of one percent tax on commercial bank assets that would raise $10 million.

This plan, which is called Taxbraker (cq), would free the normal growth in state revenues to be used for the preservation of services. Every other tax relief plan under discussion would use that revenue growth entirely for tax cutting.

The Taxbraker was designed to be both progressive—audaciously so, given the current climate in Massachusetts—and politically palatable. While guaranteeing relief to all residential homeowners and tenants, it concentrates aid in the places where poor and moderate income people tend to live.

While cutting or freezing business property taxes —and attempting to drive a small wedge between the industrial and commercial sectors—it, in fact, shifts a significant portion of the tax burden off residential taxpayers and onto corporate taxpayers. In its campaign, the coalition argues that the funding mechanism will make the tax system fairer "by closing loopholes." "You pay a sales tax when you buy a toothbrush," they say, "why shouldn't John Hancock pay a sales tax when it buys accounting services?" Or, "savings banks that give mortgages in our neighborhoods pay a tax on their assets. Why shouldn't commercial banks that export jobs out of our state pay one, too?"

The Taxbraker, which was only made possible by the classification amendment allowing different tax rates for different classes of property, is in pretty poor company in the legislature. Its competition includes King's all but defunct plan to freeze local spending, cap state spending at below inflation levels and cut services and jobs in order to fund an across-the-board tax cut.

Another contender, favored by some liberals, is a plan by the Massachusetts Taxpayers Foundation, the arm of the state's major commercial corporations, to cap spending and expand the sales tax to clothing, haircuts, movie tickets and the like. A cluster of different proposals, all going by the name of Proposition 2½, would again cut services and give relief in significant amounts only to business.

Against such opposition, the coalition is planning a campaign that relies on large numbers—massive numbers by Fair Share standards—at 42 district meetings and at the State House. As of this writing, it is uncertain how far it will get.

But it is clear that Fair Share, working on the assumption that taxes are the issue around which the fate of many other progressive efforts will turn, has positioned itself so that it can provide leadership on the issue for its natural allies and more trouble for Bay State Jarvises than they had a right to expect.

Largely because of the work of Fair Share, tax relief in Massachusetts is not a right-wing issue today—and it won't become one without a struggle. It is, as it should be, an issue through which low and moderate income people can fight for greater economic justice. The more widely that is true, the better off all of us will be.

"The Massachusetts Fair Share Tax Campaign" is reprinted by permission from Massachusetts Fair Share, 1979.

Renegade Tax Reform: Turning Prop 13 on its Head

by David Osborne

IN THE YEAR since Proposition 13 swept in from the West, the tax revolt has been seen almost exclusively as a conservative phenomenon: a rising tide of middle-class rage against four decades of New Deal, Fair Deal, and Great Society spending; a deliberate attack on the poor, the disadvantaged, the black and brown.

That perception is false—or so says the Ohio Public Interest Campaign (OPIC), the vanguard of a little-noticed but growing movement bent on turning the tax revolt on its head. Adamantly opposed to the cutbacks mandated by conservative tax-cut plans, OPIC believes the real target of taxpayers' anger is not government spending but the unfairness of the tax burden, the ability of large corporations and wealthy individuals to dodge through loopholes while the average citizen makes up the difference. And they plan to prove it with something called the Ohio Fair Tax Initiative, a measure that would cut taxes for low- and middle-income people but raise them for both the wealthy and big business.

Two states away, the Illinois Public Action Council—like OPIC a federation of citizens' groups, labor, and other organizations—is proposing similar legislation. "Our view is that tax reform is a progressive issue, not a right-wing issue," says Public Action director Bob Creamer. "People are mad about their taxes, not about abstract spending questions. The issue is who pays."

In Massachusetts, too, a broad coalition of labor, citizens' groups, mayors, and the populist Mass Fair Share organization is pushing progressive tax reform. And elsewhere groups like Oregon Fair Share, People for Fair Taxes in Washington, and the Association of Community Organizations for Reform Now (ACORN), with chapters in 14 states, are watching closely. Nationally, the public-employee unions are joining the battle wherever it erupts, and the Progressive Alliance of left-wing Democrats put together by Douglas Fraser of the United Auto Workers (UAW) ranks tax reform at the top of its agenda.

"If we can succeed in Massachusetts, Illinois, and Ohio with substantial progressive tax reform," says Creamer, "then the odds are that we're going to see lots of other people trying it across the country, in the same way that the general tax limitation movement was so radically spurred by the victory Jarvis and Gann had in California."

The progressive tax reform advocates point to the most detailed poll yet done on taxes, by Burns Roper, to support their contentions. "In the view of the American public," the poll concluded, "the major problem with the federal tax system in this country is its unfairness....A growing majority sees middle-income people as overtaxed, while upper-income people and large businesses are seen as undertaxed." (The share of federal income-tax revenues borne by business has dropped over 5 percent in the last 10 years, with a parallel shift in the property-tax burden in many states.) Those interviewed by Roper ranked "tax reform" the nation's third most pressing problem, "lowering taxes" tenth. And 76 percent agreed that tax reform meant either "making taxes fairer to all" or "tightening up loopholes," while only 5 percent felt it meant their "taxes would probably go down."

The progressives also argue that Prop 13 proved itself a poor reflection of the nation's mood at the polls last November. "Jarvis got whipped," says Jim Savarese, director of public policy for the American Federation of State, County and Municipal Employees (AFSCME), a union that has made progressive tax reform its top priority. "There were only four states that had Prop 13-style things on the ballot—meat-ax approaches. The two that lost were in Oregon and Michigan, states that are substantial. The two that won were in Idaho and Nevada—and let's face it, they're no bellwethers of public opinion in the U.S."

If the new populists are correct—and can prove it at the polls—the impact on American politics will be tremendous. A tax revolt that has in one short year cut the very legs out from under big-spending liberalism will suddenly give rise to a new, anticorporate populism, challenging Democrats to redefine their politics not to the right, but to the left. A conflict that now pits middle-class taxpayers against welfare recipients will suddenly pit the average person against the wealthy and corporate elite.

"There's no way the old liberal approach—which is to continue to raise the taxes of the middle class and continue to spend money—can continue," explains Ira Arlook, director of OPIC. "Liberals will either have to give up on the social spending commitments that have made them liberals, or they'll have to become whatever we are—progressives, populists, whatever. It's very simple, but what makes it difficult for many people who want careers as politicians is that it puts them right up against the corporations, and that threatens their political careers. What we have to demonstrate is that people like us—who are an increasing majority and who can deliver on referenda and initiatives—threaten their careers even more."

As brash as such projections may seem, OPIC just may be the organization to pull them off. In four years of existence, its founders have assembled a remarkable coalition of labor, black, Hispanic, senior-citizen, church, neighborhood, and even small-business groups, and have almost single-handedly made the issue of tax breaks for business a major one in Ohio politics.

Ohio, overall, is a low-tax state. Personal and property taxes are very low, while business taxes fall in a middle range. In per capita spending on public services—schools, roads, police, and the like—the state ranks among the lowest in the nation. In fact, the real crisis in the state is not high taxes, as it was in California, but an inability to raise enough revenue to keep the public schools open. "If we're famous for anything in Ohio," says Arlook, "it's for our school closings."

So when cities like Cleveland offer highly profitable corporations like Sohio and National City Bank tax breaks worth close to a million dollars a year over 20 years—while schools are closing for lack of revenue—residents tend to swallow hard. OPIC took on the Cleveland city council over those two "abatements"—the official name for property-tax exemptions given corporations on new or redeveloped buildings—in 1977.

Arguing that such breaks make no difference in most corporate decisions to locate—and backed up by a series of national studies supporting their point—the organization made hay out of the issue. City council meetings were packed with angry citizens; demonstrations were held in which neighborhood residents mockingly dumped garbage from their streets on prime downtown construction sites classified as "blighted areas" under the state abatement laws; and hundreds of thousands of anti-abatement leaflets were distributed.

By November of 1977 OPIC had made tax abatement a household word in Cleveland, one of two issues responsible for what the Cleveland *Plain Dealer* called "the greatest political purge in Cleveland's history," in which seven incumbent councilmen were defeated and outspoken populist Dennis Kucinich was swept into the mayor's office.

With the abatement issue igniting in other cities as well and California's Prop 13 looming on the horizon, the tax initiative was a natural. When the Jarvis-Gann landslide came in on June 7, says Arlook, "we decided we'd better jump out in front with a progressive tax-reform measure as quickly as possible, before we ended up having to fight a defensive battle against the Jarvis kind of approach. There are some other proposals in the wings, but by being first we have begun to define the terms of the debate in a way that's really crucial."

THE FAIR TAX Initiative combines two major elements: property-tax relief for low- and middle-income homeowners, renters, and farmers, and increased revenues for school funding generated by closing business-tax loopholes and making the personal and business income taxes more progressive.

The property-tax relief is delivered via a "circuit breaker," a device already employed in some form by roughly 20 states. It works like this: Any household whose income is below $30,000 a year and whose property tax (considered to be 10 percent of annual rent for renters) exceeds 2.5 percent of that income is eligible for a rebate through an income-tax credit. The amount is half the figure (60 percent for disabled and senior citizens) by which the property tax exceeds the 2.5 percent level, up to a maximum of $300. Thus a family earning $20,000 a year and paying $1,000 in property taxes would get $250 back. Someone earning $10,000 and paying $333 in monthly rent would get $75. According to OPIC, 85 to 90 percent of all households in Ohio earn less than $30,000 a year, and roughly two-thirds of those would be eligible for a rebate.

As for closing business-tax loopholes, the initiative would repeal the state laws allowing tax abatement, revoke certain exemptions from the sales tax currently granted business, and require banks and savings and loans to pay the corporate franchise (income) tax like any other business. Franchise-tax rates would be altered to lower taxes for businesses earning under $75,000 in net taxable income per year and hike them from 8 to 10 percent on income above that figure.

Personal income-tax rates, which are now graduated between zero and $40,000, but which level off at a flat 3.5 percent for any income above that line, would be graduated on up to 6 percent for those making over $50,000 a year. Thus income taxes would go up for the wealthiest 10 to 15 percent of the population.

In total, according to the state Department of Taxation, the initiative would raise approximately $562 million in new revenues in fiscal 1980, the great bulk from business. Roughly $120 million would be handed back via the property-tax circuit breaker.

When OPIC kicked off the petition drive last fall—using the slogan "We can have tax relief and keep our schools open too"—the media quickly tagged it Ohio's version of the tax revolt. The resulting bandwagon effect, combined with the broad base of organizations OPIC was able to tap, enabled it to do what many thought impossible: gather 93,000 signatures in just six weeks. Under Ohio law, any petition signed by 3 percent of the number of voters in the last gubernatorial election must be considered by the legislature. If after 120 days the petitioners are not satisfied with the General Assembly's action, they can put the proposal on the ballot with another 3 percent—in this case, 85,300 signatures.

Barring an unexpected breakdown during the 10-day grace period allowed to make up for invalid signatures among the first 93,000, the OPIC initiative should be before the legislature by early spring. Assuming that even if passed the bill will be vetoed by Republican Governor James Rhodes, the expected ballot showdown would come next November or the following June. And most people in positions to know give OPIC a fair chance to win.

"Everyone's receptive to tax relief," says Dean Lovelace, head of the Ohio Black Political Assembly. "But the seller on this initiative, from the people I collected signatures from, was that corporate loopholes would be closed. It's everyone's view that the corporate fellows tend to get off the hook—that they don't pay, and that the corporate sector can pay a lot easier than the average homeowner."

Surprisingly, the OPIC staffers report that Lovelace's experience was typical: The most attractive bait in gathering signatures was the idea of forcing business to pay its "fair share."

"The approach was in some ways new to people," says Ed Kelly, OPIC research director. "Usually, lowering taxes means cutting services. Many people were skeptical of us in a way, because they assumed our proposal would mean cutbacks. Then you'd explain the idea of raising revenues by closing corporate loopholes, and they'd say, 'OK, that sounds good.'"

Not surprisingly, big business itself

was not so pleased. "The measure goes so far that it can properly be termed 'ridiculous' and 'nonsensible,'" the Ohio Manufacturers Association (OMA) fumed in its newsletter. If it passes, Ohio "cannot possibly compete with the other industrial states in this industrial corridor....To paraphrase Cato 2,100 years ago, 'OPIC must be destroyed' if Ohio is to survive."

That said, the OMA board chairman and another active member slapped a suit on the state, arguing principally that the initiative violated the state constitution by creating different classes of property for the purpose of taxation. Though the suit was thrown out of court in February (and immediately appealed), it was a clear signal of how seriously business takes the coming battle. The OMA has in fact already warned that business will mount "an all-out and expensive" campaign if the measure is put on the ballot, with $2 million being tossed around as a minimum.

Business will clearly strive to make the key issue one of job loss, arguing that higher taxes will drive business out of Ohio. Most people believe taxes are one reason industry has left the Northeast in such droves, and breaking that impression down will be the single most important hurdle for any organization attempting to raise corporate taxes.

The facts are there, however. Study after study—whether national, regional, or local—has found tax levels to be negligible factors in corporate location decisions, insignificant compared to labor costs, union activities, transportation costs, and the like. "As one team of researchers has put it," a comprehensive Library of Congress survey concluded, "'there is little doubt that local (tax) subsidies are almost completely ineffective in influencing any regional location decisions.'" A congressional staff survey of nearly 1,300 businesses released just this January went even further, reporting that noneconomic factors like crime rates and schools are more important to corporate location decisions in urban areas than *any* financial factors,

whether labor rates or taxes.

"*Business Week* estimates that 2 to 3 percent of total corporate costs are represented by state and local taxes," says OPIC's Kelly. "And any state is going to have taxes, so you're talking about some minor percentage difference between, say, 2.8 percent in one state and 3 percent in another. It's a very minor thing.

"Any corporation is going to say they'd like low taxes, but higher on their wish list are adequate services and schools. So the idea that you're going to improve your economy by having low taxes is contradictory, because if you offer low taxes, you're going to do it at the expense of other things that are much more important in terms of actually bringing business into your community and keeping them there."

WHETHER KELLY and his colleagues can get the message across only time—and campaign funds—will tell. They do have several factors going for them, however. The widespread debate over tax abatements has already raised public awareness of the facts and anger at corporate tax breaks. The school crisis has made it painfully obvious to many that new tax revenues are necessary, and polls done by the Ohio Education Association (OEA) show that if some taxes have to be raised, the public favors business taxes by a two to one margin over any other option. And OPIC will have the credibility of industrial union leaders—always the most sensitive about job loss—willing to stand up and say the Fair Tax Initiative will not cost Ohio one job. OPIC's close alliance with labor is owed largely to a long (though as yet unsuccessful) campaign for legislation protecting workers and communities against plant closings.

On the negative side, the issue could be clouded come November by the presence of other ballot initiatives on taxes and spending. Sponsors of both a spending limitation bill and a Jarvis-type property-tax cut have talked of petition drives. And the OEA, which feels the OPIC initiative does not raise enough

new revenues for the schools, is also considering a petition drive. Ongoing discussions indicate the OEA proposal would raise perhaps a billion dollars a year in new funds, shift the property-tax burden partially onto more progressive income taxes, and also attack business-tax loopholes.

Even if the competition does emerge, however, OPIC's Fair Tax Initiative has gained the advantage of being first out of the blocks. And given the options, the OPIC measure will in many ways appear the most reasonable, cutting property taxes and generating new funds for the schools, but doing neither to the extremes desired by the Jarvis or OEA people. While the business community will surely paint the initiative as radical and dangerous, most legislators see it as a modest proposal, and if labor has a criticism—particularly public employees—it's that it doesn't go far enough.

If the proposal wins, says Mary Lynne Cappelletti, OPIC's lobbyist in the state capitol, "I think the national impact will be extraordinary. If we can win progressive tax reform in the bedrock heartland of the country, Ohio, with its diversity and its industrial base, then we really will have signaled the country that the taxpayers' revolt is a demand for progressive taxes. And that will be the clearest signal that's gone up since the lantern hung in Old North Church."

Such a signal—if indeed heard throughout the nation—would also have a direct impact on the current struggle at the heart of the Democratic Party. Should Ohio—and perhaps Illinois and Massachusetts as well—offer a reinterpretation of the tax revolt, liberal Democrats will again have some ground to stand on, some way to deliver tax relief to the hard-pressed middle and working classes without cutting back on spending for education, jobs, health, the cities, and the poor. They will have that ground, that is, *if* they are willing to slug it out with business. It's a big if, but as Jarvis and company have shown us, tax initiatives have a way of shaking things up—and quickly.

Ohio Fair Tax Initiative
We can have tax relief, if the corporations pay their fair share

Whenever 92,891 Ohioans sign initiative petitions on an issue in only 5 weeks, it's a good guess that public opinion has reached the boiling point.

The Ohio legislature has now received a strong message from its constituents in the form of the Ohio Fair Tax Initiative.

Why have Ohioans enrolled in the tax revolt?
As in other states, citizens here have taken the initiative because their elected leadership has failed to face problems which have grown worse year by year.

The Fair Tax Initiative is a big first step to resolve three pressing needs in Ohio —

- Low and middle income taxpayers, family farmers and small businesses need tax relief;

- All Ohioans need open schools and effective public services;

- We all need to have large corporations start shouldering their fair share of the tax load.

Is this Ohio's Proposition 13?
The Fair Tax Initiative will avoid the severe pitfalls of California's Proposition 13, while at the same time giving Ohioans substantial property tax relief — $150 million worth.

Proposition 13 gave a wasteful windfall — 2/3 of the relief ($5 billion) — to wealthy corporations that certainly didn't need a handout. The Ohio Fair Tax Initiative gives tax relief *only* to those who really need it — low and moderate income homeowners, renters, and family farmers. There's no hidden windfall in the Ohio Initiative.

Proposition 13 in California also didn't say who was going to pay for the tax relief it granted. As a result, many Californians who voted for it are now paying through decreased services and schools, or through an increase in other taxes and state fees. In Ohio, we can't afford to risk our already-periled schools and social service programs.

That's why the Ohio Fair Tax Initiative insures that lost revenues are recouped, primarily by closing corporate tax loopholes. In fact, the Ohio Initiative will actually *increase* overall state revenues by over $200 million a year.

Now, it's the legislature's turn
This initiative gives the Ohio legislature a unique opportunity to set a national precedent for state tax reform.

In other states, legislatures have either dragged their feet or cynically slashed state funding for schools and social services.

By following the Fair Tax mandate, Ohio can become the first state whose legislature responded to the tax revolt in a responsible way.

The less you earn, the more you pay.

For many years, low and middle income Ohioans have been carrying a disproportionate part of the overall tax burden. For an average Ohio family of four in 1974, the state and local tax burden as a percentage of income was as follows:

Adjusted Gross Income	Taxes as % of Income
$ 5,000	10.5%
7,500	9.0%
10,000	7.9%
17,500	7.7%
25,000	7.3%
50,000	7.1%

Source: **Significant Features of Fiscal Federalism—1976-77,** Advisory Committee on Intergovernmental Relations

In contrast to the warm reception given the Fair Tax Initiative throughout the state this winter, a Columbus lobby group for large corporations has wildly attacked the Ohio Public Interest Campaign.

The December 4 newsletter of the Ohio Manufacturers Association (OMA) concludes, "OPIC must be destroyed, if Ohio is to survive."

This startling announcement has been accompanied by an OMA court suit to try to prevent the Ohio legislature from having a chance to consider the Initiative. On February 5, 1979, the OMA lost its case when Judge Fred J. Shoemaker of the Franklin County Court of Common Pleas ruled in favor of the Initiative, stating:

"Therefore, the people having expressly reserved to themselves the right of initiative, it is not the function of this court to interfere with that right

and disenfranchise the voters... Plaintiff [OMA]'s request for an injunction is DENIED."

On December 22nd, the OMA had filed suit in the Franklin County Court of Appeals, asking the court to void all 92,981 signatures on technical—and unfounded—charges. The Appeals judges refused to freeze the initiative process while considering the case and speeded up the court schedule so the case could be heard promptly. Then the OMA dropped the suit and refiled it in the Common Pleas Court.

OMA's statements and actions are a chilling reminder of the power of wealthy special interests to confound the democratic process, preventing needed and popular legislation from receiving a fair hearing.

OPIC has never suggested that the OMA "must be destroyed." All we are asking is that its member corporations pay their fair share of taxes.

National Perspective:

Someone's not carrying their load:

The following table shows the shockingly low taxes which some large corporations pay to states and localities.

In Ohio, large corporations are supposed to pay 8% of their income in state taxes and 1-2% in city taxes. The state tax rates in most states are between 6% and 10%.

Unfortunately, because of loopholes and outright evasion, the real rate at which many large corporations pay is far lower.

OVERALL STATE & LOCAL INCOME TAXES PAID BY SELECTED CORPORATIONS, 1977

Corporation	Pre-tax Earnings	State/Local Income Taxes*	% of Total Income Paid in State/Local Tax
Sohio	$ 239,406,000	$ 3,500,000	1.46%
Diamond Shamrock	247,748,000	4,748,000	1.92%
Republic Steel	34,266,000	639,000	1.90%
Proctor & Gamble	867,087,000	7,546,000	.87%
Dow Chemical	841,824,000	20,900,000	2.48%
Ford	2,852,000,000	63,600,000	2.23%
General Electric	1,826,600,000	24,400,000	1.34%
ITT	675,401,000	16,885,000	2.49%
Union Carbide	594,500,000	7,400,000	1.24%
Exxon	8,151,453,000	67,000,000	.82%
Mobil	4,155,417,000	65,900,000	1.58%
Standard Oil/Ind.	2,538,138,000	14,600,000	.57%
Texaco	1,513,060,000	13,700,000	.90%

*Income taxes paid to all states and localities

Source: *Tax Notes*, Feb. 20, '78, p. 178; May 22, '78, p. 560; June 12, '78; p. 664-665; June 19, '78, p. 698-700.

"The Ohio Fair Tax Initiative" is reprinted by permission from the Ohio Public Interest Campaign, 1979.

Refashioning Ohio's Tax Structure

BY STEVE WILSON
Gannett News Service

COLUMBUS: It's called the Fair Tax Initiative, and, unless Ohio legislators come up with a more appealing plan of their own, chances are good it will be state law by this time next year.

Held up by 14 lawsuits for more than a year, the proposed tax-reform plan of the Ohio Public Interest Campaign (OPIC) is now before the Ohio legislature. Between now and June 27, legislators can debate it, amend it, praise it and malign it. But if they kill it, amend it too much or just plain do nothing, chances are excellent Ohio voters will have a chance to vote for it. And if the measure gets on the November ballot, it could be more difficult to stop than a runaway locomotive.

IN ITS own way, the Fair Tax Initiative may be to Ohio property owners what Proposition 13 was to Californians. It's a chance for some to strike back at rising property taxes and help shift the tax burden onto someone else.

The "something else" in this case is big business which, through the Ohio Manufacturers Association, was responsible for keeping the initiative out of the legislature for more than a year.

Although the battles so far have been confined to courtrooms in a series of legal maneuvers designed to keep OPIC from ever getting its plan to the legislature, the legislature has now become the battleground.

BUSINESSES, UNDERSTANDABLY, aren't too eager to have their taxes increased and are expected to fight the proposal to the bitter end. If OPIC's plan becomes law, it would close up corporate tax loopholes that have allowed big industries to avoid paying what OPIC officials say were their fair share of the tax load. It would also make the end of tax abatement as an incentive to get industries to locate in Ohio.

The plan, its supporters believe, would generate another $650 million or so in additional state revenues yearly by stepping up corporate taxes and increasing the rate of taxation on those individuals earning more than $30,000 annually. While the proposal would increase income taxes modestly for a limited number of families—$50 for someone earning $40,000—it is big business that will really pay for the proposal. OPIC estimates the higher income tax rates would affect only about 10% of the state's population. Higher corporate taxes, plus sewed-up loopholes, account for the bulk of the new revenues.

THE BENEFACTORS of OPIC's "progressive tax-reform measure" jwould be property owners with incomes of less than $30,000 annually whose property tax bills have gotten out of proportion with incomes over the years. Overall, it is expected to provide $150 million in property-tax relief to them.

Under the plan, tax credits of 50% are provided for all property taxes in excess of 2.5% of a family's income. Senior citizens would get a 60% tax credit up to the $300 ceiling. Schools, which already take a larger and larger chunk of the state's general fund, would benefit from some of the additional revenues.

While the plan doesn't appear to provide mammoth relief to anyone, it should provide enough relief to look attractive to a majority of Ohio taxpayers, even if it is far from appealing to Ohio businesses.

THE PLAN could force legislators to take action on something they've been delaying for months. If they fight it, it gives the appearance at least that they're against property-tax relief and favor big business. And, that stand would not be the most attractive to take in a legislative election year.

So, rather than try to kill OPIC's plan, legislators might be inclined to come up with one of their own—possibly one that would grant substantial property-tax relief and a little less shocking to Ohio's business community.

Either way, some margin of property tax relief seems to be in the works for Ohioans.

"Refashioning Ohio's Tax Structure" is reprinted by permission from the March 30, 1980 issue of *The Cincinnati Enquirer*.

Statistical Appendix

State and Local Government Revenues and Expenditures, Selected Fiscal Years, 1927-77

[Millions of dollars]

Fiscal year [1]	General revenues by source [2]							General expenditures by function [2]				
	Total	Property taxes	Sales and gross receipts taxes	Individual income taxes	Corporation net income taxes	Revenue from Federal Government	All other [3]	Total	Education	Highways	Public welfare	All other [4]
1927	7,271	4,730	470	70	92	116	1,793	7,210	2,235	1,809	151	3,015
1932	7,267	4,487	752	74	79	232	1,643	7,765	2,311	1,741	444	3,269
1934	7,678	4,076	1,008	80	49	1,016	1,449	7,181	1,831	1,509	889	2,952
1936	8,395	4,093	1,484	153	113	948	1,604	7,644	2,177	1,425	827	3,215
1938	9,228	4,440	1,794	218	165	800	1,811	8,757	2,491	1,650	1,069	3,547
1940	9,609	4,430	1,982	224	156	945	1,872	9,229	2,638	1,573	1,156	3,862
1942	10,418	4,537	2,351	276	272	858	2,123	9,190	2,586	1,490	1,225	3,889
1944	10,908	4,604	2,289	342	451	954	2,269	8,863	2,793	1,200	1,133	3,737
1946	12,356	4,986	2,986	422	447	855	2,661	11,028	3,356	1,672	1,409	4,591
1948	17,250	6,126	4,442	543	592	1,861	3,685	17,684	5,379	3,036	2,099	7,170
1950	20,911	7,349	5,154	788	593	2,486	4,541	22,787	7,177	3,803	2,940	8,867
1952	25,181	8,652	6,357	998	846	2,566	5,763	26,098	8,318	4,650	2,788	10,342
1953	27,307	9,375	6,927	1,065	817	2,870	6,252	27,910	9,390	4,987	2,914	10,619
1954	29,012	9,967	7,276	1,127	778	2,966	6,897	30,701	10,557	5,527	3,060	11,557
1955	31,073	10,735	7,643	1,237	744	3,131	7,584	33,724	11,907	6,452	3,168	12,197
1956	34,667	11,749	8,691	1,538	890	3,335	8,465	36,711	13,220	6,953	3,139	13,399
1957	38,164	12,864	9,467	1,754	984	3,843	9,250	40,375	14,134	7,816	3,485	14,940
1958	41,219	14,047	9,829	1,759	1,018	4,865	9,699	44,851	15,919	8,567	3,818	16,547
1959	45,306	14,983	10,437	1,994	1,001	6,377	10,516	48,887	17,283	9,592	4,136	17,876
1960	50,505	16,405	11,849	2,463	1,180	6,974	11,634	51,876	18,719	9,428	4,404	19,325
1961	54,037	18,002	12,463	2,613	1,266	7,131	12,563	56,201	20,574	9,844	4,720	21,063
1962	58,252	19,054	13,494	3,037	1,308	7,871	13,489	60,206	22,216	10,357	5,084	22,549
1963	62,890	20,089	14,456	3,269	1,505	8,722	14,850	64,816	23,776	11,136	5,481	24,423
1962-63 [5]	62,269	19,833	14,446	3,267	1,505	8,663	14,556	63,977	23,729	11,150	5,420	23,678
1963-64 [5]	68,443	21,241	15,762	3,791	1,695	10,002	15,951	69,302	26,286	11,664	5,766	25,586
1964-65 [5]	74,000	22,583	17,118	4,090	1,929	11,029	17,250	74,546	28,563	12,221	6,315	27,447
1965-66 [5]	83,036	24,670	19,085	4,760	2,038	13,214	19,269	82,843	33,287	12,770	6,757	30,029
1966-67 [5]	91,197	26,047	20,530	5,826	2,227	15,370	21,197	93,350	37,919	13,932	8,218	33,281
1967-68 [5]	101,264	27,747	22,911	7,308	2,518	17,181	23,598	102,411	41,158	14,481	9,857	36,915
1968-69 [5]	114,550	30,673	26,519	8,908	3,180	19,153	26,118	116,728	47,238	15,417	12,110	41,963
1969-70 [5]	130,756	34,054	30,322	10,812	3,738	21,857	29,971	131,332	52,718	16,427	14,679	47,508
1970-71 [5]	144,927	37,852	33,233	11,900	3,424	26,146	32,374	150,674	59,413	18,095	18,226	54,940
1971-72 [5]	166,352	42,133	37,488	15,237	4,416	31,253	35,826	166,873	64,886	19,010	21,070	61,907
1972-73 [5]	190,214	45,283	42,047	17,994	5,425	39,256	40,210	181,227	69,714	18,615	23,582	69,316
1973-74 [5]	207,670	47,705	46,098	19,491	6,015	41,820	46,541	198,959	75,833	19,946	25,085	78,096
1974-75 [5]	228,171	51,491	49,815	21,454	6,642	47,034	51,735	230,721	87,858	22,528	28,155	92,180
1975-76 [5]	256,176	57,001	54,547	24,575	7,273	55,589	57,191	256,731	97,216	23,907	32,604	103,004
1976-77 [5]	285,796	62,535	60,595	29,245	9,174	62,575	61,673	274,388	102,805	23,105	35,941	112,537

[1] Fiscal years not the same for all governments. See footnote 5.
[2] Excludes revenues or expenditures of publicly owned utilities and liquor stores, and of insurance-trust activities. Intergovernmental receipts and payments between State and local governments are also excluded.
[3] Includes licenses and other taxes and charges and miscellaneous revenues.
[4] Includes expenditures for health, hospitals, police, local fire protection, natural resources, sanitation, housing and urban renewal, local parks and recreation, general control, financial administration, interest on general debt, and unallocable expenditures.
[5] Data for fiscal year ending in the 12-month period through June 30. Data for 1963 and earlier years include local government amounts grouped in terms of fiscal years ended during the particular calendar year.

Note.—Data are not available for intervening years.

Source: Department of Commerce, Bureau of the Census.

TRENDS IN STATE-LOCAL TAX REVENUES
by Allen D. Manvel

The Census Bureau's issuance in March of its "Quarterly Summary of State and Local Tax Revenue" covering the fourth quarter of 1977 marked the 15th anniversary of this informative statistical series.

There were major changes in the mix of state-local taxes between 1962 and 1977. The financing role of the states continued to increase, so that their portion of state-local taxes grew from 49.6 to 58.1 percent. In a closely related development, property taxes, which in the main are locally-imposed, dropped from 45.8 to 35.1 percent.

Overall, state-local tax collections increased more rapidly than GNP during this 15-year interval, so that in 1977 they amounted to $97 per $1,000 GNP, as compared with $76 per $1,000 in 1962. Property tax revenue, however, grew somewhat less rapidly than GNP, so that, as shown in the accompanying chart, it amounted in 1977 to $33.95 per $1,000 GNP, as compared with $34.75 per $1,000 fifteen years earlier. The yield of state-local motor-vehicle-user taxes lagged even further behind the growth of GNP. In 1977, gasoline tax revenue amounted to only $4.96 per $1,000 GNP, as compared with $6.70 per $1,000 fifteen years before; and the yield of vehicle and operators' licenses slipped from $3.21 to $2.62 per $1,000 GNP. These are surely odd developments for a nation that is said to face a serious need for energy conservation!

Other major state and local taxes — all more directly responsive than the property tax or motor-vehicle-user taxes to inflation and real economic growth — outpaced the growth of GNP. The largest component, general sales and gross receipts taxes, went up from $11.25 to $20.52 per $1,000 GNP. An even more striking change is shown for individual income tax revenue — up from $5.66 to $16.35 per $1,000 GNP during the 15-year period. Much of this development reflects the imposition of income taxes by additional states — including, in this interval, such large states as Indiana, Michigan, Illinois, Ohio, Pennsylvania, and New Jersey. Together, individual and corporation income taxes provided 22.2 percent of all state-local tax revenue in 1977, as against only 10.6 percent in 1962.

State and Local Tax Revenue in Relation to Gross National Product, 1962 and 1977

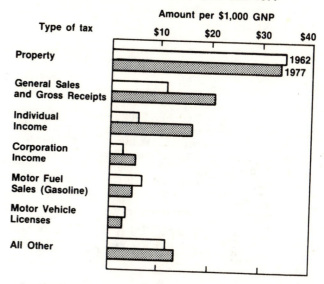

It seems highly probable that the rate of increase in property tax revenue (an average of 8.2 percent annually since 1962, but only 7.8 percent annually since 1972) has been markedly outpaced by the recent rapid rise in realty values, so that the average nationwide rate of property taxation has actually declined during recent years. Better judgment on this score should be possible later this year, when the Census Bureau is expected to report results of the taxable property values portion of the 1977 Census of Governments.

Figures that underlie the chart, and related data concerning state and local tax revenue, are as follows:

Type of tax	Amount ($ bil.) 1962	Amount ($ bil.) 1977	Percent increase	Percent distrib'n. 1962	Percent distrib'n. 1977	Per $1,000 GNP[1] 1962	Per $1,000 GNP[1] 1977
Total.............	42,738	182,903	328	100.0	100.0	$75.80	$96.75
Property................	19,593	64,177	228	45.8	35.1	34.75	33.95
General sales and gross receipts	6,341	38,798	512	14.8	21.2	11.25	20.52
Individual income .	3,191	30,907	869	7.5	16.9	5.66	16.35
Corporation income	1,342	9,709	623	3.1	5.3	2.38	5.14
Motor fuel sales	3,777	9,281	148	8.8	5.1	6.70	4.96
Motor vehicle and operators' licenses	1,809	4,958	174	4.2	2.7	3.21	2.62
All other	6,685	24,973	274	15.6	13.7	11.86	13.21

Source: Bureau of the Census, Quarterly Summary of State and Local Tax Revenue, for October–December 1963 and October–December 1977, table 1.

[1] Reflecting GNP as reported in the Economic Report of the President (January, 1978), table B-9: $563.8 billion in 1962, $1,890.4 billion in 1977, showing increase of 225 percent in this 15-year interval.

"Trends in State-Local Tax Revenues" is reprinted by permission from the May 29, 1978 issue of *Tax Notes*, Taxation With Representation Fund.

STATE-LOCAL TAX TRENDS
by Allen D. Manvel

It was pointed out in this column last week that — contrary to widespread tubthumping about an uncontrolled upsurge in property tax burdens throughout the nation — census figures show that state and local property tax collections have actually been increasing less rapidly than personal income, so that the nationwide ratio of property taxes to personal income dropped off nine percent between fiscal 1972 and fiscal 1977, from $71.50 to $65.14 per $1,000.

Unlike the property tax component, total state and local tax revenue, nationwide, has generally kept pace with changes in personal income during recent years.

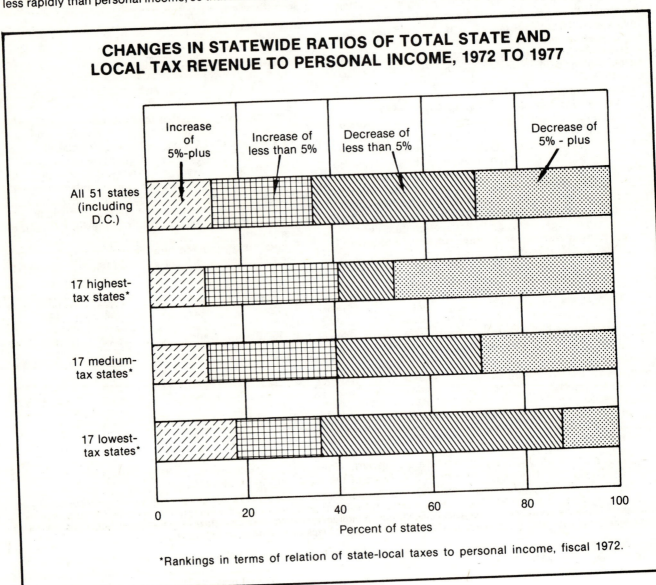

CHANGES IN STATEWIDE RATIOS OF TOTAL STATE AND
LOCAL TAX REVENUE TO PERSONAL INCOME, 1972 TO 1977

*Rankings in terms of relation of state-local taxes to personal income, fiscal 1972.

Over all, state-local tax revenue in fiscal 1977 was $128.17 per $1,000 personal income. The ratio was virtually the same five years earlier — $127.88 per $1,000 — and ranged in the intervening years only between $122.84 per $1,000 (in 1975) and $129.47 per $1,000 (in 1973).

The nationwide ratio, however, was materially affected by rising taxes in the two most populous states. In New York, the taxes/income ratio went up 12 percent, from $158 to $178 per $1,000 between 1972 and 1977. And in California the growth of tax revenue also outpaced changes in personal income, so that the ratio rose 3.4 percent, from $150 to $155 per $1,000 during the five years. In 33 of the other 48 states, however, the ratio dropped — i.e., tax revenue grew less rapidly than personal income. Moreover, as shown by the accompanying chart, this was the prevailing trend not only among the highest taxing states but also among those which in 1972 ranked relatively low or medium in the statewide relation of taxes to personal income.

It is true, of course, that like most other economic measures, state and local tax revenue has been increasing rapidly in absolute and per capita terms. The nationwide amount was $731 per capita in fiscal 1977 as against $527 five years before. This 39 percent increase directly paralleled a corresponding percentage increase in per capita personal income. The widespread hubbub about "runaway" state and local taxes seems to suggest that many people are far more aware of the increase in their tax bills than they are of the simultaneous growth of dollar income which, at least for most taxpayers in a majority of states, has made the resulting "tax load" no more burdensome than it was several years ago.

Summary statistics that underlie the chart are as follows:

Change in total state-local tax revenue per $1,000 personal income, 1972 to 1977	Number of states, grouped by 1972 tax level[1]				Percent of states, grouped by 1972 tax level[1]			
	All states	High level	Medium level	Low level	All states	High level	Medium level	Low level
Total.................	51	17	17	17	100	100	100	100
Increase of 5% or more ...	7	2	2	3	14	12	12	18
Increase of less than 5% ..	11	5	3	3	22	29	18	18
Decrease of less than 5% .	18	2	7	9	35	12	41	53
Decrease of 5% of more ..	15	8	5	2	29	47	29	12

Sources: See detailed tabulation below.

[1]Including the District of Columbia as a state.

17 highest-tax states[1]

State	State-local taxes per $1,000 income		
	1972	1977	% change
Ariz.	$137.54	$144.14	+4.8
Calif.	149.87	154.93	+3.4
Conn.	128.58	119.97	-6.7
Hawaii	139.34	140.71	+1.0
Iowa	129.51	120.25	-7.2
La.	133.65	120.91	-9.5
Maine	146.72	124.39	-15.2
Mass.	142.10	151.36	+6.5
Mich.	131.67	130.39	-1.0
Minn.	144.48	146.92	+1.7
Mont.	145.22	136.05	-6.3
Nev.	128.95	129.30	-0.3
N.Y.	157.75	176.84	+12.1
S.D.	132.48	123.46	-6.8
Vt.	170.17	151.84	-10.8
Wash.	128.54	122.34	-4.8
Wis.	160.60	143.61	-10.6

17-medium-tax states[1]

State	State-local states per $1,000 income		
	1972	1977	% change
Colo.	$126.03	$129.72	+2.9
Del.	124.08	117.96	-4.9
Fla.	115.67	104.74	-9.4
Idaho	124.37	116.97	-5.9
Ill.	122.24	118.99	-2.7
Md.	125.24	129.47	+3.3
Miss.	124.03	118.17	-4.7
Neb.	115.90	127.84	+10.3
N. Hamp.....	121.50	106.23	-12.6
N. Mex.	128.08	119.54	-6.7
N.Dak.	120.74	118.35	-2.0
Ore.	123.78	129.25	+4.4
Penn.	126.16	118.80	-5.8
R.I.	126.66	126.37	-0.2
Utah	126.20	125.88	-0.3
W.Va.	120.42	116.39	-3.3
Wyo.	125.85	154.76	+23.0

17 lowest-tax states[1]

State	State-local states per $1,000 income		
	1972	1977	% change
Ala.	$103.61	$99.96	-3.5
Alaska	102.22	234.83	+129.7
Ark.	103.58	101.78	-1.7
D.C.	103.63	130.47	+25.9
Ga.	108.84	111.50	+2.4
Ind.	115.27	105.41	-8.6
Kans.	110.99	113.24	+2.0
Ky.	107.68	112.76	+4.7
Mo.	108.08	102.60	-5.1
N.J.	106.71	126.06	+8.0
N.C.	112.52	109.83	-2.4
Ohio	101.76	99.44	-2.3
Okla.	107.67	106.53	-1.1
S.C.	110.38	107.67	-2.5
Tenn.	108.80	107.27	-1.4
Tex.	106.71	105.61	-1.0
Va.	109.15	108.69	-0.4

Sources: Bureau of the Census, *Preliminary Report, Governmental Finances in 1976-77* (September 1978), and *Compendium of Government Finances* (Vol. 4, No. 5 of the 1972 Census of Governments.

[1]The 17 "highest tax" states are those with a 1972 taxes/personal income ratio of $128 per $1,000 or more; the 17 lowest are those with a ratio of less than $116 per $1,000. The relation of taxes to (resident) personal income is a faulty indicator of the comparative level of taxation of various states. (See the Advisory Commission on Intergovernmental Relations, *Measuring the Fiscal Capacity and Effort of State and Local Areas*, 1971.) However, it is commonly so used for lack of a better recurrent measure.

"State-Local Tax Trends" is reprinted by permission from the November 20, 1978 issue of *Tax Notes*, Taxation With Representation Fund.

STATE AND LOCAL TAX BURDEN IS SURPRISINGLY UNIFORM

Few Regional Patterns Develop; Wyoming's Load Is Higher than Connecticut's

by Theodore J. Stroll

A *Tax Notes* study of average state and local tax burdens reveals that differences in tax burdens in the various regions of the U.S. are not as pronounced as is commonly believed.

Using data from the National Center for Economic Alternatives, *Tax Notes* compared the states' average tax burden as a percentage of real per-capita income. The Center developed the real per-capita income figure in cooperation with the Maine chapter of Common Cause, by adjusting state per-capita income statistics for the cost of living in each state. The initial data were supplied by the Bureau of the Census and the Bureau of Labor Statistics.

Predictably, New York, Massachusetts and California had high tax rates, ranging around 15 percent of real income, while sunbelt states such as Texas and Florida varied from eight to nine percent at the low end of the scale.

Maine, Oregon, Illinois, Colorado and Washington had similar state and local tax burdens of from 11.80 to 11.46 percent, even though they are geographically and economically diverse. Their location in New England, the Rocky Mountain plateau, the Midwest or the Pacific Northwest did not seem to make much difference. Neither did variations in per-capita income, even though Illinois, at $7,379, was the sixth wealthiest state, while Maine, at $5,572, was the poorest of all, ranking even below traditionally last-place Mississippi.

Some distortion in the rankings occurs because business taxes are included in the per-capita tax figure. In the case of Alaska, for example, property and severance taxes paid by business skew the tax burden to an improbable 32.85 percent for each Alaska native—but acutally much of Alaska's tax load is borne by oil and gas users in the lower 48 states.

Furthermore, the figures reflect averages: they fail to show the progressivity or regressivity of each state's tax system, nor do they reflect the distribution of income within states.

Tax Notes' economic consultant, Allen D. Manvel, also cautioned that comparisons of states' per-capita income, whether adjusted for inflation or not,"[do] not measure comparative revenue-raising capacity of the states." Manvel added that the lack of comparisons of revenue-raising ability is "an unfortunate gap in our data base that needs to be filled."

RANK OF STATE & LOCAL TAX BURDEN IN 1977

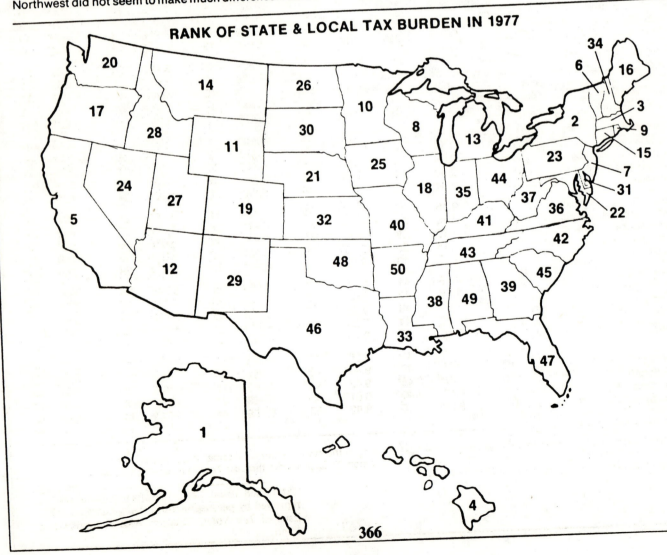

PER-CAPITA STATE & LOCAL TAX BURDEN IN 1977
Adjusted and Unadjusted for Cost of Living

State	Avg. Tax Burden (% of Real Income)[1]	Rank	Avg. Tax Burden (% of Nominal Income)[1]	Rank	1977 Real Income[2]	Rank	1977 Nominal Income[2]	Rank	1977 Avg. State & Local Taxes[3]	Rank
Alaska	32.85%	1	21.69%	1	$6,989	20	$10,586	1	$2,296	1
New York	18.70	2	16.61	2	6,696	27	7,537	12	1,252	2
Massachusetts	15.74	3	13.81	4	6,364	37	7,258	14	1,002	4
Hawaii	14.87	4	12.69	9	6,548	32	7,677	8	974	6
California	14.68	5	13.77	5	7,417	5	7,911	5	1,089	3
Vermont	14.13	6	13.91	3	5,734	48	5,823	44	810	19
New Jersey	13.08	7	11.65	14	7,118	16	7,994	3	931	7
Wisconsin	12.88	8	12.63	10	6,754	25	6,890	22	870	13
Rhode Island	12.86	9	11.70	13	6,167	43	6,775	26	793	21
Minnesota	12.77	10	12.71	7	7,093	17	7,129	17	906	8
Wyoming	12.33	11	13.06	6	8,014	3	7,562	11	988	5
Arizona	12.25	12	12.71	8	6,748	26	6,509	31	827	16
Michigan	12.05	13	11.52	15	7,285	9	7,619	9	878	12
Montana	12.03	14	12.51	11	6,367	36	6,125	34	766	24
Connecticut	12.01	15	10.98	25	7,364	7	8,061	2	885	11
Maine	11.80	16	11.48	18	5,572	50	5,734	46	658	29
Oregon	11.70	17	11.32	19	6,777	23	7,007	20	793	20
Illinois	11.65	18	11.07	21	7,379	6	7,768	6	860	14
Colorado	11.56	19	11.51	17	7,127	15	7,160	15	824	17
Washington	11.46	20	10.91	26	7,161	13	7,528	13	821	18
Nebraska	11.46	21	11.52	16	6,755	24	6,720	27	774	22
Maryland	11.41	22	11.78	12	7,820	4	7,572	10	892	9
Pennsylvania	11.26	23	10.98	24	6,841	21	7,011	19	770	23
Nevada	10.79	24	11.17	20	8,268	1	7,988	4	892	10
Iowa	10.71	25	10.89	27	6,990	19	6,878	23	749	25
North Dakota	10.71	26	11.02	22	6,369	35	6,190	33	682	27
Utah	10.63	27	11.01	23	6,134	45	5,923	41	652	31
Idaho	10.35	28	10.69	30	6,174	42	5,980	37	639	33
New Mexico	10.34	29	10.67	31	6,044	47	5,857	43	625	38
South Dakota	10.27	30	10.56	32	6,122	46	5,957	38	629	36
Delaware	10.23	31	10.77	28	8,096	2	7,697	7	829	15
Kansas	10.14	32	10.20	35	7,178	12	7,134	16	728	26
Louisiana	9.84	33	10.76	29	6,462	34	5,913	42	636	35
New Hampshire	9.80	34	9.46	42	6,306	39	6,536	30	618	40
Indiana	9.54	35	9.42	44	6,831	22	6,921	21	652	30
Virginia	9.46	36	9.83	39	7,134	14	6,865	24	675	28
West Virginia	9.36	37	10.39	34	6,642	28	5,986	36	622	39
Mississippi	9.35	38	10.48	33	5,639	49	5,030	50	527	48
Georgia	9.18	39	10.13	36	6,632	30	6,014	35	609	41
Missouri	9.17	40	9.15	47	6,641	29	6,654	29	609	42
Kentucky	9.15	41	10.11	37	6,565	31	5,945	39	601	43
North Carolina	9.06	42	9.99	38	6,543	33	5,935	40	593	45
Tennessee	8.94	43	9.75	40	6,312	38	5,785	45	564	46
Ohio	8.90	44	9.04	48	7,198	11	7,084	18	641	32
South Carolina	8.87	45	9.75	41	6,190	40	5,628	47	549	47
Texas	8.70	46	9.36	46	7,325	8	6,803	25	637	34
Florida	8.65	47	9.40	45	7,254	10	6,684	28	628	37
Oklahoma	8.48	48	9.42	43	7,056	18	6,346	32	598	44
Alabama	8.19	49	9.01	49	6,188	41	5,622	48	507	49
Arkansas	8.02	50	8.92	50	6,156	44	5,540	49	494	50

[1]"Real income" is per-capita income divided by the cost of living in the state. "Nominal income" is per-capita income.
[2]Data from National Center for Economic Alternatives, Washington, D.C., available through *Tax Notes* as Doc 79-242.
[3]Data from *The Washington Post*, 12-20-78 Doc 79-61.

"State and Local Tax is Surprisingly Uniform" is reprinted by permission from the January 15, 1979 issue of *Tax Notes*, Taxation With Representative Fund.

AVERAGE STATE AND LOCAL TAXES BY STATE

	Adjusted Gross Income										
	$10,000 -15,000	RANK	$15,000 -20,000	RANK	$20,000 -25,000	RANK	$25,000 -35,000	RANK	$35,000 -50,000	RANK	$50,000 -100,000	RANK
ALABAMA	$817	(39)	$1,094	(38)	$1,342	(38)	$1,760	(38)	$2,543	(36)	$3,381	(41)
ALASKA	1,069	(21)	1,403	(18)	1,693	(27)	2,162	(24)	3,083	(22)	4,685	(22)
ARIZONA	950	(28)	1,309	(26)	1,589	(30)	1,929	(35)	2,574	(33)	4,214	(30)
ARKANSAS	782	(44)	991	(42)	1,326	(39)	1,731	(41)	2,556	(35)	4,393	(28)
CALIFORNIA	1,232	(13)	1,657	(9)	2,090	(7)	2,700	(6)	4,045	(5)	7,432	(4)
COLORADO	1,111	(16)	1,533	(15)	1,938	(13)	2,435	(14)	3,352	(17)	4,726	(20)
CONNECTICUT*	1,321	(8)	1,586	(13)	1,699	(24)	2,042	(27)	3,408	(15)	4,993	(17)
DELAWARE†	974	(25)	1,263	(29)	1,777	(16)	2,404	(15)	3,208	(19)	6,778	(6)
DISTRICT OF COLUMBIA	1,085	(19)	1,519	(16)	1,751	(19)	2,654	(8)	3,733	(9)	6,023	(10)
FLORIDA*	715	(45)	785	(49)	991	(47)	1,305	(46)	1,565	(47)	2,502	(45)
GEORGIA	804	(41)	1,187	(33)	1,488	(34)	2,137	(26)	3,065	(24)	4,692	(21)
HAWAII	1,192	(14)	1,607	(12)	2,022	(11)	2,539	(13)	3,193	(20)	5,835	(12)
IDAHO	972	(26)	1,314	(25)	1,736	(20)	2,217	(22)	2,969	(27)	4,533	(25)
ILLINOIS	1,137	(15)	1,370	(21)	1,719	(22)	2,033	(29)	2,677	(31)	3,891	(36)
INDIANA	900	(33)	1,124	(36)	1,350	(37)	1,562	(43)	2,121	(43)	3,068	(43)
IOWA	961	(27)	1,371	(20)	1,695	(25)	2,247	(19)	2,827	(29)	4,645	(23)
KANSAS	911	(32)	1,292	(28)	1,564	(31)	2,038	(28)	2,972	(26)	3,961	(35)
KENTUCKY	1,034	(22)	1,396	(19)	1,769	(17)	2,286	(17)	3,145	(21)	4,287	(29)
LOUISIANA	557	(51)	755	(51)	913	(51)	1,102	(50)	1,612	(46)	2,234	(48)
MAINE	1,096	(18)	1,257	(30)	1,723	(21)	2,150	(25)	3,468	(13)	4,816	(19)
MARYLAND	1,468	(3)	1,839	(4)	2,212	(5)	3,040	(4)	4,014	(6)	6,072	(9)
MASSACHUSETTS	1,636	(1)	2,124	(2)	2,549	(2)	3,096	(2)	4,399	(2)	7,047	(5)
MICHIGAN	1,366	(7)	1,720	(8)	2,075	(9)	2,660	(7)	3,724	(10)	5,152	(15)
MINNESOTA	1,317	(10)	1,830	(5)	2,397	(3)	3,059	(3)	4,284	(3)	7,708	(3)
MISSISSIPPI	835	(37)	1,079	(39)	1,308	(41)	1,770	(37)	2,704	(30)	3,540	(39)
MISSOURI	947	(29)	1,256	(31)	1,557	(32)	1,935	(34)	2,481	(37)	3,771	(38)
MONTANA†	1,000	(24)	1,236	(32)	1,665	(29)	2,218	(21)	3,273	(18)	4,987	(18)
NEBRASKA	922	(31)	1,358	(22)	1,769	(18)	1,989	(31)	2,650	(32)	4,400	(26)
NEVADA*	843	(36)	854	(46)	1,016	(46)	1,250	(47)	1,622	(45)	2,419	(46)
NEW HAMPSHIRE*†	1,320	(9)	1,351	(23)	1,679	(28)	2,017	(30)	2,173	(41)	3,434	(40)
NEW JERSEY	1,400	(6)	1,771	(6)	2,055	(10)	2,582	(12)	3,606	(11)	5,464	(14)
NEW MEXICO	788	(43)	1,057	(40)	1,297	(42)	1,745	(40)	2,221	(40)	4,396	(27)
NEW YORK	1,574	(2)	2,161	(1)	2,742	(1)	3,656	(1)	5,321	(1)	10,135	(1)
NORTH CAROLINA	938	(30)	1,305	(27)	1,694	(26)	2,235	(20)	3,017	(25)	5,536	(13)
NORTH DAKOTA	792	(42)	952	(44)	1,388	(36)	1,947	(33)	2,260	(39)	3,813	(37)
OHIO	829	(38)	1,111	(37)	1,402	(35)	1,775	(36)	2,558	(34)	3,971	(34)
OKLAHOMA	692	(47)	888	(45)	1,181	(43)	1,753	(39)	2,271	(38)	3,996	(33)
OREGON†	1,099	(17)	1,631	(10)	2,085	(8)	2,647	(9)	3,744	(8)	6,357	(8)
PENNSYLVANIA	1,252	(11)	1,570	(14)	1,847	(14)	2,328	(16)	3,073	(23)	4,210	(31)
RHODE ISLAND	1,450	(5)	1,731	(7)	2,121	(6)	2,620	(11)	3,487	(12)	5,924	(11)
SOUTH CAROLINA	813	(40)	1,176	(34)	1,511	(33)	1,987	(32)	3,373	(16)	5,064	(16)
SOUTH DAKOTA*	865	(35)	1,055	(41)	1,152	(44)	1,667	(42)	1,463	(49)	2,353	(47)
TENNESSEE*	682	(49)	827	(48)	970	(48)	1,188	(49)	1,502	(48)	1,972	(49)
TEXAS*	646	(50)	839	(47)	916	(50)	1,213	(48)	1,414	(50)	1,944	(50)
UTAH	1,023	(23)	1,472	(17)	1,716	(23)	2,216	(23)	2,942	(28)	4,198	(32)
VERMONT	1,235	(12)	1,629	(11)	2,022	(12)	2,643	(10)	3,852	(7)	6,665	(7)
VIRGINIA	1,079	(20)	1,322	(24)	1,835	(15)	2,285	(18)	3,442	(14)	4,616	(24)
WASHINGTON*	866	(34)	1,137	(35)	1,325	(40)	1,507	(44)	2,128	(42)	2,562	(44)
WEST VIRGINIA	702	(46)	980	(43)	1,045	(45)	1,442	(45)	2,071	(44)	3,323	(42)
WISCONSIN	1,461	(4)	1,976	(3)	2,373	(4)	3,026	(5)	4,175	(4)	7,829	(2)
WYOMING*	691	(48)	764	(50)	969	(49)	1,065	(51)	1,090	(51)	1,433	(51)
U.S. AVERAGE	$1,131		$1,503		$1,869		$2,409		$3,368		$5,384	

Source: Internal Revenue Service

*States with no personal income tax. (New Jersey's income tax was imposed July 1, 1976; Connecticut taxes capital gains and dividends. New Hampshire and Tennessee tax income from interest and dividends.)

†States with no sales tax.

OPINION ROUNDUP

The Tax Revolt!

It is worth reminding ourselves that Americans have for a long time (probably always) been something less than wildly enthusiastic about paying taxes. In 1947, for example, Gallup found 61% of the population insisting that federal income taxes were too high. Currently, 70% of the public describe their federal taxes as too high. This particular measure suggests that some change has occurred, but that there has hardly been a massive transformation of public opinion.

Furthermore, in the *latter half of the 1960s,* there was a fundamental shift in the public assessment of governmental performance generally. Thus, Americans in unprecedented numbers began manifesting doubts about the performance of government leaders (and as well about the leadership of those who head most of the primary institutions of this society), began believing that government cannot be wholly trusted to do what is right, commenced insisting that a lot of tax dollars are wasted, and so forth. Surely, one important part of the "taxpayers' revolt" of 1978 is the widespread *decade-old* drop in confidence in public performance.

Still, it is incorrect to argue that the public has become anti-state in some single-minded fashion. Large majorities of Americans believe that we are spending the *right amount* or even *not enough* on health, education, helping blacks, urban problems, and on a host of other social needs. Something between 75% and 95% of the population endorse the present rate of spending by local government on schools, hospitals, police and fire protection, libraries, and highway maintenance. Americans are, to put it mildly, highly ambivalent about the "service state."

What do Americans want? They want lower taxes. They want government to perform better than it has. They want it to spend more prudently. And they want it to maintain a high level of public services. There is a message here, but it is a more complex one than "taxpayers' revolt" suggests.

—*Everett C. Ladd, Jr.*
Consulting Editor
Opinion Roundup

THE CHIEF VILLAINS

Question: From your personal standpoint, please tell me, for each tax that I read off to you, if you feel it is too high, too low, or about right.

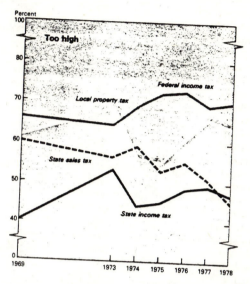

	Too high						
	1969	**1973**	**1974**	**1975**	**1976**	**1977**	**1978**
Federal income tax	66%	64%	69%	72%	73%	69%	70%
State income taxes	40	53	44	45	48	49	47
Local property taxes	62	68	56	55	61	66	64
State sales taxes	60	56	59	53	55	51	45

Source: Surveys by Louis Harris and Associates, latest that of June 15-17, 1978.

LEAST FAIR TAX GROWS MOST

Question: Thinking about ways to raise money for state and local services and programs, which one of the following three types of taxes do you think is the *fairest form* of tax? (Responses below.) I am going to read some different types of taxes. For each tell me if the amount you or your family pays has increased a great deal, a fair amount, a little bit or not at all in the past few years. If you don't have to pay this tax tell me that. (Responses below.)

The fairest tax

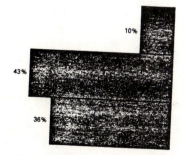

Taxes which have increased a great deal

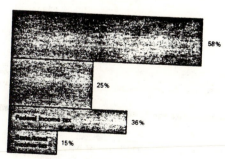

Note: Other polls confirm the property tax's low standing with the public. CBS/New York *Times* asked people which tax is "most fair": the social security tax ranked first at 24%, followed by sales (19%), state income (17%), federal income (13%), and property (10%). 53% of the nation's homeowners in the same survey agreed that property taxes had been taking a bigger portion of income in the last few years; 77% of California homeowners likewise noted a bigger property tax bite.

Source: Survey by *Newsweek*/American Institute of Public Opinion (Gallup), June 7-8, 1978.

WHERE GOVERNMENT SPENDS TOO MUCH

Question: We are faced with many problems in this country, none of which can be solved easily or inexpensively. I'm going to name some of these problems, and for each one I'd like you to tell me whether you think we're spending too much money on it, too little money, or about the right amount.

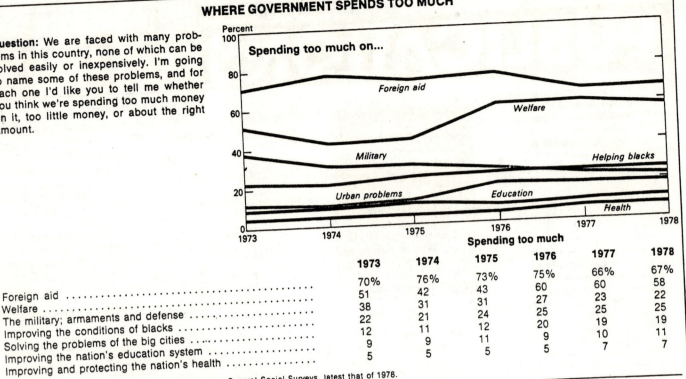

Spending too much

	1973	1974	1975	1976	1977	1978
Foreign aid	70%	76%	73%	75%	66%	67%
Welfare	51	42	43	60	60	58
The military; armaments and defense	38	31	31	27	23	22
Improving the conditions of blacks	22	21	24	25	25	25
Solving the problems of the big cities	12	11	12	20	19	19
Improving the nation's education system	9	9	11	9	10	11
Improving and protecting the nation's health ...	5	5	5	5	7	7

Source: Surveys by National Opinion Research Center, General Social Surveys, latest that of 1978.

SOLID NATIONWIDE "YES" ON PROP 13

Question: Two weeks ago, the voters in California passed Proposition 13—which reduced property taxes by more than half. Opponents of the measure said that if taxes were reduced, services provided by the local community would also have to be cut back. .... If there was a proposition like that in your area, would you vote for it, or vote against it, or wouldn't you vote?

	For	Against	Wouldn't vote	No opinion
Total	51%	24%	12%	13%
By race				
White	52	25	11	12
Blacks	43	19	22	16
By income				
Under $10,000	53	17	15	15
$10-15,000	48	23	12	17
$15-25,000	57	27	9	7
Over $25,000	55	27	8	10
By age				
18-29 years	47	25	18	10
30-44 years	54	22	13	11
45-64 years	56	23	9	12
65 years and over	48	23	7	22
By political ideology				
Liberal	57	22	12	9
Moderate	52	27	11	10
Conservative	54	23	11	12
By political party				
Republican	56	29	7	8
Independent	52	20	15	13
Democrat	49	26	11	14
By homeowner/renter				
Owner	54	25	8	3
Renter	45	18	22	15

Note: Asked of non-California residents only. Similar questions posed to national samples by other polling organizations have produced comparable results: in June, *Newsweek*/American Institute of Public Opinion (Gallup) found 57% support for such a measure; NBC News/Associated Press, 53% support; and Louis Harris, 63% support.

Source: Survey by CBS News/New York *Times*, June 19-23, 1978.

"The Tax Revolt" is reprinted by permission of the July/August, 1978 issue of *Public Opinion*, the American Enterprise Institute, © 1979.

Conference PUBLICATIONS

☐ **Capital and Communities: The Causes and Consequences of Private Disinvestment**
A groundbreaking study providing new documentation and analysis of the extent of plant closings in this country and the rising levels of joblessness and economic dislocation caused by unrestrained capital movement. The authors assess the extent of capital mobility and the social costs of unregulated private investment decisions.
By Barry Bluestone and Bennett Harrison; co-published with the Progressive Alliance. (June 1980) 50 pp.
$3.95; $5.95 Institutions

☐ **Plant Closings: Resources for Public Officials and Community Leaders**
(May 1979) 85 pp.
$4.95; $6.95 Institutions

☐ **Industrial Exodus**
Ed Kelly (1977) 30 pp.
$2.95; $4.95 Institutions

☐ **The Last Entrepreneurs: America's Regional Wars for Jobs and Dollars**
Robert Goodman (December 1979) 250 pp.
$9.95; $14.95 Institutions

☐ **The Cities' Wealth**
(1978) 85 pp.
$4.95; $6.95 Institutions

☐ **Tax Abatements: Resources for Public Officials and Community Leaders**
(May 1979) 80 pp.
$4.95; 6.95 Institutions

☐ **Economic Democracy: The Challenge of the 1980s**
Martin Carnoy and Derek Shearer (May 1980) 430 pp.
$9.95; $14.95 Institutions

☐ **Developing the Public Economy: Models From Massachusetts**
(1979) 208 pp.
$9.95; $14.95 Institutions

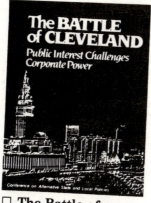

☐ **The Battle of Cleveland: Public Interest Challenges Corporate Power**
Thorough examination of the corporate/public interest conflict in Cleveland with emphasis on the election of Mayor Kucinich, how his administration resisted corporate dominance of City Hall and why he lost in his re-election bid.
Edited by Dan Marschall with the assistance of The Ohio Public Interest Campaign (March 1980) 180 pp.
$7.95; $9.95 Institutions

☐ **Public Employee Pension Funds: New Strategies for Investment**
(July 1979) 180 pp.
$9.95; $14.95 Institutions

☐ **The Shifting Property Tax Burden: The Untold Cause of the Tax Revolt**
Robert Kuttner (January 1980) 80 pp.
$3.95; $5.95 Institutions

☐ **Manual on Pay Equity: Raising Wages for Women's Work**
Thorough review of the "equal pay for work of comparable value" movement: legislative initiatives, litigation, news of organizing campaigns, comparable worth studies, collective bargaining update and the latest research. Includes proceedings from the October 1979 Washington Conference on Pay Equity, extensive resource listing, and guides to action.
Edited by Joy Ann Grune in cooperation with the Committee on Pay Equity (May 1980) 230 pp.
$9.95

☐ **Moderate Rent Control: The Experience of U.S. Cities**
John Gilderbloom (May 1980) 60 pp.
$3.95; $5.95 Institutions

☐ **Women in the Economy: A Legislative Agenda**
(1978) 133 pp.
$4.95; $6.95 Institutions

☐ **State and Local Tax Revolt: New Directions for the '80s:**
A comprehensive guide to state and local tax issues and what can be done to make these taxes more equitable. 29 chapters written and edited by nationally known progressive tax experts.
Edited by Dean Tipps and Lee Webb (June 1980) 300 pp.
$9.95; $14.95 Institutions

☐ **The Public Balance Sheet: A New Tool for Evaluating Economic Choices**
David Smith (June 1979) 20 pp.
$2.95; $4.95 Institutions

☐ **New Energy Legislation Initiatives: A State-by-State Legislative Guide 1979-1980**
(May 1980) 110 pp.
$3.95; $5.95 Institutions

☐ **New Directions in Farm, Land and Food Policies: A Time for State and Local Action**
(January 1979) 320 pp.
$9.95; $14.95 Institutions

☐ Subscribe now to **Ways and Means**, the bi-monthly magazine of The Conference featuring in-depth reporting on progressive state and local legislation, political trends and events, and news of useful publications and reports.
One year, $10, Institutions $20.

ORDER FORM

Please ship immediately the titles I've checked

Total for publications $ _____

Add 10% for postage and handling $ _____

Enclosed is my check for $ _____

- **Bulk Policy**—10 or more copies, any mix, 20% discount.
- **"Institutions"**—Applies to business and govt.

Name _____

Address _____

City/State _____

Organization _____

Send order with payment to:

Conference Publications
2000 Florida Avenue, NW
Room 400
Washington, DC 20009